ABOUT THE EDITOR

Dr Patrick Gunnigle is Professor of Business Studies at the University of Limerick, where he is also Director of the Employment Relations Research Unit. A graduate of University College Dublin and Cranfield School of Management, he has authored, co-authored or edited nine books and over forty refereed journal papers. His most recent books include *New Challenges to Irish Industrial Relations* (1995), *Personnel and Human Resource Management: Theory and Practice in Ireland* (1997), *Human Resource Management in Irish Organisations: Practice in Perspective* (1997) and *Principles of Organisational Behaviour* (1998). During the academic year 1996/97, he was a visiting Fulbright Scholar in the Department of Management, San Diego State University.

His main research interests are in the areas of trade union membership and recognition, management strategies in industrial relations, human resource management (HRM) policies and the role of HRM specialists. He has acted as a reviewer for a number of national and international journals and is a member of the Editorial Board of the *International Journal of Employee Relations*.

THE IRISH EMPLOYEE RECRUITMENT HANDBOOK

*Finding and Keeping
a High Quality Workforce*

Edited by Patrick Gunnigle

Oak Tree Press
Dublin

Oak Tree Press
Merrion Building
Lower Merrion Street
Dublin 2, Ireland
http://www.oaktreepress.com

A catalogue record of this book is
available from the British Library.

ISBN 1 86076 130 5

Printed in Britain by MPG Books, Bodmin, Cornwall

Oak Tree Press gratefully acknowledges the sponsorship of the Institute of
Personnel and Development in the production of this Handbook.

INSTITUTE OF PERSONNEL
AND DEVELOPMENT

The Institute has over 90,000 members in Ireland and the UK and is Europe's
largest professional institute for the management and development of
people. Our programmes of learning and competence accreditation are
internationally recognised and lead to highly valued professional
qualifications.

The IPD sets standards and promotes best practice in the fields of people
management and development. We express the views of the profession and
advise governments and businesses on matters relating to the management
of people at work. We provide a comprehensive portfolio of services for
members which enables them to maintain continuing professional
development throughout their working lives.

CONTENTS

PART ONE
INTRODUCTION AND BACKGROUND

Chapter 1

Chapter 2

Chapter 3

PART TWO
SOURCING A HIGH QUALITY WORKFORCE

PART THREE
PERFORMANCE MANAGEMENT

PART FIVE
THE LEGAL CONTEXT

PART SIX
EMPLOYEE WELFARE

CONTRIBUTORS

Graeme Buckingham is Senior Vice President of The Gallup Organization's Management Research Group, Europe. He was formerly Director of Personnel of Allied Breweries and Personnel Director of Gallaher Ltd. A Companion of the Institute of Personnel and Development, he has published books on pay, productivity and organisational development and numerous articles.

Con Egan is Manufacturing Manager with Kostal Ireland. He has several years' senior management experience in operations and human resource management and has worked previously with Wang Laboratories and Golden Vale. He is a graduate of the University of Limerick and has an MED with Sheffield University. He is a Fellow of the Institute of Commercial Management and a member of the Irish Institute of Training and Development and the Institution of Industrial Managers.

Thomas N. Garavan is a lecturer in human resource development and health and safety practices at the University of Limerick, a Fellow of the Irish Institute of Training and Development and a member of the American Society of Training and Development. He is the author or co-author of a number of books, including *Training and Development in Ireland* (1995), *Cases in Irish Business Strategy and Policy* (1996), the two-volume *Entrepreneurship and Business Start-ups in Ireland* (1997) and *The Irish Health and Safety Handbook* (1997).

Noreen Heraty lectures in the areas of human resource management and personnel management practice at the University of Limerick. She has co-authored a number of books, including *Principles of Organisational Behaviour* (1998), *Personnel and Human Resource Management* (1997) and *Training and Development in Ireland* (1995), and has written more than 30 book chapters and articles.

Ciara Heslin is Personnel Manager at Deutsche Morgan Grenfell, with responsibility for staff recruitment and retention, performance management and career development. She holds a B.Comm and a Diploma in Hotel Management. She was previously Personnel Manager in Jurys Kensington Hotel.

Eugenie Houston is Chief Executive of The Magic Lamp, an educational children's toy mail order catalogue. She has worked in human resource management for almost ten years, most recently as Director of Human Resources at Esat Telecom. She is the author of *Working and Living in Ireland* (1998).

Aidan Lawrence is Training and Development Manager at Hewlett Packard Manufacturing Ireland. He has seven years' experience in training and development management. He previously worked for Amdahl Ireland, York MDM Ireland and Stratus Computer Ireland.

Jennifer Lee is Group Personnel and Training Manager with Jurys Hotel Group plc, where she has worked for over six years, with responsibility for the human resource function for 17 hotels. She is an MBS graduate of the Michael Smurfit Graduate School of Business, Dublin.

Alma McCarthy is a Business Studies and French graduate from the University of Limerick, specialising in Personnel Management. She is currently studying for an MBS at the Graduate Centre of Business, University of Limerick. Her research interests include performance appraisal, reward management, and management development and training.

Gerard McMahon is a lecturer in Human Resource Management at the Dublin Institute of Technology. He is also Managing Director of Productive Personnel Ltd., specialising in the provision of advisory and training services. He has worked successfully as a trade union official, personnel advisor, lecturer, researcher, author and trainer over a 20-year period.

Orla Maher is Managing Director of Creative Asset Management Ltd. (CAM), a consulting company that specialises in human resource and strategic management. A Fellow of the Institute of Personnel and Development, she has over ten years' experience in human resource management.

Anne Morgan is a Masters in Business Studies student (MBS) at the University of Limerick. Her current research interests are in the areas of marketing and human resource management, with a particular emphasis on service quality and organisational culture.

Michael J. Morley is a Lecturer in Personnel Management and Industrial Relations at the University of Limerick. A former Irish American Partnership Scholar, his current research interests include institutional theory, the changing nature of the employment relationship and psychological correlates of expatriate adjustment. He is co-author of a number of books and a member of the editorial board of the *Journal of European Industrial Training*.

Anne O'Carroll currently works as a consultant to the Irish Hotels Federation on its Quality Employer Programme, a code of practice developed by the IHF to encourage best practice in hotels in the HR and training areas. A graduate of Hotel Management, and with an MBS in Human Resource Management and Industrial Relations, she has 15 years' experience in the hotel sector.

Karl O'Connor is Senior Manager, Training and Development, in First Active plc. He has 17 years' experience in the training and development function. In his training and development role within First Active, he won several HR best practice awards.

John O'Dowd is an independent consultant specialising in human resources. From 1997 to 1999, he was Joint Director of the National Centre for Partnership, and was previously General Secretary of the Civil and Public Service Union and a member of the executive council of the Irish Congress of Trade Unions. He is the author of *Employee Partnership in Ireland* (1998).

Bob Pattinson is Director of the Management Development Unit in the University of Limerick. He was formerly Deputy Principal of the Electricity Industry's Management College in the UK and Head of Management at Guilford College of Technology. He worked for some years with the occupational psychologists Saville and Holdsworth. He is a Fellow of the Institute of Personnel and Development.

Dermot Rush is Managing Director of Saville and Holdsworth Ltd., a consultancy specialising in the assessment and development of competent performance in the workplace. He has worked as an applied psychologist in educational, clinical and organisational settings. He also holds a Masters degree in Strategic Management and has worked in general management in the UK National Health Service.

Adrian F. Twomey is a Barrister-at-Law and a lecturer in law at the National College of Ireland, specialising in employment law and the law of contract. He previously worked for the Department of Labour and the Department of Equality and Law Reform. He co-authored *Sexual Harassment in the Workplace*, contributed to *The Challenge of Supervisory Management* and has published numerous articles in Irish legal journals.

CASE EXAMPLES

TABLES

FIGURES

FOREWORD

Today, one of the biggest single challenges facing organisations, be they large or small, is how to attract and retain quality staff at all levels. IPD Ireland is delighted to be the sponsor of this timely *Irish Employee Recruitment Handbook*, which addresses a very real need in the marketplace.

The Handbook has been written by a team of recognised experts under the skilful editorship of Paddy Gunnigle. It deals with the issues in a logical and systematic way, with a style that makes it instantly accessible to a wide readership.

The early chapters place the whole question of recruitment in context by considering the implications of globalisation on the Irish economy. This raises issues about the future of HRM and readers will be interested in the evidence that shows a strong link between HR practices and organisational performance. The section will also be of use to HR practitioners who may wish to benchmark their activities against current thinking in the field.

Having debated the strategic significance of HR, the Handbook moves on to deal with the sourcing of high quality candidates against the background of a dramatically changing labour market. It is clear that the unstructured interview as the main basis of selection is no longer sufficient and readers will be richly rewarded with exposure to new insights and techniques.

For me, a particularly valuable aspect of the Handbook is that it approaches "recruitment" from a holistic perspective. Frequently in the past, the selection process was felt to have been completed when the chosen candidate confirmed acceptance of the employment contract. All too often, however, the initial feelings of euphoria were rapidly dissipated by deficiencies in such areas as induction and socialisation, training and development strategies, employee relations and reward systems. The evidence indicates that the vast majority of employees who leave their organisations do so within a short time of joining. No employer can afford this and there are several chapters devoted to how it might be avoided.

The next section focuses attention on the institutional framework and contains valuable information on addressing the important legal issues. The final section deals with two important issues of employee welfare in the modern workplace: the balance between work and family life; and occupational health and safety.

Taken overall, the Handbook provides a most useful set of guidelines for any organisation striving to become an employer of choice in today's challenging recruitment market.

Michael McDonnell
Director,
Institute of Personnel and Development, Ireland

PART ONE
INTRODUCTION AND BACKGROUND

CHAPTER 1

INTRODUCTION: THE STRATEGIC SIGNIFICANCE OF EFFECTIVE HUMAN RESOURCE MANAGEMENT

Patrick Gunnigle

INTRODUCTION

In almost all types of organisation and sectors of the economy, we are witnessing an increasing debate on the significance of people as a critical variable in impacting on organisation performance. As a result, we have witnessed increased emphasis on attempts to align business strategies and human resource management (HRM) policies and practices. This chapter reviews some of the key developments in workforce management and considers the implications for organisations and, particularly, for personnel/ human resource (HR) practitioners.

A DRAMATICALLY CHANGED ECONOMIC CONTEXT

There is now widespread acceptance that HR management practice has undergone significant change since the beginning of the 1980s. In setting the scene for subsequent contributions to this text, it is useful to explore briefly the reasons why this change has taken place and examine the likely impact on HR management practice. In firstly looking at the period from the end of the Second World War to the beginning of the 1980s, we can broadly agree that, in most developed Western economies, national and enterprise level practice conformed towards what we have come to term the "pluralist tradition". This is based on an acceptance that a conflict of interests exists between management and labour, and a reliance on collective bargaining as the primary means of resolving these conflicting interests. In most countries, the cornerstones of this approach included trade union recognition, reliance on "adversarial" collective bargaining and some degree of procedural formalisation. In the US, we witnessed a similar picture with the development of what has been termed "post-New Deal" industrial relations. For the HR function, industrial relations became *the* priority — HR specialists were vested with the responsibility to negotiate and police agreements (Gunnigle, 1998). Industrial harmony was the objective and personnel specialists, through their negotiating, interpersonal, and procedural skills, had responsibility for its achievement. This industrial relations emphasis helped position the personnel/HR function in a more central management role, albeit a largely reactive one.

Since the early 1980s, the pluralist model has come under increasing challenge. In the US, for example, we have seen a dramatic decline in the "New Deal" industrial relations system. While developments in Western Europe have been less extreme, we have also witnessed major change in approaches to workforce management. There is general agreement that developments in the wider economic, social and political environment have been the main catalysts in stimulating change in HRM (Beaumont, 1995; Roche and Gunnigle, 1995). Of particular note in this regard is the increasingly competitive nature of product and service markets. The main sources of increased competitiveness are well treated in the literature and include: the liberalisation of European and world trade; associated deregulation in product, service and capital markets; improved communications and transport infrastructures; developments in information technology; and greater market penetration by emerging economies.

While this chapter does not allow for a comprehensive analysis of these competitive pressures, it is useful to review briefly the main dimensions of increased market competition.

Sources of Increased Competition[1]

In attempting to disaggregate the concept of increased competitiveness, we can point to three key dimensions, namely the globalisation of competition, the intensification of competition and the changing nature of competitive strategies.

Firstly, we have witnessed the *globalisation of competition*. Since the early 1980s, a key development in the macroeconomic environment is the increased trend towards the greater liberalisation of world trade. This trend has been facilitated to a significant extent by developments under the General Agreement on Tariffs and Trade (GATT) and moves towards Economic and Monetary Union (EMU). In evaluating the HRM implications, a number of issues are important. Clearly the trend towards greater trade liberalisation provides both opportunities and threats for firms: we have the opportunity for greater access to new markets but also the threat of increased market competition. In the European context, we can point to the greater competitive threat to organisations from lower-cost economies and the related dangers of organisations relocating from high-cost countries, such as Germany, to lower-cost regions. On the positive side, we find that greater trade liberalisation provides increased opportunities to develop new markets. However, in order to capitalise on such opportunities in the face of greater competition, it is likely that firms will have to improve their performance on dimensions such as unit production costs, speed to market, and customer support.

In addition to the globalisation of competition, therefore, we can also point to the greater *intensification of competition*. Again, numerous sources may be identified. In addition to traditional

---

[1] For greater detail see Sparrow and Hiltrop (1994); Roche and Gunnigle (1995).

sources of competition such as the US and Japan, we can point to increased competition from fast-developing economies such as Singapore and South Korea and other emerging economies such as China and Mexico, some of whom combine a low cost-base with strong performance on dimensions such as productivity and labour skills. Some of the countries of the former Soviet Union have undergone a period of restructuring and are likely to provide considerable competition as a result of their low cost-base, industrial tradition and educational systems with strong technical and scientific foundations.

Thirdly, we have the *changing nature of competitive strategies* as a stimulus for change in HRM. Key contemporary developments, such as increased customisation of products and services, reduced cycle time, and faster speed to market all have important implications for workforce management. In particular, such developments often require greater flexibility in employment patterns as organisations seek to align their need for workers with the level of business demand, and greater task flexibility in terms of the variety of duties which workers may be required to perform.

A related factor that has also served to stimulate change in HRM is the changing role of trade unions. In particular, we have witnessed a decline in trade union membership and influence in many Western economies, which has prompted the union movement to seek mechanisms to increase their legitimacy and representativeness at both enterprise and national level.

ORGANISATIONAL RESPONSES AND IMPLICATIONS FOR HRM

Why has HRM now emerged as a significant dimension of the debate on changes in work organisation and organisation performance? We can point to two broad stimuli. Firstly, as noted above, we have the increasingly competitive environment facing organisations and encouraging them to reconfigure their HRM policies and practices to facilitate improved performance and productivity. Secondly, we have seen some decline in the traditional, or so-called "adversarial" industrial relations model and a proliferation of different models of workforce management, including the "soft" non-union model, partnership-based approaches and hard HR approaches.

Turning to the implications for organisations, it seems that increased competitive pressures have served to focus attention on both cost *and* product innovation/quality as factors impacting on competitive positioning of firms, and to create a "flexibility imperative", whereby more and more organisations have to be increasingly responsive to consumer demand on dimensions such as customisation, quality, and support services (see Gunnigle, 1998; Roche and Gunnigle, 1995). It is further argued that these developments have all but diluted the premise that companies compete on either a price (low cost) or a product differentiation (premium price) basis. These trends mean that more and more firms — not just those that compete on the basis of low price — are striving to control their cost structures, including the labour component. Such competitive pressures are increasingly impacting on the public sector (see Hastings, 1994). Much of this change is driven by developments at EU level, particularly the removal or dilution of State monopolies. In airline travel, we have seen a significant and continuing increase in the extent of price competition. We are now witnessing a similar trend in the telecommunications sector. From a HR perspective, these changes generally herald significant organisation change and restructuring with changes in employment levels (generally reductions), employment patterns, pay and benefit systems and management–employee communications.

In responding to the challenges of increased competition, organisations appear to have followed two broad strategies. Firstly, we witnessed *widespread rationalisation*, especially in Europe during the 1980s. Common characteristics here included redundancies, contracting out or selling "non-core" activities, and "delayering", that is, reducing the number of hierarchical levels or grades in the organisation. A second common organisational response was a sharp increase in *merger, acquisition or strategic alliance activity*. A common element in these organisational responses was an increased focus on improving workforce management at the enterprise level, specifically in seeking improvements in labour productivity and reductions in labour costs. Related enterprise-level strategies include the increased use of atypical employment forms in certain sectors, improved performance management methods and initiatives to increase task flexibility.

These various developments strike at the very heart of what we have termed "pluralist" industrial relations traditions. They also explain why we are witnessing an increasing emphasis on the role of management, and particularly HR managers, in seeking to develop and change HRM arrangements in a way which serves to enhance enterprise-level performance. We now consider linkages between HRM and company performance.

BUSINESS STRATEGY AND HRM

A significant strand in the management literature over the past decade has been an increasing interest in achieving a closer alignment between business strategy and HR management. From this debate has emerged the concept of "strategic human resource management", which refers to the development of a strategic corporate approach to workforce management. In this approach, HR considerations become an integral component of strategic decision-making. It is likely that this strategic focus will continue, since workforce management considerations have been a neglected area within strategic management thinking generally. To adequately evaluate the potential linkages between business strategy and HRM, it is necessary to firstly review the nature of strategic management.

Strategic management is concerned with top-level policy decisions, which seek to position the organisation optimally to deal effectively with its environment. Strategic decisions are therefore long-term in nature, involving major resource allocation decisions which affect the future nature of the organisation and serve to guide subsequent decision-making at lower levels. We can identify three broad levels of strategic decision-making in organisations (Hofer and Schendel, 1978). *Corporate-level strategy* is essentially concerned with the question, "What business should we be in?" *Business-level (competitive) strategy* addresses the question, "How do we compete in this business?" Finally, *Functional-level strategy* focuses on how the activities of particular functions (such as the HR role) come together to support business-level strategy. These differing strategy levels are illustrated in Figure 1.1.

Figure 1.1: Levels of Strategic Decision-Making

CORPORATE STRATEGY *Multi-Business* (what business should we be in)
BUSINESS/COMPETITIVE STRATEGY *Single/Related Business(es)* (how to establish competitive advantage)
FUNCTIONAL STRATEGY (role of component parts)
Production/ Operations   Marketing   Finance   Personnel/Human Resource Management

Corporate, business and functional strategy represent different levels of strategic decision-making in an organisation. Each level involves decisions that are strategic in nature. However, decisions at higher levels, such as those at corporate or business unit level, will guide subsequent decisions on functional strategy. Purcell (1989) emphasises this point by differentiating between *upstream* (first order) and *downstream* (second/third order) strategic decisions (see Figure 1.2). Upstream decisions concern the long-term direction and nature of the organisation. Downstream decisions deal with the implications of first order decisions. Purcell argues that HR choices are made in the context of downstream strategic decisions on organisation structure. Such choices are strategic in nature since they establish the basic approach to workforce management. However, they will be heavily influenced by first and second order decisions and by broader environmental factors.

Figure 1.2: Upstream and Downstream Strategic Decision-Making

UPSTREAM			
E	FIRST ORDER	Long term direction of the firm	E
N		Scope of activities, markets, location	N
V			V
I			I
R	SECOND ORDER	Internal operating procedures	R
O		Relationships between parts of the	O
N		organisation	N
M			M
E			E
N	THIRD ORDER	(e.g.) Strategic choice in HRM	N
T			T
DOWNSTREAM			

Source: adapted from Purcell (1989)

Purcell's analysis also identifies an important contrast between highly *diversified* organisations operating in a variety of business sectors and *critical function* organisations, whose main activities are restricted to a core industry/sector. He suggests that the firms in the latter "core business" category are frequently characterised by a particular culture and value system, which may often reflect the founder's ideology. This approach is clearly evident in a number of foreign-owned organisations in Ireland, such as Hewlett Packard and Intel, but also in a number of indigenous firms, such as Superquinn. Purcell argues that a strategic planning style, considered conducive to the development of a strategic approach to HR, is more likely to develop where there is a high level of vertical integration (interdependence between business units). However, Purcell feels that organisations which emphasise long-term strategic objectives, core values and vertical linkages are becoming less common as the trend towards diversification (multi-business organisations) gathers momentum.

The Significance of Competitive Strategy
A key factor influencing the upsurge of interest in linking business strategies and HR policies is the quest for competitive advantage. The concept of competitive advantage addresses the means by which competing firms seek to gain market advantage over one another. Michael Porter (1985, 1987) has been the leading commentator in this area, arguing that the focus of strategic decision-making should be on the development of appropriate competitive strategies at the level of individual business units. Competitive strategy is concerned with achieving sustainable competitive advantage in particular industries or industry segments. Price and quality are common mechanisms by which organisations attempt to achieve competitive advantage.

Porter identifies three generic competitive strategies:

- *Cost leadership* (sometimes called *cost reduction*) involves positioning the organisation as the low-cost producer of a standard "no frills" product or service. To succeed with a cost leadership strategy, it is suggested that the firm must become *the* cost leader and not one of several firms pursuing this strategy. Cost leadership requires an emphasis on tight managerial controls, low overheads, economies of scale and a dedication to achieving productive efficiency.

- *Product differentiation*, on the other hand (sometimes called *product innovation*) requires that an organisation's product or service becomes unique on some dimension which is valued by the buyer to such an extent that the buyer is willing to pay a premium price. The basis for a differentiation may be the product or service itself, or other aspects such as delivery, after-sales service or brand image.

- A *focus strategy* involves choosing a narrow market segment and serving this either through a low-cost or a differentiation focus.

An organisation's choice of generic strategy specifies its fundamental approach to achieving competitive advantage in its particular market(s) and prescribes the broad context for policies and actions in each key functional area, such as HR management. It is suggested that different competitive strategies warrant different HR strategies, policies and practices. Of particular significance is the perceived need to match personnel selection, workforce profile and employee relations practices with the desired competitive strategy. Porter further argues that different organisation cultures are implied in each strategy and that HR policy choice is a key influence in establishing and maintaining "appropriate" corporate cultures. Thus, a key strand in the debate on competitive strategy and HR management is the idea of "policy fit". Essentially, it is argued that if an organisation is to successfully pursue a particular competitive strategy, such as cost leadership or product differentiation, it must adopt and implement a comprehensive complementary sets of HR practices (see Huselid, 1995). We can identify a number of broad areas where top management may seek to align particular HR policies and practices with their competitive strategy (see Fombrun et al., 1986):

1. *The nature of the psychological contract*: This may vary from, at one extreme, a managerial perspective that views employees in

instrumental terms and emphasises high levels of control of both employees and the work environment, to, at the other extreme, an approach that views employees as intelligent and committed beings who should be afforded challenging and meaningful work roles.

2. *Level of employee involvement*: Here organisational approaches may vary from those with high levels of employee involvement in decision-making to those where decisions are solely based on management prerogative.

3. *Internal/external labour market*: This addresses the relative emphasis on internal versus external recruitment and related differences in emphasis on employee development.

4. *Performance management*: This factor addresses extent and nature of evaluation of employee performance, incorporating the relative emphasis on group versus individual performance evaluation.

THE IMPACT ON ORGANISATION PERFORMANCE

Despite the extensive literature addressing the concept of strategy and "strategic human resource management", there has been comparatively little evidence on the extent to which HR management contributes to improvements in organisational performance. Indeed, the issue of whether, and to what extent, HR management impacts on bottom-line performance is an age-old debate that has dogged the HR role for most of its existence. It is only recently that we have seen hard evidence emerge which points to the positive impact that HR management can make to organisation performance. This evidence comes from the US and is largely attributed to the work of Mark Huselid (1995) of Rutgers University.

Huselid's work provides evidence of a positive link between particular sets — or what he terms "bundles" — of HR practices and organisation performance (as measured by productivity, employee turnover and corporate financial performance). The essence of Huselid's work is an evaluation of "high performance work systems" (including comprehensive employee recruitment and selection procedures, incentive compensation and performance management systems, and extensive employee involvement and training) and particular measures of organisation performance. Based on large-scale survey evidence on the HR practices and financial performance of a number of top US companies, Huselid (1995: 667) found a strong positive relationship between high-performance work practices and firm performance:

> Prior work in both the academic and popular press has argued that the use of High Performance Work Practices will be reflected in better firm performance. This study provides broad evidence in support of these assertions. Across a wider range of industries and firm sizes, I found considerable support for the hypothesis that investments in such practices are associated with lower employee turnover and greater productivity and corporate financial performance.

These findings are quite emphatic: there is evidence of strong and positive linkages between HR practice and organisation performance. Indeed, Huselid (1995: 667) goes on to calculate the dimensions of such linkages and argues that the "magnitude of the returns for investments in High Performance Work Practices is substantial":

> A one standard deviation increase in such practices is associated with a relative 7.05 percent decrease in turnover and, on a per employee basis, $27,044 more in sales and $18,641 and $3,814 more in market value and profits, respectively. These internally consistent and economically and statistically significant values suggest that firms can indeed obtain substantial financial benefits from investing in the practices studied.

While one may harbour reservations on the precise impact of HR practices on bottom line performance — especially the apparent precision of the financial benefits outlined above — a key contribution of Huselid's work is to demonstrate the positive outcomes of adopting particular "bundles" of HR practices, emphasising the potential benefits from investing in HR management. This contribution should not be overstated, however. While this research points to the potential performance benefits that may accrue from investment in HR, such benefits are not universally applicable. Work by writers such as MacDuffie (1995) and Marchington and Grugulis (1999) suggests that "best practice" HRM may only lead to performance improvements where employees have specific and much-needed skills/knowledge, which takes time to develop and nurture. Thus, in organisational contexts where work is more low-skilled, requisite job knowledge and skills can be quickly acquired, and replacement workers are readily available in the labour market, the application of high performance work practices may be considerably less common and, from a calculative "cost–benefit" perspective, less appropriate.

A related and important implication of Huselid's work is that it is the *linkages* between different HR practices which are important, rather than the implementation of a specific and isolated HR practice. Thus, it is the so-called "bundling" of HR practices that lead to the significant gains in organisational performance. As Guest (1998: 65) comments:

> One thing is clear from all of the research: there is no value in investing heavily in specific practices. Performance-related pay, psychometric tests in selection or extensive training will not in themselves bring bottom-line results. The key lies in having the right "bundle" of practices and the challenge for personnel managers is to find it.

Huselid's work does not identify any specific combination or "bundle" of HR practices which will most effectively improve organisational performance. Again, contingency-based approaches seem relevant: different combinations or bundles of HR practices may suit particular circumstances and company needs better than others, especially with respect to such issues as competitive strategy, organisation culture and product range. Another key factor seems to be internal fit; that is, the extent to which HR practices in one area (e.g. reward practices) complements practices in other areas (e.g. recruitment and/or employee development).

Huselid's work also addressed the role of HR practitioners in introducing high performance work practices and identifies three broad areas of competency which practitioners need to develop, namely (a) professional HR capabilities; (b) good business capabilities; and (c) change management capabilities. However, evidence to date suggests that while many HR managers demonstrate competence on the professional dimension, they may not have the requisite business and change management skills. This is clearly an important challenge facing organisations and their HR practitioners, should they seek to introduce some of the high performance work systems suggested by Huselid's pioneering work.

Developments in the Irish Context

The preceding discussion suggests that HR management represents an important area of strategic choice for organisations. HR policies and practices can have a major impact on competitive advantage, organisation structure and culture. However, the Irish research evidence presents quite a mixed picture. Gunnigle and Moore (1994) examined the level of integration between business strategy and HR policies in Ireland using data generated through the Cranfield-University of Limerick (CUL) Study. The main areas of analysis were: (a) the incidence of formal HR strategies in organisations and (b) the extent of involvement of the HR function in strategy formulation. This study found that approximately half of respondent organisations had a written mission statement or corporate strategy, while just less than one-third had a written HR strategy. In assessing the input of the HR function in the formulation of strategy, the results were quite positive. It was found that, in general, HR involvement in strategic areas has increased over recent years. Over half of the firms surveyed reported HR involvement in strategy formulation from the outset. However, although HR involvement has increased, some concerns have been raised that there has simply been greater participation at a strategic level without a corresponding increase in the all-important area of influence. In evaluating the research evidence available in the Irish context, it would appear that while some organisations appear to be successfully aligning HR policies and business strategy, this development does not seem widespread.

More detailed case study evidence on organisations which are attempting both to introduce high performance work practices *and* to evaluate their impact on organisation performance is, not surprisingly, very hard to come by. However, one exception in this respect is Allied Irish Bank. In a paper presented at the 1998 Institute of Personnel and Development Annual Conference, Mike Lewis reviewed AIB's efforts to evaluate the strategic impact of investing in people (Lewis, 1998). Lewis identified two strategic questions which AIB have attempted to address:

- Can we *prove* that investing in people increases shareholder value?

- Can we determine the return that shareholders should expect from *specific* investments?

Lewis outlined the various challenges faced by AIB in both its Irish and international markets, and also reviewed the major change initiatives implemented over a considerable period. Basing their approach on the academic and corporate research on quantifying how HR practices drive company performance, Lewis argues that AIB have gone some considerable way to proving that their investment in people has contributed to increased shareholder value. He also argued that it is possible to determine the return that shareholders should expect from specific HR investments. However, he also acknowledged that it is relatively early days. Nevertheless, the experience of AIB and other Irish organisations attempting to implement various HR changes and evaluate their impact should provide interesting insights into the debate of HR management and organisation performance.

CHANGING ROLES FOR THE HR FUNCTION

In assessing the implications of these developments for the HR function, we may plausibly argue that recent decades have witnessed considerable change in the HR role. In particular, we can point to evidence of important changes such as greater strategic integration of the HR function, a shift away from traditional industrial relations and collective bargaining to a more individual approach, a growth in atypical employment forms, and greater emphasis on other aspects of HR activity, particularly training and development.

In tracing the development of the HR function over recent decades one can identify a predictable pattern of evolution which was characterised by convergence to a prevailing orthodoxy of the HR role. This orthodoxy was based on the premise that the key employer concern in workforce management was the establishment and maintenance of stable industrial relations. Within this approach, the HR function assumed responsibility for managing relations with trade unions. Gunnigle (1998: 17) comments on this role thus:

> While more reactive rather than strategic, this *industrial relations* role was nonetheless significant: it served to both define what personnel work involved and position the personnel management function as a important aspect of the managerial infrastructure.

By the early 1980s, the dominance of industrial relations in the HR role began to unravel. We have already noted that the sources of such change may be traced to the increasingly competitive nature of product and service markets. For the HR function, these changes appear to have heralded a period which essentially appears to be devoid of orthodoxy. Rather, what we see emerging is a range of different roles for the HR function, with no one dominant model apparent (Gunnigle, 1998). Paauwe (1996: 227) captures this trend by suggesting that it is now "almost impossible to speak of *the* personnel function" but rather suggests that contingency approaches are the order of the day, with the role, and even the existence, of the HR function varying according to industrial segment, managerial philosophy, product market performance and so on. It is, however, possible to identify some of the more common models of the HR function that are apparent today. These are outlined below.

Models of the Personnel/Human Resource Function[2]

The Commitment Model
Often labelled "soft" HRM, this was the first model to challenge seriously the industrial relations orthodoxy. It is characterised by a resource perspective of employees incorporating the view that there is an organisational pay-off in performance terms from a combination of "sophisticated" personnel policies designed to develop employee commitment and emphasise the mutuality of management and employee interests. In this model, the personnel/HR function is high-powered and well-resourced with a significant change agent role. This model appears to characterise core business organisations whose competitive strategy is based on a product differentiation/premium price approach, often on a "first to market" basis. Such organisations may employ significant numbers of highly trained technical and engineering staffs whose development and retention are critical to organisational success. This model generally relies on a *union substitution* premise, al-

---

[2] This section is adapted from Gunnigle (1998), "Human Resource Management and the Personnel Function" in W.K. Roche, K. Monks and J. Walsh (eds.), *Human Resource Strategies: Policy and Practice in Ireland*, Dublin: Oak Tree Press.

though organisations with union recognition but where the union role is essentially peripheral also fall within this category.

The Transaction Cost Model

While the commitment model has received much attention, its viability has increasingly come under scrutiny in recent years. In particular, exemplars of the commitment model (e.g. Wang and Digital) experienced intense competitive pressures from low-cost producers. The transaction cost model places the workforce management emphasis on minimising operating costs. Thus, outsourcing becomes an important strategy, particularly in using contracted labour and other forms of "atypical" employment. This approach is also associated with intensification of the pace of workflow and an increased range of work tasks. This model may rely on a *union suppression* premise; often linked to the (management) suggestion that unions inhibit the development of necessary flexibility levels to ensure competitiveness. In this model the key role of the HR function is cost-effective labour supply. The HR role is essentially reactive: dealing with the operational workforce management consequences of a low-cost competitive strategy. This model is likely to prosper in more deregulated environments and, thus, poses many challenges for the European Union's "social market" philosophy.

The Partnership Model

The development of union–management partnerships has been the focus of much recent debate and is considered in depth in Chapter 14. Partnership-based models normally involve employers and trade unions entering into a set of mutual commitments by which: (i) employers recognise and facilitate worker and trade union involvement in strategic decision-making; (ii) workers/ trade unions commit themselves actively to productivity improvements; (iii) the gains of productivity improvements are shared between employers and workers; (iv) productivity improvements do not result in redundancies but rather employers actively seek new markets to keep workers gainfully employed. In essence, partnership-based approaches require that workers and trade unions actively pursue, *with* management, solutions to business problems and appropriate work reorganisation in return for greater involvement in business decisions and in the process of work reorganisation. Within this model, the HR function becomes an important strategic lever in developing the partnership agenda. It also assumes an important role in implementing a range of HR policy initiatives to underpin this new orientation, specifically in areas such as reward systems, management–employee communications, job design and employee development.

Managing without a HR Function

While the great majority of medium and larger organisations tend to have a formal HR function, it is useful to consider the option of managing without a traditional personnel function (see Paauwe 1996). As many organisations move to "leaner" and "flatter" organisation structures, it is clear that the establishment of a traditional HR function is no longer an inevitable consequence of increased organisation scale.

If we consider the option of managing without a formal HR function, there appear to be two principal ways to carry out the HR role, namely: (i) devolvement of HR responsibilities to line management (internal devolution), and/or (ii) outsourcing HR activities to external contractors (external devolution). The first route represents an extension of an ongoing debate about the optimal balance of HR responsibilities between line management and the specialist HR function. Line management have always played a key role in the execution of day-to-day HR activities. However, what is different about the internal devolution argument is the suggestion that line managers should play a greater role in policy development and interpretation, in addition to their traditional role in carrying out HR activities. This theme has developed concurrently with moves towards flatter organisation structures and team-working. Undoubtedly this development is important and will lead to a changing division of labour between HR and line management. However, it is unlikely to lead to a widespread abolition of the HR function.

Another potential threat to the existence of a formal HR function is outsourcing. The transaction cost model, discussed above, places considerable emphasis on the so-called "make or buy" decision (Gunnigle, 1998). In this model it is argued that if a particular unit does not make a demonstrable added-value contribution to the organisation when compared to outsourcing, then such services should be bought in. Two other factors make this option even more attractive: (i) on the demand side, the trend towards smaller organisation scale combined with growth of contracted-in labour means that organisations have less "employees" to manage; and (ii) on the supply side, the proliferation of "management consultants" provides a buoyant source of contracted-in HR services.

CONCLUSION: KEY AREAS OF CHANGE IN HRM

This chapter has sought to provide an overview of contemporary developments influencing workforce management and the HR role in organisations. Much of this discussion has emphasised the impact of competitive pressures on HRM and on attempts by organisations to align their business and HRM strategies more closely. The aggregate effects of such change are manifest across a range of HR activity areas. While it is not possible fully to review the extent of change that has taken place in HRM over the past two decades, it is necessary to point to some of the major areas of change and innovation. What follows, therefore, is a summary of the main changes in the nature of HR practice, grouped under traditional HRM categories, together with an outline of how the various contributions to this book address key challenges in workforce management in Irish organisations.[3]

HRM Strategy/Structure

As noted in this chapter, HRM concerns have become a more significant concern of strategic decision-makers. HRM is increasingly recognised as a key element in implementing competitive strategies. In particular, we are witnessing an increased focus on improving the performance of business units, particularly in relation to increasing productivity and reducing labour costs ("more for less" focus). We have also witnessed important changes in organisation structure, incorporating a significant emphasis on reducing bureaucracy, job grades and employment numbers. In the European Union, we find a strong trend towards rationalisation of production and logistical operations, e.g. call centres, customer support. There has also been some growth in job movement, often to low-cost regions. We have concurrently seen a growth in mergers, acquisitions and strategic alliances. This development has placed a greater HR focus on managing international/expatriate workforces and the standardisation of HR practices. Finally at this broad level, we find that flexibility is a key concern. We see a particular focus on increasing functional, numerical and financial flexibility. All three forms are not necessarily complementary, however, and one can find different management approaches among different employee categories (core versus peripheral workers) and related differences in HR approaches (soft versus hard).

Part One of this book addresses the context of HRM in Ireland. In this chapter we reviewed the strategic significance of HRM, with particular emphasis on strategy/HR linkages and the impact of HR practice on organisation performance. In the next chapter,

---

[3] For a comprehensive review of changes in HRM in European countries, see Sparrow and Hiltrop (1994).

Noreen Heraty reviews developments in the Irish labour market. This is clearly an area of immense interest to HR practitioners, both in terms of the overall supply of labour and the actual quality of labour, in terms of education, competencies, etc. In the final chapter of this section, Graeme Buckingham looks at the issue of motivating and retaining employees, with particular emphasis on the effective management of so-called "knowledge workers".

Recruitment and Selection
Part Two of this text deals with sourcing a high quality workforce. As we prepare for the new millennium, recruitment and selection are being viewed as two of the key issues facing organisations. As people are increasingly acknowledged as a key element of an organisation's competitive advantage, continuing skills shortages and the prospect of a significant decline in the number of young people — the so-called "demographic time bomb" — sees the recruitment and selection process move to the top of the personnel specialist's agenda. Recruitment and selection is thus a critical element of workforce management and we have seen considerable development in this area over recent decades. One such development has been the trend towards the deregulation of labour markets, particularly in "highly regulated" countries, such as Germany and Sweden. We have also witnessed public policy initiatives which attempt to increase incentives/ pressures to work and reduce extent and cost of welfare provision. Another important development has been changes in selection criteria. Of particular significance in this regard has been a move away from "job fit" criteria (matching needs of particular job to skills and abilities of applicants) to more amorphous "employability"/"adaptability" criterion, particularly the ability to learn new skills and adapt to different job roles over time. A third development in this area is the desire to increase labour mobility. Unlike Ireland, many European countries are characterised by ageing workforces and, consequently, face the prospect of future

labour shortages. We are therefore likely to experience more initiatives to increase labour mobility between European countries and probable growth in recruitment of non-EU workers. In some organisations, including areas of the public sector, we see some shift from an internal labour market to an external labour market focus, incorporating an emphasis on recruiting "new blood" from outside the organisation (where available). Finally, we also see a trend towards the increased democratisation of selection systems, involving greater involvement of applicants in the selection process and greater focus on "wooing" candidates into employment.

In the Irish context, recent years have seen organisations encounter increased difficulties in the recruitment and retention of staff. If the success of an organisation significantly depends on its staff, getting it right first time is of the utmost importance. Part Two of this text addresses many of the key issues which confront organisations in managing the recruitment and selection process. In Chapter 4, Gerry McMahon and Anne O'Carroll review the recruitment process, while in Chapter 5, Gerry McMahon and Jennifer Lee consider the area of employee selection. These chapters comprehensively review the varying stages and techniques in the employment process, including the vital area of selection interviewing. In Chapter 6, selection specialist Dermot Rush considers developments with respect to the use of selection tests and provides guidelines on the use of testing to aid selection decisions. Finally, in Chapter 7, Bob Pattinson considers the process by which new employees are integrated and socialised into their new organisation.

Performance Management
Part Three reviews the area of performance management. Performance management is a key variable, which impacts upon organisational effectiveness and growth. In view of the strategic pressures on organisations, it is becoming increasingly evident that organisations need to monitor performance carefully if they

are to realise improvements in productivity and growth. We can identify a number of key organisational and social variables that impact upon performance. These have been reviewed earlier and include the propensity towards organisational delayering, with its concomitant widening of spans of control; devolvement of accountability and responsibility; changing career and job expectations; the increased use of flexible working arrangements; and the greater individualisation of the employment relationship. All of these factors are impacting upon the nature of the employment relationship and are placing increasing importance on managers' ability to manage the performance of their staff and teams. However, effective performance management does not operate in a vacuum and thus must take cognisance of the related HR choices in areas such as training and development (Chapter 8) and management development (Chapter 9), both comprehensively reviewed by, respectively, Tom Garavan and Con Egan, and Tom Garavan and Aidan Lawrence. The literature on performance management reveals several terms that are often used interchangeably, such as performance appraisal, performance assessment, performance evaluation and job appraisal. In practice, we find that these terms are invariably all concerned with measuring an individual's performance in a given job against predetermined work standards and involve designing a formal system to facilitate observation, monitoring, analysis, feedback and target setting. In Chapter 10, Bob Pattinson reviews the performance appraisal process and provides specific guidelines on establishing and maintaining appraisal systems. Finally, in Chapter 11, Karl O'Connor, a leading practitioner in the area of coaching and mentoring, outlines how these techniques can be effectively implemented in a manner which benefits both the organisation and employees.

Employee Relations

Part Four reviews the area of employee relations. As we have noted earlier in this chapter, employee relations has traditionally been the most significant aspect of the work of Irish HR practitioners. Indeed, the traditional role of the personnel manager in most Irish organisations might more appropriately be described as "industrial relations manager", given their primary concern with collective bargaining and trade union interactions. While the last decade has undoubtedly witnessed some diminution of this "industrial relations" emphasis and a concomitant broadening of the HR role, employee relations, as a generic area of HR activity, remains a most critical area in workforce management. Of course, the very nature of employee relations is a source of some debate. Traditional definitions focused on the concept of *industrial* rather than *employee* relations. Such an approach reflected an emphasis on the formal regulation of the employment relationship through collective bargaining between organised employees and employers. This perspective remains significant as employers, trade unions and governments seek to develop rules and norms to govern employment relations at organisational, industrial, national and supranational levels. However, as the nature of employment has changed, the term "employee relations" has achieved increased prominence. The concept of employee relations is seen as embracing a broader scope than industrial relations, incorporating, in particular, non-union and more "individualist" approaches to management–employee relations.

A critical element in the employment relationship is the area of reward management. Recent years have seen considerable innovation in the area of pay, benefit and incentive systems. Such innovation has embraced the so-called "de-levelling" of pay systems, involving increasing the pay differentials between people at the top and bottom of organisational hierarchies. Essentially, this means that employees seen as making a greater "organisation contribution" by virtue of their technical and/or managerial competencies, are receiving much higher pay levels. Secondly, we see the greater use of contingent pay systems, particularly with respect to performance-related pay, bonuses, etc. A third important trend has been increased experimentation with reward systems, including a greater focus on the "individualisation" of rewards ("cafeteria" benefits), skill-based pay, and performance-related emphasis. Finally, we have witnessed growth in the utilisation of profit-sharing and share-ownership schemes.

In Chapter 12, Michael Morley and Alma McCarthy consider the management of rewards, with particular emphasis on the establishment and maintenance of an appropriate reward system. This chapter also addresses the various dimensions of pay, incentives and benefits as possible components of a reward package, and also considers the contentious issue of pay as a motivating factor in employment.

Another key area impacting on the nature of employee relations in organisations is management–employee communications. This area is addressed in Chapter 13 by Eugenie Houston. In Chapter 14, John O'Dowd considers the development of partnership-based industrial relations arrangements at enterprise level. This is a rapidly developing area, and John provides considerable case evidence and guidelines on the development of partnership arrangements between trade unions and employers. The final chapters of this section address two more traditional — but nevertheless critical — elements in establishing and maintaining good employee relations; namely, the management of disciplinary and grievance issues (Chapter 15, Gerry McMahon and Orla Maher) and the negotiations process (Chapter 16, Gerry McMahon and Ciara Heslin).

The Legal Context
Part Five explores the legal framework within which workforce management takes place. Two particular dimensions of employment or labour law primarily concern HR practitioners. Firstly,

we have *individual employment law*, which concentrates on the relationship between the individual worker and the employer and, secondly, we have the area of *collective labour law*, which is concerned with regulating the relationship between employers and collectivities of employees — normally trade unions. Both these dimensions are addressed in the four chapters on the legal context, written by Adrian Twomey. In Chapter 17, Adrian considers the nature of the contract of employment and the various duties and responsibilities this places on employers and employees. Chapter 18 reviews the key area of protective employment legislation and covers issues such as dismissals, redundancy and health and safety. Chapter 19 deals with collective labour law, while in the final chapter in this section (Chapter 20), Adrian deals with the issue of equality legislation and its implications for organisations.

Employee Welfare

The final section of this text (**Part Six**) addresses issues relating to employee welfare in the workplace. This is an increasingly significant concern for both managers and employees. In particular, we have witnessed initiatives that attempt both to reconcile work and family issues and to improve the organisational context within which work is carried out. On the other hand, it is argued that the period since the early 1980s has witnessed some regression in the quality of work life in many organisations. This is generally traced to intensification in the pace of work and deterioration in working conditions with regard to dimensions such as job security and reward packages. In Chapter 21, Eugenie Houston considers the issue of work and family and addresses a number of key areas including family/work conflicts, parental leave, childcare and flexible work patterns. In Chapter 22, Tom Garavan and Anne Morgan review the area of occupational health and employee welfare in the workplace. This chapter focuses on a number of dimensions of occupational health and welfare of considerable interest to organisations. In particular, it reviews the importance of managing occupational health and welfare and the potential benefits for employers and workers. It also looks at specific aspects such as smoking, alcohol misuse, drug abuse, HIV/AIDS, violence and bullying, and stress, with particular emphasis on developing and maintaining appropriate workplace policies on such issues.

References

Beaumont, P.B. (1995), "The European Union and Developments in Industrial Relations" in P. Gunnigle and W.K. Roche (eds.), *New Challenges to Irish Industrial Relations*, Dublin: Oak Tree Press in association with the Labour Relations Commission.

Fombrun, C., N. Tichy and M. Devanna (1984), *Strategic Human Resource Management*, New York: Wiley.

Guest, D. (1998), "Combine Harvest", *People Management*, 29 October: pp. 64–6.

Gunnigle, P. (1998), "Human Resource Management and the Personnel Function" in W.K. Roche, K. Monks and J. Walsh (eds.), *Human Resource Management Strategies: Policy and Practice in Ireland*, Dublin: Oak Tree Press.

Gunnigle, P. and S. Moore (1994), "Linking Business Strategy and Human Resource Management: Issues and Implications", *Personnel Review*, Vol. 23, No. 1: pp. 63–84.

Hastings, T. (1994), *Semi-states in Crisis: The Challenge for Industrial Relations in the ESB and other major Semi-state Companies*, Dublin: Oak Tree Press.

Hofer, C. and D. Schendel (1978), *Strategy Formulation: Analytical Concepts*, St. Paul: West Publishing.

Huselid, M.A. (1995), "The Impact of Human Resource Management Practices on Turnover, Productivity, and Corporate Financial Performance", *Academy of Management Journal*, Vol. 38, No. 3: pp. 635–72.

Lewis, M. (1998), "The Strategic Impact of Investing in People", Paper presented to the Institute of Personnel and Development (Ireland) Annual Conference, *People Strategies for a New Age*, Galway, April.

MacDuffie, J. (1995), "Human Resource Bundles and Manufacturing Performance: Organisational Logic and Flexible Production Systems in the World Auto Industry", *Industrial and Labor Relations Review*, Vol. 48, No. 2: pp. 197–221.

Marchington, M. and I. Grugulis (1999), "'Best Practice' Human Resource Management: Perfect Opportunity or Dangerous Illusion?", Seventh Annual John Lovett Memorial Lecture, University of Limerick, 25 March.

Paauwe, J. (1996), "Personnel Management without Personnel Managers", Chapter Six in P. Flood, M.J. Gannon and J. Paauwe (eds.), *Managing Without Traditional Methods: International Innovations in Human Resource Management*, Wokingham: Addison-Wesley.

Porter, M. (1985), *Competitive Advantage: Creating and Sustaining Superior Performance*, New York: The Free Press.

Porter, M. (1987), "From Competitive Advantage to Corporate Strategy", *Harvard Business Review*, May–June: pp. 43–59.

Purcell, J. (1989), "The Impact of Corporate Strategy on Human Resource Management" in J. Storey (ed.), *New Perspectives on Human Resource Management*, London: Routledge.

Roche, W.K. and P. Gunnigle (1995) "Competition and the New Industrial Relations Agenda" in P. Gunnigle and W.K. Roche (eds.) *New Challenges to Irish Industrial Relations*, Dublin: Oak Tree Press/Labour Relations Commission.

Sparrow, P.R. and J.-M. Hiltrop (1994), *European Human Resource Management in Transition*, London: Prentice Hall.

CHAPTER 2

THE IRISH LABOUR MARKET IN PERSPECTIVE

Noreen Heraty

INTRODUCTION

Developments in contemporary personnel/human resource management (HRM) continue to generate considerable interest in both practitioner and academic circles, as it becomes increasingly evident that firms are having to confront heterogeneous, dynamic and therefore uncertain environments. The debate on what influences HRM is a lengthy one. A considerable body of recent research (see, for example, Westphal et al., 1997; Wolf, 1997; DiMaggio and Powell, 1983) has examined how institutional arrangements, particularly those external to the organisation, can have a significant impact on internal and external labour market functioning. This research has focused on the role that, for example, the State, professional associations and awarding bodies, regulatory environments, and educational systems can play in shaping the nature and practice of management within organisations. This chapter concentrates on a key dimension of this external environment — the Irish labour market — in an attempt to understand why organisations develop the range of HRM practices that they do. Recent key determinants of Irish labour market policy, such as general overall economic performance, industrial policy, population and demographic trends, labour market participation, occupational structures and participation in education and training, are all discussed to provide a broad context within which to interpret HRM practices and outcomes. It should be noted, however, that the picture of the Irish labour market presented here reflects that which is in operation towards the end of the 1990s — as history indicates, changes in economic performance have significant impacts on labour market functioning and ultimately on the nature and practice of personnel/ human resource management.

ECONOMIC PERFORMANCE, EMPLOYMENT AND UNEMPLOYMENT

A cursory examination of Ireland's economic performance is critical to the development of an understanding of how and why the labour market operates as it does and the consequent implications for labour demands, sectoral stratification, occupational segregation and the general appeal of Ireland as a work location. This section summarily reviews the performance of the Irish economy in recent years as a backdrop to structured labour market policy and interventions.

Like most of its European counterparts, Ireland has experienced considerable variation in levels of economic activity over the past 20 years. Throughout much of the 1980s, economic growth was sluggish, inflation was high, unemployment escalated as manufacturing employment was almost halved, and Ireland's financial debt became unsustainable. As the recession receded and the global economy became more buoyant, some improvement in Irish economic activity was recorded, prompted by a devaluation of the Irish pound (1986) and a reorientation of fiscal policy to curb capital expenditure. The end of the 1980s saw some improvement in output growth rate, unemployment began to fall and both the inflation rate and the public sector deficit fell below the European average.

However, from 1994 onwards, the performance of the Irish economy has been unprecedented. Labelled the "Celtic Tiger", a number of commentators (Sweeney, 1998; Gray, 1997; CBI, 1997, 1998; FÁS, 1998; OECD, 1997b) have variously identified a range of key performance indicators of Ireland's economy over the past four years:

- Expansion of the domestic economy continues with the growth rate of real GDP averaging over 8 per cent a year (9.5 per cent in 1998) which is three to four times the EU average and makes Ireland's economy the fastest growing in the OECD. In 1998, Ireland was ranked eleventh in the World Economic Forum Competitiveness League, up from fifteenth in 1997 and twenty-second in 1996. Some slowing down is expected for 1999, although the Central Bank of Ireland (CBI) estimates that the economy will grow by a further 6.5 to 7 per cent in 1999.

- Growth in the Irish economy has been fuelled by a very rapid growth in exports of goods and services, so that Ireland's export growth rate far exceeds EU and OECD averages and is surpassed only by those of South Korea, Mexico and Poland and reflects the stronger growth in European export markets and continuing inward investment.

- The numbers at work are growing by at least 4 per cent a year (5.5 per cent in 1998) and the standardised unemployment rate has fallen below the EU average (10.2 per cent) and, at the time of writing (March 1999), stands at 7.2 per cent, which is the lowest it has been since 1979. The main increases in labour supply are concentrated among people with higher levels of qualification, while the numbers in the labour force who have not completed secondary education continue to fall. Estimates for 1999 suggest that employment will increase by approximately 3.5 per cent while the unemployment figure will drop below 6.5 per cent.

- Industrial production in Ireland has been impressively high when compared to other EU countries. The bulk of total manufacturing production, which increased by 16.9 per cent between 1997 and 1998, can be attributed to the strong performance of a small number of high-technology sectors dominated by foreign multinationals, particularly pharmaceuticals (production almost doubled between 1996 and 1997), electrical engineering, office equipment and the production of data processing machinery (including computer components). It is estimated that manufacturing output for 1999 will show a further increase of 12.5 per cent over 1998 figures.

- Traditional indigenous sector growth is more modest, at approximately 4.3 per cent (CBI, 1998), although some manufacturing production industries continue to fare poorly, reflecting, perhaps, the shift in recent years to high value-added industries for European and global export.

Table 2.1: Total Employment in Ireland, 1987–1999

Year	Total at Work	Change	Change in Non-agricultural
1987	1,090,000	+9,000	+13,000
1988	1,090,000	0	–1,000
1989	1,088,000	–2,000	+1,000
1990	1,134,000	+46,000	+39,000
1991	1,134,000	0	+14,000
1992	1,145,000	+11,000	+10,000
1993	1,152,000	+7,000	+17,000
1994	1,188,000	+36,000	+38,000
1995	1,248,000	+60,000	+59,000
1996	1,297,000	+49,000	+54,000
1997	1,338,000	+41,000	+45,000
1998*	1,385,000	+47,000	N/A
1999*	1,418,000	+33,000	N/A

*Estimates

Source: CSO Labour Force Surveys, 1987–1999.

The transformation from a relatively underdeveloped economy in the late 1950s to one capable of supporting industrial expansion and economic growth involved major changes in the structure of employment and a substantial relocation of the labour force. Trends in the sectoral distribution of employment indicate a progressive decline in agricultural and in traditional industrial employment, and a dramatic rise in the service sector, particularly private services. Between 1980 and 1996, Irish non-agricultural employment growth of 26 per cent exceeded that of the EU12 (7 per cent) and the US with 15 per cent growth (Duffy et al., 1997: 39). Of the current labour force of 1.5 million people, approximately 10 per cent are employed in agriculture, 28.8 per cent are employed in industry and the remaining 61.2 per cent are employed in services.

During 1995 and 1996, the largest share of employment creation was accounted for by the expansion of the services sector, with increases of 48,000 and 43,000 recorded respectively. This pattern was reversed somewhat in 1997, when employment creation was largely attributed to the industrial sector and particularly to the manufacturing sector (growth in employment of approximately 17 per cent) and to the building and construction sector (10,000 job increase), although employment in the services sector did also increase by 14,000. The 1997 labour force survey suggests that the overall picture of employment growth indicates that jobs in the service sector are increasing ten times faster than in industry, and almost fifty times faster than in manufacturing. However, the latest Economist Intelligence Unit (EIU, 1997) report cautions that there is a danger that the Irish economy is approaching full capacity and that there are already bottlenecks and skills shortages appearing in certain sectors. During the same period, total numbers of unemployed fell (see Table 2.2). The Irish unemployment rate in 1991 (14.5 per cent) was almost twice the then rate for the EU overall (8.2 per cent) but today, Ireland's unemployment rate of 7.2 per cent is well below the overall EU average.

Table 2.2: Employment and Unemployment, 1996–1999

(Annual average 000s)	1996	1997	1998 e	1999f
Industry	362	411	440	463
Services	809	877	928	963
Agriculture	137	135	134	130
Total Employment	*1,308*	*1,423*	*1,502*	*1,556*
Unemployment (labour force basis)	188	155	126	109
Labour Force	1,496	1,577	1,628	1,665
Standardised Unemployment Rate (SUR)*	*(11.5)*	*(9.75)*	*(7.75)*	*(6.5)*

* based on International Labour Office (ILO) definitions; e = estimate; f = forecast
Source: Central Bank of Ireland, Winter, 1997 and 1998.

It is estimated that Ireland's strong fiscal position is primarily as a result of buoyancy in tax revenue, reflecting the continued high rate of job creation and consumption growth. The sustained level of economic success in recent times is evidenced in changes in personal incomes over the last ten years or so. In 1987, incomes in Ireland were 63 per cent of those in the UK, and Ireland was recognised as one of the poorest countries in the EU. Today, Ireland has surpassed the UK and stands close to the EU average.

The main provision of current economic policy, geared towards sustaining growth and development, is detailed in the most recent programme for government and includes provision for:

- A reduction of the tax rates, both personal and corporate;

- A cap on both net current and capital spending;

- The elimination of exchequer borrowing in order to cap the public debt;

- A commitment to enter the final stage of EMU;

- Adherence to the terms of the current national wage agreement, Partnership 2000; and

- The introduction of a national hourly minimum wage.

Statutory minimum wages currently exist in 17 OECD member countries and are due to be introduced soon in both Ireland and the UK. Considerable and often contentious debate surrounds the effectiveness or otherwise of statutory minimum wages: those in favour of minimum wages argue that they provide a socially acceptable level of earnings, can help alleviate poverty and provide an incentive to work; on the other hand, it is argued that statutory minimum wages will result in fewer jobs in certain trades and sectors where employers feel unable to pay such rates. In Ireland, a national minimum wage commission has recommended that a national minimum rate should be introduced for experienced adult workers, set at two-thirds of median earnings — at current minimum rates of pay, this would imply a minimum rate of £4.40 an hour. The commission further recommended that workers under the age of 18 be paid 70 per cent of the adult rate and new entrants without experience be paid 75 per cent for the first year, 80 per cent for the second year and 90 per cent for the third year (*European Industrial Relations Review*, 1998: 33). The introduction of a national statutory minimum wage remains highly contentious and will likely be the focus of considerable discussion and negotiation between now and its targeted introduction date of 1 April 2000.

A critical objective for government now concerns the maintenance of social partnership, which arguably has been the pivot upon which economic success has been wrought (EIU, 1997). Rumblings of discontent are being heard as the perception that the benefits of economic growth are not being evenly distributed gains momentum. There is some evidence of wage drift away from the Partnership 2000 agreement — even allowing for the local bargaining clause. CSO labour market survey figures for 1998 estimate that average hourly earnings for 1998 were up by 6.8 per cent — the corresponding increase for 1997 was 3 per cent. CBI (1998) forecasts that the upward pressure on private sector wages, reflective of labour market shortages and of property prices, will result in earnings per capita rising by a further 6.5 per cent in 1999, which will intensify pressures for public sector pay rises.

INDUSTRIAL POLICY AND THE IRISH LABOUR MARKET

In the period following the foundation of the Irish Free State and until the late 1950s, the Irish economy was inwardly focused, with industrial policies concentrating on the imposition of trade barriers and the preservation of indigenous ownership of industry. However, the 1950s witnessed considerable debate concerning Ireland's poorly developed manufacturing and industrial infrastructure. There were persistent calls for greater liberalisation of trade and commerce, resulting in the development of a coherent industrial policy that focused specifically on creating a more open economy. Critical to this industrial strategy was the attraction of foreign, particularly US, investment which was actively encouraged through a progressive series of tax incentives, capital investment grants, advance factories, and so forth.

The net effect of much of this industrial policy is evidenced today in the locating in Ireland of close to one-quarter (24 per cent) of all available US manufacturing investments in Europe, and close to 14 per cent of all foreign direct investment (FDI) projects locating in Europe, even though Ireland accounts for just one per cent of the European population (*Economist*, 1997). This has led to the establishment of a significant cluster of related firms sufficient to supply each other with services (from development to distribution) and to the creation of a pool of suitably skilled labour — a further incentive for increased FDI, whereby new firms can draw upon this established integrated industry network. Since 1980, 40 per cent of all new US inward investment in European electronics has come to Ireland, while nearly one third of all personal computers sold in Europe are now made in Ireland (*Economist*, 1997). The computer software industry employs more than 15,000 people and expansion of this sector is likely to continue. Part of the reason for such high inward investment concerns the volume of government aid on offer, such as a generous subsidy programme based partly on the promise of jobs but also including, where appropriate, rent subsidies, offsets against capital investment, and a low tax rate for profits derived from "manufacturing and qualifying services" of just 10 per cent. The Irish economy is further attracting considerable new investments in international banking and financial services, food processing, pharmaceuticals and telemarketing. Foreign-owned firms are now said to account for 30 per cent of the economy and nearly 40 per cent of exports (*Economist*, 1997).

Payne (1997), commenting on the call-centre sector, notes that one-third of all US call centres in Europe are now located in Ireland. The call centre market was actively targeted, since it was felt that it would slot in well with the explosive growth taking place in both the computer and software sectors in Ireland. Call centres are a focal point that can handle everything from computer and software inquiries, to banking, hotel and airline reservations. Currently, there are approximately 50 domestic and foreign call-centre companies based in Ireland employing more than 4,000 people, and it is estimated that this sector will continue to expand.

It is evident that foreign direct investment (FDI) has made a significant contribution to the development and modernisation of the Irish economy particularly since much of our recent high growth has been driven by exports from the foreign-owned sector. It is arguable that foreign-owned firms have had a positive impact on the development of indigenous companies through the purchase of goods and services, although critics of industrial policy make a strong case for the concomitant neglect of indigenous industry. It is also apparent that FDI has played some role in the upgrading of Ireland's infrastructure and skills base. Commenting on overall economic performance, the CBI (1998) cautions that reduced corporate profitability in the US and increasing skills shortages in Ireland will likely impact on this level of FDI in Ireland over the next number of years.

CHARACTERISTICS OF THE IRISH LABOUR FORCE

An editorial in *The Economist* in May 1997 suggested that foreign companies cite a number of specific attractions of having Ireland as a European base, including the combination of English as the spoken language, with a recognised pro-European outlook, and of the well-educated workforce, particularly at the upper end. Over the past decade, the Irish workforce has become increasingly better educated and a higher proportion of young people are remaining in further education/training. These and related labour market characteristics are examined in detail here.

Demographic Trends

The population of Ireland has remained somewhat static through the 1980s and early 1990s and, although there is evidence that the population is beginning to grow again, it remains, at approximately 3.66 million people, the second lowest country population in the EU. Ireland has a relatively young population but, as in other EU member states, the number of children is falling due to a somewhat declining birth rate (see Table 2.3). However, Ireland continues to have an above-average EU birth rate. Since 1991, the overall decrease in the 0–15 age category is recorded at 34 per cent. This overall fall in the Irish birth rate has had an effect on the dependency ratio, which is estimated at about 57 per cent and is expected to fall to between 45 and 50 per cent over the next 10 years (CSO, 1995) and has some appreciable implications for some increases in overall living standards, i.e. fewer individuals in the economically inactive age group depending on those who are economically active.

Table 2.3: Population Classification by Age Group, 1971–1996

Age Group	1971	1979	1981	1986	1991	1996	% Change 1991–96
Under 1 year	64,886	71,353	73,379	61,172	53,044	48,854	–7.9
1–4 years	250,769	272,122	279,625	262,906	220,699	201,540	–8.7
5–9 years	316,940	350,140	349,487	350,650	318,503	282,943	–11.0
10–14 years	298,557	336,293	341,238	349,973	348,328	326,087	–6.4
15–19 years	267,727	317,368	326,429	331,100	335,026	339,536	+1.3
20–24 years	215,251	266,271	276,127	286,424	266,572	293,354	+10.0
25–29 years	172,993	239,425	246,053	258,439	246,321	259,045	+5.2
30–34 years	151,351	220,116	231,958	242,689	249,071	260,929	+4.8
35–39 years	149,107	178,478	193,829	229,740	237,889	255,676	+7.5
40–44 years	152,729	159,407	165,924	191,751	225,683	240,441	+6.5
45–49 years	160,124	152,441	151,850	161,740	187,762	225,400	+20.0
50–54 years	159,082	151,686	149,680	147,511	156,806	186,647	+19.0
55–59 years	154,847	154,065	149,606	142,215	142,549	153,807	+7.9
60–64 years	134,066	137,676	139,266	139,978	134,566	137,946	+2.5
65 years +	329,819	361,375	388,924	383,855	402,900	413,882	+2.72

Source: CSO Census Figures

The Irish workforce will continue to expand in the medium term as those currently of school-going age enter the labour market. However, as in many other EU countries, some evidence of the ageing of the population is beginning to emerge — i.e. the average age of the population is increasing. Between 1981 and 1996, the Irish population aged nearly three years, leading to an average

age of 33.6 in 1996 compared with 30.8 in 1981 (CSO, 1998). This is unlikely to have any impact on the short term but, as the average age of the working-age population moves closer to the 50s, then this will have significant implications for personnel policies, particularly in terms of succession planning, training/retraining, rewards and so forth. Furthermore, as the population ages, and, where the birth rate continues to fall, the dependency ration will increase as greater numbers depend on the shrinking economically active cohort. The figures here suggest, however, that a significant ageing (or "greying") of Ireland's workforce will not occur for at least another 20 years.

Migration
Net outward migration has traditionally constituted an integral feature of the Irish labour market; more than 1.2 million people have left Ireland since the foundation of the State in 1921. While the 1970s witnessed a periodical reversal of this trend, net emigration resumed through the 1980s, rising from 9,000 in 1984 to 46,000 in 1989. However, recession in the world economy, particularly in the US and the UK, stemmed the outflow in the early 1990s, and the considerable upswing in the Irish economic environment more recently has reduced the numbers migrating abroad. Indeed, latest CSO migration figures (1997) indicate that the number of immigrants into Ireland has been steadily increasing in recent years and reached a high of 44,000 in 1997.

FÁS (1996), in a review of migration trends using the 1996 census figures, note the following:

- There was a cumulative net immigration of 3,000 between 1991 and 1996 — a sharp reversal of the cumulative outflow of 134,000 between 1986 and 1991;

- The average net inflow in the early 1990s was 600 — the average net outflow in the late 1980s was 27,000, with a peak outflow of 44,000 in 1988–89;

- Most of the increases in inflows and decreases in outflows relate to movements between Ireland and the UK;

- Immigrants are typically Irish nationals who are returning migrants;

- Whole family emigration has almost ceased;

- A fall of almost 60 per cent has occurred in the level of movement to the UK, with a significant increase in the flows (in both directions) between Ireland and continental EU countries.

Overall economic buoyancy has thus resulted in a reversal of external migration — it is estimated that, in the absence of external migration, the Irish labour force has the capacity to expand by between 20,000 and 25,000 persons each year (1.5 per cent of the total labour force). Sweeney (1998) suggests that, since the 1990s, there have been many non-Irish people seeking work in Ireland and also seeking that "quality of life" which has often been cited as compensation for lower living standards. He indicates that this ephemeral "quality of life" — meaning the good social life, proximity to countryside and local amenities — is often given as the reason for staying in a country which traditionally offered few opportunities for well-qualified people to change jobs.

Labour Force Participation
While aggregate changes in the Irish labour force over the past 15 years have at times been erratic, the overall trend has been upward. In particular, there has been a steady growth of approximately 2.2 per cent per annum in the size of the labour force during the period 1992–1997, although figures for 1998 suggest an increase of 3.25 per cent. A number of diverse developments underpin this trend:

(a) Female Labour Force Participation

Overall employment expansion in the 1990s has seen very rapid growth in the numbers of women working in Ireland. Expressed as a proportion of the total female population of working age, the number of females in the labour force has increased from 34.1 per cent in 1992 to 47 per cent in 1997 (FÁS, 1998; CBI, 1998; Baker et al, 1998). Female employment in Ireland grew by 30 per cent between 1991 and 1996, while women's employment in the EU as a whole was static over the same period. Over the entire period since 1981, female employment growth (with an increase of 184,000 or 56 per cent) has greatly outpaced the expansion in male employment (up by 17,000 or 2 per cent over the same period). Speculation on the causes of this increased participation has focused on factors such as smaller family sizes, changing structure of employment demand, institutional factors, and improvements in educational attainment. FÁS (1998) note the emergence of changes in the occupational pattern of women's jobs in Ireland, where within the professional occupations, for example, women's share has increased most rapidly in the business professions and (from a much smaller base) in engineering and science. Their share has also risen, but more slowly, in education and has declined sharply among religious professionals. However, while female participation continues to increase in Ireland, the current degree of participation, estimated at about 47 per cent, remains lower than that in other EU and OECD countries.

(b) Labour Force Growth

The Irish labour force grew by an incredible 11 per cent in the five years between 1991 and 1996 (CSO Census of Population, 1996). Rapid growth in the labour force is predicted to the year 2005. The latest ESRI report (Duffy et al., 1997) predicts labour force growth of over 2 per cent between 1996 and 2005 and of 1 per cent thereafter. The factors underlying these increases in the Irish labour force, as detailed earlier, are:

- Demographic changes, resulting in a strong inflow of young people into the labour market. Significant changes are evidenced in the age structure of the population where, in 1981, 30 per cent of the Irish labour force was aged 15–24; the corresponding figure in 1997 is less than 19 per cent.

- Increasing female labour force participation, which has risen from 39 per cent of the 15–64 age cohort in 1990 to 47 per cent in 1997.

- Changing patterns of migration, with the substantial net outflows that characterised much of the 1980s contrasting with estimated net immigration of 15,000 in the year to April 1997.

- Growth of the services sector more generally, and personal services in particular, has provided greater opportunities for labour force participation. For example, the numbers employed in recreational services increased by 60 per cent between 1991 and 1996, while there was a 39 per cent increase in those working in personal services during the same period (CSO, 1996).

(c) Growth in Non-standard Employment
The growth of non-standard work forms has been observed in several OECD countries, including Ireland, since the mid- to late 1970s. The Irish Labour Market Study (1997) indicates that while the incidence of part-time work, as a proportion of total employment in the Irish economy, is relatively low when compared with other EU countries, it has increased significantly in recent years. From 1983–1993, virtually all employment creation related to part-time work, which is, perhaps, reflective of the shift to service sector employment during this period. Part-time work remains much more common among women than men (just over 5 per cent of employed males were working part-time in 1997). Just under a quarter (23 per cent) of all women in employment work part-time, and part-time work has accounted for about one-third of the in-

crease in female employment in recent years. Almost 50 per cent of females engaged in part-time work are to be found in service-type occupations, with a further 20 per cent engaged in clerical work. Nearly all the additional part-time jobs for women have been in four sectors — personal services, distribution, health and education. The increase has been more limited in sectors such as manufacturing, building and transport. The Labour Force Survey (1997) indicates that almost nine out of every ten persons working part-time are not looking for full-time work.

The current proportion of part-time work in Ireland is 12.3 per cent, indicating that part-time working is still less prevalent here than in many other EU member states. In 1996, for example, almost 70 per cent of women workers in the Netherlands, and 45 per cent of those in the UK, were working part-time. However, since 1993, the unprecedented growth in the Irish economy has resulted in the creation of mainly full-time jobs. This about-swing may be a result of the experienced expansion of manufacturing employment and the current "boom" being experienced in the building and construction industry. Overall, the increased propensity towards part-time employment may be indicative of increased flexibility in the Irish labour market. However, it remains exceptionally low by EU standards and there remains continued scope for an upward trend to continue. Temporary work, as a proportion of overall employment, currently stands at just 7 per cent.

(d) Occupational Trends

Changes in the occupational structure of the labour market are inherently associated with technological developments, product market variations, sectoral composition, and the general nature of employment practices (in terms of work structuring, composition of employment, flexibility and so forth). In 1997, a report on occupational employment forecasts to 2003 was completed jointly by FÁS and the ESRI (Duggan et al., 1997) in an effort to determine the changing pattern of occupational segregation in the Irish labour market and to identify possible variations in skill requirements across 14 broadly identified occupational classifications.

Over the period 1997–2003, it is expected that significant changes in broad occupational groupings will occur which will have appreciable impacts on the distribution of overall employment. Using data generated in the report, Table 2.4 provides details of where the strongest changes in employment distribution are expected to occur.

Table 2.4: Changes in Employment Distribution

Occupational Groups	Employment % Change 1995–2003	Distribution of Total Employment % Change	
		1981	*2003*
Agricultural Occupations	–18	15.6	7.3
Managers	+38	5.0	7.7
Proprietors in services	+31	3.3	3.4
Professional Workers	+37	9.4	14.2
Associate Professionals	+32	4.3	5.8
Clerical	+27	13.9	14.3
Skilled Maintenance	+25	4.8	4.7
Other Skilled Manual	+24	9.6	8.1
Production Operatives	+15	8.7	7.8
Transport & Communications	+21	4.4	3.9
Sales Workers	+34	6.5	8.7
Security Workers	+19	2.7	2.8
Personal Service Workers	+31	5.4	7.9
Unskilled Labourers	+7	6.4	3.3

Source: Derived from Duggan et al., 1997, pp iii–iv.

The data presented here predict that agricultural employment will continue to fall over the intervening years to 2003. The largest increases are predicted for managerial and professional occupations (categorised in the report as those workers who hold degree-level qualifications). Strong growth is also forecast for associate professions (diploma/sub-degree qualification level), for sales and personal services type employment, and for clerical work. Projected growth is also featured for skilled manual workers (both those involved in maintenance and in core production). The forecasts indicate, however, that jobs that do not require prior specialised qualifications, and that rely more on on-the-job training, or are unskilled, are less likely to experience the same level of growth as those occupations that are qualification-based/driven. When the data is viewed over a longer time period (i.e. between the years 1981 and 2003 in this instance), it is strongly evident that managerial and professional occupations have increased, and will continue to increase, their share of total employment; concomitantly, manual work is on the decrease.

Female employment is predicted to continue to rise over the next number of years, by as much as 35 per cent, which represents a rate of expansion of more than double that forecast for men. There is evidence to suggest that female participation in employment is extending out from the traditional occupations of clerical work and health-associated professions and into more business and commercial professions where they have been, and continue to remain, under-represented.

Although the data presented here represent forecasts of likely changes over the next number of years we are already witnessing some of the impacts that will be more keenly felt in times to come. Skills shortages are being reported in many technical fields, in the construction trade, in marketing/sales and in the tourism/ hospitality sector. Skilled craftspeople are in considerable demand, and participation in third level and professional education remains buoyant. It is suggested here that general education and professional education/qualifications will become, even more than heretofore, the pivot upon which the performance of the Irish labour market is determined in the years to come.

EDUCATION AND TRAINING AND LABOUR MARKET PERFORMANCE

Education and training are critical in creating and sustaining competitiveness since investment in education, training and learning add to the national stock of human capital and promote growth and employment expansion by raising national productivity. Tansey (1998) cites a number of specific advantages of improved investment in the areas of education and training:

1. Investment in education and training raise the productivity of labour directly, where more skilled workers produce greater levels of output per unit of labour input and in a more efficient manner;

2. Productivity and efficiency gains act to reduce costs of production, thereby improving the competitiveness of exports;

3. Additional relevant education can also improve the flexibility and adaptability of the labour market and thus reinforce initial productivity gains;

4. The availability of a large pool of highly qualified labour acts as a magnet in attracting new mobile foreign investment to Ireland;

5. Additional inputs of education and training act to prevent specific skill shortages and to minimise structural unemployment;

6. Investments in training, by raising productivity, lead to improvements in business profitability;

7. Education and training, targeted at those most at risk, can stem inflows into unemployment.

Given the considerable perceived benefits associated with investment and participation in education and training, the remaining sections of this chapter focus on the current institutional education and training arrangements in Ireland and the participation rates associated with them.

Participation in Education

The Irish education system has undergone significant change in the past 25 years due, in no small part, to the strongly interventionist role adopted by the Irish State in pursuit of economic development from the early 1960s onwards. In recognition of the fundamental value of a good education system to the economic and social development of a nation, free second-level education was introduced in 1966, and compulsory schooling was extended from age 14 to 15 years. Today, in Ireland, full-time education is compulsory for children aged between 6 and 15 years, and there is evidence that a new Education Bill is set to raise the school leaving age to 16 years.

Three distinct levels of schooling exist within the Irish educational system: primary level, post-primary/secondary level and tertiary or third level education. The structure of this educational system is provided in Figure 2.1.

Primary education covers a period of eight years (4–12) and is typically provided by national schools, which are state-aided parish denominational schools established under diocesan patronage. The national school curriculum typically provides instruction in Irish and English language, mathematics, social and environmental studies, art and craft, music, physical education and religious instruction. Pupils normally transfer to post-primary/secondary education at the age of 12 and as a matter of course (there are no state examinations at this level).

Two state examinations exist at second level — the *Junior Certificate* which is taken after three years of study and, in general, marks the end of compulsory schooling, and the *Leaving Certificate* (upper secondary/senior cycle), which is typically completed two years later. Traditionally, second level education was largely

Figure 2.1: The Structure of the Education System in Ireland

Typical Ages	**Levels and Institutes of Education**		
	Third Level		
23/24 22/23 21/22 20/21 19/20 18/19 17/18	Universities	Institutes of Technology	Private Colleges
	Initial Vocational Education and Training		
19/20 18/19 17/18	Post Leaving Certificate Courses	Apprenticeship Training	
	Second Level Senior Cycle		
17/18 16/17 15/16	Voluntary Secondary Schools	Community and Comprehensive	Vocational Schools
	Second Level Junior Cycle		
15/16* 14/15* 13/14* 12/13*	Voluntary Secondary Schools	Community and Comprehensive	Vocational Schools
	First Level		
11/12* 10/11* 9/10* 8/9* 7/8* 6/7*	National Schools	Private & Special Schools	
	Pre-Primary		
5/6 4/5	National Schools	Private & Special Schools	

* *Compulsory Schooling*

Table 2.5: Distribution of Students Receiving Full-time Primary and Secondary Level Education

Type of Institution	Total
FIRST LEVEL	
Aided by Dept. of Education & Science National Schools	469,628
Non-aided Primary Schools	7,004
TOTAL PRIMARY LEVEL	476,632
SECOND LEVEL	
Aided by Dept. of Education & Science	
Junior Cycle Secondary Community & Comprehensive Vocational	199,571 122,846 30,375 46,350
Senior Cycle (General)* Secondary Community & Comprehensive Vocational	151,907 98,460 21,989 31,458
VPT** Secondary Community & Comprehensive Vocational	19,706 833 1,164 17,709
Horology College (watch-making)	30
Other Courses (Institutes of Technology)	1,124
Aided by Other Departments (Agriculture/Justice)	1,565
Non-Aided Commercial	1,615
TOTAL SECONDARY LEVEL	375,518

* Comprises Leaving Certificate, Leaving Certificate Vocational Programme, Senior Certificate and Transition Year Option; ** Comprises Vocational Preparation & Training 1 (VPT1) and Post-Leaving Certificate (VPT2)

Source: Department of Education & Science Statistical Reports 1996/7

characterised as classical-academic in orientation and was generally intended to prepare students for third level education and white collar occupations (Garavan, Costine and Heraty; 1995). Vocational schools were seen to provide a more technically oriented education and practical training in preparation for subsequent employment. However, economic growth in the 1970s and 1980s highlighted the necessity to match education with the needs of the economy. Evidence of some movement away from the traditional perspective on education is emerging with a range of schools introducing what is termed a *transition year* after the Junior Certificate. This transition year is an interdisciplinary programme designed to cater both for those terminating their education after the transition year and for those progressing to senior cycle. One core objective of the transition year is to provide students with an opportunity to develop work-based skills, improve personal and interpersonal development, and explore various career choices.

Following the publication of the White Paper on Education (Dept. of Education, 1995), which echoed a persistent concern regarding the general suitability of the Leaving Certificate cycle for all students, a decision was taken to restructure the Leaving Certificate programme into three components: the established Leaving Certificate Programme, the Leaving Certificate Applied Programme and the Leaving Certificate Vocational Programme (detail on the latter of these programmes is provided in the next section under vocational education). However, the majority of senior cycle students continue to follow the mainstream Leaving Certificate Programme, which retains an emphasis on general academic education, and continues to prepare students for entry to the labour market or to third level education. In 1996, students completing second level education numbered 373,665.

Provision of public sector education at third level in Ireland is divided between three institutional sectors: (a) Higher Education Authority (HEA) Institutions comprising the Universities, National College of Art and Design, and the Royal College of Surgeons; (b) Vocational Colleges and Institutes of Technology; and (c) the Teacher Training Colleges. Arts, natural science, commerce/business and engineering are the most popular courses at undergraduate level, while postgraduate activity centres around the sciences. The distribution of students in full-time third level education is represented in Table 2.6.

Table 2.6: Distribution of Students in Third Level Education

Institution	Full-time enrolments	Part-time enrolments
State Aided		
Universities	58,090	8,426
Teacher Training Colleges	547	
Technological Colleges	41,000	12,561
National College of Industrial Relations	567	1,808
Aided by Other State Departments	758	
Non-aided		
Religious Institutions	1,254	
Royal College of Surgeons in Ireland	1,003	
Other	4,282	
Total	107,501	22,795
of which aided by State	100,204	

Source: Department of Education Statistical Report 1996/97.

Participation at third level is determined by a points system based on Leaving Certificate examination results and, while entry to some programmes of study is more difficult in terms of the number of points required, in general demand for third level education far outstrips the limited supply of places available at the various third level institutions. This high demand has led to the relatively recent addition of a further tier to the educational system — private commercial colleges (post Leaving Certificate or PLC colleges) that now also provide a range of State-certified programmes in a number of disciplines, as well as their various other programmes, many of which are not State-certified.

The total number of full-time students at third level has increased significantly over the last number of years (in excess of 40 per cent since 1990) and a number of factors are seen to have contributed to this general upsurge in participation:

- The introduction in 1968 of grants for fees and partial maintenance for eligible third level students opened up access to third level education to many students that might otherwise not have been able to afford to go to University/College.

- The raising of the compulsory school-leaving age from 14 to 15 years in 1972 has kept more students within the educational system for longer. In 1964/65, a total 51.5 per cent of 15-year-olds were in full-time education — the comparable percentage for 1996/97 was greater than 90 per cent.

- The abolition of fees for post Leaving Certificate courses in 1995 has allowed those that might not have the entry requirements for traditional third level institutions to gain an alternative third level qualification.

- The abolition of fees for undergraduate students in publicly funded third level colleges in 1995 further provided wider access to third level education.

These developments have characterised the changing face of education in Ireland. The past 30 years have been marked by increased expenditure on education, coupled with greater numbers in education and higher participation rates. Indications of those changes include the following:

- The share of publicly funded education in Gross National Product (GNP) has more than doubled, from 2.8 per cent in 1961 to 6.1 per cent in 1995, but is still low by EU standards.

- Between 1964/5 and 1996/7, the total number of students rose from 653,000 to 959,651, with a three-fold increase in those in secondary education and a five-fold increase in those in tertiary education.

- Young people are staying in the education system for longer across all levels of education, and particularly at higher education levels, and in some age groups participation rates have almost doubled in that ten-year period. For example, 66.4 per cent of 17-year-olds and 39.9 per cent of 18-year-olds were in education in 1986/7; the corresponding figures for 1996/7 are 80.6 per cent and 63 per cent respectively; 24.7 per cent of 19-year-olds and just 10.6 per cent of those aged 20 years or more were in full-time education in 1986/7, compared with 47.7 per cent and 19.1 per cent respectively in 1996/7.

However, it is evident that considerable improvements are required to ensure that Ireland's educational system can provide the qualifications and skills required for economic growth, industrial development, and individual actualisation into the new millennium. In an evaluation of participation rates in full-time education, it is evident that, while participation is virtually complete in the 5–14 year age group, outside of compulsory schooling, Ireland rates relatively poorly at the higher levels of educational attainment, particularly in completion figures for upper secondary education (see Tables 2.7 and 2.8). A combination of limited third level places and, until 1996, the prohibitive costs associated with attending third level institutions (most notably tuition fees), may partly explain Ireland's lower representation at third level

Table 2.7: Percentage of the Population who have Completed Tertiary Education by Age Group (1995)

Country	25–34	35–44	45–54	55–64
North America				
Canada	53	49	46	33
United States	34	n/a	n/a	n/a
Pacific Area				
Australia	25	28	24	17
Korea	29	16	11	7
New Zealand	24	28	26	21
European Union				
Austria	9	11	7	4
Belgium	33	27	22	13
Denmark	20	25	21	14
Finland	23	23	20	14
France	25	20	17	9
Germany	21	27	24	18
Greece	26	21	14	8
Ireland	**27**	**21**	**16**	**11**
Italy	8	11	8	4
Luxembourg	11	14	12	6
Netherlands	25	25	21	14
Portugal	14	14	10	6
Spain	27	18	11	6
Sweden	29	32	29	20
United Kingdom	23	24	21	16
Other OECD countries				
Czech Republic	12	11	11	8
Norway	32	33	27	18
Poland	15	13	14	9
Switzerland	22	23	21	17
Turkey	8	9	10	6
Country mean	23	22	*18*	*12*

Source: OECD Database.

Table 2.8: Percentage of the Labour Force 25 to 64 Years of Age by the Highest Completed Level of Education (1995)

Country	Early childhood, primary and lower secondary education	Upper secondary education	Non-university tertiary education	University-level education	Total
North America					
Canada	19	29	32	19	100
United States	11	52	9	28	100
Pacific Area					
Australia	42	31	12	16	100
Korea	39	41	x	20	100
New Zealand	36	37	16	12	100
European Union					
Austria	24	66	2	7	100
Belgium	37	32	17	14	100
Denmark	33	44	7	16	100
Finland	30	47	10	13	100
France	25	54	9	12	100
Germany	12	62	11	15	100
Greece	52	26	8	15	100

Country	Early childhood, primary and lower secondary education	Upper secondary education	Non-university tertiary education	University-level education	Total
Ireland	**45**	**29**	**12**	**13**	**100**
Italy	56	33	x	11	100
Luxembourg	63	21	x	16	100
Netherlands	31	43	a	27	100
Portugal	76	10	4	9	100
Spain	64	15	6	16	100
Sweden	24	47	14	15	100
United Kingdom	19	57	10	14	100
Other OECD countries					
Czech Republic	12	76	x	12	100
Norway	15	53	12	20	100
Poland	21	64	4	12	100
Switzerland	15	61	14	10	100
Turkey	76	15	a	9	100
Country mean	*35*	*42*	*10*	*15*	*100*

Source: OECD Database

education, while the relatively young minimum school-leaving age (15 years) might explain lower showings at second level. It must also be recognised that free second level education was only introduced in Ireland 32 years ago and thus many of the individuals represented in the figures here may not have been able to avail of either second or third level educational opportunities. Furthermore, as indicated earlier, participation rates for younger people is higher than ever before and continues to increase.

In a comparison of those who have completed third level education in the OECD countries, it would appear that Ireland fares positively against many of her EU counterparts. Here again, there is evidence of increased participation among the younger age categories, perhaps as a result of the policy changes discussed earlier.

It is interesting to note that OECD countries differ widely in the levels of educational attainment of their populations. On average, 60 per cent of adults in OECD countries have completed upper secondary education, while the proportion of the population aged 25 to 64 who have completed tertiary education ranges between 8 and 47 per cent across countries.

Today, with close to one million students participating in education in Ireland, there is little room for complacency in relation either to Ireland's educational system or indeed educational participation rates more generally. The link between education and employment is well documented, where the attainment of educational qualifications critically impacts upon one's ability to successfully gain and retain employment. The latest OECD report on education (1998) argues that many of the benefits of education cannot be quantified and that social cohesion, rather than narrow economic gain, is the greatest prize for societies in which all citizens use learning to become more effective participants in democratic, civil and economic processes. Indicators from the OECD (1995) Education Report associate higher levels of education with higher earnings, a lower chance of unemployment and more skills that yield social advantage. This link is evidenced in the most recent Irish Labour Force Survey, which suggests that individuals who possess no post-primary qualification are six times more likely to be unemployed than are those with a third level qualification. In the case of those who do find employment, the remuneration they receive is very often far lower than those with higher qualifications. Education and earnings are thus positively linked, and so the earnings advantage of increased education would appear to outweigh the costs of acquiring it.

Participation in Vocational Education and Training
The history of vocational education and training can be traced back to the guild system of the 1700s with the regulation of crafts and craft working. In later years, and particularly in Ireland, this guild system was regulated into craft apprenticeships. From a historic perspective it would appear that vocational education and training was largely limited to the apprenticeship system. Vocational educational committees (VECs) were established around the country in 1930 and were responsible for the provision of a system of continuing and technical education in their location. An emphasis was placed on "vocational training", defined in terms of full-time second level training in literacy and scientific subjects, augmented by some concentration on manual skills. Some regulation of the national training system, and the establishment of a national training authority (FÁS), provided greater impetus for the development of particular vocational programmes to provide the necessary skills for particular industry and service sectors. A summary of the types of vocational and educational programmes available, and their participation rates, is presented in Table 2.9.

Table 2.9: Vocational Education and Training Programmes, 1993–94 (105,000 participants)

Programme	%	Description
Apprenticeship	11.2	Administered by FÁS; craft qualification
Teacher Training	0.1	Non-aided sector; qualifications in Montessori education, Religious education
Business Studies Courses	1.4	Provided by private and privately funded institutions
Specific Skills Training	13.2	Run by FÁS; initial vocational education and training for employment
Business/Technical/ Secretarial	1.8	Private education/training institutes; variety of subjects
VPT-2	16.7	Follows completion of secondary education
CERT craft courses	2.1	Vocational education and training qualifications in the catering/ tourism industry
Middle Level & Higher Technical Business Skills	46.7	Run by public education system; 2-year cert/diploma courses at third level institutions
Probationer Education/ Training	1.4	Garda training colleges
General Nurse education/training	3.4	Nursing qualification
Certificate in Farming	1.7	Main education/training for those seeking a career in farming
Farm Apprenticeship Scheme	0.2	3-year programme; Cert. in Farm Management
Hotel Management Courses	0.1	Education and training for those seeking management positions in the catering/ tourism business

Source: European Commission (1997).

Vocational education has received considerable attention in recent years — many would argue that it is an area that was neglected for far too long. A 1993 NESC report argued for stronger vocational education at upper secondary level and an overall recognition of a vocational orientation at all levels of the education system to facilitate future employment growth and participation in the labour market. Some of the more widespread initiatives are reported here.

Full-Time Vocational Education
At present there are two full-time vocationally oriented education programmes available to students who do not wish to follow the traditional Leaving Certificate curriculum. They are designed to provide a more practical vocational orientation to education. Both the Leaving Certificate Vocational and Applied Programmes (mentioned earlier) form one part of the Vocational Preparation and Training Programme (VPT-1). In the new Leaving Certificate Vocational Programme, students follow a full Leaving Certificate programme including two mainstream Leaving Certificate courses in vocational/technical or business disciplines, a language, as well as work experience and enterprise modules. The Leaving Certificate Applied Programme provides greater emphasis on technical and vocational subjects, with a focus on active learning approaches to prepare students for working life (Labour Market Study: Ireland, 1997). In 1998 just over 1,700 students completed the Applied Leaving Certificate programme while approximately 6,000 students completed the vocational stream. The second stream of the Vocational Preparation and Training Programme (VPT-2) typically consists of Post Leaving Certificate courses that are designed to equip young people with the vocational and technical skills necessary for employment and progression for further education and training.

Established under the Department of Education and Science, TEASTAS is an Interim Authority that has been provided with a wide remit to develop a single and comprehensive certification framework for all non-university third level programmes, and all vocational education and training, and adult and continuing education programmes. Towards the end of 1997, TEASTAS completed a report to the Minister for Education and Science that set down its recommendations for the statutory establishment and development of a National Qualifications Scheme, a National Qualifications Authority and a National Qualifications Framework; it is expected that statutory provisions will follow in due course.

Adult and Continuing Education
Provision for adult and continuing education and training has traditionally lacked cohesive policy development and so has tended to develop in a rather unstructured and *ad hoc* fashion. More recently, however, a number of schemes have been developed to provide opportunities for those who wish to reactivate their formal education. In recognition of the importance of adult education for personal development and for overcoming disadvantage suffered during initial education, these schemes focus on the promotion of lifelong learning and continuous retraining and updating of skills. For example, the Vocational Training Opportunities Scheme (VTOS), a European Social Fund supported intervention, is designed to enable unemployed individuals who have been on the live register for at least six months to access education and training with a view to progression to employment. VTOS provides participants with an opportunity to return to full-time vocational education and training and the minimum age for participation in the scheme is 21 years. The VTOS programme is managed and delivered locally by the Vocational Education Committees (VECs) and the courses that are provided focus on the development of employment-related skills, including technological and business skills, enterprise training, project work, and personal development. VTOS was introduced on a national basis

in 1989 and participation has grown from an initial figure of 247 to in excess of 5,000 in 1997. Literacy programmes are also available through vocational educational committees; while literacy and numeracy skills are required for access to education and training, they are also perceived as critical in facilitating independent living and fuller participation in society. Area Based Partnerships provide further opportunities for skills development and retaining, and adult participation in formal third level education is facilitated through special entry requirements for mature students to undergraduate programmes.

Apprenticeship System

Training programmes employed in statutory apprenticeships are regulated by FÁS, the national training and employment agency. Apprentices are normally recruited by employers and typically undertake a four-year period of apprenticeship in one of a number of trades (see Figure 2.2).

Figure 2.2: Standards-Based Apprenticeship Trades

Carton Maker*	Stonecutter Wood Machinist
Originator*	Cabinet Maker
Bookbinder*	Brick/Stone Layer
Printer*	Sheet Metal Worker
Plasterer	Painter/Decorator*
Vehicle Body Repairer*	Agricultural Mechanic*
Aircraft Mechanic*	Refrigeration Craftsperson*
Construction Plant Fitter*	Metal Fabricator
Heavy Vehicle Mechanic*	Plumber
Toolmaker	Motor Mechanic*
Electrician*	Carpenter/Joiner
Instrumentation Craftsperson*	Fitter*
Floor/Wall Tiler	Electrical/Instrumentation*

Note: A person wishing to become an apprentice in one of the above trades marked * must pass a colour-vision test approved by FÁS.

The apprenticeship combines both on-the-job and off-the-job training, the latter provided by a FÁS training centre or educational college. Apprentices who successfully complete the programme are issued with a National Craft Certificate, a qualification that is recognised not only in Ireland but also in other EU and non-EU countries. A competency-based or standards-based model of apprenticeship has recently been introduced. For the majority of trades, this system consists of seven distinct phases and is based on the achievement of certain pre-set standards of skill and competency rather than on time served. This system facilities the progression of successful apprentices to further educational qualifications and to continue to technical level at a recognised national and international standard.

FÁS currently operates a policy that is designed to promote and encourage the entry of women into apprenticeships and has established a number of measures to facilitate female participation. In one such measure, FÁS offers a bursary to both private and public sector employers who recruit female apprentices under the Standards-Based Apprenticeship system. Up to £2,100 is paid to the employer for each female apprentice recruited. FÁS, in conjunction with the education system, further provide preparatory training for females where necessary to prepare them to train and work in what has traditionally been a male environment.

The number of apprenticeships declined quite considerably in the 1990s. This decline in recruitment can be attributed both to demand constraints in terms of curbed public sector recruitment and industrial restructuring on the one hand, and to the increased incidences of subcontracting and outsourcing on the other (Labour Market Study: Ireland, 1997). However, since 1994, there has been renewed interest in apprenticeships; in 1997, 5,300 people were registered in apprenticeships, compared with 4,200 in 1996 and about 3,000 in 1995. Recent economic buoyancy and increasing skill shortages have created significant opportunities for qualified craft and trade occupations.

NATIONAL TRAINING INFRASTRUCTURE

A cursory examination of the history of training and development in Ireland highlights a consistent focus on apprenticeship training, youth employment schemes and training for the unemployed. In view of the growing recognition of the value and economic necessity of training and development by all partners at the macro level, there is an increased impetus to provide organisational level training and development opportunities to facilitate improved organisational functioning (see Chapters 8 and 9 for greater detail on training and development).

Green (1996) argues that, in economics, skill is regarded as human capital. However, in organisational terms, this human capital is not just a technical datum about the enhanced ability of the employees. It can often represent a more favourable set of attitudes or behavioural norms, which lead employees to be more committed to the organisation. He further suggests that, when firms speak of "skill shortages", the skills they refer to are frequently as much to do with punctuality, reliability and ability to work unsupervised, as they are to do with technical skills or qualifications. Viewed in this way, training may represent more than just the acquisition of technical skills. Rather, organisation-level training and development can best be analysed as part of a broader labour management strategy that seeks to improve organisational capacity along a range of firm specific objectives.

In Ireland, as in many other countries, the greater proportion of State support for human resource development is channelled into funding for initial education and for the training/retraining of unemployed workers. Training of the employed is seen to be the responsibility of the individual organisation, since returns on investment accrue largely to both the employer and employee. Industrial training has come under the microscope in recent years as the importance of skills development as a source of sustainable domestic economic growth and international competitive advantage gains credence. However, unlike some of their EU counterparts, Irish-based companies are not required to invest a minimum proportion of annual turnover, or its equivalent, on updating the skills and knowledge of their employees, nor are they obliged to make known the amount they spend annually on the training and development function.

Fox (1995) argues that problems continuously arise in drawing up national statistics on training and development. Since organisations have differing perceptions of what constitutes training, and since many companies tend to rely on informal training strategies and mechanisms, the problems of quantifying training expenditure are further compounded. Notwithstanding such problems, attempts are made regularly, using survey-based data, to broadly assess the rate of investment and participation in training and development activities. The ESF Programme Evaluation Unit is concerned with evaluating the effectiveness of all human resource development interventions that are supported by the European Social Fund. The Unit's survey of employers conducted in 1993 reported that, while a considerable amount of training is being undertaken by organisations, much of it on-the-job and run in-house, there appear to be limited structures or systems in place to substantiate or evaluate this training.

Fox's (1995) survey of training and development activities provided further support for the contention that organisations accord priority to training and development. He reported that a total of 77 per cent of companies indicated that they conducted some form of training. Training courses were found to be the most popular intervention (43 per cent) followed closely by on-the-job training (37 per cent), and, while all occupational groupings were involved in some form of job training, technicians and associated professionals were the most likely group to participate in training activities. There emerged a relatively equal split between company specific training, which included new technology, quality and world class manufacturing (44 per cent), and general training concerned with marketing, customer services, health and safety

(48 per cent). Marked differences in the incidence of training was recorded for different company sizes, where large and medium-sized enterprises engaged in training activity to a considerably greater extent than smaller concerns. The average number of days accounted for by off-the-job training courses per employee was 1.7 — the average in smaller firms was 1.2 while that for medium-sized organisations was 1.8, and 2.0 for larger companies. Average expenditure on training and development amounted to 1.5 per cent of total labour costs for all firms — again, however, this figure was proportionately related to organisation size.

In its survey of the Irish economy, the OECD (1995) suggested that the Irish training rate was not as low as that suggested by estimates based on training costs but that Ireland fared particularly weakly in terms of the low emphasis placed on vocational education and training. O'Connell and Lyons (1995) similarly caution that the level of investment in enterprise-related training is insufficient in terms of Ireland's ability to compete effectively with other industrialised countries, and this is despite the increased investment in HRD financed by EU structural funds.

FÁS, the National Training and Employment Authority, was established in January 1988 with its activities funded by the Irish Government, the European Social Fund and the European Regional Development Fund. In 1997, FÁS's expenditure amounted to £478 million. A considerable amount of FÁS's activities are directed towards reducing unemployment and fostering community-based initiatives, through programmes such as Youthreach (for early school leavers); the Social Employment Scheme (for adult long-term unemployed); the Enterprise Programme (new business start-ups by the unemployed); and the Community Enterprise Programme (for community and co-operative groups). However, it also provides services to industry through a combination of schemes aimed at promoting training and skills development.

The Training Support Scheme (TSS) was introduced by FÁS in 1990 to encourage and promote training in small and medium-sized organisations (up to 500 employees) involved in manufacturing, internationally traded services and physical distribution. While the TSS provides graduated grant aid to eligible companies to purchase their training in the marketplace, over half of the allocation for TSS is targeted at firms employing less than 50 employees. In 1995, 2,500 organisations were granted aid under the TSS — 32,400 employees were involved and the average duration of training amounted to just under eight days per trainee (Labour Market Study, 1997).

Training Grants are administered by the State development agencies and are directed at skill needs arising from location of overseas investment in Ireland. Grants of up to 100 per cent of eligible costs are provided to carry out approved training for new employees. Average coverage of such training is about 4,500 employees per year.

The Management Development Grants scheme is a further indication of a strong national commitment to training and is operated by the development agencies and supported by the State. Grants are available to improve the management performance of firms, particularly in aspects of management information systems, strategic and business planning. The size of grants awarded varies between £2,500 and £35,000 and approximately 600 companies participate in the scheme each year.

In 1995, FÁS introduced its Training Awards Scheme and a new training quality standard "Excellence Through People" which are designed to reward and encourage high training standards and to demonstrate the link between training investment and improved business performance. In conjunction with FÁS's efforts, a new national certification authority, TEASTAS, is being established to facilitate progression to more advanced levels of education and training, as benchmarked against best practice in the international arena.

EU INITIATIVES FOR HUMAN RESOURCE DEVELOPMENT

The EU Commission supports a number of specific initiatives that are designed to improve initial and continuing vocational education and training provisions. In particular, these initiatives focus on improving the links between the education and training systems and the enterprise/industry sectors. Four programmes, in particular, have relevance here:

The LEONARDO DA VINCI Vocational Training Programme, which aims to aid member states in devising national policies on vocational education through, for example, fostering university/industry co-operation, development of language skills, vocational guidance, and improved accessing to education and training. It is estimated that, between 1995 and 1999, close to £12 million will have been received to support Irish-led projects.

The SOCRATES Programme focuses on improving the quality and relevance of education and supports initiatives such as student/staff exchanges; a system of credit/mutual recognition of qualifications between member states; curriculum development, language training, open and distance learning. Between 1995 and 1999, it is estimated that Ireland will have received about £11 million under this programme.

The EU Employment Initiative targets individuals with particular difficulties in relation to employment in the workplace, including people with disabilities, those who are disadvantaged, equal opportunities for women (NOW), and employment initiatives for young people from disadvantaged backgrounds. A total of £62 million is being made available over the lifetime of this programme.

ADAPT is a Human Resources Community Initiative supported by the European Social Fund which will operate in all member states of the European Union (EU) until the end of 1999. A key objective of the ADAPT initiative is to heighten awareness of the need for industry to adapt swiftly to changing work environments. It is designed therefore to support innovative training and human resource development projects in organisations interested in introducing progressive human resource development practices and policies that will enhance the technical competencies, skills levels and career development opportunities of their employees. A total of 79 projects have been funded to date: 44 were funded in 1996/7 and 32 are currently being funded in 1998/99. The Department of Enterprise, Trade and Employment is the National Authority for the ADAPT Initiative.

CONCLUSION

This chapter has sought to provide some insight into how the Irish labour market is constructed and determined. Significant structural, social, political and economic changes have been debated that have characterised developments in the Irish economy in recent years and that have resulted in considerable capital investment in the Irish labour market, leading to sustained employment creation combined with falling rates of unemployment and an appreciable rise in the overall standard of living. The industry and services sectors have witnessed the bulk of economic and employment growth, and Ireland is host to a significant number of foreign-owned companies, which account for a considerable proportion of overall exports and employment. The demographic profile of the Irish population is favourably disposed towards high labour market participation and it is unlikely that Ireland will experience the level of ageing of the labour force that will shortly be evidenced in many EU countries.

More recently, however, educational attainment and human capital investment are being viewed as critical determinants of positive economic growth and development. De la Fuente and Vives (1997) argue that, between 1985 and 1995, investments in human capital were the third largest identified contributor to Ireland's positive growth differential over the rest of the industrialised world, while Tansey (1998) indicates that each step up the educational ladder yields a significantly positive rate of return in terms of higher lifetime earnings. The benefits of increased educational attainment are thus spread across the whole of the economy in terms of increased productivity, increased employment and a widened tax base for the State. The educational profile of the Irish labour force has changed considerably over the last number of years, and particularly as a result of direct policy intervention to widen the provision and scope of second and third level education.

Today the quality of the Irish labour force compares very favourably with that of other EU and OECD countries, and particularly with respect to those holding a third level qualification. However, the evidence to date suggests that the provision of general vocational education is insufficient to meet the current demands of the labour market and of those participating in education. While a number of initiatives have recently been introduced, it is too early yet to make any objective evaluation of their effectiveness. Projections of occupational trends over the next five years suggest that unskilled and semi-skilled jobs will be displaced and that educational attainment and qualifications will increasingly become the criterion upon which employability is determined. There is thus a considerable danger that those who drop out of the education system before completing their formal education will become increasingly marginalised and unemployable.

In a world where the extension of knowledge and learning capacity is viewed as critical to competitive functioning, there is considerable pressure on the organisation to ensure that its internal capability can match external environmental requirements. The onus is increasingly being placed on the personnel/HR function or practitioner to ensure that the firm's labour pool has both the skills and abilities to meet organisational requirements and, furthermore, the capacity to deal with possible changes that the external environment might demand. Through most of the 1990s, the Irish labour market was characterised by an oversupply of well-educated and skilled individuals and thus organisations had considerable scope for action in terms of meeting their labour requirements. This characterisation of the labour market no longer holds true. Skills shortages are being experienced in a number of industries and sectors and many organisations, but particularly smaller firms, are finding it increasingly difficult to fill vacancies. Wage inflation is on the increase, and employees are increasingly demanding greater opportunities for knowledge expansion and competence development and are looking to the organisation to supply these opportunities. Available labour market analysis suggests that these supply and demand pressures are set to intensify in the short to medium term and these clearly have important implications for how the organisation develops and manages its range of HRM policies and practice.

References

Baker, T.J., D. Duffy and F. Shortall (1998), *Quarterly Economic Commentary*, Dublin: The Economic and Social Research Institute.

Central Bank of Ireland (1997 & 1998), Winter Report, Dublin: CBI.

Central Statistics Office Labour Market Surveys 1970–1999.

Central Statistics Office Census of Population, 1996.

de la Fuente, A. and X. Vives (1997), "The Source of Irish Growth" in A. Gray (ed.), *International Perspectives on the Irish Economy*, Dublin: Indecon.

Department of Education (1995), *Charting our Education Future*, White Paper on Education, Pn. 2009, Dublin: Government Publications Office, April.

Department of Education Statistical Reports 1994/1995.

Department of Education Statistical Reports 1995/96.

Department of Education & Science Statistical Reports 1996/7.

Department of Enterprise and Employment (1997), *White Paper on Human Resource Development*, Pn. 3381, Dublin: Government Publications Office, May.

DiMaggio, P. and W. Powell (1983), "The Iron Cage Revisited: Institutional Isomorphism and Collective Rationality in Organisational Fields", *American Sociological Review*, No. 48, pp. 147–60.

Duffy, D., J. Fitz Gerald, I. Kearney and F. Shortall (1997), *Medium-term Review: 1997–2003*, April, Dublin: The Economic and Social Research Institute.

Duggan, D., G. Hughes and J.J. Sexton (1997), "Occupational Employment Forecasts 2003", *FÁS/ESRI Manpower Forecasting Studies*, Report No. 6, November, Dublin: FÁS & The Economic and Social Research Institute.

Economist (1997), "Green is Good: Advantages of Ireland as a Host For FDI", 17 May, Vol. 343, No. 8017, pp. 21–4.

Economist Intelligence Unit (1997), "Ireland Country Report — Third Quarter", UK: EIU.

Economist Intelligence Unit (1998), "Ireland Country Report — First Quarter", UK: EIU.

Employment and Labour Market (1997), *Labour Market Studies: Ireland*, Series No 1, Brussels: European Commission.

European Commission (1997), *Key Data on Vocational Training in the European Union*, Luxembourg: Office for Official Publications of the European Commission.

European Industrial Relations Review (EIRR) (1998), Issue 296, September, pp. 33–8.

FÁS (1996), "Update on Migration", *Labour Market Data Update Paper No. 2/96*, November, Dublin: FÁS.

FÁS (1997a), "Recent Data on Long-term Unemployment", *Labour Market Data Update Paper No. 3/97*, September, Dublin: FÁS.

FÁS (1997b), "Summary Review of Labour Market Trends in 1997", *Labour Market Data Update Paper No. 4/97*, November, Dublin: FÁS.

FÁS (1998), "Women in the Irish Labour Force" *Labour Market Data Update Paper No. 5*, July, Dublin: FÁS.

Fox, A. (1995), *Training of the Employed*, Dublin: FÁS.

Garavan, T., P. Costine and N. Heraty (1995), *Training and Development in Ireland: Context, Policy and Practice*, Dublin: Oak Tree Press.

Gray, A. (1997), *International Perspectives on the Irish Economy*, Dublin: Indecon Economic Consultants.

Green, F. (1996), *Skill, Training, Organisational Commitment and Unemployment: The Economics of a Labour Management Strategy*, Discussion Paper No. 1, London School of Economics: Centre for Economic Performance.

National Economic and Social Council (NESC) (1993), *Education and Training Policies for Economic and Social Development*, No. 95, October, Dublin: NESC.

O'Connell, P. and M. Lyons (1995), "Enterprise Related Training and State Policy in Ireland: The Training Support Scheme", *Economic and Social Research Institute Policy Research Series*, No. 25, Dublin: ESRI.

OECD (1995), *Education at a Glance*, Paris: OECD.

OECD (1997a), *Economic Outlook, No. 61*, Paris: OECD.

OECD (1997b), *Economic Surveys: Ireland, 1997*, Paris: OECD.

OECD (1998), *Economic Outlook, No. 63*, June, Paris: OECD, pp. 101–4.

OECD (1998), *Education at a Glance*, Paris: OECD.

Payne, D. (1997), "Irish Answer to World's Calls", *The European*, Sept 25, p. 29.

Sexton, J.J., A. Canny and G. Hughes (1996), "Changing Profiles in Occupations and Educational Attainment", *FÁS/ESRI Manpower Forecasting Studies*, Report No. 5, November, Dublin: FÁS & The Economic and Social Research Institute.

Sweeney, P. (1998), *The Celtic Tiger: Ireland's Economic Miracle Explained*, Dublin: Oak Tree Press.

Tansey, P. (1998), *Ireland at Work: Economic Growth and the Labour Market 1987–1997*, Dublin: Oak Tree Press.

Westphal, J., R. Gulati and S. Shortell (1997), "Customization or Conformity? An Institutional and Network Perspective on the Content and Consequences of TQM Adoption", *Administrative Science Quarterly*, No. 42, June, pp. 366–94.

Wolf, J. (1997), "From Starworks to Networks and Heterarchies? Theoretical Rationale and Empirical Evidence of HRM Organisation in Large Multinational Corporations", *Management International Review* (Special Edition), No. 37, pp. 145–69.

CHAPTER 3

RETAINING, MOTIVATING AND DEVELOPING THE KNOWLEDGE WORKER

Graeme Buckingham

INTRODUCTION

There is an increasing appreciation, not least in the investment community, of the knowledge worker's value to the organisation. Identifying, motivating and retaining such talent is a strategic imperative for many companies and their personnel/human resource functions. Recent research has identified some essential factors in securing employees' commitment. It has highlighted the key role of the first line manager or supervisor in retaining and motivating the so-called "knowledge worker". Since Peter Drucker first coined the term 40 years ago, it is now appreciated that the ability of developed countries to compete internationally will depend on the applied skills and knowledge of its working population.

Human resource (HR) policies and strategies need to be reviewed accordingly to focus on a talent and recruitment strategy, and ongoing measurement, feedback and education for managers and supervisors whose challenge is to utilise and value the intellectual capital of the organisation. Knowledge workers leave managers, not companies, and it is their managers who most strongly impact their motivation and commitment. There is a growing body of evidence highlighting the impact of the first line manager on the retention and motivation of employees and the performance of the work unit.

WHY THE INTEREST IN INTELLECTUAL CAPITAL?

In March 1997, Associated Press (1997) reported from the US that:

> The Council of Institutional Investors, a powerful group of 94 pension funds that together control $1 trillion in stocks, will discuss good work place practices and how institutional investors can encourage their use at their Council's annual meeting in Washington.

Further reinforcement of the growing interest of the investment community in the quality of the workplace came almost simultaneously with an announcement that the largest US pension fund CALPERS (California Public Employee Retirement System) "is stepping up efforts to persuade companies it invests in to value employee loyalty as an aid to productivity" (Associated Press 1997).

Why in the last two to three years have such powerful investment groups begun to show this interest in companies' employment policies and practices? The answer is apparent when the market capitalisation of many companies is compared to their book values or sales revenues. Such comparison may reveal that conventional accounting measures are found wanting in providing an accurate picture of the worth of a company.

Where do Conventional Measures Fail?

Let me illustrate this with an example. While the combined 1996 sales of General Motors and Ford ($300 billion) exceed that of Microsoft, Merck, Intel and Disney, by a factor of six, the market capitalisation of this latter group of highly successful creative companies ($320 billion) is over four times larger than that of General Motors and Ford ($80 billion). Microsoft has fixed assets of only $930 million but a market capitalisation of $85 billion while IBM's asset base exceeds $16 billion but its market capitalisation is about the same. Much of this difference is to be found in the intellectual capital of these technologically and creatively innovative companies and the skills, competency and motivation of their knowledge workers.

Such comparisons led Steve Walman, the powerful US Securities and Exchange Commissioner and regulator of Wall Street's stock markets, to say that as financial statements

> ... become less and less useful and are measuring less and less of what is truly valuable in a company, then we start to lower the relevance of that scorecard.

He continued:

> What we need are ways to measure the intangibles, R&D, customer satisfaction, employee satisfaction. What we need are standards.

The implications of this new perspective from the investment community for HR policy and HR practitioners will be enormous. The human resource function will increasingly be challenged to provide measurable data on employees' retention, loyalty and productivity to satisfy company executives, who are primarily concerned with what they regard as their key priority: namely, to enhance the value of the company to the shareholder.

THE VALUE OF INTELLECTUAL CAPITAL:
THE KNOWLEDGE WORKER

It is therefore hardly surprising, given this increasing investment concern about employment policies, that the phrase "intellectual capital" is increasingly in vogue. It emphasises the worth of the trained and committed employee, particularly those with valued skills, to the organisation. This value is very different from many other assets of the company, which are to be found in the balance sheet, where the cost and value of plant, machinery and similar assets is recorded as determined by purchase price and agreed rates of depreciation and write-off.

The value of any computer bought by a company is immediately reduced on the date of purchase and continues to depreciate. By contrast, the knowledge worker, who is talented and a good fit to his or her role, appreciates in value to the company. This individual's contribution to the company increases with knowledge, experience and the assumption of increased responsibilities. He or she becomes an appreciating asset, therefore — and moreover, one that is not fixed but can walk out the door and join the competition! As Thomas Stewart (1997) observed:

> Far from being alienated from the tools of his trade and the fruit of his labour, the knowledge worker carries them between his ears.

What often occurs is that these knowledge workers become alienated by their employers and, with marketable skills and talents, vote with their feet. Where poor management creates high levels of employee wastage, the loss in competitive advantage to the company is all too apparent, as the investment community increasingly appreciates. For example, a detailed estimate of the employee wastage costs by the Corporate Advisory Board, Washington, showed the loss of an IT professional would cost the company 176 per cent of salary to find and train a replacement.

Peter Drucker has recently estimated that in the United States, knowledge workers will be the largest single group in the workforce by the end of this century. They are the creative, competitive driving force behind many companies' success, applying their education and theoretical knowledge and analytical abilities to achieve product and/or service differentiation. As Drucker has recently emphasised:

. . . the productivity of an individual, an organisation, an industry, a country, in acquiring and applying knowledge will increasingly become the key competitive factor — for career and earnings opportunities of the individual, for the performance, perhaps even the survival, of the individual organisation; for an industry; and for a country.

SOME MAJOR TRENDS IN EMPLOYMENT AND ORGANISATION

Drawing on his company's extensive and world-wide survey and talent research base, Dr Donald Clifton (1995), Chairman of the Gallup Organization, identified four major trends to which individuals and companies are having to adapt. These are:

1. New flatter organisation structures are emerging world-wide which have a focus on service;

2. The demand and use of computers as distributors of intelligence is growing geometrically.

3. The capacity for distributing intelligence brought about by computers is empowering people everywhere, with significant implications for out-of-date chain of command structures.

4. An intellectual capital is being created, which is the best measurement of the wealth of organisations and countries. This emphasises the linked importance of employee training and education and an organisation's ability to retain the knowledge worker.

It has of course been a human resources truism that companies should seek to reduce employee turnover, and that a talented, skilled, motivated workforce is one of their most important assets. Company reports pay lip service to these beliefs in thanking employees for their contribution to the company's results, often describing them as its most important resource.

And yet HR functions lack the budgets of their marketing and information technology counterparts. They struggle to provide concrete evidence that the employment policies they recommend achieve tangible results and measurably contribute to company performance and levels of service and/or product quality. Personnel and HR Managers will struggle to justify the additional resources that they seek if they fail to provide the objective measurement that both companies and investors increasingly demand. They may, as is the case in many companies, continue to remain on the periphery of strategic decision-making, rather than occupying the central role that the importance of an organisation's employees should require.

Retaining and Motivating the Knowledge Worker – Quantifying a Company's Intellectual Capital

Keith Bradley, Professor of International Management at the Open University and formerly of Harvard Business School, has estimated that in knowledge-intensive companies, the gap between balance sheet assets and the market capitalisation of such companies can be as great as 100 per cent or more. The importance of redressing this situation is highlighted by initiatives being taken by accounting bodies to establish agreed criteria on accounting for intangible assets. Thus, the International Accounting Standards Committee is shortly to publish its recommendations on such accounting standards. In the United States, the Financial Accounting Standards Board is to carry out a major research programme to clarify how intangible assets should be measured. One imagines, however, that the debate on what such measures and standards should be will last long and be hotly argued.

Meanwhile, major pieces of research are, for the first time, providing companies with the possible means of applying relevant measurement for their own requirements. Thus the University of Sheffield and London School of Economics have carried out an extensive seven-year research programme in some of Britain's most successful small and medium-sized companies and established a positive link between progressive people management practices and enhanced productivity and profits (West and Patterson, 1997).

One participating company, Keystone Values (UK) a world leader in its field, reported on its use of attitude surveys for more than a decade, during which period employee survey response rates grew from 30 per cent to 90 per cent, because employees found management taking action on the findings. This company reported that employees wanted training, fearing that they would become technically deficient as the speed of technological change increased. Having invested heavily in advanced technology training, the company was obviously concerned to retain its highly trained workforce. It found that employees wanted better communication and the opportunity for greater involvement in the workplace. Keystone uses its attitude surveys therefore as a key data source for retaining and developing employees, benchmarking its results against other companies.

MEASURING A PRODUCTIVE WORKPLACE

The challenge of linking such employee data to productive outcomes has been the focus of a large-scale research programme undertaken by the Gallup Organization, the results of which have attracted widespread attention on both sides of the Atlantic. Drawing on an employee attitude survey data base of over one million employees worldwide and using both quantitative and qualitative research methods, Gallup analysed its employee survey questions to assess employees' commitment to the company. This research focused on the responses by employees in the most productive work groups across a range of companies.

Intensive analysis identified 12 key questions that appeared to measure the commitment and motivation of employees. These 12 questions (Q^{12}) are outlined in Figure 3.1.[1]

Figure 3.1: Gallup's 12 Questions on Commitment and Motivation of Employees

---

1. Do I know what is expected of me at work?

2. Do I have the materials and equipment I need to do my work right?

3. At work, do I have the opportunity to do what I do best everyday?

4. In the last seven days, have I received recognition or praise for good work?

5. Does my supervisor, or someone at work, seem to care about me as a person?

6. Is there someone at work who encourages my development?

7. At work, do my opinions seem to count?

8. Does the mission of my company make me feel like my work is important?

9. Are my co-workers committed to doing quality work?

10. Do I have a best friend at work?

11. In the last six months, have I talked with someone about my progress?

12. At work, have I had opportunities to learn and grow?

---

[1] These 12 Statements are proprietary and copyrighted by the Gallup Organisation, Princeton. For additional information see M. Buckingham and C. Coffman (1999), *First Break All the Rules: What the World's Great Managers Do Differently*, New York: Simon and Schuster.

These twelve questions (Q^{12}) appear therefore to be a powerful way to measure the strength of a workplace. Did they work in practice? Under the supervision of Professor Frank Schmidt, of Iowa University and a world authority on meta-analysis, Gallup then undertook what is believed to be the first multi-company, multi-unit comparison of scores on these 12 questions, correlating them to productive outcomes at unit level, namely:

- Productivity
- Profitability
- Customer Satisfaction
- Employee Retention.

The data for this meta-analysis now covers over 100,000 employees employed in some 2,600 units. The principal business sectors covered are: financial services (30 per cent); healthcare (20 per cent); hospitality (18 per cent); and there are also retail, education and telecommunications organisations included in this major research programme.

The results of this study revealed strong correlations of each of the 12 questions with one or more of the business outcomes. Indeed, one question — on the relationship of the individual with his or her supervisor — related strongly to all four productive outcomes. This was of particular interest to Gallup, which in exit surveys conducted over many years with leavers, has consistently found a poor relationship with the manager or supervisor to be the most frequently mentioned reason given by people for leaving an organisation.

CASE STUDY ILLUSTRATIONS

Further confirmation of the importance of the first line manager has come from other programmes with very large US companies. For example, in a major multi-site retailer, those stores whose scores on the 12 questions put them in the top 25 per cent achieved profit and sales well above budget. Those stores whose scores put them in the bottom quartile were, on average, well below budget on both measures. The difference between the two groups ran into millions of dollars, both in sales and profit. When managers in the company were trained to take action to raise the level of scores on the 12 questions, after seven months employee wastage had reduced by 13 per cent — an average of 10 employees per store.

A very large telecommunications company measured customer satisfaction with its call centres. Detailed analysis of comprehensive data covering over 5,000 Call Centre Staff found customer satisfaction scores correlated most closely with the calibre and talent of a team's supervisor. The teams of the least talented supervisors were found to dissatisfy customers in most cases, while teams with talented supervisors who had a strong profile of relevant attributes obtained consistently high customer satisfaction scores.

THE IMPORTANCE OF THE FIRST LINE MANAGER

Good first line managers and supervisors are therefore critical to the performance of the unit, department or section for which they are responsible. The 12 questions highlight that such managers build good relations with those they supervise. They set clear and appropriate expectations, give regular praise and recognition and foster their employees' growth and development. Identifying and developing managers and supervisors with such abilities and competencies is, from this evidence, a top priority for the organisation and its HR function. Companies give much attention to identifying leadership potential and to grooming "high fliers" for career development and promotion. It would appear that, in terms of cost benefit and/or customer satisfaction and employee retention, a similar investment in selecting and developing first line managers and supervisors is equally important.

The Significance of these Findings for the "Distributed" Organisation

This emphasis is particularly significant to two types of organisation. The first is the branded distributed company, which is geographically dispersed across a large number of separate units or branches, projects a strongly defined brand image of value, service and quality. Often, large-scale advertising and expensive marketing is used to create this image. However, the delivery of the brand and the customers' experience of the advertising promise is in the hands of hundreds, or indeed thousands, of individual employees. It is they who serve the customers and either confirm or destroy much of the image created at so much expense by the company's advertising and marketing.

Delivering the Brand Promise

A few companies, notably one of Europe's top quality car manufacturers, Audi, have realised this. In the UK, Audi has linked its brand projection to developing and measuring the quality and competency of those serving its customers. Its aim — to achieve world class service standards and to convert its many customers to advocates of its brand — is critically dependent on the staff in its dealerships providing exceptional standards of service. While many companies aspire to achieve this aim, few systematically identify the systems of selection, development and measurement to attain it. Audi has put in place talent-based selection systems, short and regularly administered employee surveys and carefully designed customer satisfaction interviews to provide measurable information through which it can monitor progress towards achieving its ambitious objective of world class service quality.

Yet again, initial evidence from analysing this sophisticated inter-linked data set has revealed the critical importance of the unit manager or dealership principal in retaining employees, satisfying customers and achieving high levels of profitable sales. The best managers at this level have some special talents and drives which, in essence, combine to focus on ensuring the customer receives an exceptional experience. Such managers, for example, think, breathe and continually articulate the vital importance of service. They naturally and spontaneously build close relationships with customers and employees alike and possess a personal set of robust values that are the essential foundation for establishing trust and confidence in those with whom they deal. Such individuals, therefore, are living embodiments of the quality brand, which they sell and service. They seek to employ those with similar qualities and motivations and are prepared to spend time and effort to recruit and develop such employees.

Such individuals are not easily found but such talent exists and some organisations do spend the time and effort to seek it out. Those that do will find that their investment produces an excellent long-term return.

The Significance for Employers of the Knowledge Worker
The second type of organisation for which high quality supervision is a particular imperative is the large-scale employer of the "knowledge worker". Such employees may be chosen for their particular technical skills — for example, in information technology (IT), telecommunications, investment or engineering — or their "knowledge" may be company- or industry-specific — for example, in financial services, hotels or travel. Increased regulation by external authorities is requiring more and more investment and training by companies if they wish to sell financial services or offer the public a quality and hygienic eating experience or safe travel. Health and safety regulations or the rigorous requirements of the UK financial services regulators are cases in point. Thus, the costs companies incur to ensure their employees acquire the necessary knowledge and skills to meet such regulatory demands are often very high. Where such training fails to

satisfy the authorities, companies may face heavy fines or indeed the permanent or temporary cessation of their business.

Such companies which invest heavily in ensuring that employees have either the technical skills or industry competencies that their products, services or legislation require, have or should have particular interest in retaining and facilitating the commitment of such "knowledge workers". So, in these organisations again, the calibre and competency of managers of the "knowledge worker" is of particular importance. As mentioned earlier, when a valued employee who has acquired particular skills and great expertise leaves, the loss is considerable, and is further compounded if that person has been lured to join the competition. How then to retain and motivate such important and appreciating assets?

RETAINING AND MOTIVATING THE KNOWLEDGE WORKER: A HIERARCHY OF EMPLOYEE COMMITMENT

The 12 questions (Q^{12}) derived by Gallup from its research form a hierarchy or pyramid of four stages of employee engagement and commitment.

The starting point is to provide employees with the basic requirements to do the job (i.e. the equipment, material and technical resources and information necessary) and to ensure that each person after induction knows clearly what is required of them.

The second stage — the core of the manager's responsibilities — centres on the quality of relationship that the manager establishes with the individual employee.

The third stage is when the employee decides whether the company's purposes and their colleagues share their aspirations to commit to others and whether the organisation takes account of their views.

Finally, at the highest level of commitment, the individual seeks to grow personally, to develop, and in so doing to contribute to the company's development.

Figure 3.2: Gallup's Engagement Hierarchy

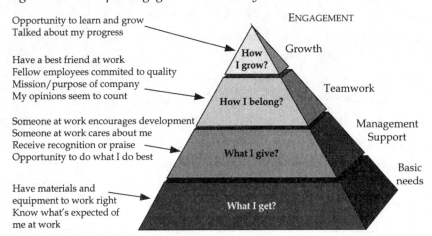

These higher stages have been, when one thinks of it, the subject of many company initiatives. Mission statements, the learning organisation, Total Quality Management programmes: all are focused on these higher stages. But employees will not reach these higher levels if they have not passed through and responded positively to the earlier stages. Employees are unlikely to commit to a mission statement initiative if expectations are not clear as to what they are being asked to contribute, if no recognition is forthcoming and no one shows a personal interest in them and their personal progress. As one couple in the licensed trade in the UK told me:

> The day the company we worked for described us as Branch No. 18, it was time to leave. No way were we going to be treated as numbers!

In an increasingly pressurised and impersonal world, people are crying out to be treated as individuals — not least at work. Put at its simplest level, this is the basic challenge for managers concerned to retain and motivate their staff.

LESSONS TO BE LEARNED FROM THE BEST MANAGERS

Gallup's research not only includes employee survey data. Over 35 years it has interviewed and analysed in-depth interviews with tens of thousands of highly rated managers from leading organisations on both sides of the Atlantic. Such interviews were developed and validated from carefully designed research programmes across a wide range of US and UK companies and focused on managers whose performance and measurable achievements placed them in the upper quartile of the companies' management.

This research covered a wide range of industry sectors and management functions. Initially, there was a large proportion of sales managers and managers in the restaurant, hotel and other hospitality companies. This range of managerial positions has widened over the years, covering not only production, IT, marketing and financial services but also large numbers of managers in the healthcare and education sectors. It represents one of the largest body of detailed source material on the essential qualities and competencies of successful managers and the concepts and management practices they employ in delivering success.

FOUR KEYS TO GOOD MANAGEMENT PRACTICE

It is a truism that the essence of management is to optimise the resources for which they are responsible to deliver a product or service which satisfies or, if possible, delights the customer or client. The human resources — the people who are the manager's responsibility — represent for many managers their most important resource in achieving this purpose. When Gallup analysed all the evidence it had collected from its huge interview database of highly rated managers, it found that, while there were many variations of management style and practice, there were four key people management activities which were common to the majority of these managers and to which they gave particular attention and emphasis. These activities are outlined in Figure 3.3.

Figure 3.3: Key People Management Activities

1. *Hiring*: the importance of recruitment.
2. *Setting Expectations*: ensuring employees know what is required of them.
3. *Motivating*: getting the best from people.
4. *Developing*: facilitating appropriate work-related growth of employees.

This is not of itself a particularly remarkable list. It forms the basis of much management training at various levels of sophistication and might be said to form the policy foundation for a proactive company's HR function. In particular, the challenge of how best to motivate and develop employees has been the subject of extensive research and many policy initiatives from job enrichment through empowerment to the current emphasis on the learning organisation — a recent response to a widespread recognition of the importance of the knowledge worker.

However, Gallup's research found that the practices of outstanding managers ran counter to the conventional human resources policies in the majority of companies. Furthermore, this separate research base confirmed and complemented conceptually the quite separate research findings from Gallup's Employee Survey database, which had identified 12 key questions as the key measures of a productive workplace.

In the majority of companies, these four key people management practices are considered and implemented according to the following precepts:

1. *Hiring*: select for skills and experience.

2. *Setting Expectations*: define the right steps, the processes the employee should follow.

3. *Motivating*: help each person overcome weaknesses and limitations.

4. *Developing*: help each person get promoted.

In stark contrast, the best managers run counter to this conventional wisdom in the way they conceive and implement these core responsibilities, as outlined in Figure 3.4.

Figure 3.4: Best Practice in People Management

1. *Hiring*: the best managers select and hire for talent.

2. *Setting Expectations*: the best managers define the required outcomes.

3. *Motivating*: the best managers focus on the individual's strengths.

4. *Developing*: the best managers help each person find the best job fit for that individual's capacities.

These differences are fundamental and therefore raise essential questions for HR practitioners and the policies they propose and implement. They suggest the need for a considered reappraisal of companies' HR policies and their conceptual foundation, because most current practices appear to run counter to those of the best managers.

So what are the lessons to be learnt in how to select, motivate and retain the knowledge worker? We now look at the four key areas in detail.

HIRING: RECRUITING FOR TALENT

All of us have been pupils at school, college or university. All of us have been taught and will recall, often vividly, our experience and evaluations of the many teachers at whose feet we metaphorically sat. We will, perhaps, remember and joke about the bad teachers — those who could not keep control and whose lessons degenerated into anarchy. Alternatively, we may have experienced the martinet who ruled the classroom with a rod of iron and who taught by rote, showing no interest in us as individuals and achieving results by force-feeding the knowledge that they wished to impart.

Conversely, for many of us there were often teachers who gave us a quite different experience, whose lessons we enjoyed and whom we remember with gratitude and sometimes affection as among the most influential individuals in our formative years. Such teachers showed an interest in us as individuals, were concerned with our personal growth and development and found appropriate ways for us to learn, creating in us enthusiasm and interest in those subjects for which we had a natural inclination.

What differentiated these two types of teacher — those we rated highly and those from whom we gained little or no benefit? All would have been similarly qualified with relevant degrees and/or teaching diplomas. They would likely, moreover, have followed similar career paths progressing from junior to more senior posts. Their CVs would probably look the same. And yet in our personal experience, their performances as teachers varied enormously. What made the difference? Clearly not their experience, nor the training that they had received, which was designed to give them the basic skills of teaching.

What differentiated the best teachers from the worst in our experience was a number of personal attributes and qualities which were strongly evident in those we rated highly and lacking in those from whom we gained little. It was these personal attributes that were what characterised the "talented teacher" and, if they were lacking in an individual, no amount of training or experience could remedy this.

We may well recall and define a number of these attributes in our best teachers. Certainly they would possess a degree of authority, an ability to command attention. They might well combine this with a real enthusiasm for their subject and thus an ability to stimulate our interest. They would be creative and imaginative in drawing on a range of information, sources and materials to aid our learning and that of our classmates.

Most importantly, perhaps, were their abilities to relate to us, their pupils. They recognised us as individuals, adjusting to our differences in ability and ways of learning, establishing a positive teacher/pupil relationship to which we would respond. They displayed a real continuing interest in our development, giving positive encouragement and constructive feedback rather than continual criticism and over-abundant use of red ink on our homework. Such teachers

> . . . take an interest in every student and display an interest in their talent and growing. They want students to discover how good they can be while in their classes (West and Patterson, 1997).

These are the talents of the best teachers and those that should be sought in those who wish to succeed in the teaching profession. Similar talents — which in essence are consistent patterns of an individual's thought, feelings and behaviour — are to be found in each and every occupation and are the bedrock on which the likelihood of success is built.

Thus, outstanding sales people combine strong influencing skills and the courage to ask for a commitment with natural relationship skills and the drive to succeed, plus the integrity on which trust and confidence is built.

Call-centre staff work in one of the fastest-growing sectors of the economy. Those who excel in their work combine a natural liking for the telephone as a method of personal communication with an extraordinary empathy, a sort of "third ear", which enables them to sense with greater perception exactly how the person to whom they are talking is feeling and to adapt their contact with the person accordingly.

The best computer programmers have an exceptional problem-solving ability and when not solving programming challenges at work, buy books of puzzles and problems to solve on trains and planes or when they take vacations.

The best chambermaids have such a natural need to put cleanliness and order into their environment that, having cleaned and dusted a hotel room so that it is spick and span, they pause at the bedroom door to admire their hard work. Incidentally, before leaving, they may well have sat in the bath to check the immaculate cleanliness of the bathroom, because this is a vantage point from which the occupant will view their room.

These are examples of qualities and attributes that characterise successful individuals in very different roles, all of which interface with the customer, client or student. It is the consistent application of these talents to which customers respond, whether accepting the sales proposition, having their telephone request dealt with well, appreciating that the computer programme delivers its promised outputs or admiring the cleanliness of their hotel suite. Talent comes in many guises but we recognise it and appreciate it when we experience it. Conversely, its absence is the source of so many of our complaints about the delivery, service and responsiveness of the companies with whom we deal.

The best managers appreciate very clearly this reality and thus their concern is to find the requisite talent in those they recruit to their team. Where their company's recruitment practices, and those of the agencies they employ, are concentrated on the skills and experience of applicants (and this is very much the norm), such managers have their own strategies and methods to identify likely talent. Some have a natural ability to identify the presence of such attributes in an applicant. This itself is a very real talent. Others appreciate that the best performers are able to or can be "incentivised" to recommend others of like ability — "the best recognise the best".

In one airline, the cabin staff were asked to rank their colleagues against a number of performance criteria, with a particular emphasis on responsible, attentive and caring customer service. There was a high degree of consistency in the ratings. Those ranked highest overall by their colleagues equally rated each other highly, recognising their own qualities in their equally highly ranked colleagues.

Increasingly, the more advanced companies have introduced recruitment and selection methods to identify such talents in key staff. Psychometric tests, assessment centres and competency-based interviews are used for making what companies regard as the more important appointments — for example, in selecting graduate trainees, senior management posts, etc. Few, however, extend such methods to selecting for the multitude of customer interfacing positions which in Western economies, with their service industry emphasis, now predominate. Here lies the challenge for future recruitment and selection policy practice for the HR function in many companies.

SETTING EXPECTATIONS:
DEFINING THE REQUIRED OUTCOMES

The influence of F.W. Taylor, the father of Scientific Management, has lasted to the end of this century and will doubtless extend into the next millennium. His focus on the importance of measurement as a mainspring of motivation has been generally beneficial. Few would disagree that "measurement improves performance". The challenge has always been to ensure that the measurement was appropriate and objective.

Equally persuasive has been Taylor's emphasis on the importance of detailed work study based on a careful analysis of the constituent elements of the job. This first ensured that no job elements are redundant and secondly sought to simplify or improve the linkages of these elements to improve productivity and provide a sound basis for work measurement.

What is Competency?

Over the years, the application of Taylor's work study concepts extended from manufacturing into clerical activities, spanning Organisation and Methods processes and then into managerial roles. Thus, over time companies adopted, often at the urging of their HR functions, more and more complex systems of job definition and description. This approach reached its current zenith with the extensive use of competency-based systems in defining managerial, technical and similar roles. Such systems are used for defining recruitment requirements, performance appraisal, remuneration systems (both for evaluating a job's worth and determining merit or performance increments) and identifying training and development needs.

However, there appears to be no clearly agreed definition of a "competency" and certainly the competencies of similar jobs are defined very differently by companies in the same business sector. In some sectors such as financial services, competencies serve as the basis for defining minimum standards established by regulatory authorities to safeguard the consumer. In other industries, they serve to specify the essential requirements to ensure safe working practices as required — for example, by health and safety regulations.

As "*de minimis*" standards, basic definitions of competency are clearly essential. However, where used more extensively for assisting managers and employees to achieve high levels of performance, their value is more open to question. Firstly, many competency-based systems are excessively elaborate and bureaucratic. Job competency definitions for management positions can run to several pages with a plethora of detailed definitions and requirements. Secondly, the definitions of competencies are often confused, failing to distinguish between personal qualities seen as desirable in the job-holders, the knowledge they should possess and the skills they should acquire. In one extreme example, I have even seen the ethical standards required defined by a competency consultancy with a set of specified levels to which the job-holder should aspire to achieve over time. How one develops more integrity and ethical behaviour in an individual is a question that the prison services have grappled with for two or more centuries. It is at best naïve to include it in a managerial competency process.

The emphasis of such competency systems is on the processes within the job which in combination define how the job is performed. A detailed competency definition is like a car's workshop manual, with the job-holder and their boss regarded as mechanics who together should understand in detail the various components of the job and fine-tune them to achieve optimum performance.

The Importance of Outcomes

This essentially mechanistic approach is rejected by the best managers. They recognise instinctively that it is not the detail of the process that determines job performance, but the outcomes achieved by the individual. They ask fundamental questions: "What is the individual paid to do?" and "Can such outcomes be defined clearly and objectively so the job-holder knows what is expected?" Their job analysis then consists of defining simply those key activities undertaken regularly each hour or day or week by the individual which contribute to that expected outcome. Furthermore, these best managers appreciate that, subject to legislative or regulatory requirements, their employees, if talented and a fit for the job, should be encouraged to find their own paths to meet and if possible exceed their expectations. Their management philosophy therefore is not one of prescription and control but of facilitation informed by a willingness to delegate and to put trust in those working for them. Indeed, as managers they see themselves as partners in helping their staff achieve standards of excellence, always however making clear what is expected of them.

"By their fruits ye shall know them": this is the philosophy espoused by the best managers who appreciate the individual differences in those for whom they are responsible, and also their common need to assert their identity, and manage accordingly. In any age where the fear of being treated as a cog is anathema to the knowledge worker in particular, the best managers have an important lesson for their organisations and for HR policy.

MOTIVATION: FOCUSING ON STRENGTHS

Some years ago, we presented some comprehensive findings on the qualities and attributes characteristic of highly rated managers to the HR function of a large UK retailing organisation which wished to take new management initiatives. At the end of a long presentation discussing and illustrating what we had identified from research to be the strengths of excellent managers, we invited questions. A hand was quickly raised by one individual: "What do you do about the weaknesses?" was the question. There, we thought, perhaps unkindly, speaks a member of the training function!

It is a pervasive feature of western cultures to concentrate on identifying, communicating and then trying to remedy people's weaknesses. Philosophically, Jean Jacques Rousseau has been perhaps the most influential thinker of the last three hundred years in laying these foundations of thought. His belief that mankind's natural goodness has been distorted by society strongly influences our practical efforts to remedy both the way our environment is organised and our individual limitations and the cultural influences seen as their causation.

Poverty, prejudice and discrimination all restrict the growth, development and fulfilment of the individual. And yet history to a remarkable degree is the story of individuals overcoming such restrictions to leave their mark on the world. Gandhi, Martin Luther King, Nelson Mandela, Joan of Arc, the Apostles, and so on, all triumphed over adversity to make their impact on the world.

Building on Strengths

The source of their achievement and ability to succeed against all odds came not from their environmental restrictions nor from their personal limitations, but from unusually powerful motivation and other personal qualities that each possessed. While we recognise and accept the importance of such talents in those who have achieved greatness, we fail to extend this understanding to the work environment. While we appreciate the exceptional abilities of world class artists and sporting champions, organisations do not formally develop and implement policies that focus on identifying and developing the individual talents and strengths of their employees. These, it is agreed, can take care of themselves; company interventions must be concentrated on identifying and taking action on what limits and restricts an individual in performing in their role.

Given the *ad hoc* process of recruitment and selection, many of these efforts endeavour to correct poor selection decisions. As already discussed, if an individual is a poor fit to the demands of the job, training, appraisal and counselling are unlikely to achieve results and represent a poor investment of time and resources.

More fundamentally, high performance is not achieved by the individual working exclusively on what is lacking. It is achieved by what they possess in good measure — those relevant personal attributes that the individual spontaneously calls on to satisfy the demands of the job. The best managers intuitively appreciate this fact and play to it, but they are in a minority. Ask one hundred managers which is more important in creating a top performing team — talent or motivation — and the great majority will answer "motivation". There is a widespread belief that anyone can excel at anything if only they really work at it and receive the best training and development. Our common sense may tell us that, however hard we try, few of us can ever be champion golfers, prima ballerinas, successful presidents or world class surgeons;

and yet our management policies and training practices run counter to such critical thinking.

Furthermore, it is only a minority of managers who devote more time and effort to their more successful and talented subordinates. The majority focus most of their time and energies on the weaker members of their team. In seminars, we ask sales managers to list their sales team members by performance and then by the amount of time they, the manager, devote to each. Overwhelmingly, when then asked to link the names in the two lists, the lines cross. The poor performers get most of their managers' attention.

Excellence in many walks of life is achieved by balancing talent — the strengths of the person — with rigorous and continual training both off and on the job. The acquisition of skills and honing them through learning and practical experience is a process with no end, as the examples of great pianists or master craftsmen demonstrates. Training investment gets its best return, therefore, when it builds on talent, not when it tries to inject it into an individual.

Thus, the best managers are always seeking glimpses of excellence in those they work with and are often skilled at talent-spotting. Their high-performing teams are not achieved by chance but by recruiting those with potential and then spending time and effort on nurturing. Such managers perceive the uniqueness of each person and play to it, both in their focus on drawing out the special abilities of the individual and in giving appropriate and regular recognition and positive feedback. "By their strengths will I grow them" is their motto, and they apply it in their successful practice of management.

FINDING THE RIGHT FIT:
THE FOUNDATION FOR DEVELOPMENT

A General Manager of a highly successful multinational was appointed to take responsibility for the company's business in a major Western European country. He described assessing his sales organisation and reviewing, in particular, one of his sales managers whose performance was barely adequate. Checking back, he found that the manager had previously had an exceptional record of sales success in a technically complex and demanding market as a sales consultant with the company. In a long review meeting, the General Manager asked the Sales Manager when he had felt most fulfilled and successful in his career and the latter described with enthusiasm his previous sales role. "How do you feel now?" asked the General Manager and his subordinate admitted to being anxious, feeling highly stressed and lacking sleep through worry. The upshot of a long, sensitively handled discussion was that the Sales Manager agreed to revert to his former role and within six months was again receiving recognition as a star of the sales team.

The Peter Principle — The Tendency to Over-promote

It is now thirty years since Peter and Hull's (1970) idiosyncratic and entertaining book, *The Peter Principle*, was published and spent nine months on the US bestsellers list. It touched a nerve of all employed in organisations — both large and small. Why? Because it so succinctly defined the perceptions and experience of those in employment work. The Peter Principle was short and to the point, proclaiming that:

> In a hierarchy, every employee tends to rise to his level of incompetence.

The authors modestly claimed that this principle was "the key to an understanding of all hierarchical systems and therefore to an understanding of the whole structure of civilisation", and went on to add a corollary to the Principle, namely that:

> In time, every post tends to be occupied by an employee who is incompetent to carry out his duties.

This corollary has serious implications for the organisation in that the stronger this tendency, the greater the likelihood of organisational dysfunction. Conversely, the less this tendency is evident, the more likely it is that the organisation has the people resources to succeed, other things being equal.

It is evident that the impact of the Peter Principle increases in relation to the level in the organisation. Whereas an incompetent retail salesperson will annoy or upset a relatively small number of customers, an incompetent chief executive can destroy a whole company.

In the earlier illustration, the General Manager, on taking responsibility for his organisation's new branch, found evidence of the Peter Principle in his sales organisation. A talented leader, his response was not to issue warnings or fire the Sales Manager, but to reposition him and set him up for success. His response typifies the approach taken by excellent managers that Gallup has studied. They are all too aware of the Peter Principle and the cultural and organisational pressures that encourage it — the promotion ladder, the benefits package, the career planning process.

While all these are necessary and, if properly designed, relevant to the planned development of a company's human resources, they tend to dominate the criteria by which success is determined and judged, often providing the only real recognition and feedback that an individual receives. Thus, in many organisations, if you are not promoted, you have failed. Such failures in the managerial echelons lead to the widely reported mid-life crises of the 40-year-old manager who suddenly finds that the board appointment to which they have aspired has become a mirage.

What is the Right Fit?

The best managers fight against these cultural pressures which encourage promotion to levels of incompetence — their emphasis being to try and ensure a good fit of each individual to their role. Many have a real ability to perceive the uniqueness, that individual combination of talents and limitations that those working for them possess. Such managers are continually reviewing their organisation and the demands made on it and seeking to position individuals to best effect, so setting them up for success and fulfilment.

These managers have a number of strategies to combat the insidious pressures of the promotion ladder. Where they can, they influence their company's remuneration policies, and press for open-ended incentive arrangements, outcome-related, which allows conventional differentials to be eroded. They themselves are prepared to see their exceptional performers earning more than they themselves, where it is clearly and objectively warranted.

When considering promotions and when doubts exist in their minds, the best managers will recommend trial periods with the opportunity for the individual to revert to their previous role, if the move does not prove to be an appropriate one. Thus, one highly successful and entrepreneurial Chief Executive was pressed by his Finance Director to appoint him as Managing Director of a newly acquired subsidiary. Doubting the likelihood of success but not wanting to lose the undoubted financial skills of his colleague, the Chief Executive gave the Finance Director the opportunity to run the subsidiary, but without a formal appointment or widespread announcement. When, as the Chief Executive half-expected, his colleague admitted within the year that he was struggling, as results were beginning to demonstrate, he was able to revert to his previous role as Finance Director, without loss of face. His move was seen within the company as a short-term measure, to evaluate the financial viability of the new business.

One of the benefits of the flatter and less hierarchical structures, which have been widely established in organisations on both sides of the Atlantic, has been some reduction in the pressures that make the Peter Principle such a widely observed phenomenon. However, whether companies, and in particular their HR functions, have developed appropriate responses to the loss of promotion opportunities, by introducing more imaginative recognition, reward and development programmes and processes, is open to question. It should be a priority if highly competent and experienced employees are to be retained. In particular, those with especially valuable skills and expertise need to be treated and recognised as professionals, with appropriate treatment and conditions to establish their status and importance to the success of the organisation.

CONCLUSIONS

There appears to be a basic truth in the research which Gallup undertook with the best managers and within its extensive employee survey database. These research programmes were separated by more than a decade and drew on different sources. The first was a qualitative, clinical analysis of what could be learned from carefully structured interviews with thousands of successful and highly rated executives and managers. The later research into Gallup's employee survey data combined qualitative and quantitative analysis, culminating in a comprehensive meta-analysis which produced statistically significant correlations of the 12 questions (Q^{12}) to productive outcomes at workplace level.

What was particularly intriguing about both sets of research was the conceptual cohesion and consistency that emerged. Here apparently were some basic truths about how to manage and motivate the individual — a clear but simple blueprint for the manager, teacher or indeed any individual responsible for aiding the growth and development of another individual.

A Formula for Management

These findings, derived empirically from all this research, can be expressed by a simple formula (as an aid to recall):

$$T \times (R_1 + E + R_2) = P_3$$

Where:

> T is a person's talent;
>
> R_1 is the quality of the relationship of the manager, teacher, etc., with the person;
>
> E is the Expectation made of the person;
>
> R_2 is the Recognition and Reward given when expectations are met or exceeded; and
>
> P_3 is Per Person Productivity (or growth)

This formula was first derived from the analyses of interviews with the "best managers". Subsequently, the employee survey research produced the Q^{12} questions as the "drivers" of a committed and retained workforce. Several of these questions are congruent with the formula. They ask the individual if the supervisor cares, if expectations are clear, if recognition is regularly given to the individual and so on.

Such questions, and the measurement that confirms their relevance, highlight the central importance of the manager or supervisor in gaining the commitment of employees. It is the manager who establishes the basis of the relationship of the employee with the organisation. It is the manager who is the key factor in establishing the company's culture. It is the manager who the disgruntled employee leaves and for whom the committed employees stays. It is the manager who should be the primary focus of companies concerned to retain and motivate the knowledge worker.

The Implications for HR Policy

This data and the conclusions drawn from it highlight the challenge for the HR function. Can it accept the need to question con-

ventional wisdom and established practice, and become the cata-
lyst for fundamental change both in philosophy and policy determination? Having interviewed hundreds of HR managers in
recent years, we would not be confident that most appreciate such
a rethink is required. Most companies and their HR departments
will continue to follow the well-tried paths — recruit for skills,
define the processes, try to remedy weaknesses and maintain the
promotion ladder as the primary path for growth and achievement.

However, some of the world's leading companies are moving
in the direction to which this research points. In particular, they
increasingly recognise the fundamental importance of talent and
the crucial role of the manager in motivating and retaining the
appreciating asset who is the knowledge worker. Sometimes the
data is so strong that such conclusions are inescapable. For example, in a recent UK study across a large distributed organisation,
Gallup found strong correlations between the talent and capability of the unit managers, the motivation and commitment of employees and the sales performance of the retail unit. In a very
large US fast food restaurant chain, where the brand, the product
and the facility is virtually identical nationwide, customer satisfaction scores, from a meticulously derived sample of customers,
followed a bell curve distribution across the range from high levels of satisfaction with the product and service offering to strong
dissatisfaction. The principal explanation for such variation was
concluded to be the ability and talents of the restaurant manager,
who is the lynch pin in providing the brand offering of this restaurant chain.

If the knowledge worker is most likely to leave an organisation
because they are poorly managed, the lesson is clear. It should be
a priority for the organisation and its HR function to select and
develop its management cadre with particular emphasis on the
first line manager and supervision. There are now simple and objective ways to measure how well the manager motivates those for

whom they are responsible and to improve standards over time through regular feedback and training. It is likely to be an investment with a very high return if planned and implemented with care and if properly researched. Those companies that follow such a strategy are likely to be the ones that retain their best employees and through them achieve improving levels of customer service and profitable growth. It remains to be seen how much value organisations put on their knowledge workers as appreciating assets in allocating funds and resources to achieve these objectives.

References

Associated Press Report, 19 March 1997.

Buckingham, M. and C. Coffman (1999), *First Break All the Rules: What the World's Great Managers Do Differently*, New York: Simon and Schuster.

Clifton, D.O. (1995), "Creating Intellectual Capital", *Teacher Education and Practice*, Vol. II, No. 2.

Drucker, P. (1995), *Managing in a Time of Change*, London: Butterworth Heinemann.

Peter, L.J. and R. Hull (1970), *The Peter Principle*, London: Pan.

Stewart, T.A. (1997), "Intellectual Capital: The New Wealth of Organisations", New York: Doubleday.

West, M. and M. Patterson (1997), "Profitable Personnel", *People Management*, 8 January.

PART TWO
SOURCING A HIGH QUALITY WORKFORCE

CHAPTER 4

THE RECRUITMENT PROCESS

Gerard McMahon and *Anne O'Carroll*

INTRODUCTION

As we enter the new millennium, recruitment is arguably the single biggest challenge facing personnel and human resource specialists. Skill shortages and forecasts of a huge drop in the number of people available for work point to rapidly deteriorating recruitment prospects. The outlook may be especially bleak for those employers who are failing to change their ways and look to new sources and methods of recruitment, as well as more innovative forms of employment.

Of course, recruitment persists in eras of both scarce and abundant labour supply. Whilst the Ireland of the 1980s was characterised by an oversupply of labour, the Ireland of the late 1990s — and into the new millennium — seems to be characterised by quite the opposite — a scarcity of labour. It is already evident that such shortages will be particularly acute in some sectors of the market, such as information technology and engineering. In the era of labour oversupply, with more applicants chasing fewer vacancies, recruitment tends to be less problematic. The advantage of an abundance of applicants is that it allows the employer to demand higher qualifications and more relevant experience. However, there is a danger that the process is neglected in an era of abundance, so that the organisation ends up with the right quantity of staff, but not the right quality. In the "scarcity" scenario — with severe shortages of certain types of skill — there is a shift in power to those looking for work, particularly those with skills that are in high demand. Consequently, employers must find ways of maximising the size of their applicant pool, probably at the expense of competitors. Potential options in this regard include attractive publicity material, good salaries, fringe benefits and working conditions. For example, organisations such as Jefferson Smurfit, Waterford Crystal, Qualcast, Guinness, IBM and Iona Technology have undertaken the "Quality Ireland Programme" — with its emphasis on staff motivation, development, remuneration and advancement — for the purpose of making themselves more attractive in the labour market.

However, a less apparent option is the application of professional recruitment techniques. For example, it is well known that the quality of a firm's recruiting process has a big impact on whether candidates pursue their applications with employers (Dessler, 1994). If you're not getting the right number of applicants, then the result is likely to involve either a lowering of your selection standards, or a failure to fill vacancies. With a growing economy, and a strong product or service market, the former route tends to be the most attractive. However, in the longer term, it may be an extremely problematic route. This chapter attempts to highlight the various recruitment options open to employers, their respective merits and demerits, and best practice in regard to same. It provides instruction in how to undertake a job analysis, and compile a job description and person specification; identifies the most appropriate media through which to advertise specific vacancies; and offers guidelines on how to present such advertisements.

WHAT IS RECRUITMENT?

It is quite common for the practice of "selection" to be totally subsumed within the term "recruitment". We would be better served by a less all-embracing definition of recruitment as:

the activity that generates a pool of applicants, who have the desire to be employed by the organisation, from which those suitable can be selected (Lewis, 1985).

Professional recruitment practice necessitates the compilation of job analysis documentation. Job analysis is a key function in personnel or human resource management. It is an essential foundation for many of the processes that underpin personnel/human resource management practice in organisations, including not only recruitment, but also selection, performance appraisal, training and development, job evaluation and health and safety.

Ideally, job analysis should comprise the following components:

- *Job Description*: a statement of the component tasks, duties, objectives, standards and environmental circumstances of the job;

- *Job Specification*: a specification of the knowledge, skills and attitudes (KSA) required to perform the job effectively;

- *Person Specification*: details on the ideal kind of person required to perform the job effectively.

Of particular relevance to the recruitment process are the *job description* and the *person specification* documents, while the job specification tends to find greater use in the training process (see Chapter 8).

What is the Job Description?
Compiling a job description is a useful mechanism for ensuring that there is in fact a vacancy, rather than a gap because another employee is not doing their job properly. The items listed in Table 4.1 constitute a comprehensive account of any job, which can be flexibly adapted to suit varying requirements of particular posts and organisations.

Table 4.1: Components of a Job Description

Component	Description
1. Basic Details	Exact title and grade, location, numbers in the job.
2. Purpose	Objectives and relationship to the aim of the organisation.
3. Tasks	Main tasks and key areas. Occasional tasks. Secondary duties. Hours of work.
4. Standards	Standards for effective performance of tasks. Criteria or competencies indicating that tasks or the job have been or can be effectively performed.
5. Responsibilities	Position of job in organisation structure. Managers/supervisors to whom jobholder is accountable. Subordinate staff for whom jobholder is responsible. Responsibilities for: (a) Finance; (b) Materials, equipment, etc.; and (c) Classified information.
6. Physical and Social Environment	Particular features of work environment (e.g. sedentary, static/mobile, indoor/outdoor, dirty, hazardous, etc.). Contacts with others (e.g. small/large groups, isolated, external contacts, etc.).
7. Training and Education	Training planned to bring new jobholders to required levels of performance (e.g. induction programme, job rotation, visits, external courses, etc.). In-job training and educational courses normally associated with the job.
8. Advancement	Opportunities for promotion and career development.
9. Conditions of Employment	Salary and other emoluments and benefits.
10. Trade Unions/ Associations/ Institutions	Appropriate unions or staff associations. Closed shop conditions. Membership of institutions/ organisations.
11. Job Circumstances	Aspects of the job commonly accepted as pleasant/unpleasant, easy/demanding, etc.

Whilst such a rigorous description of the job serves many purposes, one could argue that it creates a "working to contract" dilemma, whereby jobholders may seek to adhere strictly to the explicit and published job requirements, and refuse to go "beyond contract". Those organisations espousing "high-performance work systems", "blame-free cultures", "high trust philosophies", "total quality customer service", "continuous improvement" and "world class manufacturing", generally expect staff to be willing to go "beyond contract" in the performance of their duties. Therefore, more flexible job descriptions, which are not linked to one specific task, are becoming more common. On the other hand, some organisations simply prefer to add an all-embracing sentence to their job contracts or descriptions. This may serve as a safety net, covering:

> any other duties which management deem appropriate from
> time to time.

Beyond such precautions, it is hard to see how one might assemble a photofit of the "ideal" person for the job, in the absence of a description of the job. Having assembled the job description, one may proceed to the drafting of the person specification.

What is the Person Specification?
A person specification covers three main areas of requirement for effective performance of the job: physical, intellectual and personality attributes. In practice, it is useful to distinguish between those attributes which are considered to be essential and those considered to be desirable. The next chapter, which deals with effective employee selection, provides a practical example of a person specification.

Many organisations now utilise a system whereby they initially establish whether or not the candidate meets all of the essential requirements. If so, a weighting system is generally applied to the various criteria or requirements and the candidate is then scored on these. For example, *attainments* (or *experience*) might be adjudged to be twice as important as *physical make-up*. Accordingly, it would command twice as many marks in the overall scoring system. This facilitates a comparative assessment where there is more than one candidate.

The person specification headings and descriptions outlined in Table 4.2 (based upon the renowned "Seven Point Plan" — see Rodger, 1970) are intended therefore as a discipline to ensure that recruiters systematically ask themselves questions about potential jobholders.

Table 4.2: Components of a Person Specification

Component	Description
1. *Physical Make-up*	Health, physique, appearance, bearing, speech
2. *Attainments*	Education, qualifications, experience, training
3. *General Intelligence*	Fundamental intellectual capacity
4. *Special Aptitudes*	Mechanical, manual dexterity, facility in the use of words or figures
5. *Interests*	Intellectual, practical — constructional, physically active, social, artistic
6. *Disposition*	Acceptability, influence over others, steadiness, dependability, self-reliance
7. *Circumstances*	Availability, mobility

Note that a number of these criteria may be amalgamated into "competencies" — that is, behaviours that are adjudged to be critical to the successful performance of the job (e.g. teamwork, client care, communication). An increasing number of (predominantly public sector) organisations are displaying a preference for this approach, which is reviewed in Chapter 5.

SOURCES OF RECRUITMENT

Having ascertained what kind of job you are trying to fill (i.e. the job description), and the type of person likely to perform it effectively (i.e. the person specification), one may progress to the next phase of the recruitment process. According to both Curnow (1989) and Gunnigle et al. (1997b), a number of strategies are adopted in an effort to facilitate this recruitment process. For example, many Irish-owned organisations are investing heavily in retraining as a means of aiding their recruitment drive, while others have improved their remuneration package, targeted international recruits or sought to improve their corporate image. The earmarking of pools of labour that were traditionally ignored is also becoming more apparent (e.g. older and retired people and "return to work" mothers). Even the unemployment pool is being revisited, via State incentives encouraging the long-term unemployed back to work through tax breaks and wage subsidisation incentives.

Utilising the internal labour market for recruitment purposes appears to be the most popular method at all managerial levels (see Table 4.3), whilst consultants tend to be used most frequently for the filling of the more senior management positions. At clerical and manual levels, the preference also appears to be to advertise internally first (Gunnigle et al., 1997a).

Table 4.3: Usual Methods for Filling Vacancies (%)

	Senior Management	Middle Management	Junior Management
Internally	57	75	77
Recruitment Consultants	52	38	22
National Newspaper	47	49	37
Prof. Magazine	12	13	5
Interntl. Newspaper	12	7	2
Word-of-mouth	7	10	14

Source: Gunnigle et al., 1997b.

In this section, the pros and cons associated with the main recruitment sources are set down. Whilst some other options exist (e.g. unsolicited enquiries, previous applicants and employees, outplacement consultants, recruitment fairs and publications), the following represent the more common routes. The importance of this search process is well encapsulated in the statement from Brian Bramhall, Personnel Manager at Loctite (Ireland), that:

> a company should be like a leading Premier Division club — whoever does the job best should be hired, no matter how far you have to go to find them.

However, if the company is a second or third division club, it may be argued that they shouldn't recruit a Premier type high-flier, as they may leave quickly, perhaps taking many of the organisation's clients with them!

1. Internal Advertisement

Advantages

- It is a motivator, encouraging staff development within the organisation, as the existing staff can see that there are real succession plans and promotion or transfer opportunities available to them. Indeed, access to this source is often obligatory under some union–management agreements.

- If an internal candidate is appointed it is cost-effective, reducing the need for external advertising/sourcing and entailing a shorter induction period.

- The employer will know the candidates' strengths, weaknesses and behaviour, thus significantly reducing the "gamble" normally associated with recruitment decisions.

- By providing the relevant information to employees, they can act as recruiters. Some organisations even have formal reward systems for staff who introduce successful candidates to them.

Furthermore, there are indications that the "word-of-mouth" or "grapevine" source unearths employees who stay longer and are less likely to be dismissed (Kirnan et al., 1989).

Disadvantages

- Internal candidates cannot be compared with outsiders who might be interested in the vacant post. Consequently, the "ideal" outsider doesn't get the chance to apply and is lost to the organisation.

- Reliance on this source militates against the introduction of new perspectives and fresh ideas to the organisation from the outside.

- The successful candidate, having secured an internal promotion, may have difficulty with old colleagues.

2. Vacancy List On/Outside Premises

Advantages

- It is an economical way of advertising, particularly if the noticeboard or advertising space is near a busy thoroughfare (e.g. outside the staff canteen, at the corner shop, on the supermarket's notice board).

Disadvantages

- Only a few people are likely to see the vacancy list, and it is generally a more viable/realistic option for more junior posts.

- It is normally only possible to put the barest information on the notice or postcard.

3. Advertising in National Press

Advantages

- Reaches large numbers quickly.

- Some papers are the accepted medium for search by those seeking particular posts.

- The typesetting quality is usually good and there is advertisement size flexibility.

- Can serve as a useful vehicle for public relations.

Disadvantages

- It can be costly. For example, using late 1997 prices, the cost of a full-page advertisement in the *Irish Independent* was approximately £15,000, and approximately £17,000 in the *Sunday Independent*. Broadly proportional rates apply for smaller sizes.

- Much of this cost is "wasted" in reaching inappropriate people.

- There is considerable competitive clutter on the appointments pages, with a brief period of exposure.

- If the post has not been open to internal applicants, they may resent it.

4. Advertising in Local Press

Advantages

- Lower costs.

- More likely to be read by those seeking local employment.

- Little delay or "wasted" circulation.

- Can serve as a useful vehicle for public relations.

Disadvantages

- Does not appear to be used by many job seekers (e.g. professional workers) when looking for a post.

- In a large urban area (e.g. Dublin), it may be difficult to identify the most appropriate "local" press.

- Many interested and more suitable candidates are not aware of the vacancy.

- If the post has not been open to internal applicants, they may resent it.

5. Advertising in Professional/Technical Journals

Advantages

- Reaches the specific sector of the population having the required expertise — there's a compact and homogeneous readership.

- The typesetting quality is often good and there is advertisement size flexibility.

- Relatively inexpensive due to the smaller circulation.

Disadvantages

- Their infrequent publication causes lead time delays. For example, the advertising copy may be required six weeks before the actual publication or appearance of the advertisement.

- Wide geographic circulation — which usually cannot be used to limit recruiting to a specific area.

- If the post has not been open to internal applicants, they may resent it.

6. Employment Agencies, Executive Search and "Head-hunters"

Advantages

- Good agencies will properly test and screen possible candidates before recommending them for interview — so your time and effort is saved.

- They are an established method for filling certain vacancies (e.g. secretarial posts), and can provide applicants at short notice.

- Agencies that specialise in temporary workers can provide cover for coping with unexpected absences (e.g. through illness), workload peaks, once-off or temporary requirements for skills (e.g. installation of specialist equipment), or new developments in the organisation of work.

- They provide an opportunity to elicit candidates anonymously. In some cases, this will suit particular employers (such as those attempting to "poach" the ideal employee who works for your competitor). This may be particularly common when the skills and experience needed are possessed by just a few fairly easily identifiable people. Furthermore, recruitment agencies/consultants may have many contacts, and can be adept at identifying qualified candidates who are employed, but not actively seeking to change jobs.

- It gives the employer the chance to avail of the expertise of a specialist/consultant in an area of the labour market where they may not have ventured previously (e.g. when filling a senior post where the vacancy rarely arises). Consequently, they can save a lot of time.

Disadvantages

- Such is the proliferation of these agencies in recent years that it may be hard to decide which one(s) to use. For simplicity, they may be categorised into (i) those dealing with contract and temporary staff, (ii) general/permanent staff, (iii) specialist permanent staff and (iv) executive search and selection consultancies. However, there may often be some overlap in an agency's core market.

- They can be costly. For example, agencies for general/ permanent staff tend to operate on a commission basis with fees of 8–15 per cent of the basic salary. Agencies for specialist/permanent staff normally charge between 12 per cent and 20 per cent. The cost of an executive search programme typically ranges from 33 per cent (of the total remuneration package) to conduct the search in Ireland, to 50 per cent for an international search.

- They can produce staff who are likely to stay only for a short while. This may be the nature of the source's applicants (e.g. secretarial staff), or the recruit may remain on the "head-hunter's" list and be hunted again!

- They may not always be trusted by employers. Related to this is the fact that some such agencies may be more interested in their fee, and persuading the employer to hire a candidate, rather than finding one that will really do the job.

- Potential candidates who are not on the agencies' books, or are outside the "head-hunters" network, are excluded.

- Such agencies or consultants are only as good as the executive or consultant assigned to the activity. If an employer is to maintain a satisfactory relationship with one of these agencies, it is advisable that they put time and effort into meeting with several agency executives, choosing one that best serves the organisation's needs, and developing that relationship over time.

- If the post has not been open to internal applicants, they may resent it.

7. Government Agencies, Job Centres (FÁS/CERT/Manpower)

Advantages

- Applicants can be selected from nation-wide sources with convenient, local availability of computer-based data.

- Can produce applicants quickly.

- Because such centres often place workers for the acquisition of on-the-job experience as part of their agency training programme, it gives employers the opportunity to preview, prior to making a job offer.

Disadvantages

- Registers are mainly of the unemployed, rather than of the employed seeking a change.

- Some of the "applicants" may not be genuinely interested in getting back to work, and employers might possibly end up with applicants who have little or no real desire to obtain immediate employment.

8. Visiting Second and Third Level Institutions

Advantages

- Some institutions specialise in educating and training people for particular industrial sectors or occupations (e.g. the College of Catering, Dublin Institute of Technology, for hotel and catering staff; the College of Marketing, Dublin Institute of Technology, for marketing and promotion/sales staff). Such institutions are an important source of "raw" recruits to be developed by the employer — including management trainees as well as professional and technical employees. Accordingly, some employers develop good relationships with those offering relevant specialisms (e.g. accountancy and legal practices).

- Can provide a regular annual flow of interested enquirers/applicants.

- Have a measurable standard of performance, intellect and knowledge.

- Inexpensive and administratively convenient, via the usage of the free services of the college/school's careers office, or via the relevant Student's Union.

- The Colleges' work experience programmes offer the chance to preview potential employees (e.g. the co-operative education programme at the University of Limerick).

Disadvantages

- Interviewees may be enquirers rather than genuine applicants.

- The interview schedules can be expensive, time-consuming and exhausting.

- The recruits tend to lack experience, leaving recruiters without a work history as a guide to the applicants' suitability.

- Career prospects — and therefore movement within the organisation — are of paramount importance to graduates and many school leavers. This can create competitive "Dutch Auction" type situations.

9. Aertel/Teletext, TV and Radio Advertising

Advantages

- The Teletext option is relatively cheap. In the case of Aertel, at September 1997, the cost was approximately £300 per page per month.

- An employer's Teletext page can be updated immediately.

- The TV and radio options are exclusive and high-impact, making it difficult for audiences to ignore — and they immediately reach prospects who are not actively seeking a job change.

Disadvantages

- The Teletext option is still a relatively new recruitment source. Accordingly, in addition to its novelty, it will not be available to all potential recruits.

- The TV and radio option is costly, and as a consequence, not a recognised source of advertising.

- The details which can be given via the TV and radio option are necessarily brief.

- The TV and radio option lacks permanence, so prospects cannot refer back to it. This is a particular drawback when your desired audience is not tuned in for those critical 15 or 30 seconds.

10. The Internet

Advantages

- It is a convenient desktop method of sourcing applicants, which is likely to become common practice in the future. This is particularly apparent in the information technology arena, where it makes sense for companies seeking young computer-literate graduates to target them through a medium they understand and are comfortable using.

- Employment agencies are increasingly recognising its value as a means of advertising their Curriculum Vitae lists under specific industry and job type headings. Consequently, it will prove valuable to employers for accessing the agency databases. Likewise, the average corporate web site now includes an appointments section, with a simple e-mail response facility to make it as easy as possible for applicants to apply.

Disadvantages

- The Internet option is still a relatively new recruitment medium. Accordingly, it will take some time before it is fine-tuned to meet employers' needs.

- It can be a cumbersome and frustrating process, lacking appropriate classifications and user-friendly techniques.

RECRUITMENT ADVERTISING

The Advertisement

Whatever recruitment source is used, some form of hard copy job advertisement will normally be required. The job advertisement used in the recruitment exercise conveys images of the organisation, its products and its overall philosophy. For example, Mercury Communications recognised that recruitment advertisements provide a general impression of the company and "send out messages to potential employees, clients, customers, partners and shareholders" (Industrial Relations Services, 1994.)

It is the advertisement that attracts applicants in the first place. If it is well designed and conveys a realistic and accurate image of the employer and the job to be filled, it will normally succeed in encouraging people to apply. If it is badly designed, with typographical errors and conveys an image of a boring, drab and lifeless entity, it will generally succeed in putting off suitable candidates. The reality is that, in an era of skill shortages, employers must brush up their own Curriculum Vitae for the recruitment "beauty contest" in which candidates may often be in a position to choose for whom they wish to work.

The aim of the effective job advertisement is to meet the so-called AIDA criteria. That is, firstly, the advertisement must attract *attention*. This is best achieved by avoiding close print and maximising the use of wide borders, graphics, colour and vacant spaces. Secondly, it should develop *interest* in the job (e.g. "this is an opportunity of a lifetime"). Thirdly, the employer should create the *desire* factor, by amplifying the interest and adding extras in terms of job satisfaction, career development, travel, etc. Finally, the advertisement should instigate *action* — as the would-be applicants are advised of their next move (e.g. "ring for an application form").

To "attract attention", a headline is most commonly used — one which is meaningful to the candidate and "shouts" from the page. It is usual to have the job title as the main heading. However, the headline must catch the candidate's eye as they scan the page. It must be capable of being read in a fraction of a second, and absorbed by suitable candidates, so that they are seduced into stopping and reading further. The employer's name rarely achieves this! Though the "heading" is of the utmost importance, many job advertisers use headings that are both vague and misleading. The title of the job should be familiar, or relate to positions that the prospective candidate(s) may already hold. According to a Price Waterhouse survey, the job title and salary are the prime incentives to read and respond to an advertisement (IPM Digest, 1989).

The lead-in paragraph is critical, and will determine whether the job seekers will bother to read the rest of the advertisement. Consequently, this paragraph requires care, so that it highlights the appeal of the job, excites suitable candidates to read further, yet at the same time puts off unsuitable applications. Clearly then, the recruitment advertisement should tell the person more about the company than just the job it is offering. The potential recruit — having been initially attracted to reading the text — should have their interest further aroused with information on the employer, the job and the requirements of and for the job. In conveying the message, one should not assume that the employer is well known. Even if they are, the potential applicant is likely to have a different perspective on the organisation, either positive or negative, before reading the advert. It is up to the advertiser to make its position known — in terms of what it does, how big it is, whether it is part of a group, its position in the market, its growth potential, future prospects/projects, etc.

Against this, however, advertisements should not be over-burdened with irrelevant details. Subjects such as holidays/hours, equipment/technology, relocation expenses/fringe benefits, etc. may generally be left for discussion at a later stage.

How To Say It

Advertisements should be written for, and speak the language of, the applicant. This can be checked by getting the opinion of someone on a similar level to read over the draft before going to print. The sequence of the text should be arranged so that the information that will hold the potential applicant's attention is placed in the most prominent position (or at the beginning of the advertisement). The following is a possible list of the ingredients of a successful advertisement:

1. *Heading*: this can be the job title or other means of identification.

2. *The Company*: name and address; what it does; size/location; market position; future prospects; interest factors.

3. *The Job*: duties/responsibilities; interest factors.

4. *Requirements*: essential/preferred; education/qualifications; experience; special aspects.

5. *Incentives*: remuneration, working conditions; prospects/development/training, etc.

6. What is the next step:

    a) "Write/ring for application form and further particulars."

    b) "Applications in writing stating full details of . . ."

    c) "Call for interview between [state times] on X day."

    d) "Phone to arrange interview."

Design Guidelines

When designing and placing an advertisement, it is sensible to minimise the content and stick to the point. There are a number of guidelines which will help the employer in this respect (Plumbley, 1985). For example, sentences should be kept short — 15 words being the ideal. There should be plenty of paragraphs, with just one or two key thought-provoking sentences therein. Given the amount of information to be put into the advertisement — as set out in the list above — and the space limitations, its drafting can be a difficult task. However, a lot can be said in a few well-chosen words — a type of shorthand that a prospective candidate will relate to. There is no need for long, descriptive sentences.

Position on the Page

When placing an advertisement in a newspaper or journal/magazine, the best position is considered to be the top corner, outside right of the right hand page, marked "A" at Figure 4.1 below.

Figure 4.1: Where to Place the Advertisement

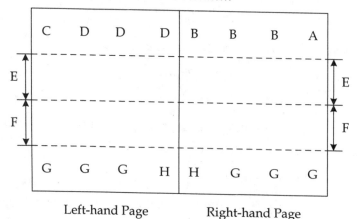

Left-hand Page   Right-hand Page

Source: Ray (1986)

Any position along the top of the right hand page is also adjudged to be a good one — marked "B" below. The next best would be the top corner of the left-hand page, marked "C". This is followed by any top position on this page, marked "D". The next best is any position above the halfway fold (horizontal), marked "E". This is preferred to placing the advertisement below the halfway fold — marked "F" and "G". The least desirable position is marked "H".

Whilst one may get a response no matter where the advertisement is placed, it has been established that response levels are affected by the position of the advertisement on the page (Ray, 1986). If one gives the newspaper or magazine enough notice of your intention to advertise, a space can normally be reserved.

To assess the effectiveness of the different media, it is necessary to keep a record showing the number of respondents to the advertisement, where it was placed, and what it cost. Where several advertisements for the one post are placed, it is not uncommon to see a request that candidates quote the source or "Reference Number" when replying. This enables the organisation to determine the number of applicants who saw the advertisement in the different publications involved. So advanced has information technology become that it can now be used to analyse responses to advertisements, and identify which media have been the most useful in generating high-quality and relevant applications (Industrial Relations Services, 1994).

What's The Law?

It is critically important that organisations take all reasonable steps to avoid any form of discrimination in advertisements on grounds of sex or marital status. Under the Employment Equality Act, 1977, advertisements which state a preference for persons of a particular sex or marital status are illegal. Also, where the job title connotes a particular sex such as "waiter", "salesgirl" or "postman", or where the job has traditionally been associated with one sex only — such as "fitter" — the Employment Equality Agency advises that the advertisement make it clear that the position is open to males and females. Specific guidelines designed to help the employer avoid discrimination when wording or framing job advertisements is set down below. New legislative initiatives, under the Employment Equality Act, 1998, promise to extend such prohibition to include discrimination on the grounds of family status, sexual orientation, religion, age, disability, race and membership of the travelling community.

What You Can Do to Avoid Discrimination when Framing a Job Advertisement

- Advertisements for jobs should be worded so that they do not directly or by implication discourage persons from applying because of their sex, sexual orientation, disability, membership of the travelling community, age, race, creed, family or marital status. Use words that have no gender (e.g. person, applicant, operator, machinist, sales representative).

- Avoid any distinctions, exclusions or preferences regarding who may apply or concerning terms and conditions of employment. Any distinctions should be based on the inherent requirements of the job.

- Do not include in the advertisement any qualifications that are not essential for the job (e.g. "minimum height"), where the number of one sex or marital status who are able to comply with the requirement is substantially greater.

THE APPLICATION FORM

Poorly designed application forms may put off suitable applicants, or fail to provide the assessors with information necessary for the selection process. The more effective application forms ensure that the information sought ties in with the person specification and/or core competencies required for the job in question. That is, for each competency, applicants are asked to provide examples of their track record in the area, or of how they have dealt with specific situations (e.g. motivation, influencing skills). Where employers avail of an application form in the recruitment process, the items that should be considered for inclusion in the form are:

1. Job title;

2. Applicant's full names, address and telephone number;

3. Education (including full-time, part-time training courses);

4. Academic qualifications;

5. Professional qualifications;

6. Present employment;

7. Previous employments in chronological order;

8. Main current interests, pursuits and achievements outside work;

9. Health;

10. Court convictions (convictions other than for minor offences, e.g. car-parking, etc.);

11. Additional information (any information not covered in the form which the applicant considers relevant to their application) e.g. driving licence;

12. Referees;

13. Source of information about the vacancy.

A sample model application form, for use in the hotel/guesthouse industry, designed by the Irish Hotels Federation, is included for specimen purposes as Figure 4.2.

Figure 4.2: Sample Employment Application for the Hotel/Guesthouse Industry

---

APPLICATION FORM – CONFIDENTIAL

Thank you for applying for a position at our hotel/guesthouse. We are pleased that you have chosen us and we would be grateful if you would assist us by fully completing the information below.

Name: _____

Position Applied For: _____

Home Address: _____

_____

Telephone No: _____

Employment History

Name & Address of Present Employer	Date Started	Gross Salary	Reason for wishing to Leave

Telephone No: _____

Briefly Outline your
Duties & Responsibilities: _____

_____

_____

Previous Employment

Name & Address of Previous Employer(s)	Dates From–To	Position	Salary	Reason for Leaving

General Education

Name and Address of School	Dates of Leaving	Examination Results Junior/Leaving/ Other (List subjects and grades)

Training, Professional or Other Trade Qualifications

Name & Address of Institution(s)	Course Followed	Year Obtained	Qualifications Obtained

Interests/Sports/Hobbies

_____

_____

_____

Medical Information

Please list any serious illnesses or accidents

_____

_____

Have you attended hospital within the last 2 years?

Yes ❑   No ❑

Are you willing to undergo a medical
examination by the hotel doctor?   Yes ❑   No ❑

General Information

Have you been convicted of a criminal offence?

Yes ❑   No ❑

If yes, please give details _____

_____

How soon would you be able to take up a new appointment?

_____

Are there any circumstances which would prevent you working the hours?

_____

_____

In which language(s), apart from English, can you conduct
business?

_____

Referees

Names and Addresses (preferably previous employers) whom we can contact for a reference.

Name	_____	Name	_____
Address	_____	Address	_____
	_____		_____
	_____		_____
Tel No.	_____	Tel No.	_____

If you are still at or have just left school/college, give the name of your head teacher/tutor and the name and address of your school/college.

Name	_____
Address	_____
	_____
	_____
Phone No.	_____

I declare that the information contained in this form is true and complete. I understand that if it is subsequently discovered that any statement is false or misleading, I could be liable to be dismissed by the hotel/guesthouse.

Signature _____ Date _____

Thank you for taking the time to complete
this application form

Source: *Quality Employer Manual*, Irish Hotels Federation, Dublin, 1997.

PROFESSIONAL PRACTICE

In 1978, the Institute of Personnel Management — now the Institute of Personnel and Development — launched a Recruitment Code designed to promote high standards of professional recruitment practice, by encouraging recruiters to adhere to common guidelines. Beyond standards of common courtesy, the Institute contend that the way in which candidates are treated reflects on an employer's public relations image. The key obligations suggested in the Code are set down in Figure 4.3.

Figure 4.3: Key Recruitment Obligations from the Institute of Personnel and Development's Recruitment Code

---

- Job advertisements should state clearly the form of reply desired; in particular, whether this should be a formal application form or by curriculum vitae. Preferences should also be stated if hand-written replies are required.

- An acknowledgement or reply should be made promptly to each applicant by the employing organisation or its agent. If it is likely to take some time before acknowledgements are made, this should be made clear in the advertisement.

- Applicants should be informed of the progress of the selection procedures, what these will be (e.g. group selection, aptitude tests), the steps and time involved and the policy regarding expenses.

- Detailed personal information (e.g. religion, medical history, place of birth, family background) should not be called for, unless it is relevant to the selection process.

- Applications must be treated as confidential.

Source: Institute of Personnel and Development Code of Professional Conduct, *The Recruitment Code 1978–90.*

CONCLUSION

Recruitment paves the way for selection procedures by producing candidates who appear to be capable of performing the required tasks of the job from the outset, or of developing the ability to do so within an acceptable period of time. The achievement of this objective depends very much on how professionally the job analysis documentation has been prepared, the advertisement designed and the right sources tapped.

References

Curnow, B. (1989), "Recruit, Retrain, Retain: Personnel Management and the Three Rs", *Personnel Management*, Institute of Personnel Management, November, pp. 40–4.

Dessler, G. (1994), *Human Resource Management*, Englewood Cliffs, NJ: Prentice Hall International Editions.

Gunnigle, P., N. Heraty and M. Morley (1997a), *Personnel and Human Resource Management: Theory and Practice in Ireland*, Dublin: Gill and Macmillan.

Gunnigle, P., M. Morley, N. Clifford and T. Turner (1997b), *Human Resource Management in Irish Organisations: Practice in Perspective* Dublin: Oak Tree Press.

Industrial Relations Services (1994), "The Changing Face of Recruitment Advertising", *Industrial Relations Services Employee Development Bulletin*, No. 49, London.

IPM Digest, (1989), "How Job Adverts Work — and Why", *IPM Digest*, No. 282, London: Institute of Personnel Management.

Kirnan, J.P., J. Farley and K. Geisinger (1989), "The Relationship between Recruiting Sources, Applicant Quality and Hire Performance: An Analysis by Sex, Ethnicity and Age", *Personnel Psychology*, Vol. 42, pp. 293–308.

Lewis, C. (1985), *Employee Selection*, London: Hutchinson & Co.

Plumbley, P. (1985), *Recruitment and Selection*, London: Institute of Personnel Management.

Ray, M. (1986), *Recruitment Advertising*, London: Business Books Ltd.

Rodger, A. (1970), *The Seven-point Plan*, Third Edition, London: National Institute of Industrial Psychology.

CHAPTER 5

GETTING THE RIGHT PERSON: SCREENING APPLICANTS AND GUIDELINES FOR EFFECTIVE SELECTION INTERVIEWING

Gerard McMahon and *Jennifer Lee*

INTRODUCTION

We have seen in the previous chapter how the recruitment process seeks to identify a pool of applicants suitable for employment in the organisation. This chapter addresses the equally critical area of employee selection; that is, the use of particular selection techniques or processes for the purpose of deciding to which of these people the organisation wishes to make offers of employment.

Since the interview is a most favoured selection technique among Irish employers, it is therefore likely to continue to take centre stage in the selection process drama. Along with the application form and reference checks, the selection interview is the most commonly used means of attempting to "identify the right person for the job" (Gunnigle et al., 1997; McMahon, 1988). Realistically, it is difficult to conceive of many scenarios where a person might be selected for employment without some form of face-to-face assessment — either formal or informal — taking place. Accordingly, this chapter addresses the key features associated with effective applicant screening and selection interviewing.

How Do You "Screen" Applications?

Having received the applications by the due date, the onus is on the employer to decide which candidates to invite to the next stage of the recruitment and selection process. This task should be based upon a rigorous comparison of the information provided by candidates with the criteria that the job demands.

As noted in the preceding chapter, the "person specification" is an invaluable tool in this regard. Dale (1995) contends that there is an inherent tendency to compare applicants against each other rather than against the job requirements, and for the shortlister's biases and heuristics to provide the underlying rationale determining suitability. Accordingly, she has devised the example of a vacancy for an Office Manager, presenting a short-listing matrix based upon the person specification in order to facilitate a more informed final decision (see Figure 5.1). This is a useful model for the "professional" practitioner on which to base their "who will we call to interview?" decision.

To help develop a more systematic approach, it is appropriate to conduct a preliminary sift of the applications on this basis, producing three categories of applicant, namely those deemed: (i) suitable; (ii) not suitable; and (iii) marginal. Having decided to invite the "suitable" category to the next phase of the process, effort can be concentrated on which of the "marginal" group to accept for this next hurdle. The importance of this stage of the procedure should not be underestimated. In deciding that an applicant is unsuitable, based entirely on documentary evidence, one should be as certain as possible about the reason(s) for rejection. Ultimately, it is a decision-making process that may have to be defended in court.

Figure 5.1: Indicative Shortlisting Matrix for Office Manager's Position

Criteria	Candidate			
	1	2	3	4
Attainment				
Successful Completion of Further Education Course	Yes	Yes	Yes	Yes
Some Job-Related Management Training	Yes	No Evidence	No Evidence	Yes
Experience				
IT Office Applications	No Evidence	Yes	No Evidence	Yes
Customer Service	Yes	Yes	Yes	Yes
Staff Training and Supervision	Yes	No Evidence	No Evidence	Yes
Record Maintenance	No Evidence	Yes	Yes	Yes
Abilities				
Communication Skills	Untidy Application	Yes	Application Badly Produced	Yes
Leadership Skills	Trainer With No Supervisory Responsibilities	No Evidence	No Evidence	Yes
Planning & Organisation	Poor Organisation of Information on Form	No Evidence	Application Badly Produced	?
Training & Instructional Skills	Yes	No Evidence	No Evidence	Yes
Aptitudes				
Customer-Focused	No Evidence	Yes	No Evidence	Yes
Accuracy	No Evidence	?	Application Badly Produced	Yes
Concern For Quality	Untidy Application	Yes	Application Badly Produced	Yes
Interests				
Involved with People	Yes	Solitary Interests	No Evidence	Yes
Learning & Self-Development	No Evidence	Yes	No Evidence	Yes

Source: Dale (1995)

THE INTERVIEW

As noted earlier, the interview is usually the central part of the selection process. It is generally the primary forum whereby the relative suitability of the candidate for the job is assessed by the organisation's representatives.

Are There Interview Pitfalls?

Despite the popularity of, and faith invested in, the interview, there is considerable research evidence to suggest that it has some serious limitations as an effective selection technique. The main question to be asked when choosing a selection method is:

In the absence of direct evidence, what predictive methods will provide the next best evidence of suitability for employment?

To be fully effective, the methods need to satisfy the conditions of *reliability* and *validity*.

A *reliable* test is one that gives consistent measurements at different times and in different circumstances with different subjects; e.g. a ruler or a weighing scales. However, the selection interview cannot always be said to reliable, as one is measuring human characteristics. No two interviewers will generally interpret and assess information in the same way and even the same interviewer will reveal fluctuations in interpretations of data and assessments over a period of time.

A *valid* test is one that measures what it purports to measure; e.g. a measuring tape. The interview cannot always be said to be a valid test of candidates' suitability for employment for the following reasons:

- It is a contrived, interrogative conversation, involving a meeting, usually between strangers and rarely lasting for more than an hour. It is, therefore, an artificially distorted and fairly stressful situation, despite the sometimes best efforts of the interviewers to reduce the anxiety levels.

- It can't really assess the relevant areas that comprise suitability for employment (e.g. ability to effectively meet the requirements of the job over a period of time; personality and disposition to work constructively with new work colleagues; capacity for self-development and the potential to assume wider responsibilities).

- It may reveal that the "all singing all dancing" interviewee is presentable, fluent and quick-thinking at the interview, but to suppose that this pattern of behaviour will persist in the very different circumstances of work, over a long period of time, would be an unwarranted assumption.

What Does the Research Tell Us?

The available survey evidence, in respect of the value of the selection interview, offers little cause for comfort. In one survey of an interviewing system for postgraduate selection, a comparison was made between the progress and careers of the selected candidates with those rejected at various stages of the selection procedure, but who had gone on to equivalent careers elsewhere (see Reading, 1983). No significant differences between these two groups emerged. A further comparison of the subsequent careers of students accepted for training on the basis of interviews with those accepted before or without interview revealed no significant differences between the two groups.

This study also examined the way in which the impact of information can vary, depending on the stage at which it arises in the process. It revealed that the initial ratings, given on the basis of the application form and first appearance/impressions, predicted the final outcome in 85 per cent of the total cases (see Reading, 1983). Other research reviews (see, for example, Anderson, 1992; Judge and Ferris, 1994; Bratton and Gold, 1994) noted the following findings with respect to the selection interview:

- People are not good at recalling accurately what they have heard in the interview;

- The evaluation of one candidate is often affected by contrasts with earlier interviewees;

- The interviewer's capacity to come to a sensible decision can be hampered by the proportion of time they spend talking, as opposed to listening and learning;

- Visual and non-verbal cues are very important, and interviewers can often respond subconsciously to them;

- Interviewers interpret and use information differently, depending on what each interviewer is looking for in, or thinks about, the candidate;

- Interviewers often respond disproportionately favourably to those qualities of a candidate which are attitudinally, sexually, and racially or culturally similar to their own;

- People use stereotypes of various sorts. The variety of a candidate's attributes is simplified and distorted by the interviewer's inability to recognise relevant attributes; their tendency to focus excessively on a general picture of a good employee and to ignore more specific and more pertinent qualities; and their judgements are often excessively coloured by one or two striking attributes of a candidate, i.e. the "halo" or "horn" effect.

Related to these deficiencies is Rowan's (1990) findings that only a small proportion of Irish organisations undertake interview training. This is an alarming discovery, given that the value of training in increasing the predictive value of the interview has long been established. Studies carried out in the Unites States in the 1940s and 1950s revealed that when highly trained interviewers conducted comparable interviews in search of precisely defined objectives, they came close to complete agreement in their assessment of candidates. Their estimates of candidates' abilities were also shown to be accurate by evidence of subsequent performance on the job (Rowan, 1990).

The relatively poor validity of the selection interview is well reflected in the scale presented in Figure 5.2. This reveals that — despite the interview's popularity — it offers little better than chance prediction of job performance. Nevertheless, Anderson and Shackleton (1993) contend that the practice has received a lot

Figure 5.2: Predictive Ability of Selection Methods

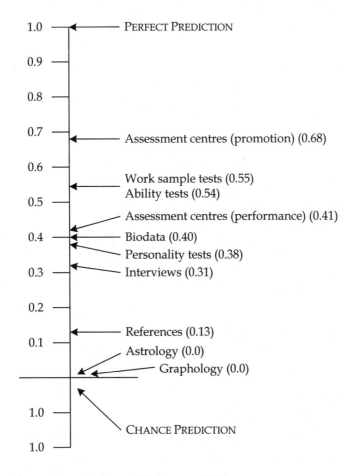

Source: Adapted from Makin and Robertson (1986)

of bad press, and that panel, structured and successive interviews help minimise many of these limitations, thus increasing the method's reliability and validity. Furthermore Wiesner and Cronshaw (1988) emphasise the point that where interviews are structured — based on the job analysis, standard job situations and behaviours — the interview's value at predicting future job performance improves. Hence the increased usage of job behaviour or competency-based screening and interviewing, for example, in the Irish public sector (e.g. Irish Civil Service Commission, Dublin Corporation). Beardwell and Holden (1997) contend that the structured interview has twice the predictive accuracy (at 0.62) of the unstructured interview (at 0.31). These structured mechanisms are addressed below.

Why Interview?
Given the host of pitfalls and limitations associated with the practice, one can legitimately inquire as to why employers rely so heavily on the interview. The main reasons include:

- *Tradition/Face-to-face contact*: It is likely that managers would lose confidence in the whole recruitment and selection process if it did not contain some form of face-to-face assessment. It is standard practice, and traditionally seen to play a key role in deciding which of several candidates is the most appropriate to fill the relevant vacancy. It is a standard part of our ritual behaviour. That is, it is akin to an initiation ceremony whereupon the outsider displays him/herself before the organisation's representatives, and has traditionally played a key part in the whole employment process. Furthermore, candidates normally like the chance to "state their case", and the opportunity to "sell themselves", which more objective selection techniques (such as selection tests) may deny them. There are few experiences in the job-hunting process as frustrating as taking the time and expense associated with submitting an

application form or curriculum vitae, and not even being invited to support it at an interview.

- *Communication*: It provides an opportunity for the organisation to give the candidate information on both the position
  and the organisation itself. In the case of a highly suitable
  candidate, it offers the organisation a chance to attract the
  candidate, by "marketing" both the post and the organisation.
  In an increasingly tight labour market, this facility is becoming
  more prevalent. Furthermore, before the contract of employment comes into force, the parties generally need to meet each
  other to "tune in" and begin the process of induction/
  socialisation. The interview also allows the interviewer to test
  the interpersonal relations between the candidate and the person to whom the candidate, if successful, will report.

- *Flexibility*: Effectively conducted interviews are a flexible way
  of gathering information, filling in gaps, developing points of
  interest and logically concluding the employment process.
  They also allow the candidates to explore issues of interest or
  concern with the potential employer.

- *Limited Options*: Despite extensive research on selection techniques, the discovery of a fool-proof means of accurately forecasting subsequent job performance has yet to be found (see
  Figure 5.2 above).

Which Type of Interview?
To facilitate the "right decision", one should decide which "type"
of selection interview to use. Selection interviews can be conducted in many different ways. However, the four most widely
used approaches are: biographical; behavioural/competency;
situational; and combination-type interviews.

The *biographical* interview is essentially an exploration of the
interviewee's past experiences, and is based on the premise that
past behaviour enables one to predict future behaviour. That is,

the best predictor of what you're going to do in the future is what you've done in the past. Accordingly, the interview is likely to focus on the interviewee's past employment, education and leisure interests, enabling a comprehensive picture of the interviewee's development to be drawn up. However, a key limitation of this approach arises from the difficulty of linking the interview information to job-relevant criteria. This gap can allow the interviewers' subjectivity to affect decisions detrimentally.

The *behavioural* or *competency* type interview entails a series of structured questions, designed to elicit information on specific "behaviours" or "competencies" which are relevant to effective performance on the job. Questions are based upon an objective analysis of the job, and can be seen to be directly relevant to the job's demands. So if it entails a lot of teamwork, initiative or leadership, the interviewers would explore evidence of the candidates' ability in these areas, based on their track record. This interview type is also based on the assumption that past performance is the best indicator of future performance. Normally, then, the candidate is asked a list of predetermined questions and expected to provide behavioural evidence as proof of each competency. It should be a consistent process whereby all of the interviewers are working from the same list of questions, allowing the responses to be evaluated on rating scales for the relevant competencies. This approach provides little scope for a candidate's "impression management" tactics. However, where interviewees frequently encounter this interview type, it becomes easier for them to "fake" answers. Given that a high proportion of candidates openly admit to lying at interviews, the danger of synthetic behavioural evidence does seem real (Fletcher, 1996). Furthermore, to cover a range of relevant competencies properly, such interviews are likely to take up a considerable amount of time. There is also a danger that, if used in isolation, key aspects of the interviewee's past may be overlooked.

The *situational* interview entails posing hypothetical job-related questions, and evaluating the responses against a set of sample answers (e.g. "What would you do if . . . ?"). Because of this interview type's potential in minimising bias and illegal discrimination, it is often used by employers in Northern Ireland. As with the behavioural or competency type interview, this format enjoys a high level of predictive validity. However, it assumes that the candidate's intentions are related to their actual behaviour — rather than reflecting their problem-solving skills! It should also be noted that — like the aforementioned behavioural interview — the time and expense of devising, running and scoring the interviews can be very resource-intensive.

As these interview options each have their own pros and cons, there is considerable merit in the view that interviewers should deploy a *combination* of all three. This would entail primary reliance on the biographical approach, supplemented by a range of appropriate "behavioural" and "situational" questions. The obvious disadvantage with this approach, however, is the time constraint.

How Many Interviewers?
Deciding on the number of interviewers is one of the most vexing questions facing selection specialists. This issue has been carefully examined by Plumbley (1985), who contends that, for certain types of appointment, there are advantages to having more than one interviewer present. This approach certainly reduces the scope for bias and subjectivity. However, the one-to-one situation is generally preferred, as rapport is established more easily and it allows the interviewer to be more flexible in approach. Candidates respond more freely in an informal atmosphere, and this is more likely to be created in the one-to-one scenario. It can also make fewer demands on management time, since the second interviewer(s) might only meet those applicants who have survived the preliminary interview.

Panel interviews, with up to five assessors, tend to be used at the final short-list stage for more senior positions, when a range of departments need or want to be identified with the eventual appointment. They are especially common in the public sector. This approach certainly reduces the scope for bias and subjectivity, allows experts in the relevant areas to pursue pertinent matters and requires the interviewee to present themselves just once to the key decision-makers. However, too often a "strong" personality on the interview board can dominate the others, or some interviewers show off to impress their colleagues. Furthermore, the formality of the arrangement reduces the scope for real rapport and flexibility, with the possibility of overawing and inhibiting the candidate from talking freely. On occasion, panels of more than five interviewers are deployed. Fortunately, these are quite rare, and tend to be more of a convenient vehicle for introducing the final candidate(s) to a full committee, with the effective choice having already been made by a sub-committee (e.g. the appointment of trade union officials, or staff to Credit Union offices).

In summary, it seems that the fewer the number of interviewers the better, and where more than one interview can be arranged (for the other organisational representatives to evaluate the candidate), the best of both worlds may be secured.

What about Interviewing by Telephone?

The telephone interview is attracting increasing interest from large employers (Fletcher, 1997). It is a useful way of cutting down on applicant travel costs, and is generally considered to be quite a cost-effective approach. Not being able to see the candidate should mean that the interviewer will be less influenced by appearance, and perhaps less biased or susceptible to "halo" or "horn" effects. On the other hand, it could mean that the candidate's voice, and in particular any regional accent, has a greater impact (negative or positive). Furthermore, candidates often seem ill-prepared for the experience — it's not what they are generally used to. Nevertheless, preliminary research suggests that it can be a useful mechanism, though there is no evidence on the extent to which it can predict future performance. Indeed, it seems likely that it will become an increasingly common element in selection procedures.

What's the Law on Interviewing?[1]

An effective selection procedure will result in the appointment of the best-qualified and most suitable candidate for the job. Ideally, the selection process will be driven by the key job analysis components (i.e. the job description and the person specification), as opposed to bias on the basis of the candidates' sex or marital status. To highlight this danger, it is important that all interviewers — and not just personnel/HR practitioners — be aware of the impact of the Employment Equality Act, 1977 (see Chapter 20). Under this Act, discrimination on the basis of sex or marital status is prohibited: in advertising, by an employment agency on behalf of an employer; in the arrangements which an employer makes to recruit new employees; and in the opportunities for promotion offered by an employer to employees. New legislative initiatives, under the Employment Equality Act, 1998 (which repeals the 1977 Act), promise to extend such prohibition to include discrimination on the grounds of family status, sexual orientation, religion, age, disability, race and membership of the travelling community (see Chapter 20 for greater detail).

Under Sections 2(a), 2(b) and 2(c) of the 1977 Act, discrimination was taken to occur:

a) Where by reason of his/her sex, a person is treated less favourably than a person of the other sex;

b) Where because of his/her marital status a person is treated less favourably than another person;

---

[1] For a more detailed review of equal opportunities legislation, see Chapter 20.

c) Where a person is obliged to comply with a condition of employment which is not essential to the job, but with which a substantially greater proportion of persons of the other sex or of a different marital status is able to comply.

Anyone who considers that they have suffered unlawful discrimination has the right to have their case investigated by the Labour Court.

What Is All This "Direct" and "Indirect" Discrimination About?
Discrimination on the grounds of sex or marital status is illegal. This discrimination may be direct or indirect. For example, it is clearly *direct* where an employer recruits persons of one sex only for work that could be done by either sex. Yet it could be *indirect* if, for example, candidates were required to have qualifications which were more likely to be held by persons of one sex. Whether or not an employer intends to discriminate is irrelevant. If a non-essential requirement (which may be a condition laid down for the job, a practice or part of the recruitment/promotion procedure) has the effect of discriminating against the majority of persons of one sex or marital status, then there is indirect discrimination.

What Questions Can I Not Ask?
Consequently, care should be taken in the course of the selection interview that questions which are actually discriminatory, or which could give rise to an inference of discrimination, are not posed. Questions relating to sex, marital status, family responsibilities, reactions of spouse, etc., should be avoided. They are likely to be taken as an indication that the applicant must satisfy conditions which may not apply to single people or persons of a different sex.

It is worth listing some of the questions posed at interviews in the past which have been held to be discriminatory. They include:

- Asking a married woman if she realised the effect the job would have on her marriage — "you'll never see your husband" — and placing a restrictive note on her application form as regards the type of work for which she was suitable;

- Asking how many children a female candidate had and how she would have them minded;

- Asking the age of a child and what the candidate's husband thought about the job;

- Asking the candidate (a single female) if she was thinking of getting married;

- Asking the candidate (a married female) whether or not she intended having any children;

- Asking the candidate (a married female) who takes care of the children when she is working;

- Asking the candidate (a married female) about her husband's availability to share the child-minding responsibilities;

- Asking the candidate (a married female) how much night duty she had done since her child was born;

- Asking the candidate (a married female) how much maternity leave she had taken.

In addition, the Labour Court has adjudged the following selection practices, in specific circumstances, to be discriminatory:

- Imposing maximum age limits;

- Setting minimum height requirements;

- Requiring persons to be prepared to be mobile throughout the country;

- Restricting an applicant pool to the output of a particular training school, or to those qualifying in a particular year;

- The refusal of employment on the grounds of pregnancy.

What is the Recommended "Code of Practice"?

An effective route for minimising the prospect of being hauled through the courts and the media for such discriminatory practices is proposed in the Employment Equality Agency's Code of Practice on equality of opportunity. In relation to selection interviews, it recommends that:

- Where possible, interview boards should not be comprised of persons of one sex only, and all persons who conduct or participate in interviews should always be carefully trained in the avoidance of discrimination.

- Where practicable, records of interviews should be kept, showing clearly why applicants were or were not selected.

- Questions should refer to the requirements of the job. Care should be taken that questions relating to marriage plans, family planning intentions, children, etc., not be asked. Where it is necessary to assess whether personal circumstances will affect performance of the job (e.g. where the job involves anti-social hours or extensive travel), relevant questions, where they are deemed absolutely necessary, should be asked equally of married, single, male and female candidates, and the answers should be evaluated on the same basis for each.

- In all cases, an interviewer should explain why a particular question is being asked, if its relevance might not be immediately obvious.

Given the legislative extension provided for in the 1998 Act, it is likely that this area will prove to be a minefield for employers in the future. Furthermore, as the Freedom of Information Act, 1998, has already obliged some public sector employers to explain their screening and selection decisions, the onus to deploy objective and job-related criteria more rigorously will weigh heavily on them.

Once decisions on the interview type and panel size have been taken, the interviewers can reflect on the crucial stages of the process: what should happen *before, during* and *after* the interview.

What Should I do before the Interview?

1. *Study all of the available information: the application forms, the job description and the person specification.* The person specification details the main "person" requirements for effective performance of the job (e.g. experience, qualifications). In practice, it is useful to distinguish between those attributes considered to be essential and those considered desirable. A weighting system can also be applied to the various requirements and the candidate may then be scored on these. For example, "experience" might be adjudged to be twice as important as "qualifications" (see Figure 5.3 below). Accordingly, it would command twice as many marks in the overall scoring system. This facilitates a comparative assessment where there is more than one candidate, and is strongly recommended. Some organisations, such as the North Eastern Health Board, take a somewhat more rigorous approach. For example, under the heading of education, specific scores are allocated or weighted according to the standard and level of qualification — differentiating between Junior and Leaving Certificate grades, certificates, diplomas, postgraduate qualifications, pass and honours marks. Such an approach to the assessment of interviewees is a valuable way of minimising biases, as it clearly specifies — before one meets any of the candidates — exactly what's being looked for, and what marks are available under the various criteria. Once the interviewers know where the "goalposts" are, they can aim accordingly, and are less likely to be led astray by the host of limitations associated

Figure 5.3: Person Specification – Sales Merchandiser

Candidate's Name: _____			
Criteria	**Maximum Available**	**Minimum Essential**	**Candidate's Score**
1. *Physical* (e.g. health, appearance, speech)	10	5	
2. *Education/Training* (e.g. Leaving Cert, certificate, diploma, primary degree, secondary degree, relevant training, clean licence)	15	5	
3. *Experience* (e.g. work experience, sales environment exposure, sales work)	40	10	
4. *Special Aptitudes* (e.g. verbal ability, numeracy)	10	5	
5. *Disposition* (e.g. personal impact/interaction, persuasiveness, stability, dependability, motivation)	25	10	
6. *Interests* (e.g. leisure, social)	20	10	
7. *Circumstances* (e.g. availability/flexibility, mobility)	30	20	
Total Available Score	150	**Candidate's Score:** ___	

Source: Productive Personnel Ltd. (1998)

with the interview as a selection device (e.g. the glittering Curriculum Vitae or the favourable impression made by the "all singing, all dancing" interviewee). As noted above, some employers prefer to rely on a behavioural/competency or structured-type interview, with its associated scoring system.

2. *Agree the coverage plan (i.e. who will cover what and when).* This ensures that all relevant matters will be dealt with in turn, whilst allowing important deviations from the "main road", as required. A comprehensive structure can facilitate flexibility, by ensuring that all the important issues will be addressed, when appropriate.

3. *Appoint a chairperson.* As noted above, the fewer the interviewers the better, but in the event of there being more than one, it is the chair's responsibility to co-ordinate the board's activities, and to ensure that all interviewers know the (agreed) ground rules and their specific role in the process.

4. *Allow adequate time.* Given the huge financial investment associated with so many appointments, and their impact on organisational morale and success, it is worth getting it right. Would you really expect to predict a candidate's performance in the job over the next 40 years on the basis of a 20-minute interview? The cost implications, particularly in relation to the danger of selecting an unsuitable candidate, are significant in this regard. On an average salary of £20,000 per annum for 40 years, plus pension costs, employer's Pay Related Social Insurance, recruitment and training costs, etc., the investment/employment cost could easily surpass £1 million.

5. *Get the climate and physical setting right.* Prohibit interruptions and distractions. Organise the seating arrangements to minimise the confrontational 90-degree facial angle. Avoid the physical and psychological (desk) barrier if possible.

6. *Prepare for note taking.*

What Should I do during the Interview?

1. *Establish rapport.* It is important that the interviewer(s) gets the candidate talking at the very beginning. This entails nothing more complex than "breaking the ice", as you try to relax the interviewee. The bottom line here is that if you can't get him/her to talk about their home town, a sporting event, a soap opera, the weather or some topical yet "neutral" item — it's hard to see how you'll get him/her to talk about the more crucial issues affecting job suitability. A preliminary examination of the CV should give you some ideas of what the candi-

date is interested in. The Civil Service Local Appointments Commission's "Notes for Members of Interview Boards" provides the following advice:

> The first few minutes are critical to the success of the interview. This is not the most appropriate period for judging a candidate and the chairman who normally talks to candidates first should concentrate on putting them at ease.

Furthermore, your reputation as an employer will be affected by how you conduct the interview. This reputation should enhance your prospects of getting the best person, rather than dissuading people from applying, or from taking up the offer.

2. *Outline the purpose and structure of the interview.* This allows everybody to know what the game plan is, and the candidate can relax, knowing where he/she is being taken, when and by whom. Having set down the coverage plan, the interviewer can retain control of the proceedings. This is relevant with the "rambling" or talkative interviewee, or where they persist with questions before being formally invited to pose them.

3. *Clear the fact that there will be (discreet) note-taking.* Subsequently, you shouldn't feel embarrassed when making notes, which will help you to make your assessment when the candidate has left the room.

4. *Follow the agreed coverage plan.* Don't engage in the potentially disconcerting practice (for the interviewee) of criss-cross questioning. This is also unfair and confusing for the interviewer who is pursuing a particular line of questioning.

5. *Listen as much as possible.* This is central to the art of good interviewing, which entails up to 80 per cent listening, as you elicit enough relevant factual information upon which to base a selection decision. By asking appropriate open (e.g. why? what? how?) and probing questions, inside the agreed agenda, the interviewer can direct discussion to the most relevant is-

sues. Minimise the use of closed-ended questions (which are usually answered with "yes" or "no" or limit the information passing to the interviewer — as they don't encourage interviewees to open up). Whilst leading questions (e.g. aren't you a conscientious person?), and multiple questions, tend to serve little purpose, relevant behavioural and situational questions have considerable merit.

6. *Clarifying and reflecting are also useful techniques for getting the interviewee to elaborate.* "Reflecting" merely entails repeating the interviewee's comment in a questioning tone.

7. *Maintain eye contact and give appropriate positive feedback.* This entails verbal and non-verbal contact to demonstrate your interest in the interviewee, and encourage him/her to talk and discuss issues openly. As with the "rapport" feature, this may eventually sway the interviewee's decision to accept your job offer.

8. *Take your time, and don't be afraid to use "silence", when appropriate.* Whilst many interviewers are embarrassed by "silence", it may fit in the circumstances. Observing the interviewee's body language should tell you whether they're reflecting on your question, or puzzled by it!

9. *Treat all candidates equally.* As detailed above, discrimination on the grounds of gender, marital status, family status, sexual orientation, religion, age, disability, race or membership of the travelling community is legally prohibited.

10. *Invite questions/comment.* Having checked that his/her colleagues have no further questions, the chairperson should invite the candidate to ask questions and volunteer any additional information they wish.

11. *Be prepared to summarise.* A good, confident, experienced and alert chairperson will briefly summarise the key features on

the credit and debit side of the interviewee's candidature. This requires considerable tact and diplomacy, but should ensure that the interviewee is not rejected on the basis of inaccurate information or omissions. By allowing the candidate to respond to this, the interview board can feel pleased that they gave each interviewee a fair and adequate opportunity to make their case in respect of the key assessment criteria. It should also help minimise the employer's vulnerability in the event of a court action.

12. *Advise the candidate of the next stage and timescale.*

What Should I do after the Interview?

1. *Assess the candidate against the person specification immediately.* In 1992, Nenagh Urban District Council was found to be in breach of equality law by failing to use the person specification in the correct manner. Their approach, of firstly deciding their preference between two candidates, and subsequently completing their scoring to reflect this preference, cost the council £8,000 and led to much unwanted publicity.

2. *Strive for objective assessment.* To minimise the impact of the most senior interviewer, or a dominant personality, the panel may opt to work out their scores and supporting/explanatory comments individually. Having calculated the average score of each interviewee at the end of the whole process, they may then proceed to discuss and review their final results. The equity associated with such an approach is relevant, given the aforementioned need to take decisions that can be defended in court. Other interview panels prefer to discuss and agree a score for each interviewee immediately after they have left the room.

3. *Concentrate on solid facts of past behaviour.* This advice is based on the premise, once again, that the best indicator of what

you'll do in the future is what you did in the past. Whilst it's not foolproof, it is more reliable than "gut instinct".

4. *Incorporate information from the other selection techniques used.* As detailed above, because of the limitations of the interview as a selection device, it is important that information elicited through other techniques is used to inform the selection decision. This is particularly pertinent in relation to selection tests (see Chapter 6).

5. *Advise the candidate of the outcome when appropriate.*

CONCLUSION

The selection decision is arguably the most important HR decision taken by an employer. The interview is an integral part of this process. Given the stakes, its importance should not be underestimated. The consequences are immense. Aligned with a professional approach to the recruitment phase, it can make a significant contribution to finding the best person for the job. Its inherent pitfalls, however, explain the rising popularity of selection tests. Whether used in isolation or in conjunction with these options, the bottom line remains the same. Like the loaded gun, it is not an instrument to leave in the hands of the untrained! The next chapter considers another key selection technique: selection tests.

References

Anderson, N. (1992), "Eight Decades of Employment Interview Research: A Retrospective Meta-Review and Prospective Commentary", *The European Work and Organisational Psychologist*, No. 2.

Anderson, N. and V. Shackleton (1993), *Successful Selection Interviewing*, Oxford: Blackwell.

Beardwell, I. and L. Holden (1997), *Human Resource Management: A Contemporary Perspective*, Second Edition, London: Pitman Publishing.

Bratton J. and J. Gold (1994), *Human Resource Management: Theory and Practice*, London: Macmillan.

Dale, M. (1995), *Successful Recruitment and Selection: A Practical Guide for Managers*, London: Kogan Page.

Fletcher, C. (1996), "Using Past Behaviour as a Guide to Potential", *People Management, Journal of the Institute of Personnel and Development*, 21 March.

Fletcher, C. (1997), "Just How Effective is a Telephone Interview?", *People Management, Journal of the Institute of Personnel and Development*, 26 June.

Gunnigle, P., M. Morley, N. Clifford and T. Turner (1997), *Human Resource Management in Irish Organisations: Practice in Perspective*, Dublin: Oak Tree Press, Irish Studies in Management.

Judge, T. and G. Ferris (1994), "The Elusive Criterion of Fit in Human Resources Staffing Decisions", *Human Resource Planning*, Vol. 15, No. 4.

Makin, P. and I. Robertson (1986), "Selecting the Best Selection Technique", *Personnel Management, Journal of the Institute of Personnel Management*, November.

McMahon, G. (1988), "Personnel Selection in Ireland: Scientific Prediction or Crystal Ball Gazing?" *IPM News*, Vol. 3, No. 3, October.

Productive Personnel Ltd. (1998), *Successful Selection Interviewing Course Notes*, Dublin: Productive Personnel Ltd.

Plumbley, P. (1985), *Recruitment and Selection*, London: Institute Of Personnel Management.

Reading, T. (1983), "How Interviews Fail", *Personnel Selection and Interviewing*, The Open University Open Business School, Book 1 - P673, The Open University Press.

Rowan, M. (1990), "Boardroom Theatrics", *Management, Journal of the Irish Management Institute*, November.

Wiesner, W. and S. Cronshaw (1988), "A Meta-analytic Investigation of the Impact of Interview Format and Degree of Structure on the Validity of the Employment Interview", *Journal of Occupational Psychology*, No. 61.

CHAPTER 6

USING SELECTION TESTS AND OTHER OBJECTIVE ASSESSMENT TECHNIQUES

Dermot Rush

INTRODUCTION

This chapter deals with the use of psychometric tests and other objective assessment techniques and their role in the selection process. It takes forward the discussion of the previous chapters and reviews how current "best practice" has developed to the point where more than one assessment technique is typically deployed in the selection process. While the interview is still the most popular selection method, it is increasingly being complemented by the use of other more objectively structured techniques including psychometric tests, simulation exercises and custom-designed application forms.

The aims of this chapter are:

- To define the main categories of assessment methods that are used to complement the interview;

- To describe the rationale and uses of these methods;

- To give practical examples of how the methods are deployed;

- To identify leading edge trends in method development;

- To give guidelines on how to choose, deploy and evaluate methods used against quality assurance criteria.

ORIGINS OF OBJECTIVE ASSESSMENT

The use of structured assessment methods goes right back to biblical lore when Gideon chose his regular army by observing the vigilance of applicants after a long desert march. His criteria were simple: those who retained a grip on their spears while drinking at a water hole were accepted while those who cast their weapons aside were discarded.

This early example illustrates one of the fundamental characteristics of sound assessment methods, which is:

> *To take a sample of job-relevant candidate behaviour*
> *and to compare this against a standard.*

DEFINITION OF TERMS

A simple definition of a test is "a standardised sample of behaviour which can be described by a numerical scale or category system" (Cronbach, 1984: 9). Psychological or "psychometric" tests aim to maximise objectivity by standardising all aspects of the assessment process, as illustrated in Figure 6.1.

Figure 6.1: Standardisation of Testing

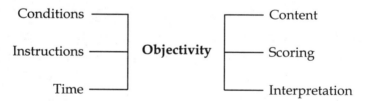

WHAT ARE THE COMMONLY USED OBJECTIVE ASSESSMENT METHODS?

While there are a multiplicity of structured assessment methods now in use, the most commonly used methods may be categorised as: (i) general intelligence tests; (ii) aptitude tests; (iii) attainment tests; (iv) personality questionnaires; (v) interest inventories; (vi) simulation exercises; and (vii) assessment centres. These are briefly considered below.

General Intelligence Tests

General intelligence tests measure overall or general mental ability by combining sub-scores across a range of discrete tasks. The most popular intelligence tests, such as Wechsler Adult Intelligence Scales combine scores of verbal intelligence and performance intelligence to give an overall IQ score.

Aptitude Tests

Aptitude tests measure specific abilities by testing items of graded difficulty. Typical examples would be tests of Numerical Critical Reasoning, Spatial Reasoning, Code Checking, and Mechanical Reasoning.

In comparison to intelligence tests, aptitude tests or cognitive ability tests are more frequently used for selection purposes for the following reasons:

- Intelligence tests only give a global measure of intellectual capability. In fact, two individuals can achieve the same IQ score but can have completely differing patterns of subscores (i.e. one may have strong verbal intelligence and the other have strong non-verbal intelligence and vice versa.

- Aptitude tests, on the other hand, are measures of differential ability, which means that they can measure individual sub-skills in isolation. This allows testing to be more specifically focused on the critical abilities required for a particular job. For example, a data entry job may require specific skills in code checking, following instructions and classification, while a senior management role will require high-level verbal and numerical critical reasoning skills.

Attainment Tests

Attainment tests measure acquisition of previously taught content and can include reading tests, maths tests, tests of rules or specific job content. Typically such tests are used in selection to assess baseline technical knowledge.

Personality Questionnaires

Personality questionnaires measure an individual's typical or preferred style of behaviour and ideally should focus on work-relevant areas such as relationships with people, task approach, emotional balance and drives.

Interest Inventories

Interest inventories measure an individual's vocational or career interests. Care must be taken to ensure that these instruments are updated in pace with changes in career behaviour and how work is configured (for example, teleworking is a more common feature nowadays than even ten years ago).

Simulation Exercises

The term "simulation exercise" covers a wide range of methods whose common feature is that a live behavioural response to a presented situation is elicited and then scored by a structured scoring system.

Assessment Centres

Contrary to their name, assessment centres are not a physical place but a sophisticated and comprehensive assessment method incorporating the use of a range of the above measurement methods with groups of candidates and multiple raters.

While all these methods share the common features of being pre-designed, administered in a consistent way and scored against a standard scoring key, they actually do differ in the level of subjective judgement involved and in the latitude of their scoring. Typically, simulation exercises are not fully psychometric measures and they are often used in a more diagnostic manner.

THE EFFECTIVENESS OF DIFFERENT ASSESSMENT METHODS

There is a considerable body of research, which has been built up over the years, on how effective each of the main assessment methods is. Table 6.1, based on work by Smith and Robertson

(1989), illustrates the effectiveness or validity of the main selection methods.

Table 6.1: *Validity of Selection Methods*

Selection Methods	Range of Validity Values
Work Sample	.38–.54
Ability Composite	.53
Assessment Centre	.41–.43
Supervisor/Peer Evaluation	.43
General Mental Ability	.25–.45
Bio-data	.24–.38
References	.17–.26
Interviews	.14–.23
Personality Assessment	.15
Interest Inventory	.10
Hand Writing Analysis	0

N.B. Figures are expressed as co-relations on a decimal scale from 0 to 1 where 1 represents a perfect concordance between assessment scores and subsequent job performance.

Source: Smith and Robertson (1989).

These research findings point to three main conclusions:

1. There is a high degree of consensus about the relative effectiveness of different methods.

2. It is usually possible to generalise the effectiveness of methods across jobs with roughly similar characteristics. The benefit to practitioners is that they can apply current best practice in test use in most situations without having to enter into a test design and validation process from scratch.

3. In selection for critical roles it makes sense to use a combination of assessment methods to achieve a more comprehensive view of candidates. Combining assessment methods can lead to greater reliability and accuracy of candidate measurement.

FREQUENCY OF USE OF METHODS

Research on selection practices in Irish organisations shows that the use of objective assessment techniques is increasing while at the same time there is still an alarmingly high reliance on the use of more subjective methods (Porteous and Hodgins, 1995; also see Gunnigle et al., 1997: see Table 6.2 below).

Table 6.2: Utilisation of Selection Methods by Organisation Size

Selection Method	Organisation Size		
	Small *(n=42)*	*Medium* *(n=94)*	*Large* *(n=95)*
Structured Interview	23 (55%)	70 (74%)	83 (87%)
Unstructured Interview	20 (48%)	38 (39%)	27 (28%)
Cognitive Ability Tests	1 (2%)	11 (12%)	36 (38%)
Personality Tests	5 (12%)	11 (12%)	34 (36%)
Bio-data	1 (2%)	2 (2%)	4 (4%)
References	27 (64%)	71 (75%)	80 (84%)
Assessment Centre	0 (0%)	2 (2%)	8 (8%)
CV/Application Form	34 (81%)	87 (93%)	91 (96%)

Source: Porteous and Hodgins (1995), p. 397.

SETTING A CONTEXT FOR THE USE OF TESTS AND OTHER STRUCTURED ASSESSMENT METHODS

First Principles: Establishing the Purpose of Assessment in Selection

Structured assessment methods are used in selection for one of four main purposes.

1. To improve the chances of identifying the best person for the job
The use of structured and scientifically based assessment methods is mainly justified by the increased likelihood that they provide means of identifying candidates who will be significantly more effective than the norm for the job. The research on the effectiveness of each method (illustrated in Table 6.1 above), shows that while better methods will give better prediction, we are still a long way short of being able to perfectly predict job performance from test results. However, as can be seen from Table 6.1 above, aptitude tests and other structured assessment techniques will achieve double the predictive power of more traditional interview and CV-based approaches to selection.

2. To identify candidates who have an acceptable level of capability
This is a more conservative approach where we are using assessment techniques to ensure that candidates have, as a minimum requirement, the essential mental problem-solving characteristics required for acceptable baseline job performance.

3. To eliminate potential mistakes and poor performance
This approach takes the "fail safe" concept one step further and it sets out to identify and test those human qualities that are most likely to contribute to significant or " mission critical" mistakes in the workplace.

Case Example 6.1: The Cost of Poor Performance

In the micro-chip industry a combination of poor code checking ability and lack of attention to detail can result in a highly qualified graduate routing "work in progress" incorrectly at a resultant scrap and rework cost of $250,000 per mistake made. The remedy is specific testing of candidates for these critical attributes.

The fail-safe approach will identify desirable and "danger zone" profiles for a critical job and evaluate candidates very stringently against these criteria.

4. To assess candidate's fit to the wider context of a job
Structured assessment techniques can give valuable data on the "goodness of fit" between an individual and the wider context of a job. Going beyond the mental ability to do a job well, we can also assess other personal characteristics that will have an impact on job performance, such as:

- How well the individual's preferred style of leading others will fit with the values and culture of the prospective employing organisation.

- Whether the individual will have a sufficiently resilient behavioural style to cope with a highly intense demand level in a particular role.

- How comfortable someone with a very innovative and change-oriented way of thinking will be working in a tightly controlled and role-following managerial environment.

When one considers the costs that arise from selection errors (such as poor performance level, retraining costs, low morale, severance and further recruitment), it makes sense to ensure that selection procedures are as objective, structured and broad-ranging as possible.

The Increasing Demand for Standards of Practice and Compliance with Legislation
In addition to these reasons, we find that with the introduction of recent legislation on Employment Equality and Freedom of Information, there is a growing imperative on employers to ensure that the selection methods they use are transparent, objectively grounded and free of bias.

In addition to the effectiveness arguments based on validity research, it is clear that appropriately chosen structured assessment methods will meet these acceptability criteria to a greater extent than the traditional CV, interview and reference check based systems, where greater subjectivity often comes into play. This is particularly the case where large-volume recruitment programmes are held, with many candidates not even being progressed to a full individual face-to-face interview.

The Second Issue to Consider: What are the Sources of Performance Differences between Individuals

Traditionally, recruiters have focused on Knowledge, Skills, and Attitudes (KSA) as the main qualities underpinning differences in job performance, with motivation being an additional but highly elusive factor to consider. Since the 1980s, however, there has been a growing interest in the competency-based approach to performance. This approach springs from the seminal work done by Boyatzis (1982) in the US on the characteristics associated with effective management performance. Put simply, he defines "competency" as:

> A job competency is an underlying characteristic of a person in that it may be a motive, trait, skill, aspect of one's self-image or social role or a body of knowledge which he or she uses.

Competencies are the qualities that underpin effective role performance. Fundamentally, the competency approach directs our attention to a much wider range of human factors that influence job performance, with a particularly critical emphasis on learned behaviour as a key predictor of future performance.

A rule of thumb for effective selection would be to ensure that there are in place means of assessing four main areas:

1. The individual's thinking capabilities and their capacity to structure task delivery;

2. The individual's capacity to work well with and through other
   people — the area loosely dubbed interpersonal skills;

3. The individual's personal values, motives, commitment;

4. Their level of relevant work knowledge and technical skill.

EXAMPLES OF BEST PRACTICE

Starting in the Right Place

The first step in the effective development of tests and other objective assessment methods is to make sure that you are starting in
the right place.

   Starting in the right place entails being absolutely clear about
the role requirements of the job that you are selecting for. Definition of role requirements typically involves the conduct of some
form of job or role analysis. Role analysis involves answering a
series of fundamental questions, such as those in Table 6.3.

Table 6.3: Role Analysis

Area of Enquiry	Job Analysis Methods
1. What are the main tasks in the job? Which are most frequent? Which are most critical?	Tasks Analysis and Observation
2. What are the most critical situations in the job and the main pressure points?	Structured Interview and Employee Debriefing
3. How do really effective performers differ from the average in their job behaviour?	Structured Enquiry with Managers and Customers
4. How is the job likely to change over the next five years (e.g. with new technology or changes in structures, processes/products and customers)?	Future focused interview with senior managers and planners in the organisation

A comprehensive job analysis will usually more than repay the
effort and resources involved, particularly if it is conducted as a
participative and collaborative enquiry process with the job hold-

ers and the direct manager of the job. Indirect benefits include greater insight into how the job needs to be structured and supported as well as valuable data for the design of training and development interventions.

Case Example 6.2: Using Job Analysis for Restructuring Work

In the chemical industry, Olin Chemicals BV, a bulk manufacturer, was experiencing severe competitive pressures with a consequent emphasis on the need to get a greater productivity return from its relatively compact but highly traditional workforce.

A job analysis conducted prior to the recruitment of a new shift team provided the following picture of performance requirements for operating team members.

Old Requirements	New and Future Requirements
A. Task Capabilities	
• *Ability to follow instructions* • *Basic numeracy* • *Reliability and work discipline* • *Broad-based technical awareness*	• *Ability to think in system terms and anticipate problems* • *Numerical evaluation for statistical process control and other tracking* • *Schedule planning and monitoring* • *Problem-solving skills* • *Broad-based technical awareness*
B. Interpersonal Skills	
• *Team-playing skills* • *Communication skills*	• *Acting as a role model or example for others* • *Team-playing skills* • *Communication skills* • *Coaching and development skills*
C. Personal Qualities	
• *Calm under pressure* • *Pride in the job*	• *Willingness to take the initiative* • *Resilience under pressure* • *Achievement orientation*

The above data provided a valuable contribution to the induction, training and performance management system in the organisation as well as shaping the selection criteria for the new recruitment process.

Getting the Right Balance between Effectiveness and Efficiency in High Volume Recruitment

Recruitment planning often involves finding the right balance between the ideal best practice assessment approach and the realistic resources available to run the selection process.

In a situation where it is not possible to deploy the most comprehensive assessment process desirable due to very large candidate numbers, then it is imperative that the most effective screening methods are deployed at the first stage of the competition. This will ensure that the selection process achieves a good balance between effectiveness and efficiency in that:

Valuable management resources, which usually constitute a significant opportunity cost in large recruitment competitions, are only committed to interviewing those candidates where it has already been established that they have the required baseline capability to do the job well.

For this reason, many large organisations that regularly run high-volume selection programmes deploy psychometric tests as an initial screening stage. Table 6.4 illustrates the benefits of this approach in a health service context.

Building as Comprehensive a Picture as Possible

In some recruitment situations there is an extra emphasis on building the fullest picture possible of the candidate as a whole person. Two such situations are graduate recruitment and selection into senior management or professional positions.

In graduate recruitment programmes, organisations are trying to identify the candidate's potential to fill a broad spectrum of future roles rather than focus on their "goodness of fit" to one specific role. In this context, multiple assessment methods are usually deployed so that:

- A fuller picture of candidate capability is built incrementally across stages of the selection programme, with evidence from

Table 6.4: Use of Aptitude Tests in a Large Volume Recruitment Screening Competition

Job Role: Clerical/Administration	Sector: Health Boards
Traditional Recruitment Process using Screening Interviews	**Improved Process using Aptitude Tests**
Candidate Numbers: 3,000	
Screening Method	
Panel interview lasting no more than 15 minutes. Two-member panels from middle management grades. Four to six panels working in parallel. Criteria not fully specified, i.e., "General Suitability" used as a heading.	Screening method using tests of reasoning, clerical skills and work style with these; criteria based on job analysis. Candidates tested in groups of 100 over a 2½-hour session. Testing conducted by trained personnel.
Time to run screening	
12 weeks to complete the entire screening programme.	Two weeks to complete the entire screening programme.
Benefits	
• All candidates seen face-to-face, but the assessment method has low validity.*	• All candidates are screened using the most valid single assessment method. • The time and manpower required to run the screening process have been significantly reduced.
Costs	
• There is a massive opportunity cost in running a large-volume interview process. Conservative costs of the interview panel time alone work out at around £54,000 plus the logistical and administrative costs. However, the greater cost is the reduced availability of managers for other essential work. Average cost per candidate works out at approximately £22.00.	• The costs are for test materials, test venues and trained testers. In this case, in-house invigilating staff were trained for the competition. Total costs including analysis and reporting of results come to £30,000. Average cost per candidate worked out at approximately £12.00.

* See research evidence on validity of methods cited earlier.

each individual method being used to further augment the picture of the candidate;

- The combined methods give a higher predictive power;

- The in-depth picture gained on successful candidates can be used as the initial foundation for induction and placement experiences that will give the best learning and development to the new entrants.

Assessment centres are the best example of a multiple assessment process. Assessment centres have the following characteristics:

- The assessment criteria are defined in a rigorous way (usually through role analysis);

- The assessment methods are tightly mapped against these criteria;

- More than one assessment method *and* more than one assessor are deployed for each criterion area;

- Candidates typically go through the assessment process in groups, with a full integration session following each assessment programme.

Well-run assessment centres typically achieve higher validity or accuracy of measurement than any other assessment method. They are a resource-intensive process and their use has often been confined to selection for more senior roles in an organisation. However, a more searching cost–benefit analysis will show that assessment centres can give added value to selection for team leader and supervisory roles. This is particularly so where modern work processes have pushed down the central responsibility for customer retention, service levels and current resource usage to these layers of the business.

The Irish Trade Board (now part of Enterprise Ireland) uses an assessment centre format combined with a very detailed application form in a good example of best practice in graduate recruitment; see Case Example 6.3.

Case Example 6.3: Graduate Selection at the Irish Trade Board

---

The Irish Trade Board uses a sophisticated screening and final assessment process to select for its highly prestigious marketing internship programme.

The programme attracts a high-volume candidature of talented graduates, while the varied demands of the programme make it imperative to get a broad view of the individual's potential.

1. The screening process comprises a structured application form, which includes a section for evidence of specific competencies relevant to the programme. Candidates are also interviewed on campus using a structured format, which again is largely competency-focused. Both the application forms and interview are scored against pre-set criteria and candidates must exceed a threshold score to proceed to the final selection.

2. The short-listed candidates are taken through a half-day assessment centre where they undertake a number of simulation exercises comprising:

- A group exercise with a marketing theme. (60 minutes duration)
- A one-to-one telephone role-play based on a realistic client scenario. (30 minutes duration)
- An In-tray exercise, tapping planning analysis, problem-solving and communication skills. Again, this exercise is based on a realistic Trade Board scenario. (60 minutes duration)

The candidate's performance is evaluated by a team of trained assessors and scores are allocated across competency criteria with the aid of behavioural rating scales.

The benefits of this very structured assessment process are:

1. Managers in the operational areas report higher satisfaction ratings with the calibre of the graduates taken onto the programme;

2. Placement and induction planning is now directly shaped by the comprehensive assessment data available on the graduates;

3. All candidates can receive specific feedback on their current strengths and weaknesses.

Using Personality Questionnaires as Diagnostic Tools in Selection

The competency-based approach to human resource management has re-focused our attention on the contribution that personality style makes to effective job performance. Personality question-naires can give valuable insight into the likely "goodness of fit" between an individual and the specific characteristics of a role. In a nutshell, personality profiling can help to assess the extent to which the candidate's preferred ways of thinking and behaving fit comfortably with factors such as:

- Specific role criteria such as a critical need for self-discipline, decisiveness or innovation;

- The demand level and pressure points of the job;

- The preferred management style of the candidate's potential boss or superiors;

- The values and culture of the organisation.

A good example of this is in an internal promotional context, as outlined in Case Example 6.4 below.

Case Example 6.4: Avoiding the Peter Principle, or "Hindsight is an Exact Science"

An absolutely outstanding salesman in the consumer goods sector was promoted to the position of national sales manager. Within a twelve-month period, sales performance was in decline and team morale was plummeting.

As part of a problem-solving intervention, the new manager's personal-ity style was profiled using the Occupational Personality Questionnaire (OPQ). His preferred style of behaviour made for interesting analysis when compared to the demands of his new role.

Strong personality characteristics on OPQ	*Relevance to new management role*	*Relevance to previous sales role*
(I) Relationship with people		

• *He scored strongly as an extroverted individual with:*
 	
  ◊ *A strong orientation to control others*
 	
  ◊ *A penchant towards influencing and a strongly independent point of view*
 	
• *He was less likely to consult others before forming an opinion*
 	
• *He had a strong need for personal recognition of his achievements*
	• *His style emphasised being in control and putting forward his own views rather than listening to the proposals of others*
	
	• *He needed to get a lot of personal recognition for achievements rather than sharing these with his team*
		• *Strongly influential personal selling style based on charisma and a dynamic approach*
		
		• *It was natural and appropriate to look for personal recognition as an individual sales performer*

(II) Thinking Style		
• *He was more strongly oriented towards data rather than people issues*	• *He was less sensitive to picking up individual and group morale nuances, but good at tracking sales trends*	• *He was excellent at pricing and product performance knowledge*
(III) Emotional Balance		
• *He was emotionally very wrapped up in his work whilst at the same time being quite tough-minded about setbacks or criticism* • *He tended to very easily adopt a critical view of the performance of others*	• *He took the success of the entire sales function as his own personal responsibility* • *He also tended to shrug off negative feedback or disappointments and not consider the sensitivities of his team to setbacks*	• *He was able to persevere when selling situations were tough* • *He shrugged off disappointments and redoubled his efforts*
(IV) Drives and Energies		
• *He was extremely competitive by nature and disliked losing* • *He was very strongly career- and achievement-oriented* • *He was used to making up his mind quickly*	• *He tended to push his own views and ideas as the best way forward in every situation* • *He tended to quickly adopt a strong position and then would stubbornly defend it*	• *He was able to turn his competitive energies outwards to securing business opportunities against tough competition* • *He was able to close deals quickly and respond to customer priorities*

The personality profile clearly illustrated that many of the individual's strongest personality traits were very well suited to his previous sales role but were actually maladaptive in his new management role. After a period of reflection, the manager agreed to revert to a specialist sales role (albeit at senior status and remuneration level!). Within months, the upward graph of sales performance had been re-established.

This example will sound a familiar chord with many personnel practitioners, as it could be seen as a classic example of the "Peter Principle", where able individuals are promoted to one level above their natural competence. In actuality, it illustrates how very successful performers often have a very strong personality fit with the demands of a particular type of role. Career planning for the mutual benefit of the organisation and the individual should take serious account of such strong patterns of personality style, when addressing the provision of both promotional opportunities and recognition.

Linking Assessment to Development Planning

At a time when organisations are rightfully concerned to get the "best bang for their buck", the investment in objective assessment techniques for selection can also be channelled into training and development applications. In effect, an organisation can improve cost efficiency, not only in selection but also in training and development programmes, by a careful investment in objective assessment methods.

A variant of the multiple assessment process is the "development centre" approach, where participants engage in a range of assessment centre exercises for the purpose of identifying development needs. There is a significant action learning element involved in these programmes and the objective assessment of performance in realistic scenarios leads to very powerful behavioural feedback and the generation of personal insight.

The following case study illustrates how First National Building Society used the development centre approach to conduct a developmental audit of its management team (see Chapter 9).

Case Example 6.5: Development Centres at First National Building Society

---

First National Building Society initiated a Development Centre programme for its management grades in 1994, with the objectives of: (i) establishing a baseline of current capabilities; and (ii) providing a starting point for focused personal development of performance.

The assessment process consisted of a highly interactive 1½-day programme for groups of six to eight participating managers. These exercises included:

- *A pre-centre 360° competency audit*

- *At the Centre:*

    ◊ *Tests of verbal and numerical critical reasoning*

    ◊ *An In-tray Exercise, which is a case study involving management of an operational branch network*

    ◊ *A Group Exercise involving a team problem-solving task*

    ◊ *A Performance Coaching Exercise involving a scenario where a subordinate has performance difficulties*

    ◊ *A One-to-One Customer Encounter Exercise revolving around quality and sales issues*

    ◊ *Personality Profiling using the Occupational Personality Questionnaire (OPQ).*

The table below illustrates how the exercises map onto the target competencies for assessment.

Competency Clusters	360° Comp. Inventory	In-tray	Group Exercise	Apt. Tests	OPQ	Perform. Coach.	Cust. Exerc.
Commercial Acumen	X	X	X	X			X
Team Skills	X		X			X	
Service Focus	X				X		
Selling/ Customer Skills	X				X	X	X
Task Management	X	X		X			

During the centre process, candidates were encouraged to learn from their performance at individual and group debriefing scenarios.

The development centre was followed up by individual action plans, which were agreed by the participating managers and their direct superiors.

The reported benefits of the programme include:

- *Channelling of the bulk of training resources into the development of competencies that have proven business relevance;*

- *Individually tailored development programmes (over 50 underway at the last count);*

- *A number of managers who were relatively unknown to senior executives have subsequently accelerated their progress within the organisation;*

- *A participant satisfaction rate of over 90 per cent (despite over 65 per cent reporting that the centre was the most challenging training event that they had ever experienced).*

The First National case study illustrates many best practice features of development centre programmes. Such programmes will facilitate ongoing development when they include the following features:

- The process must be anchored by a set of well-defined and business-relevant competencies;

- The same level of assessment rigour must be used as in assessment centres for selection;

- The exercises should include a debriefing component to give participants the opportunity for active learning during the centre process itself;

- Participants receive individual feedback whereby their profile of current strengths and weaknesses is compared against a standard (which may be job-level specific or be strategically pitched at the demands of work at one level higher than the participants currently work at);

- The use of senior managers as assessors and facilitators during the development centre programme should be actively encouraged.

FUTURE TRENDS IN SELECTION METHODS

The development of selection and assessment methodologies continues to evolve and we can identify some of the key emerging trends under the following headings:

- Development of new methods;

- Development of delivery systems;

- Development of practitioner expertise;

- Quality of assurance.

Development of New Methods

Other chapters have alluded to the development of structured and situational interview techniques as a means of improving the poor validity of traditional selection interviewing. Another development has been the design of *situational inventories* as a new form of structured assessment.

In essence, a situational inventory replicates the best design features of a well-constructed situational interview and embodies these in a paper-and-pencil format, which allows for simultaneous administration to large groups of candidates. Candidates are presented with a number of scenarios, derived from authentic job content, and are asked to select their most likely response from a set of defined options. Candidates' response preferences are evaluated against the standard of response displayed by competent job performers.

The Civil Service Commission has been a pioneer in the use of these techniques in Ireland (see Case Example 6.6 below).

Case Example 6.6: Use of Situational Inventories in the Civil Service Commission

The Civil Service Commission sought to improve the breadth of assessment when very large numbers of candidates were being screened at the preliminary stages of the Garda Entrance Competition. It replaced the traditional numerical and general knowledge written examinations with a specially designed situational inventory based on real-life examples of typical situations that a garda encounters on the job.

A typical item from the inventory would take the following format:

"You are on duty at a public event when a number of youths use abusive language in the presence of other members of the public. A woman brings their behaviour to your attention. How would you deal with this situation?

"Pick one of the five actions below as your preferred response:

1. *Tell the women not to be alarmed and to do her best to ignore it.*

2. *Approach the youths and take their names and addresses.*

3. *Caution the youths to tone down their language and behaviour.*

4. *Decide, as it is a festive occasion, to let the matter go.*

5. *Acknowledge her concerns and promise to intervene if the abusive language continues."*

The introduction of this new selection method has had the following benefits:

1. *It enables a large number of candidates at the first screening stage to be assessed on a broader and more relevant range of competencies than would be measured by aptitude tests alone.*

2. *The patterns of candidate scores show that this assessment method is free from gender bias.*

3. *Candidates' initial response to this assessment method has been to rate it as both relevant and fair.*

Another new methodology has been the development of *competency inventories* or *competency rating scales*. These are instruments that focus on the measurement of specific competency areas. They can best be understood as seeking to measure the observable effects of an individual's behaviour at work — in contrast, for example, to a personality questionnaire, which measures the individual's preferred style in a way that is less directly linked to the observable effect of their behaviour. Some features of these emerging competency instruments are:

•   They range in technical sophistication from psychometric scales to simple behaviour rating / attribution scales;

•   They can be used in single or multiple rater formats.

The multiple rater format is increasingly used to give individuals 360° feedback on their current performance from a range of raters, including boss, colleagues, subordinates and even customers.

Most typically, they are used for performance review or development applications, although they can also make a contribution to internal selection processes.

Case Example 6.7: Using 360° Assessment for Succession Planning

A large commercial organisation, Eireco, used a competency inventory to help identify individuals who were showing the capability to move into roles of greater responsibility. It used an instrument called the Director's Development Audit (DDA), which assesses board-level competencies under four domains: Strategy, People Skills, Operational Skills and Culture Building, as in the model below.

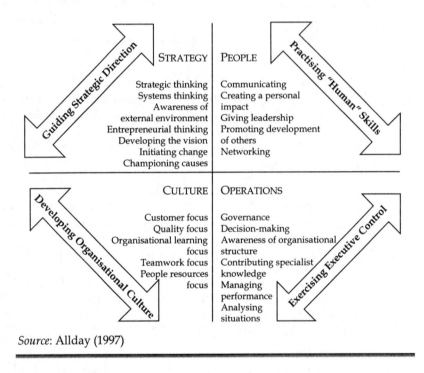

Source: Allday (1997)

A third trend is the movement towards *computer-assisted testing* (CAT). This type of format can make the testing process more interactive or dynamic in nature. It is possible, for example, to programme a computerised test so that it moves through levels of item difficulty in correspondence with the respondent's accuracy of response. This gives the potential to test for a much wider span of ability on a single test. Other uses of computerised testing are to assess speed of learning on a new task.

Another development of note is the launching of the *ABLE series of tests*, which are designed to measure learning aptitude in a number of job-relevant contexts. While extravagant claims have been made for these tests, it is probably too early to identify their distinctiveness from mainstream aptitude tests.

These methods also show promise in the area of assessment of learning potential. A further application which is gaining ground is the use of *interactive simulation exercises* which can be built on a software platform so that the task demands change in accordance with the respondents' behavioural strategies.

Another trend is the *embedding of competency assessment within the application form* itself. These applications can range from asking the respondent to cite examples of competency evidence in an open-ended format to weighted application blanks which ask for evidence of competency in pre-formatted areas and allocate a fixed score based on a predetermined weighting of the criteria.

All five of the above method developments share common characteristics in that:

- They seek to capture evidence of specific competencies or capabilities within a pre-structured format;

- They have an in-built and predetermined scoring system;

- They require a considerable amount of set-up and design work, which can be quite specialised and resource-intensive;

- They provide the potential for very high running gains in both the efficacy and consistency of assessment programmes.

New Delivery Methods

The major progress in delivery methods has been the *automation* of testing by transferring paper and pencil tests onto computerised on-screen formats.

Personality questionnaires, competency inventories and some simulation exercises are relatively easily transferred onto an on-screen modality, but care needs to be taken with the computerisation of aptitude tests, where presentation, structure and scoring issues may well arise.

Perhaps the greatest benefit in the computerised delivery of tests is that it allows remote delivery or multiple-site delivery whilst maintaining centralised control over administration protocols and data interpretation. In the future, more and more organisations will be able to deliver sophisticated assessment and selection programmes at multiple locations without the need for a concomitant increase in personnel and administrative manpower.

Development of Expertise

Whereas the domain of objective assessment and testing was previously the exclusive territory of specialist recruiters and psychologists, the trend is now towards making these best practice methods available in a more user-friendly way to a broader range of personnel.

There is growing emphasis on ensuring that front-line personnel practitioners are trained to a proficiency level in the administration and interpretation of tests and other structured assessment methods.

There is also a growing trend towards further involvement of line management in the selection process. Key features of this more empowered selection approach are:

1. Line managers being centrally involved in the definition of selection criteria based on comprehensive role and performance analysis;

2. Line managers becoming involved in the design of the assessment process guided by an expert practitioner;

3. Line managers being trained to the level where they can provide a core assessor input for simulation exercises and structured interviews.

There are a number of training courses available in Ireland which train personnel practitioners to a professional standard (see list of contact addresses at the end of the Chapter).

A critical consideration in the devolution of objective assessment skills is to ensure that high standards of objectivity, accuracy and professionalism are maintained. Central to this issue is the formal training and certification of assessors, and the current minimum standards here should be regarded as the British Psychological Society's Level A & B Standards of Competence, which have been adopted by the Institute of Personnel and Development as the appropriate benchmark standard for practitioners.

Quality Assurance of Selection Methods

The need for stringent quality assurance of selection methods has never been greater.

Table 6.5 illustrates the competing forces which recruiting organisations must accommodate to, in order to achieve the best balance between efficacy and accountability.

While recruiting organisations have to steer a difficult course between these competing best practice demands, there are some clear guidelines to assist them. Quality assurance in the use of objective assessment methods is fundamentally reducible to a small number of core good practice points:

1. Using rigorous role analysis to specify selection criteria;

2. Accurate matching of assessment methods to selection criteria;

3. Discipline in the conducting of the selection process;

4. Well-thought-through evaluation and decision rules;

5. Subsequent follow-up of candidate performance on the job.

Table 6.5: The Demands to be Reconciled in Achieving Best Practice in Recruitment

Demands for cost-effective recruitment process mainly driven by pragmatic organisational needs	Demands for objectivity, transparency and fairness mainly driven by ethics, accountability and legislation
• The need to select candidates accurately but quickly • The need to minimise the cost of recruitment, as in: 　◊ Screening methods rather than face-to-face assessment 　◊ Minimising opportunity costs of manager's time • Minimising the time and resources spent on giving feedback to unsuccessful candidates • The need to ensure confidentiality and non-disclosure of company-specific competencies and performance criteria	• The need to assess all candidates equally • The need to ensure candidates get the best/broadest opportunity to show their capabilities • The need to give adequate and clear information about the detail of the selection process and the criteria for evaluation and decision-making • The need to positively design equality of opportunity features into the selection process • The need to treat all candidates with equal respect, including the right to feedback on negative decisions • The need to keep adequate and clear records of all stages of the recruitment process, including candidate data and evaluation criteria

Figure 6.2 illustrates key guidelines with respect to quality assurance in objective assessment.

Figure 6.2: The Quality Assurance Guide in Objective Assessment

---

1. Start in the Right Place
   Rigorous role profiling / job analysis.
   Specific competency definitions.

2. Make an Informed Methods Choice
   Ensure testing methods are criterion referenced.
   Ensure methods have a sound technical base.
   Ensure methods meet feasibility criteria
   (i.e. you have the resources to deliver).

3. Ensure Discipline in Methods Use
   Use multiple methods wherever possible.
   Design stages to ensure front-end adequacy of assessment.
   Ensure that all recruiters and assessors are fully trained.
   Pre-design the evaluation and decision criteria.
   Brief Candidates as fully as possible.

4. Monitor Effectiveness
   Collect on the job performance data subsequently.
   Review methods compliance to best practice.
   Collect participants' feedback.
   Refine methods on a continuous basis.

5. Work to Achieve a Value Added Impact
   Use the assessment data developmentally.
   Use analysis and observation skills on the job.
   Give developmental feedback to all internal candidates.

References

Allday, D. (1997), *Check–a–Board: Helping Boards and Directors to Become More Effective*, Institute of Management Foundation in conjunction with Saville and Holdsworth, London: The Institute of Management.

Boyatzis, R.E. (1982), *The Competent Manager: a Model for Effective Performance*, NewYork: Wiley.

Cronbach, L.J. (1984), *Essentials of Psychological Testing*, New York: Harper and Row.

Gunnigle, P., M. Morley, N. Clifford and T. Turner (1997), *Human Resource Management in Irish Organisations: Practice in Perspective*, Dublin: Oak Tree Press.

Porteus, M. and J. Hodgins (1995), "Selection Trends in Irish Organisations", *Irish Journal of Psychology*, Vol. 16, No. 4.

Smith, M. and I. Robertson (1989), *Advances in Selection and Assessment*, New York: Wiley.

Contact Addresses: Further Information

(Providers of Testing and Assessment Products, Professional Training and Consultancy)

AXION,
Woodbank,
Saval Park Road,
Dalkey,
Co. Dublin.
Tel/Fax: (01) 285 5771

ETC Consult,
17 Leeson Park,
Dublin 6.
Tel: (01) 497 2067/497 1749
Fax: (01) 497 2518

Oxford Psychologists Press (OPP),
(Publishers of the new ABLE series),
Lanbourne House,
311–321 Bambury Road,
OX2 7SH,
United Kingdom.

Pearn Kandola Ltd.,
18–19 Harcourt Street,
Dublin 2.
Tel: (01) 475 3931
Fax: (01) 475 3215

Psychological Consultancy Service Ltd. (PCL),
101 Sorrento Road,
Dalkey,
Co. Dublin.
Tel: (01) 285 9400
Fax: (01) 285 9632

Saville and Holdsworth Ireland Ltd. (SHL),
24 Priory Hall,
Stillorgan,
Co. Dublin.
Tel: (01) 288 3550
Fax: (01) 288 3668

CHAPTER 7

SOCIALISATION AND INTEGRATION OF NEW EMPLOYEES

Bob Pattinson

INTRODUCTION

The previous chapters have outlined the care and attention that organisations must take to analyse jobs, search the employment market, attract potential candidates, systematically select the person for the job in a fair and equitable manner, and Chapter 17 emphasises the need to provide the successful applicant with a legal and psychological contract. All of these steps cost considerable amounts of money and by the time the new member of staff arrives for the first day's work, a substantial investment of time and money will already have been made. If the new recruit leaves within the year, all this effort will have been wasted, and the organisation faces the task of repeating the cycle again.

This chapter examines the practical steps that organisations can take to improve the socialisation and integration of new employees so that both the new employee and the organisation benefit.

Fowler (1983) illustrates the importance of this induction process when he observes:

> When organisations invest in new equipment they usually spend a good deal of time and money ensuring that it is properly installed, and that it is quickly brought up to the planned performance levels which justified its acquisition. Preventative maintenance systems are operated to avoid breakdowns. De-

tailed performance and cost records are kept of servicing, re-
pairs and down-time.

This care and attention to new equipment is unhappily in
stark contrast to the haphazard manner by which new employees are often inducted into their jobs.

Table 7.1 below summarises the reasons why organisations
should take the socialisation and integration processes seriously
by providing formal induction procedures.

*Table 7.1: Advantages of Effective Socialisation and Integration of New
Employees*

Advantages to the Employee	Advantages to the Organisation
• Reduces the stress of starting a new job • Makes the employee feel valued and important • Helps the learning process for the employee • Enables the employee to settle in more quickly • Creates a positive attitude and motivates employee commitment • Reinforces the professional image gained in the recruitment and selection process	• Helps the employee to reach maximum efficiency as fast as possible • Reduces employee turnover • Improves morale • Aids working relationships • Assists in the recouping of the investment made in the recruitment and selection process

Starting a new job is often exciting and challenging but it may also
be quite stressful. Marks (1974) refers to:

the culture shock, the feeling of inadequacy any of us might
suffer on entering the company of strangers who all appear to
know how to behave towards each other, according to a code
which is unknown to us. The shock is particularly severe
when, in addition to learning the appropriate social responses,
the stranger is expected to contribute to a shared task in which
the other members of the group are all apparently carrying out
their allotted roles with ease and confidence.

Kahn (1964), in his survey of 725 male industrial workers in the US, found several forms of role conflict and role ambiguity which relate to the need for some form of induction:

- 35 per cent worried about the lack of clarity with regard to the scope and responsibilities of the job;

- 32 per cent suffered tension due to uncertainty about how their managers viewed them;

- 29 per cent were concerned about what their co-workers thought of them.

Mullins (1998) draws attention to induction and socialisation programmes as one of several human resource management initiatives for reducing stress at work.

One of the dangers for organisations that organise professional recruitment and selection procedures is that, unless the socialisation and integration of new employees continues in the same vein, new starters suddenly find themselves being treated much less importantly than when interviewed for the job. Such ambiguities can quickly lower expectations, reduce morale and possibly lead to an early exit from the organisation. This problem of the early leaver has been around for a long time. Fowler (1983) reports studies showing that, in the early 1980s, it was quite common amongst factory workers for between 40 and 50 per cent of employees to leave within three months. For higher skilled groups, it takes the employee longer to assess the organisation before deciding whether to leave or stay, often being closer to one year rather than three months. Some Irish food plants seeking seasonal workers for a three- to four-week employment period find that employees will often leave within two days, despite interactive efforts at the recruitment and selection stage.

Fowler (1983) identifies three major problems with early leavers: *cost; bad publicity;* and *disillusioned ex-employees*. Figure 7.1

shows the possible costs of losing a series of employees within three months.

Figure 7.1: Costs of Early Leavers

Computer Programmer		
Salary		£18,000
Recruitment Costs:		
Agency fee	£1,800	
VAT	£378	
Time	£500	
Expenses	£200	
	£2,878	£2,878
Leaves after two months but takes another month to get a replacement; so, in addition to the further cost of £2,878 there is a loss of output for one month.		£2,878
Replacement leaves within three months. Takes two months for the next replacement.		£2,878
Total costs for the year **(excluding loss of three months' output)**		£ 8,634

Obviously, these costs increase substantially if employee turnover is widespread across jobs within the organisation.

The bad publicity factor that arises from early leavers stems from the leavers blaming the organisation for the failure to stay and quickly a company may gain an impression of being a poor employer, difficult to work for. In the present competitive environment market such a poor reputation may adversely affect recruitment of replacement staff.

Finally, disillusioned ex-employees may themselves lose out from what could have been a rewarding experience if the socialisation process had been better handled.

Heraty and Morley (1997) note that in the Cranfield-University of Limerick survey of Irish companies, one key problem is the mismatch of employee expectations about the job and career prospects and the reality of the situation, and this is a main contributor to the "induction crisis".

So far we have explored some of the problems associated with early leavers and looked briefly at the advantages of effective socialisation and integration of employees. It is now appropriate to examine how organisations can plan and design the socialisation and integration process. Figure 7.2 shows four key steps within the process.

Figure 7.2: Four Key Steps in the Socialisation and Integration of New Employees

---

1. **Pre-Employment Information**

    - Conditions of employment
    - Job description
    - Company literature
    - Starting instructions

2. **Planning the First Day**

    - Initial reception
    - Introduction to the workplace
    - Introduction to the organisation

3. **Learning the Job**

    - Job descriptions
    - Job specifications
    - Work procedure manuals
    - Role of the supervisor, mentor and training instructor

4. **Getting to Know the Organisation**

    - Induction process
    - Induction manuals

PRE-EMPLOYMENT INFORMATION

It is important to note that the socialisation and integration of new employees is not something that begins on the first day at work. The employee's perception of the organisation would start to be moulded when the job advertisement was first noticed, and reinforced by the treatment received during the recruitment and selection process.

Once the successful candidate has agreed to accept the offer of employment, there are four practical steps the organisation might take:

1. *Conditions of Employment*: Whilst it is necessary from a legal perspective to issue a formal contract of employment, it is also helpful to provide new starters with an explanatory booklet covering all important conditions of service, including pensions information. This can be written in an easy-to-read style and provides a friendlier outline of what the company offers than perhaps the more formal, legalistic contract of employment.

2. *Job Description*: The job description may already have been given to candidates for the post at the recruitment stage to aid self-selection by candidates before applications were received for shortlisting. Heraty and Morley (1997) suggest that organisations can reduce the risk of an "induction crisis" by developing a "realistic job preview" that describes the job and the company as seen by those who work there. This then helps potential job applicants to self-match their skills and ambitions against job and organisational realities.

   If this process has not already been done, it is not too late to send out the job description and company literature at this stage. The job description will certainly help the new recruit understand the breadth and depth of the job and, as we shall see later under "learning the job", it may also help in training.

3. *Company Literature*: A general booklet about the company can help the new recruit begin to gain insights into the nature and size of the organisation and begin to build a sense of commitment to the company. Content should include the following:

- History of the company;

- Nature of the products and services provided;

- Geographical spread of the company;

- Organisation chart;

- Type of customers;

- Current development plans.

An easy-to-read style with plenty of photographs, maps and diagrams can make this a document that the new recruit would be proud to show to their family and friends, some of whom could be potential recruits in future years.

4. *Starting Instructions*: It is vital to provide the new employee with relevant information to help them arrive in a comfortable and relaxed manner on the first day. Table 7.2 on the following page provides a useful checklist.

PLANNING THE FIRST DAY

The aim of the first day is to help the employee begin to relax into the organisation and the job. It is vital that the new employee sees the normal workspace as early as possible, so they at least have somewhere to hang their coat. At all costs, bombarding the new employee with excessive amounts of information must be avoided. The induction process consists of two main elements:

1. *Induction to the job*: this needs to be done fairly quickly but might be spread over up to three months;

2. *Induction to the organisation*: this might be spread over six to twelve months in some organisations.

Table 7.2: Checklist of Starting Instructions

Item	Description
Starting Time	It is often best for the new employee to start a little later than the normal starting time on the first day, as this allows those staff welcoming the newcomer to have sorted out their own jobs before focusing on the induction process.
Location	A map of the location of the building and the reception helps.
Contact Person	The name of the first person who is going to be meeting the new employee.
Transport	Details of bus routes or trains near to the location. If travelling by car, where the car can be parked.
Documents	A reminder of the documents required, such as: <ul><li>P45</li><li>Signed copy of the contract of employment</li><li>Copies of educational and training qualifications</li><li>Birth and marriage certificates for pension schemes.</li></ul>
Security	Security pass to enter the site or building.
Clothing	A reminder of any rules on clothing at work or details about any protective clothing/equipment to be collected on the day.
Catering	Details of the company's catering facilities.

Thus, the first day can concentrate on the essential items required to start doing the job and finding one's way round the organisation as soon as possible.

Three core activities on the first day are:

1. The initial reception

2. Introduction to the workplace

3. Introduction to the organisation.

The Initial Reception

As discussed earlier, the starting instructions should tell the new employee where and to whom to report. Before meeting the person responsible for the first day's induction, the new employee needs to get past security and report to the company's reception area. Again, the starting instructions must cover these points.

To create a warm and friendly reception for the newcomer, it is helpful if security staff and the receptionist know that the new employee is coming. The job satisfaction of front-of-house staff also may be improved by being involved more closely in this induction process.

Fowler (1983) suggests a five-point checklist for the reception process, as shown below in Figure 7.3.

Figure 7.3: Checklist for the Initial Reception

1. Ensure that the people at the first point of contact (i.e. receptionist, security staff) know of the new employee's arrival and what to do next.

2. Set an arrival time that avoids the risk of the starter turning up before the reception, security, office staff.

3. Train reception staff to be friendly, efficient and helpful towards new starters.

4. If the new starter has to go to another location immediately after reporting, provide a guide unless the route to the other location is clear-cut.

5. Avoid keeping the new starter waiting in order to prevent undue nervousness or apprehension.

Introduction to the Workplace

Ideally, the person who conducted the selection interview with the new employee (normally the departmental manager) should be available to give an initial welcome to the new employee. Seeing a familiar face in a sea of strangers can be very reassuring to new staff. It is also important that the newcomer's supervisor (if not the departmental managers) meets the employee next. Again, it would have improved the selection process if the supervisor had been involved in the final selection decision and thus had already met the new employee. The time spent by the departmental manager on induction need not be long, but in terms of establishing relationships, it is time well spent.

It is helpful if the supervisor is trained in how to induct the new employee to the workplace. Certainly, the initial meeting between the two participants is very important in terms of beginning to cement together a working relationship. This stage should not be rushed, should be kept relatively informal and may include tea or coffee.

As a general principle, it is best to let the supervisor show the employer around the workplace early in the procedure so that the newcomer begins to get their feet under the table and to gain some level of psychological security in a strange environment.

Later in the day, the supervisor may take the new employee to the human resources management section to deal with various documentation. The supervisor can also cover the do's and don'ts of the job and the organisation.

In addition to the supervisor, it is often helpful in the induction process to have a mentor, someone chosen from the work team who will act as a friend and guide to the newcomer during the early days of the induction process. When the supervisor shows the new employee round the workplace, one of the first team members to be met should be the mentor.

The use of a mentor helps the supervisor to spend quality time on the induction process without reflecting the other demands of the job. There is a case for the mentor to have short service and thus have experienced the induction process relatively recently. As such, they should have ready empathy with the latest recruit, understand the key anxieties of joining this new organisation, and be quite capable of advising on how to quickly get a feel for the job and the organisation.

The following basic information is often required from the mentor on the first day:

- Location of entrances and exits;

- Routes to and from the restaurant, lavatories, car park, first aid post, changing rooms, etc.;

- Location of vending machines, water fountains, etc.;

- Tips about the organisation's culture and practices, e.g. raffles, who sits where in the restaurant.

The involvement of the manager, supervisor and mentor is summarised in Table 7.3 below.

Table 7.3: Respective Roles of the Manager, Supervisor and Mentors in the Induction of the New Employee

Role	Duties
Manager	• Meet the new employee at the start • Provide a bridge to the selection process • Put the newcomer at ease and introduce to the supervisor
Supervisor	• Build up a rapport with the newcomer • Introduce the new employee to the work team, starting with the mentor first • Cover some of the dos and don'ts of the job and the organisation
Mentor	• Act as a friend and guide • Give a geographical tour • Advise about getting on in the job and the organisation • Remember what it is like to join the organisation

Introduction to the Organisation

Many larger organisations run induction courses designed to help new entrants learn about the multifarious activities of the organisation so that they have a better idea of where their own work team fits in. Such courses will be discussed later in the chapter. On the first day, the new employee needs to get to grips with the organisation on a number of essential items, which are usually dealt with by the human resources department:

- Handing over the P45 tax form;

- Signing documentation for various items such as locker keys, safety equipment and clothing;

- Receiving copies of employee handbooks, health and safety literature;

- Providing information for personnel records including details of next of kin, details of own car if used for work, birth and marriage certificates for pension schemes;

- Receiving information on trade union membership.

Some organisations have a short video on the company and this can be viewed by the newcomer whilst various documentation is being sorted out. Raychem, for example, have produced an excellent video on the total quality management system used in their Shannon plant, which is also very useful for induction programmes, as it provides an overview of the company's values, range of products and different stages in the production process. As mentioned earlier, some of the introduction to the organisation can be carried out by the mentor, especially the practical issues of finding the way round the organisation and learning the basics of the informal rules and regulations. The immediate supervisor has responsibility for explaining the formal rules of the section or department in which the new employee is placed and, normally, the human resources department handles the corporate issues.

LEARNING THE JOB

Whether or not the new employee is experienced in the work of the job already, or is a completely inexperienced recruit, there is always an element of learning the job to be done by any new member of staff. As mentioned earlier, a copy of the job description helps both the inexperienced and the experienced recruit to understand the overall scope of the job. When the job description has been broken down into a more detailed job specification, there is great benefit in the new employee being given a copy so that they are more aware of the detailed requirements of the job in terms of skills, knowledge and attitudes.

Figure 7.4 provides an example of part of a job specification for a production supervisor's job in respect of the task of motivating staff.

Figure 7.4: Job Specification for a Production Supervisor

Task: To motivate the work team		
Knowledge	*Skills*	*Attitude*
• Aware of several theories of motivation	• Able to set clear targets	• Approachable
• Understands the core dimensions of a job that motivate employees	• Provides regular, systematic feedback to staff	• Firm
• Appreciates the fact that different people are motivated in different ways	• Can conduct effective performance appraisal reviews	• Assertive
	• Capable of coaching employees	• Positive

Work procedure manuals are also very helpful to new starters. If the job description and the job specification outline the duties, responsibilities and key requirements in terms of skill, knowledge and attributes, the procedure manuals let the newcomer know how to carry out the various tasks.

Figure 7.5 shows a procedure manual for handling external mail in a revenue collection section.

Figure 7.5: Procedure Manual for Handling External Post

---

1. Each of the five Revenue teams take responsibility for the morning post in the following sequence:

   Monday: Team A   Thursday: Team D
   Tuesday: Team B   Friday: Team E
   Wednesday: Team C

2. One member of each team to collect the post from security at 08h45.

3. Teams to process post before 09h30.

4. Each team to open envelopes, pin cheques to covering letter, etc., and date stamp each item.

5. All items to be placed into alphabetical order in five folders to match the name allocations and team as follows:

Team A	Names A–E
Team B	Names F–I
Team C	Names J–M
Team D	Names N–R
Team E	Names S–Z

6. Folders of mail to be circulated to each team by 09h35.

Manuals explaining the operation of equipment such as computers, printers, telephones, faxes, photocopiers, lathes, CNC machines, etc., should also be available for new starters to examine once they have received a demonstration on how to operate the equipment.

Three people are normally involved to help the new starter learn the job:

- Supervisor

- Mentor

- Training instructor.

The supervisor has a key role in managing the learning process, checking up on progress, and arranging coaching sessions as appropriate. Whilst the supervisor should ideally be a qualified training instructor, demands of time may restrict their availability for training new staff.

The mentor may be able to carry out some of the more basic training instructions, but a specialist training instructor may be needed for more advanced operations. In some companies, the new operators would be trained away from the normal workplace over the first two days so that they develop sufficient speed to keep up the line when they start for real on the third day. This allows the new person to receive higher quality training inputs without the undue embarrassment of others observing the simple mistakes made at the start of learning any new task.

In some industries such as electronics, training instructors would provide initial instruction and then on-line coaching to new starters for several weeks until the operator reached a pre-determined level of job performance.

As a general principle, unless simulation training is taking place off-the-job, it is advantageous for the new employee to begin to learn the job during the first day in the new job.

GETTING TO KNOW THE ORGANISATION

Once the new employee gets to know the supervisor and the work-team, starts to learn the job, and can find their way around the immediate workplace, it is now opportune to learn more about the organisation.

The degree of formality given to this task will depend largely on the size of the organisation and on the number of new employees starting at any one time. For example, if a company is recruiting a batch of 20 new graduates, there are several advantages in starting the entire group on the same day:

- Saves time by avoiding repetition;

- Helps to reduce individual anxiety about being the latest stranger in the company, as one is a member of a group of newcomers;

- Ensures consistency of information given to all new starters;

- Allows members of the induction group to build up a degree of team spirit which may help them to network later in their careers in the company;

- Facilitates the opportunity to deal with a wider range of organisational issues earlier in the organisational life of the new starter;

- Makes a more formal induction programme much more cost-effective;

- Provides participants in the process with better insights into the potential variety of work that their different colleagues will be doing in the organisation.

As mentioned earlier, it is important not to overload new starters with too much information; newcomers are often anxious to get to grips early on with their workplace rather than learning about the history of the organisation. For organisations taking on batches of recruits, there are distinct advantages in covering all the organisational issues at the start. However, where newcomers join individually and over a longer period of time, the essential organisational information is usually covered in an employee handbook, and the more general items are covered after about three months when there are sufficient newcomers to warrant a formal induction course.

In either case, an induction manual is extremely useful in several ways in that it:

- Allows all new starters to receive the same information;

- Provides a helpful source of information to be used later in the career;

- Provides supervisors with a checklist of items to cover in the face-to-face sessions;

- Allows supervisors to focus on the key points, knowing that the details are all written in the handbook.

Figure 7.6 shows the typical content used in an induction manual.

Figure 7.6: Content of an Induction Manual

1. Brief outline of the history, scope and nature of the organisation
2. Basic conditions of employment — hours of work, holidays, pension scheme, etc.
3. Pay — pay scales, when paid and how, deductions, queries, etc.
4. Sickness — notification of absence, certificates, pay
5. Leave of absence
6. Work rules
7. Discipline procedure
8. Grievance procedure
9. Promotion procedure
10. Union and joint consultation arrangements
11. Education and training facilities
12. Health and safety arrangements
13. Medical and first aid facilities
14. Restaurant and canteen facilities
15. Telephone calls and correspondence
16. Travelling and subsistence expenses

In many organisations, the key points of the above material would often be covered in a one-day induction programme. Table 7.4 shows the induction programme for a hospital.

Table 7.4: Day One of an Induction Programme for a Nurse Starting in a Regional Hospital

Time	Activity	Notes
Pre-Course		
	A letter has been sent two weeks before the starting date, detailing the time and place of the induction course, with a copy of the job specification.	This will help to alleviate some of the fears of the unknown.
Induction Course		
08h50	Reports to Reception.	Receptionist informed that the nurse will be coming to her for first day. The nurse is requested to start an hour later than other staff so that people are not too busy on arrival.
09h00	Interview with Director of Nursing.	An early attempt to focus on the job in hand.
09h30	Meeting with her managers, the Ward Sister. Explanation of the role of the Ward, key policies and procedures.	A chance to meet some of the team in an informal setting.
10h00	Tour of Ward and coffee with available colleagues, including the mentor.	Mentor saves the Ward Sister's time.
10h20	Mentor takes the nurse on a tour of the hospital and points out key items listed on the induction checklist.	Use of checklist ensures all key points are covered.

Time	Activity	Notes
11h00	Visit to Personnel Office to deal with paperwork, including copy of induction handbook and health and safety statement and procedure.	Mentor leaves nurse to Personnel Officer to cover hospital policies.
11h30	Mentor collects nurse and leaves her in an interview room to read the induction handbook.	Allow the nurse time to absorb the flow of information.
12h00	Ward Sister spends 20 minutes dealing with any questions on the handbook and then goes through the key points of the manual using an induction check-list.	Lets the nurse raise questions. Checklist ensures the standardisation of the induction process.
12h30	Tour of Ward, meeting other colleagues and patients.	Provides opportunity to view work environment and meet colleagues.
13h00	Lunch with Director of Nursing, Ward Sister and Mentor.	Provides an opportunity for socialisation with a small group of key people.
13h45	Starts Ward duties, working with mentor.	Encourages immediate involvement in the work of the Ward.
16h45	Meeting with Ward sister to discuss the first day.	Helps to monitor day one of the induction process.
17h00	End of shift.	

CONCLUSIONS

This chapter emphasises that there are real benefits to organisations that take the socialisation and integration of employees seriously:

- Reduced stress and anxiety for employees;

- Increased employee commitment;

- Faster learning of the job;

- Improved efficiency;

- Helps to avoid the "induction crisis" of early leavers and associated costs.

Four steps are outlined for structuring the socialisation and integration process:

1. Pre-employment information;

2. Planning the first day;

3. Learning the job;

4. Getting to know the job.

It was stressed that the flow of information should be sequenced to avoid overloading the newcomer with excessive information at the start. Induction manuals are helpful in this regard.

Finally, a checklist for managers is shown below in Figure 7.7, which summarises seven key points to help the socialisation and integration of employees.

Figure 7.7: Checklist for Managers to help Organise the Socialisation and Integration of New Employees

1. Conduct an initial "get acquainted" interview on the first morning. If possible, be the person to meet the new employee on their arrival; if not, ensure that someone responsible meets them.

2. Give the employee information about the organisation and be prepared to discuss any queries.

3. Discuss with the employee information about the work, duties to be carried out, work rules that exist with regard to standards of work, safety (employee's own and that of others), etc.

4. Introduce the new employee to colleagues.

5. Arrange for any initial training that has to be carried out.

6. Check on the employee's progress, with regular visits to make sure that the new employee is fitting in, and show that you are available to discuss any problems.

7. Listen to the new employee's needs and find out their feelings on the work so that problems can be identified and sorted out at any early stage.

References

Fowler, A. (1983), *Getting off to a Good Start: Successful Employee Induction*, London: Institute of Personnel Management.

Heraty, N. and M. Morley (1997), "Training and Development" in P. Gunnigle, M. Morley, N. Clifford and T. Turner, *Human Resource Management in Irish Organisations: Practice in Perspective*, Dublin: Oak Tree Press.

Kahn, R.L. et al. (1964), *Organisational Stress*, New York: Wiley.

Marks, W. (1974), *Induction: Acclimatising People to Work*, London: Institute of Personnel Management.

Mullins, L.J. (1998), *Management and Organisational Behaviour*, London: Pitman.

PART THREE
PERFORMANCE MANAGEMENT

Chapter 8

Designing, Delivering and Managing Training and Development Activities

Thomas N. Garavan and *Con Egan*

Introduction

Training and development is generally considered a key element of a successful human resource management strategy. Despite such recognition, there is evidence of major gaps in training performance in Irish companies. At its worst, training is viewed as an isolated programme of activities put together with little or no understanding of the needs of the business or trainees, and with no attempt to determine the value of the training. Training at its best in Irish companies is viewed as a set of processes aimed at continuously improving employee performance and organisational effectiveness.

This chapter considers the training and development process as it should be managed in the ideal situation. Unfortunately, for many Irish firms, ideal conditions do not exist. There is often insufficient finance, time or training resources, and often a general lack of commitment to training and development as a key human resource management activity. The chapter is structured as follows:

1. It explains some of the concepts and terms associated with training and development;

2. It outlines the role of training and development and how that role has been changing in recent years;

3. It explains alternative ways of organising the training and development function and their respective advantages and disadvantages;

4. It outlines alternative but potentially synergistic approaches to training and development;

5. It explains the processes of training design and training evaluation.

TRAINING AND DEVELOPMENT TERMINOLOGY

Training and development has its unique terms and concepts. It is important to have a good understanding of these at the outset because they influence the process of training management within organisations. These are presented below.

Learning

The term learning means a relatively permanent change in cognition (i.e. understanding and thinking) that results from experience and that directly influences behaviour.

KSAs (Knowledge, Skills, and Attitudes)

Learning can be separated into different categories. Traditionally, these categories are knowledge, skills and attitudes (KSAs) for the purposes of labelling the different types of learning outcomes.

Knowledge

This category of learning refers to the information we acquire and place into memory, how it is organised into the structure of what we already know, and to our understanding of how and when it is used. Thus, knowledge can be seen as composed of three distinct but interrelated types: declarative, procedural and strategic (Kraiger, Ford and Salas, 1993).

- *Declarative Knowledge*: a person's store of factual information about a particular subject matter. Evidence of factual learning exists when the learner is able to recall and/or recognise specific blocks of information.

- *Procedural Knowledge*: the person's understanding about how and when to apply the facts that have been learned. It assumes some degree of factual knowledge, since some information must be known about an object or activity before rules for its use can be developed. It allows trainees to understand the underlying rationale and contingencies surrounding potential courses of action so they can apply their factual knowledge appropriately. This type of knowledge reflects how the facts are stored in memory and what types of linkages are formed with other knowledge the trainee has acquired.

- *Strategic Knowledge*: The highest level of knowledge is strategic knowledge. This is used for planning, monitoring, and revising goal-directed activity. It requires acquisition of the two lower levels of knowledge (facts and procedures), which are internalised as complex mental models. Strategic knowledge consists of the person's awareness of what he or she knows coupled with the internal rules for accessing relevant facts and procedures to be applied toward some goal. When this type of knowledge is the focus of training or education, it is often called a "learning how to learn" programme.

Skills

Skills can be defined as the capacities needed to perform a set of tasks that are developed as a result of training and experience (Dunnette, 1976). A person's skills are reflected by how well they are able to carry out specific actions, such as operating a piece of equipment, communicating effectively, or implementing a business strategy.

Attitudes

Attitudes are reflections of an employee's beliefs and opinions that support or inhibit behaviour (Oskamp, 1991). In a training context, the concern is about employees' attitudes that are related to job performance. Examples would be employees' beliefs about management, trade unions, empower-ment, training and how satisfying various aspects of the job are. These beliefs and opinions create associations between objects and events that can modify positive or negative feelings (called affect) that the person attaches to the objects and events. Thus, changing a person's beliefs or opinions can change how he or she feels about a particular object or event, making it more or less desirable.

Training, Development and Education

The terms "training", "development" and "education" are used in various ways. Training is often described as focusing on the acquisition of KSAs needed to perform more effectively in one's current job.

Development is used to refer to the acquisition of KSAs needed to perform in some future job. Training is a set of activities, and development represents the desired outcome of those activities. Training is the systematic process of attempting to develop KSAs for current or future jobs; development refers to the learning of KSAs.

Education is typically differentiated from training and development by the types of KSAs developed. Whereas training is generally seen as the development of job-specific KSAs, education is viewed as the development of more general KSAs, related (but not specifically tailored) to a person's career or job.

Competency

The term competency is generally used to denote an area of personal capability that enables an employee to perform a job. It will give an indication of knowledge, skills, behaviour and personal characteristics required.

THE ROLE OF TRAINING AND DEVELOPMENT IN IRISH ORGANISATIONS

Many Irish organisations have a centralised training function. Training is typically part of the personnel/human resource (HR) department, along with other human resource management activities such as recruitment, selection, reward management and industrial relations. The training department is generally mandated to improve the organisation's effectiveness by providing employees with the competencies that will improve their current or future job performance. The focus of training is generally on the development of job-related knowledge, skills and attitudes. The development component will usually address the personal needs of employees, and help them to learn, to grow and to cope with the issues that are important to them. It is generally recognised that effective training and development strategies are those that meet the needs of the organisation while simultaneously responding to the needs of individual employees and that take into account the wider organisational context.

Two examples that illustrate this point are demonstrated in Case Examples 8.1 and 8.2.

Case Example 8.1: Training in Action – Performance Appraisal

The supervisors in a large German-owned Irish electronics company were continuously asking the training officer to help them do a better job of conducting performance appraisal interviews. The supervisors were generally using a "tell and sell" approach. This would involve telling the employee the problems they had observed and trying to sell the employee a corrective action plan. This constantly led to arguments about the accuracy of the appraisal and the appropriateness of the corrective action proposed and employees had generally negative perceptions of the problem.

In response to these problems, the training officer organised a two-day off-site workshop focusing on performance appraisal interviewing skills. The trainer emphasised a joint problem-solving approach in which the supervisor and employee come to agreement on the problem and identify ways of solving it. The workshop cost the company £2,800 and an evaluation taken immediately after the training showed that supervisors had positive perceptions of the approach, understood it and were willing to use it. They believed their problems with performance appraisal were over. However, follow-up evaluations and discussions with employees months later revealed that none of the supervisors were using the problem-solving approach.

Some weeks after the workshop, the HR department issued a policy modifying the performance appraisal procedure. The new policy mandated that the official performance appraisal documentation, with the supervisor's signature, be forwarded to HR before any formal interview process took place. This had the effect of making the supervisor's appraisal official, without any input from the employee. Consequently the supervisor was required to justify it to the employee. They had now to convince the subordinate that the appraisal was accurate. Supervisors were using the "tell and sell" approach.

Case Example 8.2: Training in Action — Developing Teamwork and Problem-Solving

---

The managing director of a large US-owned electronics company operating in Dublin believed that the creation of employee problem-solving teams would improve quality in the company. All employees were provided the opportunity to participate in team-building and creative problem-solving training. Fifty percent of the employees, including the Managing Director and the management team, signed up for the training. The training involved ten three-hour sessions facilitated by an external facilitator. Employees, working on common processes within their respective departments, were grouped into teams for three weeks of team-building training and seven weeks of problem-solving training.

The problem-solving training process involved each team identifying a problem in its area of operation and working through this problem as it proceeded through each step of the training. Team members reacted positively to the learning opportunities and on completion of training each team had made significant progress towards solving the problem it was working on.

A report was made by the General Manager to Corporate Headquarters in the US on the success of the training.

Nine months later, analysis showed that only one team was still in operation, from a start-up situation of 20 teams. Some teams had fallen apart because workloads prevented them setting time aside for meetings. Some team leaders complained that little recognition was given where teams actually solved problems. Employees who were not part of the training process resisted making changes to work processes. There was also evidence that non-training employees ridiculed employees who participated in the training and perceived that they were getting preferential treatment from supervisors.

Both of these scenarios illustrate some important lessons about how training and development operates in organisations. Both illustrate that training and development was successful in developing new competencies but it failed to consider fully the context and the motives of the employees. This failure prevented the knowledge, skills and attitudes from becoming integrated into day-to-day operations and the wider organisation culture. In the first scenario, training addressed the needs of the supervisors but was rendered unsuitable by the organisation's HR policies. More systematic training needs analysis might have led to a more appropriate intervention to deal with the policy change, or it may have helped to modify its effects.

In the second scenario, training and the organisation's requirements to develop team-building problem-solving skills were addressed but failed to take account of factors in the wider organisational system, including peer acceptance, workload and cultural influences. This resulted in low transfer to day-to-day organisational practice and produced conflict.

There is increasing evidence, in the Irish context, that training is, however, moving away from a primary focus on enhancing employees' specific skills to a broader focus on creating and sharing knowledge. This trend was illustrated in both scenarios above.

Three dimensions of the changing training role are worth highlighting:

1. *A skills and knowledge orientation*: Traditionally, training was viewed by many Irish companies as a means of "teaching" employees specific skills and behaviours. Training will continue to make this contribution in the future. However, a skills and knowledge orientation is based on the premise that business conditions are predictable, that the company can manage these factors and that the company has the capacity to control and predict the knowledge and skills needs of employees in the future.

2. *Linking Training to Business Needs:* There is considerable evidence that many organisations experience unpredictability in their external environment. This places significant demands on the training function to deliver training on an "as-needed" basis to help employees deal with specific business problems as they occur, assuming that training is the appropriate solution. The business strategies that organisations pursue have important implications for training practices. Training issues vary greatly from one strategy to another. Irish companies that focus on niche markets, for example, may need to emphasise up-to-date skills for their existing workforce. Companies placing emphasis on internal growth may need to emphasise issues such as cultural training, technical competence and interpersonal competence. Table 8.1 provides a summary of the implications of generic business strategy for training strategies and activities within an organisation.

Table 8.1: Linkages between Generic Strategy and Training and Development Activities

Strategy	Emphasis	How Achieved	Key Issues	Training Implications
Concentration	Increase market share	Improve product quality	Skill currency	Team building
	Reduce operating costs	Improve productivity or innovate technical processes	Development of existing workforce	Cross-training
	Create or maintain market niche	Customise products or services		Specialised programmes
				Interpersonal skills training
				On-the-job training
Internal Growth	Market development	Market existing products / add distribution channels	Create new jobs and tasks	Support or promote high-quality communication of product value
	Product development	Expand global market	Innovation	Cultural training
	Innovation	Modify existing products		Help in development of organisational culture that values creative thinking and analysis
	Joint ventures	Create new or different products		Technical competence in jobs
		Expand through joint ownership		Manager training in feedback and communication
				Conflict negotiation skills

Table 8.1 (continued)

Strategy	Emphasis	How Achieved	Key Issues	Training Implications
External growth (acquisition)	Horizontal integration Vertical integration Concentric diversification	Acquire firms operating at same stage in product market chain (new market access) Acquire business that can supply or buy products Acquire firms that have nothing in common with acquiring firm	Integration Redundancy Restructuring	Determining capabilities of employees in acquired firms Integrating training systems Methods and procedures of combined firms Team building
Disinvestment	Retrenchment Turnaround Divestiture Liquidation	Reduce costs Reduce assets Generate revenue Redefine goals Sell off all assets	Efficiency	Motivation, goal setting, time management, stress management, cross-training Leadership training Interpersonal communications Outplacement assistance Job-search skills training

Source: Garavan, 1987: pp. 17–31.

3. *Creating and Sharing Knowledge*: A number of Irish-based companies believe that the development of the organisation's intellectual capital is the key to gaining competitive advantage (see also Chapter 3). Intellectual capital is generally defined as cognitive knowledge, advanced technical skills, creativity, and systems understanding. There is evidence to suggest that training departments in Ireland have tended to concentrate on developing cognitive and advanced skills. However, some commentators argue that the major contribution of training in the future may lie in achieving a greater understanding among employees of the manufacturing and service processes and the interrelationships between departments and business units. Training can also contribute to motivating employees to be innovative and service conscious. Training in such a situation is viewed as a strategy to create and share knowledge.

BENEFITS OF TRAINING AND DEVELOPMENT TO ORGANISATIONS AND EMPLOYEES

Training as a vehicle for human resource development is concerned with improving the skills of employees, enhancing their capacity to cope with changing demands in the workplace and creating and sharing knowledge. A summary of argued benefits of training and development, as identified by a number of commentators, is outlined below (see Reid and Barrington, 1997; Armstrong, 1992; Garavan et al., 1995).

- Training allows employees to get to grips with job requirements quickly, and by improving the knowledge and skills, allows job holders to improve the quantity and quality of output with fewer mistakes and less waste/rework. Enhancing the skill base of employees can lead to job enrichment, with benefits to both the individual and the organisation.

- Where effective training leads to increased competency in the workforce, this reduces the extent of management time spent dealing with tasks related to remedial or corrective effort.

- Training is generally perceived as a valuable process when the organisation wishes to introduce changes in working methods and wants to equip employees to cope with change. Training may be used as a confidence-building exercise in a change management programme, and address issues such as the reasons for change, potential benefits and downsides, and the necessary skills required to participate effectively in the change process.

- Training can be significant in a public relations sense in that it has value in projecting a positive image to prospective employees.

- Where training incorporates a safety dimension, the outcome may be favourable in terms of health and safety at work.

- Training can have a favourable impact on staff turnover. It may also serve to reduce the extent of recruitment and/or redundancy (through retraining).

- The motivational impact of training can be considerable. Workers may feel a sense of recognition because they are sent on a training programme, and after training they may be motivated to acquire new skills, particularly when rewards follow on from the acquisition and use of skills.

- The value of training in a communication context is considerable when core values, such as those related to product quality and consumer service, are disseminated to employees, with the hope that they will be internalised and operated upon.

- Identification with the organisation can be fostered when a better understanding of mission statements and corporate objectives is achieved through an induction and socialisation programme (see Chapter 7).

- Training aimed at operationalising certain management techniques (such as TQM) can generate certain desirable outcomes, such as analytical, problem-solving and presentation skills.

- Training can act as a signal to employees that the company believes they are important.

- Training can provide an effective channel for two-way communication, especially if "workshops" are used to bring managers and employees together to discuss organisational issues and develop plans jointly to deal with them.

- Training can enable people to exercise greater responsibility, and can enlarge their portfolio of skills which they can use both to their own advantage and that of the company.

- Training can enhance the employability of employees and improve their future employment possibilities.

ORGANISING THE TRAINING FUNCTION

A number of options are open to the training function in terms of its general organisation and structure. The structure of the training function has important consequences for how training as a significant HR activity contributes to the business. Five basic models of the training function may be identified as follows: the faculty model, the customer model, the matrix model, the corporate university model and the virtual training model.

Faculty Model

Training departments organised on the basis of a faculty model look a lot like the structure of a college. The training department is headed by a manager with a staff of experts who possess specialist knowledge on particular topics or skill areas. These experts develop, administer, and update training programmes; for example, sales trainers are responsible for sales skills training. This is quite a common model in Irish companies.

The faculty model has several strengths. First, training staff are generally experts in the area they train in. Second, the training department's plans are easily determined by staff expertise. The content and timing of programmes are determined primarily by their availability and the expertise of the trainers. Organising by the faculty model also has some disadvantages. Companies using the faculty model may create a training function in which the expertise does not meet the needs of the organisation. Trainers in a faculty model may also be unaware of business problems or unwilling to adapt materials to fit business needs. This can result in de-motivated trainees who fail to learn because the programme content lacks meaningfulness for them. To overcome the disadvantages of the faculty model, the training specialist will need to survey training customers frequently to ensure that the programmes offered are meeting their needs. Expert trainers also need to ensure that they adapt programme materials so that they are meaningful for participants.

Customer Model

Training departments organised according to a customer model are responsible for the training needs of one division or function of the company. For example, trainers might be responsible for training related to information systems, marketing or operations. This model addresses a major problem of the faculty model. Training programmes are developed more in line with the particular needs of a business group, rather than on the expertise of training personnel. Trainers in this model are expected to be aware of business needs and to update programmes and content to reflect them. If needs change such that training is no longer available from a source inside the company, the trainers may use external consultants.

There are several disadvantages of this model. First, trainers have to spend considerable time learning the business function before they can be successful trainers. Second, a large number of programmes covering similar topics may be developed by customers. These programmes may also vary greatly in effectiveness. It may be difficult for the training manager to oversee each function to ensure that a common instructional design process is used or the company's quality philosophy is consistently emphasised in each programme. This type of structure is likely to be unattractive to trainers who consider presentation and teaching to be their primary job function. In a customer model, trainers are likely to be employees from a functional area (e.g., manufacturing engineers) who have functional expertise but lack training in instructional design and learning theory. Consequently, the training may be meaningful to employees but poor from a design perspective.

Matrix Model
A matrix model involves trainers reporting to both a manager in a training department and a manager in a particular function. The trainer has the responsibility of being both a training expert and a functional expert. One advantage of the matrix model is that it helps ensure that training is linked to the needs of the business. Additionally, the trainer gains expertise in understanding a specific business function. Because the trainer is responsible to the training manager, it is likely that the trainer will stay professionally up-to-date. A major disadvantage of the matrix model is that the trainer is likely to have more time demands and conflicts because of the need to report to both a functional manager and a training manager.

Corporate University Model (Corporate Training Universities)
An emerging model for organising training is termed a "corporate university model". The corporate university model differs from the other models in that the client group includes not only em-

ployees and managers but also stakeholders outside the company, including colleges and universities. Training functions organised around a university model tend to offer a more comprehensive range of programmes than functions utilising other models. Important elements of culture and values tend to be emphasised more often in the training programmes of corporate universities than in the other models. The university model centralises training to make sure that the best training practices are disseminated across the company and it is argued that the model enables the company to control costs.

There are no examples of such arrangements in Ireland. However, Motorola, which has facilities in both Dublin and Cork, operates such a model in the US. Motorola University is an excellent example of the university model. It was created in 1989 and includes 110 full-time and 300 part-time staff. Curriculum is arranged by function: engineering, manufacturing, sales, and marketing. However, the curriculum for technical and business skills (basic maths, electronics, accounting, etc.) is developed in partnership with community colleges and technical schools.

Virtual Training Organisation Model
Hewlett Packard and Apple, among others, now organise their training function so that they can respond quickly to client needs and provide high-quality training services. A virtual training organisation model operates according to three principles. First, employees (not the company) have primary responsibility for learning. Second, the most effective learning takes place on the job, not in the classroom. Third, for training to translate into enhanced job performance, the manager–employee relationship is critical. For employees to use training content on the job, they are responsible for learning the course content and understanding how it may be applied to their work. Managers are responsible for holding employees accountable to use training on the job and for removing obstacles that might interfere with the learning process.

A virtual training organisation (VTO) is characterised by five competencies: strategic direction, product design, structural versatility, product delivery and accountability for results. Strategic direction is defined as a clearly described goal and direction for the department, and a customer focus that includes customising training to meet customer needs and continuously improving programmes. Compared to a traditional training department, a virtual training organisation is more customer-focused. It takes more responsibility for learning and evaluating training effectiveness, provides customised training solutions based on customer needs and determines when and how to deliver training based on these needs. The most noticeable difference between a VTO and a traditional training department is its structure. The traditional training organisation tends to operate with a fixed staff of trainers and administrators who perform very specific functions such as instructional design. The number of trainers in a VTO varies according to the demand for services. The trainers have both specialised competencies and the capacity to act as internal consultants. As consultants, they may provide advice on the assessment of training needs, the design of programmes and evaluation activities.

APPROACHES TO TRAINING AND DEVELOPMENT IN ORGANISATIONS

A number of options are open to Irish companies to facilitate the effective training and development of staff. Four particular approaches are highlighted: a systematic and planned approach; a policy of continuing development; a performance-based approach; and a learning organisation approach.

A Planned Training Approach

A systematic training approach is specifically designed to meet defined needs. It is planned and provided by people who know how to train, and the impact of training is carefully evaluated. It is based on a simple model of defining training needs, identifying a training approach, implementing training and finally conducting a systematic evaluation.

The process of planned training consists of the following steps:

1. *Identify and define training needs*: This involves analysing corporate, team, occupational and individual needs to acquire new skills or knowledge, or to improve existing competencies (competence is defined as the ability and willingness to perform a task). The analysis covers problems to be solved, as well as future demands. Decisions are made at this stage on the extent to which training is the best and most cost-effective way to solve the problem.

2. *Define the learning required*: It is necessary to specify as clearly as possible what skills and knowledge need to be acquired, and what attitudes need to be developed in order to perform the job effectively.

3. *Define the objectives of training*: Learning objectives are set which define not only what has to be learned, but also what trainees must be able to do after the training programme.

4. *Plan training programmes*: These must be developed to meet the needs and objectives. They will consist of an appropriate format, a range of methods and learning tactics.

5. *Decide who provides the training*: The extent to which training is to be provided from within or from outside the organisation is decided. At the same time, the division of responsibility between the training department, line managers or supervisors and individuals has to be determined.

6. *Implement the training*: Ensure that the most appropriate methods are used.

These issues will be considered in more detail later in this chapter, when issues related to the delivery of training are discussed.

A Continuing Development Approach

Planned training is a necessary element of effective human performance, but a philosophy of continuing development argues that training is not just something provided for people by the organisation at the start of their employment or at occasional points in their career. Rather, it should be regarded as a continuous process, with less emphasis on formal instruction and an increased requirement for trainees to take responsibility for their own learning, with help and guidance from their managers.

If learning in an organisation is to be fully beneficial to both the organisation and its employees, the following conditions should be met:

- The organisation should have some form of strategic business plan. It is desirable that the implications of the strategic plan, in terms of the skills and knowledge of employees who will achieve it, should be spelled out.

- Managers must be ready, willing and able to define and meet needs as they appear. All learning needs cannot be anticipated; and organisations must foster a philosophy of continuing development.

- As far as practicable, learning and work should be integrated. This means that encouragement must be given to all employees to learn from the problems, challenges and successes inherent in their day-to-day activities.

- The impetus for continuing development must come from the top management team (the board of directors, for example). The top management team must regularly and formally review the way the competencies of its management and workforce are being developed. It is important, too, that one senior executive is charged with responsibility for ensuring that continuous development activity is being effectively undertaken.

- Investment in continuing development must be regarded by the management to be as important as investment in research, new product development or capital equipment. It is not a luxury that can be afforded only in the good times. Indeed, the more severe the problems an organisation faces, the greater the need for learning on the part of its employees and the more pressing the needs for investment in learning.

A Performance/Competency-Based Approach

A performance/competency-based approach to training relates specifically to performance requirements of the individual or organisation. For individuals, this may mean filling gaps between what they know and can do, and what they should know and be able to do. However, simply concentrating on filling the gaps may allow organisations to fall into a trap of adopting a "deficiency model" of training, which implies that training is only about putting things right when they have gone wrong.

A performance/competency-based approach places emphasis on core competencies. It argues that learning should be more concerned with identifying and satisfying development needs: multi-skilling, fitting people to take on extra responsibility, providing for management succession and increasing all-round competence within the organisation.

The approach starts from an analysis of the competencies required for successful performance — present and future — identifying the areas in which competencies need to de developed and implementing strategies to develop these competencies.

A "Learning Organisation" Approach

A "learning organisation" has been defined by Pedler et al. (1988) as "an organisation transforming itself". Handy (1994) describes a learning organisation as one that both learns and encourages learning in people. It creates space for people to question, think and learn, and constantly reframes the world and their part in it. The learning organisation, according to Handy, needs to have a formal way of asking questions, seeking out theories and reinforcing them. Members of the organisation must be encouraged to challenge traditional ways of doing things and to suggest improvements.

All successful companies are good at doing certain things. This is their knowledge and skills base. This base must be developed to match changing conditions. Learning is not just the acquisition of new knowledge, but rather, a collective process of observation, experimentation and experience, which can be mobilised to deal with new opportunities or threats.

What needs to be learned cannot always be taught. Training and development programmes must therefore help people to learn from their experience. Learning cannot be left to chance. The characteristics of a learning organisation generally include the following:

- Encouraging people to identify and satisfy their own needs;

- Providing individuals with regular views of performance and learning needs;

- Providing feedback on performance and achieved learning;

- Providing new experiences from which people can learn;

- Facilitating the use of training on the job.

DESIGNING TRAINING PROGRAMMES

Five main issues are included in the training design process: organisational/policy issues; the identification of training needs; selecting an appropriate training design; delivering the training; and training evaluation.

Organisational/Policy Issues

There will always be a number of organisational constraints which will influence decisions on the design of training and development activities. Some of these constraints derive from organisational policies, the priorities of the key stakeholders and the power position of training and development specialists. Others will have been negotiated or agreed by the training and development specialist when identifying the particular training and development needs. Specific elements of the organisational context are worth mentioning.

Policy and Planning Context

This refers to the existence of policies and plans relating to the provision of training and development. These policy constraints may be externally or internally imposed. They may be well formulated and written or they may be unwritten and unplanned. These policies may set limits on the types of training and development activities that are acceptable. Training and development plans set out specific commitments to training and development activities within a given time period. Any training intervention undertaken will usually have to fit within the plan. It is accepted, however, that there may be no written plan as such, so that all training activity is essentially reactive. Case Example 8.3 presents an example of a training and development policy.

Case Example 8.3: Example of a Training and Development Policy

---

Preamble

This training and development policy defines the scope and responsibility of training throughout the company, taking into account the goals of the overall organisation. The reason for having such a policy is to clarify the company's position with regard to training and development, and to provide a set of guidelines so that training and line staff can carry out their day-to-day training responsibilities. Furthermore, the policy will establish a framework within which more detailed training plans can be developed. It will give direction to and create a goal for all who participate in or are affected by training.

The training and development policy has been prepared by the Training Manager in consultation with Department/Function Heads. The job of coordinating the development of the policy is the responsibility of the training manager.

Training and Development Goals

All employees will be trained to a level of competency that will allow them to achieve maximum contribution in their work, with a commitment to continuous improvement in efficiency and quality. In this process, it is the company's objective to encourage and develop employees' potential, leading to their personal development and growth.

General Goals and Objectives

- *Training, like any other organisation activity, is to help achieve the goals of the organisation. It has no value unless it helps eliminate deficiencies and achieve the organisation's goals.*

- *To train and educate all newly recruited employees in the process, structure and philosophy of the company as well as to prepare them thoroughly in a specific skill so that they may quickly and productively perform their assigned job following the training.*

- *To upgrade and improve, where necessary, the knowledge, skills and attitudes of all existing employees, which would include introduction to new techniques and procedures.*

- *To implement, as appropriate, job rotational training and development, in order to create a pool of experienced and motivated employees capable of filling the company's immediate and long-range transfer, departmental back-up and staff promotion needs.*

- *To upgrade and improve, where necessary, the knowledge and managerial skills (decision-making, delegation, organising, controlling, etc.) of existing supervisors and managers.*

- *To train selected personnel in supervisory and managerial skills, as appropriate, in order to fill promotional vacancies from within, wherever possible.*

- *As a result of the training and employee development programmes, to motivate employees to a greater sense of belonging and identification with the company, its ideals and aspirations, and thereby create job satisfaction and organisational commitment.*

Who will Conduct the Training

- *For training to be an effective and ongoing part of the organisation's structure, it is imperative that it be considered a "team effort", involving not only the training staff but supervisors and managers as well. Training is a continuous responsibility of line management and can never be totally delegated to a separate training function.*

- *Dependent on the type and location of training, it may be carried out by a training instructor, an experienced employee, a supervisor, manager or external specialist as required.*

- *The preparation and supply of training materials, the co-ordination and planning of programmes are primarily the responsibility of the training department.*

Training and Development Process

- *The training manager will carry out an identification of training needs for all employees in consultation with department supervisors and managers, which will form the basis of a training programme and will be updated as the need arises.*

- *The individual(s) needing training are identified, and their present competencies are determined. The difference between those competencies and what is actually necessary for the job is the "gap" which the training and development activity must fill.*

- *The most appropriate type of training required will be determined: formal (classroom) or on-the-job; training at an outside school, institution, parent plant or consultant organisation. If the training is to be in-company, a decision will be made as to who will carry it out − training instructor, experienced employee, supervisor, manager or any combination thereof.*

- *Finally and probably most importantly, on-the-job application of the competencies acquired must begin immediately after the training ends. The measure of training is the success achieved in transferring the learning into actual job performance. The training department in conjunction with line management will "follow up" and "review" training* to measure its effectiveness and if necessary modify and determine future course content and training approaches.

- *All training will be practical, job-related and skill-oriented, and will use the most modern and efficient training methods to achieve its objectives.*

Who is Responsible for Training?

- *Supervisors, line managers and the training manager have major roles in managing and delivering training. Each line manager and supervisor must accept the development of his or her people as a prime responsibility, include it in their objectives and be willing to be appraised on the basis of how well the goals have been achieved.*

- *The training nomination procedure, both for in-house and outside courses, can be initiated by either employees or their supervisor or manager, with further approval required of the training department and perhaps personnel or administration.*

Resources Allocated

- *The company's commitment to training is demonstrated by the provision of a modern training facility. Training facilities will be continuously upgraded and improved.*

- *The company provides a substantial financial allocation to training annually, based on the projected training needs for that year.*

- *The training manager will continuously assess recent developments, methods and new technology in the world of training and adopt as required to maintain a vibrant, worthwhile training function.*

Training and Development Needs Context

Any training and development intervention undertaken should be in response to specifically identified training needs. These needs may have been identified as part of an organisational review or they may have been identified at occupational, job or individual level. The nature of the needs identified will shape the structure, learning methods and delivery of the training and development.

Resource Context

There are three resource bases that may place constraints on the training and development specialist. First, a certain level of financial resources may be allocated to training and development within the organisation. All training provided must fit within this budget. Physical resource limitations, related to the availability of training facilities, programme materials and accommodation, may also be a constraint. Irish organisations vary considerably in their allocation of dedicated space to training and development. Organisations may use colleges, training centres and hotels as venues for training and development. In other cases, on-the-job training may be more appropriate. Other physical resource limitations may include the availability of computer terminals and special learning packages. A third resource limitation relates to specialist training expertise. This may be available internally or it may have to be bought in.

Stakeholder Context

The priorities and expectations of the different stakeholders involved may significantly shape the type and nature of the training intervention provided. These stakeholder expectations may be explicit or implicit and an effective trainer should be aware of them when designing the intervention.

Power/Political Context

The training and development department is not immune to power and political considerations. The introduction of a training and development programme, as well as its content and methods, may be subject to scrutiny within and outside of the organisation. Buckley and Caple (1992), for example, suggest that senior managers can become suspicious of discussion periods included in the design of training programmes. These may be viewed as an opportunity on the part of the trainees to criticise the style of management, the values espoused in the organisation, etc. The significance of power has five major implications:

1. It may determine the amount of co-operation the training and development specialist gets from line managers;

2. It may influence the extent to which participants will actually attend training programmes provided by the training department;

3. It will determine the amount of resources that the function can secure;

4. It will determine the amount of commitment given by senior management within the organisation;

5. It may determine the innovativeness of the interventions adapted by the training and development function.

Time Context

Some commentators would contend that time is one of the greatest constraints. Buckley and Caple (1992) suggest that training and development specialists may experience time constraints in three ways:

1. There is the issue of how soon the training programme can be delivered;

2. There is a major issue of how much time there is available to design the training programme and select the appropriate materials;

3. There is also a balance to be achieved between the length of time people can be away from the workplace to attend training and development programmes and the length of time required to achieve the learning objective.

Identifying Training Needs

Training and development needs can be assessed at an organisational, job/occupational, and/or individual level and this tripartite classification forms the framework for training needs analysis (TNA). The methods and data sources used for assessing each level differ slightly, but since the process for identifying needs is broadly the same, they will be dealt with collectively here. Though TNA is often reactively triggered by a shortfall in expected performance, it should also be used to explore ways of improving performance in general, as well as proactively assessing future needs.

The first stage of TNA involves the collection of comprehensive data on:

- The external (political, economic, social, technological, legal and competitive) environment — drawn from environmental-scanning or "horizon-watching" activities which should be conducted on an ongoing basis;

- The organisation's internal environment — strategy, structure, technology, managerial style, culture, working conditions, as well as information on employee's aspirations, knowledge and skills, particularly in relation to their current roles.

Perhaps the best source of data will come directly from employees themselves. Observation, key informant interviews, group discussions and questionnaires are some of the other methods that may be used to assess training needs. In addition, much valuable data will already be available within the organisation. This data can be used to assess the current performance levels and capability of the organisation in relation to its present and future needs. These include business and strategic planning documents incorporating human resource and succession plans, and an array of data captured within management information systems — sales, labour turnover figures, sickness and absence records, number and nature of accidents, quality measures, etc. Data from performance appraisal systems, probationary reports and exit interviews can support the needs identification process at an individual/group level.

These sources of information, combined with an assessment of the environment, offer measures of current and future business performance needs on the one hand and, on the other, current performance and capability levels at an organisational, occupational/group and individual level. Comparing the two helps identify exactly where performance and capability gaps currently exist or are likely to arise, and specify the exact nature of these gaps. Once identified, the next stage is to assess the extent to which training and development interventions might effectively address these gaps — whether the performance gap is attributable to a deficiency in knowledge, skills or attitudes. This is not always the case and separating cause from effect is critical at this stage. The root cause of performance problems may well lie in physical working conditions — equipment failure, social/psychological factors (such as poor manager–employee relationships), and/or the nature of the employment contract (such as employees having to work long hours for little pay, few holidays and/or on temporary contracts). In such cases, non-training solutions are more likely to be effective.

Table 8.2 presents some specific reasons why an employee may not perform to an acceptable level. Alternative options, which can in themselves have developmental consequences and address performance gaps, include, for example, work redesign, organisational restructuring, requirement and/or redeployment. Training interventions should only be considered when a genuine training need has been identified.

Table 8.2: Sources of Unsatisfactory Employee Performance

Managerial and Organisational Shortcomings	Individual Employee Shortcomings	External Shortcomings
Lack of proper motivational environment	Lack of motivation	Family problems
Personality conflicts with boss and/or co-worker	Laziness	Morals and values that conflict with organisational expectations
Inappropriate job assignment	Poor personality	
	Job dissatisfaction	Labour market conditions
Improper supervision	Failure to understand job duties	
Lack of knowledge or skills	Chronic absenteeism	Government action
Failure to establish duties	Alcoholism and drug problems	Union policies and procedures
Poor planning of a change process	Mental illness	
Poor person/job fit	Chronic physical illness/injury	

Training Design and Delivery

Having identified a training need(s) and the target population, the training solution must be designed. Identifying clear objectives of the training intervention is critical. Binsted (1982) states that by clearly defining both the present state and the desired state of the target learners, the "growth" required to get from the former to the latter will become apparent. This required growth — the gap between present and future states — forms the basis for training design and informs other design and delivery issues, including the following:

- Content of the training intervention (what is to be learned);

- Sequence of learning activities (general, then particular; concrete, then abstract; doing, then thinking);

- Place (on- or off-the-job);

- Trainers (tutors, line managers);

- Time (when the training intervention will take place and how long it will last);

- Media (computer-based training, video) and methods (lecture, group discussion);

- Reinforcement tactics (handouts, texts, questions and answers).

Approaches to training delivery can be viewed in terms of a continuum. At one end of the spectrum is the "packaged" traditional approach, where a body of knowledge and/or specific skills to be learned are carefully predetermined by the organisation and the training programme is delivered in a formal manner by subject matter "experts", usually off-the-job, and often to a large number of employees. At the other end is a more informal "organic" experiential approach, with learning arising on-the-job or even "through" the job, facilitated (often by a line manager or mentor) rather than directed by a subject matter expert, with the individual negotiating and owning learning outcomes. Between these two extremes are a whole range of training delivery methods to choose from, including lectures, computer-based training, demonstration, individual or group projects and assignments, group discussions, role-playing, case studies, coaching, counselling and mentoring.

The objectives of the training intervention are the key considerations when selecting methods, as are related decisions such as whether the training intervention will occur on- or off-the-job, and whether internal or external HRD consultants will manage its design and/or delivery — so called "make or buy" decisions. Numerous constraints will influence the selection, not least resource constraints in terms of time and money available, the urgency and importance of the training needs, the availability of expertise within the organisation and, last but not least, the characteristics of the learners themselves, their motivation and willingness to learn, and their preferred styles of learning.

Training and Learning Evaluation

Training and learning evaluation represents the final stage of a training cycle. Evaluation serves a number of different purposes. Easterby-Smith (1994) highlights the following:

- *Proving*: the worth or impact of a training programme;

- *Improving*: ensuring that the learning intervention has improved performance;

- *Learning*: evaluation viewed as part of the learning process itself, to be fed back into the proceeding training cycle to foster continuous improvement;

- *Controlling*: ensuring that individual trainees are performing to standard.

Reid et al. (1992) draw on the evaluation models suggested by other theorists and suggest five different levels at which training can be evaluated:

- Level 1: Reactions of trainees to the training programme;

- Level 2: Whether trainees learned what was intended;

- Level 3: Whether the learning transfers back to the work environment;

- Level 4: Whether the training has enhanced departmental performance;

- Level 5: The extent to which the training has benefited the organisation.

Though not made explicit in this list, a major objective of evaluation is also to determine the bottom-line impact of training and development investment — whether benefits derived warrant the financial costs incurred. This is often difficult to assess, given that not all benefits can be easily translated into financial terms, that benefits may accrue over the long rather than the short term, and that consequently it is difficult to prove that changes, for better or worse, are directly attributable to the training intervention. However, such financial assessments are imperative to demonstrate the strategic impact of training and development and to persuade organisations of the value of investing in HRD. Figure 8.1 contains an example of a reaction evaluation form.

Figure 8.1: A Sample Reaction Evaluation Form

Course Title _____	Course Code _____
Course Location _____	Staff No. _____
Dates From _____	To _____

To enable us to evaluate the effectiveness of this programme of training, please complete this questionnaire. We would ask you to be as honest/ accurate as you can in your answers. It should take approximately 15 minutes to complete.

Please tick relevant boxes:

1. Did you enjoy the programme?

Very enjoyable	Enjoyable	Don't Know	A Little	Not Enjoyable
❏	❏	❏	❏	❏

2. How would you rate the learning environment in terms of the following?

Rating: 7 = Excellent 1 = Very Poor

	1	2	3	4	5	6	7
a) Location	❏	❏	❏	❏	❏	❏	❏
b) Training Room	❏	❏	❏	❏	❏	❏	❏
c) Documentation	❏	❏	❏	❏	❏	❏	❏
d) Training Aids	❏	❏	❏	❏	❏	❏	❏
e) Canteen	❏	❏	❏	❏	❏	❏	❏
f) Other	❏	❏	❏	❏	❏	❏	❏

3. What did you consider the most useful part(s) of the programme? Give a brief explanation.

_____

_____

_____

4. What did you consider the least useful part(s) of the programme? Give a brief explanation.

_____

_____

_____

5. Did the programme meet your identified needs?

A Lot	Some	Don't Know	A Little	None
❏	❏	❏	❏	❏

6. Indicate your level of agreement with the following statements:

a) I found the trainer approachable and helpful

Agree Strongly	Agree	Not Sure	Disagree	Disagree Strongly
❏	❏	❏	❏	❏

b) I consider the trainer knowledgeable on the subject covered

Agree Strongly	Agree	Not Sure	Disagree	Disagree Strongly
❏	❏	❏	❏	❏

c) I consider the trainer's presentation skills to be effective

Agree Strongly	Agree	Not Sure	Disagree	Disagree Strongly
❏	❏	❏	❏	❏

d) I found the trainer's style appropriate to the training audience

Agree Strongly	Agree	Not Sure	Disagree	Disagree Strongly
❏	❏	❏	❏	❏

e) I was exposed to a wider range of learning methods

Agree Strongly	Agree	Not Sure	Disagree	Disagree Strongly
❏	❏	❏	❏	❏

f) The trainer encouraged learner participation

Agree Strongly	Agree	Not Sure	Disagree	Disagree Strongly
❏	❏	❏	❏	❏

g) I am now better informed on the subject matter of the programme

Agree Strongly	Agree	Not Sure	Disagree	Disagree Strongly
❏	❏	❏	❏	❏

7. Below are listed sets of words which may be used to describe the trainer; please rate the trainer on a scale from 1-7.

	1	2	3	4	5	6	7	
Approachable	❏	❏	❏	❏	❏	❏	❏	Unapproachable
Helpful	❏	❏	❏	❏	❏	❏	❏	Unhelpful
Intelligent	❏	❏	❏	❏	❏	❏	❏	Lacking intelligence
Interesting	❏	❏	❏	❏	❏	❏	❏	Uninteresting
Articulate	❏	❏	❏	❏	❏	❏	❏	Inarticulate
Concise	❏	❏	❏	❏	❏	❏	❏	Rambling
Relevant	❏	❏	❏	❏	❏	❏	❏	Irrelevant
Considerate	❏	❏	❏	❏	❏	❏	❏	Inconsiderate
Directive	❏	❏	❏	❏	❏	❏	❏	Consultative
Friendly	❏	❏	❏	❏	❏	❏	❏	Unfriendly
Supportive	❏	❏	❏	❏	❏	❏	❏	Non-Supportive
Professional	❏	❏	❏	❏	❏	❏	❏	Unprofessional

8. How were your skills enhanced in the following areas?

	A Lot	Somewhat	Don't Know	A Little	Not at All
Communications	❏	❏	❏	❏	❏
Negotiations	❏	❏	❏	❏	❏
Leadership	❏	❏	❏	❏	❏
Team Work	❏	❏	❏	❏	❏
Planning	❏	❏	❏	❏	❏
Scheduling	❏	❏	❏	❏	❏
Problem Solving	❏	❏	❏	❏	❏
Other	❏	❏	❏	❏	❏

9. How would you rate the programme design under the following criteria:

1= Very Ineffective 5 = Very Effective

	5	4	3	2	1
Ease of Learning	❏	❏	❏	❏	❏
Participant Involvement	❏	❏	❏	❏	❏
Appropriate to Subject Matter	❏	❏	❏	❏	❏
Interesting Content	❏	❏	❏	❏	❏
Clear Objectives	❏	❏	❏	❏	❏
Good Use of Time	❏	❏	❏	❏	❏
Pace of Learning	❏	❏	❏	❏	❏

10. What changes if any, would you make to the programme and why? Give a brief explanation.

_____

_____

_____

_____

CONCLUSIONS

Effective training and development is concerned with enhancing organisational performance through the systematic training and development of staff. The design of training and development activities is a complex process but it is often approached as a simple task of filling in the blanks in a timetable. There are, however, many factors that influence the training management and training design process, including resource and time constraints, the policy content, power and political issues and the level of training expertise within the organisation. Many of these factors are highly interconnected and demand the ability continually to reassess previous decisions and makes changes as necessary. Training and development activities that follow the guidelines set out in this chapter have the ability to achieve tangible results in terms of performance and organisational effectiveness.

Training and development activities in organisations can take different forms and possess varying degrees of sophistication. The function can be organised along different lines and the most appropriate structural form is determined by organisational characteristics and the level of maturity of the training function within the organisation. The most typical structural designs include a faculty model, a customer-oriented model, a matrix design, a corporate university design and, more recently, a virtual training model has become popular.

One of the more effective approaches to training and development is embodied in a planned model. It offers the organisation a systematic, planned approach to identifying and responding to training and development activities. Continuing development is seen as a sophisticated approach in which all employees become agents rather than objects of learning.

The training design process involves consideration of a range of issues, including assessment of the organisational context; the identification of the core competencies and needs; the specification of learning goals; and a range of decisions related to the selection of a training structure, learning methods, reinforcement tactics and evaluation methods.

References

Armstrong, M. (1992), *Handbook of Personnel Management Practice*, Fifth Edition, London: Kogan Page.

Bee, F. and R. Bee (1994), *Training Needs Analysis and Evaluation*, London: IPM.

Bennett, R. (1991), "The Effective Trainer Checklist" in J. Prior (ed.), *Handbook of Training and Development*, Aldershot: Gower.

Binsted, A.S. (1982), "The Design of Learning Events: Parts 1 and 2", *Managerial Education and Development*, Autumn–Spring, pp. 25–41.

Buckley, R. and J. Caple (1992), *The Theory and Practice of Training*, London: Kogan Page.

Burgoyne, J., M. Pedler and T. Boydell (1994), *Towards the Learning Company: Concepts and Practices*, London: McGraw-Hill.

Collin, A. (1994), "Learning and Development" in I. Beardwell and I. Holden (eds.), *Human Resource Management*, London: Pitman Publishing.

Dunnette, M. (1976), "Aptitudes, Abilities and Skills" in M. Dunnette (ed.), *The Handbook of Industrial and Organisational Psychology*, Chicago: Rand McNally.

Easterby-Smith, M. (1994), *Evaluating Management Development, Training and Education*, Aldershot: Gower.

Garavan, T.N. (1987), "Strategic Human Resource Development", *Journal of European Industrial Training*, Vol. 15, No. 1, pp. 17–31.

Garavan, T.N., P. Costine and N. Heraty (1995), *Training and Development in Ireland: Context, Policy and Practice*, Dublin: Oak Tree Press.

Gilley, J.W. and S.A. Eggland (1989), *Principles of Human Resource Development*, Reading, MA: Addison-Wesley.

Gross, D. (1994), *Principles of Human Resource Management*, London: Routledge.

Handy, C. (1994), *The Empty Raincoat: Making Sense of the Future*, London: Hutchinson.

Harrison, R. (1990), *Principles of Human Resource Development*, London: Routledge.

Keep, E. (1989), "Corporate Training Strategies: The Vital Component?" in T. Storey (ed.) *New Perspectives on Human Resource Management*, London: Routledge.

Keep, E. and K. Mayhew (1995), "Training Policy for Competitiveness: Time for a New Perspective?" in H. Metcalf (ed.) *Future Skill Demand and Supply*, London: Policy Studies Institute.

Kraiger, K.J., J. Ford and E. Salas (1993), "Application of Cognitive, Skill-based and Affective Theories of Learning Outcomes to New Methods of Training Evaluation", *Journal of Applied Psychology*, Vol. 78, No. 2, pp. 311–28.

Maguire, M. and A. Fuller (1996), "Lifelong Learning and Professional Development" in I. Woodward (ed), *Continuing Professional Development: Issues in Design and Delivery*, London: Cassell.

Oskamp, S. (1991), *Attitudes and Opinions*, Upper Saddle River, NJ: Prentice Hall.

Pedler, M., J. Burgoyne and T. Boydell (eds.) (1988), *Applying Self-Development in Organisations*, Hemel Hempsted: Prentice Hall.

Pettigrew, A.M., G.R. Jones and R.P. Reason (1982), *Training and Development Roles in their Organisational Setting*, Sheffield: MSC.

Rae, L. (1995), *Techniques of Training*, Aldershot: Gower.

Reid, M.A. and H. Barrington (1997), *Training Interventions*, Fourth Edition, London: Institute of Personnel and Development.

Sloman, M. (1994), *A Handbook for Training Strategy*, Aldershot: Gower.

Stewart, J. and J. McGoldrick (1996), *Human Resource Development: Perspectives, Strategies and Practice*, London: Pitman Publishing.

Thompson, R. and C. Mabey (1994), *Developing Human Resources*, Oxford: Butterworth-Heinemann.

CHAPTER 9

MANAGEMENT DEVELOPMENT: PRACTICES, POLICIES AND IMPLEMENTATION

Thomas N. Garavan and *Aidan Lawrence*

INTRODUCTION

There is a general recognition that managers represent a particularly important human resource because they hold the key to unlocking the potential of other factors of production. Many commentators are, however, critical of Irish company investment in management development and for those who make such an investment, there is evidence of reliance on conventional programme-based approaches. It appears that management development in Irish organisations is perceived as an activity designed to ensure that the organisation has the required management talent to face present and future challenges. As such, management development tends to focus on improving the performance of existing managers, giving them scope for personal growth and development, and taking proactive steps for the future replacement of managers. It is also concerned with equipping managers to fulfil the managerial role, in terms of compliance with organisational rules, policies and practices, and facilitating managers to meet the operational requirements of the business.

This chapter considers the nature of management development and in particular the issues that a company should consider when implementing effective management development programmes. In doing so, it focuses on the following issues:

- The nature and scope of management development;

- The objectives of an organisation's management development efforts;

- The distinction between formal and informal approaches to management development;

- The range of approaches that organisations can adopt to achieve their management development goals;

- The range of policy issues that an organisation should consider when implementing management development activities;

- The evaluation of management development activities.

DEFINING MANAGEMENT DEVELOPMENT AND RELATED CONCEPTS

The question of "what constitutes management development" has yet to be answered definitively. Many definitions exist but they generally have a similar focus. For example, Ashton et al. (1975: 16) define management development as:

> a conscious and systematic process designed to control the development of managerial resources in the organisation for the achievement of organisational goals and strategies.

Mumford (1993: 10) defines management development as:

> an attempt to improve managerial effectiveness through a planned and deliberate learning process.

These definitions highlight that the development of managers within an organisation should enable it to become more effective in achieving its goals.

But what are those "organisational goals" that drive the need for more effective managers? Storey (1989a) suggests three possible organisational goals. The first is the "management of change": It is argued that the environment in which organisations interact is fast changing and this impacts upon the organisation as a whole. Management acts as a buffer against such change. The second objective is to use "management development as a tool in pursuit of quality, cost reduction and profitability through excellence". In these circumstances, the organisation's priority is to attempt to differentiate itself from its competitors by providing a product or service that is considered a leader in its field, with its competitive advantage derived from high quality service, excellence or low cost. Finally, the "nature and aims of management development may be seen to extend to a close involvement with the changing wider role for line managers in organisations". This goal reflects an approach which has as a strategy the greater need for line management involvement in the day-to-day functioning of the organisation, while more senior managers are involved in formulating the strategic priorities of the organisation.

In order to fully explain the contribution of management development, a number of other terms require definition, such as "manager" "management", "development" and "management development". They find broad and varied definition and interpretation within companies, so it is important to consider their nature and scope.

Managers and Management
"The one thing that organisations ignore at their peril, however difficult it is, is to seek some definition of what they expect managers to do" (Sisson and Storey, 1993: 7). This comment is made in the context that it is the perspective organisations hold on management and the role of managers that informs and shapes management development activities and the level of investment in such activities by the organisation. Sisson and Storey further ar-

gue that implicit, if not explicit, in many discussions of managers and management appears to be a view that what constitutes the managerial task is pretty self-evident. Traditionally, the model of management espoused in business schools was strongly influenced by the work of the classical management school. This static perspective essentially viewed management in terms of a closed system, concerned with specific activities and responsibilities such as planning, organising, leading, etc.

More contemporary perspectives place emphasis on what managers do in practice, rather than on what the theories and principles of management advocate. Such an approach highlights the reactive, social, behavioural, complex, fragmented and dynamic nature of the "management" task. Some theorists have developed classifications of the various aspects of managerial work, Mintzberg (1973), for example, identifies ten roles that managers perform within organisations and that have found general acceptance. Table 9.1 presents an explanation of these roles.

Development
Development is a concept which is difficult to define. Garavan (1997: 4) suggests that notions of development embrace both "the outer reality of the environment and organisational goals and the inner reality of the employee's emerging self". Pedler (1995) suggests that development is making the most one can out of opportunities in both the inner and outer spheres, while Baum (1995) views development as a process that is not constrained by the formal features of the organisation. The notion that development focuses more on the learner than on the learning *per se* is now generally accepted by practitioners and academics.

Table 9.1: Management Roles According to Mintzberg

Role	Activities
Interpersonal: *Figurehead*	Meeting the routine, obligatory, social and legal duties required of the head of the unit. Examples: attendance at social functions, meeting with politicians, buyer, or suppliers.
Leader	Maintaining, developing, and motivating the human resources necessary to meet the needs of the unit.
Liaison	Developing and maintaining a network of individuals outside the unit in order to acquire information and action of benefit to the unit.
Informational: *Monitor*	Searching for and acquiring information about the unit and its environment so that the manager becomes an information centre for the unit and the organisation. Derives from liaison and leader roles.
Disseminator	Distributing selected information to others within the unit or organisation, some of which has been transformed through integration with other information.
Spokesperson	Distributing selected information to others outside the unit regarding plans, values, activities, etc. of the unit and conveying the appropriate image of the unit.
Decisional: *Entrepreneur*	Proactively developing and adjusting the unit to take advantage of existing opportunities or meet anticipated threats in the environment. Actions are based on inferences and conclusions drawn from the evaluation and integration of information gathered in the monitor role.
Disturbance Handler	Reacting to meet the immediate demands of the unit. Examples of demands: a wildcat strike, loss of a major customer.
Resource Allocator	Evaluating and choosing among proposals; integrating and authorising activities and resource utilisation.
Negotiator	Bargaining to acquire the resources to meet the needs of the unit and organisation.

Source: Mintzberg (1973).

Management Development

Traditional definitions of management development tend to place emphasis on conscious intent as an essential feature, emphasising the formal, planned and deliberate aspects of the management development process. Recent definitions, however, suggest management development is more generic, encompassing both education and training, and formal and informal learning processes. For example:

- Mumford (1993) stresses a holistic perspective involving a continuous, ever-changing process and informal, unplanned experiences;

- Lees (1992) suggests that management development is the entire system of corporate activities with the espoused goal of improving the performance of the managerial resources in the context of organisational and environmental change;

- Storey (1989) suggests that management development includes those processes which enhance managerial capabilities whilst leaving scope for discretion, creativity and flexibility;

- Torrington and Hall (1998) emphasise that management development places a focus on the future. Managers are therefore developed for future roles as much as for what they are presently doing.

In summary, it can be argued that the overall focus of management development is to move managers from a point of blindness about their development to a point where they not only understand and have the skills to be more effective but that they also have the capacity to change their approach to the role, increase their overall contribution to the organisation's success and their own career self-reliance.

THE SCOPE OF MANAGEMENT DEVELOPMENT IN ORGANISATIONS: RATIONALE FOR INVESTMENT

For the purpose of this Chapter, it is assumed that management development is primarily aimed at ensuring that organisations have a supply of effective managers to meet present and future needs. Management development focuses on improving the performance of existing managers, providing opportunities for growth and development and making a contribution to effective succession management within the organisation. Management development is therefore greatly concerned about ensuring alignment with the organisation's business objectives, reinforcing the organisation's espoused culture and values, and equipping individual managers with the capability to operate business processes effectively.

Management development activities can therefore range from formal to informal approaches. Formal approaches to management development include the following:

- *Development on the job*, through coaching, counselling, monitoring and feedback by managers on a continuous basis associated with the use of performance management systems to identify and satisfy development needs. This can also be supported by the role played by peers in providing feedback, sharing experiences and practices and clarifying development needs.

- *Development through work experience*, which includes job rotation, job enlargement, taking part in project teams or task groups, "action learning" and secondment outside the organisation. Participation on "change experiences" significantly enhances the development gained from work experience.

- *Formal training*, by means of internal or external courses which are used to teach new skills or help people to acquire additional knowledge, but aim to supplement experience rather than replace it. Other areas could include the following: clarification and appreciation/understanding of the role of manager, reinforcement of organisational values and the provision of new understanding and perspectives.

- *Structured self-development,* by following self-development programmes agreed with the manager or a management development adviser — these may include guided reading or the deliberate extension of knowledge or acquisition of new skills on the job. They could also include the pursuance of a relevant third level academic qualification and the use of 360° feedback tools as a means of identifying and prioritising development needs.

Formal approaches to management development are based on the identification of development needs through a performance management system or an assessment centre process. The approach may be structured around a list of competencies which have been defined as being appropriate for managers in the organisation. Case Example 9.1 outlines Hewlett Packard's approach to management development.

Case Example 9.1: Management Development at Hewlett Packard Manufacturing, Ireland

---

Values

Hewlett Packard has always held its organisational values as a critical factor in its business success. These values are enshrined in what is known as the HPWAY. Essentially, the values emphasise the need for each employee to:

- *Have trust and respect for individuals;*
- *Focus on a high level of achievement and contribution;*
- *Conduct business with uncompromising integrity;*
- *Achieve common objectives through teamwork;*
- *Encourage flexibility and innovation.*

Accordingly, one of the core objectives of any development programme or activity at HP is to reinforce these organisational values.

Objectives

In 1997, one year after the establishment of HP Manufacturing in Ireland, a Management Development programme was designed and put in place. This programme of development has four over-arching objectives:

- Values: *To reinforce the HPWAY in terms of values, practices, priorities, policies and procedures;*

- Role: *To develop a clear alignment between the business requirements and the management/supervisors' perception and understanding of their role;*

- Competencies: *To significantly enhance management competency to enable the achievement of business goals in line with the cultural values;*

- Development: *To enhance individual manager/supervisor self-development opportunities, and to develop a strong commitment to employee development through role modelling.*

These top-level objectives have in turn been broken down into specific development objectives for each of the three levels of management in the organisation, namely, supervisors, managers and functional/senior managers — the aim being to provide the necessary and relevant development opportunities targeted to the specific management audience.

Development Approaches

In terms of approaches to management development, the following represent the primary and most frequently used:

- Development Workshops, *with the emphasis being on the development of understanding, skills and a reinforcement of values, i.e. performance management, coaching, behavioural interviewing, safety, employment law.*

- *Each manager/supervisor works with their respective manager to create a* Development Plan *that focuses on the year ahead. The objective is to define the development needs and experiences required to fulfil the requirements of the current position, plan for future changes in the role, and agree a path forward to satisfy the individual career aspirations.*

- *A core element of HP's people management system is the* Performance Management *process. Each individual is managed by objectives, provided with constructive feedback and recognised for their contribution. This process also enables a level of reflective learning and future planning about the application of learning through practical work experiences.*

- *Every six weeks, managers and supervisors are invited to attend a* Managers' and Supervisors' Forum. *The focus of these developmental events revolves around specific areas of current interest to managers and supervisors (e.g. pay for performance, business initiatives and strategies, employee survey scores). The event is attended by all members of the management team and normally lasts for six hours.*

- *All managers and supervisors receive* Coaching *from their respective immediate managers, the aim being to listen to issues and challenges and enable the individual supervisor or manager to develop a path forward. All managers receive coaching skills training to ensure that they are effective in the role of coach.*

- *Individuals or groups of managers and supervisors will be assigned to significant organisational* Projects and Assignments, *the objective being twofold: firstly, to achieve an improvement in the business; and secondly, to broaden the experience of those participating. Typically, the projects are cross-functional and involve the management of a change within the organisation.*

- *A core element of any manager or supervisor's development is the learning achieved through* on-the-job training. *Typically, this involves a collaborative effort where the individual's manager prepares a development plan and the individual's peer group plays an active part in coaching and developing.*

- *The use of 360° Feedback tools and self-development planning is being explored as a means to provide individuals with a "safe" process to gather feedback, identify development priorities and seek development. The process is voluntary, with the emphasis being placed on the individual to decide what areas of feedback they need to work on, and who would be the best resource to support their development. The tool used seeks to inform an individual on their areas of strength, areas of capability, and the areas of specific weakness.*

Informal approaches to management development make use of the learning experiences which managers encounter during the course of their everyday work. Managers are learning every time they are confronted with an unusual problem, an unfamiliar task or a move to a different job. They then have to evolve new ways of dealing with the situation. They will learn if they analyse what they did to determine how and why it contributed to its success or failure. This reflective learning will be effective if managers can apply it successfully in the future.

While experiential learning is probably the most powerful form of development for managers, it is important to recognise that a range of environmental factors may inhibit its effectiveness. Of greatest significance is the organisation's culture. Many organisations do not "value" experiential learning and accordingly little time is provided to managers to reflect on the learning gained from experience. Important metrics used to determine how the organisation values experiential learning include the following:

- *Positive experience learning* is valued and opportunities identified to reapply the learning;

- *Negative experience learning* is valued as an opportunity to learn from mistakes and to avoid the use of blame.

- *Time* is provided to reflect on experience.

- The use of *post-mortems and reviews* is viewed as a highly valuable tool in improving future organisational performance and increasing the role of organisational learning.

This is potentially one of the most powerful forms of learning. The question arises: can anything be done to help managers make the best use of their experience? This type of "experiential" learning comes naturally to some managers. They seem to absorb unconsciously, as if by some process of osmosis, the lessons from their experience, although in fact they have probably developed a capacity for almost instantaneous analysis, which they store in their mental databank and can retrieve whenever necessary.

Many managers, however, find it difficult to conduct this sort of analysis or simply do not perceive it to be an important part of the learning process. Consequently, formal approaches to management development are necessary. However, in implementing such formal approaches a lot of emphasis is placed on the manager accepting responsibility for the development process. This may happen in a number of ways:

- Emphasising self-assessment and the identification of development needs by getting managers to assess their own performance against agreed objectives and to analyse the factors contributing to effective or less effective performance — this can be provided through a performance management system;

- Getting managers to produce their own development plans;

- Encouraging managers to discuss their own problems and opportunities with their bosses or colleagues in order to establish for themselves what they need to learn or be able to do.

Table 9.2 presents three forms of management development found in organisations.

Lees (1992) suggests ten rationales for investment by organisations in management development. While the most overt of these may be "to directly improve managerial functioning and thereby corporate performance", management development can also be driven by reasons which reflect social, political, emotional, environmental or symbolic concerns. These are important to many organisations.

Table 9.2: Approaches to Management Development

Informal Managerial *Accidental Processes*	Integrated Managerial *Opportunistic Processes*	Formalised Development *Planned Processes*
Characteristics		
• Occurs within manager's activities • Explicit intention is task performance • No clear development objectives • Under-structured in development terms • Owned by managers	• Occurs within managerial activities • Explicit intention is both task performance and development • Clear development objectives • Structured for development by boss and subordinate • Planned beforehand and/or reviewed subsequently as learning experiences • Owned by managers	• Often away from normal managerial activities • Explicit intention is developed • Clear development objectives • Structured for development by developers • Planned beforehand and/or reviewed subsequently as learning experiences • Owner more by developers than by managers
Outcomes		
• Learning real, direct, natural unconscious and insufficient	• Learning real, direct, conscious, more substantial	• Learning may be real (through a job) or detached (through a course) • Is more likely to be conscious, relatively infrequent, contrived.

Source: Mumford, 1993.

Functional Performance

A functional performance rationale has as its aim the direct improvement of managerial functioning and ultimately corporate performance. It views management development as "a conscious and systematic process designed to control the development of managerial resources in the organisation for the achievement of organisational goals and strategy" (Easterby-Smith et al., 1975: 17). Functional performance represents the mainstream business approach to management development in Ireland. From a developmental perspective, the functional performance rationale can provide relatively objective data relating to the achievement or non-achievement of business or individual objectives.

Agricultural

An agricultural rationale focuses on the perceived need to cultivate and grow managers internally. It differs from the functional performance rationale in that the development of managers is assumed to take place mainly on the job and responsibility for development is placed firmly on managers themselves. An agricultural rationale perceives management development as a somewhat haphazard, one-to-one process involving natural learning-type activities, many work-based experiences and much informal learning.

Functional-Defensive

A functional-defensive rationale suggests that the purpose of management development is to build up a reservoir of knowledge and potential skills within the organisation, just in case such competencies should ever be required in the future to effectively manage the external environment or major organisational change.

Socialisation

In this situation, management development is concerned with the socialisation of managers to match a corporate value system and ethos. This is a common purpose in many non-union companies. Storey (1989) argues that it may be concerned with "attitudinal structuring", with "the diffusion of company values" and with "forging a common identify and approach". It is also advocated, for example, that "management development . . . has . . . the primary task of maintaining organisational order" (Lawrence, 1977). It could also be argued that, in this era of increasing complexity in decision-making, the role of management judgement is even more significant. It requires managers to have a sound understanding of, and alignment to, the organisation's core values and over-arching objectives.

Political Reinforcement

According to the political reinforcement perspective, management development acts as an extension of the organisation's political order; the organisation becomes tightly coupled and is designed to reinforce a partisan, internal perception of how organisational performance is to be improved, and management development is used to reinforce the political credibility of those who are shaping the organisational vision. Management development is, therefore, as much concerned with the regulation, as with the realisation, of management potential. To a degree, many management development processes follow such a rationale. Management education, for example, perpetuates the view of management as a rational order and generally serves to reinforce the status of management as an elite social grouping.

Organisational Inheritance

Within an organisational inheritance rationale, management development is perceived as the key to organisational succession and career fulfilment, and is illustrated in particular through such rituals as performance appraisal, assessment centre processes, development centres and succession management activities.

Environmental Legitimacy

An environmental legitimacy rationale suggests the notion of mimetic isomorphism — that is, the signalling of conformity with environmental myths and the conferring of legitimacy on the organisation from external stakeholders. Organisations generally desire to be well-respected and valued by customers, suppliers and professional bodies. Management development may be viewed as one means of achieving this. The objective may be to cultivate a professional stereotype of management activity, with much public demonstration of career and succession planning and the creation of positive publicity about same.

Compensation

A compensation rationale advocates that management development can offer some form of compensation from the deprivations of employment and work. Rather than trying to remedy the corporate causes of employee alienation, the solution is to use management development as a substitute and hope that it reduces employee turnover and other exit behaviours.

Psychic Defence

Those who suggest a psychic defence rationale advocate that management development activities can help to reduce the anxieties that managers experience arising from career-related issues such as limited opportunities for promotion or other forms of advancement. The periodical enactment of ceremonies and rituals within organisations may serve to reduce the fear of disorder and chaos, by giving the appearance of an ordered system of managerial succession. Management development activities represent one such ritual that may have value in reducing fears about careers.

There is evidence in the Irish context that management development may be used for a range of purposes. Figure 9.1 presents the perceptions of some Irish companies on the contribution of management development.

Figure 9.1: Contribution of Management Development – Some Irish Research Findings

---

- Management development contributes most to continuous process improvements, improved customer satisfaction and cost reduction.

- Irish companies utilise individual manager development, project/team work and succession planning as major career planning activities.

- Irish companies spend on average two per cent of payroll on management development activities; directors receive an average of three days per annum of management development, senior managers six days and middle managers/supervisors nine days.

- Very few Irish companies use overseas placements and assignments as part of their management development activities.

- Management development can make a significant contribution to the competitive advantage of the organisation.

- There is increasing evidence of the use of mentoring and peer learning processes as a fundamental component of management development.

- Management development is increasingly concerned with the reinforcement of corporate values and their espousal in management practices.

- Managers are participating more in decisions about their development.

Source: Walsh, Finchan and Anderson, 1998; Garavan, 1998.

DELIVERY OF EFFECTIVE MANAGEMENT DEVELOPMENT: SOME ISSUES

A number of organisational and HRM issues impinge on the effective delivery of management development. These issues include selection, identification of development needs, competencies, choice of delivery strategies, rewards, succession planning and performance management. They require careful consideration by organisations and we will outline each one in turn.

Formulation of Management Development Policy

The effective implementation of management development in organisations requires a clear statement of management development policy. When formulating such a policy, it is important to consider the following issues:

- How will development plans and activities relate to business goals and strategies, human resource planning processes and wider HRM issues?

- Who will have responsibility for the development of managers within the organisation?

- Does the organisation have a clear picture of the characteristics of effective managers within the organisation?

- Will the organisation adopt a competency approach and how will these competencies be defined?

- What is the nature of the organisation's value system in respect of management?

- How will individual managers' needs be accommodated within a wider management development approach?

- How will management succession planning and rewards issues be addressed?

An effective policy statement can provide a clear expression of the organisation's commitment to the management development process and set out a clear framework within which management development initiatives can take place. Case Example 9.2 presents an example of a management development policy statement.

Case Example 9.2: Management Development Policy Statement in Kostal Ireland

---

Kostal Ireland Management Development Policy Statement

Kostal accepts that it is the company's responsibility to provide every manager with the opportunity to maximise their ability and potential so that performance is maximised.

- *Our policy requires that in each department we will create an environment in which all managers contribute to the objectives of the business to their optimum ability;*

- *We will provide an organisational structure within which the responsibilities of each manager will be clearly defined;*

- *We require management to be committed to the objective of their job and to their development as managers;*

- *We will support and fund appropriate external management development initiatives where such activities meet the development needs of the particular manager.*

Human Resource Planning and Selection

Effective management development requires the organisation to plan for the right number of managers, with the appropriate competencies to be available when required. Effective human resource planning can make a major contribution by assessing existing managerial talent and identifying future requirements. Organisations have a range of assessment options available, including assessment and development tactics, performance management processes, personnel files and discussions with senior managers.

Success in managerial work depends on the possession of a range of social skill competencies and personal qualities. Therefore, considerable attention needs to be paid to selection in order to ensure an appropriate managerial pool. This will entail the specification of measurable selection criteria and their systematic implementation across the organisation (see Chapters 4 and 5). It will also require the development of appropriate selection methods to identify those competencies and personal qualities effectively and accurately.

A related selection issue is the manager's readiness for management development. Some managers may demonstrate arrogance and simply resist management development initiatives. Others may be ignorant about their development needs. Others still may have reached a stage where they are knowledgeable about their role but recognise significant gaps. Some individual managers may be at a point of performing effectively in the sense of compliance and doing all of the necessary tasks, but nothing over and above that. They could benefit significantly from a management development initiative. Managers who have fully participated in management development may serve as role models, and others may have the capacity to develop and coach other managers.

Analysis of Development Needs
Effective management development requires the careful and systematic assessment of individual development needs. This process has traditionally been carried out in an *ad hoc* and often piecemeal manner (Doyle, 1995). Increasingly, organisations are using performance appraisal as a mechanism to identify the skills and behaviours required to meet business objectives (Storey, 1989, Mumford, 1993). The resultant needs analysis, forming the basis of an agreed personal development plan, is then regularly reviewed and modified according to changing circumstances. Particular issues in the context of appraisal revolve around its purposes, the methods used, the skills and subjectivity of the appraisers; the danger of it becoming a ritualistic process; and the

difficulty in striking a balance between a control-led and a development-led approach (see Chapter 10).

The performance appraisal process is typically focused on past performance, behaviours and practices observed by the reviewing manager. Therefore, it is critical that feedback from customers, peers and subordinates be sought as a means of ensuring a more holistic view of the individual's performance and their development needs. The use of questionnaires and semi-structured interviews can help this process. It is also agreed that the act of appraisal should be conducted separately from the act of development planning. This would address the concern that managers being appraised would seek to justify past performance or role development gaps to avoid negative perceptions or possibly lower levels of reward. The separation of the discussion on development plans helps to foster greater honesty and to minimise the tendency to be judgmental, and provides a greater opportunity to focus on the future.

There is evidence that some Irish companies, especially US-owned multinationals, are now using development centres. Development centres enable companies to assess the competencies and abilities of a managerial pool against a particular benchmark. They usually consist of a specification of the criteria necessary for success in a managerial role, the implementation of psychometric tests, games, simulations, in-tray exercises, interviews, the professional assessment of each manager and the provision of structured feedback and guidance to managers. They are generally conducted off-site and their basic philosophy is the use of multiple methods, criteria and assessors to identify development potential and the needs of managers. The assessors will usually produce a comprehensive report on each manager.

Managerial Competencies
The identification of competencies needed for effective performance must, in one form or another, play a major role in any man-

agement development initiative. Storey (1989) suggests that a competency-based approach to management development has gained in popularity and "work on refining competency profiles is currently at the cutting edge of activity". Competency-based systems of training and development are now quite a common feature of organisations (O'Donnell and Garavan, 1997). Jones and Woodcock (1985) suggest that the term "competency" subsumes the traditional categories of knowledge, skills and attitudes and implies effectiveness, while Boyatzis (1982) defines job competency as "an underlying characteristic of a person which results in effective and/or superior performance in a job".

The competency approach seeks to develop managers through workplace activities, with the focus on the manager's ability to perform and deliver predetermined outcomes, rather than on the achievement of specific knowledge and qualifications. The Management Charter Initiative (MCI) in the UK has sought to establish a generic set of standards and qualifications based upon the areas of activity which the majority of managers would be expected to perform competently (Miller, 1991). Doyle (1998) suggests, however, that many companies feel the imperative to continue to devise their own framework within their unique organisational context.

However, competency-based programmes, and in particular those that are of a standardised format, have attracted considerable criticism both in philosophical and practical terms. These criticisms arise on the basis that competency-based programmes are too functional and behavioural in orientation (Stewart and Hamlin, 1992); are too bureaucratic and overly simplistic; place too much emphasis on analysing competencies into distinct and separable parts; and are too individualistic and unable to cover all types of relevant behaviour or mental activity adequately (Ashworth and Sexton, 1990). Hence, Canning (1990) suggests that they are unable to take account of the complex, contextual, contingent and ever-changing nature of the managerial role. Despite such criticisms, their popularity continues to grow.

Performance Management and Reward

There is a close link between management development and performance management processes (also see Chapter 10). A well-designed performance management system can provide a mechanism to identify development needs, to provide feedback to the manager on performance and to reward personal development and achievement. Some Irish organisations are now rewarding the attainment of enhanced competencies, have implemented performance-related pay and have successfully implemented a range of rewards, including profit-sharing schemes, bonuses, shares, all with the aim of reinforcing high performance criteria.

Promotion and Succession Planning

Closely related to performance and reward issues are those of promotion and succession planning. Management development has a major political dimension, in that for many managers it sets up expectations of promotion and advancement. Mumford (1993) argues that management development will only be effective if the organisation carefully considers issues concerning career paths, opportunities for promotion and other forms of progression. The availability of such progression and promotion opportunities will, however, depend on the age structure amongst existing managers, issues related to downsizing, restructuring and the extent to which the organisation uses novel horizontal progression strategies such as secondments, special projects and assignments.

In terms of career planning, it is argued that managers will in the future become increasingly responsible of their careers. There is evidence that managers are as much concerned with the development of their employability as with vertical career progression. Table 9.3 provides a summary of the elements of successful management development.

Table 9.3: Elements for Successful Management Development:
A Checklist of Questions

Element	Characteristics
Purpose	• Why is the organisation investing in management development? • What is the emphasis given to organisation needs versus individual needs? • How will the conflict between individual and organisational needs be resolved?
Context	• Within what cultural context will management development take place? • What is the current climate and ethos of the organisation? • What structural changes are envisaged within the organisation? • What is the dominant HRM philosophy and set of strategies in operation?
Relevance	• Have the management development needs been correctly identified? • Have the managers themselves made a contribution to the needs identification process?
Time	• How much time will be given to the management development initiative? • How will the management development strategy affect the managers' commitment? • How will the management development initiative affect the core task of management?
Focus of Initiative	• Does the management development initiative seek to develop new values and attitudes? • Does the management development initiative seek to develop technical, financial, business or interpersonal skills? • Is the initiative concerned with the implementation of structural and/or technological change?
Strategies	• What are the most cost-effective and appropriate management development strategies available? • What scope is available to accommodate individual learning priorities? • What role will the individual manager have in the selection strategies? • Should management development occur on the job, off the job, in an academic context or some combination?

Element	Characteristics
Development Population	• Is it older managers seeking new challenges and redevelopment? • Is the focus on graduate highfliers on fast-track development programmes? • Is the concern with engineers and technical specialists seeking to acquire management skills or expand their cross-functional capabilities? • Is it senior managers seeking to enhance strategic management skills? • Is it middle or junior managers seeking to broaden functional skills or acquire new ones?
Resources	• What financial investment will be required by the organisation? • What demands will the management development initiative make of specialist training and development staff?
Evaluation	• What criteria will be used to assess the effectiveness of management development? • What techniques or approaches will be used to assess the effectiveness of management development? • Who will carry out the evaluation process? • What role will participating managers have in the evaluation process?

APPROACHES TO MANAGEMENT DEVELOPMENT

Education and Training

A training programme will usually be a key feature of most formal programmes of management development, and such programmes may be standard offerings by specialist bodies or consultants, or in-house programmes developed to meet the organisation's own specialist needs (see Chapter 8). Increasingly, these options are being combined so that there is the possibility of an externally provided programme tailored to suit an organisation's particular needs. There are five variations of this approach.

First, there are *pre-experience courses*. These consist of full-time education programmes leading to an academic qualification with a management science or business studies label and are undertaken by young people as a preliminary step to a career. They are often described as "vocational" and intended to be a practical preparation for a management-type occupation. The sandwich programme that incorporates periods of work in the "real" world introduces what might be seen as greater reality to the learning process, but they can rarely provide any meaningful experience in, and practice at, managerial work. Such programmes provide an education, normally based on a study of the academic disciplines of economics, mathematics, psychology and sociology and incorporating some work in the more specialised disciplines like industrial relations and organisational behaviour, as well as an introduction to practical areas like accounting, marketing, personnel and production. The learner hopefully will emerge with a balanced understanding of the workings of business, and they will have some useful blocks of information. The learner should also have developed maturity and the ability to analyse, evaluate and debate. However, they will not be trained to be a manager.

Second, there are *post-experience programmes*. These may consist of full-time or part-time education, usually leading to a certificate, diploma, degree or master's degree with a management or business orientation and undertaken during a career. The main difference is not only that learners are older, but that they study on the basis of experience they have acquired and with the knowledge of the work to which they will return. Participants may be seconded or supported on a part-time basis by their employer at a time when they already hold a management post. The material on the programme may not be very different from that of the pre-experience programme, but the learner's perception will be very different and the application of any new insights or skills will be more immediate.

The third category can be generally described as *consultancy-type programmes*. These may vary from a half-day to several weeks in length, and they are usually run by consultants or professional bodies. They have the advantage of bringing together managers from varying occupational backgrounds and are not, therefore, as introspective as in-house programmes. Such programmes are popular for current issues and new developments. They are, however, relatively expensive and may be superficial, despite their value as sources of knowledge and the swapping of experiences among programme members. These consultancy-type programmes can prove valuable to individuals with specialist development needs related to the role they fulfil within the organisation. Such programmes can also provide individuals with the opportunity to interact with individuals in similar professions and provide the possibility of longer-term networking. It should, however, be recognised that consultancy-type programmes will only provide an individual with the opportunity to increase their contribution to the organisation where senior management are open to allowing the manager use the new knowledge or skill to influence organisational thinking and practice. Often managers attend consultancy-type programmes and struggle to implement new-found ideas and insights. This can result in a certain amount of cynicism about the priority and usefulness of such development when they return to the organisation. The most valuable programmes of this type are those that concentrate on specific areas of knowledge, like developing interviewing or disciplinary skills. Managers need not only to find an interpretation of new developments, but they also need to share views and reactions with fellow managers to ensure that their own feelings are not idiosyncratic or perverse.

A fourth education and training programme type strategy consists of *in-house programmes*, which are often similar in nature to consultancy programmes. Such in-house programmes are often run with the benefit of some external expertise, but this is not always the case. In-house programmes can be particularly useful if the training needs relate to specific organisational procedures and structures, or if they are geared to encouraging managers to work more effectively together. The disadvantage of in-house programmes is that they often suffer from a lack of breadth of both content and input from managers. There is no possibility of learning from people in other organisations. The use of in-house programmes can help target the development process by addressing a given business need and this in turn can enable a more focused evaluation of the results. Typically, such in-house programmes are less expensive and can provide experienced managers with the opportunity to participate in or lead the development of less experienced managers, provided more experienced managers act as tutors and/or mentors.

A fifth variant is represented by *outdoor-type courses* (sometimes known as outward-bound). Outdoor courses attempt to develop such skills as leadership, getting results through people, self-confidence in handling people, and increasing self-awareness through a variety of experiences, including outdoor physical challenges. Outward-bound courses are popular and their value is assumed to hinge on their separation from the political and organisational environment within which the managers operate. A natural, challenging and different environment is assumed to encourage individuals to forsake political strategising, act as their "real" selves and be more open to new ideas. The challenge in using outward-bound development is to transfer the learning experience to a change in approach or behaviour in the workplace. As a socialisation process, outward-bound programmes can be particularly effective in helping managers to get to know each other in an environment where the power dynamics are absent or of little value.

Action Learning

Reg Revans, the originator of action learning, as a Professor of Management in the 1970s, had become increasingly disenchanted with the world of management education which he saw developing around him. He believed that managers did not need education, but the ability to solve problems (Revans, 1980, 1982). Action learning focuses on real problems that enable managers to question the conditions that have led to these problems and to generate solutions that can be implemented and translated into action within the organisation. The process of action learning consists of a number of elements:

- A learning set is established consisting of a group of five or six managers.

- Participants work to test and question each other until the problem is much clearer. This process of analysis may take a considerable amount of time (sometimes months) to complete.

- The set will usually have a facilitator whose role is to manage process issues such as conflict and lack of progress.

- The process is underpinned by a series of open exchanges, which provides for both mutual criticism and mutual support.

- The process is inherently active in that managers must not only understand, but must also be committed to their choices of action.

Revans's approach, therefore, is essentially to organise exchange, so that a managerial experience in one organisation is transplanted to another to solve a particular set of problems that are proving baffling. The participant brings a difference of experience and a freshness of approach. Managers work on a significant problem for a period of months, having many sessions of discussion and debate with a group of other individuals similarly planted in unfamiliar organisations, with a "knotty" problem to solve. The learning stems from the immediate problem that is presented, and from all the others that emerge, one by one, in the steps towards a solution. This presents a need that the participant must satisfy and learning is related to what they discover from other perspectives. Figure 9.2 presents a summary of the principles of action learning.

Figure 9.2: Revans's Principles of Action Learning

> - Management development should be based in real-life work projects;
> - Successful projects should be owned and defined by senior managers;
> - Managers must aim to make a real return on the cost of the investment;
> - Managers should work together and learn from each other;
> - Management development activities based on action learning principles must achieve real action and change;
> - Managers must understand the content and process of change;
> - Managers must be fully committed to taking action;
> - Managers must drive the content of the action learning set.

Coaching

Coaching is an informal approach to management development based on a close relationship between the developing manager and a manager who is experienced in management. The manager, as coach, helps trainees to develop by giving them the opportunity to perform an increasing range of management tasks, and by helping them to learn from their experiences. Both parties work to improve the manager's performance through asking searching questions, discussion, exhortation, encouragement, understanding, counselling, and providing information and feedback. It is essential that the coach is someone who has experienced what the trainee is now learning. Coaching creates the possibility of a highly focused and participative development planning process, where the individual's relationship with the organisation, the operation of process and interpersonal relationships are viewed from a holistic perspective. Critical to the success of coaching is the use of positive reinforcement and constructive feedback: these provide both opportunities for reflective learning and the prioritisation of development needs.

The coach, as the immediate manager of the learner, is also in an excellent position to provide the appropriate learning opportunities in terms of new/challenging tasks, membership of working parties and committees, secondments, deputising and so on.

The area of coaching is addressed in considerable detail in Chapter 11.

Mentoring

Mentoring is seen as offering a wide range of advantages for the development of a manager. The mentor will occasionally be the individual's immediate manager, but more often they are a more senior manager in the same or a different function. Kram (1983) identifies two broad functions of mentoring: first, career functions, which are those aspects of the relationship that primarily enhance career advancement; and second, psychosocial functions, which are those aspects of the relationship that primarily enhance a sense of competency, clarity of identity and effectiveness in the managerial role. A possible third function of mentoring relates to the rapidly changing and increasingly complex environment that managers are required to operate within. The role of mentor as "listener" and friend is often critical for a manager to enable the process of coping with such challenges and stresses. Failure to cope will often result in a lack of development. There is a more significant emphasis placed on the mentoring relationship than on the coaching relationship, on career success, and managers are selected for mentoring because, among other things, they are effective performers, perhaps from a similar background and know the potential mentors socially (Kanter, 1977). There are advantages in the relationship for mentors as well as managers. These include reflected glory from a successful manager, the development of mentors throughout the organisation, and the facilitation of their own promotion by adequate training of a replacement.

The area of mentoring is addressed in detail in Chapter 11.

Peer Relationships

Although mentor–protégé relationships can lead to high levels of career success, not all developing managers have access to such a relationship. Supportive peer relationships at work are potentially more available to the individual and offer a number of benefits for the development. The benefits that are available depend on the nature of the peer relationship. Kram and Isabelle (1985) have identified three groups of peer relationships which are differentiated by their primary development functions and which can be expressed on a continuum from "information peer" through "collegial peer" to "special peer".

Peer relationships most often develop on an informal basis and provide mutual support. Some organisations, however, formally appoint an existing employee to provide such support to a new member of staff through their first 12–18 months in the organisation. Such relationships may continue beyond the initial period. The name for the appointed employee will vary from organisation to organisation, and sometimes the words "coach" "buddy" or "mentor" is used (see Chapter 11). Cromer (1989) suggests many advantages of peer relationships organised on a formal basis and highlights the skills and qualities sought in peer providers, which include accessibility, empathy, organisational experience and proven task skills. It could be argued that development through peer relationships should be a relatively systematic process as with other professions within organisations. While it is critical that the peer providing coaching be skilled and experienced, it is equally important that the development role they are required to fulfil is viewed as a legitimate activity within the organisation and is accordingly reflected in their performance goals.

Natural Learning

Natural managerial learning is learning that takes place on-the-job and results from managers' everyday experiences of the tasks that they undertake (Garavan, 1987). It differs from action learning in that action learning activities are group-based and focus on specific organisational problems. Natural learning is even more difficult to investigate than either coaching, mentoring or peer relationships, and yet the way managers learn from everyday experiences, and their level of awareness of this, is very important from a management development point-of-view.

Burgoyne and Hodgson (1983) suggest three levels of learning. The first level is when the manager takes in some factual information that has an immediate relevance but does not have any long-term effect on their view of the world in general. At the next level, the manager learns something that is transferable from one situation to another — they have changed their understanding about a particular aspect of their view of the world in general, this aspect being situation-specific. For example, managers use critical incidents to add to their personal stock of knowledge and from this select models when dealing with future situations. In some cases, managers specifically set aside time for reflective learning so that they can derive insights and new approaches for use in the future. Some managers also learn through deliberate problem-solving. Level three learning is similar to level two, but not as situation-specific.

Self-Development

To some extent, self-development may be viewed as a conscious effort to gain the most from natural learning in a work situation. The emphasis in self-development is that each manager is responsible for, and can plan their own development, although they may need to seek help when working on some issues. Self-development involves managers in analysing their strengths, weaknesses and the way that they learn, primarily by means of questionnaires and feedback from others. This analysis may initially begin on a self-development programme, or with the help of a facilitator, but would then be continued by the manager back on the job. From this analysis, managers plan their development goals and the way they hope to achieve these, primarily through development opportunities within the job. When managers consciously work on self-development, they use the learning cycle in a more conscious way than when involved in a natural learning process. They may also be in a better position to seek appropriate opportunities and help from their superior. It is important to recognise that a true commitment to self-development requires a manager to put him/herself at risk. It is easier to be arrogant or self-justifying than it is to admit to a lack of competencies. Therefore, a manager's request for coaching and development must be viewed as something to be encouraged and should not be viewed as a reason for a low performance.

Many of the activities included in self-development are based on observation, soliciting feedback about the way they operate, experimenting with different approaches and, in particular, reviewing what has happened, why and what they have learned.

Self-Development Groups
Self-development or management learning groups are another way in which managers can support their development. Pedlar (1986) suggests that, typically, a group of managers is involved in a series of meetings where they would jointly discuss their personal development, organisational issues and/or individual work problems. Groups may begin operating with a leader who is a process expert, not a content expert, and who acts primarily as a facilitator rather than as a source of information. The group itself is the primary source of information and as their process skills develop they may operate without outside help. The content and timing of meetings can be very flexible, although clearly if they

are to operate well, they will require a significant level of energy and commitment.

Self-development groups can be devised in a variety of situations. Such groups can be part of a formal educational course, where a group of managers from different organisations come together to support their development. They may constitute the whole of a self-development programme, or they can be an informal group within a particular organisation. Irrespective of how the group originates, it is important that they understand what every member hopes to get out of the group, the role of the facilitator (if there is one), the processes and rules that the group will operate by and how they agree to interact. A critical success factor for self-development groups lies in the creation of a climate of trust and a common objective to the effect that each manager will learn each other's best practices. Support and sponsorship from senior management is vital and often senior managers will be invited to participate in group discussions, particularly around issues of senior management expectations and business priorities.

Learning Contracts

Garavan and Sweeney (1994) suggest that there is evidence of an increasing use of learning contracts in a management development context. They are used within more formalised self-development groups; on other management programmes; as part of mentoring or coaching relationships; or in working towards competency-based qualifications. These contracts represent a formal commitment by the learner to work towards a specified learning goal, with an identification of how the goal might be achieved. Boak (1991) suggests that such contracts should include:

- An overall development goal;

- Specific objectives in terms of skills and knowledge;

- Activities to be undertaken;

- Resources required;

- Method of assessment of learning.

The value that individual managers gain from learning contracts is dependent on their freedom to participate, their identification of the relevant development and learning goal and the importance and value they ascribe to achieving them. Commitment is necessary for a learning contract be effective, because ultimately it is down to the individual learner to make it happen.

ADVANTAGES AND DISADVANTAGES OF MANAGEMENT DEVELOPMENT STRATEGIES

The following pages present the advantages and disadvantages of a range of management development strategies, with a short description of each strategy.

In-house Development Programmes

These are courses organised by internal or external trainers and conducted internally.

Advantages	Disadvantages
• Develops in-company knowledge and skills • Establishes/maintains organisational culture, norms, formal practices • Useful with geographically dispersed units	• May not be company-specific, but merely an imported package not adapted to the unique needs of the organisation • Can pass along organisation's mythology about how managers should behave, rather than testing its assumptions

External Development Programmes

Managers are sent to outside courses, for special training and/or academic degrees. Trainers are external to the organisation.

Advantages	Disadvantages
• Increased sensitivity to events in the external environment	• May not be relevant to organisational needs
• Develops emotional resilience	• Is often expensive
• Cross-cultural impact	• May be fashionable rather than usable
• Bridges gaps between organisations	• May be seen as a holiday or reward rather than task-focused
• Introduces new ideas and approaches	• May be difficult to apply to organisation
• Challenges organisational assumptions	• Can create barriers in the organisation

Training Centres

These are organisation-oriented training facilities usually restricted to in-house training.

Advantages	Disadvantages
• Facilitates the full development of in-house training capabilities	• To be cost effective, must be used often
• Provides maximum control over training site and schedule	• May become an empire and the focus of organisational policies
• Highlights training as a legitimate activity within the organisation	• May become an ivory tower
• Potentially holds expenses down	• May become an organisational burden
• It can become a forum for ideas, materials and expertise for management development within the organisation	• Requires management
	• Keeps trainers isolated from organisational environment
	• May add travel expense

Consultants

Outside trainers to help design, run and assist in evaluation of programme practices.

Advantages	Disadvantages
• Can be employed to expand internal resources	• Can be sensitive to nuances of organisational culture
• Often bring new ideas and fresh approaches	• Are often expensive
• Can challenge current management practices	• No ongoing responsibility within the organisation
• No vested interest in management behaviour and can give their best professional judgement	• Sometimes circumvent rather than support internal training staff
• Can help train internal trainers	• May foster dependency in the interest of follow-on business
• Can be scheduled flexibly	
• Can bring objectivity to programme evaluation	

Group Training Programmes

These are in-house, system-wide, small-group-oriented training programmes (e.g. Managerial Grid, Coverdale, T-groups, Transactional Analysis, Assertion Training).

Advantages	Disadvantages
• Can inculcate common concepts and language	• Can be threatening
• Utilise group skills of managers	• Can be inappropriately and excessively personal
• Often require managers to stretch themselves personally	• Can be manipulative
• Promote togetherness, break down barriers	• Can damage individuals
• Usually intense and personal	• Can promote dysfunctional organisational norms
	• Require specialised skills on the part of trainers
	• Often faddish or trendy
	• Can become quasi-religious

Outdoor Management Development Programmes

Programmes designed to develop such skills as leadership, self-confidence and self-awareness through a variety of experiences including outdoor physical challenges (e.g. on rivers, lakes and in the hills and mountains).

Advantages	*Disadvantages*
• Can simulate conditions where teamwork and collaboration are necessary	• There is limited evidence of effective learning transfer to the workplace
• It is hoped that a natural and challenging environment will encourage managers to forsake political strategies	• They do not necessarily provide a de-politicised environment as claimed in the literature
• Participants may be more open to new ideas	• They are expensive to run and questions have been raised about the ethics of the activities included in such programmes
• Have capacity to lay the foundations for effective teamwork	

Performance Review

This involves regularly scheduled appraisals of employee job performance; they generate growth plans for individuals in terms of competency and responsibility.

Advantages	*Disadvantages*
• Provides for individual goal setting	• Managers often lack the necessary skills to make it effective
• Better manager–subordinate communication	• May not be carried out honestly and openly
• Improved interpersonal relationships	• May become bureaucratic and time-consuming
• Promotes better career guidance/planning	• May be perfunctory without data-gathering or planning
• Puts manager in position of developing subordinates	• Sometimes not goal-oriented but retrospective
	• If confused with salary review, feedback can be ineffective

Career Development

Counselling service for employees to manage their own careers within the organisation; may involve courses, private consultations and vocational testing.

Advantages	Disadvantages
• Helps develop responsibility in self-management • Provides data to training managers of reversal management development • Provides data for individual choices • Facilitates proper employment of people • Pressurises managers to be developmental	• Can raise false expectations • Opportunities may be insufficient • Can lead to dissatisfaction and seeking alternative employment • Can put emphasis on individual needs at the expense of organisational needs

Job Rotation

This involves shifting managers and potential managers systematically through various jobs to develop skills, technical expertise and perspective.

Advantages	Disadvantages
• Can give wide experience • Can generate a positive sense of perceptiveness and "worldliness" • Helps gain new ideas, skills and expertise • Can help challenge the existing order • Can generate interdepartmental cross-fertilisation	• Individuals must make frequent, often stressful job adjustments • Can interfere with hanging organisational processes • May result in individuals coping more than learning • Can be seen as a threat or nuisance by managers

Secondments

These are temporary assignments, usually within other organisations.

Advantages	Disadvantages
• Cross-pollination of ideas • An influx of skills can be effected where they are needed • Can have a cross-cultural impact • Potential for rapid problem-solving in host organisation • Development of wider perspective	• Often met with resistance on both sides • Generate entry/re-entry problems • Frequently viewed administratively as a nuisance • People are often given inappropriate assignments

International Assignments

Secondment across national boundaries. This is an area of management development that is likely to become more prevalent. Advantages and disadvantages are the same as for secondment, in addition to the following:

Advantages	Disadvantages
• Foster better international understanding and contacts • Helps shape the organisation structure by ensuring the right people are developed • Permits organisational decentralisation and differentiation while also ensuring conformity with the centre's key aims and values	• Language and cultural difficulties • Expense • Applicability of learning to own country

Mentoring

Assigning more senior managers to assist new managers in growing into the jobs. The relationship is not usually between the individual and their immediate boss. Mentoring is about relationships rather than activities.

Advantages	Disadvantages
• Involves senior management in management development • Can provide practical guidance • May improve performance review systems • Improves "up-down" communication • Can make provision for ombudsman services	• Consumes expensive senior management time • May generate insubordination • Can inadvertently elicit jealousy by perceived elevation of "mentee" status • Can become political in orientation

Counselling

This involves personal development help for employees in their personal concerns.

Advantages	Disadvantages
• Helps organisation become sensitive to individual needs • Promotes appropriate employment • Bridges personal/organisational goals • Can help maintain rapport with employees • People treated more humanely through this orientation • Fosters family spirit • Reduces people seeking other employment • May uncover organisational problems	• Requires special training • May make people vulnerable • Can create dependency • Conditions of confidentiality — may be manipulated • May undermine performance review • Can be resented • Requires privacy; may threaten it • Often not asked for even when needed • Time consuming

Coaching

On-the-job, job-specific, individualised instruction and assistance by supervisors and/or trainers. It involves "improving the performance of someone who is already competent rather than establishing competency in the first place".

Advantages	Disadvantages
• Job-relevant	• Assumes the job makes sense
• Requires the coach to relate to individual needs and readiness	• May be too here-and-now oriented
	• Heavily dependent on the manager's training skills
• Facilitates two-way communication and relationships	• Many managers find it easy to avoid
	• Difficult to monitor
• Generates learning that is immediately applicable	• May be inefficient
	• Takes time away from the normal work flow
• Highly goal-oriented	• Organisational power structures suggest that there may be a need for additional support from a professional counsellor
• Easily linked to performance review	
• Requires managers to be developmental	

Organisational Role Analysis

Clarifying managers' roles within the organisational context.

Advantages	Disadvantages
• Provides clarity in responsibilities	• Can be impersonal, rigid, competitive
• Fosters negotiation	
• Helps manage redundancy of functions	• Can foster independence rather than interdependence
• Can uncover system problems	• May fail to take personal feelings and aspirations into account
• Helps implement organisational change	
• Identifies deviant performers	• Time-consuming
• Easily linked to performance review	• May generate resistance

Learning Contracts

A formal commitment by the learner to work towards a specific learning goal with an identification of how the goal might be achieved.

Advantages	Disadvantages
• Can facilitate the identification of an overall development goal • Put onus on the individual learner to clarify goals • Involve all the relevant parties in the development process	• Require a high level of commitment to be effective • There may be resistance from managers to make contractual-type commitments • Require a culture of openness and collaboration to be effective

Task Force/Project Groups

These are cross-departmental groups that study organisational problems and/or carryout special assignments.

Advantages	Disadvantages
• Cross-pollination • Operational skills applied • New experience • Promotes "we" attitude • Fosters inter-team relations • Improves organisation's fire-fighting ability • Highly task-focused • Improves communication, diagnostic, judgmental, evaluative and political skills	• May mirror organisational instability • Can disrupt functional work teams • Can reduce unworkable solutions • May generate non-committal outcomes • Outcomes must be sold to decision-makers • Requires advance experience of teambuilding • Can disrupt the system

Seminars/Workshops

These are teach-each-other events for pooling experience.

Advantages	Disadvantages
• Pools experience • Develops interpersonal support • Uses resources well • Flexibility scheduled • Develops managers' training and communication skills • Exchange of ideas	• Practice is time-consuming • Requires skills that many managers do not have • Ineffective consulting models, such as extensive advice-giving, may be used • May distract from manager's own goal attainment • Can be seen as interference and/or threat • Often not asked for by those who need it most

Action Learning

Experiential learning, based on the concept of the learning cycle and around the principles of action learning.

Advantages	Disadvantages
• Managers learn about themselves, their job, about team managers, and how to improve things and make changes • Leads to developments such as learning contracts, learning communities and learning organisations • Rooted in the everyday reality of what managers do and how they behave	• A time-consuming process • Commitment may decline over the period of the project • May have difficulty finding an appropriate project • Unpopular in academic circles

Self-Development Groups
Involves a group of managers in a series of meetings to discuss personal development issues.

Advantages	Disadvantages
• Can be implemented effectively within many types of organisation • Involve self-management activities • May help clarify personal goals and priorities • May change individual attitudes and behaviour	• May need facilitation to be effective • Group may lack the information and/or expertise to operate • Require a significant level of energy and commitment • Must have a clear understanding of what they can and cannot achieve

Peer Relationships
Supportive peer relationships designed to provide information, confirmation, emotional support, feedback and friendship.

Advantages	Disadvantages
• Demands relatively little commitment but can offer many benefits • Not all developing managers have access to a mentor relationship but have access to peers • The relationship may be informational, collegial or special in orientation • Can often develop on an informal basis and provide important initial support	• The peer must have accessibility and empathy • The peer will require a good organisational knowledge and proven task skills • Peers contribution to development may not be appreciated • Often work better in an informal rather than formal capacity • There may be some confusion with coaching and mentoring relationships

THE EVALUATION OF MANAGEMENT DEVELOPMENT: A PROBLEMATIC ISSUE

Evaluation is a necessary process to establish whether management development is effective in meeting individual and organisational priorities, to enable judgements to be made about cost-effectiveness, and to aid organisational learning and improvement processes. Although management development absorbs real and substantial costs, systematic evaluation rarely occurs within organisations. Making connections between investment in management development, future management performance and organisation success is extremely difficult. Evaluation activities tend to focus heavily on training and education, and are primarily concerned with measuring the inputs, process and immediate outcomes rather than the longer-term impact of management development activities.

Approaches to evaluation vary from those that are objective, rigorous and scientific to those that are pragmatic and subjective. A systematic, holistic perspective on evaluation places emphasis on the extent to which development activities fit with individual needs and the organisational context; how far new behaviours have been applied in the workplace; and whether new behaviour corresponds with the organisation's culture and values.

Smith (1993) identifies a number of problems with the evaluation of management development that companies should have knowledge of:

- *Choice of Methods*: The potential exists for complex evaluation studies. The range of instruments available is considerable, each having unique benefits, depending on the objectives of the exercise. The requirement that measurement incorporate emotional, attitudinal and behavioural changes alongside more quantitative measures, such as financial performance and technical competency, necessitates the use of carefully constructed and focused methodologies incorporating more qualitative approaches. Such approaches demand time, commitment and particular competencies that the company may not possess.

- *Integrating the Methods*: Evaluation processes need to be developed as an integral part of the management development process. Many organisations, in seeking to provide a generic design and delivery, de-couple the management development process from the individual manager's unique context (Mole, 1996). However, given that evaluation operates in a highly complex and subjective environment with diffuse targets, the effectiveness of management development cannot be accomplished by using a single method (Endres and Kleiner, 1990).

- *Maintaining Objectivity*: Whatever method of evaluation is chosen, outcomes must be judged within the context in which they are embedded. Given the subjective and interpretative nature of evaluation, it is not unexpected that it is prone to bias and manipulation and becomes an arena for political games (Currie, 1994). Therefore, it is difficult to isolate the evaluation processes from the real constraints and politics of the organisation in which they are taking place.

Table 9.4 presents a list of criteria that may be used when evaluating the success of management development initiatives.

Table 9.4: Evaluating Management Development — Examples of Criteria

Evaluation Criteria	Indicators	Measurement Approach/Strategy
Stakeholder: Senior/Functional Management		
Reinforcement of organisation cultural values / business priorities	• Effect on bottom line business result • Management development activities reflect core values and mission • Efficiency and effectiveness of managers at all levels • All formal management development activities incorporate cultural fit issues	• Corporate survey of employee opinion • Reaction evaluation questionnaires • Indicators for market share, sales and turnover
Understanding by management of business requirements	• Knowledge of business requirements • Clarification of role in respect of business requirements	• Corporate survey of employee opinion • Focus group discussions • Performance management results
Enhanced managerial competence	• Increased skills, knowledge and competence • Improvements on specific business metrics	• Performance management results
Enhanced self-development opportunities	• Favourable reports by managers of commitment to management development • Decrease in number of managers citing lack of development as reason for leaving	• Turnover figures compared with relevant benchmarks • Number of internal promotions • Number of external opportunities • Exit interviews • Benchmark survey with network partners

Table 9.4 continued

Evaluation Criteria	Indicators	Measurement Approach/Strategy
Stakeholder: Senior/Functional Management (continued)		
Demonstrated positive commitment to employee development	• Improvements in the quality and quantity of development plans for employees • Favourable perception of commitment of organisation to development • Better retention of employees • Decrease in number of employees citing lack of development as reason for leaving	• Number of development plans prepared • Snapshot survey of quality of development plans • Corporate survey of employer opinion • Exit interviews • Benchmark survey with network partners
Stakeholder: Training and Development Department		
Management development objectives achieved	• 90% favourable rating at end of development activities • Self-reports of satisfaction by participating managers • Level of certification • Clearly identified development paths	• Reaction evaluation questionnaires • Interviews with managers
Management development providers meet quality requirements	• 90% rating score of either very good or excellent • Professionalism of management development providers • Providers' understanding and reinforcement of core values	• Reaction evaluation sheets • Interviews with providers (internal or external)
Management development delivered in a cost-effective manner	• Delivered within budget allocated • Cost per head cheaper than total reliance on external provision	• Assessment of budgets

Table 9.4 continued

Evaluation Criteria	Indicators	Measurement Approach/Strategy
Stakeholder: Training and Development Department (continued)		
Attendance by managers at formal management development activities	• Full attendance at all formal development activities • Level of support and involvement of mentors and facilitators	• Results of attendance
Stakeholder: Participating Manager		
Perception that management development programme is relevant	• Favourable reports in employee opinion survey • 90% of ratings either good or excellent on part programme evaluation	• Corporate employer opinion survey • Reaction evaluation questionnaire
Objectives of specific development efforts achieved	• Promotion prospects enhanced • Greater number of career objectives • More educational opportunities	• Self-reports by managers • Performance management process
Improved performance / employability	• Ratings of performance • Outputs from job • Increased employability	• Performance management process • Superior evaluations • 360° Feedback
Management development delivered in an effective manner	• Operated within budget • Operated on schedule	• Self-reports
Greater understanding of managerial role/ competency	• Certification • Capacity to adapt to change • Enhanced interpersonal competencies • Greater self-confidence as manager	• Self-reports

CONCLUSIONS

Management development represents an important activity for Irish companies, but one where there is considerable under-investment. It does not, however, consist solely of management education and training. It is a more complex set of activities that requires consideration of management development needs, manager expectations, the cultural, structural and political features of the organisation and a whole host of management issues related to the identification of development needs, selection, reward, performance management, promotion and succession management/career issues.

Effective management development requires a close link to, and support of, the organisation's business strategy. Enhancement of the business is generally considered one of the most important justifications for investment in management development. To be successful, management development initiatives require the participation of a range of stakeholders, including individual managers, their immediate boss and other training and development specialists within the organisation. It may also involve collaboration with external consultants and colleges. It requires the selection of a range of management development strategies. This selection process will depend on the development needs of managers and their learning preferences. It must also reflect the reality of managerial work within the organisation and the organisation's culture.

The evaluation of management development is problematic. Many organisations undertake fairly superficial evaluation, concentrating on immediate reactions. Very few organisations attempt to assess the level of managerial learning or the extent to which investment in management development impacts on the bottom line. It is clear that stakeholders may have different perceptions and articulate different priorities and criteria to assess the impact of management development and its contribution to organisational effectiveness.

References

Anthony, P.D. (1986), *The Foundations of Management*, London: Tavistock.

Ashton. D., M. Easterby-Smith, and C. Irvine (1975), *Management Development: Theory and Practice*, Bradford: MCB.

Ashworth, P.D. and J. Sexton (1990), "On Competence", *Journal of Further and Higher Education*, Vol. 14, No. 2, pp. 8–25.

Atkinson, J. and N. Meagher (1986), *Changing Patterns of Work: How Companies Introduce Flexibility to Meet Changing Needs*, London: Institute of Manpower Needs, Falmer.

Baum, T.(1995), *Managing Human Resources in the European Tourism and Hospitality Industry: A Strategic Approach*, London: Chapman and Hall.

Beck, J and C. Cox (1984), *Management Development: Advances in Theory and Practice*, London: Wiley.

Beck, J.E. (1994), "The New Paradigm of Management Education", *Management Learning*, Vol. 5, No. 2, pp. 231–47.

Beddows, P.L. (1994), "Management Development", *Journal of Management Development*, Vol. 13, No. 7, pp. 40–7.

Binstead, D., R. Stuart and G. Long (1980), "Promoting Useful Management Learning: Problems of Translation and Transfer" in J. Beck and C. Cox (eds.), *Advances in Management Education*, Chichester: John Wiley and Sons.

Bloom, B.S., M.B. Englehart, W.H. Hill and D.R. Krathwohl (1956), *Taxonomy of Educational Objectives: The Classification of Educational Goals Handbook 1: Cognitive Domain*, New York: Longmans Green.

Boak, G. (1991), *Developing Managerial Competencies: The Management Learning Contract Approach*, London: Pitman.

Boyatzis, R. (1982), *The Competent Manager: A Model for Effective Performance*, New York: Wiley.

Boydell, T. and M. Pedler (1981), *Management Self-Development*, Aldershot: Gower.

Buckley, K. and N. Kemp (1989), "The Strategic Role of Management Development", *Management Education and Development*, Vol. 20, No. 1, pp. 157–74.

Burgoyne, J. (1988), "Management Development for the Individual and the Organisation", *Personnel Management*, 20–24 June.

Burgoyne, J.G. and C.L. Cooper (1976), "Research on Teaching Methods in Management Education: Bibliographical Examination of the State of the Art", *Management Education Review*, Vol. 16, No. 4, pp. 95–102.

Burgoyne, J.G. and V.E. Hodgson (1983), "Natural Learning and Managerial Action: A Phenomenological Study and Field Study", *Journal of Management Studies*, Vol. 20, No. 3, pp. 26–41.

Burgoyne, J.G. and R. Stuart (1991), "Teaching and Learning Methods In Management Development", *Personnel Review*, Vol. 20, No. 3, pp. 27–33.

Canning, R. (1990), "The Quest for Competence", *Industrial and Commercial Training*, Vol. 22, No. 5, pp. 22–6.

Constable, L. and T. McCormick (1987), *The Making of British Managers*, London: BIM.

Cornwall, M. (1981), "Putting into Practise: Promoting Independent Learning in a Traditional Institution", in D.J. Boud (ed.), *Developing Autonomy in Student Learning*, London: Kogan Page.

Cromer, D.R. (1989), "Peers and Providers", *Personnel Administrator*, Vol. 34, No. 5, pp. 85–6.

Cunnington, B. (1985), "The Process of Educating and Developing Managers for the Year 2000", *Journal of Management Development*, Vol. 4, No. 5, pp. 66–79.

Currie, G. (1994), "Evaluation of Management Development: A Case Study", *Journal of Management Development*, Vol. 13, No. 3, pp. 22–6.

Davis, T. (1990), "Whose Job is Management Development: Comparing the Choices", *Journal of Management Development*, Vol. 9, No. 1, pp. 55–70.

Denning, R.W., D.E. Hussey and P.G. Newman (1987), *Management Development: What to Look For*, London: Harbridge House Europe.

Digman, L.A. (1978), "How Well Managed Organisations Develop their Executives", *Organisational Dynamics*, Autumn, pp. 63–80.

Doyle, M. (1995), "Organisational Transformation and Renewal: A Case for Reframing Management Development?", *Personnel Review*, Vol. 24, No. 6, pp. 6–18.

Doyle, M. (1998), "Management Development" in I. Beaudwell and L. Holden (1998), *Human Resource Management: A Contemporary Perspective*, Second Edition, London: Pitman Publishing.

Easterby-Smith, M. (1994), *Evaluation of Management Training, Education and Development*, Aldershot: Gower.

Easterby-Smith, M., D. Ashton and C. Irvine (1975), *Management Development: Theory and Practice*, Bradford: MCB.

Endres, G. and B. Kleiner (1990), "How to Measure Management Training and Effectiveness", *Journal of European Industrial Training*, Vol. 14, No. 9, pp. 3–7.

Engestrom, Y. (1994), *Training for Change: New Approach to Instruction and Learning in Working Life*, Geneva: International Labour Office.

Fulmer, R.M. (1992), "Development Challenges for the 1990s", *Journal of Management Development*, Vol. 11, No. 7, pp. 4–10.

Fyfe, T.W. and R. Richardson (1974), *Educational Technology*, Dundee: College of Education.

Gage, N.L. and C. Berliner (1979), *Educational Psychology*, Chicago: Rand McNally, 2nd Edition.

Garavan, T.N. (1987), "Promoting Natural Learning Activities within the Organisation", *Journal of European Industrial Training*, Vol. 11, No. 7, pp. 18–23.

Garavan, T.N., P. Costine and N. Heraty (1995), *Training and Development in Ireland, Context, Policy and Practice*, Dublin: Oak Tree Press.

Garavan, T.N. (1997), "Training, Development, Education and Learning: Different or the Same?" *Journal of European Industrial Training*, Vol. 21, No. 2, pp. 39–50.

Garavan, T.N. (1998), "Management Development: Current Trends and Issues", *Annual Review of Training & Development*, Bradford: MCB University Press.

Garavan, T.N. and P. Sweeney (1995), "Supervisory Training and Development: The Use of Learning Contracts", *Journal of European Industrial Training*, Vol. 18, No. 2, pp. 17–27.

Handy, C. (1987), *The Making of Managers*, Report for the NEDO, the MSC & BIM on Management Education, Training and Development with the US, Germany, France, Japan and the UK, London: National Economic Development Office.

Harrison, R. (1993), *Developing Human Resources for Productivity*, Geneva: International Labour Office.

Hayes, R.H. and W.J. Abernathy (1980), "Managing Our Way into Economic Decline", *Harvard Business Review*, Vol. 28, No. 4, pp. 16–22.

Hendry, C. and A. Pettigrew (1986), "The Practice of Strategic HRM", *Personnel Review*, Vol. 15, No. 5, pp. 3–8.

Hendry, C., A. Pettigrew and P. Sparrow (1988), *The Role of Education and Training in Employers' Skill Supply Strategies*, Sheffield: Training Agency, Coopers and Lybrand.

Hitt, W.D. (1987), "A Unified Development Programme", *Journal of Management Development*, Vol. 6, No. 1, pp. 43–53.

Hopfl, H. and F. Dawes (1995), "A Whole Can of Worms! The Contrasting Frontiers of Management Development and Learning", *Personnel Review*, Vol. 24, No. 6, pp. 19–28.

Huczynski, A. (1983), *Encyclopaedia of Management Development Methods*, Aldershot: Gower.

Hussey, D.E. (1985), "Implementing Corporate Strategy Using Management Education and Training", *Long Range Planning*, Vol. 18, No. 5, pp. 34–41.

IRDAC (1991), *Skills Shortages in Europe*, London Industrial Research and Advisory Committee of the Commission of the European Communities, London: IRDAC Opinion.

Jones, J.E and M. Woodcock (1985), *Manual of MD, Strategy Design and Instruments for Programme Improvement*, Aldershot: Gower.

Kanter, R.M. (1977), *Men and Women of the Corporation*, New York: Basic Books.

Kotter, J.P. (1982), *The General Manager*, Glencoe: Free Press.

Kram, K.E. (1983), "Phases in the Mentor Relationship", *Academy of Management Journal*, Vol. 26, No. 4, pp. 17–33.

Kram, K.E. and L.A. Isabelle (1985), "Mentoring Alternatives: The Role of Peer Relationships in Career Development", *Academy of Management Journal*, Vol. 28, No. 1, pp. 14–36.

Lawrence, G.L. (1977), "Management Development . . . Some Ideals, Images and Realities", *Journal of European Industrial Training*, Vol. 1, No. 2, pp. 21–5.

Leavitt, H. (1986), *Corporate Pathfinders: Building Vision And Values Into Organisations*, New York: West Publications.

Lees, S. (1992), "Ten Faces of Management Development", *Journal of Management Development*, Vol. 23, No. 2, pp. 89–105.

Litt, G. (1982),"Management Development as the Key to Organisational Renewal", *Journal of Management Development*, Vol. 1, No. 2, pp. 26–34.

Mabey, C. and G. Saleman (1995), *Strategic Human Resource Management*, Oxford: Blackwell.

Mangham, I.L. and M.S. Silver (1986), *Management Training: Context and Practice*, Pilot Survey Commissioned by ESRC and Department of Trade and Industry, Bath: School of Management, University of Bath.

Manpower Services Commission (1985), *A Challenge to Complacency: Changing Attitudes to Training*, Sheffield: Manpower Services Commission.

Margerison, C. (1991), *Making Management Development Work*, Maidenhead: McGraw-Hill.

McClelland, S. (1994), "Gaining Competitive Advantage through Strategic Management Development", *Journal of Management Development*, Vol. 13, No. 5, pp. 4–13.

Miller, L. (1991), "Managerial Competencies", *Industrial and Commercial Training*, Vol. 23, No. 6, pp. 1–15.

Mintzberg, H. (1973), *The Nature of Managerial Work*, New York: Harper and Row.

Mole, G. (1996), "The Management Training in Industry in the UK", *Human Resources Management Journal*, Vol. 6, No. 1, pp. 19–26.

Morgan, G. (1986), *Images of Organisations*, London: Sage.

Morris, J. (1971), "Management Development and Development Management", *Personnel Review*, Vol. 1, No. 1, pp. 30–43.

Mumford, A. (1986), *Handbook of Management Development*, London: Gower.

Mumford, A. (1993), *Management Development: Strategies for Action*, London: IPD.

Nadler, C. and Z. Nadler (1992), *Every Manager's Guide to Human Resource Development*, San Fransisco, CA: Jossey-Bass.

Newstrom, J. (1986), "Leveraging Management Development through the Management of Transfer", *Journal of Management Development*, Vol. 5, No. 5, pp. 33–45.

O'Donnell, D. and T.N. Garavan (1997), "New Perspectives on Skill, Learning and Training: a Viewpoint", *Journal of European Industrial Training*, Vol. 21, No. 4, pp. 131–7.

Pedler, M. (1974), "Learning in Management Education", *Journal of European Training*, Vol. 3, No. 1, pp. 182–94.

Pedler, M. (1978), "Negotiating Skills Training: Part 4 — Learning to Negotiate", *Journal of European Industrial Training*, Vol. 12, No. 1, pp. 20–5.

Pedler, M. (1985), "Self-Development", *Training Officer*, Vol. 21, No. 7.

Pedler, M. (1986), "Management Self-Development", *Management, Education and Development*, Vol. 17, No. 1, pp. 26–31.

Pedler, M. (1995), "Applying Self-Development in Organisations" in C. Mabey and P. Iles (eds.), *Managing Learning*, London: Routledge in Association with the Open University.

Preston, D. (1993), "Management Development Structures as Symbols of Organisational Culture", *Journal of Management Development*, Vol. 22, No. 1, pp. 24–33.

Rae, L. (1986), *How to Measure Training Effectiveness*, Aldershot: Gower.

Reid, M. and H. Barrington (1994), *Training Interventions*, London: Institute of Personnel Management.

Report and Recommendations of the Advisory Committee on Management Training (1998), *Managers for Ireland: The Case for the Development of Irish Managers*, Dublin: The Stationery Office.

Revans, R.W. (1980), *Action Learning*, London: Blond and Briggs.

Revans, R.W. (1982), *Origins and Growth of Action Learning*, Bromley: Chartwell and Bratt.

Salaman, G. (1995), *Managing*, Buckingham: Open University Press.

Schon, D.A. (1988), "Developing Effective Managers: A Review of the Issues and an Agenda for Research", *Personnel Review*, Vol. 17, No. 4, pp. 3–8.

Sisson, K. and J. Storey (1993), *Managing Human Resources and Industrial Relations*, Milton Keynes: Open University Press.

Smith, A. (1993), "Evaluation and Effectiveness", *Journal of Management Development*, Vol. 12, No. 1, pp. 20–33.

Stewart, J. and B. Hamlin (1992), "Competence-Based Qualifications: The Case against Change", *Journal of European Industrial Training*, Vol. 16, No. 7, pp. 21–32.

Stewart, R. (1994), *Managing Today and Tomorrow*, Basingstoke: Macmillan.

Storey, J. (1989a), "Management Development: A Literature Review and Implications for Future Research — Part 1", *Personnel Review*, Vol. 18, No. 6, pp. 3–19.

Storey, J. (1989b), "Management Development: A Literature Review and Implications for Future Research — Part 2", *Personnel Review*, Vol. 19, No. 1, pp. 3–11.

Storey, J., C. Mabey and A. Thomson (1997), "What a Difference a Decade Makes", *People Management*, June.

Stuart, R. (1986), "Social Learning", *Management Decision*, Vol. 24, No. 6, pp. 16–23.

Thomson, A., J. Storey, C. Mabey, C. Gray, E. Carmer and R. Thomson (1997), *A Portrait of Management Development*, London: Institute of Management.

Tijmstra, S. and K. Kasler (1992), "Management Learning for Europe", *European Management Journal*, Vol. 10, No. 1, pp. 26–41.

Torrington, D. and L. Hall (1998), *Human Resource Management*, Fourth Edition, London: Prentice Hall Europe.

Van Wart, M., N.J. Cayer and S. Cork (1993), *Handbook of Training and Development for the Public Sector*, San Fransisco, CA: Jossey-Bass.

Walsh, J.S., M. Finchan and P.H. Anderson (nd), *Management Development in Ireland: A Critical Appraisal*, (In Press).

Watson, T. (1994), *In Search of Management*, London: Routledge.

Wesley, E.B. and S.P. Wronski (1965), *Teaching Social Sciences in the High Schools*, New York: D.C. Heath and Company.

Whitley, R. (1987), *On the Nature of Managerial Tasks and Skills*, Manchester: Manchester Business School.

Yeomans, W. (1989), "Building Competitiveness through Human Resource Development", *Training and Development Journal*, October, pp. 77–82.

Zenger, J. (1985), "Training for Organisational Excellence", *Journal of European Industrial Training*, Vol. 9, No. 7, pp. 3–8.

CHAPTER 10

PERFORMANCE APPRAISAL

Bob Pattinson

INTRODUCTION

It is likely that some form of appraisal of performance takes place in all organisations. Management may note that employee X is frequently a few minutes late, takes more days' sickness than the average employee, and is not so effective in dealing with customers. On the other hand, employee Y is always on time, is quick to learn new methods, develops an easy rapport with customers, and is keen to take on new responsibilities. Based on these observations, management make decisions about which employees are to be developed, trained, promoted or terminated. These decisions are made behind closed doors without any input from employees.

Many organisations formalise this process of assessing performance by developing common criteria which managers and supervisors can use to help appraise employee performance, to identify training needs and to listen to suggestions on how the employee can improve overall job performance. These schemes, in which employees receive regular feedback and may contribute to the assessment process, may be described as an open forum of appraisal.

Gunnigle et al. (1997) report that about 70 per cent of managerial employees in Ireland are subject to an appraisal system, with corresponding figures of 60 per cent, 55 per cent and 30 per cent for professional/technical, clerical and manual employees respectively. Twice as many private sector organisations have appraisal schemes than do public sector organisations, and the larger the organisation the more likely it is that there will be an appraisal scheme. Union membership may also influence the use of performance appraisal schemes, with non-union companies more likely to have systems in place, especially those covering manual and to a lesser extent clerical employees.

This chapter outlines the performance appraisal process, examines why organisations use performance appraisal schemes, the costs of appraising and not appraising and the benefits of the schemes to the organisation, managers and employees. It also looks at the shift towards the use of target-setting and competency analysis in the appraisal process.

THE PERFORMANCE APPRAISAL PROCESS

The full sequence of steps in the appraisal process may be summarised diagrammatically in Figure 10.1 below.

Figure 10.1: The Performance Appraisal Process

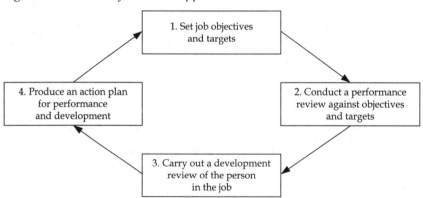

The main tasks in each of the above four steps would normally be conducted by the manager and employee jointly, as shown in the following table:

Table 10.1: Key Tasks in the Four Appraisal Steps

Steps	Tasks
1. Set objectives and targets	• Establish job objectives • Set specific targets • Outline the actions needed if the targets are to be achieved
2. Conduct a performance review against objectives and targets	• Review job performance against the initial objectives and targets throughout the year at set intervals, such as monthly or quarterly • Explore areas where performance is below standard and seek ways of improving same
3. Carry out a development review of the person in the job	• Identify training and development needs of the individual against the knowledge, skill and attitude requirements of the job • Assess performance against specific skills criteria such as planning and organisation, teamwork, flexibility, etc. • Explore future career development plans
4. Produce an action plan for performance and development	• Agree specific job improvement plans, such as reducing materials wastage by 2 per cent over the next year • Plan training and development events to meet skills gaps, such as completing a PowerPoint training course to help develop particular skills • Schedule dates for interim reviews in order to make appraisal become an ongoing activity rather than an annual check-up

Performance appraisal is just one component in the performance management process, which involves several human resource management activities. Figure 10.2 shows the linkages between performance appraisal and these other activities.

Figure 10.2: How Performance Appraisal Links to Other Activities in the Management of Performance

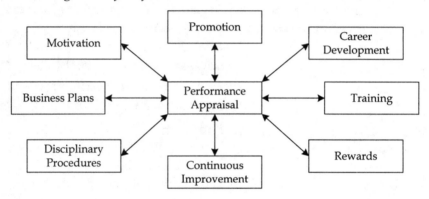

It can be seen that performance appraisal is a critical activity that provides eight important two-way linkages:

1. *Business Plans*: The plans of the organisation can be reflected in the individual employee's targets, e.g. to reduce materials wastage by 2 per cent over the next year. Employee feedback may also assist future business plans, e.g. suggestions on new working methods, new product ideas, ways of overcoming operational difficulties in the workplace.

2. *Motivation*: James (1988) suggests that motivation is a key benefit of appraisal schemes in that people work, learn and achieve more when they are given:

   • Feedback on the results of their performance;

   • Clear, attainable goals;

   • Involvement in the setting of tasks and goals.

3. *Promotion*: Evidence from performance appraisal can help to identify potential and highlight people with the right mix of abilities, skills and knowledge required in higher level jobs.

4. *Career Development*: Appraisal provides employees with the opportunity to express a view on their own career development and to work with their manager in setting up personal development plans.

5. *Training*: Performance appraisal is ideal for identifying gaps between the job requirements and the employee's own level of knowledge, skills and experience. More emphasis is being given to examining levels of competency in core skills; examples of this will be provided later.

6. *Rewards*: In Ireland, merit/performance-related pay tends to be the most commonly used incentive, with performance appraisal being the main mechanism for the review process. In addition to linking appraisal to financial rewards, employees may also benefit from non-monetary rewards such as feedback on performance, recognition for achievements, and the opportunity to plan career development.

7. *Continuous Improvement*: Many organisations have moved towards a total quality management culture, which is built on the principle of continuous improvement. This is now being reflected in performance appraisal systems, with an emphasis being given to seeking the ideas of employees on how to improve both individual and organisational performance. Competency-based systems also stress the drive towards individual continuous improvement.

8. *Disciplinary Procedures*: While performance appraisal schemes are designed primarily for the positive reasons shown above, nevertheless, when performance is unsatisfactory, the appraisal interviewer may trigger off the initial discussion of why performance needs to be improved. If no improvement is achieved

within a specific time period, the employee may be taken into the first stage of the disciplinary procedures. An example will be given later of a formal Performance Improvement Plan (PIP) used by one large electronics company to tighten the link between the appraisal and disciplinary processes.

Several of the above eight factors may be seen in the reasons why Irish organisations set up performance appraisal schemes. The main reasons, from two recent surveys, are shown in Table 10.2.

Table 10.2: Why Organisations use Appraisal Schemes

McMahon and Gunnigle (1994)		Gunnigle et al. (1997)	
Reasons	*Percentage of Organisations*	*Reasons*	*Percentage of Organisations*
Improve future performance	98	Individual training needs	70
Provide feedback on performance	96	Career development	52
Agree key objectives	95	Promotion potential	51
Identify training needs	95	Individual payment by results	45
Strengthen employee commitment/ motivation	89	Organisational needs	43
Improve communication	84	Organisation of work	35
Assess promotion potential	82		

The top three factors in each of the two surveys show some interesting differences in emphasis. The first survey shows that organisations place priority on performance and objectives, which tend to relate to the needs of the business, whereas the second survey's top three tend to stress the individual in respect of training needs, career development and promotion potential. When examining specific schemes later in the chapter, it will be worthwhile reflecting on how these two trends are found in actual practice.

BENEFITS OF PERFORMANCE APPRAISAL

There are many benefits of performance appraisal. Table 10.3 summarises the range of benefits identified by Pattinson (1995) for the organisation, for managers conducting the appraisals, and for employees.

Table 10.3: Benefits of Performance Appraisal

Benefits to the Organisation
• Helps to improve performance throughout the organisation
• Improves the fit between organisational objectives and the individual's own targets and action plans
• Creates a more open climate in which performance issues can be discussed
• Enhances the process of identifying training needs
• Helps with human resource planning by highlighting areas of strengths and weaknesses across the organisation
• Provides a more accurate basis for assessing the potential of individuals

Benefits to the Manager

- Chance to listen to the employee and talk about how they see their job, the things they enjoy or dislike in the job, their hopes and fears for the future

- Opportunity to motivate the employee by recognising achievements and giving praise for work well done

- Forum for joint input into new targets and action plans

- Time to examine training and development needs and to relate them to the needs of the organisation

- Chance to hear the employee comment on how they see their own strengths and weaknesses, and to provide own feedback to them accordingly

- Opportunity to discuss how performance could be improved

- Helps to focus on developing long-term potential

Benefits to the Employee

- Opportunity to express own views

- Chance to discuss individual strengths and weaknesses

- Mechanism for identifying own training and development needs

- Can help to clarify own role and priorities

- Provides a forum for discussing working relationships

- Helps to focus on future career development

- Opportunity to provide feedback to the manager about the job and the organisation

- Chance to gain recognition for achievement of targets and for work well done

- Joint input to future objectives, targets and action plans

Earlier in this chapter, it was noted that although assessment of job performance takes place in some shape or form in all organisations, not every organisation has an open appraisal scheme. Without doubt, the time taken to set up a scheme and to conduct interviews is a real opportunity cost to an organisation, but there are costs associated with not providing employees with regular feedback and performance review. Table 10.4 outlines the respective types of costs associated with providing an appraisal scheme on the one hand and not having a scheme on the other.

Table 10.4: Examples of Costs Associated with Providing a Formal Scheme and Not Having a Scheme

Costs of Formal Schemes	Costs of Not Appraising
• Time spent on the design of the formal system of appraisal • Providing interviewing skills training for managers • Time spent carrying out interviews, writing appraisal reports, setting targets • Meeting training and development needs arising out of the appraisals	• Increased labour turnover due to poor feedback and low motivation • Few people capable of taking higher level posts due to lack of development • Poor levels of work performance due to lack of feedback and encouragement • Low focus on priorities due to failure to set objectives and targets

DEVELOPMENTS IN APPRAISAL SCHEMES

McMahon and Gunnigle (1994) suggest that there are two main reasons why performance appraisal schemes tend to be less effective in practice than they should be in theory:

- Failure to define the objectives of the appraisal process;

- Lack of fit between the appraisal scheme and the operations of the organisations.

To overcome these two weaknesses, a number of Irish organisations have given considerable time to agreeing the objectives of the performance appraisal scheme, and linking the schemes strongly to the day-do-day operations of the business.

One example is the scheme used by Green Isle Foods, which has the following objectives:

Figure 10.3: Objectives of the Performance Management Scheme at Green Isle Foods

---

1. Link business objectives to role specifications and work targets of each staff member.

2. Link career aspirations to organisational needs.

3. Provide regular feedback against targets and develop tailor-made performance and improvement plans.

4. Develop skills and competencies to meet role specifications and work targets.

5. Allow for staff feedback where management support is needed.

6. Reward senior performance via merit payments.

The above scheme is a good example of an open scheme in that employees contribute to the setting and reviewing of targets, the identification of training and development needs, and making suggestions on general performance issues.

Four key features of this scheme are the use of the following mechanisms:

1. *Briefing Meeting*: held two weeks before the performance appraisal interview;

2. *Preparation Form*: to be completed by both the managers and the team member as a means of tuning up for the interview;

3. *Target Setting*: not only are targets set, but the level of likely outcome is classified into five categories;

4. *Competencies*: core competencies are provided with five behavioural anchored rating scales so that the manager and the employee can assess current skill levels and agree personal development plans to enhance a range of skills.

Figure 10.4 outlines how the briefing meeting is conducted.

Figure 10.4: Conducting the Briefing Meeting

The manager performs this fifteen-minute activity either as a one-to-one interview or in a weekly team meeting. Key actions are for the manager to:

- Explain the purpose of the scheme;

- Decide the complete cycle of events;

- Express own commitment to the scheme and its outputs;

- Outline the structure of the interview;

- Give examples of likely outcomes such as setting new targets, designing personal development plans, etc.;

- Circulate and discuss the preparation form and competencies;

- Deal with any queries;

- Recommend team members to complete the preparation form as a means of tuning in for the appraisal interview;

- Arrange the schedule of the performance appraisal interviews.

The preparation form is a simple form comprising one sheet of A4. The first side requests the team member to rate the job performance against targets that were set at the beginning of the review period in five performance categories, of which the middle one is the one the organisation sees as meeting the performance requirements. The five categories are:

1. *Unacceptable*: performance way below the expected level;

2. *Marginal*: performance marginally below the expected level;

3. *Satisfactory*: achieving the expected level of performance;

4. *Good*: exceeding the expected level;

5. *Excellent*: far exceeding the expected level.

The above are the guidelines on the five categories, and in practice each team member agrees specific targets with the manager, broken down into the five categories, as shown in the following example.

Figure 10.5: Sample Target Setting

Target Area: To reduce wastage in production area X.

- *Unacceptable*: No change or a disimprovement in the current wastage rate of 7.5 per cent.

- *Marginal*: Wastage reduced to between 7 and 7.4 per cent.

- *Satisfactory*: Wastage reduced to between 6 and 6.9 per cent.

- *Good*: Wastage reduced to between 5.5 and 5.9 per cent.

- *Excellent*: Wastage reduced to below 5.5 per cent.

The second side of the preparation form requests the team member to assess their own level of competency across six core competencies, which are:

1. *Planning and Organising*: the ability to identify the required elements to carry out the job effectively and achieve planned goals, and to bring these elements together in the most productive way to achieve the goals.

2. *Problem Analysis*: the ability to resolve routine problems in a capable and competent manner.

3. *Relationships*: the ability to relate well to supervisors, peers and external contacts.

4. *Reliability*: the degree to which the individual endeavours to fulfil the requirements of the job, even in difficult circumstances. The extent to which the person regularly attends work and is punctual.

5. *Teamwork*: the ability to contribute constructively to the effective functioning of a team, to give support to other team members, and to ensure that required team tasks are delivered on time.

6. *Versatility*: the ability and willingness to undertake a range of tasks/jobs, which may lie outside the usual role.

Each of these six competencies are set out in the same five categories used for target setting, this time as behavioural anchored rating scales. Details of the competency "Teamwork" are shown in Figure 10.6.

Team members do not show the preparation form to their managers but are encouraged to complete it to aid their contribution to the appraisal interview.

The format of the preparation form is the same for the performance appraisal form, with the latter having an additional two sides of A4. The first side focuses on areas for improvements in job performance and is reproduced in Figure 10.7 with a sample plan shown.

Figure 10.6: Teamwork Competency

Appraisal	**Competency: Teamwork** *Ability to contribute constructively to the effective functioning of a team, give support to other team members, and to ensure that required team tasks are delivered on time.*
Far Exceeds Requirements	Sets an example to others as an excellent team player. Often takes a leadership role, contributes enthusiastically to problem-solving, and helps others to solve problems. Demonstrates a high degree of team-building skills.
Exceeds Requirements	Is a strong team player, taking the lead at times in the meetings, building positive relationships with all members, and ensuring that any individual tasks are completed ahead of the team schedule.
Successfully Meets Requirements	Is willing to play an active part in teams, contributing to problem-solving and decision-making, and taking responsibility for delivering own tasks on time to meet the team's schedule. Gets on well with most team members and makes an effort to give support to others.
Partially Meets Requirements	At times appears to be a relevant team member, holding back from giving full support to the team, and on occasions failing to deliver team tasks on time. Could improve at problem-solving in the team and make more effort at interpersonal skills.
Fails to Meet Requirements	A poor team player, making little effort to contribute to the task and social aspects of team-work, and failing to support other team members in the combined efforts to get the job done on time. At times can be hostile to other team members and negative on problem-solving efforts.

Figure 10.7: Areas for Improvement in Job Performance

Where improvements are required, outline what is needed and the actions necessary to achieve the improvements in performance	
Improvement Required	*Actions to Achieve Improvement*
1. Several delays have occurred in production scheduling due to inadequate knowledge of the computer software.	1.1. Arrange for three 60-minute sessions with the Master Scheduler over the next three weeks. 1.2. Check the schedules each day for the next three weeks.
2. Wastage still above 7 per cent, as against the company average of 5.7 per cent.	2.1 Check on the work practices being used in the preparation area. 2.2 Hold a team briefing on ideas for ending wastage. 2.3 Display weekly wastage rates on team notice board.

The second side of the appraisal form covers two items:

a) *Personal Development Plan*: from the list of competencies, no more than three may be used to design an action plan for personal development.

b) *Personal Ambitions – Concerns or Issues*: the team member may raise any items under those three headings and space is provided to record the item and to outline the action plan agreed to address them.

Finally, a separate A4 sheet is used to plan out next year's targets, again using the five categories of performance against targets. Both parties keep copies of these sheets so that team members can assess their own performance against the pre-set categories.

Managers and supervisors in Green Isle have exactly the same appraisal system with the addition of three further competencies, one of which includes responsibility for developing staff.

As part of the evaluation of the effectiveness of this scheme, Pattinson (1997) carried out a survey of managers and supervisors conducting the interviews and a sample of team members being appraised. A summary of these results is shown in Table 10.5.

Table 10.5: Feedback on the Effectiveness of the Appraisal System

Content of Questionnaire Items	% Response
Managers' and supervisors' feedback on performance review system	
Most interviews worthwhile with some benefits to both parties	97
In many cases it was not too difficult to break the ice at the start and get a response	91
I am reasonably comfortable with the thought of conducting next year's interviews	91
The majority of interviews were straightforward to conduct and few posed major difficulties	89
It was relatively easy to give feedback to all employees on observation of their performance	82
Some useful progress was made with the majority of employees in exploring areas where targets had not been met and in identifying steps to improve performance	79
Team members' feedback on performance review system	
Gained some useful feedback on job performance/ job objectives clarified	94
Positive feedback on job performance	92
Put at ease at beginning of the interview	91
Encouraged to set targets for next year	88
Interview had a logical structure and the manager/ supervisor was skilful in conducting the interview	88
Given quite a lot of feedback on how the manager/ supervisor observed my job performance	84
I am quite comfortable about next year's interview	78

PERFORMANCE IMPROVEMENT PLANS

A number of Irish companies have devised performance improvement plans (PIP) to deal with employees who are marginal performers. Such plans provide a bridge between performance appraisal and the disciplinary procedures, with feedback, training and coaching being the meat in the sandwich between appraisal and discipline.

The mnemonic "SPECIFIC" summarises the aims and structure of PIP as shown in Figure 10.8 below:

Figure 10.8: Performance Improvement Plan (PIP)

"SPECIFIC" means:	
Systematic:	Monitoring of performance by manager
Philosophy:	Provide coaching first; discipline is the last resort
Equity:	Use the "red hot stove" principles
Coaching:	Provide specific guidance and advice; offer opportunities to improve
Immediate:	Take action as soon as performance falls below standard
Feedback:	Give specific examples of where performance needs to be improved
Involve:	Individuals in developing the PIP performance targets
Constructive:	Be positive and constructive throughout the process and ensure confidentiality

Six Objectives of the New Performance Management Scheme

1. Link business objectives to role specifications and work targets of each staff member;

2. Link career aspirations to organisational needs;

3. Provide regular feedback against targets and develop tailor-made performance and improvement plans;

4. Develop skills and competencies to meet role specifications and work targets;

5. Allow for staff feedback where management support is needed;

6. Reward superior performance via merit payments.

Under the normal performance appraisal process, as shown in the earlier example of Green Isle, employees may be satisfactory performers or better in most of their targets or developing required competencies, with perhaps marginal or unacceptable performance in one or perhaps two areas. The appraisal process allows both parties to look at improvement areas and to design suitable action plans and personal development plans. Further coaching may also be necessary.

If there is no improvement within six months of the performance appraisal review after receiving training and coaching, then the PIP would come into play, as shown in Figure 10.9.

Figure 10.9: Structure of the PIP Process

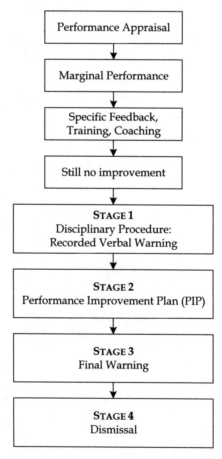

Figure 10.10 below shows the recommended actions for managers to take in PIP interviews.

Figure 10.10: Key Steps for Managers to take in all PIP Interviews

> 1. Give reasons why performance is below standard
>
> 2. Seek suggestions on how the gap can be filled
>
> 3. Set goals to improve performance
>
> 4. Agree actions to help achieve goals
>
> 5. Review performance against goals and actions
>
> 6. Warn employee of results of failure to improve

It should again be noted that most performance issues are dealt with in the day-to-day working relationships, but some specific issues can be revealed at performance reviews. The PIP process provides a formal mechanism for completing the appraisal cycle by dealing with issues.

CONCLUSIONS

This chapter has provided a framework of the four key steps in carrying out performance appraisal.

1. Set job objectives and targets;

2. Review performance against these objectives and targets;

3. Review the development of the person in the job;

4. Produce action plans for job improvements and personal development.

It has been stressed that, to be effective, appraisal schemes need to be truly open systems, with full participation of both the manager and the employee in each of the above four steps. Feedback from the manager is a vital component in the appraisal process and this is one of the main reasons why many companies establish performance appraisal schemes.

Several benefits of performance appraisal were identified for the organisation, the manager and the employee. The costs of having such schemes and not having them were also outlined.

The example of the Green Isle Foods scheme shows how business objectives can be controlled down the organisation to individual targets, and that the latter can be pre-set at different performance levels. From a motivational perspective, this enables employees to monitor their own performance during the review period and to actively seek help from the manager if their performance appears to be slipping. It also takes away the possibility of any surprises at the annual performance review.

The use of an agreed set of competencies allows employees to assess their own level of skill, receive feedback from the manager and develop action plans to improve specific skills. One advantage of this method is that high, average, and low performance can all strive to improve their skills using this approach.

Finally, marginal performers may find the Performance Improvement Plan (PIP) a useful extra form of care and attention to improve their contribution to the business via extra coaching and training. From the company's perspective, it also provides a bridge to the disciplinary process should there be no improvement after training and coaching.

References

Gunnigle, P., M. Morley, N. Clifford and T. Turner (1997), *Human Resource Management in Irish Organisations: Practice in Perspective*, Dublin: Oak Tree Press.

James, G. (1988), *Performance Appraisal*, Occasional Paper No. 40, London: ACAS Work Research Unit.

McMahon, G. and P. Gunnigle (1994), *Performance Appraisal: How to get it Right*, Dublin: Productive Personnel Limited in association with the Institute of Personnel and Development.

Pattinson, R. (1995), *Performance Appraisal*, Unit 2 of *Motivating the Team*, Module 7 of Distance Learning Certificate in Health Services Management, University of Limerick.

CHAPTER 11

COACHING AND MENTORING: AIDS TO THE DEVELOPMENT OF PERFORMANCE

Karl O'Connor

INTRODUCTION

Coaching and mentoring are two words that increasingly appear in management language and literature. They are developmental practices that focus on assisting managers or team leaders to help realise the full potential of their staff. The two terms are sometimes used interchangeably but have distinct differences, which we will explore in this chapter.

Many leading international companies have introduced these practices and there is concrete evidence that they have helped managers and staff to improve performance. Coaching and mentoring can help people to build, share and apply knowledge and skills. Both the individual and the organisation can reap the resulting dividend. Irish organisations, both in the private and public sectors, are paying more attention to the relevance of these developmental practices. Indeed, both the Irish Management Institute and the Institute of Public Administration have recently introduced programmes that focus on unlocking people's potential, including coaching and mentoring. Furthermore, in recognition of the growth of these practices and with the objective of promoting their further use, the Institute of Personnel and Development has published several guides on coaching and mentoring from Clutterbuck's (1985) *Everyone Needs a Mentor* to Cunningham et al. (1998), *Exercises for Developing Coaching Capability.*

Aim

This chapter will explore the definitions of coaching and mentoring and their use in Irish organisations. It will highlight the advantages and disadvantages of these techniques. Some models will be featured and case studies of their application will be cited.

COACHING V MENTORING

There is widespread confusion as to what constitutes coaching and the difference between this concept and mentoring. Indeed, as already noted, many people use these terms interchangeably. For example, Clutterbuck (1985: 1) states:

> In spite of the variety of definitions of mentoring (and the variety of names it is given, from coaching or counselling to sponsorship) all the experts and communicators appear to agree that it has its origins in the concept of apprenticeship. In the days when the guilds ruled the commercial world, the road to the top in business began in an early apprenticeship to the master craftsman . . . [when an] older, more experienced individual passed down his knowledge of how the task was done and how to operate in the commercial world.

Parsloe (1995: 25) makes a clearer distinction between coaching and mentoring, namely:

> . . . coaching is the responsibility of a line manager who has an immediate and day-to-day accountability for the learner's performance . . . [while] a mentor is rarely a learner's line manager. A mentor can be described as someone who acts as a friend and trusted counsellor. Mentors have protégés rather than learners and will therefore aim to develop a special kind of relationship.

The word "mentor" originates from Greek mythology when Odysseus, before setting out on a long journey, entrusted the education of his son to his old friend Mentor and exhorted him to "tell all you know". Megginson and Clutterbuck (1995: 13) define mentoring as, "off-line help by one person to another in making significant transitions in knowledge, work and/or thinking". In this context, "off-line" means that the mentoring relationship is not between the boss and their immediate subordinate.

For this chapter we have taken the term mentoring to refer to giving advice and guidance on career planning, providing a role model or helping newcomers to settle into an organisation. In this regard, the mentor can highlight, for example, cultural issues and invisible roadblocks, which the organisation chart cannot do. Coaching, on the other hand, focuses on what Gallwey (1975) described as the unlocking of a person's potential to maximise their own performance where the individual learns from within themselves rather than being taught. Gallwey urged coaches to help performers remove internal obstacles to their own performance which would result in an unexpected natural ability to surface on the part of the individual without the need for further technical advice from the coach. In essence, the focus for the coach is to develop practical strategies and approaches for the learner, to become more aware of their performance and themselves and to acquire knowledge and skills in a planned and structured way.

It should be stated, however, that coaching is not simply training under a new guise. Training concentrates on helping the trainee to acquire the relevant knowledge, skills and attitude in order to reach a standard of performance. Coaching is more powerful and can help the trainee to exceed the standard. Salisbury (1994: 3) notes:

> Once you have delivered training and people have been given the opportunity to reach the standard, there comes a cut-off point when further training just will not work. The challenge is that cut-off point is different for every person. A manager working as a full-time coach will know when it is time to move from training to coaching. Only by working with people

on a one-to-one basis can a manager hope to understand what motivates an individual and what tack to take — training or coaching.

The coach's timeframe for working with the individual tends to be days, weeks or months, while the mentor's focus tends to be on the protégé's development over a longer period in their career or life. There are similarities between the two practices and the effectiveness of both coaching and mentoring will depend on the manager's beliefs about the individual and their future potential. Whitmore (1992: 12) states that unless the manager

> believes that people possess more capability than they are currently expressing, he will not be able to help them express it. He must think of his people in terms of their potential, not their performance.

The respective strengths and weaknesses of both coaching and mentoring as developmental tools are summarised in Tables 11.1 and 11.2.

Table 11.1: Coaching — Benefits and Obstacles

Benefits	Obstacles
• Performance improvement	• Time
• Wide application — motivation, team-building to change management	• Hierarchical status (manager perceived as more important than coach)
• Encourages effort and continuous improvement	• Culture of organisation, e.g. autocratic style less democratic
• Learner-focused	• "Tell" style of management preferred
• Learner feels more valued	• Coaching seen as soft option
• Learner takes personal responsibility	• Executive reluctance to "buy-in"
• Can free up manager/coach for more strategic issues	

Table 11.2: Mentoring – Benefits and Obstacles

Benefits	Obstacles
• Improved succession planning • Improved relationships/ communication • Improved self-confidence/ motivation • Sharing of experience with protégé • Satisfaction of helping a person to learn • Assist in career development • Better induction	• Exposure to new ideas/ perspectives • Time • Unclear mentor–protégé roles • Lack of commitment • Organisation culture • Personality clashes • Resentment from protégé's line manager

COACHING: FROM SPORT TO BUSINESS

While the origins of mentoring can be traced back to ancient Greece, coaching owes a lot to modern sports.

Coaches in the sporting world have fine-tuned their coaching skills to ensure their athletes win, set records or at least achieve their best results. In the same way that athletic coaches help their teams or individuals to achieve excellent performances, workplace coaches need to help their teams and individual team members to reach their potential and deliver a personal best. The sports coaching model has been embraced by business and it has become increasingly common for sports coaches to share their learning with the business community. For example, at recent business seminars, the Irish rugby coach Warren Gatland presented his methodology, while the quality association Excellence Ireland used the expertise of the national sports coaching centre (based in the University of Limerick) in a conference. Similarly, Guinness helped to organise a mentoring workshop focusing on a dialogue between sport, business and enterprise, while First Active plc drew an analogy between the very effective methods of the 1996 All-Ireland winning Wexford team champion coach, Liam Griffin, and the need for its managers to introduce performance coaching with their staff.

Tennis expert Tim Gallwey helped start the sports and business debate in the 1970s when he made the insightful comment on performance barriers that "the opponent inside one's own head is more formidable than the one the other side of the net".

It should be noted that, in sports, the coaches to the top players are often not as skilled in their performance as the people being coached, yet they can bring out the best in their performance. Where there are internal obstacles, sports coaches can help their people to remove or reduce these blockages and release their natural ability. They typically work in two ways: psychological and technical. The psychological focus involves the coach encouraging, challenging, motivating and obtaining commitment from the athlete to try a new technique and to keep practising. On the other hand, the technical input comes when the coach adds value by giving feedback on how the athlete is approaching their task. Both of these coaching approaches were evident in Liam Griffin's Wexford hurling team's preparation for the All-Ireland Championship. With regard to the psychological coaching, for example, Griffin was very motivational to the players and used a sports psychologist in the process. His technical coaching involved gathering statistics for every player following a game, looking at, for example, the number of shots on goal and the "hit rate" of the player. These statistics were then displayed and discussed with the player in order to agree with them the standard of their current performance and the performance gap between the level and their desired standard of performance.

There are obvious parallels for business managers and how they manage or coach their staff. In this chapter, we will draw on some further insights from Wexford's Liam Griffin and his successful coaching methodology, which he also tries to apply in the management of his hotels.

Use in Ireland

The most recent Irish research into the use of coaching and mentoring in business was conducted by Cranfield-University of Limerick (CUL) in 1995 (Gunnigle et al., 1997). It found that both coaching and mentoring were the least popular training delivery mechanisms among respondent companies, although their usage had increased since the early 1990s, especially by large organisations. Heraty and Morley (1997) refer to research that highlights the critical contribution that coaching and mentoring can make to strategic employee development (see, for example, Wexley and Latham, 1991), and suggest that their lower usage as development practices stems from what they perceive as "the large commitment of time and resources" required.

It will be interesting to assess future research on how these same organisations have addressed their perceived sizeable need for more training and development in people management and supervision. This is one key area where coaching and mentoring can help managers and team leaders to unlock their staff potential. The Institute of Public Administration addressed this theme in their 1998 annual personnel conference and endorsed coaching as one approach that can add value in the people management area (see O'Connor, 1998).

The growth of call centres in recent years also appears to have triggered greater use of coaching. In the Voluntary Health Insurance (VHI), for example, following intensive customer service operator telephone training, a coach is deployed to work with the newly trained employees back on the job. Typically, a coach in these circumstances will listen to how an operator handles the customer call and reviews with the operator standard coaching questions, such as "what went well", "what could have been better" and "how the operator intends to handle the next call" (and apply their learning from the coaching review). The coach in these circumstances can also give the staff the opportunity to listen to good and bad pre-recorded examples of customer service and then encourage the operator to evaluate the calls along the standards which have been set.

As already noted, there are many examples of organisations that have embraced either coaching, mentoring or both developmental techniques. Many of these organisations are in the process of monitoring, or have been able to monitor the added value that these approaches have resulted in and can reinforce the view that the benefits outweigh the obstacles. With regard to coaching, organisations such as the British-American Tobacco Company have initiated a world-wide programme for its managers in order to help them become effective developers of people. Similarly, many leading financial service organisations such as Abbey National plc, Woolwich plc, Ulster Bank, AIB, Bank of Ireland and First Active plc are training their managers in performance coaching techniques.

Mentoring is widely used internationally, to the extent that there exists a European Mentoring Centre. This Centre, based in London, promotes best practice for the use of mentoring in business, the public service, education and community. Case studies of mentoring in action can be found in Megginson and Clutterbuck (1995), and include, for example, the Institute of Management, Asda Superstores, ICL Learning Consultancy and Aer Rianta.

University College Dublin (UCD), as part of its MBA course, has a personal development programme which includes mentoring, where course participants can interact with prominent business leaders. Oliver Tatton, former Chief Executive of An Bord Tráchtála (which is now part of Enterprise Ireland) experienced both sides of the mentoring relationship. He stated that:

> during my own studies, I found this type of contact very useful and still carry many of the insights gained then with me now. From a mentor's point of view, it is always an interesting exercise to articulate the way you practise business to a group

> like this. Minimal preparation is required which suits a busy schedule. (UCD Highflier, 1998: 2)

Before drawing on other case study evidence, it is appropriate in the first instance to examine the process of coaching and mentoring.

THE PROCESS OF COACHING

There are different models of performance coaching available in business. John Whitmore (1992: 147) outlined one popular model, which is based on:

- *Context*   Awareness and Responsibility

- *Skill*   Effective Questioning

- *Sequence* **G** – Goals (for future performance)

  R – Reality (of current performance)

  O – Options (to close the gap)

  W – Will (to commit to a relevant action plan).

Salisbury (1994), a management consultant who participated in a coaching course using the above model, developed a further methodology which he called POWER coaching. He successfully introduced this coaching model into Abbey National plc and he is helping to introduce it into several organisations in the UK and Ireland. We will now focus on the constituent parts of this coaching model, namely:

- **P** – Purpose

- **O** – Objectives and options

- **W** – What is happening now

- **E** – Empowerment

- **R** – Review

Purpose

In a coaching relationship, it is important to define the purpose of the coaching session between the coach and the individual in the first instance before agreeing the objectives. For example:

- How much time have we got?

- What is the purpose of this session for you?

- What are you looking for from me?

It is very important for the individual to spell out what exactly they see as the purpose of the coaching session rather than for the coach to prescribe it. However, if the person being coached encounters difficulties answering these questions, the coach can, through empowering questions, help the individual to clarify the purpose and address the other areas of the coaching session. By helping the performer to find their own answers in this way, the coach creates an atmosphere of individual ownership, helping the person to learn rather than having to teach them. Invariably, people find that the answer lies within themselves and the coach adds value by helping the person through questioning to find the answers in their own head.

Objectives

It is vital for the individual to identify their objective(s) or goal(s). The most effective people and organisations have clearly identified goals. When coaching, it is however important to differentiate between *end goals* and *shorter-term performance goals*. For example, to use our previous sporting example, the Wexford hurling team in the 1996 All-Ireland championships had an end goal of outright victory but they also had shorter-term performance goals such as minimising the number of frees awarded against them in championship matches. Performance goals are within the performer's (or team) control, while end goals are seldom absolutely within their grasp. End goals provide important focus and the effective coach needs to keep a keen eye on the ultimate destination for the performer. The coach can keep the performer on track and help them to measure progress, but the goals must be relevant, realistic and owned by the individual. Indeed, the well-known mnemonic SMART will help to focus both the coach and performer when setting goals, namely that they should be:

- **S** — Stretching and Specific
- **M** — Measurable
- **A** — Achievable
- **R** — Relevant
- **T** — Time-related

In reality, the goals which are also written down help to ensure clarity for performer and coach.

A trusting and honest relationship is fundamental between coach and performer if real progress is to be made towards the achievement of goals. In the Wexford team's journey towards their All-Ireland victory, the team coach, Liam Griffin, laid the foundation of their success on team trust and honesty among all the players and his coaching relationship with them. This trusting relationship facilitated constructive feedback on match performance, which helped the players to identify the current standard of their performance in regard to agreed goals and to agree performance improvement goals. It is also the basis for performers to become more aware of their true current performance and helps them to take personal responsibility for their actions and not blame others or the team or organisation for their own failings.

The coach can ask many questions in order to help the performer to identify their objectives, such as:

- What is your ultimate goal?
- How realistic is that objective?

- What do you want to achieve in the short term?

- When do you need to achieve this goal by?

- How will we measure your progress?

- How will you feel when you achieve your goal?

- What would the goal achievement bring to the team? To the company?

In asking these types of questions, the effective coach needs to become a motivator and to build enthusiasm for the personal benefits the learner will gain from becoming a better performer.

Once the goal(s) have been agreed with the coach, it is essential to establish what the current reality is for the performer.

What is happening now?
Once the coach and performer have begun with the end in mind, they need to establish the current level of performance of the individual. Once again, the coach needs to ask powerful, non-judgemental questions, which help to raise the awareness of the performer and increase their focus on the gap that exists between reality and the desired level of performance. At the same time, the coach also needs to pay close attention to the answers and to explore the detail with the individual if the responses aren't specific enough. Reality check questions could include:

- What is happening now?

- What has been done so far?

- What are the current results?

- What stopped you from achieving more?

- What are the barriers in relation to your goal?

- What, if anything, have you done to overcome these obstacles?

- What would you do differently now?

- What are the opportunities open to you in relation to your goal?

- On a scale of one to ten, how would you rate your current level of performance?

These types of open questions are asked in a spirit of partnership between the coach and the individual in order to encourage the respondent to dig deep within themselves before providing the answers. Indeed, individuals are often their most own most powerful and insightful critic. Bivens (1996) highlights the power of this type of questioning as opposed to the "tell" style in which we have been brought up:

> we are a society of "tell-aholics". We have been rewarded by our parents, our teachers, and especially our corporations for knowing and telling the answer. Every time we tell associates our answer, we rob them of the opportunity to grow, learn, and become more independent. The single most important thing a coach does is to help raise the awareness of the performer and increase his focus.

The traditional "tell" style of questioning would be more prescriptive, such as saying to the individual, "Your current level of performance is . . .", instead of asking them to reflect on it, as in the questions set out above. This directive or tell style works best when the individual is new to the job and needs to be shown the basics of the task in hand. The coach's questioning style in the POWER model leads to greater empowerment.

Empowerment

> Empowerment is the placing of the responsibility for the performance on the individual. If the coach is also the manager, that does not mean that the manager abdicates responsibility. The manager remains accountable for overall results and the performance of the team. At the moment of execution of the coaching plan by the individual, it is the person being coached who is responsible. (Salisbury, 1994: 92–3)

Empowerment is a key ingredient in coaching, allowing individuals to work as adults and helping the team and the organisation to benefit from people taking greater responsibility for their own actions. People who are empowered in a coaching situation identify what options they can take in order to close the gap between the current reality of their performance and their desired performance. One First Active plc manager, Kevin Slattery, in an interview with the *Sunday Business Post* (1997) described some of the benefits of coaching and empowerment, which he said give people the chance to expand their skills and take on more responsibility:

> we needed to appoint a new sales co-ordinator . . . now I spend half an hour a week working with this individual, looking at the issues, discussing job needs and agreeing a structure. . . . I am not the individual who drives it, it is the individual who must appreciate the importance of this coaching. I realise that some company managers would say they don't have the time to spend helping staff in this way. But if I can get people to a certain standard, we can divide the workload and make it easier to achieve our objectives.

Empowering questions in a coaching context could include:

- What are the different alternatives?

- What else could you do to improve your performance?

- Which would give the best result?

- What would you do differently if you could start all over again?

- How much trust do you have in your ability to do it?

- On a scale of one to ten, what is the likelihood of your succeeding with this idea?

- What are the advantages of this proposal?

- What are the disadvantages of this proposal?

- Would you like a suggestion?

- What plan of action will you implement?

- How can the coach help you?

The coach needs to practise very good interpersonal skills when helping the individual through these empowering questions and also when giving feedback. It is advisable to start positively and to ask "What worked?" This provides a solid basis to explore what *didn't* work. The exploration of events must always focus on the process or performance and not on the individual. A more open review should ensue, rather than triggering defensiveness on the part of the individual. The question of what would you do differently opens the way for ideas and tends to produce more actionable initiatives than if they were prescribed by the coach.

Review

Following an agreed action plan, the coach should then observe the individual carrying out some of the tasks. This will test the commitment of the performer to the action plan and provides the coach with an opportunity to observe the performer. In First Active plc, following an intensive training course for managers in a new mortgage sales system, each individual worked with a personal coach and endeavoured to implement their new skills and knowledge back on the job. The coach would observe the individual manager operate the new customer-focused system and then would initiate the review by asking the person to assess their own performance in the first instance. Typical questions in the review process include:

- What were you trying to achieve?

- What worked well for you during your performance?

- What could have gone better?

- What would you do differently the next time?

- What are the next steps in your plan of action?

The coach will observe the performer and compare their performance against an agreed standard. The coach will give constructive feedback to the performer as part of this review process. In First Active's case, the coach reviewed the progress of managers in several role-play situations before sitting in with the manager in a "live" customer mortgage interview.

Reviews should not be one-off. Once again, the sporting world teach us that practice makes perfect. Wexford's hurling success in 1996 was built on very hard work both on and off the field, leading to continuous improvement, with the coach making invaluable input on an ongoing basis. The responsibility to perform rests with the performer. Coaching helps the performer to reach new heights by helping them to realise their inner potential. Only the individual has the power to unleash that strength or, as Argyris (1962) put it, "No-one can develop anyone apart from himself. The door to development is locked from the inside."

Case Example 11.1: High Performance Coaching in Irish Fertiliser Industries

---

Frank Brennan, Human Resource Manager of Irish Fertiliser Industries, described how Richardson's Fertiliser Industries in Belfast developed leadership skills through high performance coaching.

The company devised a survival and development strategy for the whole business including Richardson's in 1994/95. In effect, the new strategy focused on a major cost reduction programme and an expansion of production capacity. However, the company was quite traditional (e.g. command and control structure, formal communication lines) and senior management felt that there was not enough time to engage in management development or team-building exercises.

Brennan's belief was that "what was needed was a novel and very high-powered intervention that could have an early impact, particularly with senior managers". Using external consultants, the company turned to high performance coaching which it felt could help the Belfast plant.

"Firstly, it provided the ultimate flexibility of one-to-one coaching, structured around the varying job needs of every manager. Secondly, this one-to-one approach would eliminate the problems of dealing with two groups of managers – those steeped in the organisation culture and those new to the organisation. Thirdly, it provided high intensity with the prospect of rapid movement for each individual, eliminating the requirement for the Group tutor to "wait for the slowest". Finally, it dealt with basic behaviour of each manager as a person, dealing with their individual preoccupations, beliefs, ambitions, etc."

The performance coaching worked effectively in the plant because it started with the individual and used process tools (e.g. mind mapping, visioning) that prompted people to take charge of their own work and to become more flexible. People were able to empower themselves to aspire to behaviour changes they did not think possible. Performance coaching was able to link individual needs to corporate demands and even the sceptics were won over.

The programme delivered results and helped managers to keep major projects to budget and introduce more flexible work practices. ISO 9000 status has also been achieved.

Source: Brennan, 1998.

MENTORING

As with coaching, the relationship between the mentor and their protégé can be both formal and informal. As already noted, the mentoring relationship can be highly beneficial for those who participate in it. Some organisations have introduced formal mentoring schemes to assist in the development of potential high-flyers, while others try to link new staff up with a *buddy* (or partner) who will look after them and share their organisational experiences with the new entrants. With regard to the buddy system, a case in point was in one of American Express's UK offices where new graduates were linked up with an experienced graduate who acted as their mentor and took responsibility for regular monthly meetings where advice and counsel was available to them.

In the Irish context, more companies are trying to introduce formal mentoring programmes. First Active plc, for example, introduced a fast-track management development programme in 1998 for recently appointed branch managers, which included a formal mentoring system between participants and experienced colleagues and executives. The structure of IBM's current formal mentoring programme is outlined in Figure 11.1.

Figure 11.1: Mentoring in IBM

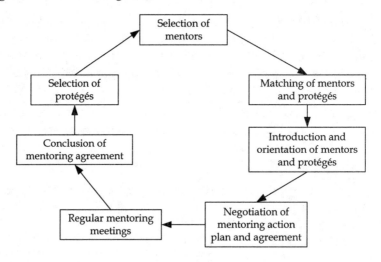

Source: Poynton and Dirks, 1998.

In general, however, research undertaken by Sweeney (1993) highlighted that most mentoring schemes were still informal.

Clutterbuck (1985: 4) highlights that part of the appeal of mentoring is that

> it makes sense of networks and resources that already exist and operate within the firm. Part is also that, in a time of increasing strain on training and development resources, anything that pushes the burden of developing managerial talent back onto the more experienced managers and away from the training department is a good thing.

In the London and Manchester Assurance organisation, executive managers act as mentors to the business regions and in particular to the branch manager running the region. This produces an interesting mix of different central functions spending time in the field, listening to and helping sales managers improve themselves and their businesses.

Mentoring has wide application and is practised in all types of organisations. In a guide called *Starting Your Own Business* by Immink and O'Kane (1997: 108), mentoring is recommended as one positive business development practice which entrepreneurs can usefully use, where mentors make available their experience and expertise to small businesses. There are several mentor schemes available from Enterprise Ireland, Dublin Chamber of Commerce through to the City/County Enterprise Boards and the Area Partnership Companies. When profiled in *Business Plus* magazine, one Irish entrepreneur, Sean Walsh, managing director of Millbrook Studios, a video production company, credited his mentor with helping him to turn his business around. He chose to work with a mentor outside his company whose wide-ranging business experience helped him to focus on his key business goals and develop more commercial acumen (Neary, 1999).

Mentoring has also found favour with the growth of vocational qualifications. This trend is particularly evident in the UK, where candidates follow a formal programme of development and gather evidence to prove competence to a standard required for the National Vocational Qualification (NVQ). The mentor's role in these circumstances is to provide help and support to candidates in order for them to gather the necessary evidence. AIB has embraced the NVQ concept for several hundred new employees recruited in 1998. As part of their own formal induction to the company, AIB has introduced the mentoring role to assist trainees in gathering the necessary evidence to prove their competence on the job.

Some professional bodies, such as the Institute of Personnel and Development (Ireland) have also turned to mentoring for students. In 1996, the IPD launched a special mentoring programme for undergraduates taking the HRM option in Dublin City University. Since then:

> the programme has exceeded expectations and has established itself as an important element in the professional development of tomorrow's human resource executives. (IPD, 1997)

THE PROCESS OF MENTORING

The classic five-step process of a mentoring session is set out in Figure 11.2 below.

Figure 11.2: Steps in the Mentoring Process

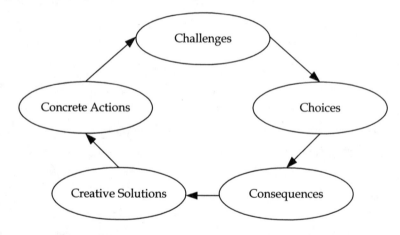

Source: Pegg, 1998

The mentor's role can help the protégé to focus on each of these stages in order to come up with a realistic action plan to address the challenges facing the individual.

Mentoring can help organisations to retain employees even during a difficult economic cycle. For example, Digital, the US computer company, has "downsized" in recent years, and yet it tried to maintain a diverse workforce in the US during its massive redundancy programme. In this regard it focused, for example, on limiting the loss of new college recruits and minority groupings through the introduction of a mentoring programme. Managers volunteered to serve as mentors at Digital, and they received a half-day's training to help equip them for this new role. These manager volunteers agreed to meet with their protégés once a month for one year. One result of this programme of mentoring was that Digital cut turnover from 30 per cent among new college graduates to 15 per cent.

In an Irish survey of chartered accountants reported in *Equality News*, the importance of mentoring for career development was highlighted; 72 per cent of respondents agreed that having an influential mentor is critical to career development and to promotion to partner (Barker and Monks, 1998: 5).

Case Example 11.2: Mentoring for Women in Aer Rianta

Aer Rianta, which manages three international airports, has used mentoring to help manage diversity. It launched a formal programme in 1993 to help women break the glass ceiling into senior management.

The idea for the pilot scheme followed a review of the company's equal opportunities policy (which had helped more women to progress, mainly to the lower managerial ranks). Aer Rianta was keen to develop its women managers further and create a more gender-balanced management profile. It was recognised that, although mentoring occurred almost naturally and informally for men, a formal programme targeted at the new women managers would assist their development, training and promotion prospects.

With the support of Derek Keogh, the company's chief executive, and Sheila Flannery, manager of equal opportunities development, the mentoring programme was initiated for 18 women managers who were mentored by senior managers in the company. These mentors and their protégés volunteered to participate in the programme. Separate half-day training courses were provided for both mentors and their protégés. Individual training needs analysis was undertaken with the women and helped them to identify their personal objectives for the mentoring pilot. Sheila Flannery and a colleague tried to match mentors to the needs of the women partici-

pants. *She asked the protégés who they would prefer to be mentored by and endeavoured to meet their first preferences.*

Although both parties were given diaries to record their experiences, most participants did not use them, instead finding their own ways to progress the mentoring relationships. The programme was tracked in several ways; for example, through feedback from participants on training courses and through the equal opportunities officer. A formal review took place several months later with the European Mentoring Centre.

Writing in Equality News *(September 1995), Sheila Flannery noted that the review:*

> *. . . revealed that both the women managers and their mentors had similar expectations of the programme from the outset. Women expected, first and foremost, that their mentors would share with them their own experiences of management. After that, they wanted their mentor to be a listening ear; somebody who would be a counsellor and sounding board on a variety of issues; and someone who would give encouragement. Following the first ten months of the programme, the women expressed that they had more realistic expectations and felt they had undergone a maturing process which had seen them learn political skills faster than would have been possible outside of the mentoring process. Some of the difficulties experienced were in the setting of clear objectives at the outset, and the time commitment was a problem for some. Some people found it slow in the beginning because it took time to establish a relationship of trust and openness. (Flannery, 1995)*

Following the positive review of the programme, both the mentors and their protégés agreed that a successful mentoring relationship required a number of factors. These were:

- *Commitment and encouragement;*
- *Trust and confidentiality;*
- *Openness, questioning and feedback;*
- *Clear objectives;*
- *Time (for meetings, follow-up and for the mentoring process to develop);*
- *Development of a career path;*
- *Sharing of experience.*

The mentoring scheme worked well and helped many of the women to gain greater confidence. Since the scheme was initiated, a number of the women have been promoted.

Reflecting on the success of the programme, Sheila Flannery believed that the mentoring scheme provided a management development tool to benefit both women and men as well as harnessing the skills and experience of managers throughout the organisation. She also noted that it took longer than expected to build rapport in cross-gender mentoring. Finally, Sheila indicated that the time required for a successful mentoring scheme is significant and not to be underestimated: "it takes a lot of time to keep in touch with people on an individual basis and this needs to be planned into the programme at the start" (Megginson and Clutterbuck, 1995: 152).

CONCLUSION

Many European organisations are actively recruiting people not just on the usual terms and working conditions but also on the basis of a development package (Holbeche, 1998). Practices such as coaching and mentoring can benefit both the employee and the organisation. Where there is a tight labour market supply, as is currently the case in Ireland, organisations that invest in their people development can fare better in attracting and retaining staff than institutions that see such practices as simply a cost. This type of investment can help to make the organisation stand out in the eyes of potential employees and to become more an employer of choice in the marketplace. Indeed, Holbeche (1998) suggests that organisations increasingly recognise that their future success will to a large extent depend on how well they develop their current employees and how successfully they attract future employees because they are good developers of people.

Coaching and mentoring are developmental practices that produce concrete results.

There is evidence in recent times of a move in business to link coaching and mentoring closer to the goals of organisations. In this context, the terms used to describe these development practices tend to be *performance coaching* and *business mentoring*. Similar skill sets are required, and the focus is on both organisational outcomes and personal improvement. This orientation helps to explain in part the reasons behind the success of the "Investors in People" award scheme in the UK, where the human resource developmental practices are aligned with business. There is early evidence of a similar trend in Ireland, with the "Excellence Through People" award where, as in the example of First Active plc, the business plan and the training and development plan must be inextricably linked.

This chapter has highlighted some cases where the benefits arising from the introduction of coaching and mentoring outweigh the drawbacks. The Cranfield-University of Limerick research (Gunnigle et al., 1997) highlighted a perceived need for organisations to train and develop their people in the skills of people management and supervision. Coaching and mentoring can add to the number of arrows in the quiver by helping organisations to address this need and to maintain competitive advantage. These are not flavour-of-the-year practices, but have been with us in varying guises for some time. Indeed, in the case of mentoring, we owe a debt to ancient Greece. The introduction of coaching and/or mentoring, however, requires time, commitment and other resources. The challenge for organisations is to look harder at these initiatives as contributors to future success in attracting and retaining their employees.

References

Argyris, C. (1962), *Interpersonal Competence and Organisational Effectiveness*, New York: Irwin Dorsey.

Barker, P. and K. Monks (1998), "Women in Accountancy", *Equality News*, summer.

Bivens, B. (1996), "Coaching for Results", *Journal for Quality and Participation*, June.

Brennan, F. (1998), "High Performance Coaching: Irish Fertiliser Industries", Paper: Institute of Personnel and Development Conference (Ireland), March.

Clutterbuck, D. (1985), *Everyone Needs a Mentor*, London: Institute of Personnel and Development.

Cunningham, I. and G. Dawes (1998), *Exercises for Developing Coaching*, London: Institute of Personnel and Development.

Flannery, S. (1995), "Mentoring for Women Managers in Aer Rianta", *Equality News*, September.

Gallwey, T. (1975), *The Inner Game of Tennis*, New York: Random House.

Gunnigle, P., M. Morley, N. Clifford and T. Turner (1997), *Human Resource Management in Irish Organisations: Practice in Perspective*, Dublin: Oak Tree Press.

Heraty, N. and M. Morley (1997), "Training and Development" in P. Gunnigle, M. Morley, N. Clifford and T. Turner (1997), *Human Resource Management in Irish Organisations: Practice in Perspective*, Dublin: Oak Tree Press.

Holbeche, L. (1998), *Motivating People in Lean Organisations*, Oxford: Butterworth-Heinemann.

Immink, R. and B. O'Kane (1997), *Starting Your Own Business*, Dublin: Department of Enterprise, Trade and Employment and Oak Tree Press.

IPD News (1997), "IPD Student Mentoring Programme 1997", May.

Megginson, D. and D. Clutterbuck (1995), *Mentoring in Action*: London: Kogan Page.

Neary, C. (1999), "Get Mentoring", *Business Plus*, January.

O'Connor, K. (1998), "Unlocking People Potential", paper presented at the Institute of Public Administration Conference, Dublin, March.

Parsloe, E. (1995), *The Manager as Coach and Mentor*, London: Institute of Personnel and Development.

Pegg, M. (1998), "The Power of Mentoring", *TMI Tempus*, Issue 13.

Poynton, R. and S. Dirks (1998), "New HR Tools and Applications: IBM" Paper presented to the Institute of Personnel and Development Conference (Ireland), October.

Salisbury, F. (1994), *Developing Managers as Coaches*, Berkshire: McGraw Hill.

Sunday Business Post (1997), "First National: Getting It All Together", Excellence through People supplement, 14 December.

Sweeney, M. (1993), "The Use of Mentoring in Management Development", University of Limerick, degree thesis.

UCD Highflier (1998), "MBA Mentor Programme established by Alumni Association", November.

Wexley, K. and G. Latham (1991), *Developing and Training Human Resources in Organisations*, New York: Harper-Collins

Whitmore, J. (1992): *Coaching for Performance*, London: Nicholas Brealey Publishing Ltd.

CHAPTER 12

THE MANAGEMENT OF REWARDS

Michael Morley and *Alma McCarthy*

INTRODUCTION

The pivotal nature of the reward package with all its costs and "knock on" implications throughout the organisation means that the devising/implementing and/or altering of pay structures is an assignment which many managers approach with considerable wariness. This task — the establishment and maintenance of an appropriate reward system — which has proven difficult for many organisations, is the central theme of this chapter. Pay, incentives and benefits as possible components of the reward package are defined along with the objectives and scope of reward management. The importance of pay as a motivator is also briefly explored. Issues in the design of an effective reward system are considered and the meaning, purpose and methods of job evaluation are set down and reviewed. Finally, the choice of pay, incentives and fringe benefits available to organisations and their relative usage are presented and examined.

THE IMPORTANCE OF THE REWARD PACKAGE

As a key human resource management activity, it involves balancing labour costs and establishing fairness towards employees and has proven significant in determining the organisation's ability to attract and retain employees, in developing strategy, and in influencing performance in the workplace (Levine, 1993; Gomez-Mejia and Balkin, 1992; Quarstein et al., 1992). The reward system therefore represents "a major mediating mechanism between the requirements of those planning the organisation and the desires and interests of the employees" (Bowey, 1975: 57). The body of evidence on the perceived importance of reward policies and practices and their links to organisational outcomes, though controversial, is beginning to grow, largely as a result of the recognition that compensation practices must be relevant to a world of increasing competition and an increasing awareness of the contribution of labour productivity to organisation performance (Lowery et al., 1996; Wood, 1996; Williams and Dreher, 1992; Sanfilippo and Weigman, 1991). In a recent review, Grace and Coughlan (1998) identify a number of the key trends that have forced managers to review their traditional reward systems including:

- The impact of new technologies which have reshaped jobs;

- Adjustments in the composition of skills and in the calibre of employee required;

- The technology revolution and the growing services sector;

- The potential competitive advantage that employees can bring to an organisation;

- De-layering/introduction of flatter organisation structures, incorporating less emphasis on hierarchy and greater emphasis on role flexibility.

Whatever the direction of these innovations, pay, incentives and benefits are of central importance to employees and organisations alike and subsumed under the label "reward management" are a myriad of objectives relating to human resource plans (Mahoney, 1989a); business strategies (Mahoney, 1989b); high performance and continuous improvement (Kessler and Purcell, 1991; Gerhart and Milkovich, 1990); the satisfaction of individual needs and wants (Marsden and Richardson, 1994; Quarstein et al., 1992);

cultural maintenance and the promotion of teamwork (Markham, 1988). High or low pay, the nature of incentives and the range of fringe benefits provide valuable insights into the corporate approach to HR and how the reward package is structured and applied will have a major impact on employee performance and organisational outcomes (Milkovich and Newman, 1990).

Thus, the management of rewards is more than just the direct wages and salaries paid. Additional direct payments in the form of bonuses and other incentives are used extensively. The cost of employee benefits is on the increase for many employers. These benefits represent a type of indirect reward because employees receive the value of the benefits without getting direct cash payments. Overall, the complete reward package is now often one of the largest costs faced by employers with many organisations having labour costs at or above 50 per cent of all operating costs. The recent Employee Participation in Organisational Change survey reports the findings of an investigation carried out across ten countries of the EU. It is reported that public service organisations have very high labour costs, as 40 per cent of the respondents indicated that labour costs constituted over three-quarters of total costs. Private firms indicated that their labour costs were a smaller proportion of overall costs (45 per cent reported that labour costs were between 25 and 50 per cent of overall costs) (EFILWC, 1999).

THE SCOPE AND OBJECTIVES OF THE REWARD PACKAGE

Central to an organisation's approach to human resource management is the reward package (Feldman and Doerpinghaus, 1992; Williams and Dreher, 1992). As an aid to deciphering the many objectives underlying this package, Gunnigle et al. (1997) note that three aspects are worth distinguishing at the outset, namely *pay*, *incentives* and *benefits*. Pay refers to the basic wage or salary that an employee receives. An incentive refers to the rewarding of an employee for effort that results in performance above normal performance expectations. Benefits refer to indirect rewards, such as health insurance and pension entitlements, associated with organisational membership. In establishing a remuneration system, an organisation must weigh up the motivational aspects of a performance-related scheme against its drawbacks in terms of operational and other difficulties. With reference to incentive approaches, which emphasise tailored rewards based on performance indicators as a means of increasing motivation, it is not axiomatic that higher motivation will follow. This is a complex research area and the accumulated evidence supports at least as much conjecture as it does conclusive proof. Such schemes have numerous drawbacks in terms of design, operation and potentially negative side-effects. For this and other reasons, many organisations continue to use standard pay rates which do not vary according to performance.

However it is constituted, the reward package is important to the organisation for a number of key reasons. Critical among these is the fact that it serves to attract potential employees. Taken together with the organisation's human resource plan and its recruitment and selection activities, the reward package and its mix of pay, incentives and benefits serves to attract suitable employees. It also assists in the retention of good employees, provided that the package is perceived to be internally equitable and externally competitive. In relation to internal equity, rewards must be seen as fair when compared to others in the organisation. The criteria for the allocation of rewards should be equitable and clear. These should be communicated and accepted by all parties and applied consistently throughout the organisation. In terms of external competitiveness, the package must be seen as fair when compared to those offered for comparable work outside the organisation. It may also serve to motivate employees (see section on pay and motivation). More broadly, it constitutes a core aspect of the human resource and business planning process. Concomitantly, it is important to employees because it provides the means to satisfy basic needs for survival and security, and may also allow them satisfy less tangible desires for personal growth and satisfaction. Thus, the objectives of an effective reward system encapsulate the identification of prevailing market trends, balancing individual needs with organisational needs and/or constraints, ensuring fairness, equity and trust, inducing and rewarding higher levels of performance and working within the law.

Figure 12.1: Components of the Reward Package

	Total components	

Non-monetary rewards	Monetary rewards
• Job security • Status symbols • Task self-rewards • Praise • Recognition	

Indirect rewards (benefits)	Direct rewards

Public protection (legally required)	Private protection	Paid leave	Life events	Basic salary	Performance-based pay
• Social insurance • Unemployment • Disability	• Pensions • Savings • Supplemental unemployment insurance	• Training • Work breaks • Sickness days • Holidays • Personal rest periods	• Legal advice • Elder care • Day care • Counselling • Perks • Moving	(including shift pay and premium pay)	• Share options • Bonuses • Day care • Merit incentives

Source: Adapted from Schuler, 1995: p. 384.

PAY AND THE MOTIVATION CONTROVERSY

The utility of using pay to motivate and promote performance has been a subject of debate for many years, with empirical and theoretical support for both sides of the argument (Levine, 1993). Most managers instinctively believe that money is a motivator, even though empirical evidence to support this is far from conclusive (Fowler, 1991; Goffee and Scase, 1986). Indeed, failure of such schemes, in some instances, to fulfil their potential has been attributed to a flawed theoretical base, which in many cases serves to undermine effectiveness by demotivating employees (Pearse, 1987; Sargeant, 1990).

Perhaps the key point to be drawn from the available evidence is that pay is a complex, multi-faceted issue which serves as both a tangible and intangible motivator, offering intrinsic and extrinsic rewards. Thus, the applicability of pay-related incentive schemes across a wide range of organisational contexts is difficult to generalise on and is largely dependent on organisational circumstances, employee profile and prevailing conditions.

Kohn (1993) suggests that punishment and rewards are two sides of the same coin. Rewards have a punishment effect because they, like outright punishment, are manipulative. "Do this and you'll get that" is not very different from "Do this or here's what will happen to you". In the case of incentives, the reward itself may be highly desired, but by making that bonus contingent on certain behaviours, managers manipulate their subordinates, and that experience of being controlled is likely to assume a punitive quality over time. Similarly, others have argued that just because too little money can irritate and de-motivate, this does not mean that more money will bring about increased satisfaction, much less increased motivation. Doubtless, pay is important to employees. It provides the means to live, eat, and achieve other personal or family goals. It is a central reason why people hold down and move between jobs. However, a key question is not the importance of financial incentives *per se*, but whether they motivate employees to perform well in their jobs.

Once an individual has been attracted to the organisation and the job, the role of money as a motivator is debatable. Clearly money, or the lack of it, can be a source of dissatisfaction, grievance, etc. However, if the employee is reasonably happy with their income, does that income induce them to perform at high levels of performance? Many of the theoretical prescriptions suggest that money is important in satisfying essential lower-order needs, such as basic physiological and security needs. This line of argument suggests that once such lower-order needs are satisfied, it is factors intrinsic to the job that are the prime motivators, especially at the self-actualisation level. Others suggest that money is important at all levels and may be a prime motivator where it is a valued outcome and where there is an obvious or tangible link between effort, performance and the achievement of greater financial reward.

During the 1960s and 1970s, many organisation behaviour theorists emphasised the importance of job enrichment and organisation development and it became somewhat popular to discount the importance of money as a motivator (Biddle and Evenden, 1989). The current emphasis on performance, productivity and cost reduction has tended to focus on primary job values like employment security, benefits and, more particularly, the pay package. Most managers will agree that remuneration — especially the money element — has an important role in motivating employees. However, it is only one factor in the total motivation process. Clearly many people are not primarily motivated by money but by other factors such as promotion prospects, recognition or the job challenge itself. All employees do not have a generalised set of motives. Rather, an organisation's workforce will be comprised of people with varying sets of priorities relating to different situations and work contexts resulting in differing employee motives and goals. These motives and goals will vary both between employees and among individual employees over time. For example, a young single person may prioritise basic income and free time and the job itself may not hold any great interest. Later, that person, now married and with a mortgage, may be more concerned with job security and fringe benefits such as health insurance and a pension plan.

Arguably, there are four key issues that should be considered when exploring the extent to which employees are motivated by pay:

1. Firstly, it is clear that employees must value financial rewards. If people are paid at a very high level, or simply not concerned

with financial rewards, higher pay will have little incentive value for employees. At this stage other factors related to the job and work environment must have the potential to motivate employees.

2. Secondly, if money is a valued reward, employees must believe that good performance will allow them realise that reward. This suggests that pay should be linked to performance and differences in pay should be large enough to adequately reward high levels of performance. This approach obviously rejects remuneration systems which reward good, average and poor performance equally, such as regular pay increments based on seniority.

3. Thirdly, equity is an important consideration. Employees must be fairly treated in their work situation, especially in terms of the perceived equity of pay levels and comparisons with fellow employees. They will be keen that rewards (pay, incentives and benefits) adequately reflect their input (effort, skills, etc.). Should employees feel they are not being treated fairly on these criteria, performance levels may fall.

4. Finally, employees must believe that the performance levels necessary to achieve desired financial rewards are achievable. The required performance criteria and levels should be clearly outlined and communicated to employees. Organisations must also ensure that employees have the necessary ability, training, resources and opportunity to achieve such performance levels. Otherwise, employees will either not be able, or else not try, to expend the necessary effort.

Thus, from the motivational perspective, effective payment systems should have the following characteristics:

- Be objectively established;
- Clarify performance levels required and rewards available;

- Reward the achievement of required performance levels adequately and quickly;

- Ensure employees have the ability, training resources and opportunity to achieve required performance levels;

- Recognise that financial incentives are only one source of motivation and that jobs should be designed in such a way as to ensure employees can satisfy other needs through their work (e.g. achievement, challenge);

- Take regular steps to identify employee needs and ensure these can be satisfied within the organisational environment.

Even where these factors are present, success is not guaranteed. For example, an incentive scheme based on production figures may be established to encourage employees to achieve high performance levels. However, unofficial norms established by the work-group may dictate "acceptable" performance levels and ensure this is not exceeded through various social pressures. Equally, such an approach may signal to employees that management are clearly in charge and may either lessen employee feelings of control and competency or encourage conflict over the standards set.

It should always be appreciated that while pay is an important source of employee motivation, it is not the only one. To motivate effectively, financial incentives should be structured in such a way as to highlight the link between effort, performance and subsequent reward. The pay system should adequately reward good performance and be equitable in the eyes of employees. The remuneration system should be viewed as part of a total motivational process which allows for individual differences and provides motivational opportunities through additional extrinsic and intrinsic factors, particularly self-fulfilment.

DETERMINING THE RELATIVE WORTH OF A JOB

Following on from our discussion on motivation, important considerations in the design of an organisation's reward system will be the relative emphasis on extrinsic versus intrinsic rewards, the role of pay and whether it is contingent upon individual performance and its compatibility with the organisation's business goals and other personnel policies (see Gunnigle et al., 1997a). This latter issue is particularly significant, as it is widely argued that an organisation's reward system should complement overall business objectives and other HR policy choices. Decisions on an organisation's cost structure and market strategy will influence the reward strategy. A high-volume, low-cost strategy may constrain the organisation's ability to provide expansive rewards. On the other hand, a product innovation strategy may require a comprehensive reward system to attract and retain high calibre staff. The reward system must also "fit" other personnel/HR decisions. Recruitment and selection will provide a particular workforce profile and the reward system must cater for their various needs. The reward system may also complement personnel/HR practices in areas such as employee development and promotion.

Of primary importance is the establishment of basic pay levels for various jobs. Here again the organisation must be aware of the need to establish pay equity and organisations typically go to great lengths to ensure that base rates are internally equitable and competitive within the market. This initially applies to *external comparisons* with pay levels in other organisations. Comparable pay rates influence an organisation's ability to attract and retain employees. Suitable comparable organisations should be chosen both to maintain pay competitiveness and to keep wage costs at reasonable levels. Pay levels will be influenced by factors in the broader business environment such as:

1. *Economic Climate*: Here factors like levels of inflation, disposable income and industrial activity will exert both direct and

indirect influences on payment levels by affecting employment levels, demand, consumer price indices, etc.

2. *Labour Market*: The state of the labour market will be influenced by general economic factors. It will also depend on labour supply/demand for certain skills and local factors like the level of company closures, emigration, etc. Information on local and national pay rates may be obtained through wage surveys of comparable organisations.

3. *Government Policy*: The government will exert considerable influence on pay levels both indirectly (fiscal policy) and directly through what it pays its own employees (state, semi- state sector), national pay guidelines, minimum pay levels (Joint Labour Committees), and legislation (e.g. equal pay).

4. *Trade Unions*: Through collective bargaining, trade unions will seek to improve or, at least, maintain their members' earning levels. Such claims will generally be based on comparability, differentials and cost of living increases.

Pay levels will also depend on factors relating to the organisation itself. Managerial philosophy and style in managing employees will impact upon approaches to the supervision, development and payment of employees. The organisation's competitive position will influence its ability to reward employees. These factors help determine the organisation's position as low, high or average payer, which in turn will influence the choice of comparable organisations for pay purposes.

Organisations must also endeavour to maintain *internal equity* in deciding differential pay rates for different jobs. The establishment of an internal pay structure involves deciding the relative value of jobs within an organisation and results in the creation of a hierarchy of job grades. The perceived equity of internal job grades will likely impact upon employee performance and commitment.

Establishing equitable and consistent pay rates and differentials between jobs is an important step in developing an effective compensation system. Management will want to ensure that jobs which contribute most to the organisation are rewarded appropriately. They will also be keen to ensure that conflict over pay and job grading is kept to a minimum by establishing an equitable and consistent system for grading jobs and determining differentials. Aspirations for pay equity can be partially satisfied by ensuring that pay rates are competitive in comparison with other organisations. Before this, however, the organisation should establish an acceptable mechanism for internally grading and evaluating jobs.

The initial stage in establishing the relative worth of jobs involves analysis of job content. This is typically achieved through systematic job analysis, which attempts to provide detailed information on the duties, demands, responsibilities, and skills of the various jobs in the organisation. Such information may then be used to establish the organisation's grading structure and decide related pay levels through some method of job evaluation.

METHODS OF JOB EVALUATION

While job evaluation is typically characterised as being concerned almost exclusively with the methodology used to establish the comparative worth of jobs within an organisation, it should also, according to Armstrong and Baron (1995), be concerned with the making of decisions on what people should be paid for the work they do. Gunnigle et al. (1997a) suggest that as a technique for determining the relative worth of jobs within an organisation, so that differential rewards may be given to jobs of different worth, it represents an attempt to measure a job's value to the organisation and then assign a base pay level that is reflective of that value. It seeks to provide a rational basis for the design and maintenance of an equitable and acceptable pay structure and to help in the management of the relativities existing between jobs within the organisation. In this way, it enables more consistent decisions to

be made on grading and rates of pay and has the potential to establish more equitably the extent to which there is comparable
worth between jobs so that like pay can be provided for like work.
It operates by focusing on and assessing job content and placing
jobs in a hierarchy according to their contribution to the attainment of overall business objectives. As an area of activity it is,
however, problematic. Its critics say that, as it assesses the job
rather than the jobholder, it fails to recognise the contribution of
the individual. It has been suggested that it leads to an inappropriate focus on promotion whereby people are led to believe that
a job is more important than the individual in the job. It also demonstrates an inability to keep pace with high speed organisational
changes and emergent employee roles. Gunnigle et al. (1997a: 129)
cite the potential for error in human judgements that form a central part of the process as perhaps one of its greatest drawbacks.

> Despite some of the obvious benefits of job evaluation . . . it is
> not infallible. It attempts to create a consistent and equitable
> system for grading jobs. However, it depends on the judge-
> ment of people with experience and training, requiring them
> to make decisions in a planned and systematic way, and the
> results do not guarantee total accuracy.

Selecting the right job evaluation method is crucial if the resulting
pay frameworks are to be consistent with an organisation's
structure, style and values. There is, therefore, no one best approach. Rather, each organisation must assess its own specific requirements and set these against the range of potential methods
available.

Job evaluation schemes are commonly classified into *non-
analytical schemes* and *analytical schemes*. Non-analytical schemes
involve making comparisons between whole jobs without analysing them into their constituent parts or elements. Among the
main schemes under this heading are *job ranking, job classification*
and *paired comparison*. Analytical schemes involve jobs being broken down into a number of critical factors which are then ana-

lysed and compared, using a quantitative measure. Among the main analytical methods are *points rating, Hay method* and more recently, *competency-based* job evaluation. We now turn to a description of the non-analytical and analytical schemes mentioned.

Job Ranking

Ranking is the simplest method of job evaluation. It aims to evaluate each job as a whole and determine its place in a job hierarchy by comparing one job with another and arranging them in perceived order of importance, their difficulty, or their value to the organisation. No attempt is made to quantify judgements. A ranking table is then drawn up and the jobs thus ranked are arranged into grades. Pay levels are then agreed for each grade. Sometimes a single factor such as skill is used; alternatively, a list of factors such as skill, responsibility, complexity, physical demands, etc., is used. The following table highlights some of the commonly cited advantages and disadvantages of job ranking as a method of job evaluation.

Table 12.1: Advantages and Disadvantages of Job Ranking

Advantages	Disadvantages
• It represents an almost intuitive or instinctive valuation of the job • It is clear, intelligible and readily understood • Provided agreement can be got on the rank order of jobs in the hierarchy, it is quick and cheap to implement • It can prove useful as a means of checking the results of more sophisticated methods	• There are no established principles for assessing • Ranking is rarely acceptable as a method of evaluating comparable worth in equal-value cases • Those involved in the process need to be knowledgeable on all jobs that are being analysed • Ranking is likely to be extremely difficult when a large number of jobs are being analysed • Arriving at an acceptable ranking for jobs in widely different functions where the demands made upon the job holder vary may be difficult

Job Classification

This method is more complex than job ranking in that classes or grades are established and the jobs are then placed into the grades. Thus it begins, not by ranking jobs, but by agreeing a grading structure. Initially, the number of job grades and particular criteria for these grades are agreed, so that for each job grade there is a broad description of its key characteristics. The number of grades is usually limited to between four and eight, between each of which there are clear differences in the demands made by any job in its respective grade. In establishing the grades, benchmark jobs considered to be particularly characteristic of each job grade are chosen, and using detailed job descriptions, all other jobs are evaluated by comparison with both the benchmark jobs and the criteria for each job grade. Evaluated jobs are then placed in their appropriate grades.

Table 12.2: Advantages and Disadvantages of Job Classification

Advantages	Disadvantages
• Its simplicity and the ease with which it can be understood • Greater objectivity than job ranking • Standards for making grading decisions are provided in the form of the grade definitions	• The basis of the job evaluation is either one factor or an intuitive summary of many factors • It is difficult to apply with more complex jobs where duties and skills do not fit neatly into one grade but overlap with other grades • It may not be able to cater for a wide range of jobs or for senior jobs where grade descriptions have to be very general • Because it is not an analytical system, it is not effective as a means of establishing comparable worth and is unacceptable in equal-value cases

Paired Comparison

More sophisticated than the previous two methods, the paired comparison approach is based on the premise that it is more reasonable to compare one job with another than to consider a larger number of jobs together. The method requires the comparison of each job individually with every other job, until one builds up a rank order of jobs. When a job is deemed to be of higher worth than the one with which it is being compared, it is awarded two points. If it is deemed to be of equal worth, it receives one point and if it is found to be of less worth, it receives no points. The points are then totalled for each job and a rank order is produced.

Table 12.3: Advantages and Disadvantages of Paired Comparison

Advantages	Disadvantages
• It is easier to compare one job with another at a time which results in greater overall consistency	• It relies on whole/complete job ranking which is difficult • There is a limit to the number of jobs that can be ranked

Points Rating

Points rating is a widely used method of job evaluation. It involves breaking down each job into a number of component job factors and then analysing these separately defined factors, which are assumed to be common to all jobs. Gunnigle et al. (1997a) suggest that it is based on the assumption that the degree to which differences in the job factors arise will accurately reflect the actual difference between total jobs. The selection of the job factors is critical. Benge (1944), who first promulgated the method, suggested that it should be limited to the following five factors which he believed were the universal factors found in all jobs: skill requirements; mental requirements; physical requirements; responsibility and working conditions. Each of these job factors may then be broken down into a number of sub-factors. Thus, the sub-factors of responsibility might well include financial, quality, equipment and materials, training and others. Once the factors and sub-factors have been agreed, point values are then allocated.

Table 12.4: Points Rating Job Evaluation

Factor	Level				
	1 *Minimum*	*2* *Low*	*3* *Moderate*	*4* *High*	*Total* *points*
Responsibility					*200*
(a) Financial	10	20	30	40	
(b) Quality	10	20	30	40	
(c) Equipment	10	20	30	40	
(d) Training	10	20	30	40	
(e) Other	10	20	30	40	
Working conditions					*100*
(a) Hazardous	15	30	45	60	
(b) Unpleasant	10	20	30	40	

Source: Gunnigle and Flood, 1990: p. 132.

In the example shown here, responsibility is twice as important as working conditions, while in relation to working conditions, hazardous conditions get more points than those that are simply rated as unpleasant. The various jobs may then be evaluated and placed in their appropriate grades. This can be done by either taking one factor and evaluating its significance in all jobs under consideration, or taking each job and evaluating it in terms of all job factors. The former approach is recommended, as it concentrates on the comparable worth of jobs in terms of a specific factor and this information can be brought together at the end to give a total picture of relative job worth.

Table 12.5: Advantages and Disadvantages of Points Rating

Advantages	Disadvantages
• It is systematic and analytical in the sense that it compares jobs on a factor-by-factor basis • The standards of comparison are clearly defined	• It is complex and difficult to understand • It can be time-consuming and expensive • Although analytical, it still relies on a deal of subjective judgement • It may be impossible to put numerical values on different aspects of jobs since skills are not always quantifiable in this way, particularly when comparing the skills demanded by jobs of often disparate demands and responsibilities

Hay Method

The Hay method or plan is one of the most widely used job evaluation methods and is generally classified as a points-factor rating. Traditionally associated with managerial and professional jobs, it is becoming more widely used for technical, clerical and other positions. The method relies on three primary factors: know-how, problem-solving and accountability.

It combines aspects of points rating and factor comparison. Point values are established for each job using the factors set out in the table and jobs are compared to one another on each factor. Points-factor schemes of this kind are popular because people generally feel that they work.

Figure 12.2: Primary Factors in the Hay Method

Problem-solving	Know-how	Accountability
The amount of original self-starting thought required by the job for analysis, evaluation, creation, reasoning, and arriving at conclusions	*The total of knowledge and skills, however acquired, needed for satisfactory job performance (evaluates the job, not the person)*	*The measured effect of the job on the company goals*
Problem-solving has three dimensions:	Know-how has three dimensions:	Accountability has three dimensions:
• The degree of freedom with which the thinking process is used to achieve job objectives without the guidance of standards, precedents or direction from others.	• The amount of practical, specialised or technical knowledge required.	• Freedom to act, or the relative presence of personal or procedural control and guidance, determined by answering the question, "How much freedom has the jobholder to act independently?" For example, a plant manager has more freedom than a supervisor under his or her control does.
• The type of mental activity involved; the complexity, abstractness or originality of thought required.	• Breadth of management, or the ability to make many activities and functions work well together; the job of company president, for example, has greater breadth than that of a department supervisor.	• Dollar magnitude, a measure of the sales, budget, value of purchases, value added or any other significant annual money figure related to the job.
Problem-solving is expressed as a percentage of know-how, for the obvious reason that people think with what they know. The percentage judged to be correct for a job is applied to the know-how point value; the result is the point value given to problem-solving	• Requirement for skill in motivating people.	• Impact of job on dollar magnitude, a determination of whether the job has a primary effect on final results or has instead a sharing, contributory or remote effect.
	Using a chart, a number can be assigned to the level of know-how needed in a job. This number – or point value – indicates the relative importance of know-how in the job being evaluated.	Accountability is given a point value independent of the other two factors.

Note: The total evaluation of any job is arrived at by adding the points for problem-solving, know-how and accountability.

Source: Schuler, 1995: p. 395.

Table 12.6: Advantages and Disadvantages of the Hay Method

Advantages	Disadvantages
• The wide acceptance of the approach • Evaluators are forced to consider a range of factors and thus avoid over-simplifications • A higher level of objectivity than other approaches • Many external comparisons are available because of the widespread adoption of the method	• The degree of complexity • Because of its standardised nature, it may not reflect an organisation's real needs • Despite the impression of objectivity, human judgement is required in the process

Competency-based Job Evaluation

Variously referred to as competency-based, skill-based or knowledge-based, the emphasis is on an evaluation of the individual who performs the job and their competencies and performance abilities rather than on the job title or grade itself. Thus, if the previously described job evaluation methods had at their core the principle of "paying for the job", competency-based evaluation has as its central tenet "pay for the person". Armstrong and Baron (1995) argue that competency-based job evaluation is growing in importance because much greater significance is now attached to knowledge work in organisations and more emphasis is being placed on flexibility, multi-skilling individual/team autonomy and empowerment.

Armstrong and Baron (1995) highlight three approaches to developing competency-based job evaluation:

1. Take an existing analytical scheme and modify the factor plan to make it more competency-related by reference to an existing competency framework;

Table 12.7: Comparison of Conventional Job Evaluation and Competency-based Job Evaluation

Component	Skill-based Evaluation	Job-based Evaluation
1. Determination of job worth	Tied to evaluation of skill blocks	Tied to evaluation of total job
2. Pricing	Difficult because overall pay system is tied to market	Easier, because wages are tied to labour market
3. Pay ranges	Extremely broad; one pay range for entire cluster of skills	Variable, depending on type of job and pay grade width
4. Evaluation of performance	Competency tests	Performance appraisal ratings
5. Salary increases	Tied to skill acquisition as measured by competency testing	Tied to seniority, performance appraisal ratings, or actual output
6. Role of training	Essential to attain job flexibility and pay increases for all employees	Necessitated by need rather than desire
7. Advancement opportunities	Greater opportunities; anyone who passes competency test advances	Fewer opportunities; no advancement unless there is a job opening
8. Effect of job change	Pay remains constant unless skill proficiency increases	Pay changed immediately to level associated with new job
9. Pay administration	Difficult, because many aspects of pay plan (training, certification) demand attention	Contingent on complexity of job evaluation and pay allocation plan

Source: Adapted from Schuler, 1995: p. 398.

2. Take existing competency frameworks and adapt them to develop a competency-based scheme;

3. Conduct a special analysis of generic and job-specific competencies to produce a competency framework and develop a scheme from this analysis.

Among some of the competencies likely to be considered in any of these approaches are interpersonal skills, communication skills, reasoning and critical thinking ability, technical knowledge, business knowledge, decision-making ability, team-working and leadership skills, resource management capabilities and planning, organising and problem-solving abilities.

Table 12.8: Advantages and Disadvantages of Competency-based Job Evaluation

Advantages	Disadvantages
• It provides a framework for relevant ongoing employee development	• The competency movement has been accused of being vague in its terminology
• It can assist in making the organisation more flexible through an ever-expanding focused skill base	• It can be as complex and difficult as any other form of job evaluation

WHICH JOB EVALUATION METHOD SHOULD BE CHOSEN?

It follows from our discussion above that whichever form of job evaluation is chosen will have a large impact on pay structures and employee relations generally. It is essential, therefore, that due care is taken when deciding which method to use. Fowler (1996) suggests that a job evaluation scheme needs to be determined primarily by setting the characteristics of different methods against the organisation's circumstances and objectives. In this respect, he suggests that the following questions are useful:

1. Is the principal aim to meet the requirements of equal pay legislation?

2. How many different jobs are there to be evaluated?

3. How complex is the pay structure?

4. What are the factors or characteristics to which the organisation wishes to allocate monetary value within the pay structure?

5. Is the scheme intended for making market comparisons?

6. Is there an advantage in using a computerised system?

Gunnigle et al. (1997b) highlight the necessity for advice and participation. They argue that the introduction of job evaluation can be a complex process and thus it is often useful to seek expert advice and guidance at the initial stages. This expert would usually be responsible for advising on the technical aspects of the scheme and assisting in decisions on the type of scheme to use, the establishment and composition of overseeing committees, the training of job analysts and communicating the details of the scheme to all concerned. In relation to participation, they suggest that staff should be kept adequately informed at all stages in the process. It is vital that those who will be most directly affected by the scheme should know its objectives, its content and how it will operate. Middle management and supervisors are critical here. They will play a vital role in implementing the scheme, so it is imperative that they understand it and appreciate their role in its operation.

THE REWARD PACKAGE: PAY, INCENTIVES AND FRINGE BENEFITS

Determining the worth of a job and setting down basic pay levels are critical aspects of the process of establishing a pay system. Choosing the actual payment system is the other critical aspect. In this section, our attention turns to the practicalities of choosing different payment methods, incentive schemes and fringe benefits which can be offered to employees. In several instances, examples of companies that have adopted the various schemes are highlighted.

The choice of compensation system is an important consideration for organisations. It will partially reflect the corporate approach to personnel management and impact on areas such as employee relations, supervisory style and employee motivation. The particular package offered will be determined by a variety of factors related to the organisation, the general business environment and the workforce. In relation to choices of payment schemes, Mooney (1980) feels these are related to characteristics of the organisation and the product. In particular, he identifies the significance of:

- *Company Ownership*: Mooney feels that a continuing influx of foreign companies will increase the utilisation of performance-related bonus schemes.

- *Size*: Performance-related schemes are more common in larger organisations while small firms tend to rely on flat rate only.

- *Technical System*: Organisations operating large batch production techniques — which are common in Ireland — are more likely to use performance-related payment systems.

- *Labour Costs*: Mooney feels this is the most important factor influencing the choice of payment system. Flat rate only or company-wide schemes dominate in capital cost-intensive organisations, while individual or group incentive schemes are popular in organisations with high labour costs.

Overall, as with other aspects of personnel management, the corporate approach to compensation should complement the organisation's strategic business goals, personnel philosophy and other personnel activities.

There are numerous options with regard to the type of pay, incentive and benefits package an organisation might adopt. The more common types of payment systems are discussed below. Benefits available in Ireland are then considered. The Irish Business and Employers Confederation (IBEC) recently published a report which presents the findings of a survey carried out among its member companies in April 1997. The purpose of the report was "to explore the extent and coverage of the various reward/payment schemes . . ." (IBEC, 1998: IV). Surveys were sent out to 923 companies in a variety of sectors and the response rate was 34 per cent. Throughout the following section, there will be references made to some of the findings of this survey, especially with regard to the extent that the various types of payment systems are in use in Ireland.

PAYMENT SYSTEMS

In this section, the various payment systems and their characteristics are outlined. Where appropriate, examples of organisations that have these systems in place are highlighted. The purpose of this section is to provide a general overview of the various approaches that organisations can take where pay, incentives and fringe benefits are concerned, and to outline the current trends and developments in reward management in Ireland. Gunnigle et al. (1997a, 1997b) have clearly set down some of these schemes and this section draws upon and extends this work, namely, the treatment of more recent innovations and developments such as broadbanding, competency/skill-based pay and recent statutory provisions in maternity, adoptive and parental leave.

Flat Rate Systems
Flat Rate Only
Flat rate pay systems are the most basic and easily understood payment systems that an organisation can adopt. A traditional approach to reward management, flat rate pay schemes pay a per-

son for time on the job and no incentive is provided for actual performance. They are popular because of their simplicity and ease of administration. They are particularly useful for managerial and administrative jobs where specific performance criteria are difficult to establish. They help attract employees to join the organisation but their motivational potential in encouraging good performance is thought to be limited. In Mooney's (1980) study of wage payment systems in Ireland, he found the flat rate system by far the most popular, particularly for indirect employees (i.e. administrative and support staff). However, he also found that the utilisation of approaches which combine the flat rate with incentive payments based on some measure of performance was on the increase. A more recent study carried out by the European Foundation for the Improvement of Living and Working Conditions in 1996 reports that fixed pay is still the most popular method of payment across the EU (EFILWC, 1997).

Annual Hours Contract

As with the flat rate only system, this is based on the premise that one is paid for the time spent on the job. However, in this instance working time is organised on an annual rather than on a weekly basis. Thus, the annual hours contract will specify the number of hours to be worked in the year rather than the week. Originally developed in Scandinavia, O'Sullivan (1996) notes that it is increasingly regarded as an important alternative to the standard 39-hour week plus overtime in Ireland.

The distribution firm, Allegro Ltd., implemented an annualised hours system in late 1997. There is mention of more companies introducing annualised hours but these have not been reported formally as yet (Sheehan, 1997a).

Figure 12.3: Methods for Calculating the Annual Hours Contract

---

There are two ways of calculating the contract, both producing the same result:

(1) Standard working week formula:

Calendar year:	52.18 weeks (inc. leap year)
Annual leave:	4 weeks
Public holidays:	1.8 weeks
Average working week:	46.38 weeks × 39 hours
Annual hours:	**1,808.82 (net basic working hours)**

(2) Annual working formula:

In a complete calendar year, there are an average of 365.25 days, which comprise 8,766 hours.

Example:

Employee works 39 hours a week.

$$\frac{39 \times 365.25}{7} = 2{,}035 \text{ hours a year}$$

Less annual and public holidays:	2,035
20 days' annual leave:	7.8 × (20)
9 public holidays:	7.8 × (9)
	– 226.2
Employee available to work:	**1,808.8 hours per year**

Source: O'Sullivan, 1996: p. 21.

O'Sullivan cites a number of advantages to be gained from this approach. From the company's perspective, there will often be an improvement in unit costs and productivity; the elimination of large-scale overtime; a closer match between output and demand; and a reduction in absenteeism. From the employee's perspective, the benefits include improved basic pay; stability of earnings; and increased leisure time. The disadvantages cited by O'Sullivan include the necessity to recoup monies owing to the organisation if an employee leaves during the year; the necessity for reorganisation, cultural and value changes that are congruent with this approach.

Incentive Systems

Ireland has, in recent years, seen a number of shifts in the application of incentive schemes as a cure for low productivity. This change has stemmed from a preoccupation with the productivity bargaining of the 1960s, measured day work in the 1970s to PRP in the 1980s (Grafton, 1988). As the operating environment became ever more complex during the 1980s, organisations turned increasingly to performance appraisal and merit pay (Randell, 1994). Fowler (1988) suggests that a number of organisations are moving towards the evaluation of employee performance against specified objectives and using this as a basis for deciding on merit awards. He also notes the extension of performance-related pay systems into the public sector, the use of performance appraisal for all grades of employees and attempts to move away from regular increments to increases based on some evaluation of individual performance. The use of incentives is not a new phenomenon with performance-related pay schemes having formed a significant part of the traditional remuneration package in many organisations. McBeath and Rands (1989) define Performance Related Pay (PRP) as "an intention to pay distinctly more to reward highly effective job performance than you are willing to pay for good solid performance", the objective of which should be to develop a productive, efficient, effective organisation (Hoevemeyer, 1989).

Performance-based incentive schemes in an organisational environment fulfil a number of functions, the key ones being:

- To ensure an adequate supply of skilled and trained employees in response to fluctuating labour demands. While choice is more repressed in turbulent economic circumstances, individuals making an employment decision will look not only at the terms of employment, but also at the total remuneration package, including variable and incentive pay.

- To elicit from employees, both individually and collectively, performance that reinforces the strategic direction of the organisation. Thus, one of the key underlying assumptions is that pay has the potential to motivate.

There are benefits and drawbacks associated with the use of performance-based pay. It is suggested that there is a positive correlation between variable individual incentive payments and improvements in costs and quality. However, McBeath and Rands (1989) also point to potentially adverse effects on attitudes to work and employee relations. A continuing problem in merit-based pay is finding an acceptable mechanism to assess performance equitably and consistently. Otherwise, merit-based payments can lead to problems as a result of resentment to managerial control or inequity/inconsistency in performance evaluation. A key factor seems to be the extent of employee involvement, with schemes requiring extensive consultation having a greater chance of success. There are a number of factors identified in the literature which underpin successful merit-based reward systems:

- Equitable mechanisms for performance measurement incorporating performance appraisal;
- Consistency of rewards among individual employees;
- Managerial flexibility to link reward decisions to organisational needs in order to attract and retain employees;
- Simple to understand and apply;
- Good basic compensation package;
- Clearly defined employee development policy.

It is important that management clearly outline key performance criteria and reward employees accordingly. Employee acceptance of merit-based pay will depend on perceived equity in performance evaluation. It demands a climate of trust and fairness — the main responsibility for whose development lies with management.

Trade unions may often be opposed to payments based on individual performance, preferring collective increases achieved through management–union negotiations. Grafton (1988) feels that schemes which operate merit increases in addition to general salary awards are less likely to cause employee opposition, as they operate as a discretionary element which does not cut across the collective bargaining role of the trade union. In an appropriate organisational climate, merit-based pay can be effectively used to augment negotiated pay and benefit increases and stimulate improved employee and organisational performance. There are various forms of incentive-based pay and these are discussed in turn below.

Flat Rate plus Individual PRP
Gunnigle et al. (1997b) note that support for contingent payment systems is based on the concept that it is fair and logical to reward individual employees differentially, based on some measure of performance. While this principle is rarely a source of contention, problems may arise in attempting to develop reliable and acceptable mechanisms for evaluating employee performance. These include the limited criteria used (e.g. work study), inconsistency of application (e.g. performance appraisal), or bias/inequity in employee evaluations. A more fundamental issue may be resentment towards the exercise of managerial control via performance measurement and reward distribution, which is inherent in many "reward-for-performance" approaches. Notwithstanding this, many commentators suggest that individually rewarding performance has a strong motivational impact. Payment is related to

the individual employee's contribution; required performance levels and related financial rewards are specified and these are achievable immediately after these performance criteria have been met. McMahon (1998) attributes performance-related pay's rising popularity to "attempts to change organisational cultures in the direction of commercial, customer, quality or performance considerations" (pp. 247–8). The IBEC survey reports that 57 per cent of respondent companies have individual performance-related pay systems in operation (IBEC, 1998).

It seems logical to base pay upon performance. "In fact, the principle of merit pay is so logical that it seems almost ludicrous to criticise it" (Meyer, 1975: 39) since if "two individuals are performing the same job and one is substantially more effective than the other, the person with the superior contributions should surely be paid more" (Lowery et al., 1996: 27). However, despite the popularity that individual PRP schemes have achieved in the recent past they do, according to Appelbaum and Shapiro (1991), potentially have a number of flaws. Firstly, they result in a preoccupation with the task at hand and do not relate individual performance to the larger company objectives. Secondly, they work against creating a climate of openness, trust, joint problem-solving and commitment to organisational problem-solving. Thirdly, they can divide the workforce into those supporting the plan and those against the plan, which may create adversarial relationships. Among the other defects identified are improper design and implementation, practical difficulties in paying for individual performance, a possible lack of conviction on the part of workers that pay is really linked to performance and inadequate or inappropriate objectives, criteria and measures (Lowery et al., 1996).

Case Example 12.1: Individual PRP at Dell, Bewley's and Marks and Spencer

There are a number of firms that reward employees on the basis of their performance. Dell Computers have an end-of-year review which examines an employee's performance and pay increases are awarded on merit (O'Reilly, 1998). Also, Bewley's have recently introduced a performance-related pay system which provides for a pay increase of about 5 per cent for new entrants (Higgins, 1998a). Almost 1,000 employees at Marks and Spencer have recently backed a new performance-related pay system. This new system means that a top rate of £7.20 per hour will be paid for "exceptional" performers, which represents an increase of 8.5 per cent on the previous rate of £6.64 per hour (Frawley, 1998a).

Flat Rate plus Group/Team-based PRP

The greatest problem associated with individual PRP schemes is not, therefore, that they won't work, but rather, that they will focus the attention and effort in a direction which does not aid the achievement of the strategic goals of the organisation. In recognition of these and related problems, many organisations have turned to group/team bonus schemes. Armstrong et al. (1996) argue that there is growing scepticism regarding individual PRP and the growing trend is to reward teams or groups of employees rather than individuals.

Payment systems which pay a flat rate plus an incentive based on group/team or sectional performance are used where it is difficult to measure individual performance or to avoid some of the harmful side-effects of individual-based schemes while providing some incentive related to a measure of performance. Daly (1989) defines group bonus schemes as "the application of payment by results schemes to a group or team where the bonus payments are divided among team members on a pre-agreed basis". The figure that IBEC give for the extent that team-based pay is used in Ireland is 6 per cent (IBEC, 1998). As with individual schemes, there are a wide range of schemes from which an organisation may choose, but Ost (1990) feels that all incentives based on group or team work are subject to a number of guiding premises, namely:

- They always have one or more explicitly stated unit or firm-level performance goals that can only be achieved through teamwork;

- A team-based incentive system always contains a reward component that is contingent on the successful achievement of those goals;

- The reward must be perceived by the employee as resulting from contributions that they have made;

- The reward must be perceived as a fair reward;

- The behaviours and rewards offered must clearly signal what is meant by good performance.

Case Example 12.2: Team-Based PRP at IBM Ireland and in the UK

IBM Ireland paid an average bonus of about £2,400 to eligible employees in 1996. These bonuses were related to individual team and business unit performance (Higgins, 1997f). In the UK, organisations such as Lloyds Bank, Portsmouth Hospitals, NHS Trust and Sun Life pay team bonuses only. Others such as Norwich Union and Pearl Assurance pay both team and individual bonuses (Armstrong et al., 1996).

Piecework

This involves payment solely by performance. While it remains popular in specific areas (e.g. seasonal work in agriculture, outworkers) it is unacceptable to many employees and their organisations, since it provides no guarantee of a minimum income to satisfy basic requirements for both individual and societal well-being. However, 30 per cent of respondents to the IBEC survey reported that their pay system was based on piecework (IBEC, 1998).

Gainsharing Schemes

Gunnigle et al. (1997a) outline the main characteristics of gain-sharing schemes. They explain that these systems incorporate arrangements which reward employees for improvements in corporate performance through profit-sharing, share ownership or some other compensation mechanism. Gainsharing schemes differ from more traditional profit-sharing arrangements insofar as they link rewards based on corporate performance to changes in managerial philosophy and style which incorporate greater employee influence, involvement and participation. The direct effects of such schemes on employee motivation are believed to be poor because of their weak relationship with individual performance and lack of immediacy. However, they are seen as having important long-term benefits in increasing employee participation, awareness and commitment.

Most gainsharing schemes involve either profit-sharing or employee share ownership. Profit-sharing is a scheme under which employees, in addition to their normal remuneration, receive a proportion of the profits of the business. Profit-sharing may take a number of forms and it is largely at the discretion of the employer and employees to decide to what measure of profit the incentive should be tied, what percentage should be allocated and how it should be administered to employees. The IBEC survey reports that 22 per cent of respondents reported the existence of gain-sharing and profit sharing schemes in their company (IBEC, 1998).

Employee share ownership schemes involve the allocation of company shares to employees according to an agreed formula. Interest in Ireland in employee share ownership schemes has traditionally been relatively low (Long, 1988). The growth, small though it has been, is rooted in the Finance Acts of 1982–1984, which were driven by governmental commitment to "ensuring the success and efficiency of Irish industry and the prosperity and security of Irish workers for the future" by developing employee shareholding. More recent changes however, have served to undermine further the already narrow base of share ownership in Ireland. Bertie Ahern, the then Minister for Finance, removed tax incentives for employee share schemes. While resultant action was a dilution rather than removal, employees and employers may be more reluctant to adopt such schemes in what could be described as "an atmosphere of uncertainty".

Gainsharing arrangements, incorporating either profit or equity sharing, are generally linked to organisational attempts to increase employee involvement and commitment. Armstrong and Murlis (1988) enumerate a number of objectives underlying such schemes:

- To encourage employees to identify themselves more closely with the company by developing a common concern for its progress;

- To stimulate a greater interest among employees in the affairs of the company as a whole;

- To encourage better co-operation between management and employees;

- To recognise that employees of the company have a moral right to share in the profits they helped to produce;

- To demonstrate in practical terms the goodwill of the company to its employees;

- To reward success in businesses where profitability is cyclical.

Such schemes have become particularly popular in Britain and the US and have been linked to corporate successes on such criteria as market share, profitability and quality.

Case Example 12.3: Profit-Sharing at Henniges Elastomers, Taconic International, Union Camp and Dell Computers

There are many examples of organisations who have introduced gainsharing or profit-sharing schemes recently. Some commentators have suggested that the increase in gainsharing schemes can be associated with Chapter 9, more commonly referred to as the Partnership Chapter, of the Partnership 2000 agreement. For example, Henniges Elastomers, a German-owned automotive components firm located in County Mayo, has recently agreed to a gainsharing scheme which will come into play once there are significantly increased levels of performance at the plant (Higgins, 1998b).

Taconic International, Mullingar, has introduced a gainsharing scheme with effect from January 1998 (Higgins, 1998c). Taconic will base the gainsharing scheme on four criteria: first, the amount of scrap produced; second, the amount of late orders processed; third, the operating income; and fourth, the number of goods returned by customers. Union Camp, the Meath-based packaging manufacturer, also has a gainsharing scheme in place which makes two payments to employees in January and August of each year (Higgins, 1998d). Dell Computers is another company that has a programme in place where all permanent staff are eligible for profit-sharing, which is based on the company's performance (O'Reilly, 1998).

Case Example 12.4: Share Ownership at Dell Computers, Athlone Extrusions, Telecom Éireann and Campbell Bewley

Another form of gainsharing is employee share ownership. Along with the profit-sharing scheme at Dell Computers there is also a scheme in operation whereby employees can buy company shares at a reduced rate (O'Reilly, 1998). Athlone Extrusions, a plastics firm, offers an employee share ownership programme to employees, who own almost 8 per cent of the company (Higgins, 1998e). Negotiations at Telecom Éireann between management, unions and various other parties resulted in the agreement of the employee share ownership plan (ESOP) in March 1998 (Sheehan, 1998). Under the terms of the ESOP agreement, employees are to receive a shareholding of 14.9 per cent in the company. Irish Life have a share option scheme for staff which allows them to purchase 475,000 shares in five years' time at a price of £6.12 (Frawley, 1998b). It has been reported that the Campbell Bewley group are to offer free shares worth almost £2 million to those employees who have more than two years' service (Higgins, 1998j).

Competency/Skill-based Pay

The concept of skill-based pay is not particularly new, though organisations are now more readily endorsing skill and competency as a factor in determining employee pay (Murray and Gerhart, 1998; Vogeley and Schaeffer, 1995). Prominent examples of companies that have gone this route include Lapple in Ireland and, internationally, Procter and Gamble which has implemented such plans in some 30 plants and Polaroid which is attempting to become the first corporation to pay virtually all employees through skill-based plans. Lawler et al. (1992) reported that 51 per cent of large organisations were using skill or knowledge-based pay programmes in at least small portions of their organisations. An innovative reward system, it promotes workforce flexibility by rewarding individuals based on the number, type, and depth of skill mastered. Therefore, while the traditional job-based pay programmes have largely only considered the attributes of the task to be completed, skill/competency-based pay programmes have emphasised and sought to reward the work-related attributes of employees. According to O'Neill and Lander (1994), while relatively limited in application, it has been used for years under names such as pay for knowledge, competency pay, pay for skills and multi-skilled pay. While there may be slight technical differences in these terms, they are generally used interchangeably. Skill-based pay is a payment system in which pay progression is linked to the number, kind and depth of skill which individuals develop and use and the practice differs significantly from the reward systems discussed above, which calculate base pay according to the specific job and/or the employee's/team's performance. Armstrong and Baron (1995) highlight that it involves paying for the horizontal acquisition of the skills required to undertake a wider range of tasks, and/or for the vertical development of the skills needed to operate it at a higher level, or the in-depth development of existing skills. In this way, competency/skill based pay is directly linked to competency/skill based job evaluation described earlier and through paying for attributes such as knowledge and skills, an attempt is being made to direct the attention of employees to developmental opportunities and to encourage skill-seeking behaviour. In terms of operation, there will usually be a basic job rate for the minimum level of skills. Above this level, individuals will be paid for new skills acquired which assist them in performing their job as individuals or members of a team.

In evaluating the issue of linking competency and performance against objectives, Vogeley and Schaeffer (1995: 75–9) argue for a "change in philosophy" from one based on paying for "position" to an approach based on paying for "people". They suggest that linking competencies and objectives to pay can be achieved in four stages as follows:

1. Rating the employee's demonstrated competencies;

2. Rating the employee's achievement of objectives;

3. Plotting the ratings on an X- and Y-axis; and

4. Determining where the employee can be paid relative to the market.

Vogeley and Schaeffer (1995) propose the use of a "competencies and objectives grid" to aid managers vested with responsibility for deciding on pay levels for employees (relative to the "going rate" in the labour market). This approach, as outlined in Figure 12.4, utilises a five-point scale to identify the "level of competencies and achievement of objectives". This scale may be used to assess both the competency level of employees and their success in achieving previously agreed objectives, and culminates in a two-part score: competency levels (on the X-axis) and achievement of objectives (on the Y-axis). As we can see from Figure 12.4, employees rated as meeting all of the required competencies and objectives achieve a score of 3 on both dimensions. Thus, the "standard performer", who meets the competencies and objectives expected, will achieve an aggregate score of 6. Such performers will then be paid at the going rate in the labour market. Employees achieving scores of less than 6 are paid below the market level and those with scores greater than 7 are paid above the market level.

Figure 12.4: Linking Competency and Performance against Objectives

		1	2	3	4	5
OBJECTIVES	5 *Exceeds all objectives*	6	7	8	9	10
	4 *Exceeds most objectives*	5	6	7	8	9
	3 *Meets all objectives*	4	5	6	7	8
	2 *Meets some objectives*	3	4	5	6	7
	1 *Meets few objectives*	2	3	4	5	6
		1 *Meets few competencies*	2 *Meets some competencies*	3 *Meets all competencies*	4 *Exceeds most competencies*	5 *Exceeds all competencies*

COMPETENCIES

Key: ▨ Payment at market/going rate

▯ Payment below market/going rate

▰ Payment above market/going rate

O'Neill and Lander (1994) cite four major reasons for the increasing adoption of competency/skill-based pay:

1. The need to develop and maintain productive efficiencies through increased output, often combined with a leaner workforce and fewer levels of supervision;

2. The need to make more flexible utilisation of the existing workforce to cover absenteeism, turnover and production bottlenecks;

3. The need to support new technologies such as computer-aided manufacturing and new value systems such as total quality management;

4. The need to build higher levels of involvement and commitment, increase teamwork and provide more enriched jobs that provide greater reward opportunities for employees.

Table 12.9: A Comparison of Traditional and Skill/Competency-based Pay Systems

Traditional	Skill/Competency
Pay based on the current job that the employee performs	Pay based on the width and breadth of skills that the employee can perform
Multiple job classifications and rigid work rules	Typically less than four job classifications needed
Focus on formal feedback mechanisms one or two times per year that may not be directly tied to salary or career progression	Informal and formal feedback provided on an on-going basis. Feedback directly tied to salary or career progression
Employee involvement and job rotation not required	Requires job rotation and employee involvement systems
Jobs tend to be highly specialised and repetitive	Jobs allow greater task variety and decision-making autonomy

Source: Adapted from Recardo and Pricone, 1996: pp. 16–22.

Case Example 12.5: Skill-Based Pay at Lapple Ireland and Harty Steeline

Lapple Ireland, a Carlow-based engineering firm, recently agreed a deal with the unions to introduce a new pay system based on "skill points", which provides for an extra £3 per week for each skill achieved (Higgins, 1998f). "The skill-based system was devised by Lapple itself and a list of 25 different skills/competencies were drawn up. Each of the employees is guaranteed the opportunity to achieve at least three of these each year for the first two years of the five-year scheme" (Higgins, 1998f: 11). The Dublin-based sheet metal fabricator, Harty Steeline, is another company that has in-

troduced a skill-based pay system. The deal stipulates that the workers will receive an increase of 4 per cent in basic pay when they achieve all of a number of separate skill modules and there is provision for an increase of 0.8 per cent of basic pay per module (Higgins, 1998k).

Although skill/competency-based pay plans vary according to their objectives and components, all, according to Recardo and Pricone (1996), have the following key similarities. They typically exclude managers and cover hourly production as well as a number of white-collar staff groups (e.g. finance, engineering, management information systems and customer services). Most plans also contain a detailed curriculum of education to facilitate new skill acquisition. The more effective plans use small group improvement activities to promote improved understanding of the overall business and to facilitate desired employee behaviours. Many plans also use a structured process to certify the skill mastery of employees.

A concept that is closely related to skill- or competency-based pay is *broadbanding*. Broadbanding has been defined by Tyler (1998) as the elimination of all but a few, usually between three and ten, comprehensive salary bands. It therefore represents a compensation management strategy that involves consolidating several salary grades into fewer, wider pay bands. The bands have minimum and maximum monetary amounts. Hequet (1995) claims that broadbanding is one of the fastest growing compensation schemes in the US. He cites a study carried out by the American Compensation Association, which found that 78 per cent of the 116 respondents used broadbanding. One of the reasons for the growth in broadbanding is the trend towards delayering and flatter organisational structures (Sheehan, 1997d). Examples of companies that are using broadbanding in Ireland include IBM and Nortel. The IBEC survey reports that 11 per cent of the companies surveyed have skill-based, competency-based or broadbanding pay systems in operation (IBEC, 1998).

Case Example 12.6: Experts Differ Regarding Broadbanding

Broadbanding compresses numerous salary grades into fewer, wider pay bands. Those involved in the process articulate different benefits:

According to Dan Gilbert, a compensation consultant at General Electric Co., "Broadbanding has freed General Electric Co.'s employees and managers to use their talents where they are most needed for organisational success. Broadbanding reinforced the linkage between our internal culture and the external, competitive environment".

Susan Dempsey, a senior compensation analyst at Philip Morris Management, argues that "Pay systems are most effective when they support, rather than lead, organisational change. Consequently, unless appropriate performance-management structures, managerial empowerment, top management commitment and overall organisational readiness are in place, Philip Morris Management is not likely to implement broadbanding".

Kenan Abosch, a principal at Hewitt Associates, suggests that, from a manager's perspective, broadbanding can enhance the ability to compensate people for what they bring to the organisation beyond their job descriptions.

Source: Based on Compensation Report, *HRFocus*, August 1994.

The following Table provides some evidence of the increased popularity of incentive schemes in many Irish organisations.

Table 12.10: Use of Incentive Schemes in Ireland (%)

	Management		Prof/Technical		Clerical		Manual	
	1995	*1992*	*1995*	*1992*	*1995*	*1992*	*1995*	*1992*
Share options	23.0	22.8	13.8	13.6	11.5	9.2	9.6	8.8
Profit sharing	19.2	15.8	13.4	12.3	12.6	10.5	10.0	10.1
Group bonus	21.1	14.9	15.7	12.7	16.1	11.0	15.3	14.0
Merit/PRP	51.3	49.1	44.8	42.5	36.8	29.4	15.3	13.2

Source: Gunnigle, Morley, Clifford and Turner (1997)

The growth of incentive schemes in Ireland has been inexorably linked to the trend towards relating pay more closely to performance. However, the take-up of incentive schemes is correlated with organisational ownership. Thus, in the Irish context, US-owned organisations on the whole appear far more likely to utilise incentives than their counterparts, particularly Irish indigenous organisations, who demonstrate a low take-up across the range of incentives (Gunnigle et al., 1997a).

Overall, it is evident that incentive schemes may take a number of forms and the question facing most organisations is not which type of incentive scheme to pick but rather, which package of methods will be most successful in fulfilling the organisation's strategic goals. In implementing incentive schemes, Balkin and Gomez-Mejia (1987) highlight a number of issues that must be addressed:

1. The number of different forms to offer;

2. The relative importance of each form;

3. The proportion of the workforce to which each form may be applicable.

The responses to the above questions will be determined by the objectives of the incentive system itself and whether the organisation sees enhanced performance, cost containment or employee retention as the overriding objective of the incentive system. It must be realised, however, that while incentive schemes represent a potentially effective tool, they are not a panacea for all organisational ills. Incentive schemes will only fulfil their true potential if existing barriers to individual/group/organisational effectiveness have been removed. Such schemes do not represent a mechanism for compensating wage differentials, nor for overcoming inadequacies in the production system.

FRINGE BENEFITS

Gunnigle et al. (1997b) note that, in general, fringe benefits (both statutory and voluntary) are estimated to constitute an additional 25–30 per cent on top of basic weekly pay for manual grades. For clerical, administrative and managerial categories, a figure of 15–35 per cent should be added. However, the percentage add-on is primarily related to the level of fringe benefits voluntarily agreed at company level, particularly items such as company cars, pensions, health/insurance cover, and sickness benefit and can, therefore, vary considerably between organisations.

The nature of fringe benefits provided to employees also varies considerably between organisations and are normally the result of voluntary agreements between employees (or their representatives) and management. Major differences also exist between blue- and white-collar workers. Some general guidelines on the nature of fringe benefits in Irish organisations are outlined below. (See also Chapter 18 for further details on legal requirements with regard to leave and Chapter 21 for family-friendly initiatives, particularly with regard to childcare.)

Maternity/Paternity/Adoptive Provisions

Female employees are entitled to a minimum period of 14 weeks' unpaid maternity leave, in accordance with the terms of the Maternity Protection of Employees Act, 1981, and the Worker Protection (Regular Part-time Employees) Act, 1991, during which leave a social welfare benefit is available. Amendments to the maternity legislation in the form of the Maternity Protection Act (1994) were introduced to satisfy our obligations under EC Directive 92/85. While many of the entitlements provided by the Maternity Protection Act, 1994, already existed under the Maternity Protection of Employees Act, 1981, there were significant changes with regard to who is covered by the Act, provision for payment for the time-off for natal care visits and health and safety leave provisions under certain circumstances. In terms of leave coverage, any individual under a contract of employment is entitled to protection under the Maternity Protection Act, 1994. This includes apprentices, employees on probation and employment agency workers. The Act entitles a pregnant employee to 14 weeks' consecutive leave, with a minimum of four weeks' leave before the last day of the expected week of confinement and a minimum of four weeks' leave after the last day of the expected week of confinement. There are exceptional provisions for early, late and still-births.

The Adoptive Leave Act, 1995, entitles female employees and, in certain circumstances, male employees, to employment leave for the purpose of child adoption. It provides for a minimum of ten consecutive weeks of adoptive leave. Notice of at least four weeks must be given in writing to the employer of the employee's intention to take adoptive leave. The employee is entitled to additional adoptive leave for a maximum period of four consecutive weeks, commencing immediately after the end of the adoptive leave.

The Parental Leave Act, 1998, was introduced to implement Council Directive 96/34/EC of June 1996 on the framework agreement on parental leave concluded by UNICE, CEEP and the ETUC. According to this Act, an employee who is the natural or adoptive parent of a child shall be entitled to leave from their employment for a period of fourteen weeks. The child for which leave is being sought must be born or adopted on or after 3 June 1996. Parental leave must be taken before the child in question reaches his/her fifth birthday. Notice of intention to take parental leave must be given in writing at least six weeks before the anticipated commencement date.

The Parental Leave Act, 1998, also makes provision for *force majeure* leave with pay, where the employee is entitled to employment leave for urgent family reasons such as injury or illness of a family member. An employee is entitled to *force majeure* leave if the person who is ill or injured is: a person of whom the employee is a parent or adoptive parent; the spouse of the employee or a person with whom the employee is living as husband and wife; a person to whom the employee is *in loco parentis*; a brother or sister of the employee. With regard to *force majeure* leave, the employee must give notice to the employer that they have taken *force majeure* leave as soon as possible after taking the leave. *Force majeure* leave can consist of one or more days on which, but for the leave, the employee would be working in the employment concerned, but will not exceed three days in any period of twelve consecutive months or five days in any period of 36 consecutive months.

Case Example 12.7: Paternity Leave at the ESB

The ESB introduced a Paternity Leave scheme in 1997 which entitles fathers to three days' paid paternity leave at the time of the birth or adoption of a child (Sheehan, 1997c). The leave will be paid when the following conditions are met: the three days must be taken consecutively, either immediately after the birth or adoption of the child or immediately after the child's release from hospital.

Childcare Facilities

A small number of Irish organisations provide childcare facilities for staff. Currently, there are about 50 state-financed nurseries sponsored by local health boards, mostly for families with special needs. There are four semi-state nurseries in Dublin and approximately ten in third-level educational institutions.

Career Breaks

Provision for career breaks is rare in Irish private sector organisations. However, career break schemes are becoming increasingly widespread in the public sector. Where schemes exist in the private sector, they are normally shorter than those available in the public sector — generally one to two years.

Case Example 12.8: Career Breaks in the Civil Service

An example of a career break scheme in operation is the civil service, where civil servants will be able to take two career breaks of five years each under a revised scheme agreed recently between the Department of Finance and the public sector unions. If the employee wants to avail of the second career break, they must return to work for a period at least equal to the length of the first break (IRN, 1998). The minimum career break is six months and can be extended in blocs of six months not exceeding five years.

Holidays

The great majority of organisations provide annual leave entitlements greater than the statutory minimum of 15 days. This may vary from 18 to 23 days, with the average being 20 days per annum. Legislation provides for eight public holidays per annum. Some companies also grant Good Friday, which is not a public holiday, as a privilege day off.

Additional Holiday Pay/Bonuses

Practice varies enormously on this issue. However, many larger private sector companies make such payments. These are typically in the form of either additional holiday pay (from one to several weeks' pay), end-of-year bonus (Christmas bonus – one to several weeks' pay) and discretionary payment/gifts for special occasions (service, marriage). For example, Intel usually pays an employee cash bonus twice-yearly. For the second half of 1997, the bonus was 13.5 days' pay for eligible employees (Higgins, 1998h). The IBEC survey found that 37 per cent of respondents have a system of pay bonuses which are related to company performance and 4 per cent responded that they had Christmas and annual bonuses in operation (IBEC, 1998).

Managerial Incentive Schemes

A large number of organisations operate incentive bonus schemes for managerial grades. However, there are considerable variations in the level of payment and the grades involved. Typical criteria for basing incentive payment upon include company performance (particularly profitability), sales or output.

Sick Pay

There is no legal obligation on organisations to provide sick pay to employees. However, a large number of organisations provide some kind of sick pay scheme during defined periods of absence from work due to illness or injury. The 1997 IBEC Annual National Survey for the Manufacturing and Wholesale Distribution Sectors reported that 74 per cent of companies surveyed indicated that manual workers were paid when out sick and 87 per cent indicated that staff grades were paid when out sick (IBEC, 1997).

Case Example 12.9: Sick Pay at Arlington

Arlington, the Portarlington-based cosmetics and jewellery manufacturer, introduced a new sick pay scheme in 1997, which provides 25 days of sick pay cover in the first year of the scheme at 90 per cent of the difference between social welfare and normal net pay for all full-time employees with more than one year's service. It is expected to increase to 30 days per calendar year if the scheme proves to be working well. (Higgins, 1997b)

Sick pay schemes normally provide that once a particular service requirement is fulfilled, employees receive full pay (inclusive of social welfare payments) for a finite period (which may vary from a few weeks to a year). It is normal practice for employers to take into account the total benefit payable to employees from Social Welfare, as well as income tax rebates, in calculating how much the company should pay to make up the total employee benefit during periods of absence due to illness or injury. This may be achieved either by paying the total benefit through payroll and recovering social welfare cheques from employees or by paying a "top up" element with the employee retaining social welfare benefits.

Health Insurance

The State provides free health care to persons on very low incomes via the "medical card" system. There is no legislative requirement on employers to provide employees with the coverage of a private medical employment scheme. However, health insurance is available to individuals through the Voluntary Health Insurance Board (VHI), BUPA Ireland and other providers.

Canteen Facilities

There are no statutory requirements for the provision of canteen facilities. However, the Safety in Industry Act, 1980, requires that "where more than five people are employed, there must be adequate provision for boiling water and taking meals". In practice, the majority of larger employers provide some form of canteen facilities. These may be subsidised by up to half the economic costs of meals. Tea/coffee facilities may also be provided at a subsidised rate.

Sports/Recreation Facilities

These are typically restricted to larger organisations, who may contribute towards some of the cost of their operation.

Company Cars

The majority of larger organisations provide company cars for senior management and, in some instances, for sales staff. The cost of such cars varies considerably according to range, but is normally from IR£11,000 to IR£26,000. Where cars are supplied, the company normally pays for insurance, tax, petrol and service. Where employees use their own cars on company business, firms normally pay a mileage allowance, typically varying from 25p–60p per mile, depending on engine size. Company cars are taxed as benefits-in-kind at a cash equivalent of 20 per cent of original market value. This is reduced where the employee pays the cost of fuel (3 per cent), insurance (2 per cent), service (2 per cent) and tax (0.5 per cent).

Pension and Death-in-Service Schemes

There is no legislative requirement on employers to provide employees with a pension scheme. However, most larger organisations have pension schemes, particularly for managerial grades. It is becoming increasingly popular to provide death-in-service benefits to employees in conjunction with the pension scheme. The majority of these schemes are contributory. Most schemes are based on a normal retirement age of 65, although some are based on retirement at 60. Seventy-seven per cent of respondents to IBEC's 1997 survey indicated that staff grades were covered by a pension scheme and 69 per cent of companies stated that manual workers were covered by a pension scheme. The normal rate of employee contribution was 5 per cent of annual earnings. Company pension schemes are governed by the Pensions Act, 1990.

Case Example 12.10: Pension and Death-in-Service Benefits at Glen Dimplex, Tente Ireland and Leonische Ireland

---

The Glen Dimplex Company, Bitech Engineering, has a pension scheme whereby the employer and the employee pay equal contributions of 2.1 per cent of annual salary. The pension contribution is 2 per cent and the extra 0.1 per cent relates to a death-in-service benefit (Higgins, 1997c). Tente Ireland, a German-owned furniture-making company, has a similar pension scheme in operation, to which the employer and the employee contribute 3 per cent of annual salary. This scheme also provides a death-in-service benefit to the value of the retirement fund at the date of death and twice the worker's annual base salary (Higgins, 1998i). Leonische Ireland, a cable manufacturer located in Birr, offers a death-in-service benefit of three times the annual salary for its employees, which is paid subject to the basic pay at the time of bereavement (Higgins, 1997d).

In Ireland, the State provides a basic pension at age 65. This is related to means, but is independent of income and is non-contributory. There is no income-related state pension scheme. Private occupational schemes provide earnings-related pensions to supplement state entitlements, and the State actively encourages the introduction of such schemes through various tax concessions. The Pensions Act, 1990, is designed to protect the rights of members of private occupational pension schemes. It provides for the control of private schemes through a regulatory body, the Pensions Board, and deals with funding, benefits and information disclosure in relation to private occupational pension schemes.

Other Benefits

Some companies give employees a discount on the company's products or services, or occasionally provide them free of charge (see Case Example 12.11). Few companies provide employees with low interest or interest-free loans. Some companies are beginning to pay bonuses to employees who recommend suitable candidates for vacant positions within the firm. The bonus is paid after a number of months have elapsed, if the new recruit has proved satisfactory. For example, Tellabs, the Shannon-based telecommunications equipment manufacturer, has introduced a new scheme where employees who recommend new recruits who subsequently prove satisfactory are entitled to a lump-sum bonus of between £500 and £3,000, depending on the position the candidate filled (Higgins, 1997e).

Case Example 12.11: Discount Schemes in the Retail Sector

In the retail sector in recent times, there have been novel incentives introduced for employees. For example, Tesco Ireland introduced a scheme for its 7,000 employees whereby they receive a discount on purchases within the store to the value of 10 per cent (Sheehan, 1997b). In 1998, Dunnes Stores, one of Tesco's leading rivals, introduced a similar scheme, offering employees with over one year's continuous service a discount of 15 per cent on purchases within the store. The maximum weekly spend for which the discount applies is £100 (Frawley, 1998c).

In relation to the evidence on the use of benefits in Ireland, the Cranfield-University of Limerick study indicates an increase in the utilisation of non-money benefits (Gunnigle et al., 1997b). Such an increase, however, has not been universal. Privately owned organisations, particularly of US and UK origin, were far more likely to have such schemes in operation than public and indigenous companies. Recognition of a trade union was also found to have an impact, with those organisations not recognising unions reporting a much greater tendency to include non-money benefits in the reward package than those organisations in which there was a union presence.

Table 12.11: Change in the Use of Non-Money Benefits (%)

	Ireland	Britain	United States
Increase	15.6	35.7	31.3
Decrease	0.7	–	2.1
No change	79.4	64.3	62.5
Don't know	4.3	–	4.2
	n = 141	*n = 14*	*n = 48*

Source: Gunnigle, Heraty and Morley (1997).

CONCLUSION

This chapter has focused on the area of reward management. An organisation's reward package is seen to consist of pay (base wages), various incentives (performance-related rewards) and fringe benefits. Organisations will provide various mixes of these three components in order to attract, retain and motivate their employees. While developing an effective reward package can prove a rather difficult task, if the reward package satisfies basic needs, as well as being flexible enough to meet individual employee needs, and has equity, fairness and trust as its central tenets, it can be effective.

Job evaluation is the most common method of determining the relative worth of jobs, and a variety of analytical and non-analytical schemes are available. With the exception of competency-based approaches, job evaluation techniques focus solely on the job, rather than on the individual performing it.

Numerous options are available to an organisation in the type of pay, incentive and benefits package it might adopt. Control over costs remains fundamental. While flat rate systems still prevail, various individual and group/team incentive schemes have grown in popularity in recent years, largely in response to competitive pressures. The survey carried out by IBEC in 1997 reports that there is a growing trend to reward employees on the basis of performance rather than on a fixed-rate system. With such a development, it is necessary to consider the potential drawbacks of adopting performance-related pay as outlined earlier, especially with regard to individual PRP, and to realise that PRP is not a panacea.

References

Appelbaum, S. and B. Shapiro (1991), "Pay for Performance: Implementation of Individual and Group Plans", *Journal of Management Development*, Vol. 10, No. 7.

Armstrong, M. and A. Baron (1995), *The Job Evaluation Handbook*, London: Institute of Personnel and Development.

Armstrong, M. and H. Murlis (1988), *Reward Management: A Handbook of Salary Administration*, London: Kogan Page.

Armstrong, M., L. Curry and M. Thatcher (1996), "How Group Efforts Can Pay Dividends", *People Management*, Vol. 2, No. 2, pp. 22-7, January.

Balkin, D. and L. Gomez-Mejia (1987), *New Perspectives on Compensation*, Englewood Cliffs, NJ: Prentice-Hall.

Beer, M., B. Spector, P. Lawrence, D. Mills and R. Walton (1985), *Human Resource Management: A General Manager's Perspective*, New York: Free Press.

Benge, E. (1944), *Job Evaluation and Merit Rating*, Washington: US National Foreman's Institute.

Biddle, D. and R. Evenden (1989), *Human Aspects of Management*, London: Institute of Personnel Management.

Bowey, A. (1975), "Installing Salary and Wage Systems", in A. Bowey (ed.), *Handbook of Salary and Wage Systems*, London: Gower.

Casey, B. (1994), "Employers' Provision of Pensions and Sick Pay: Evidence from the 1990 Workplace Industrial Relations Survey", *Applied Economics*, Vol. 26, No. 3, pp. 229–38.

Compensation Report (1994), "Expert Opinions Differ Regarding the Benefits of Broadbanding", *HRFocus*, August, Vol. 71, No. 8, pp. 14–15.

Daly, A. (1989), *Pay and Benefits in Irish Industry*, Dublin: Federation of Irish Employers.

EFILWC (1997), *New Forms of Work Organisation: Can Europe Realise its Potential?*, Dublin: European Foundation for the Improvement of Living and Working Conditions.

EFIWLC (1999), *EPOC: Direct Employee Participation in the Public Services*, Dublin: European Foundation for the Improvement of Living and Working Conditions.

Feldman, D. and H. Doerpinghaus (1992), "Missing Persons No Longer: Managing Part-time Workers in the 1990s", *Organizational Dynamics*, Vol. 21, No. 1, pp. 59–73.

Fowler, A. (1988), "New Directions in Performance Pay", *Personnel Management*, November.

Fowler, A. (1991), "Performance Related Pay", *Personnel Management Plus*, June.

Fowler, A. (1996), "How to Pick a Job Evaluation System", *Personnel Management*, Vol. 42, No. 3, 8 February.

Frawley, M. (1998a), "Marks and Spencer Set New PRP Rate for Retail Sector", *Industrial Relations News (IRN)*, No. 16, 23 April, pp. 14–15.

Frawley, M. (1998b), "Irish Life's New Share Option Scheme for Staff", *Industrial Relations News (IRN)*, No. 27, p. 3, 9 July.

Frawley, M. (1998c), "Dunnes 15 per cent Discount Scheme Aimed at Retaining Staff", *IRN*, No. 38, p. 5, 8 October.

Gerhart, B. and G. Milkovich (1990), "Organizational Differences in Managerial Compensation and Firm Performance", *Academy of Management Journal*, Vol. 33, pp. 663–91.

Goffee, R. and R. Scase (1986), "Are the Rewards worth the Effort? Changing Managerial Values in the 1980s", *Personnel Review*, Vol. 15, No. 4.

Gomez-Mejia, L. and D. Balkin (1992), *Compensation, Organizational Strategy and Firm Performance*, Cincinnati, OH: South-Western Publishing.

Grace, P. and A. Coughlan (1998), "Reward Systems and Reward Strategies" in W. Roche, K. Monks and J. Walsh (eds.), *Human Resource Strategies: Policy and Practice in Ireland*, Dublin: Oak Tree Press.

Grafton, D. (1988), "Performance-related Pay: Securing Employee Trust", *Industrial Relations News (IRN)*, No. 44, 17 November.

Gunnigle, P. and P. Flood (1990), *Personnel Management in Ireland: Practice, Trends and Developments*, Dublin: Gill and Macmillan.

Gunnigle, P., P. Flood, M. Morley and T. Turner (1994), *Continuity and Change in Irish Employee Relations*, Dublin: Oak Tress Press.

Gunnigle, P., N. Heraty and M. Morley (1997a), *Personnel and Human Resource Management: Theory and Practice in Ireland*, Dublin: Gill and Macmillan.

Gunnigle, P., M. Morley, N. Clifford and T. Turner (1997b), *Human Resource Management in Irish Organisations: Practice in Perspective*, Dublin: Oak Tree Press.

Hequet, M. (1995), "Not Paid Enough? You're Not Alone", *Training*, Vol. 32, No. 11, November, pp. 44–55.

Higgins, C. (1997a), "Tarkett: New Gainsharing Scheme", *Industrial Relations News (IRN)*, No. 24, 19 June, p. 2.

Higgins, C. (1997b), "Arlington's New Sick Pay Scheme Covers 300 Workers", *Industrial Relations News (IRN)*, No. 47, 11 December, p. 3.

Higgins, C. (1997c), "Glen Dimplex Firm Introduces New Pension Scheme", *Industrial Relations News (IRN)*, No. 13, 27 March, p. 9.

Higgins, C. (1997d), "Leonische Ireland Agrees Death-In-Service Benefit", *Industrial Relations News (IRN)*, No. 39, 16 October, p. 5.

Higgins, C. (1997e), "Tellabs £3,000 Recruitment Incentive Part of a Wider Scheme", *Industrial Relations News (IRN)*, No. 24, 22 May, p. 6.

Higgins, C. (1997f), "IBM Pays Average Bonus of £2,400", *Industrial Relations News (IRN)*, No. 13, 27 March, p. 5.

Higgins, C. (1998a), "Bewley's Performance Pay Provides Up to £5.50 Per Hour", *Industrial Relations News (IRN)*, No. 29, 23 July, p.5.

Higgins, C. (1998b), "Henniges Agrees Gainsharing, Leave Improvements", *Industrial Relations News (IRN)*, No. 12, 19 March, p.3.

Higgins, C. (1998c), "Taconic Introduces Gainsharing Scheme", *Industrial Relations News (IRN)*, No. 44, 20 November, p.3.

Higgins, C. (1998d), "Union Camp Agreed Gainsharing, Teamworking, Pay Increase", *Industrial Relations News (IRN)*, No. 5, 29 January, p. 3.

Higgins, C. (1998e), "Athlone Extrusions: Share Scheme Exceeds Expectations", *Industrial Relations News (IRN)*, No. 6, 5 February, p. 2.

Higgins, C. (1998f), "Lapple Ireland: Skill-Based Pay, P2000 'Plus' Deal Agreed With SIPTU", *Industrial Relations News (IRN)*, No. 35, 17 September, pp. 11–12.

Higgins, C. (1998g), "Parental Leave Legislation: Amendments", *Industrial Relations News (IRN)*, No. 36, 24 September, pp. 12–13.

Higgins, C. (1998h), "Intel Workers to Get 13.5 Days Pay as Bonus", *Industrial Relations News (IRN)*, No. 4, 22 January, p. 7.

Higgins, C. (1998i), "Tente Introduces New Pension Scheme", *Industrial Relations News (IRN)*, No. 10, 5 March, p. 7.

Higgins, C. (1998j), "Campbell Bewley Provides £2m Share Bonus", *Industrial Relations News (IRN)*, No. 25, 25 June, p. 5.

Higgins, C. (1998k), "Harty Steeline Agrees Skill-Based Pay, WCM", *Industrial Relations News (IRN)*, No. 3, 15 January, p. 8.

Hoevemeyer, V. (1989), "Performance Based Compensation: Miracle or Waste", *Personnel Journal*, July.

IBEC (1997), *Annual National Survey on Pay and Conditions of Employment for the Manufacturing and Wholesale Distribution Sectors*, Dublin: IBEC.

IBEC (1998), *Survey of Reward/Payment Schemes*, Dublin: IBEC.

Industrial Relations News (IRN) (1998), "Civil Servants Can Now Extend Career Breaks by a Further 5 Years", *Industrial Relations News (IRN)*, No. 32, 27 August, p. 3.

Kessler, I. and J. Purcell (1991), "Performance Related Pay: Objectives and Application", *Human Resource Management Journal*, Vol. 2, No. 3, pp. 16–33.

Kohn, A. (1993), "Why Incentive Plans Cannot Work", *Harvard Business Review*, September–October.

Lawler, E., S. Mohrman and G. Ledford (1992), *Employee Involvement and Total Quality Management*, San Francisco: Jossey Bass.

Levine, D. (1993), "What Do Wages Buy?", *Administrative Science Quarterly*, Vol. 38, No. 3, pp. 462–84.

Long, P. (1988), "A Review of Approved Profit Sharing (Trust) Schemes in Ireland and the UK", Dissertation, Dublin Institute of Technology.

Lowery, C., M. Petty and J. Thompson (1996), "Assessing the Merit of Merit Pay: Employee Reactions to Performance Based Pay", *Human Resource Planning*, Vol. 19, No. 1, pp. 26–38.

Mahoney, T. (1989a), "Multiple Pay Contingencies: Strategic Design of Compensation", *Human Resource Management*, Vol. 23, No. 3, pp. 337–47.

Mahoney, T. (1989b), "Employment Compensation Planning and Strategy" in R. Gomez-Mejia (ed.), *Compensation and Benefits*, ASPA/BNA Series No. 3, Washington, DC: Bureau of National Affairs.

Markham, S. (1988), "Pay-for-Performance Dilemma Revisited: Empirical Example of the Importance of Group Effects", *Journal of Applied Psychology*, Vol. 73, No. 2, pp. 172–80.

Marsden, D. and R. Richardson (1994), "Performing for Pay? The Effects of Merit Pay on Motivation in a Public Service", *British Journal of Industrial Relations*, Vol. 32, No. 2, pp. 219–42.

McMahon, G. (1998), "Managing Reward Systems for Effective Perform-ance", in W. Roche, K. Monks and J. Walsh (eds.), *Human Resource Strategies: Policy and Practice in Ireland*, Dublin: Oak Tree Press.

McBeath, G. and N. Rands (1989), *Salary Administration*, 4th edition, London: Gower.

Meyer, H. (1975), "The Pay for Performance Dilemma", *Organisational Dynamics*, Vol. 3, No. 1, pp. 39–50.

Milkovich, G. and J. Newman (1990), *Compensation*, Homewood, IL: Irwin.

Mooney, P. (1980), *An Inquiry into Wage Payment Systems in Ireland*, Dublin: Economic and Social Research Institute/European Foundation for the Improvement of Living and Working Conditions.

Murray, B. and B. Gerhart (1998), "An Empirical Analysis of a Skill-Based Pay Program and Plant Performance Outcomes", *Academy of Management Journal*, Vol. 41, No. 1, pp. 68–79.

O'Neill, G. and D. Lander (1994), "Linking Employee Skills to Pay: a Framework for Skill-Based Pay Plans", *ACA Journal*, Winter.

O'Reilly, A. (1998), "Dell's 'High Interaction' HR Model", *Industrial Relations News (IRN)*, No. 41, 29 October, pp. 24–7.

O'Sullivan, C. (1996), "Time Ripe for the Irish Annual Hours Contract?", *IR Data Bank*, Vol. 14, February.

Ost, E. (1990), "Team-based Pay: New Wave Incentives", *Sloan Management Review*, Spring.

Pearse, J. (1987), "Why Merit Pay Doesn't Work: Implications for Or-ganisation Theory" in D. Balkin and L. Gomez-Mejia (eds.), *New Perspectives on Compensation*, Englewood Cliffs, NJ: Prentice-Hall.

Quarstein, V., B. McAffee and M. Glassman (1992), "The Situation Oc-currences Theory of Job Satisfaction", *Human Relations*, Vol. 45, No. 8, pp. 859–74.

Randell, G. (1994), *Performance Appraisal in Personnel Management: A Comprehensive Guide to Theory and Practice in Britain*, Oxford: Blackwell.

Recardo, R. and D. Pricone (1996), "Is Skill-based Pay for You?", *SAM Advanced Management Journal*, Vol. 61, No. 4, pp. 16–22.

Sanfilippo, F. and G. Weigman (1991), "A Compensation Strategy for the 1990s", *Human Resource Professional*, Vol. 4, No. 1, Fall.

Sargeant, A. (1990), *Turning People On: The Motivation Challenge*, London: Institute of Personnel Management.

Schuler, R. (1995), *Managing Human Resources*, 5th edition, St. Paul: West Publishing.

Sheehan, B. (1997a), "1997 in Review: Looking Back on a More Turbulent Year", *Industrial Relations News (IRN)*, No. 48, 18 December, pp. 14–17.

Sheehan, B. (1997b), "Quinnsworth Staff to Get Novel 10 per cent Discount on Purchases", *Industrial Relations News (IRN)*, No. 34, 11 September, p. 2.

Sheehan, B. (1997c), "ESB Introduces Paid Paternity Leave Scheme", *Industrial Relations News (IRN)*, No. 31, 21 August, p. 8.

Sheehan, B. (1997d), "'Broadbanding' Pay System Encourages 'Sideways' Movement", *Industrial Relations News (IRN)*, No. 6, 6 February, p. 17.

Sheehan, B. (1998), "Telecom: ESOP and Partnership Deal Promise a Radical Departure", *Industrial Relations News (IRN)*, No. 14, 2 April, pp. 12–16.

Tyler, K. (1998), "Compensation Strategies can Foster Lateral Moves and Growing in Place", *HR Magazine*, Vol. 43, No. 5, April, pp. 64–71.

Vogeley, E. and L. Schaeffer (1995), "Linking Employee Pay to Competencies and Objectives", *HRMagazine*, Vol. 40, No. 10, pp. 75–9.

Williams, M. and G. Dreher (1992), "Compensation System Attributes and Applicant Pool Characteristics", *Academy of Management Journal*, Vol. 35, No. 3, pp. 571–96.

Wood, S. (1996), "High Commitment Management and Payment Systems", *Journal of Management Studies*, Vol. 33, No. 1, pp. 53–78.

CHAPTER 13

ESTABLISHING AND MAINTAINING EFFECTIVE COMMUNICATIONS

Eugenie Houston

UNDERSTANDING WHAT WE MEAN BY COMMUNICATION

As organisations become increasingly fast moving, the need for effective employee communications has never been greater. Key issues involve determining who is responsible for employee communications; devising and implementing a formal communications policy; and setting a communications budget. First, however, we must ask: what is communication? It is about getting the right information to the right people at the right time. There have been an increasing number of articles written about "knowledge management", which has been defined as the management of the information, knowledge and experience available to an organisation — its creation, capture, storage, availability and utilisation — in order that organisational activities build on what is already known and extend it further (Mayo, 1998). Mayo highlights three driving forces behind the development of the term knowledge management: namely, an interest among organisations in capturing their intellectual assets; a focus on the learning organisation; and the increased use of information technology. Later in this chapter, we will look at some examples of the use of information technology as a communications tool.

A survey of 430 organisations across the US and Europe revealed that organisational culture and people's commitment are the two major barriers to *knowledge transfer* (Skyrme and Armidon, 1997), while Chase (quoted in Mayo, 1998), having surveyed UK best practices, concluded that the most commonly experienced obstacles include:

- The culture of the organisation;

- Lack of senior management commitment;

- Lack of time;

- Lack of rewards and recognition;

- Lack of ownership;

- Lack of skills.

McGuckian (1998) points out that the results are not very different to studies on potential barriers to *effective communications* carried out in the 1980s and early 1990s (Saunders, 1984; Smith, 1990), namely that the most commonly reported obstacles to successful communications include:

- The culture of the organisation;

- Lack of senior management commitment;

- Lack of time;

- Fear of leakage;

- Lack of ownership;

- Lack of skills.

Despite the use of different terminology and the distinction between communication and knowledge management outlined above, the analysis on trends in knowledge management and communication highlighting the convergence of the two makes a powerful argument that knowledge management is "a rose by any other name" and that knowledge management is effectively the same thing as communication. The differences between the two could, of course, equally be argued. Attention is drawn here to the common ground so that readers new to the area of employee communications will not see communication and knowledge management as totally unrelated areas, since it makes sound commercial sense for the human resource professional to have input into both.

If communication is about getting the right information to the right people at the right time, then it is about the transfer of knowledge. Knowledge is generally categorised into three areas:

- Internal knowledge of an organisation, which includes patents, documentation, processes, systems and culture;

- External knowledge, which includes brands, customer feedback, relationships and reputation;

- Employees' knowledge — the people available to the organisation, their education, skills, experience.

To facilitate effective communications, you must generally facilitate open access to any of these types of knowledge to those who need or want it, obviously within reason and with due regard to sensitive corporate negotiations, for example. In other words, getting the right information to the right people at the right time. Depending on the size of your organisation and the resources available to you for communication, you may select any of a number of options to achieve this objective. As you work towards this, it is worth remembering that one of the greatest assets your organisation has are its human assets, that is, employees' knowledge (see Chapter 3). A great deal can be gained by accessing the tacit knowledge of employees, the kind of knowledge which an individual gains through experience, by making mistakes and learning from them. This type of knowledge is unlikely to be accessed electronically but by creating a communications environment based on trust, motivation and informal dialogue. The Employee Relations Index described later in this chapter provides a straightforward yet highly effective mechanism for creating that environment.

Clearly, all of the categories of knowledge are highly relevant to employees and organisations in creating a learning environment and information technology plays an increasingly important role in facilitating this knowledge transfer. The key point to remember in establishing and maintaining effective communications is that one of the most critical factors impacting upon the success or failure of communications is the people; people need to see that the benefits of actively participating in a learning organisation exceed the investment of time and personal risk involved. An important step towards creating that level of trust is to evaluate closely confidential or commercially sensitive information and determine whether it really is all that confidential. The less secrecy that pervades within an organisation, the higher the potential for effective communication. While there may be valid commercial reasons for secrecy, this is one example of how the culture of an organisation may present a barrier to effective communication.

EMPLOYEE COMMUNICATIONS IN IRELAND

Anybody working in the human resources area will be aware through their work of the increased attention that has been paid to communication in recent years. This trend is borne out by research carried out between April and June 1997 by Drury Communications in conjunction with IPD Ireland. This benchmarking survey provides a clear picture of the current state of play in internal communications in Ireland. Thirty companies and 1,350 of their front-line employees participated in the exercise, which used a two-tiered questionnaire approach: a detailed questionnaire for the manager responsible for communications within the organisation and a shorter, anonymous questionnaire for the employees.

The benchmarking exercise sought to establish the extent to which clear communication objectives were set, where the responsibility for communications lay, staffing levels, budget allocation and training levels.

Figure 13.1: Survey on Internal Communications − Results

The National Survey on Internal Communications was conducted by Drury Communications in conjunction with IPD Ireland between April and June 1997 among 30 companies and 1,350 front-line employees. The findings of this benchmarking survey show that in these organisations:

- Around £113 per employee is spent on internal communications each year;

- Responsibility for internal communications is mostly based in the human resources function and at a senior level;

- Fewer than half of managers are required to set aside more than two hours per month to communicate;

- Two-thirds of employees are told how the organisation is performing on at least a quarterly basis;

- Team briefings are used more than newsletters;

- Communications skills training is a key strategy;

- Use of measurement techniques tends to be limited;

- Employees feel that they are kept informed about their job, but do not know what is happening in other areas of their organisations;

- Employees do not feel encouraged to contribute to any part of the organisation beyond their direct job.

The results show that, in the majority of companies surveyed, the responsibility for employee communications lies with the human resources department. In 18 of the 30 companies, the person with responsibility for internal communications reported directly to the CEO, indicating the strategic role of communications. Most of the companies dedicated half of one full-time position to internal communications. The ratio of internal communicators to employees varied greatly, depending on the size of the organisation, averaging 1:812.

The companies indicated that their communications activities included providing information, involving employees, damage control, leading change, team building, boosting morale, contributing to strategy and writing and editing communications materials. The participating companies suggested that they would ideally like their roles to include helping to steer corporate goals and to gain commitment to those goals; providing communications skills; providing coaching/role-modelling in communication for both management and employees.

In most of the organisations surveyed, the day-to-day responsibility for internal communications is the domain of the line manager. Of the 30 organisations, 22 stated that they require their line managers to set aside time formally on a monthly basis to communicate with their employees, varying from two to ten hours per month. Organisations establishing a communications programme from scratch should certainly include this as a positive practice.

To show your organisation's commitment to employee communications, you need to have an internal communications policy and make employees aware of this. Of the 30 organisations benchmarked, only five had a formal internal communications policy in place that was communicated to all employees. A further ten had a formal policy in place but had not communicated it and almost half of the companies had no policy in place at all. It is difficult to see how communications objectives can be achieved without a policy in place.

Once a policy is in place, the next step in to ensure that adequate financial resources are available. The benchmarking survey found that an average of IR£113 (€143.51) is spent on communications activities each year, with organisations spending between IR£10,000 and IR£50,000 each year.

Figure 13.2: Key Tasks in Implementing a Communications Programme

---

- Set objectives
- Seek employees' input
- Define communications policy and communicate to all employees
- Agree budget
- Ensure all team leaders and line managers are clear about their objectives
- Provide communications training

DEFINING A COMMUNICATIONS PROGRAMME

Step 1

The first step to establishing an effective communications programme for your organisation is to assess the current state of communication. You may find the following checklist helpful.

Figure 13.3: Communications Check-Up

		Yes	No	Sometimes	Don't Know
1.	Are your employees aware of the aims and objectives of the organisation and do they support them?	❑	❑	❑	❑
2.	Are your employees aware of their own role in meeting the aims of the organisation?	❑	❑	❑	❑
3.	Do all employees have access to managers through a well-established procedure when they want to ask questions or make changes?	❑	❑	❑	❑
4.	Is staff turnover higher than desirable in any part of the organisation?	❑	❑	❑	❑
5.	Is absenteeism higher than might be reasonably expected?	❑	❑	❑	❑
6.	Do formal grievances or complaints frequently occur without management knowing about them well in advance?	❑	❑	❑	❑
7.	Are employees happy to approach their immediate manager when they have a problem?	❑	❑	❑	❑
8.	Is communications regarded as an integral part of each line manager's role?	❑	❑	❑	❑
9.	Do managers feel comfortable with their given roles in communications?	❑	❑	❑	❑
10.	Do senior managers have a good insight into the operational difficulties faced by staff?	❑	❑	❑	❑

		Yes	No	Sometimes	Don't Know
11.	Does the organisation encounter widespread resistance to necessary changes?	☐	☐	☐	☐
12.	Do most people rely on the grapevine to hear about what is happening in the organisation?	☐	☐	☐	☐

Source: Effective Employee Communications, IBEC/Drury Communications Ltd. (1996)

This checklist will give you a good idea of the current status of communications within your organisation.

Step 2

The next step is to find out directly from employees what they think. Remember, your communications programme needs to gain their trust, motivate them to participate and communicate. Depending on the size of your organisation, there are numerous options to choose from. Bearing in mind that evaluation needs to be ongoing and improvements measurable, the following employee attitude survey, the Employee Relations Index (ERI), is a very strong starting point and is used in many companies. My experience of using it to start formalised communications programmes at both UPS and Esat Telecom was that it is a simple idea that generates a very high level of trust and results, provided the agreed action steps are taken.

The survey is anonymous and comprises 16 statements. You can substitute the questions with others appropriate to your organisation. A scale of 1–5 is used with 1 representing "strongly disagree" and 5 representing "strongly agree".

Figure 13.4: Employee Relations Index

	Employee Relations Index					
	For each statement, please circle the response that mostly accurately reflects how you feel	Strongly Disagree	Disagree	Hard To Decide	Agree	Strongly Agree
1.	Management want to know about service & operational problems so they can be fixed.	1	2	3	4	5
2.	Management is sincere in its attempts to understand the employee's point of view.	1	2	3	4	5
3.	Management provides recognition for employees who do a good job.	1	2	3	4	5
4.	Management will act on many of the important issues identified by this survey.	1	2	3	4	5
5.	[Company name] treats its employees with respect.	1	2	3	4	5
6.	The procedures for job openings are fair.	1	2	3	4	5
7.	Management creates an environment of openness and trust.	1	2	3	4	5
8.	[Company name] gives prompt answers to my problems/requests.	1	2	3	4	5
9.	I am aware of the procedure for promotion.	1	2	3	4	5
10.	I have received adequate training to use the tools provided to carry out my job.	1	2	3	4	5

	Strongly Disagree	Disagree	Hard To Decide	Agree	Strongly Agree
11. The reasons for changes in policies and procedures are adequately explained.	1	2	3	4	5
12. I am informed on a timely basis about changes that affect me.	1	2	3	4	5
13. The people in my work area co-operate to get the job done.	1	2	3	4	5
14. I have enough opportunities to let management know how I feel.	1	2	3	4	5
15. [Company name] is receptive to ideas that would improve our business.	1	2	3	4	5
16. I know how well my area achieves its business goals.	1	2	3	4	5

A positive selling point with regard to the ERI is that the results are measurable, so that continuous improvement or disimprovement can be monitored. Once you have analysed the results, select the three best and three worst practices and communicate these to employees at focus groups. It is very important to be completely honest with employees about the results of the survey so they understand nothing is being hidden. This will help build trust in the communications process and in the communicators.

Allow about an hour for each focus group, with between eight and twelve participants. The human resources professional should facilitate these sessions. However, it needs to be clear that the focus group is a meeting between the manager and employees. If it can be arranged for the Chief Executive or other directors to participate in at least some of the focus groups, this can send a

powerful message to employees about the company's commitment to communication.

Be sure to state clearly the purpose of the focus group: to
communicate the results of the survey, concentrate on the three
best and three worst practices and to hear directly from the employees their suggestions for change. Emphasise that employees
are expected to take ownership for ensuring that the suggestions
are followed up. At the end of the meeting, summarise who
agreed to take ownership for which actions and the agreed time-
frame, publish the action plan within as short a time-frame as
possible — ideally the next day — and then ensure the follow-up
takes place and is communicated. The Employee Relations Index
can be repeated periodically, every six months or annually, allowing sufficient time in between for the agreed actions to be
completed.

Figure 13.5: Benefits of using Employee Relations Index

- Effective evaluation of current level of communication

- Survey anonymous

- Results measurable

- Results provide quantifiable basis for focus group discussions

- Emphasis is on line managers and employees taking responsibility for action plans

---

Step 3

Having heard directly from employees what their concerns are
and equally importantly what their proposed solutions are, you
should now define your organisation's internal communications
policy and communicate it. You could, of course, complete this
before the Employee Relations Index and present it as a *fait accom-
pli*; however, you are likely to find a much higher level of com-

mitment and trust on the part of employees if they feel they have had some input into it. You can then find yourself in the position of communicating positive changes, such as the introduction of the policy, *as a result of employee feedback.* The following case example shows a sample communications policy. Important points to note when drafting such a policy are included here in boxes at the right-hand side.

Case Example 13.1: Sample Communications Policy in Company A

Our communications objectives are:
- *To establish a communications structure that ensures all employees are informed in a timely manner;*
- *To establish a forum to elicit employees' suggestions and ideas for improving business processes.*

We often say how important teamwork is at Company A. Each individual has valuable experience, skills and knowledge which can benefit their colleagues and the company. Our communications policy is structured in a way that allows you plenty of opportunity to participate as a team member and to share and gain the information you need when you need it. Here are some of the ways in which you can participate:

Open Door Policy
There are very few secrets at Company A. Information is freely available to you and you are free to ask any questions you may have at any time.

> *Keep in mind that concerns about commercial sensitivity and lack of time for communication can lead to a perception of secrecy.*

Work Teams
Briefly describe your organisation's team structure, if applicable.

> *Cross-functional teams are a way of transferring tacit knowledge*

Recommend-a-Friend
Because you are a valued employee, we recognise your contribution in recommending candidates for employment with Company A. You will be rewarded for recommending a candidate who is subsequently hired by the

> *The Drury/IPD benchmarking survey showed that employees do not feel encouraged to contribute to any part of the organisation beyond their own job – this is one solution.*

company. Details are available from your team leader or manager or on the Intranet.

One-on-Ones

These are face-to-face meetings which you schedule regularly with your manager, or other team leader colleagues and for which you set the agenda. The purpose is to discuss concerns or ideas, improve the quality of feedback and ensure open, honest and regular communication.

> *International studies show that just 41% of employees believe communication to be two-way (IBEC/Drury, 1996).*

Employee Relations Index

The Employee Relations Index (ERI) is a means of gathering employee feedback (similar to the way we use customer satisfaction indices) within the company. The ERI will take place at least once a year when you will be invited to participate in an anonymous survey. The results of this survey will be used as the starting point for a series of focus group discussions. The purpose of the ERI is to provide you with a forum for raising comments, opinions and ideas and for proposing solutions to any concerns. Focus groups should conclude with agreed action plans for follow-up by named individuals or groups.

> *Studies on the success of communications show that 69% of managers and 43% of employees believe that management within an organisation will act on employees' ideas (IBEC/ Drury, 1996).*

> *To maintain effective communications, employee feedback must be acknowledged and followed up; if an idea cannot be actioned, say so. If it can, link the credit back to its source.*

Staff Meetings

Each manager or team leader will meet regularly with their team to provide up-to-date business information and other relevant information and to provide an opportunity to respond to queries regarding individuals or the team.

> *90% of employees indicate their immediate manager as their preferred source of information (IBEC/Drury, 1996). The Drury/IPD survey found that 73% of organisations require managers to set aside time every month for communication.*

Employee Lunches

On a regular basis a group of individuals from different departments will be invited to meet with [one of the functional directors, COO, CEO] over lunch to exchange ideas and experiences.

> *Include this as a budget item. Schedule and publish the dates in advance. Perhaps hold a competition for employees to suggest a name for regular lunch meetings.*

Communications Meetings

Every quarter, all employees will come together to hear an update on how the company is performing. The Chief Executive/ General Manager will give you a summary of Company A's progress and its business plans. Please don't hesitate to ask any questions you may have.

> *Quarterly communications meetings provide a good opportunity to dispel any perception of excessive secrecy within an organisation. Consider using video conferencing for employees in other locations.*

Corporate Events

Company A is proud of its corporate sponsorship. Current sponsorship includes events such as [include event names]. Our corporate sponsorship provides an opportunity to show the high standards at Company A and from time to time you may be asked to participate in these events.

> *Another opportunity to provide employees' scope for involvement outside their normal job. Examples include UPS' involvement of employees at the Olympics. At Esat Telecom, employees participate d in the company's TV advertisements.*

Employee Presentations

This is an opportunity for you to present to a cross-functional group of colleagues on a project you have worked on.

E-mail

In addition to the various meetings at which you will participate, you will also receive additional information on what is going on through regular e-mail notices. Please don't hesitate to ask your manager if you have any questions about these.

> *Studies show that employees are suffering e-mail overload. See the section on training below.*

Intranet

Not all companies have yet developed an Intranet site for employees. Others are already at advanced stages, such as Dell who use their Intranet to manage employee benefits. If your organisation does not yet have an Intranet, this is a good opportunity for an IT-led cross-functional team.

TRAINING

Once a solid communications programme has been established, it needs to be maintained. There are several points to bear in mind in maintaining communication — it needs to be timely and relevant and commitments made need to be met. By providing team leaders and line managers with the necessary skills to communicate effectively, you will increase the sustained effectiveness of your communications activities. The Drury/IPD survey found that two-thirds of the organisations who responded provide formal communications training, mainly to supervisory and middle management groups. The training most commonly given was to provide skills in leadership, facilitation, presentation, writing and in the use of communications technology such as e-mail.

A separate report, called *Nil By Mouth*, compiled as a result of a joint study by Investors in People UK and Andersen Consulting, warns that failing to adapt to the use of e-mail, the Internet, intranets and video-conferencing could mean a drop in productivity and disenfranchised employees. It indicates that three-quarters of all communications are now conducted electronically, but that many employees suffer from information overload from the excessive volume of unnecessary, badly written messages. The report states that fewer than half of employees have been trained in communicating electronically and that just 27 per cent had received training in how to handle information overload.

However, organisations using electronic communication in Ireland seem to be getting the balance right. As with all of its other employee practices, Intel Ireland's *Circuit* Intranet site strikes a good balance of content, up-to-date information, business and local site news. The intranet is accessible to all employees and training is available to everyone in how to use it. AIB's intranet achieves the same objective. Amdahl Ireland has recently changed its communications process from one which had an emphasis on management and communications meetings to a process using an intranet to consolidate information in a communications database supported by scheduled interactive sessions with employees.

Case Example 13.2: Amdahl's Internal Communications Process —
Summary

- *To deliver information directly to managers and employees both in-house and off-site primarily through e-mail;*
- *To arrange meetings as required to clarify and reinforce critical messages such as significant policy changes;*
- *To allow employees view a repository of information on various business and employee relations matters (policies, pensions, benefits) on a communications database;*
- *To receive employee inputs along with concerns/issues/fears and provide prompt closure, facilitated by HR, through a communications database;*
- *To provide facility for employees to raise questions with closure facilitated by HR. Questions and answers (anonymous) accessible on a communications database by all employees;*
- *To provide interaction with employees through scheduled coffee sessions run by HR; coffee sessions for assignees/ business travellers in customer sites run by senior managers. Open issues raised transferred to communications database, closure facilitated by HR;*
- *To provide quarterly platform for managers and other key personnel to interact and promote dialogue on business matters.*

Reproduced with the permission of Amdahl Ireland

There are many reasons why Amdahl's process is successful. Amdahl has a track record of successful and effective internal communications, as is evident from its low turnover of staff. The process is clearly documented and communicated to all employees; consequently, both managers and other employees understand exactly what is expected. Electronic communications are well and clearly written and the human resources department ensures that training is provided in this. All of the information transferred, including questions raised by employees, is centralised in the communications database where questions and answers are presented on an anonymous basis. It is also worth noting that the forerunner to the communications database was the HR electronic post box, so employees were already accustomed to raising questions electronically and had a high level of trust in the way their questions were handled. Further, the responsibility for facilitating the process is clearly defined and resides with HR. Finally, a balance between technology and human interaction has been found. While communication is primarily transferred electronically, this is supported by face-to-face interaction. Overall, Amdahl's internal communications process is an excellent example of best practice in employee communications.

COMMUNICATING MAJOR CHANGE

Two of the biggest changes that an organisation may have to communicate are often redundancies or change of ownership. In either case, it is possible to retain employee support but this largely depends on what is communicated and the manner of the communication. If your organisation has to communicate downsizing, then those staff members who are involved in internal communications must be involved at the earliest possible stages of initiatives. Rumours usually start well before an organisation is ready to communicate its proposals and often attract media attention. It is essential that employees hear information from their employer, even if it is bad news, before they see it on television or read it in the papers. The recent Fruit of the Loom example, where an uncertain future was played out in the media for quite a long time before concrete information was forthcoming, is a case in point.

Ideally, organisations should keep their employees appraised if the company is in difficulties. That way, the likelihood of a shock announcement can be reduced. If bad news is likely, it is better to explain in advance the business case for the uncertainty, outlining what options are being considered and what the likely outcomes

may be. It is important to explain how the news impacts individuals. The following example of Finelist does not relate to
downsizing but to the merger of two organisations; however, the
organisation's template for communicating major change could be
adapted to many other situations.

Case Example 13.3: Communicating the Merger at Finelist

*One of the most common failures of any acquisition or merger is the failure
to integrate two organisations together quickly enough. Communications
plays a very important role in a merger. It is vitally important to plan the
stages of communications in advance. Best practice on how to achieve this is
best illustrated by an example, one of the best of which is that of Finelist
Group plc. Finelist in the UK's leading distributor, retailer and marketer of
automotive products to trade and retail customers. The Group has grown
organically and by making strategic bolt-on acquisitions. It comprises some
800 sites, 8,000 employees within five divisions and a turnover in excess of
St£500 million.*

*The moment an acquisition is agreed, Finelist's acquisition team springs
into action. Having acquired more than 60 companies in the past four years,
the rapidly expanding company has developed a well-polished 100-day action plan. Their key objectives are to ensure that employee morale does not
go into a tailspin and to communicate the message that it is business as
usual. Finelist always endeavours to complete a deal on a Friday, so that the
acquired company's employees will start the week under new ownership.
Within an hour of the takeover, Finelist's chairman, Chris Swan, and his
integration team go on site at the headquarters of the newly acquired company. Their purpose is to introduce Finelist, reassure key management staff
of their intentions and explain the benefits of being part of the group. They
recognise that it is much more difficult to rebuild low employee morale than
to prevent it from happening. The employees of the newly acquired company
are invited to the meeting under the guise of a sales or promotions meeting,
or something that is familiar to them.*

*On the first day, employees are given a take-away video about how their
company will fit into Finelist's plans and a leaflet welcoming their company
to the group. This gives them something to take home to their families. It includes a question-and-answer section reassuring all staff that they will continue to be employed on the same terms as before. The leaflet also sets out*

the employment benefits of the takeover. Presentations are made to groups of 15 to 20 staff by human resources managers. Finelist finance department specialists establish links to the acquired company's accounts department to enable performance data to be included in the daily group trading report from Day 2. During Days 3 to 5, there are one-to-one meetings with all staff. Letters are sent to all suppliers explaining the change of ownership and customers are sent a notification together with a special-offers leaflet bearing the unchanged company name. Any change of trading name is delayed until the last phases of the 100-day programme, by which time customers and employees have been reassured that the changes are positive. The company describes Days 6 to 100 as a period of handholding and reports that, having won the confidence of new employees, they are invariably very helpful. At the end of the 100-day period, the newly acquired company can generally be taken off the company's weekly review of new acquisitions.

Finelist's Questions and Answers Leaflet

Why does Finelist want to purchase Bancrofts?
Finelist is rapidly growing in a changing market. It is growing organically and by acquiring good businesses. By good business we mean those that complement and strengthen our existing activities. These businesses have quality workforces and can benefit from the resources provided by Finelist. As well as being a well-established and well-respected business, Bancrofts clearly meets these criteria.

What will happen to jobs?
All employees will continue to be employed as prior to the acquisition, on continuous employment and on the same terms and conditions. We expect the business to continue in the same manner as before it was part of the Group. However, Finelist's profitable growth and expansion will also mean many more career development opportunities for employees.

What can I say to customers and suppliers?
All major customers and suppliers will be contacted with a prepared statement. From the customer's point of view, it should be "business as usual".

When will I get paid?
You will continue to be paid under your existing agreement and there are no plans to change this at present.

What shall I do now?
Business as usual. Concentrate on offering a good service to your customers. Keep working, secure in the knowledge that Finelist is acquiring Bancrofts because it believes it to be an excellent business.

Note: *include in your Q&A sheet the contact names and numbers of those responsible for handling employee and press queries.*

Reproduced with the permission of Finelist Group plc.

Communicating Change Requires

- Good information, obtained in advance

- Thorough planning

- Focused, dedicated resources at the highest level

- Demonstrable commitment to employees, featuring personal, professional communication

CONCLUSION

The examples and case studies examined in this chapter are intended to provide you with a choice of options to select from in establishing your organisation's communications programme. Perhaps the best advice if you are establishing a communications programme from scratch is to keep it relatively simple; to maintain the interest of your employees, it is crucially important to deliver on what you set out to achieve. It is well worth taking a long-term view as you select the elements of your communications programme, as your activities will need to be sustainable. In view of the results of studies showing that employees prefer communication to be two-way, it may be best from the outset to involve employees as much as possible. In summary, you need to establish a budget for your communications activities; seek regular employee feedback to ensure that your communications programme is meeting its objectives; ensure that communication is two-way, timely and relevant; and accept that the forum which your organisation selects now may change as the level of communication within the organisation grows.

References

Drury Communications/IPD (1997), *National Survey on Internal Communications*, Dublin: Drury Communications (also reported in *IPD News*, Vol 4., No. 4.

IBEC/Drury Communications (1996), *Effective Employee Communications: A Practical Handbook on Communicating at Work in Ireland*, Dublin: IBEC/Drury Communications.

Mayo, A. (1998), "Memory Bankers", *People Management*, Vol. 4, No. 2.

McGuckian, R. (1998), "When Thoughts Run Free", *Decision Magazine*, Vol. 3, No. 4.

Saunders, G. (1984), *The Committed Organisation: How to Develop Companies to Compete Successfully in the 1990s*, Aldershot: Gower.

Skyrme, D. and Armidon, D. (1997), *Strategic Communications Management*, Issue 4, p. 5.

Smith, A. (1990), "Bridging the Gap between Employees and Management", *Public Relations Journal*, November, pp. 20–1.

Whitehead, M. (1998), "Managers Encouraged to Rage against the Machine", *People Management*, Vol. 4, No. 20.

CHAPTER 14

INDUSTRIAL RELATIONS PARTNERSHIP AT THE LEVEL OF THE WORKPLACE[1]

John O'Dowd

INTRODUCTION

Partnership is the current preferred approach to workplace industrial relations — at least at the level of public rhetoric — of Irish governments, employer and trade union organisations as well as a range of other public bodies such as Forfás and the Labour Relations Commission. Serious doubt has been cast on the extent to which the practice matches up to the rhetoric (Roche and Geary, 1998). There is, however, no questioning the fact that in many organisations, in both the private and public sectors, employers and trade unions have taken to this new approach as a way of improving upon their traditional adversarial relationships. As might be expected with any significant industrial relations development, there is a growing international and Irish academic literature on partnership, including surveys and case studies (see

---

[1] This chapter is based on a previous work, *Employee Partnership in Ireland: A Guide for Managers* (O'Dowd, 1998a) as well as on my experience since 1997 as a Joint Director of the National Centre for Partnership which was established to facilitate partnership in the private and public sectors (NCP, 1998). This experience has included working as a consultant and facilitator to organisations that were engaged in the design and implementation of partnership systems.

references). The principal questions addressed in this literature are:

- What is partnership and how does it work?

- What different forms of partnership are there?

- What conditions give rise to the adoption of partnership strategies on the part of employers and trade unions?

- What are the outcomes of partnership for employers and trade unions?

There is also a growing popular or "how to" literature on partnership; for example, the guidelines produced by the Irish Business and Employers' Confederation (IBEC, 1998), the Irish Congress of Trade Unions (ICTU, 1997) and the Irish Productivity Centre (IPC, 1998). In addition, both ICTU and IBEC have allocated specific responsibility for partnership development to senior executives in the light of their commitment to partnership in Partnership 2000. They are also co-operating in a number of EU-funded initiatives through the Irish Productivity Centre and on their own. It is not the objective of this chapter to provide a comprehensive discussion of the literature, but rather to provide an overview of some of the main arguments and findings coming from the academic research while concentrating on a "how to" approach to partnership development.

DEFINITION OF PARTNERSHIP

The term "partnership" is used in Ireland in a broad sense within the field of industrial relations. The term does not imply any fixed agenda or institutional arrangement. Partnership is voluntary and not statutory. There is evidence of several contrasting approaches to partnership within both private and public sectors. Partnership may involve direct forms of employee involvement such as teams and project groups, as well as indirect forms such as joint steering groups and other forms of joint consultation and decision-making. Most of what we know of workplace partnership in Ireland comes from unionised organisations. While partnership was confined until recently, for the most part, to private companies and commercial state companies, there is currently a remarkable growth of partnership arrangements in the civil service, local government and the health sectors.

Trade unions are inclined to use the term "partnership" as applying only in the context of trade union recognition. Employers, on the other hand, while acknowledging pluralist forms of partnership, maintain that there can be "partnership" between employers and employees without trade union involvement. The difference in emphasis derives from the interest position of each side. However, the language of Partnership 2000, the current national agreement on pay and social and economic development, which strongly promotes the adoption of partnership approaches to management–union–employee relations within the workplace, is deliberately non-explicit in respect to collective representation as a prerequisite for partnership. In this agreement, partnership is defined (page 62) as

> an active relationship based on recognition of a common interest to secure the competitiveness, viability and prosperity of the enterprise. It involves a continuing commitment by employees to improvements in quality and efficiency; and the acceptance by employers of employees as stake holders with rights and interests to be considered in the context of major decisions affecting their employment. Partnership involves common ownership of the resolution of challenges, involving the direct participation of employees/representatives and an investment in their training, development and working environment.

It is this latter reference to "employees/representatives" which leaves open the possibility of partnership in both union and non-

union settings, a point which is confirmed in the guidelines produced by IBEC (1998).

Looked at as a specific approach to organisational change in
unionised settings, partnership may be contrasted with more traditional approaches such as managerial prerogative, collective
bargaining and direct employee involvement (Roche et al., 1998).
Indeed, Cooke (1990: 3) defines partnership in terms of its separation from collective bargaining, as:

> co-operative efforts between union representatives and plant
> management that are outside traditional contract negotiations
> and contract administration.

Partnership is perhaps best seen not so much as a complete alternative to collective bargaining but rather as a system that includes
new forms of employee and trade union involvement in problem-
solving and decision-making alongside collective bargaining.

In a review of industrial relations models in Ireland, Roche
(1998) describes partnership as a process that challenges traditional collective bargaining as the dominant form of workplace
governance. It embraces a wider agenda of issues, including business and product plans, the design of production systems and
work organisation. It focuses on problem-solving within a consensus decision-making framework and it involves employee and
trade union acceptance of employer productivity goals, thus
questioning the traditional adversarial assumption that the interests of employers and employees are fundamentally in conflict.
Table 14.1 provides a summary of the main differences between
the traditional collective bargaining approach and the new partnership approach.

Table 14.1: Differences between Traditional Collective Bargaining and Partnership Approaches

	Traditional Collective Bargaining System	**Partnership Approach**
Goals and Objectives	Focus on areas of conflict and disagreement	Focus on common goals
Participants	Dominated by "professionals", such as personnel officers and union officials	Includes the IR "professionals", but in addition a broad range of managers and employees
Focus	Pay and work condition issues	Organisational improvement and development; a "gain-sharing" approach to pay and work conditions
Process	Two sides bargaining across a table	A group problem-solving around a table separate from collective bargaining
Ethos	Adversarial	Co-operative
Typical Outcome	Decisions relating to economic or power issues	Decisions relating to organisational improvement and new ways of working

Source: O'Dowd (1998a)

FACTORS INFLUENCING DECISIONS TO OPT FOR PARTNERSHIP

What factors have influenced the adoption of partnership by employers and trade unions? Not surprisingly, the international literature identifies a range of factors, both internal and external to organisations, as potential influences on employers and trade unions. The main emphasis is on the nature of competition, on the internal features of the bargaining relationship and on the strategic choices of employers in the industrial relations and human resource management areas.

The kinds of factors that are cited as potential influences on the adoption of a partnership strategy by employers and trade unions include:

- The requirements of new manufacturing processes and technologies;

- Presence in international markets;

- Supportive public policies, legislation and the authority of state industrial relations institutions;

- Employee and management perceptions of the effectiveness of the current bargaining system;

- Corporate values;

- Trade union values and strategies.

Current research into the incidence of partnership in Ireland, however, suggests the absence of any strong patterns of association between the factors discussed in the international literature, which is mainly American and is almost exclusively based on manufacturing industry, and the presence of partnership arrangements in Irish workplaces (Roche et al., 1998). It is necessary, therefore, to treat with caution findings from the US or elsewhere when considering the development of partnership in Ireland and the conditions likely and not likely to support its growth.

Nevertheless, it is worth pointing out some of the key arguments arising from this literature. Cooke (1990) maintains that the decision to co-operate must satisfy two general conditions. Firstly, management, the workforce, and union leadership must perceive that the benefits from proposed joint programmes outweigh the costs. Potential benefits include increased productivity for employers, enhanced rewards from gainsharing for employees and greater input into management decisions for the union. Potential costs include perceived loss of authority for management, loss of employment due to productivity increases for employees, and perceived co-optation by management for unions. Secondly, each party must perceive that the net benefit from co-operation is greater than the net benefit derived from the exclusive utilisation of relative power through collective bargaining and conflict. Table 14.2 summarises the main potential benefits and costs of partnership.

Table 14.2: Potential Costs and Benefits of Partnership

Potential Benefits	Potential Costs
• Improved organisational performance • Lower costs • Improved communications and relationships with employees and the union • Fewer grievances and disputes • Stronger commitment to company goals • Reduced absenteeism and turnover • Increased organisational flexibility • A better approach to change	• The cost of training managers, employees and union representatives • Perceived loss of authority and status of managers • Perceived loss of authority and status for union representatives • Loss of employment for middle-managers and supervisors • The amount of scarce time spent in new activities and bodies • Wider implications for the organisation, such as new reward systems

Source: O'Dowd (1998).

My own experience of working with organisations in both the private and public sectors that are developing partnership indicates that the introduction of partnership certainly can be related to the external and internal pressures generated by particular competitive environments. At the same time, there has to be a management and trade union *decision* to go down this road. In the case of Irish plants of multinational companies, there is pressure to compete for scarce resources with other plants and there are cases, such as Bausch and Lomb, where Irish plants have gained a competitive edge by developing co-operative relations between local plant management and trade unions. The vulnerability of such plants to external decision-making can create the basis for management and unions to "circle the wagons" through a partnership agreement. In the financial services sector, partnership is being developed in a context of considerable mergers and acquisitions activity. AGF-Irish Life Holdings and Royal Sun Alliance are cases in point. In the state financial sector, the publicity surrounding the proposed merger of ACC Bank and Trustee Savings Bank has stressed the importance of a partnership approach.

In the case of state companies such as Telecom Éireann, ESB, RTE, An Post and others, there is increasing pressure to restructure and to reduce costs in the context of loss of monopoly status, developing competition and, most recently, preparation for partial privatisation through strategic alliances and public flotation. In the fully funded public services, the development of partnership may be viewed as a response to the "new public management" agenda (O'Dowd and Hastings, 1998; Roche, 1998). A history of damaging industrial relations can also provide the impetus towards partnership, as is seen in such different organisations as AIB and the Western Health Board. Indeed, one of the most powerful forces influencing the adoption of partnership can be a common perception among managers and union representatives that their current bargaining system, even where there are few actual disputes, is simply ineffective in meeting their separate and mutual interests.

DIFFERENT FORMS OF WORKPLACE PARTNERSHIP

The international literature on forms of partnership is not extensive at this stage of its development. Cutcher-Gershenfeld and Verma (1994), in a widely quoted study, have categorised what they regard as the three main innovations in workplace governance this century as a "non-union high commitment system", statutory works councils and what they term "joint union–

management governance". They define "joint union–management governance" as:

> . . . an ongoing formal process where workers and their immediate supervisors or union and management leaders bear joint responsibility for making decisions. The scope of decision-making may be narrow (i.e. it may involve a single issue) or it may be broader, covering a whole range of issues.

Writing in the Irish context, Roche and Turner (1998) pick up this theme of joint governance. They identify three broad forms of partnership. These are described as "joint decision-making models", a "consultation-focused model" and "transitional models". In the "consultation-focused" model, the employer seeks to involve the union and employees in management plans through increased flows of information. This is done without any new joint management–union bodies and without any new ground-rules which would give unions additional rights of co-decision over any areas of company policy. The increased flows of information take place alongside collective bargaining. This form of partnership may be accompanied by the introduction by the company of various forms of direct employee involvement such as teams, project groups, appraisal systems, etc.

The "joint decision-making model" is a form of "joint governance" in which "collective bargaining channels continue to co-exist with the joint structures, but the lines between the two channels may become blurred in ways that neither party finds unacceptable" (Roche and Turner: 1998: 18). "Joint governance" is a form of partnership that may develop in situations where there is a strong trade union and where competitive pressures force the parties into acceptance that current adversarial approaches are no longer viable from an employer or employee perspective.

The "transitional models" include instances where partnership emerges in the form of "new procedural ground-rules for the conduct of dialogue, the purpose of dialogue and the scope of dialogue" (Roche and Turner, 1998). These instances involve the exploration by management and trade unions of new possibilities while existing realities are dealt with through the collective bargaining system. The authors stress that these models are tentative and not mutually exclusive.

Gunnigle (1998) categorises partnership arrangements along a number of dimensions — level of trade union involvement, level of involvement in strategic decision-making, and level of sophistication of new institutional arrangements, if any. Using these dimensions, he identifies three models. "Strategic union–management partnerships" are characterised by institutional arrangements that involve unions in both strategic and operational decision-making. This usually involves worker directors and below-board representation. The most significant instances are in the state companies, Telecom Éireann being a recent case in point (Telecom Éireann, 1997). "Operational union–management partnerships" are characterised by union acceptance of change in work practices in return for participation in operational decision-making, such as changes in work organisation. The crucial difference between this model and the former is that there is no scope for worker or union involvement in strategic decision-making. Gunnigle's third model is "operational employee–management partnership", which is found in the non-union sector and which bears the main hallmarks of union–management partnerships but without trade union involvement.

THE INCIDENCE OF PARTNERSHIP IN IRELAND

The most authoritative research available indicates that partnership is only found in a minority of organisations in Ireland (Roche and Geary, 1998). A survey of companies across industrial sectors (including commercial state companies but excluding construction) established a number of figures that are worth citing (see Table 14.3).

Table 14.3: Incidence of Different Forms of Employee and Representative Involvement in Unionised Irish Organisations

Form of Involvement	Incidence (% of workplaces)
Total Quality Management	71.1
Team work	59.0
Quality circles	15.0
Ad hoc task forces	45.5
Joint consultative committees/works councils	12.7
Partnership as a means of introducing change in cases of:	
• Changes to work practices	20
• Changes to payment systems	17
• Changes to working time arrangements	16
• New products and services	8
• Setting business targets	3
• Formulating plans for mergers and acquisitions	1

Source: Roche and Geary (1998)

The survey findings show quite a high incidence of TQM, team work and *ad hoc* task forces but a lower incidence of quality circles and works councils. The exercise of managerial prerogative emerged as the most common approach to organisational change, with direct employee involvement being preferred by management to new forms of trade union and employee involvement under the heading of "partnership". It remains to be seen to what extent the figures for partnership will have increased as a consequence of Partnership 2000 and the various promotional activities undertaken by government, the National Centre for Partnership and IBEC and ICTU themselves. Anecdotal evidence from conferences and specialist publications such as *Industrial Relations News* indicates some increase in the incidence of partnership agreements in unionised firms and in the commercial state companies, but no figures are available. The UCD survey (Roche and Geary, 1998) did indicate an increased intention on the part of managers to use both partnership and direct employee involvement for handling operational changes.

THE OUTCOMES OF PARTNERSHIP

Outcomes may be looked at from the perspectives of employers, employees, trade unions and the state. Criteria for effectiveness could include:

- *For employers*: economic performance as measured by cost reductions, improvements in productivity and absence of disputes;

- *For employees*: greater job security, better pay and conditions, more satisfying work, including training and personal and professional development;

- *For trade unions*: more information and influence within the workplace and more satisfaction among members; at the national level, a more positive image of trade unions in a dynamic economy;

- *For the State*: a more competitive economy, modernised public services, less industrial conflict and an image that is attractive to foreign investors.

Unfortunately, there is no comprehensive research on such issues in Ireland. Certainly, the European Foundation's EPOC project (EFILWC, 1997) indicated a very high level of satisfaction among Irish managers with direct forms of involvement when these were introduced in co-operation with trade unions. Three sets of indicators were used in the measurement of economic effects. These were: *economic* (cost reduction, reduction of throughput time, improvement of quality of product or service, increase in output), *labour cost variables* (decrease in sickness, decrease in absenteeism), and *employment levels* (reduction in number of employees, reduction in number of managers).

In the perception of the managers who responded, all forms of direct participation had a strong economic impact — in the case of quality, nine out of ten respondents reported so. Around a third of respondents reported a reduction in absenteeism and sickness. In around a third of cases, there was a reduction in the number of employees and managers. In addition, the greater the scope of direct participation, measured in terms of a wider coverage of issues in which employees were involved, the stronger was the positive impact on economic performance.

Multiple forms were reported as more effective than single forms — respondents with five or six forms consistently reported greater effects than those with one or two forms (EFILWC, 1997: 110–14). This finding is supported by extensive research in the US. Pil and McDuffie (1996), for example, in a study of the automobile industry, refer to what has become known as human resource "bundling"; that is, the combined application of a range of "high-involvement" work practices such as work teams and problem-solving groups. However, the incidence of multiple forms of involvement in Ireland was comparatively low. While four out of five workplaces practised at least one form of direct participation, only four per cent practised six forms.

The EPOC survey examined the effects of union participation in the introduction of direct employee involvement. Two major questions arose: to what extent are unions at present involved in the introduction of direct participation and how useful do employers find such involvement? With the exception of Portugal, Ireland had the highest figure for the "no participation" category of employee representative involvement in the introduction of direct participation. However, on the positive side, the combined figure for employee representative involvement — 66 per cent — indicated a high level of employer willingness to involve unions in such activities. On the issue of usefulness, 74 per cent of employers in Ireland considered it either "useful" or "very useful" to have trade union involvement in the introduction of direct participation.

These findings are supported by a number of US studies. Cooke (1992, 1994), for example, surveyed managers of union and non-union companies on the effects of participation programmes on product quality improvement. He concluded that, among union firms, those with jointly administered programmes achieved significantly greater improvements in product quality than did those firms with more traditional adversarial relationships (that is, with no participation programmes). He also concluded that firms with programmes solely administered by management fared no better than the firms that had no programmes at all. In addition, the gains associated with jointly administered programmes in unionised firms were at least equal to the gains associated with participation programmes in non-union ones. Other studies have come to broadly similar conclusions on the positive impact of trade union involvement in the introduction and administration of participation programmes; for example, Schuster (1983), Havlovic (1991), Ichniowski et al. (1996) and Pil and McDuffie (1996).

As well as formal research evidence, there are the self-reports given in the form of case studies at management conferences. At several such conferences in Ireland in recent years, managers have presented case studies of various forms of partnership including *direct forms* such as teams and suggestion schemes; *indirect forms* such as consultative bodies and joint productivity groups; and *financial forms* such as employee share ownership. These case studies have highlighted the positive economic effects of the innovations concerned and have indicated higher levels of employee effort, commitment and contribution of ideas and solutions to production problems. However, it might be argued that such case studies are highly selective and do not account for cases of failure — and doubtless there are such.

DEVELOPING PARTNERSHIP

If the management of an organisation want to develop partnership, how can they set about doing so? This section suggests some broad advice based on the experiences of a number of organisations in Ireland.

Initial Discussions

Senior managers and senior union officials will usually have some informal, and perhaps confidential, discussions about the possibility of partnership. This will involve some discussion of the key problems facing the organisation, what might be achieved through partnership that is not presently being achieved, what the likely responses of the workforce and management would be to such an initiative, and how it might be progressed. In the case of AIB, for example, the initial discussions were at the level of the bank's Secretary, Kevin Kelly, and the general secretary of the Irish Bank Official's Association, Ciarán Ryan. The two leaders met a number of times and agreed that there had to be a better kind of relationship than that prevailing in the wake of the 1992 national bank strike. Together they created a framework within which a group of management and union representatives could then begin working together on issues outside the arena of pay and conditions through a joint working party.

It is frequently the case that a senior manager — usually the HR person — and the senior full-time official will readily see the potential for their respective interests in a partnership approach, but the difficulty may lie in convincing others on each side. In such cases, an outside "expert" may be invited to make a presentation to the parties on partnership including the achievements of other organisations. Or an external facilitator may be used to independently chair some initial discussions as a way of moving the agenda forward.

A Working or Steering Group

Where a decision has been made to explore partnership further or to develop a system for the organisation, the next step is usually the setting up of a working group, frequently called a "steering group". The group will comprise of senior managers, union officials and lay representatives from the organisation. This group will usually be given some broad mandate arising from the initial discussions, perhaps in the form of a letter or a note of discussions. The group will, however, usually be given a fairly free hand as to how precisely it will carry out its work. Two important issues at this stage are time-scale and resources. The group will need to know how long it has to complete its work and what resources will be made available in terms of time (release of group members to attend meetings, visit other organisations, consult internally, carry out research, draft documents, etc.) and other resources such as full-time administrative assistance.

The steering group may identify issues that are of concern to the parties and project groups may be set to work on these issues. In this case, the role of the steering committee will be to oversee the work of the project groups. Alternatively, the steering group may focus on the development of partnership as a formal system and may leave the actual addressing of current problems aside until the new systems have been put in place.

What exactly the steering group does and how long it takes will vary from case to case. In RTE, for example, a steering group was given full-time release for three months and they were able to do work that would have taken considerably longer in other organisations. A part-time group working over a greater period might very well have cost the organisation more than the cost of the release of the personnel involved in the steering group.

The operation of two distinct steering groups, one in Allied Irish Bank and the other in the Western Health Board, are set out below to illustrate the variety of approaches available (see Case Examples 14.1 and 14.2).

Case Example 14.1: Joint Working Group in the Western Health Board

---

The Board received a report from the Advisory Service of the Labour Relations Commission that was critical of its industrial relations and personnel practices and structures. The management and unions decided to establish a joint process through which they would implement the LRC's recommendations for improvement. They established a "plenary group" consisting of some 40 managers and representatives from across the organisation. The function of this group was to determine some broad terms of reference for a smaller "working group" of 14 managers and representatives which would work together to prepare an implementation report. Given the background of poor relationships and the lack of experience of working together management and unions decided to use the services of an external facilitator.

The role of the facilitator was to help the working group to develop objectives around the LRC report, to develop an effective way of working together and to help develop the trust that would be vital to the achievement of significant improvements in management–union–employee relationships. The facilitator chaired the meetings of the working group as well as the plenary group.

As a work plan emerged, it became necessary to divide the tasks between two sub-groups, which then met without the facilitator at times agreed by themselves. The sub-groups would then meet in a joint session to co-ordinate and discuss each other's work. This form of working proceeded for some months. A report was produced that contained significant new draft procedural agreements and the group circulated the report to all employees for information and to the management and unions for a formal response. At this stage, the group decided to give itself a name and they chose the title "Round Table" to indicate the joint problem-solving character of their approach, as opposed to the "arms' length" approach typical of adversarial industrial relations. Subsequently, the group organised a conference on workplace partnership for some 150 employees with outside speakers as a way of showing that the kinds of effective, co-operative relationships that prevailed in other organisations were also possible in this one.

The group proceeded to design and implement partnership arrangements on a pilot basis in a number of workplaces. They also intervened in a serious industrial dispute that threatened the stability of the Round Table and facilitated a settlement.

Case Example 14.2: Joint Working Party in Allied Irish Bank (AIB)

In the wake of the 1992 bank strike, the management and the Irish Bank Officials' Association (IBOA) agreed to search together for a better way of conducting their relationships than the prevailing adversarial approach. In 1994, they established a Joint Working Party to address issues of mutual concern outside the collective bargaining agenda. The group was initially comprised of union representatives and managers from outside the industrial relations area. The group worked without any external assistance. Work began on a range of significant organisational change issues such as new banking services and new opening arrangements, as well as on the design of a new working relationship between the parties, including a more efficient system of industrial relations. Through the Joint Working Party, the management gave much more information to the IBOA representatives than would traditionally have been the case. The group visited a number of banks in the UK and Denmark to see what best practices were as regards the management of change and the involvement of employees in the change process.

While the core industrial relations issues such as pay continued to be handled through the collective bargaining system, the improved relationships that developed through the Joint Working Party "spilled over" into the bargaining system and earlier agreements were made to the benefit of both sides. The Joint Working Party undertakes communications with the IBOA representatives and with managers throughout the organisation. The group recently agreed a set of principles or high-level objectives to govern their future working. These principles included: organisation prosperity; job security; management of change; negotiation and agreement; enhancing the quality of the work environment; development of a co-operative culture; mutual problem-solving; recognition of the IBOA's role within the bank; and a professional approach to staff relations.

Three Strands of Activities

Not everything is done through a steering group or even jointly between the management and unions: each side still has considerable work to do on their own. Both management and unions, for example, have to brief their own principals and have to manage their "constituencies" on an ongoing basis. In addition, the effectiveness of the joint activities may depend on the extent to which the parties have considered issues in depth from their own perspectives. For example, when the steering group is seeking to establish a set of objectives for partnership, it will be important for the two sides to have given thought to what they each wanted to get out of any new relationship. There is a danger of agreeing superficially on some bland objectives that will not sustain the relationship when it comes under pressure, as it inevitably will. External facilitation can be a big help in bringing conflicting objectives to the surface and in dealing with them in a constructive way.

Setting Objectives

This is a critical area of activity for the steering group. Two sets of objectives arise: objectives for the steering group and objectives for the partnership system. Either set of objectives may involve an element of bargaining, as neither side is likely to produce objectives that are entirely acceptable to the other. Also, a set of objectives that focused exclusively on the interests of either management or unions would not motivate the other side for long. Each side may, therefore, have to live with certain objectives that would not be their own priorities. What is important is that there be sufficient common ground upon which to develop a workable partnership.

Setting objectives is not always as easy as it may seem and there can sometimes be a reluctance on the part of the management and union personnel involved to go beyond "motherhood and apple pie" formulations. In such cases, a facilitator may devise some means other than plenary discussions that will encourage the parties to consider in some detail their own objectives as a lead-in to discussion of joint objectives. Case Example 14.3 below describes how this has been done in a number of cases.

Case Example 14.3: Establishing Objectives in a Management–Union Group

---

The management and unions in a company decided to explore the possibility of partnership. Each side came to the process with a reasonably open mind. They decided to convene a meeting of management and union representatives and to ask a facilitator to attend the session, which was to be open-ended. The discussion ranged over a variety of issues and it was agreed that a further meeting would be convened at which the issue of objectives for partnership would be discussed.

At the next meeting, the facilitator suggested, in the absence of any detailed preparation having been done by the parties, that they would, in the first instance, meet separately in sub-groups to consider what they each thought the objectives of a partnership might be. Each side worked separately with a flip-chart for about an hour. They then reconvened and presented their views to each other, putting their points of view on the wall on chart paper.

Next, they looked at the two positions to see to what extent there was common ground and to what extent each side was prepared to agree to objectives that did not feature on their own list. A participant put up some fresh paper and together they considered the two sets of objectives. They reached agreement on what common objectives could be written on the fresh paper. Each side was prepared, through further discussion, to accept certain objectives that were not on their list but not others.

Rather than engage in a long argument, they agreed to settle on the list of common objectives as a working document that would inform their work but which could be amended in the light of subsequent discussions or experience.

Objectives can be framed in general or specific terms. Sometimes they will be framed in general terms on the understanding that partnership working groups will then take the objectives and flesh them out in the context of particular issues or parts of the organisation. Clarity is, however, important. If the objectives are not clear, then how can the parties decide which forms of employee involvement to use; or what training to provide; or whether or not the objectives have been achieved? Measurable objectives, whether developed centrally or locally, are easier to monitor and evaluate and will be of help to the parties in deciding whether the system is working well or badly and where.

Communications

A key issue for steering groups is whether or not they should communicate with the wider audience. This is usually advisable, as there can be suspicion and concern as to what the group might be doing. Groups may prepare joint presentations for workplace meetings or workshops. In Tara Mines, for example, the company arranged presentations and workshops on partnership and change for all of the employees using company speakers, as well as external presenters from the National Centre for Partnership and other bodies. Steering groups may prepare joint publications as their preferred means of communication. In RTE, the management and union representatives on the Partnership Steering Group jointly prepared and delivered a Powerpoint presentation to all sections of the organisation. They also produced two glossy bulletins during their three-month existence and conducted an extensive survey using the services of the ESRI. Such activities require resources. Steering groups usually see benefits in keeping the wider organisation up-to-date with what they are doing.

Data Gathering

Steering group members usually find it useful to meet representatives of other organisations to discuss why and how they developed partnership. The steering group may subdivide into twos and threes for this purpose. Data-gathering can also be extended to information on other issues, such as changes in reward systems, staffing levels, performance standards, operational issues, etc. One particular benefit for older organisations is that this can help to broaden the perspective of steering group members beyond their own organisation. In general, it is easier to get to grips with issues such as the separation of partnership from collective bargaining through practical examples in other organisations than through theory alone. In the case of An Post, the management and union representatives who were charged with the design of a partnership system for the organisation invited a number of well-known organisations from both the private and public sectors to make presentations to the group on how they had gone about the development of partnership.

Decision-making

Decisions within steering groups are usually made on a consensual basis. A consensus decision is one that all are prepared to live with and implement. It may not be everyone's first choice, but at the same time no one has fundamental difficulties with it — otherwise it would not be a consensus decision. Consensus protects the parties from decisions with which they could not live. In the case of Tara Mines, the principle of consensus was written into the terms of reference of the Joint Working Group that designed the partnership agenda and processes.

Ongoing Change

Life goes on within the organisation as the steering group is doing its work. The parties to a steering group usually have some understanding as to how the ongoing change and industrial relations agendas will be managed as a new partnership system is being designed and developed. This is important, as employees, conscious that a new approach is being espoused, may expect management behaviour to change overnight. This is not realistic. It is essential, however, that some ground rules be agreed as to how significant change issues will be handled during the development of partnership. Such ground rules should be to the benefit of the organisation, in that they should minimise the possibility of adverse employee reaction to changes. There should be agreement that there will be no surprises for employees and representatives as far as management announcements of changes are concerned.

If anything, management should ensure that representatives are informed in advance of any significant announcements.

In RTE, the management and unions agreed that, during the course of the Steering Group phase of development, any ongoing or new change issues that had the potential to give rise to conflict would be referred to the Managing Director of Organisation Development, who had overall responsibility for the personnel and industrial relations areas, and the Secretary of the Trade Union Group. The objective of the referral was for the two to decide what process should be used to pursue the change item in question; for example, a working party or a conventional management–union meeting.

Industrial Relations

It will also be the case that ongoing industrial relations issues will continue to be handled through the existing machinery. The parties do, however, need to be careful that the kinds of low level conflict that are "normal" in organisations do not cause damage to what the steering group is attempting to achieve. Greater effort will need to be put into the resolution of issues to avoid this.

A Formal Agreement

The outcome of the steering group's work may be a formal partnership agreement, which will require ratification in the normal way through senior management and the workforce. Some of the standard elements of partnership agreements are:

- The objectives of the partnership agreement and the underlying principles;

- The range of issues appropriate to the new system;

- The structure, composition and operations of any new bodies set up under the agreement;

- The relationship between the new bodies and the collective bargaining system;

- The facilities that will support the new system, including training and facilitation;

- Mechanisms for resolving differences that may arise through the partnership system;

- Review and termination clauses.

Training and Facilitation

New partnership training products are now becoming available to meet the needs of organisations that are seeking to develop partnership. One such product is the National Centre for Partnership's *Working Together* programme, which is aimed at newly formed partnership groups (O'Dowd, 1998b) and which was developed initially for the public sector. Similar products are being finalised for use in the private sector.

One of the central features of partnership training is that the management and union representatives are trained jointly. Given the different objectives and methods of operation of partnership and collective bargaining, it stands to reason that the kinds of behaviours that are appropriate in a collective bargaining forum, such as withholding information, bluffing and making threats, will not transfer to a partnership forum. New behaviours and skills must be learned by the participants if the new systems are to work effectively. These behaviours and skills include information sharing, listening, problem-solving and consensus decision-making. Table 14.4 below gives an outline of the two-day interactive training programme titled *Working Together*.

Table 14.4: Partnership Training Programme of National Centre for Partnership

Module	Content
Partnership	• The concept of partnership • The objectives • How it works • Benefits • Cases • Partnership and collective bargaining • Setting objectives • Barriers to development
Group Development	• What is a group? • The individual and the group • Group development • Positive and negative behaviours • Group roles
Consensus Decision-making	• What is consensus decision-making? • Benefits and techniques • Practical exercises
Communications	• Principles of effective communication • Barriers to communication • Developing a communications strategy

It is important that the training should be delivered by competent trainers, but also by trainers who are familiar with the management–union context and who are acceptable to employees as well as to managers.

Many steering groups use an external facilitator to assist them with their work. A facilitator can provide a useful service by assisting the group to form as a group, to overcome initial differences, to discuss and agree objectives, and to develop a work plan for the period of its operation. A facilitator may also bring considerable experience of how other organisations have developed partnership systems. It is important for a group using a facilitator to ensure that the person is acceptable to the entire group and has an understanding of the union–management context of industrial relations as well as being skilled in the techniques of facilitation.

CONCLUSIONS

What are the prospects for a wider development of partnership as a dominant Irish model of industrial relations and what issues are likely to arise for those organisations that have already embarked on the partnership road? The history of Irish industrial relations since the 1980s has been one of "fragmentation" into distinctive approaches, including the continuation of the adversarial approach and the development of new approaches, such as the non-union HRM approach favoured by many multinationals, particularly those of US origin (Roche, 1996). Partnership, while being the espoused policy of government and the social partners, is only one of a number of new industrial relations approaches available to organisations. A review of the operations of Partnership 2000 and all the instruments used to influence the uptake of partnership at workplace level will reveal some important lessons that may then be integrated into a successor agreement to the current one. It is unlikely, given the benefits already being experienced in a number of organisations in the private and public sectors, that, in the event of there being no follow-up national programme, there will be no follow-up on partnership at workplace level. It is likely that government and the social partners will devise additional means of supporting those employers and trade unions who have decided to place partnership at the centre of their future strategies.

For individual organisations, the problem will be one of sustaining the level of commitment by managers, employees and representatives that is required to keep joint working alive. This will require considerable attention by all concerned to ensure that the partnership agenda remains relevant to the current interests of the parties, so that practical benefits continue to be achieved. An issue of interest will be the extent to which organisations, as they grow in confidence, will transfer more of the traditional collective bargaining agenda into a partnership framework for discussion and resolution. At present, there is considerable caution on both the employer and trade union sides on this issue and the continuation of existing bargaining and dispute resolution systems is seen as an important "safety net".

Nevertheless, for partnership to justify its existence, there will have to be evidence of movement towards less adversarial bargaining approaches. The exploration of new bargaining approaches, such as interest-based bargaining, may provide fruitful opportunities in this respect. In the public sector, it is ironic that the development of partnership in areas such as health and local government is being accompanied by the highest ever level in recent years of adversarial behaviour at national level on the pay of powerful groups such as nurses and fire-fighters. It remains to be seen whether meaningful local partnerships can take root in such a national setting. Also, the emergence of new adversarial forces in "partnership" companies such as the ESB will fuel scepticism among employers and trade unions towards the new approach.

While the current approach to partnership is based firmly within the voluntary tradition, this may not continue to be the case if decisions already made by the European Commission to legislate for national systems of employee involvement are implemented. Whatever the future may hold, the age-old problem of developing industrial relations and human resource strategies that will enhance the performance of organisations in both the public and private sectors will endure and the overwhelming likelihood must be that no single new strategy will dominate the practices of organisations within the near future.

References

Cooke, W.N. (1990), *Labor–Management Co-operation: New Partnerships or Going Around in Circles?*, Kalamazoo, MI: Upjohn Institute for Employment Research.

Cooke, W.N. (1992), "Product Quality Improvement through Employee Participation: The Effects of Unionisation and Joint Union–Management Administration", *Industrial and Labour Relations Review*, Vol. 46, No. 1, pp. 119-34.

Cooke, W.N. (1994), "Employee Participation Programs, Group-based Incentives and Company Performance: A Union–Non-union Comparison", *Industrial and Labour Relations Review*, Vol. 47, No. 4, July.

Cutcher-Gershenfeld, J. and A. Verma (1994), "Joint Governance in North American Workplaces: A Glimpse of the Future or the End of an Era?", *International Journal of Human Resource Management*, Vol. 5, No. 3, pp. 547–80.

D'Art, D. (1992), *Economic Democracy and Financial Participation: A Comparative Study*, London: Routledge.

Department of An Taoiseach (1991), *Programme for Economic and Social Progress*, Dublin: Stationery Office.

Department of An Taoiseach (1997), *Partnership 2000*, Dublin: Stationery Office.

European Foundation for the Improvement of Living and Working Conditions (EFILWC) (1997), *New Forms of Work Organisation: Can Europe Realise its Potential?* Dublin: EFILWC.

Forfás (1996), *Shaping Our Future: A Strategy for Enterprise in Ireland in the 21st Century*, Dublin: Forfás.

Gunnigle, P. (1998), "More Rhetoric than Reality: Industrial Relations Partnership in Ireland", *Economic and Social Review*, Vol. 28, No. 4, pp. 179–200.

Havlovic, S.J. (1991), "Quality of Work Life and Human Resource Outcomes", *Industrial Relations*, Vol. 30, No. 3, pp. 469–79.

Ichniowski, T., T.A. Kochan, D. Levine, C. Olson and G. Strauss (1996), "What Works at Work: Overview and Assessment", *Industrial Relations*, Vol. 35, No. 3, pp. 299–333.

Irish Business and Employers' Confederation (IBEC) (1998), *Guidelines for the Development of Partnership in Competitive Enterprise*, Dublin: IBEC.

Irish Congress of Trade Unions (ICTU) (1993), *New Forms of Work Organisation: Options for Unions*, Dublin: ICTU.

Irish Congress of Trade Unions (ICTU) (1995), *Managing Change: Review of Union Involvement in Company Restructuring*, Dublin: ICTU.

Irish Congress of Trade Unions (ICTU) (1997), *Partnership in the Workplace: Guidelines for Trade Unions*, Dublin: ICTU.

Irish Productivity Centre (IPC) (1998), *Building Partnership*, Dublin: IPC.

Kochan, T.A. and L. Dyer (1976), "A Model of Organisational Change in the Context of Labor–Management Relations", *Journal of Applied Behavioural Science*, Vol. 12, No. 2, pp. 59–78.

Kochan, T.A., H.C. Katz and R.B. McKersie (1989), *The Transformation of American Industrial Relations*, New York: Basic Books.

Kochan, T. and P. Osterman (1994): *The Mutual Gains Enterprise*, Boston, MA: Harvard Business School Press.

Labour Relations Commission (LRC) (1996), *A Strategic Policy*, Dublin: LRC.

Marchington, M., A. Wilkinson, P. Ackers and J. Goodman (1994), "Understanding the Meaning of Participation: Views from the Workplace", *Human Relations*, Vol. 47, No. 8, pp. 867–93.

McKersie, R.B. (1996), "Labour–Management Partnerships: US Evidence and Implications for Ireland", *Irish Business and Administrative Research*, Vol. 17, pp. 1–13.

National Centre for Partnership (NCP) (1999), *Partnership at Work, Issue 1*, Dublin: NCP.

National Economic and Social Council (NESC) (1996), *Strategy into the 21st Century*, Dublin: NESC.

Nissen, B. (1997), *Unions and Workplace Reorganisation*, Detroit, MI: Wayne State University Press.

O'Dowd, J. and T. Hastings (1997), "Human Resource Management in the Public Sector", Working Paper, Dublin: Centre for Employment Relations and Organisational Performance, Graduate School of Business, University College Dublin.

O'Dowd, J. (1998a), *Employee Partnership in Ireland: A Guide for Managers*, Dublin: Oak Tree Press, Irish Management Briefings.

O'Dowd, J. (1998b), *Working Together: A Training Programme for Partnership in the Public Sector*, Dublin: National Centre for Partnership.

Olney, S.L. (1996), *Unions in a Changing World: Problems and Prospects in Selected Industrialised Countries*, Geneva: International Labour Office.

Osterman, P. (1994), "How Common is Workplace Transformation and Who Adopts it?", *Industrial Relations*, Vol. 47, No. 2, pp. 173–88.

Pil, F.K. and J.P. McDuffie (1996), "The Adoption of High-Involvement Work Practices", *Industrial Relations*, Vol. 35, No. 3, pp. 423–55.

Regini, M. (1995), *Uncertain Boundaries: The Social and Political Construction of European Economies*, Cambridge: Cambridge University Press.

Roche, W.K. (1996), "The New Competitive Order and the Fragmentation of Employee Relations in Ireland", Working Paper, Dublin: Centre for Employment Relations and Organisational Performance, Graduate School of Business, University College Dublin.

Roche, W.K. (1998), "Between Regime Fragmentation and Realignment: Irish Industrial Relations and Human Resource Management in the 1990s", *Industrial Relations Journal*, Vol. 29, No. 2.

Roche, W.K. and T.A. Kochan (1996), "Strategies for Extending Social Partnership to Enterprise and Workplace Levels in Ireland", unpublished draft paper, Dublin: National Economic and Social Council.

Roche, W.K. and J.F. Geary (1998), "Collaborative Production and the Irish Boom: Work Organisation, Partnership and Direct Involvement in Irish Organisations", Working Paper, Dublin: Centre for Employment Relations and Organisational Performance, Graduate School of Business, University College Dublin.

Roche, W.K., J.F. Geary, T. Brannick, J. Ashmore and M. Fahy (1998), *Partnership and Involvement in Irish Workplaces*, Report presented to the National Centre for Partnership, Dublin: Centre for Employment Relations and Organisational Performance, Graduate School of Business, University College Dublin.

Roche, W.K. and T. Turner (1998), "Human Resource Management and Industrial Relations: Substitution, Dualism and Partnership" in W.K. Roche, K. Monks and J. Walsh (eds.), *Human Resource Management Strategies: Policy and Practice in Ireland*, Dublin: Oak Tree Press.

Schuster, M. (1983), "The Impact of Union–Management Co-operation on Productivity and Employment", *Industrial and Labour Relations Review*, Vol. 36, No. 3, pp. 415–30.

Streeck, W. (1992), *Social Institutions and Economic Performance: Studies of Industrial Relations in Advanced Capitalist Economies*, London: Sage.

Telecom Éireann (1997), *The Telecom Partnership A Framework Agreement for the Transformation of Telecom Éireann into a World Class Telecommunications Business*, Dublin: Telecom Éireann.

CHAPTER 15

THE EFFECTIVE MANAGEMENT OF DISCIPLINARY AND GRIEVANCE ISSUES AT WORK

Gerard McMahon and *Orla Maher*

INTRODUCTION

Formal procedures for the resolution of disciplinary and grievance matters are now a standard feature of the great majority of
workplaces. Whilst such procedures may be no panacea, they do
provide a framework, or guide, for employers and employees —
aiding clarity, control, direct communication and consistency of
treatment on these matters. It is now widely accepted that, apart
from considerations of natural justice and equity, the maintenance
of a good industrial relations atmosphere at workplace level requires the installation of, and adherence to, acceptable discipline
and grievance procedures. Established and shared procedures
serve as a beacon for an environment of open and positive communication.

However, these procedures are no substitute for the astute deployment of interpersonal skills, flexibility, sensitivity and creativity when handling "people" problems. Accordingly, this
chapter outlines the procedural and practical imperatives associated with effective discipline and grievance handling at work.

THE DISCIPLINARY PROCEDURE

Purpose

The primary purpose of a disciplinary procedure is to *help* the employee whose conduct or performance falls below organisational standards to improve. For example, this is an explicit feature of the Irish Hotels Federation's (IHF) recommendations for employers in the hotel and guesthouse sector (IHF, 1997). Whilst you also wish to maintain compliance with organisational rules and standards, the "help" focus should significantly influence the manner and tone of your investigation and subsequent actions. In practice, then, the actual disciplinary interview must allow the employee to present their point of view and give a comprehensive picture of the case. Through a constructive discussion of the issues, you should be able to assess culpability, to decide on appropriate action and attempt to effect the desired change in the employee's behaviour.

In the interest of good people management practices, the procedure should be in writing, and in a language and format that is easily understood. The consequences of a departure from the company rules and standards should be set down as clearly as possible. Copies should be given to all staff and included in any induction programme for newcomers.

It is also recommended that disciplinary procedures should be drafted so as to cover as many specific situations as possible, yet remain flexible. This may seem paradoxical, but in practice, it isn't (see Case Examples 15.1 and 15.2). Of course, breaches of regulations should be treated similarly, and must be seen to be so treated. However, the procedures should be sufficiently broad to countenance mitigating circumstances, which can render situations that are ostensibly alike to be treated differently.

Case Example 15.1: Disciplinary Procedure for Jurys Hotel and Towers

It is agreed that the primary aim of this disciplinary procedure is to help the member whose behavioural conduct or performance falls below Company requirements where the necessary improvement has not been achieved.

Disciplinary problems require immediate management attention and can usually be corrected by an early approach to a member. Where disciplinary measures are required, it is agreed that the following procedures shall apply in all cases and are designed to ensure consistency of treatment in similar situations.

Stage I: Counselling

A verbal, non-recorded counselling shall, in the first instance, be arranged with the member by the member's Head of Department (i.e. Head Chef, Bar Manager, Head Porter, Embassy Head Waiter, Coffee Dock Head Waiter, Steward, Assistant Accountant or Assistant Engineer).

Stage II: Recorded Verbal Warning

A verbal recorded warning shall be given to the member in the presence of a member of the Section Committee or Shop Steward by the Departmental Manager and Personnel Manager, in the event of any other breach of conduct or any aspect of work or conduct that requires improvement.

Stage III: Written Warning

In the event of a subsequent breach of conduct, or of the required improvement not taking place, a "written warning" will be issued to the member and a copy of same will be sent to the Shop Steward. This letter should inform the member that they may be given a "final written warning" if the required and specified improvements are not forthcoming.

Stage IV: Final Written Warning

Should the required improvement(s) not take place, or if a further breach of conduct occurs, the member will be given a "final written warning", stating that if the required improvement does not take place the member will be suspended. A copy will be sent to the Shop Steward and Union Official.

Stage V: Suspension
In the event of any further breach of conduct or of required improvements not taking place, the Company will suspend the member and issue them with the final document, making it clear that the member's employment will be terminated if the required improvements are not forthcoming.

Stage VI: Dismissal
The member will be dismissed in the event that the conduct or performance has not improved to the required level following the warnings set out above. The final decision to dismiss will not be taken by the member's immediate superior, but only by the General Manager after consultation.

a)   *With the exception of the habitual offenders, it is agreed that should the member's conduct improve to the required standard or should the specified improvement in the member's particular aspect of work take place for at least the periods set our hereunder, the member shall revert to the disciplinary stage immediately before the stage at which they were most recently disciplined:*

Stage II	*6 months without further warning*
Stage III	*6 months without further warning*
Stage IV	*6 months without further warning*
Stage V	*9 months without further warning*

b)   *It is agreed, with the exception of Stage I above, that a member under this procedure should always be accompanied by a Shop Steward or Section Committee Representative. It is further agreed that in a case where the Shop Steward or Section Committee Representative may be involved in disciplinary measures, they shall be accompanied by a Union Official. The Company will regard breaches of discipline/ unacceptable conduct as related.*

Breach of Serious Rule/Gross Misconduct
Where summary action under this heading may be required, immediate suspension pending investigation shall attach to the alleged breach of the most serious rule/gross misconduct. The main examples under this heading are set our below, and in such cases the following steps shall apply:

- *Step A: The member will be suspended by the senior manager on duty and sent home pending further investigation of the alleged offence (with pay to the end of the shift).*

- *Step B: Following investigation, the member will be met by the Divisional Manager in the presence of the member's Shop Steward/Union Official and any charges will be put to them at such meeting.*

- *Step C: Following investigation and meeting, the member may be dismissed/suspended/warned in writing, as appropriate, without recourse to the normal procedure set out above, in the event of Gross Misconduct being established, and the provisions at Clause (a) above, shall not apply.*

In the event of disagreement at any stage of this procedure, it is agreed that the provisions of the Grievance/Disputes Procedures will be fully utilised in the interests of maintaining good industrial relations.

Examples of Gross Misconduct

The parties to this agreement agree that it is impractical to list every possible item of gross misconduct. However, as an example, the following breaches of good conduct would render a member liable to disciplinary action by the Company:

- *Falsification of information supplied on the employment application form, references;*

- *Falsification of Company records including personnel, timekeeping, clock-cards, stock records, medical certificates, qualification certificates;*

- *Reporting for or being at work under the influence of alcohol or unprescribed drugs or having same on the premises;*

- *Fighting, theft or fraud;*

- *Wilful failure to follow cash register/credit card procedures;*

- *Wilful damage to company/other employees' property;*

- *Possession of an offensive weapon on company property;*

- *Indecent behaviour;*

- *Wilful violation of safety rules.*

Case Example 15.2: Disciplinary and Grievance Procedure at New Ireland Assurance

---

The objective behind these procedures is to resolve grievances which staff might have, and to deal with disciplinary issues, at the earliest possible moment.

Grievance Procedure

1. Issue should be raised by employee for resolution at the first supervisory level;

2. If unresolved, issue should be raised at Head of Department/Line Management level (District/Area Manager in the field);

3. If the grievance remains, it should be raised at Senior Management level for resolution and, if necessary, it may be referred to an agreed third party at this stage.

Disciplinary Procedure

1. Counselling interview between Supervisor/Manager and staff member;

2. Verbal warning outlining improvement required and outcome if not achieved;

3. Written warning stating shortfall and outlining required improvement and indicating that the next offence could lead to suspension or dismissal;

4. Suspension or dismissal. (If suspension, the staff member should be made aware that not meeting the required improvement will lead to dismissal.)

Note: Staff members are entitled to (union) representation at all of the above stages of both procedures.

Misconduct

In the event of serious misconduct, the employee may be dismissed summarily without recourse to the disciplinary procedure. Termination for any other reason is subject to the provisions of the Minimum Notice and Terms of Employment Act, 1973.

The Counselling Interview

According to Gunnigle et al. (1995), when issuing warnings, the managerial approach should be remedial rather than penal, except in the most extreme circumstances. Therefore, managers should be primarily concerned with encouraging improvements in individual conduct rather than simply imposing sanctions. Sample disciplinary procedures along these lines agreed by the Jurys Hotel and Towers, with the Services, Industrial, Professional and Technical Union (SIPTU), and New Ireland Assurance Co. plc with the Manufacturing, Science and Finance Union (MSF), are outlined in the Case Examples above. It is interesting to note the labelling of Stage 1 of these (and many other) organisations' disciplinary procedures as "counselling". Such an approach is certainly less intimidating for all parties than the normal alternative of a disciplinary verbal warning. This increasingly common "counselling" label fits more easily with the aforementioned "help" focus, and lends itself more to the deployment of a manager's interpersonal skills than does the "verbal warning" label. The North Eastern Health Board's disciplinary procedure also provides parties with considerable scope and flexibility in this regard. Under their Stage 1, it is stipulated that "a number of verbal warnings should be given". In this regard, it is interesting to note that the majority of larger Irish companies provide a counselling service for their employees. Most of these companies offer a service covering work performance and behaviour, and personal problems — including alcohol and drug issues (*Industrial Relations News*, 1996; see also Chapter 22). Tackling performance or behaviour matters from a counselling as opposed to a punitive perspective reflects a more informed disciplinary approach. When staff support is required in terms of flexibility, options to work evenings or weekends, or to defer holidays, this supportive approach is more likely to win that extra effort.

When the more punitive approach is required, warnings have to be issued (see the earlier Case Examples). This raises the vexed question of how long such a warning should remain "alive". Hawkins (1979) suggests that verbal warnings remain on an employee's record for six months, written warnings for 12 months and, for very serious offences, a period of two years or more (see Case Example 15.1 for comparative purposes). Many organisations do not specify limits, but, in practice, allow warnings to lapse after a reasonable period of satisfactory performance.

The Legal Angle[1]
According to the Code of Practice on Disciplinary Procedures, issued by the Department of Enterprise and Employment in 1996:

> in any enterprise or organisation, it is important that procedures . . . exist and that the purpose, function and terms of such procedures are known and clearly understood by management, employees and trade unions.

Given the requirements of the Unfair Dismissals Acts, 1977–1993, the necessity for employers to have a disciplinary procedure is evident. Section 14 of the Act requires that, within 28 days of taking up a job, an employee must be advised of the procedures that will be used for dismissal (see Chapters 17 and 18). Though the absence of such a procedure does not automatically make a dismissal unfair, the experience from the Employment Appeals Tribunals' (EAT) case precedents is that it often does.

Two key requirements of direct relevance to disciplinary interviewing, which are well established in the Irish Constitution and in our case law, relate to the "investigation" and "hearing" elements of the process. An inadequate investigation of the situation on the part of the employer may give rise to a dismissal or disciplinary action being deemed unfair. Accordingly, a reasonable and fair investigation of the matter should be undertaken by the employer prior to a decision to dismiss or discipline. The employer is also obliged to put the relevant case to the employee,

---

[1] For greater detail see Chapter 18.

thus allowing them to respond. A refusal to allow representation at such meetings is also likely to render a disciplinary or dismissal decision unfair. According to the aforementioned Code (Department of Enterprise and Employment, 1996), representation by an "employee representative" includes a colleague of the employee's choice and an authorised trade union, but not any other person or body unconnected with the enterprise (e.g. a solicitor). The Code also emphasises the "principles of natural justice" and their implications for the disciplinary interview (see Figure 15.1).

Figure 15.1: The Principles of Natural Justice in the Management of Discipline

---

The procedures applied must comply with the general principles of natural justice and fair procedures, which include:

- That details of the allegations or complaints be put to the employee concerned;

- That the employee concerned be given the opportunity to respond fully to any such allegations or complaints;

- That the employee concerned be given the opportunity to avail of representation;

- That the employee concerned has the right to a fair and impartial determination of the issues being investigated, taking into account the allegations or complaints themselves, the response of the employee concerned to them, any representations made by or on behalf of the employee concerned and any other relevant or appropriate evidence, factors or circumstances.

These principles may require that the allegations or complaints be set out in writing, that the source of the allegations or complaint be given or that the employee concerned be allowed to confront or question witnesses.

Source: Department of Enterprise and Employment (1996).

The two key elements of these provisions are that, firstly, details of the allegation must be put to the employee; and secondly, they should be given the chance to respond to the allegations. Failure to adhere to these "golden rules" is likely to render the relevant disciplinary action void, and frequently leads to unfair dismissal determinations.

Appealing the Disciplinary Action

It is not necessary for disciplinary procedures to provide for an appeal against dismissal within the company. Such appeals may materialise at the EAT or even at the Labour Relations Commission (LRC) or in Court. An appeal against any lesser sanction should be through the organisation's grievance procedure (see Case Example 15.1). It is important that the management representative hearing the appeal has not been involved in any way in the decision to discipline; otherwise there is an infraction of another principle of natural justice — that one cannot be a judge in one's own case. Should it occur, it may also render a dismissal technically unfair.

THE DISCIPLINARY INTERVIEW

Disciplinary interviewing is often as stressful and daunting a task for the manager or supervisor as it is for the employee concerned. The fear of making a mess of it, damaging a good working relationship, or being found guilty of unfair dismissal, is enough to seriously damage your health! To alleviate this anxiety, and secure the best outcome for all concerned, practical advice for the conduct of the successful interview is now offered. To get the best out of the disciplinary procedure, it is advisable that interviewers adhere to the following recommendations, which are categorised into the *before*, *during* and *after* stages of the interview.

Before the Disciplinary Interview

1. Decide on the best time for the interview. This should be close to the incident. However, a "cooling off" period may be required, to ensure that parties approach the interview rationally rather than emotionally. The logic of this approach will be self-evident, for example, when the individual in question is suspected of being under the influence of alcohol or drugs. However, it also enables you to do the all-important investigative preparatory work.

    If the offence is adjudged to be of a serious nature, it is recommended that the employee be advised immediately of the situation in the presence of their representative, given a chance to respond and suspended pending investigation into the alleged misconduct (see Case Example 15.1 – Step A). This should be with pay. When a thorough investigation is completed, the interview can proceed.

2. Research carefully and confidentially. Check out the facts of the case (*who, where, when, why, how, it is or I think it is*), and the required and average performance standards on the job. Rigorous preparation will help you avoid "getting egg on your face". Indeed, it may turn out that, having completed the investigation, no action is required, or one settles for an informal counselling session.

    Some organisations encourage their supervisors to review the range of relevant documents on the employee's personal file (previous warnings, training received, appraisal records, etc.), the disciplinary procedure and relevant precedents at this point. However, the purpose of an initial interview is investigative. Therefore, little is served by pre-checking the employee's previous discipline record. To do so leaves one open to an accusation of bias in the handling of the interview. In any case, most supervisors will be aware of the previous record without the need to check. If so, they should consciously set that knowledge aside.

Of course, as outlined above, the potential of the counselling interview must not be damaged by reference to the disciplinary procedure. In the event of Stage 1 of your procedure being a "counselling" interview, you may opt to resort to it after a real "counselling" interview has been convened and failed — as the identical or a similar offence is repeated.

3. Plan the interview structure and your key questions. Write down all of the facts and be prepared to substantiate them.

4. Decide on the personnel to be involved. Where issues have reached a serious stage, at least two management representatives should be present. This allows your version of proceedings to be substantiated, ensures that you are not outnumbered, and facilitates the correct and consistent application of rules and procedures. You should also be clear as to who has the authority to formally warn or dismiss staff. The aforementioned Code (1996) also recommends that the employee concerned be allowed to confront or question witnesses.

5. Advise the interviewee of the time, place and purpose of the interview and their representation entitlement.

6. Allow enough time — since one never knows what will surface in the course of such a delicate, yet potentially explosive meeting — and prohibit interruptions. Ensure that the physical layout of the room is appropriate to the purpose of the meeting.

During the Disciplinary Interview

1. Don't be cosy, yet don't be rude — strike the right balance. In any interview, the interviewee deserves a fair hearing. You don't want to intimidate the employee to the extent that you

only hear their side of the story when it's told by their legal representative at the EAT! At that stage it's too late, and may be too costly for your organisation — not to mention your own career prospects! Don't allow personalities to influence your investigation; "be hard on the problem and easy on the person".

2. Remain calm throughout the meeting, whatever the provocation or personal jibes. This should help you to see the key issues in a more objective light.

3. Deliver your opening statement. This can take the form of advising those present that it is a disciplinary interview, the stage of the procedure you're at, your role relative to the procedure and the function of the other people present (i.e. representatives, witnesses, etc.). The structure of the meeting should then be outlined.

4. The structure of the meeting entails the aforementioned opening statement, stating your position and posing questions. The employee and their representative will then reply, question witnesses and produce their own witnesses. You can then further question the employee and their witnesses. The employee should be encouraged to highlight any issues they consider important, including any mitigating circumstances. There may also be adjournments, to facilitate reflection and further inquiries.

5. Use open-ended questions to elicit information, and probing and closed-ended questions for clarification and to eliminate evasiveness. Your questioning and presentation of the case should be neutral, creating an invitation to respond. By the end of the meeting, you will want to have established what happened to whom, where, when, how and why. You also need to be able to differentiate between facts and assumptions (i.e. *it is or I think it is*).

6. Determine whether there is any mitigating evidence. The action you take depends on the circumstances and the seriousness of the offence. When determining the action to be taken, the test of "reasonableness" must be borne in mind, and should take account of these mitigating factors. This means that every situation must be evaluated on its own merits, taking account of these special considerations. The final management decision must reflect such considerations, or else it is likely to fail the "test of reasonableness" when applied by the Rights Commissioner, the EAT or the LRC.

7. Summarise, to ensure that everyone understands the key issues, and then adjourn the meeting. Prior to an adjournment you should summarise the situation. This summary should reflect the key points of your original case, the employee's reply, the changes to your original case that have arisen during the meeting, the circumstances pertaining to the case as it now stands, and the matters for investigation during the adjournment. Adjournments should always be for the minimum amount of time necessary to allow for any checks that have to be conducted and for you to confer, consider all of the issues and decide your action. Reconvene the meeting and convey your decision.

8. At the end of the formal disciplinary meeting, summarise the outcome and action to be taken — warn or withdraw. Should the evidence point toward disciplinary action, management's position should be explained to the employee, who should be made fully aware of their shortcomings and management's concern. The nature of the improvement and the means for its achievement should be outlined, as should the consequences of future transgressions. Management must ensure that the employee fully understands the discipline imposed and the right of appeal.

9. If it is established that you have no case, the employee should be provided with a full explanation as to why it is not being taken any further. This explanation should be neither defensive nor apologetic. An effectively handled withdrawal from the disciplinary process can enhance the image of the organisation, and its disciplinary system, as investigative-oriented and fair.

After the Disciplinary Interview

1. Write up your records, advise the relevant personnel and send copies to the appropriate parties (e.g. Personnel Department, the employee, the representative). Accurate records should be kept of all disciplinary issues. The more detail the better, but in particular the record should set down dates, parties involved, the original case, the changes to that case, your action and its relationship to previous actions, and the particular circumstances of the case and how they affected the final action. The operation of an effective system requires the maintenance of adequate records. As the unfair dismissals legislation places the burden of proof primarily on the employer, management must be able to substantiate their case with adequate documentary evidence.

    At the counselling stage, a brief note on the issue, the individual concerned and the date and nature of the discussion would suffice. At verbal, written and all subsequent stages, the records should be more elaborate — including reference to what has been done "to put things right".

2. At the end of the disciplinary interview you will have outlined the nature of the improvement required and the means for its achievement. You should subsequently monitor the employee's performance or conduct, in an attempt to ensure that it does not recur.

3. Work at trying to prevent relationship(s) deteriorating. Disciplinary action can be a source of discomfort, disrupted relationships and resentment. Whilst your final action may be fair and reasonable in the circumstances, it is unlikely to endear you to staff. Your action should be followed up, to ensure that the problem does not arise again. You should not gloat over your handling of the problem, but make positive efforts to consolidate the relationship.

4. Wipe the slate clean in due course (if appropriate). Warnings should remain on an employee's record for as long as is consistent with the nature of the offence, in accordance with organisational rules and practice. Minor warnings tend to have a shorter time scale than those relating to more serious issues (see Case Example 15.1).

Be Cautious

A note of caution for HR specialists with responsibility for discipline administration is to be aware of possible bias on the part of supervisors or managers who bring such problems to your attention. In practice, the difficulty is often not one of finding out how "procedurally fair" the warning/suspension has been, as much as finding out how "unfair" or "unreasonable" it has been. That is, no matter how well trained one is in this area, bias on the part of the supervisor/manager is a real danger. Consequently, it is up to the HR practitioner to be alert to this tendency. A useful guide in this regard may be to apply the so-called "3Rs":

1. *Readiness*: prepare for the investigation. Gather as much background information as possible. Prod and prod again, as you give the supervisor/manager as much "attention" as the alleged offender.

2. *Rights*: get both parties to state their case and listen to both sides, and then listen again! Active listening will entail not just listening to what is being said, but to how it is being said,

what is not being said and observing the body language accompanying the statements.

3. *Reasonableness*: get all of the facts and seek out mitigating circumstances, rather than waiting for them to jump out at you at a later stage. Now you can feel more confident that you'll pass the "test of reasonableness".

GRIEVANCE PROCEDURE

The terms "disputes procedure" and "grievance procedure" are sometimes used interchangeably (see Case Example 15.1 earlier). The distinction is that the latter refers more to an individual employee grievance, and the former to a claim initiated by the whole workforce or a work group. The main aim of a grievance procedure is to settle the grievance fairly, and as near as possible to the point of origin (see Case Example 15.3).

Case Example 15.3: Sample Grievance Procedure at the North Eastern Health Board

The objective of the grievance procedure is to enable grievances to be dealt with promptly and fairly with no disruption, if possible, in patient care.

It is the Board's view that the most satisfactory way in which good working relationships are promoted is through consultation with employees and through the resolution of grievances as close as possible to the point of origin.

The Board believes that the procedural arrangements for the resolution of grievances should vary, having regard to whether the grievance relates to:

- *The employee's existing working conditions, duties etc.; or*

- *A fundamental change in the working conditions of employees or the manner in which the service is being provided.*

Existing Working Conditions/Work Practices
It is considered that a grievance should be defined as a complaint which has been formally presented to a management representative or to an employee representative.

While the issues listed hereunder are not intended to be exhaustive, grievances at local level normally relate to the following issues:

- *Rostering, shift working, weekend work, work breaks, overtime and deputising arrangements;*

- *All forms of leave, i.e. annual, sick, special, compassionate, maternity, study, etc.;*

- *Errors in pay, methods of payment of various allowances and premium payments;*

- *Duties and responsibilities of various grades of staff;*

- *The safety of the working environment.*

Where an employee considers that a complaint concerning issues regarding existing working practices/procedures has been ignored or unfairly dealt with, or where there is a difference in interpretation of the work practices/ duties or rules, the grievance procedural machinery should be invoked.

Grievance Procedure
Stage 1
Any grievance or dispute which arises at the workplace should be discussed, in the first instance, between the employee(s) and the immediate supervisor, i.e. nursing officer, ward sister, assistant staff officer/staff officer, etc. If either party considers it necessary/appropriate, they may involve the shop steward or union/staff association official.

Stage 2
If agreement cannot be reached, the matter should be referred to the appropriate management at local level at the earliest opportunity but in any event not later than one week following the completion of Stage 1. At this stage, the grievance may be in writing. If either party considers it necessary/ appropriate, they may involve the shop steward or union/staff association official. It should be noted that, for group disputes, Stages 1 and 2 may be combined.

Stage 3
If agreement cannot be reached at local level, local management should clarify the issue in dispute and refer it to the Programme Manager/Functional Officer as appropriate. At this stage, the Personnel Officer should also be advised by local management of the issue in dispute. The union/staff asso-

ciation should forward to the Personnel Officer a statement of its position on the matter in dispute.

Management will then arrange a meeting with the employee (or committee if it is a group dispute) and the official representative as soon as is reasonably practicable.

Stage 4
Should the parties fail to agree, the grievance may be dealt with as follows:

- *By reference to the machinery established under the Industrial Relations Act, 1990 (i.e. Labour Relations Commission, Labour Court);*

- *Under the Scheme for Conciliation and Arbitration for grades which have access to it;*

- *By appeal to the Chief Executive Officer;*

- *Ad hoc arbitration by agreement.*

Note: An employee may under certain circumstances appeal to the Minister for Health; see Health Act, 1970.

Where the grievance concerns existing work practices and conditions and is being processed under the grievance procedure, the status quo will be maintained until the issue is determined.

When a supervisor gives an instruction to an employee to carry out a particular task or function, which in the opinion of the supervisor is appropriate duty for that grade of staff, and where the employee does not believe that this is the case, the employee should carry out the instruction under protest until the end of the shift or tour of duty and so advise the supervisor, who will arrange to have the matter processed under Stage 2 of the Grievance Procedure. While the grievance is being processed, the employee, or employees of the same grade, will not be asked to carry out the particular duty/instruction.

Grievances Arising from Planned Changes in Working Conditions or the Manner of Providing Services
On occasions, because of budgetary matters, rationalisation of services or development of services, it may be necessary to introduce fundamental change in the organisation. The Board accepts that change can be traumatic for employees and supervisors; therefore it should be aware that:

- *There may be a fear of change per se because change can mean uncertainty;*
- *There may be fears about the economic effects of change in terms of earnings, benefits, job security and career prospects;*
- *People are often uneasy about having to learn new skills, assume different responsibilities, meet higher standards or work with new colleagues in a new setting;*
- *Individuals or groups may have status fears about the effect of a proposed change;*
- *There may be confusion about the nature of the proposed change and the underlying objectives, creating an environment of rumour and suspicion.*

The board will endeavour to address these fears by:

- *Providing full information at an early stage about proposed anticipated changes including the reasons, objectives and means involved;*
- *Consulting extensively with affected parties;*
- *Being frank about the problems and dangers posed by the proposed changes;*
- *Creating an atmosphere of trust;*
- *Trying to reach agreement with staff associations in relation to the proposed changes.*

In view of the Board's commitment to an approach which allows for consultation, explanation and participation, it is expected that in return employees and their representatives would be willing to engage in meaningful discussions and not to engage in precipitative action while discussions are under way. Therefore, it is envisaged that, when change is being discussed, several meetings would be held locally with staff and their representatives.

If local meetings fail to resolve the issues, it would be a matter for either party to request that the grievance procedure outlined at Stage 3 be invoked.

Grievances are inherent to the workplace. Issues such as pay, working conditions and practices, discrimination, job security and rules and regulations are frequent sources of employee grievance.

Consequently, managers should be aware of, and confident in, their role as effective grievance handlers, and of the positive contribution that they can make to good employee relations. Poor grievance handling can lead to low morale, low output, high labour turnover, high absenteeism and the loss of mutual confidence and trust at the workplace. It may also give rise to frustration, which permeates through to other staff and promotes an uneasy working environment. In 1996, a Council for the Education, Recruitment and Training (CERT) survey discovered that employees in the hotel and catering industry considered their relationship with their employer to be highly important, and were much more likely to stay if good relationships exist (CERT, 1996).

The bottom line is, if you repeatedly fail to address grievances, you lose staff, and you lose the respect of those who stay. The grievance process is the all-important "safety-valve", for releasing the tensions and pressures that build up at the workplace. Indeed, such a process is even more important in non-union firms, where employees are likely to have less internal support in the processing of issues. In fact, it appears that a number of the larger non-union plants place considerable emphasis on the rapid and effective handling of employee grievances (e.g. the so-called "open door" policy).

It is advisable that the effective manager keep so close to their staff that grievances are not allowed to fester. Therefore they are less likely to suddenly "blow up". When they arise, they are speedily addressed. Most grievances emerge slowly and quietly in the course of normal working, and only take the form of a sudden, emotional "blow-up" if the earlier warning signals have been ignored. Allowing grievances to grow and eventually escalate out of all proportion can be very costly and cause unnecessary damage to working relationships.

"Status Quo" Clause

As noted above, the main aim of the grievance procedure is to ensure that issues raised by employees are handled properly and settled fairly, and as near as possible to their point of origin. Of course, most grievances should be handled by the immediate supervisor, without recourse to a formal procedure. In the event that they are not resolved at this level, the procedure follows an upward path from one organisational level to the next (see Case Examples 15.2 and 15.3 earlier). Where grievances cannot be resolved within the workplace, it is normal to provide for the referral of the matter to an outside agency (e.g. Labour Relations Commission, Labour Court). Furthermore, it is common practice to include a provision that no form of industrial action will be taken until the procedure has been fully exhausted. This provides ample opportunity to settle issues, either through direct discussion, or by availing of a third party. A sample grievance procedure detailing this approach, at the North Eastern Health Board, is outlined in Case Example 15.3 above.

One of the most interesting features of the sample procedure in this Case Example is the inclusion of a "status quo" clause. According to Wallace (1987), though there is no real evidence on the incidence of "status quo" clauses in Irish procedure agreements, it would seem that they are quite rare. It may be argued that this is a deficiency, as it fails to address an area with considerable potential for conflict in industrial relations. The main reason that this issue is avoided is, according to Hawkins (1979), that management's ability to manage would be hampered. This dilemma is also reflected in the area of job descriptions. The preparation of a rigorous job description may serve many purposes in the recruitment, selection and training arenas. However, it may also create a "working to contract" dilemma, whereby jobholders abide by the explicit and published job requirements, but refuse to go "beyond contract". Those organisations espousing "high-performance work systems", "blame-free cultures", "high-trust philosophies", "total quality customer service", "continuous improvement" and "world class manufacturing", expect staff to be willing to go "beyond contract" in the performance of their duties. As a result, more flexible job descriptions, which are not linked to one specific task, are becoming more common. The application of a "status quo" clause would be quite alien in such environments. By the same token, the application of a clause facilitating the intervention of a third party in the resolution of disputes may also be resisted in some of these organisation types — with their non-union policies — for its threat to "management's right to manage" (e.g. the 1998 Ryanair dispute).

The Legal Angle[2]
Most large and medium-sized organisations have some process in place for the resolution of employee complaints. These processes may range from an informal "open door" policy to a very formal grievance procedure. However, the legal implications of the grievance-handling process were brought home forcibly in Britain recently, where an Industrial Tribunal held that an employer's failure to provide and apply a grievance procedure amounted to a breach of the employment contract. This entitled the employees to resign and subsequently successfully claim constructive dismissal. The Appeals Tribunal agreed, holding that it was an implied term in any employment contract that employers should reasonably and promptly give employees an opportunity to obtain redress of any grievance (McMullen, 1996).

THE GRIEVANCE INTERVIEW

The key face-to-face interaction in the management of grievances takes place at the grievance interview. Its first objective is to learn from the interviewee the true nature of their grievance. The apparent grievance may not be the real one. If there really is a prob-

---

[2] For greater detail see Chapter 18.

lem, agreement should be reached on a solution which both parties can deliver. If this is not possible, the first meeting should ensure that the grievance is progressed to the next stage in the procedure as expeditiously as possible. To get the best out of the grievance procedure, it is advisable that interviewers adhere to the following recommendations, which are again categorised into the *before*, *during* and *after* stages of the interview process.

Before the Grievance Interview

1. As most grievances are resolved informally, an informal meeting or preliminary interview, without employee representation, is worth the effort. If it fails, parties can resort to the appropriate first stage of the grievance procedure.

2. As an interviewer, you have less control over the timing than in any other kind of interview. When the grievance is brought to your attention, you must decide whether you can deal with it immediately. If you defer it for a short while, the angry interviewee may cool down. However, a long delay will lead to further frustration, and perhaps to the employee seeking satisfaction through the union, or from a higher level of management. So it is recommended that, if at all possible, you listen to the employee's grievance there and then. However, it may not be advisable to answer it on the spot. You may need time to reflect, investigate and decide what to do about it. Agree a time for reporting back, and adhere to it.

3. Be clear about your authority in relation to possible solutions. What are you empowered to give or concede? Consult other people as necessary, and check out the feasibility of the possible solutions. Will you establish a precedent via a concession? Are there others with a similar grievance? How do any of the possible solutions fit with organisational policy? The experience of the Personnel Department should be invaluable in informing you on these matters.

4. If you have the opportunity to plan the course of the interview, do so. Concentrate on reviewing what you already know or surmise about the nature of the grievance, and consider ways in which you can draw out further information.

5. Allow adequate time for the meeting. Given the potential impact on the individual's morale, and their preparedness to bring it to your attention, it is worth taking the time to hear what they have to say.

6. Get the climate and physical setting right. Prohibit interruptions and distractions. Organise the seating arrangements. Avoid the physical and psychological (desk) barrier if possible. Prepare for note-taking and to deploy counselling, problem-solving and negotiation skills as required.

During the Grievance Interview

1. Outline the purpose and structure of the interview, and clear the (discreet) note-taking.

2. Be careful to focus on the problem and the solutions, not the personality.

3. By asking appropriate open (e.g. *why? what? how?*) and probing questions, you can direct the discussion to the most relevant issues. A fair decision can only be based upon a fair assessment of all the facts. Minimise the use of closed-ended questions, as they don't encourage people to open up. However, they are useful for dealing with evasiveness and omissions. Leading questions (e.g. "Aren't you an honest woman?") and multiple questions tend to serve little purpose. In short, effective questioning can unearth the "real" grievance, as opposed to the stated one. It should also help you to differentiate between the causes and the symptoms.

4. Maintain eye contact and give appropriate positive feedback (verbally and non-verbally) to show your interest in the inter-

viewee, and encourage them to talk (and open up). It is wiser
to try and establish all of the facts at this point, than to have
them thrust at you in a more adversarial setting like the Labour Court.

5.   Clarifying and reflecting are useful techniques for getting the
     interviewee to elaborate, and to think twice about what they
     have just said. "Reflecting" merely entails repeating the inter-
     viewee's comment in a questioning tone.

6.   Listen. The atmosphere of grievance interviews can be
     charged with emotion. The pressure for it may have built up
     over a long time and it is upon you that the person has chosen
     to vent their feelings. The emotions can range from annoy-
     ance, anger, frustration and exasperation to despair. You may
     have to face shouting, abuse or even tears! Remember, you
     cannot resolve the problem until the emotions have subsided.
     Encourage the interviewee to say what's on their mind, whilst
     showing sincere concern at their dissatisfaction. You may not
     agree with what they have to say, but it is important that you
     understand the facts and the feelings associated with the issue.
     Don't underestimate the therapeutic value of letting them "get
     it off their chest". In some instances, this alone may resolve the
     grievance!

     Responding impulsively, or prejudging the issue without
     having the full facts, is dangerous. It may well be appropriate,
     therefore, to adjourn the meeting to allow you to check the
     matter out thoroughly. At the end of this meeting, summarise
     the facts and the action you'll take. Get back to the employee
     as quickly as possible.

7.   When you have heard everything that the interviewee wishes
     to say, summarise the key points of the grievance to their sat-
     isfaction. Now they know that you've been listening, and you
     know that you have all of the relevant facts, allowing you to

proceed to the "solution" stage. You cannot attempt solutions until the problem has been clearly defined and agreed by both parties. Help the interviewee to suggest their own solution(s) to the problem.

8. At the reconvened or first formal meeting, reiterate the facts of the matter and the common ground (e.g. "what did we agree with regard to . . .?"). By focusing initially on what you agree upon, the points of contention can be isolated. Discuss these points and the possible solutions. It may help to adopt a process of elimination, starting with the "worst" solution and moving to the "best".

It is likely that you will have to state and explain the organisation's position. Don't be afraid to do this, but invite the employee to question and comment upon it. Ensure that you understand each other's point of view. Though your position may not be accepted, it should be understood. If the final outcome is a negative one, the next stages in the procedure should be outlined. Your decision should be definite, detailed and clear. Explain and justify it. It's very important to try and explain the reasons for your decision, as it may make it more acceptable to the interviewee, and spare your boss the trouble of having to repeat it.

After the Grievance Interview

1. Write up the record of the interview. This is especially important if it is to be appealed to the next stage. Such information can also help to provide management with useful data on trends and the effectiveness of the procedures.

2. If you are able to meet the interviewee's request, do so and let them know as soon as possible. However, you should ensure that the settlement fully addresses and resolves the matter, as opposed to placing a "band-aid" over a sore spot which is likely to fester again.

3. If necessary, ensure that the next stage of the procedure is activated.

BULLYING AND SEXUAL HARASSMENT PROCEDURES[3]

In more recent times, the issues of bullying and sexual harassment at work have become more prominent, and are receiving a level of attention which they long deserved. Awareness is increasing of the need to balance "management's right to manage" with providing employees with a respectful and dignified working environment. Stemming from this is an increasing trend to provide employees with a grievance channel that recognises the particular sensitivities associated with bullying and sexual harassment situations. Sample procedures for dealing with these matters, deployed at New Ireland Assurance Co. plc, are outlined in Case Examples 15.4 and 15.5.

Case Example 15.4: Anti-Harassment Policy at New Ireland Assurance

New Ireland Assurance Company is committed to protecting the dignity of staff and preserving the right to equitable treatment. Incidents of harassment are unacceptable to this philosophy.

Disciplinary action will be taken against those whose behaviour is contrary to this policy. Depending on its severity, harassment could constitute gross misconduct and could lead to dismissal.

Allegations of harassment will be dealt with in an objective and sensitive manner and the utmost confidentiality will be preserved for both parties involved.

What is Harassment?
Harassment is behaviour which is unwanted, unreciprocated and offensive to another. It takes many forms and includes physical, verbal and non-verbal conduct.

---

[3] See Chapter 21 for additional detail of the legal context.

It is not only limited to conduct at the workplace. Actions which occur outside the workplace may also be covered, i.e. Company functions, Company business, etc.

Examples of harassment can include:

- Physical aggression to another;

- Shouting at a colleague;

- Abusive language/insults;

- Criticising a colleague in front of others;

- Sexual harassment – verbal and non-verbal, i.e. lewd comments, gesturing or displaying pornographic material;

- Indecent exposure or sexual assault;

- Harassment of another due to race, religion, ethnicity, sexual orientation, membership or non-membership of a trade union;

- Boycotting a colleague.

Procedures

What to do if you feel you are being harassed:

Many people subjected to harassment do not complain because they feel embarrassed, they are worried they may be victimised or they don't want to get the other person into trouble.

New Ireland Assurance Company guarantees that all complaints will be taken seriously and investigated swiftly and that all parties involved will be treated with respect.

Complaints should be made either to your direct manager (in confidence), or to a member of the Personnel Department. An investigation will ensue, on a confidential basis which is sensitive to the rights of both the alleged victim and the alleged harasser.

Stage 1

Many incidents of harassment can be dealt with effectively in an informal way, as often the harasser has no idea of the impact or effect their behaviour is having on others. Once it is drawn to their attention, the behaviour ceases. You may find it difficult to broach this subject personally and if this is the case you should seek the assistance of a colleague or a member of the Personnel Department for advice and/or assistance.

Stage 2

If appropriate, you should register a formal complaint against the alleged harasser. Your complaint should be put in writing to the Personnel Officer, outlining the nature of the complaint. In cases involving a senior member of staff, the Personnel Officer's place may be taken by the Head of Personnel.

- *The formal complaint will be treated as a disciplinary issue and will be investigated following New Ireland's disciplinary procedure.*

- *The investigation will be confidential, thorough and objective. It will be carried out with sensitivity and with due respect for the rights of all parties involved. Where it is necessary to interview witnesses, the importance of confidentiality will be emphasised. It will be explained to witnesses that any breach of confidence would constitute gross misconduct and would itself be subject to disciplinary action.*

- *Both parties involved will have the right to representation (union or non-union) at all stages of the investigation, if so desired.*

Case Example 15.5: Sexual Harassment Policy at New Ireland Assurance

---

What is Sexual Harassment?

Sexual harassment has been defined as conduct towards another person which is sexual in nature or which has a sexual dimension and is unwelcome to the recipient.

It is not only limited to conduct at the workplace. Actions that occur outside the workplace may also be covered e.g. Company functions, Company business, etc.

Examples of harassment can include:

Verbal

- *Requests or demands for sexual favours;*
- *Suggestive remarks;*
- *Degrading abuse or insults;*
- *Jokes or tricks of a sexual nature.*

Physical

- *Gesturing of a sexual nature;*
- *Unnecessary touching;*

- *Indecent exposure;*
- *Actual assault, up to and including rape.*

Visual

- *Displaying of pornographic material in the workplace.*

Sexual harassment can be imposed by either sex upon another and can include harassment of a person due to sexual orientation/sexual preferences.

Company Policy

The company is committed to protecting the dignity of staff and preserving their right to equal treatment. Sexual harassment is unlawful and discriminatory and will not be condoned by the company.

Instances of sexual harassment will be treated as serious misconduct and as such will have appropriate disciplinary responses which, depending on the gravity of the offence, could include dismissal.

Dealing with Sexual Harassment

Allegations of sexual harassment will be dealt with in an objective and sensitive manner and the utmost confidentiality will be preserved for both parties involved. All complaints will be fully investigated and no employee will be victimised for making a complaint.

Complaints of sexual harassment should be made either to your direct manager (in confidence) or to a member of the Personnel Department. An investigation will ensue, on a confidential basis, sensitive to the rights of both the alleged victim and alleged instigator.

Both parties involved will have the right to representation, at all stages of the investigation if so desired.

CONCLUSION

In conclusion, it should be emphasised that grievance and disciplinary procedures are merely a facilitator of effective people management practices. Where line management have not been trained in their practical application, or the interpersonal skills associated with successful line management are neglected, or the basic employee relations climate is poor, the procedural framework is likely to be of little use, as it institutionalises the conflict, and serves to aggravate issues far beyond what they warrant.

To ensure the effective management of disciplinary and grievance matters, the personnel and training function should equip line managers with adequate skills and knowledge to carry out their role effectively. This is particularly important, given that most of the issues arise and are handled at the shop-floor level by line management. Personnel can actively guide such development through in-service training seminars and case-by-case counselling — effectively ensuring that the overwhelming majority of such cases never go beyond the shop-floor. In an era of total quality management and labour and skill shortages, personnel would do well to recognise employees as another type of customer. Indeed, it may be argued that customer-employee service is effectively the personnel department's primary *raison d'être*. Improving this process, so that employee disciplinary and grievance issues are addressed and resolved effectively, is a central means of enhancing this service. Managers should be encouraged to depersonalise disciplinary and grievance matters, viewing them as opportunities to review and improve their operations, rather than as opportunities for retaliation.

The personnel/HR function also has an important role to play in establishing disciplinary and grievance policy and related procedures, and in monitoring their application throughout the organisation. In the long term, it should monitor them from a number of viewpoints — such as the impact on employees' behaviour, trends and consistency in incident sources, types and treatment, and the effectiveness of grievance handling and of the various forms of disciplinary action. Failure to do this may cost the organisation right across its staff recruitment, retention and employee relations functions.

References

Council for the Education, Recruitment and Training (Hotel Industry) (1996), *Towards Successful Recruitment and Retention*, Dublin: CERT.

Department of Enterprise and Employment (1996), *Code of Practice: Disciplinary Procedures*, Dublin: Department of Enterprise and Employment.

Gunnigle, P., G. McMahon and G. Fitzgerald (1995), *Industrial Relations in Ireland: Theory and Practice*, Dublin: Gill and Macmillan.

Hawkins, K. (1979), *A Handbook of Industrial Relations Practice*, London: Kogan Page.

Irish Hotels Federation (1997), *Quality Employer Manual*, Dublin: IHF.

McMullen, J. (1996), "A Grievance Procedure is Implied in Contracts" in *People Management, Journal of the Institute of Personnel and Development*, 11 January.

Industrial Relations News (1996), "Majority of Companies Provide Counselling Service", *Industrial Relations News*, No. 38, 10 October.

Wallace, J. (1987), "Procedure Agreements and their Place in Workplace Industrial Relations", *Industrial Relations in Ireland: Contemporary Issues and Developments*, Dublin: Department of Industrial Relations, University College, Dublin.

CHAPTER 16

NEGOTIATIONS:
HOW TO GET THE BEST DEAL

Gerard McMahon and *Ciara Heslin*

INTRODUCTION

Negotiations take place when two or more parties meet, aiming to win as much as they can from their counterparts, while giving away as little as possible. Everyone is a negotiator, at least in some of their activities. You've been negotiating since you first looked for pocket money, swapped comics or sweets, and cried in the cot! You've engaged in "purposeful" persuasion and constructive compromise — the essence of negotiation. Many of us spend a considerable amount of our time trying to persuade others about things. It is a type of a battle, in the sense that we're pitting our wits against each other, whilst bringing in the heavy artillery in the shape of sanctions, if and when required.

This chapter outlines the conventions, process, personality attributes, team roles, stages, strategies and "tricks" associated with effective negotiation. They should be applied whether one is negotiating pension entitlements with a new recruit, the release of hostages with dangerous terrorists, pay levels with a trade union or remuneration packages to retain key staff in a union or non-union environment.

NATIONAL PRACTICE

For the Personnel or Human Resources Manager, whilst many terms and conditions of employment tend to be negotiable, the most contentious tend to concern pay. Pay determination in Ireland is diverse, with a host of formal systems being pursued at various levels, as outlined in Table 16.1. For example, with managerial categories, pay is often decided at an individual one-to-one level. In contrast, for manual categories, pay is largely decided at national level (e.g. via Partnership 2000 or similar national level agreements). The development of collective bargaining practices in Ireland — as reflected in negotiations between workers and their unions, and employers and their organisations — can be categorised into a number of distinct phases. These start in the late nineteenth century to 1941, as trade unions struggled to establish themselves, from 1941 to 1946, when pay negotiations were effectively frozen by Government statute, the wage rounds from 1946 to 1970, the national wage agreements from 1971 to 1981, the return to decentralised bargaining between 1982 and 1986, and the current period of national bargaining, starting with the Programme for National Recovery in 1987 up to the current Partnership 2000 agreement. The details of these developments are well traced in Gunnigle et al. (1995).

Table 16.1: Levels of Basic Pay Determination

	Management	**Prof./Tech.**	**Clerical**	**Manual**
National/ Industry-wide	34.5	40.2	53.6	62.1
Regional	0	0.8	4.6	8.8
Company/ Division	31.4	26.4	23.8	11.9
Establishment	10.3	14.9	13.0	10.0
Individual	44.4	28.7	20.7	6.1

Source: Gunnigle, Morley, Clifford and Turner, 1997, p. 159.

So influential have these national deals been that various sources estimate that there was up to 95 per cent adherence to their terms between 1987 and 1996 (i.e. the Programme for National Recovery, the Programme for Economic and Social Progress and the Programme for Competitiveness and Work). The key questions now are whether this can be maintained with Partnership 2000, and whether such national level agreements can prevail in the new millennium. Because of their flexibility, via the provision of "local" bargaining clauses, the increasingly complex agenda of negotiation in Ireland, and the emergence of a burgeoning non-union sector, the Personnel/HR Manager still needs keen negotiation skills. Not everyone is ideally suited to the task. So what type of personality makes for a good negotiator? We consider this and related issues in the next section.

THE EFFECTIVE NEGOTIATOR'S PERSONALITY

In listing the attributes of a good negotiator, one may end up with a picture of superman or superwoman. Nevertheless, it is useful to identify the key attributes of a good negotiator. You can then assess whether you are suited to a central role in this process, what you need to develop or whether it is a job best left to a colleague. The effective negotiator is:

1. Constantly aware, able to listen to others, with an imaginative and quick mind;

2. Flexible, so that if the initial plan doesn't work, you are prepared to abandon it and make a new course;

3. Cool — since an emotional negotiator is easy prey for your counterpart;

4. Approachable, able to make, accept and maintain contacts;

5. Capable of keeping your distance, stepping back and coldly assessing how things are progressing;

6. Able to listen to, and look at, issues from the other side's viewpoint — to put yourself in their shoes;

7. Able to withstand the physical and emotional demands of the process.

NEGOTIATING ROLES

Even if you don't fit this particular mould, there may be other valuable roles that you can play on the negotiation "team". Like any team, the best negotiation team comprises a number of roles, ideally involving different people performing tasks for which they are best suited. Though negotiations often entail a one-on-one exchange, with the individual performing a variety of team roles, we find that in more consequential exchanges, such as political, boardroom or union–management encounters, a negotiation team will be formed. This normally comprises the following roles:

The Lead

The lead negotiator or spokesperson takes charge of the negotiation on behalf of their side. This person has the main responsibility for presenting their arguments and countering those coming from the other side. A good lead negotiator will require little support from their side, except where they invite the summariser or other team member(s) to contribute on a specific issue. Good leaders will control the team performance on their own, so as to enable a sharper and more focused edge on their side's objectives, arguments, tactics and strategy. They may not be the most senior person in the group, but should be considered the most fitting against the personality attributes detailed above.

The Summariser

This person's main tasks are to ask questions, to seek clarification, to summarise and, when necessary, to buy time for the lead negotiator. With the lead negotiator engrossed in the presentation of arguments, the summariser can look at the big picture, and take a more strategic view of what is going on. This will give the lead negotiator time to gather their thoughts, so they can make a fresh attack on the other side. However, at no time should the summariser attempt to take over the leadership. A good summariser will recognise when the lead negotiator needs help and will provide it.

The Observer

Not all in attendance at negotiations need to participate actively. There is an important role to be played by those observing. As they are less emotionally involved in the exchanges, they are better positioned to evaluate the situation as it unfolds. They can read the more subtle nuances of the negotiations, including the use of certain phrases and body language. For example, according to Denny (1994), there are about 700,000 body language signals and about 40,000 words and sounds. However, on a day-to-day basis, we only use 4,000 of these words! It appears that whenever the body language information is in conflict with the verbal information, the body's signal is invariably correct. Most people can control what they say, but with 700,000 body language signals, it is practically impossible to control real feelings!

For example, in 1972, the Provisional Irish Republican Army (IRA) insisted on the release of Gerry Adams from prison to take part in negotiations with the British Government. On release, Adams was advised by his colleagues that his role was that of observer. He was instructed not take part in the direct negotiations, but to observe the meaning of what was said as much as to listen to the words (Coogan, 1996).

The Specialist

The particular specialist to be invited on to the negotiation team depends on the issue under negotiation. The more common specialists used would have particular strengths in areas such as corporate strategy, accounts or the commercial viability of the enterprise, the law, pensions or remuneration. Put simply, they are there to provide expert advice when needed. They rarely contribute to the bargaining, but do provide valuable assistance and clarification when preparing for negotiation and during the adjournments.

However, the great danger with the deployment of specialists in the negotiation process is that, despite their expertise, they are oblivious to the charades and peculiarities of negotiation, and may unwittingly serve to hand the advantage to their opponent. Accordingly, the lead negotiator should keep the specialist "under wraps" until such time as they are needed. At this point, the lead will invite them to make an input, knowing what they will contribute and what they will say in response to questions from the opposing team.

The Recorder

Recording equipment is not normally tolerated at negotiation sessions. Consequently, the recorder's job is to take a written record of proceedings at the meetings. This is often an underrated function, but it can be of considerable help in more detailed and complex negotiations. Good notes are invaluable between meetings, to help the team shape its next position or strategy. For those embarking on a personnel career, it is a good location from which to learn both the blunt and the more subtle skills of the negotiation process.

NEGOTIATING: PROCESS AND CONVENTIONS

The process of negotiation consists of three elements. Firstly, both teams, or negotiators, state their *opening bargaining positions*. Secondly, they *probe* weaknesses in the bargaining position of the other team and try to convince them that they must move from their present position to a position closer to what their opponent wants. Thirdly, they both *revise* their original bargaining position, in light of information gleaned and reactions observed, so that, if push comes to shove, the ground chosen for future exchanges will be as favourable as possible.

Negotiations are described as a game, in the sense that both sides are trying to win. But — like any game — there are various conventions or rules which the parties tactically adopt or recognise. Interestingly, these conventions, and the associated ritualistic behaviour or charade, while appearing bizarre to newcomers (like the aforementioned specialist), have the benefit of reducing anxiety for the main players. They help create an atmosphere of trust and understanding, which is essential to the maintenance of the type of stable bargaining relationship that benefits both sides in the long term. With these "unwritten rules", both sides know what to expect, and so move along a familiar road until agreement or a temporary compromise is reached.

Figure 16.1: Characteristics of the Three Outcomes of Negotiations

---

1. Win/Win (both parties gain)

Achieved by joint decision-making and discussion

- Both parties needs are met;
- The decision is not unacceptable to anyone;
- It requires two-way communications;
- The emphasis is on a flexible approach;
- The concentration is on objectives;
- A long-term relationship is maintained.

2. Win/Lose (one party wins, the other party loses)

- The creation of a "them and us" distinction;
- Energies are directed only towards victory;
- Parties have only one point of view;
- There is a strong emphasis on immediate solutions, regardless of whether the long-term objectives are met;
- Too many personal conflicts exist;
- Emphasis is on short-term concerns, the long-term relationship is forgotten.

---

3. Lose/Lose Characteristics (both parties lose)

- Neither party achieves their objectives;
- Disillusionment with the negotiating process as a whole;
- Frustration of both parties;
- Loss of respect/trust;
- The long-term relationship is soured;
- No solutions are generated.

It is essential that parties involved in negotiations know and understand these traditions and rituals, as failure to adhere to them can lead to a hardening of positions, increasing the likelihood of breakdown and a "lose/lose" situation (see Figure 16.1). These conventions are understood and accepted by experienced and responsible negotiators. However, they are rarely explicitly stated by the parties and may even be broken in the heat of the moment. Armstrong (1984) and Salamon (1992) have identified some of these conventions:

1. Agreement is the aim. On issues in which a precedent for negotiating or meeting has been set, there should be a willingness to meet the other party. The absence of this precedent may prevail where management decide that some term or condition of employment is "non-negotiable". Its absence is also at the heart of trade union recognition disputes, such as the notorious 1998 Ryanair dispute, where the company refused to recognise the Services, Industrial, Professional and Technical Union (SIPTU).

    If the parties do engage in negotiations, both parties are using the process in the hope of coming to a settlement. Focusing on the common ground may help in the maintenance of a constructive climate. For example, both union and staff may need constant reminding that both sides have a vested interest in developing a flexible, productive and profitable company.

This is the win/win scenario, the best of the three possible outcomes of the process (as set down in Figure 16.1). Reflecting this approach in respect of Coillte's organisational change programme, Paul Cassidy, then Director of Human Resources, warned:

> . . . change programmes must have a balance of gain for all who are involved. . . . You cannot force things down people's necks.

This perspective is also accepted on the trade union side, as John Tierney, National Secretary of the Manufacturing, Science and Finance Union (MSF) observes:

> MSF has no difficulty with change, but we demand the right to negotiate it — that is our policy. Any union that does not take an interest in where the industry is going or where the company is going within that industry is not looking at the real agenda.

2. The wish of both teams to reach a mutually satisfactory conclusion does not preclude the threat or use of industrial sanctions. Furthermore, attacks, hard words, threats and (controlled) losses of temper are also perfectly legitimate tactics to underline determination to get your way and to shake the opponent's confidence. However, as noted by Patricia King, Branch Secretary with SIPTU, the essential thing is to judge carefully when industrial action will deliver and when it will not — when it will help to progress matters, as opposed to regress them.

But these "weapons" are treated by both sides as legitimate tactics and should not be allowed to shake the basic belief in each other's integrity or desire to settle without taking drastic action. For example, trade unions frequently threaten various forms of industrial action; employers threaten lay-offs, closure or wage cuts; dissatisfied individuals may threaten to leave the company; whilst the Government's threat, in 1969, to apply statutory control over all pay rises served to bring about the first ever national level wage agreement.

As in real life, threats may be counter-productive if used regularly in negotiation. If a threat is made, it should only be as a last resort and the negotiator must be prepared to carry it through, conscious of the consequences. If your bluff is called and you can't deliver — whether it be boardroom support or workers on the picket line — your credibility is undermined and irreparable damage may be done to your bargaining strength and the overall relationship for the future.

3. It is normally management's responsibility to organise the physical setting for the negotiations. In so far as it is possible, management should ensure that their counterparts (e.g. union negotiators) have the same facilities as themselves. The psychological gurus contend that the traditional face-to-face negotiations, with both principal negotiators sitting directly opposite each other, encourages a combative atmosphere, whereas a roundtable setting encourages a less formal, collaborative style of discussion. This explains the tendency of many senior managers to deploy a round table in the corner of their office.

4. Off-the-record discussions are mutually beneficial as a means of "feeling the way", probing attitudes and intentions and smoothing the way to a settlement. Your counterpart may be prepared to be more forthcoming informally, outside the pressure of the negotiating forum. But such exchanges should not be referred to specifically in the formal negotiating sessions, unless both sides agree in advance. All major negotiations entail an element of this, though politicians and trade union officials may not acknowledge them, for fear of losing face with their constituents.

5. Each party should be given an opportunity to state its position and will normally be prepared to move from this. If they refuse, they can be accused of imposing rather than negotiating. The negotiations proceed as the teams alternate offers and counter-offers, eventually leading to a settlement. As outlined above, the process entails movement towards rather than away from the other party. If it doesn't, the negotiations are likely to break down. For example, reflecting this movement, in 1998, the Garda Representative Association (GRA) opened negotiations with a demand for a pay rise of 39 per cent, subsequently took industrial action in support of their claim at less than half of this figure, and eventually settled for a figure of less than one third the original amount demanded!

6. Adjournments are taken by mutual agreement. The main purpose of an adjournment is to review and assess progress against your prepared objectives, and to assess your opponent's objectives or latest offer/proposal. They provide an opportunity to update strategy. A request for an adjournment is normally granted and the duration mutually agreed. On resumption, the party that requests the break speaks first. It is an invaluable part of the negotiation process, allowing the teams to revisit their strategy, demands and tactics.

    The number and frequency of adjournments will depend upon the complexity and stakes of the exercise and normal practice in this context. Industrial relations negotiations might adjourn more frequently than commercial negotiations — but this is not necessarily so. For example, major take-over or contract negotiation may be spread, of necessity, over many meetings.

7. Concessions, once made, are not withdrawn. Nor are firm offers withdrawn, although it is legitimate to make and withdraw conditional offers. Thus, once an offer has been made, it should not be withdrawn unless it is conditional at the time of

making or the circumstances surrounding it have radically and visibly changed.

8. Third parties should not be brought in until both parties are agreed that no further progress can be made without them. In some instances, employers refuse such intervention — arguing that it interferes with "management's prerogative to manage". Whilst the 1998 Ryanair dispute is one such prominent case, Michael Collins' refusal, in 1922, to retain a "third party" system for the Irish public service (installed by the British), started a long and bitter battle with the unions which ran to 1950, bringing down a Fianna Fáil government in the process, in 1938.

    The other end of this third party extreme is that some negotiators almost see their involvement as inevitable. For example, according to Seán Healy, former Director of the Labour Relations Commission's Advisory Service:

    > We identified 60 major companies and their trade unions which were using the service on a continuous basis without perhaps looking to themselves to resolve issues. Many of the issues which were coming forward were minor and could or ought to have been settled at local level. (Sheehan, 1996a)

9. Negotiators may make the agreement conditional upon its acceptance by their principals (e.g. top management, the workforce, the company board). This may arise, for example, where the management team has (conditionally) granted concessions outside what they've been authorised to concede. It is a practice which has earned the personnel profession the tag "messenger boy", but is also an integral feature of trade union operations, as they often put offers to the membership. For example, in 1997, recommendations from their union leaderships to accept offers arising from pay negotiations were

rejected by the memberships of the Irish Nurses' Organisation, the Civil and Public Service Union, the Association of Secondary Teachers of Ireland and the Teachers' Union of Ireland.

STAGES OF NEGOTIATION

Ultimately, the key criteria for successful negotiations are information and power. These will be reflected in, and conditioned by, such factors as:

- The relative strength of your case and that of your counterparts;

- The relative power of the employer vis-à-vis the union/employee;

- The size of the union's/employee's claim and whether it is realistic;

- The likely target and minimum acceptable offer set by the union/employee;

- The amount of room for negotiation that management want to allow;

- Management's ability to pay/concede the request;

- The going rate/practice elsewhere, nationally agreed norm or the rate of inflation (in the case of a pay claim).

Although pay decisions are now largely taken at national level, between government, employers and trade unions, personnel/ HR practitioners continue to negotiate. It is an integral feature of the job. Whether you're negotiating on the local "discretionary" pay claim provided for in the national agreements, about the pay of a benchmark group of workers, a middle manager's bonus, career prospects or even your own job title, you'll get the best deal if you break the process into four stages: *preparing; opening; negotiating;* and *closing*.

The Preparatory Stage

It is generally argued that what you have done before you arrive at the negotiation table will show when you get there. A well-prepared negotiator will direct events while a poorly prepared negotiator may only react to them. It is in the preparation phase that you decide what needs to be achieved and how to achieve it. Good preparation involves researching and assembling all relevant information and structuring it in a logical manner. An analysis should take place of all the options and alternatives available, thus ensuring that you know the costs, implications, advantages and disadvantages of each in advance, rather than when it's too late and the agreement is signed.

Information: Strengths

Identify your strengths, which will include facts to support your case. For example, to assess an individual's or trade union's claim, a lot of data needs to be assembled and assessed. Information about pay levels and increases and conditions in other employments, Labour Court decisions, the Consumer Price Index and other national industrial/economic trends and relevant matters may be crucial. Such data can be secured by members of the Irish Business and Employers Confederation (IBEC), including:

- A wide range of schedules of current pay rates and conditions of employment for different categories of workers;

- Regional/industrial survey breakdown reports on the above;

- Occasional analyses and weekly listings of wage round settlements;

- All relevant economic and social statistics from national and international sources.;

- Recent Labour Court and Employment Appeals Tribunal decisions on pay and relevant conditions of employment.

Some trade unions also provide their constituents with such key data. When negotiating pay rates, rises and job perks with managerial categories, sources such as the Irish Management Institute and Inbucon have a ready bank of relevant comparative data which can prove invaluable if deployed properly.

In pay negotiations, there is often a "going rate" at which comparable employments are settling. Negotiations on wages, for example, often take place in a climate of precedent: where are other similar employments settling? This was the defining feature of pay bargaining in Ireland over the 1946–82 period. Despite some recent success in restricting it, over the 1997–98 period a spiral of repercussive claims, offers and awards followed the nurses' pay award (e.g. paramedics, prison officers, civil service clerical grades, gardaí). For example, in 1998 the GRA were able to present evidence in support of their demand for a pay rise, showing that numerous other comparable groups had enjoyed a better relative pay performance e.g. the British police, Garda sergeants, chief superintendents, Garda commissioners, prison officers, civil service departmental secretaries, administrative officers, executive officers, staff officers, clerical officers, custom and excise officers (McMahon, 1996). Attempting to stem the tide in the course of the negotiations with the gardaí, the Taoiseach, Bertie Ahern, explained that:

> ... for us to go up to a figure like 15 per cent would mean that every public servant in the country would come back in with a substantial pay increase demand. (Cusack, 1998a)

Support for your negotiating position may also be derived from previous agreements, custom and practice, previous statements from opponents and evidence. It may also be derived from the level of public support for your case (e.g. the nurses in 1997), the capacity to disrupt business or societal functioning (e.g. power workers or transport staff versus biscuit makers), the employer's ability to relocate the business elsewhere or the individual's ability to attract other job offers.

Information: Weaknesses

The sensible negotiator will also note the main weaknesses in their position. In attempts to recruit and retain a quality workforce, the main weaknesses might be the tightness of the labour market, with more lucrative and better job opportunities available elsewhere. Related to this may be the inflexibility of your organisation's wage structure. The opponents are likely to raise these points, so a prepared response is required if you don't want to be "hung out to dry". This means that you should have an idea of what they will say or do should the weaknesses be raised. It is not your job to raise these weaknesses, thereby making your opponent's case for them. However, in certain cases where it is obvious that they are going to be raised, you may be able to downplay them by introducing them and responding to them yourself.

Of course, expectations as to how trends will develop are often a crucial factor in negotiations. For example, if the current (1999) level of economic growth were to slow significantly or indeed to regress, the question might not be "how do we get and keep our key staff?", but "how do we get rid of the workforce at minimal cost and disruption?". The overriding impact of this "contextual" influence is repeatedly emphasised by organisations such as the Economic and Social Research Institute, which, in 1997, warned that the biggest domestic danger to continued economic growth is an excessive rise in expectations, which could feed into wage inflation or excessive demands on the Exchequer.

Negotiation Objectives

The first priority at this preparatory stage is to establish your objectives. Everything follows from this. Parties should arrive at the negotiating table with a clear idea as to the level of priority and price that these objectives have. Assign relative priorities to the objectives and question how realistic they are. There is little to be gained from aiming at the unattainable. You should also try to estimate the likely priorities in your opponent's objectives. It is often difficult during the negotiations to establish what their priorities really are. Indeed, they may make a considerable effort to conceal the fact that they have any priorities and will attempt to persuade you that everything they demand is of equal importance. The negotiator cannot complain at this form of bluff, but should be prepared to respond in a similar fashion.

Remember, the overall objective is to get as much of your package of demands as possible, by settling as close to your ideal as possible. But the very existence of a range of possible settlements between your ideal and your limit means that some of your objectives are less important than others, and that a number of fallback positions exist. So start out by making a list of your objectives — all of them, even those which are more implicit that explicit (e.g. to keep your job, retain key staff, keep the existing business, get a discount for multiple job advertisement placements, preserve the status quo, secure flexibility, pay cut/rise and so on). This list is the ideal solution — what you would like to achieve. Many of the items on the list may be things that you already enjoy; the rest remain to be achieved. Recognise that in any negotiation all issues may be revisited and it is possible to lose some items which previously have been taken for granted. It's no problem if the overall trade is beneficial.

It is now time to identify the "must achieve" objectives. This is sometimes called the "bottom line", "fallback" or limit position. These are the objectives that you must secure agreement on. For example, in a typical wage negotiation the employee, union or representative body making the claim, and the Personnel Manager or employer/manager faced with it, will define three things in advance:

1. The ideal settlement point they would like to reach;

2. The minimum they will accept or (from the employer/ manager's perspective) the maximum they would be prepared to concede;

3. The opening claim which will be most likely to help achieve the target, or (from the employer/manager's perspective), the opening offer they will make to provide them with sufficient room to manoeuvre in reaching their target.

The difference between the union's claim and the employer's offer is the negotiating range. If your maximum exceeds their minimum, this is the settlement range.

Negotiation Strategy

Negotiation strategy is important to the attainment of the best deal (McMahon, 1997). As noted above, the strategy should clearly be designed to achieve the target settlement, with the maximum you are prepared to concede, or the minimum you are prepared to accept, being the fallback position. To deliver on this, it helps to decide two things:

1. The ideal route and stages to be followed when moving from the opening to the closing offer or demand;

2. The negotiating package to be used in reply to whatever package your counterparts have put forward. There is much to be said for having in reserve various conditions (like a shopping list), which you can ask your counterparts to deliver in return for your concessions. You might, for example, ask for an extended period before the next pay settlement, in return for an increase in your offer.

Summary for Preparatory Work

To finalise your preparation for negotiation, where a staff member or union has made a claim, Armstrong (1984) and McDonagh (1995) urge consideration of the following questions:

- Is the claim legitimate?

- What will it cost?

- Is there a precedent within the organisation or the industry?

- What is normal practice within the industry?

- Is there a likelihood of an unacceptable knock-on effect for other individuals or groups in the organisation if a concession is made?

- Is management on weak ground in relation to any of the issues likely to arise?

- Is the claim compatible with the terms of Partnership 2000 or the prevailing national agreement?

- If there is a breakdown, what will the consequences be? Will sanctions be applied?

- Will you lose key member(s) of staff, can you replace them and what will this do to your business?

- Is there likely to be a dispute if you do not agree to the demands?

- Can the other side prevent or obstruct the implementation of your proposals for change?

- What would the Labour Court recommend if you have to go there?

- What are your objectives, and what strategy offers the best prospects of delivering them?

- What arguments will be used in supporting your case?

- What are the arguments and counter-arguments that your opponent is likely to use?

- What data do you need to support your case?

- Are you the sole negotiator or will there be others on your negotiating team?

- Have you briefed and rehearsed the members of your negotiating team on their roles, and the negotiating objectives, strategy and tactics that are to be adopted?

Having satisfactorily addressed these questions, you're now ready to enter the fray.

The Opening Stage

The main purpose of the opening stage is to reveal the broad outline of your position, whilst gathering as much information as possible about the opponent's. The more extreme the opening positions, the more time and effort it will take to discover if agreement is possible. Nevertheless, the opening salvos in this game of charades should not deceive you as to what the final shape of things to come will be. For example, predicting the emergence of Partnership 2000, industrial relations expert Brian Sheehan opined:

> Most observers of the industrial relations scene can already envisage the shape of what might emerge from the forthcoming talks on a new national programme to replace the PCW . . . (but) all of the main players will want to be seen to play "hard to get" in the talks. (Sheehan, 1996b)

According to Armstrong (1984), the best tactics to deploy when opening negotiations are:

1. Open realistically and move moderately;

2. Challenge your opponent's position as it stands; do not destroy their ability to move;

3. Explore attitudes, ask questions, observe behaviour and, above all, listen in order to assess your opponent's strengths and weaknesses, their tactics and the extent to which they may be bluffing;

4. Make no concessions of any kind at this stage;

5. Be non-committal about proposals and explanations (don't talk too much, but encourage your opponent to respond to all of your queries).

Firmness at this point can provide a negotiating platform for later flexibility. The higher your platform, the more the opponent has to do to get agreement to compromise. However, the danger here is that the firmer you are, the greater the chance of failure to agree. Firmness can be taken as a sign that you are not willing to negotiate and the opponent may exercise the costly and disagreeable option of imposing sanctions, to weaken resolve and force flexibility upon their counterpart (as the nurses and the gardaí did with the Government in 1997 and 1998 respectively). Alternately, they may simply decide not to do business at all, and to take their custom, product, service or labour elsewhere. Some negotiations don't get beyond the opening. They break down because tension is heightened by the behaviour of the parties toward each other. Instead of coming closer together, they move farther apart, resulting in breakdown. The consequence of this may be a lost order, failed take-over, closure, a strike, a lock-out, the departure of a valued staff member or the relocation of the business.

The opening proposals of one side in a negotiation exercise may be on the table before the first meeting. Unions often send their claim to the employer in advance. Naturally, this claim is expected to represent their most ambitious position (their ideal). The task now is to try and establish the negotiating margin available.

The Negotiating Stage

After the opening moves, the main bargaining phase begins. At this phase, the gap is narrowed as parties try to persuade their opponent that their case is sufficiently strong to force the opponent to close at a less advantageous point than planned. This negotiating stage is about exchanging — something gained for something given. It is the most intense stage of the whole process, and both parties have to pay close attention to what they are doing. Ill-judged concessions by one party can make the difference between a successful and a disastrous outcome.

The best way to avoid the disaster is to lead with conditions. Get them up front. Tell the opponent what you will give them in return for your condition(s). A proposal, then, in this context, is a movement towards, if not into, the negotiating arena. Responses to tentative proposals provide information about each other's strength of commitment to the issues in dispute. The parties "stalk" around each other at this point, trying to size up the possibilities.

It is generally argued that you should always make proposals conditional: "If you will do this, then I will consider doing that." The key words to remember are: "*if . . . then . . .*" Astutely presented offers are conditional: "*If* you are *prepared to do* such and such, *then* we are *prepared to consider doing* this and that." (Note how you present your condition first, and make it a specific "to do" — as opposed to "consider doing" — and how your offer is a tentative "consider doing"). Don't make a one-sided concession. Always trade for concessions from the other party: "If I concede X then I expect you to concede Y." On occasion, negotiators will be able to concede some demand to their counterpart. However, it is wiser to link the issue to something that you want a concession on in return. Related to this, good negotiators negotiate on the whole package. They don't allow their opponent to pick them off item by item. They keep all of the issues alive and open, so as to extract the maximum benefit from any potential trade-offs at the final hurdle. Having listed your priority objectives at the preparatory stage, you now try to trade what is "cheap" for you in return for your priority objectives.

Signalling

Signalling is an inherent part of the negotiation process. A signal is a means by which parties indicate their willingness to negotiate on something. Listen to the language used. Somewhere, tucked away in a long sentence, you may hear a qualification used. For example, instead of "We will never agree to what you are proposing", the words "In its present form" might be added. Such disarming innocence, yet so vitally important for the progress of the negotiations! The negotiator is telling the opponent to amend their offer in some way, thus creating the possibility of agreement. But remember that the signal is not just a movement by the party sending the signal; it is a call for the other party to respond. For example, in 1998, in the course of an impasse in the negotiations between the Government and the GRA, the Taoiseach successfully signalled an attempt to get the talks reopened, by stating that there was room to negotiate a "fairly substantial increase" for gardaí, so long as it remained within the public sector pay parameters.

The Closing Stage

When and how you close is a matter of judgement, and depends on the assessment of the strength of both cases, together with the determination of both parties to see it through. Armstrong (1984) suggests various closing techniques:

1. Make a concession from the package, preferably a minor one, which is traded off against an agreement to settle. The concession can be offered more positively than in the negotiating stage: "If you will agree to settle at X, then we will concede Y."

2. Do a deal: splitting the difference, or bringing in something new, such as extending/shortening the settlement time-scale, agreeing to back payments, phasing increases, making a joint declaration of intent to do something in the future (e.g. introducing flexitime, job sharing, a productivity plan). For example, the eventual settlement of the Partnership 2000 pay agreement entailed a concession by the union side of a clause that payment (of the 2 per cent under the local bargaining wage clause) required "verified progress" on the productivity-oriented Strategic Management Initiative for the public sector.

3. Summarise what has happened to date, emphasise the concessions that have been made and the extent to which you have moved, stating that you have reached your final position. Do not make a final offer unless you mean it. If it is not really your final offer and your opponent calls your bluff, you may have to make further concessions and your credibility will be undermined. Your opponent will, of course, attempt to force you into revealing the extent to which you have reached your final position. Do not allow them to hurry you, and try not to present it as your final offer unless you are confident that it will be accepted, and that they know the consequences of rejecting it.

4. Apply pressure, through a threat of the dire consequences that will follow if your final offer is not accepted.

5. Give your opponent a choice between two courses of action: "You can have X or Y, but not X and Y."

This closing stage is a dangerous time for negotiators. There may be a high degree of euphoria, as the tensions of the previous steps dissipate in the natural relief of arriving at agreement. It can put you off guard. If you are keen to get agreement, and relieved to get it, it is easy to neglect the finer details of what has been agreed. This can cause endless trouble later on, when the agreement is implemented, and each side has its own version of what was agreed. Then the charges fly, of "cheating", "dirty tricks", "foul play" and so on. The emotional heat caused by feelings such as these can take a long time to overcome. People may really believe something was agreed when it was not. This "disagreement about the agreement" is especially prevalent in workplaces characterised by low-trust relations. It leaves human resource managers and trade union representatives operating as quasi-legal experts, as they devote their time to putting the most favourable interpretation on an agreement, regardless of the intent or the long-term relationship with their negotiation opponents. The "decommissioning impasse" in the Northern Ireland peace process in 1999 is a good example of this.

So the final agreement should mean exactly what it says. It should be specific and, where appropriate, have a timescale for implementation. There should be no trickery in the wording, and the terms agreed should be implemented without amendment. Failure to deliver on this during the 1979–81 National Understandings (under which government, employer associations and unions determined national pay increases and economic and social issues), led to them being labelled "notional" understandings and "national misunderstandings", and the demise of such agreements for nearly five years. So this hostility can transpire even at the most senior levels, as John Dunne, Director General of IBEC complained bitterly about the trade union side's approach to both the PCW and Partnership 2000:

> People did not really read the [PCW] document in the way in which it was intended and, therefore, they believed it could deliver more than it could. . . . A deal is a deal. We have advised our members to operate in accordance with the terms of Partnership 2000 as agreed between IBEC and ICTU. . . . We will expect and accept nothing less . . . [for] the union to fully honour the original commitments. (Sheehan, 1997)

So the best way to avoid this unpleasantness is to make sure — before you leave the negotiation table — that everybody is absolutely clear as to what has been agreed. For example, at the close of the Garda pay negotiations in 1998, the Deputy General Secretary of the GRA cautioned:

> We have agreed to try and draw up a document to clearly set out what each other is saying. At least there won't be any misunderstanding at a later stage. Our difficulties all along . . . have been confusion at the end of some process. We have left the official side with the task of clearing up what we believe they are saying . . . (Cusack, 1998b)

In direct negotiations, management should summarise, finalise and confirm the agreement. This summary should be agreed by all concerned and commitment given to implement it fully. It will help if specific dates are set for the implementation of its various aspects, confirmed in writing and signed by both parties.

Figure 16.2 presents an indicative checklist to facilitate effective negotiations.

Figure 16.2: Summary Checklist for Effective Negotiations

Preparing your Case
- Get the facts and check them;
- Look at agreements, practices, policies and entitlements;
- Work out objectives and prioritise them;
- Decide on key arguments and counter-arguments;
- Work out opening, interim and fallback positions.

Teamwork
- Arrange a pre-negotiation meeting for an informal exchange and soliciting of information;
- Choose a main speaker and allocate roles to other team members;
- Agree strategy, arguments and tactics and brief/rehearse team members.

Meeting Your Counterparts
- Never disagree in front of your counterparts;
- Use adjournments when needed;
- Steer discussion to your strongest points;
- Look for your counterpart's offers/concessions;
- Make sure there's an agreed written record.

Reporting Back
- Keep the board/top management, or your members, in touch;
- Consult them before accepting or making final offers.

CONCLUSION

It should be borne in mind that, while a successful outcome is important to the negotiators, so also is the maintenance of the relationship between the parties for the future. Playing it hard may achieve satisfactory results in the short term, but will undermine the relationship in the medium and long term. Playing it soft runs the risk of doing a bad deal. Negotiators can avoid indulging in "positional bargaining" by separating the people from the problem, focusing on common interests as opposed to extreme positions, generating a variety of possibilities for any given problem, and attempting to apply objective standards (Fisher and Ury, 1986; see Figure 16.3). Emotions should be kept out of the process. These often become entangled with the merits of the problem. Taking firm positions tends to make this worse, because peoples' egos become identified with their positions. Therefore every effort should be made to regard "the problem" as everybody's to solve.

Of course, the best way to handle workplace problems, and issues of dispute, is by prevention. This can be achieved by commitment to good communication (see Chapter 13). Building good personal relationships, trust levels and knowing the other side are

Figure 16.3: Negotiating Techniques (Indicative)

Problem		Solution
Positional Negotiating: Which Game Should You Play?		Change the Game. Negotiate on the Merits.
Be Soft?	**Be Hard?**	**Be Principled**
Participants are friends	Participants are adversaries	Participants are problem-solvers
The goal is agreement	The goal is victory	The goal is a wise outcome reached efficiently and amicably
Make concessions to cultivate the relationship	Demand concessions as a condition of the relationship	Separate the people from the problem
Be soft on the people and the problem	Be hard on the problem and the people	Be soft on the people, hard on the problem
Trust others	Distrust others	Proceed independent of trust, unless your past relationship suggests otherwise
Change your position easily	Dig in to your position	Focus on interests, not positions
Make offers	Make threats	Explore interests
Disclose your bottom line	Mislead as to your bottom line	Avoid having a bottom line
Accept one-sided losses to reach agreement	Demand one-sided gains as the price of agreement	Invent options for mutual gain
Search for the single answer: the one they will accept	Search for the single answer: the one you will accept	Develop multiple options to choose from. Decide later.
Insist on agreement	Insist on your position	Insist on objective criteria
Try to avoid a contest of will	Try to a win a contest of will	Try to reach a result based on standards independent of will
Yield to pressure	Apply pressure	Reason and be open to reason. Yield to principle, not pressure.

Source: Fisher and Ury (1986)

key factors. Even when problems do come to the negotiating table, progress will be more easily achieved if the parties have a good personal relationship based upon mutual respect and trust. Successful negotiation will contribute in a very central way to the attraction and retention of the type of staff you want, and in some way to the goals of long-term harmony in the primary relationship and long-term survival of the business.

References

Armstrong, M. (1994), *A Handbook of Personnel Management Practice,* Second Edition, London: Kogan Page.

Coogan, T.P. (1996), *The Troubles,* London: Arrow Books.

Cusack, J. (1998a), "Ahern clears way for talks to break impasse on Garda pay", *The Irish Times,* 16 June.

Cusack, J. (1998b), "Garda pay dispute could end today after new offer", *The Irish Times,* 17 June.

Denny, R. (1994), *Speak for Yourself,* London: Kogan Page.

Gunnigle, P., G. McMahon and G. Fitzgerald (1995), *Industrial Relations in Ireland: Theory and Practice,* Dublin: Gill and Macmillan.

Fisher, R. and W. Ury (1986), *Getting to Yes,* London: Hutchinson.

Gunnigle, P., M. Morley, N. Clifford and T. Turner (1997), *Human Resource Management in Irish Organisations: Practice in Perspective,* Irish Studies in Management Series, Dublin: Oak Tree Press.

McDonagh, K. (1995), "Preparing for Successful Negotiations: Part 2", in *Industrial Relations Data Bank: Human Resources,* Vol. 13, No. 301, January, Dublin: Irish Business and Employers Confederation.

McMahon, G. (1996), "Claim by the Garda Representative Association for a Pay Increase", September, Dublin: Garda Representative Association.

McMahon, G. (1997), "Pay Strategy", Presentation to the Garda Representative Association Central Executive Committee, November, Dublin: Garda Representative Association.

Salamon, M. (1992), *Industrial Relations: Theory and Practice,* Second Edition, New York: Prentice Hall.

Sheehan, B. (1996a), "The Sean Healy Interview", *Industrial Relations News*, No. 43, 14 November.

Sheehan, B. (1996b), "National Talks to Commence as Parameters of New Pact Emerge", *Industrial Relations News*, No. 39, 17 October.

Sheehan, B. (1997), "A Deal is a Deal, says IBEC's John Dunne", *Industrial Relations News*, No. 19, 15 May.

PART FIVE
THE LEGAL CONTEXT

CHAPTER 17

THE EMPLOYMENT CONTRACT

Adrian F. Twomey

INTRODUCTION

The relationship between an employer and an employee derives
legal status by virtue of the fact that it is based on contract. Although many employers and employees quite innocently believe
that they are not parties to any contracts because they have signed
no written agreements, the general rule that should be remembered in such circumstances is that if one is in paid employment,
then one almost always has an employment contract of some sort
(Meenan, 1994).

Employment contracts, like most other contracts, need not necessarily be entered into in writing. In fact, in most instances, at
least part of the contract will be agreed verbally, with no written
evidence of the contract's terms being created by the parties. The
ambit of the employment contract is not, however, limited simply
to those terms and conditions that are expressly agreed by the
employer and the employee. Rather, employment contracts will
also contain terms implied into them by the judiciary (through the
common law), by the Oireachtas (through legislation or statute)
and, indirectly, by collective bargaining agreements. In that context, the aims of this chapter are to:

- Outline the nature of the two different types of employment
  contract and the tests used to distinguish between them;

- Outline the different sources of the terms in employment contracts;

- Examine the main rights and responsibilities of employees arising from their employment contracts; and

- Briefly examine the concept of fixed-term contracts.

THE TWO TYPES OF EMPLOYMENT CONTRACT

There are essentially two kinds of contract under which one may "employ" a worker: "contracts of service", under which PAYE workers are employed, and "contracts for services", under which one employs independent contractors. So, as Lord Denning explained in *Stevenson, Jordan and Harrison Ltd.* v *MacDonald and Evans* ([1962] 1 ILR 107), "a ship's master, a chauffeur and a reporter on the staff of a newspaper are all employed under a contract of service, but a ship's pilot, a taximan and a newspaper contributor are employed under a contract for services".

It is important for an employer to be able to determine whether they are employing an individual under a contract of service or under a contract for services, for four main reasons:

1. Persons employed under contracts of service are protected by a range of statutory provisions, such as those discussed in Chapter 18. In contrast, the rights of independent contractors are generated almost exclusively by the express terms contained in their contracts. So, for example, an individual who is employed under a contract of service can accumulate entitlements under the Minimum Notice and Terms of Employment Act, 1973, or the Redundancy Payments Acts, 1967 to 1979, whereas an individual who is employed under a contract for services cannot do so.

2. Employers can be held legally liable on foot of unlawful acts committed by their employees, whereas they are usually not responsible for those committed by independent contractors.

3. Persons employed under contracts of service pay tax on a PAYE basis, whereas independent contractors pay tax on a self-assessment basis.

4. Persons employed under contracts of service qualify for a broader range of social welfare benefits.

Employment contracts can be extremely complex. For that reason, the courts have found it difficult to define and distinguish between contracts of service and contracts for services. They have, however, formulated a number of tests for assisting them in the task of distinguishing between the two types of contracts. The three main tests are outlined below.

The Control Test

The traditional English method of identifying a contract of employment was to consider the degree of control that the employer has over the employee. As Whincup (1980: 6) explains:

> [t]he basic proposition is quite straightforward — the more control A exercises over B's work, the more likely A is to be the employer and B his employee.

According to Drake (1981: 6), the control test essentially involves asking four questions about the contract in question:

- Can the "employer" tell the worker what to do?

- Can the "employer" tell the worker how to do it?

- Can the "employer" tell the worker when to do it?

- Can the "employer" tell the worker where to do it?

If the answer to all four questions is "yes", then the test suggests that the contract is one of service. If not, then the worker should be classed as an independent contractor.

Despite the simplicity and ease of use of the control test, it has, for some years, been regarded as unreliable (particularly in cases involving highly skilled workers). For that reason, the courts have attempted to develop a number of more sophisticated tests in order to better analyse the contractual status of more complex modern employment relationships.

The Integration Test

The second standard test is the integration test, which was developed in England by Lord Denning. As Denning himself explained, in *Bank voor Handel en Scheepvaart NV v Slatford* ([1953] 1 QB 279):

> the test of being [an employee] does not rest nowadays on a submission to orders. It depends on whether the person is part and parcel of the organisation.

In other words, the application of the integration test involves assessing whether the worker is integrated into the business or is merely an accessory to it.

The integration test is rarely used by judges nowadays because it is inherently difficult to apply. It has, however, been used on a number of occasions by Ms Justice Carroll in the Irish High Court. In the case of *re Sunday Tribune Ltd.* ([1984] IR 505), for example, Carroll J was required to determine the status of the contracts of a number of the newspaper's journalists. One of the journalists had written a column for 50 of the 52 weeks in the previous year. She had also taken part in editorial conferences and had received holiday pay. Carroll J held that the journalist in question was "an integral part of the business" and was, therefore, employed under a contract of service.

The Mixed Test

The third and final test is the mixed or multiple factors test, which essentially involves the consideration by the court of all relevant factors. The mixed test is generally regarded as having originated in the English case of *Readymixed Concrete (SE) Ltd.* v *Minister of Pensions and Social Security* ([1968] 2 QB 497). In that case, McKenna J stated that a contract of service exists if the following conditions are satisfied:

- The worker agrees that, in return for a wage or other remuneration, they will provide their own work and skill in the performance of some service for their employer;

- The worker agrees, expressly or impliedly, that in the performance of that service, they will be subject to the employer's control; and

- The other provisions of the contract are consistent with its being a contract of service.

The mixed test, therefore, demands that one look not only at the degree of control exercisable by the employer, but also at all other relevant factors. According to Barron J (*McDermott* v *Loy*, unreported, High Court, 29 July 1982), the following questions are among those which should be asked by a court applying the mixed test:

- Are the workers in business on their own account?

- Do they provide their own equipment?

- Can they employ their own assistants?

- What degree of financial risk do they take themselves?

- Are they members of a trade union?

- To what degree are they responsible for investing and managing resources?

- What opportunity do they have to make a profit?

In recent years, the courts have usually preferred to employ the mixed test when assessing employment contracts because of its inherent flexibility. Both the control and integration tests have, however, been applied in cases over the last decade and, for that reason, should not be ignored.

Case Example 17.1: Contracts of Service and Contracts for Services — The Denny Case

---

The case of Henry Denny & Sons (Ireland) Ltd. t/a Kerry Foods *v* The Minister for Social Welfare *((1998) IR 34) concerned the nature of the employment of Ms Sandra Mahon by Kerry Foods as a demonstrator of their products in supermarkets.*

In 1988, Ms Mahon had contacted Kerry Foods looking for work as a demonstrator. She was interviewed and her name was included on a panel of approximately 70 demonstrators used by the company. Ms Mahon was given a one-year fixed-term contract, which was subsequently renewed on an annual basis by the company. According to Keane J:

> *The manner in which Ms. Mahon's services were availed of by the Appellant was as follows. The particular retail store which required one of the Appellants' food products to be demonstrated got in touch with the local customer service manager of the Appellants and asked for such a demonstration specifying the day or days upon which it was required. Three or four days before the date of the proposed demonstration, the manager would telephone a demonstrator on the panel to enquire whether or not the demonstrator was available to provide her services on the particular day at the particular shop. Generally speaking, neither the demonstrator nor the Appellant knew prior to this time whether or not a demonstration was to be given at any particular shop or store during the immediately following weekend. If the demonstrator was available, it was agreed that the service should be provided. The demonstration was carried out without any supervision by the Appellants.*

This last comment would seem to suggest that the company exercised little control over Ms Mahon. In fact, the Court subsequently acknowledged that there was "no continuous and direct supervision". On the other hand, the demonstrators were sent a circular letter, which gave them detailed instructions as to how their jobs should be done.

Ms Mahon's contract expressly stated that she was not an employee of Kerry Foods and would be providing her services as an independent contractor. The contract pointed out that this fact had "implications in the area of employment legislation". The contract also required that demonstrators wear a uniform provided by Kerry Foods, present themselves for work at the times and in the locations specified by the company. The contract itself expressly provided that:

> The demonstrator is and shall be deemed to be an independent contractor and nothing in this agreement shall be construed as creating the relationship of master and servant or principal and agent.

Despite this statement, the Supreme Court held that Ms Mahon was employed under a contract of service. In arriving at his decision, Keane J explained that:

> ... while each case must be determined in the light of its particular facts and circumstances, in general a person will be regarded as providing his or her services under a contract of service and not as an independent contractor where he or she is performing those services for another person and not for himself or herself. The degree of control exercised over how the work is to be performed, although a factor to be taken into account, is not decisive. The inference that the person is engaged in business on his or her own account can be more readily drawn where he or she provides the necessary premises or equipment or some other form of investment, where he or she employs others to assist in the business and where the profit which he or she derives from the business is dependent on the efficiency with which it is conducted by him or her.

The company's aims in attempting to classify Ms Mahon's employment as being pursuant to a series of rolling one-year contracts for services are relatively easy to ascertain. If they had been successful in persuading the court that such was the case, their demonstrators would have had almost no statutory rights and could have been easily dismissed. The decision of the Supreme Court has almost exactly opposing effects. The judgment of Keane J, in particular, spells out a number of clear warnings for employers. Particularly noteworthy is his very clear emphasis of the fact that labelling a contract as one "for services" does not necessarily mean that it will be construed as such by the courts.

THE TERMS OF THE EMPLOYMENT CONTRACT

Very often, employees feel that the only terms and conditions contained in their contracts are those set out in any formal written document presented to them by their employers at the time at which they commenced employment. In actual fact, like any other kind of contract, an employment contract can contain a considerable number of different kinds of terms. Obviously, it will contain terms that have been expressly agreed, either verbally or in writing, by the employer and employee. Such express terms will, for example, usually include terms relating to the employee's rate of pay, hours of work and annual leave entitlements.

All contracts of service will, however, also contain a wide range of what are referred to as "implied terms". Such terms are implied into contracts by the law, on foot of common law rules, legislative provisions and collective bargaining agreements.

EXPRESS TERMS

The terms of employment contracts that are expressly agreed between employers and employees will obviously vary from contract to contract, depending on the nature of the job. It is, for that reason, impossible to draft a definitive model contract. Among the terms that will typically appear in employment contracts, however, are the following:

- The names of the employer and the employee;

- The employer's address;

- Either the place of work or a statement specifying that the employee is required or permitted to work at various places;

- The job title or a description of the nature of the work for which the employee is employed;

- The date of commencement of the contract;

- The expected duration of the contract or, if the contract is for a fixed term, the date on which the contract expires;

- The rate or method of calculation of remuneration;

- The length of the intervals between the times at which remuneration is paid;

- Details in relation to any other benefits and/or expenses;

- Details relating to hours of work;

- Provisions in relation to overtime;

- The times and duration of rest periods and breaks;

- Any requirements in relation to medical examinations;

- Any terms or conditions relating to incapacity for work due to sickness or injury and paid leave;

- Any terms or conditions relating to pensions and pension schemes;

- Details of the employee's holiday entitlements;

- The period of notice which the employee is required to give before leaving (or the method for determining that period);

- The period of notice which the employee is entitled to receive, or the method for determining that period;

- A reasonable restraint of trade clause (if such is required);

- Requirements in relation to confidentiality;

- Any provisions in relation to relocation;

- A statement setting out the employer's right to require the employee to relocate or travel periodically (if necessary);

- Details of the employee's rights and responsibilities in relation to any equipment or other property being made available to them by the employer;

- Any specific provisions in relation to health and safety which may be required (such as a contractual requirement to comply with an employer's no-smoking policy);

- A reference to any collective agreements (such as one relating to disciplinary and dismissals procedures) which directly affect the terms and conditions of the employee's employment;

- Any requirement in relation to trade union membership;

- The age at which the employee will be expected to retire (if appropriate);

- Provisions relating to subsequent amendments of the contract;

- An acceptance clause.

Such a contract will typically be signed and dated by, or on behalf of, the parties, with copies being retained by both the employer and the employee.

TERMS IMPLIED BY THE COMMON LAW

The courts will not readily imply terms into contracts of service on the basis that it is, in general, a matter for the parties themselves to determine the scope or ambit of the contract. A number of terms are, however, regularly implied into contracts of service by the courts. As Lord Justice Stephenson explained in *Mears* v *Safecar Security Ltd.* ([1982] IRLR 183) contracts of service must:

> . . . by their nature and subject matter [contain or impose] certain obligations, and those obligations the law will impose and imply. . . . But the term must be a necessary term. . . . It is not enough that it would be a reasonable term.

It is, therefore, not sufficient for the party seeking to have a term implied into the contract simply to argue that the term is more convenient than a term expressly agreed by the parties or that it is consistent with the other terms of the contract. Rather, one has to prove that the parties must have intended to imply the term into the contract. In that context, even the commonly implied terms outlined below can be supplanted or displaced by a term expressly agreed by the parties.

IMPLIED TERMS THAT IMPOSE DUTIES ON EMPLOYERS

A significant number of the terms regularly implied into employment contracts by the courts impose duties on employers. The main duties so implied are discussed below.

Duty of Employer to Maintain Employee

Employers are obliged to maintain their employees for a reasonable period once they have hired those employees. In other words, the employer must give the employee some time to settle into the job and reach peak performance level. The period of time in question will vary from job to job.

Duty of Employer to Pay Employee Agreed Wages

Employers are obliged to pay their employees their agreed wages. They are not, however, obliged to provide the employees with work. In *Collier* v *Sunday Reference Publishing Co. Ltd.* ([1940] 2 KB 647), Asquith J illustrated that point well, explaining that "[p]rovided I pay my cook her wages regularly she cannot complain if I choose to take any or all of my meals out".

There are, however, two specific exceptions to this general rule. The first of these exceptions is where the employee is paid on a commission or piece-rate basis and so needs work in order to earn a living. The second exception is where the employee is highly skilled and needs to work in order to practise and maintain their particular skill or expertise. In that context, an actor was held to be such a skilled worker in *Herbert Clayton and Jack Waller Ltd.* v *Oliver* ([1930] AC 209) whereas it was held in *Turner* v *Sawdon and Co.* ([1901] 2 KB 653) that there was nothing unique about the talents of a salesman which required that he be provided with work.

Duty of Employer to take Reasonable Care for the Safety of the Employee

Employers have a duty to take reasonable care for the safety of their employees. The employer is not, however, to be regarded as an insurer. Their duty is not to protect at their peril all of their employees against all hazards of the employment. Rather, they will have discharged their duty if they do what a reasonable and prudent employer would have done in the circumstances. The duty in question is essentially comprised of four main elements:

1. To provide a safe place of work;

2. To provide proper plant and equipment;

3. To provide a safe system of work; and

4. To provide competent staff.

Safe Place of Work
The employer must ensure that a reasonably safe place of work is provided and maintained for the benefit of the employee. The extent to which an employer must protect an employee from injury on premises not under the employer's control is somewhat less certain. Obviously, there have to be limits to the employer's duty in this regard. As Pearce LJ has observed in the English Court of Appeal:

> if a master sends his plumber to mend a leak in a respectable private house, no one could hold him liable for not visiting the house himself to see if the carpet in the hall creates a trap (*Wilson* v *Tyneside Window Cleaning Co.* [1958] 2 QB 110).

It seems that no hard and fast rules have been articulated on this question, and that the courts have generally been content to regard it as a question of fact.

Proper Plant and Equipment
The employer has a duty to take

> . . . reasonable care to provide proper appliances and to maintain them in a proper condition, and so to carry on his operations as not to subject those employed by him to unnecessary risk (Budd J, *Burke* v *John Paul & Co. Ltd.* [1967] IR 277: 281).

In *Deegan* v *Langan* ([1966] IR 373), for example, the Supreme Court imposed liability on an employer who supplied his employee, a carpenter, with nails of a type that the employer knew were apt to shatter when struck by a hammer.

Safe System of Work

As McLoughlin J explained in *Kinsella* v *Hammond Lane Industries Ltd.* ([1958] 96 ILTR 1):

> If an accident causes injury to a workman and the accident results from a risk of an unsafe system of work, against which the employer should have [taken], but did not take, reasonable precautions to guard, then the employer is liable for damages.

Competent Fellow Employees

Employers owe their servants a duty of care to select competent fellow employees. Before an employer will be held liable for having failed to provide competent staff, it must be shown that the employer had reason to be aware of the negligent employee's incompetence. If, however, a worker has a previously undetected propensity for mischief and engages in skylarking, the employer will not usually be responsible for resulting injuries if the incident was an isolated one.

Duty of Employer to Treat Employees with Trust and Confidence

As Carr and Kay (1994: 75) note, courts and tribunals have, in recent years, "developed a wide and somewhat indefinite mutual obligation upon each party to a contract of employment to treat the other with trust and confidence". So it was that in 1978, the English Employment Appeals Tribunal held, in *Courtaulds Northern Textiles Ltd.* v *Andrew* ([1979] IRLR 84) that

> ... there is an implied term in a contract of employment that employers will not, without reasonable and proper cause, conduct themselves in a manner calculated or likely to destroy

or seriously damage the relationship of trust and confidence between the parties (Carr and Kay, 1994: 75).

Three years later, in *Woods* v *W.M. Car Services (Peterborough) Ltd.* ([1982] ICR 666), Lord Denning recast the nature of the duty somewhat, stating that:

> It is the duty of the employer to be good and considerate to his servants. Sometimes it is formulated as an implied term not to do anything likely to destroy the relationship of confidence between them.

Duty of Employer to Indemnify Employees

According to Carr and Kay (1994: 78), an "employer is under an obligation to indemnify his employees in respect of any expenses incurred in performing their duties. . . ." In other words, it is generally the case that if an employee personally incurs a cost in doing work for his employer (such as paying for raw materials or tools out of his own pocket), then he is entitled to be recompensed by the employer.

Duty of Employer to Inform Employees of their Rights

In *Scally* v *Southern Health & Social Services Board* ([1991] IRLR 525) the House of Lords held that employers are under a duty to inform employees of the steps which they need to take in order to benefit from rights or entitlements which have not been negotiated directly with them.

The plaintiffs in the Scally case were four doctors who were employed by Health and Social Services Boards in Northern Ireland. Under 1974 Regulations, such employees were given the right to purchase "added years" of pension entitlements on highly advantageous terms. That right could, however, only be exercised within a limited time period. In such circumstances, the House of Lords held that there was an implied obligation on the employer to bring the term of the contract to the employee's attention. The

Court added, however, that such a duty to inform would only be imposed on employers where:

- The terms of the contract of employment have not been negotiated with the individual employee but result from negotiation with a representative body or are otherwise incorporated by reference;

- A particular term of the contract makes available to the employee a valuable right contingent upon action being taken by him to avail himself of its benefit; and

- The employee cannot, in all the circumstances, reasonably be expected to be aware of the term unless it is drawn to his attention.

Duty of Employer to Take Reasonable Care in Preparing References

There is no general obligation on employers to provide character references to or on behalf of employees. As the House of Lords explained in *Spring* v *Guardian Assurance plc* ([1994] 3 All ER 129), however:

> an employer is under a duty to a departing employee, or indeed to any person who had been working for him, to take reasonable care in the preparation of a reference, and is liable for pecuniary loss suffered by the employee as a result of an inaccurate and negligently prepared reference (Milmo, 1994: 1477).

The plaintiff in the Spring case had been employed by Guardian Royal Exchange Assurance as a sales representative but was dismissed. When he applied for jobs with other companies, those companies sought references from Guardian Royal Exchange. The references provided by the defendants stated that Spring was "a man of little or no integrity and could not be regarded as honest". In finding for the plaintiff, Lord Woolf went so far as to hold that:

it is necessary to imply a term into the contract that the employer would, during the continuance of the engagement or within a reasonable time thereafter, provide a reference at the request of a prospective employer which was based on facts revealed after making those reasonably careful inquiries which, in the circumstances, a reasonable employer would make ([1994] 3 All ER 129: 179).

IMPLIED TERMS THAT IMPOSE DUTIES ON EMPLOYEES

The main duties of employees that are implied into contracts of employment by the courts are:

- A duty to be ready and willing to work;

- A duty to use reasonable care and skill;

- A duty to obey lawful orders;

- A duty to take care of the employer's property;

- A duty to act in good faith.

Duty of Employee to be Ready and Willing to Work

The primary duty that an employee is implicitly deemed to owe to his employer is:

to present himself at work, in accordance with the contract of [service], and to work at the direction of the employer in return for the implied obligation of the employer to pay wages as agreed (Carr and Kay, 1994: 56).

An employee who fails to turn up for work is, therefore, acting in breach of contract.

Duty of Employee to use Reasonable Care and Skill

The duty to use reasonable care and skill in the performance of duties under an employment contract has two aspects:

- A duty not to be unduly negligent; and

- A duty to be reasonably competent.

Therefore, if an employee is negligent in the performance of their work, they may be regarded as being in breach of contract. This is particularly true if there has been a pattern of negligent conduct by that employee or if the single act of negligence is particularly serious. In *Lister* v *Romford Ice and Cold Storage Co. Ltd.* ([1957] AC 555), for example, a lorry driver, employed by the company, carelessly reversed his lorry and injured a fellow employee, who was in fact his father. The employers paid damages to the father but claimed an indemnity from the son on the grounds that he had broken an implied term of the contract of employment: the duty not to be negligent in the performance of the work. It was held that the employee would be liable because of the breach of the implied duty.

Even where there is no negligence on the part of the employee, mere incompetence in and of itself may constitute a breach of the contract of employment, particularly if the employee has professed their ability to do the work in question.

Duty of Employee to Obey Lawful Orders
Employees are under a duty to obey all the lawful orders of their employer. A failure to do this is a breach of the contract of employment and may, in certain circumstances, justify summary dismissal. However, it must be established that the order lies within the scope of the contract of employment. In *Price* v *Mouat* ((1862) 11 CB 508), for example, a lace-salesman was ordered to "card" (pack) lace. He refused to do so and was dismissed without notice. The dismissal was held to have been wrongful because the order was not one that was within the scope of the contract.

On the other hand, in the Irish case of *Waters* v *Kentredder Ireland Ltd.* (UD 3/1977) the claimant was employed as a skilled operator to retread or remould tyres. His function was solely that of operating a retreading machine. One of his fellow employees had died, and the other employees had agreed to carry out that employee's functions. After some time, the claimant had an argument with the employer, refused to comply with the said arrangement any longer, and was duly dismissed. The Employment Appeals Tribunal held that the terms of the claimant's contract of employment had been varied by conduct and implication. Hence the refusal was one to obey a reasonable order within the altered terms of employment, and so the dismissal was not unfair.

The only circumstances in which an employee may be justified in refusing to obey an order that is apparently within the scope of their employment are:

- Where the employer orders the employee to do something which would constitute a criminal offence; or

- Where such an order involves exceptional danger for which the employee is not given extra payment.

Duty of Employee to Take Care of the Employer's Property

An employee is under an obligation to take reasonable care of his employer's property. In *Superflux* v *Plaisted* (*The Times*, 12 December 1958), for example, the defendant had been in charge of a team of vacuum cleaner salesmen and had negligently allowed 14 cleaners to be stolen from his van. He was held to have been in breach of his contract of employment. In such circumstances, an employee will be regarded as being under an obligation to indemnify the employer for the loss sustained.

Duty of Employee to Act in Good Faith

The duty of an employee to act in good faith can be viewed as being comprised of four distinct sub-categories:

1. A duty not to make a secret profit;

2. A duty to disclose relevant information to the employer;

3. A duty not to act to the detriment of the employer; and

4. A duty not to disclose confidential information.

The last-mentioned of these duties is discussed in greater detail below.

Duty of Employee Not to Disclose Confidential Information

The nature of the employee's duty not to disclose confidential information has been clearly defined by the courts in a number of cases. In *Bent's Brewery* v *Hogan* ([1945] 2 All ER 570), for example, Lynskey J opined that:

> [I]t is quite clear that an employee is under an obligation to his employers not to disclose confidential information obtained by him in the course of and as a result of his employment.

The basis of this implied duty is that the information is in the nature of a property right, which cannot be taken from the employer without his consent.

In *Faccenda Chicken Ltd.* v *Fowler* ([1986] ICR 297) the company sought an injunction to restrain Fowler and a number of other former employees who had formed a rival company, from using "confidential" information which they had acquired whilst working for the company. The information included purchasing requirements of customers, pricing structure and marketing strategy. There was no express term limiting the disclosure of information. The Court of Appeal held that while an employee remains in the employment of an employer, the duty of confidentiality forms part of the more general duty of good faith and fidelity. The duty also extends to ex-employees, but in a more limited form. In that context, it only covers trade secrets, designs, special methods of construction and other information that is of a "sufficiently high degree of confidentiality as to amount to a secret".

As the decision in the *Faccenda Chicken* case makes clear, the duty on the employee does not extend to all information obtained in the course of their employment. The critical question, then, is whether the information in question will be regarded by the law as being "confidential" in nature. Perhaps the clearest definition of what constitutes confidential information is that elaborated by Megarry VC in *Thomas Marshall Ltd.* v *Guinle* ([1979] 1 Chancery 227: 248):

> First, that the information must be information the release of which the owner believes would be injurious to him or of advantage to his rivals or others. Second, the owner must believe the information is confidential or secret. Third, the owner's belief under these headings must be reasonable. Fourth, the information must be judged in the light of usage and practices in the particular industry concerned.

TERMS IMPLIED BY LEGISLATION

As has already been pointed out, contracts of service are affected by a broad range of statutory provisions, which imply into them a considerable number of largely protective terms, often referred to as "workers' rights". These protective terms cover matters such as holiday and maternity rights, minimum notice, dismissals and employment equality. The various statutes in question are discussed in detail in Chapters 18 and 20.

FIXED-TERM CONTRACTS

In recent years, it has become increasingly commonplace to find employers offering potential employees alternatives to the traditional employment contract in order to satisfy a number of the employers' objectives in recruiting. One of the most commonly used of these alternatives is the fixed-term contract (a contract of service with a fixed duration or lifetime). The periods of such contracts vary widely, in that the period of a fixed-term contract may be as short as a matter of days or as long as a number of years. A large proportion, however, last for just under one year. Such contracts would seem, at least on a *prima facie* basis, to enable the employer to terminate the worker's engagement with a considerable degree of ease. It is, however, clearly the case that workers employed under fixed-term contracts of service are covered by the bulk of existing protective employment legislation. Once the worker has given a period of unbroken service equivalent to that required by the Act in question, they qualify for its protection.

The question that would seem to be causing most confusion among employers in respect of fixed-term contract workers and protective legislation relates to the renewal of fixed-term contracts (Twomey, 1998). If, for example, one employs an individual under a nine-month fixed-term contract and offers a second such contract to the worker on the expiry of the first, is the worker then protected by the Unfair Dismissals Acts, 1977–93 (which require, in most instances, that the employee have completed at least one year of continuous service)? The answer to such a question is relatively clear. As Madden and Kerr (1996: 126) explain:

> . . . continuity is not broken by the dismissal of an employee followed by their "immediate re-employment". Tribunals have [however] had some difficulty with this issue and the cases generally turn on their particular facts rather than through the application of legal principle. In *Howard* v *Breton Ltd.* (UD 486/1984) [for example] a dismissal followed by re-employment on new conditions a week later was considered sufficiently immediate to preserve continuity. . . .

Effectively, the Tribunal is attempting to establish whether or not the termination of the employment relationship is genuine rather than simply a ruse on the part of the employer aimed at avoiding the application of protective legislation. Any such ploy will inevitably be regarded as a somewhat cynical attempt to circumvent the legislation. The Tribunal is not, however, simply seeking to "catch out" employers. In *Mulhall & Sons Builders* v *Dunphy* (UD 710/1981), for example, the Tribunal was again faced with a situation where there had been a short break in the employment. In that case, however, the employee was proved to have been actively seeking work elsewhere during the break in employment.

In such circumstances, the logical implication is that when the employment relationship was terminated there was no intention to resume it again so quickly. The termination, therefore, could not be construed as a ruse to avoid the application of the legislation.

In respect of the Unfair Dismissals Acts, the matter was put beyond any doubt by section 3(c) of the Amendment Act introduced by Mary O'Rourke TD in 1993. The paragraph in question provides that, where an employee is re-employed by the same employer within 26 weeks of the dismissal, there is no break in the continuity of employment if the dismissal was designed to avoid liability under the legislation.

CONCLUSION

In drafting employment contracts, one needs to bear a number of factors in mind. Firstly, one must remember that the decision as to whether or not to offer a contract of service (as opposed to a contract for services) will have significant implications for both parties at a later stage.

Secondly, one must remember that almost all employment contracts are comprised of terms emanating from a variety of sources. It is certainly the case that any written contract will be supplemented by terms verbally agreed by the parties, terms implied by their conduct and terms implied by both the common law and legislation. Collective bargaining agreements may also lead to the amendment of employment contracts. For that reason, the legal implications of collective bargaining are examined in Chapter 19.

Despite these complexities, it should be remembered that ultimately the courts, in interpreting contracts, seek to give effect to the intentions of the parties. In that context, the function of an individual charged with drafting an employment contract is simply to clearly and comprehensively express the intentions of the parties. If such clarity and comprehensiveness is achieved, the contract will usually prove to be a source of reassurance and certainty, rather than a source of problems, for the parties.

References

Carr, C.J. and P.J. Kay (1994), *Employment Law*, 6th Edition, London: M+E.

Drake, C.D. (1981), *Labour Law*, 3rd Edition, London: Sweet & Maxwell.

Madden, D., and T. Kerr (1996), *Unfair Dismissal: Cases and Commentary*, 2nd Ed., Dublin: IBEC.

Meenan, F. (1994), *Working within the Law*, Dublin: Oak Tree Press.

Milmo, P. (1994), "Liability for References", (1994) *New Law Journal* p. 1477.

Pitt, G. (1995), *Employment Law*, 2nd Edition, London: Sweet & Maxwell.

Twomey, A.F. (1998), "Terms of Engagement", *Gazette of the Incorporated Law Society of Ireland*, May, 30.

Whincup, M. (1980), *Modern Employment Law: A Guide to Job Security and Safety*, 3rd Edition, London: Heinemann.

Further Reading

Fennell, C. and I. Lynch (1993), *Labour Law in Ireland*, Dublin: Gill and Macmillan.

Forde, M. (1991), *Industrial Relations Law*, Dublin: Round Hall Press.

Forde, M. (1992), *Employment Law*, Dublin: Round Hall Press.

Forsaith, J. and N., Townsend (1997), *The Personnel Administration Handbook*, London: Institute of Personnel and Development.

Irish Business and Employers Confederation (IBEC), (1996), *A Guide to Employment Legislation*, 6th Edition, Dublin: IBEC.

von Prondzynski and McCarthy (1989), *Employment Law in Ireland*, 2nd Ed., London: Sweet & Maxwell.

Wayne, N. (1980), *Labour Law in Ireland: A Guide to Workers' Rights*, Dublin: Irish Transport and General Workers Unions (ITGWU).

Wedderburn, Lord (1986), *The Worker and the Law*, 3rd Edition, London: Pelican.

CHAPTER 18

PROTECTIVE LEGISLATION AND EMPLOYMENT RIGHTS

Adrian F. Twomey

INTRODUCTION

The basic principles of Irish employment law have changed quite dramatically over the last 30 years, due, in large part, to a considerable degree of legislative activism in the area since the establishment of the Department of Labour in 1966. Despite the formal abolition of that Department in 1993, the pace of reform of employment law has been maintained by virtue of the combined efforts of the Departments of Enterprise, Trade and Employment, and Justice, Equality and Law Reform (Twomey, 1997).

This period of legislative activism has resulted in the introduction of a statutory "floor" of basic employment rights. For that reason, this chapter pays particularly close attention to the primary pieces of employment legislation enacted by the Oireachtas since the Department of Labour began to make its mark with the introduction of the Redundancy Payments Act in 1967. In particular, this chapter aims to outline the main statutory rights (and corresponding duties) of employees in relation to:

- Statements of conditions of employment;

- Wages, wage slips and deductions from wages;

- Working hours;

- Holidays and other leave;

- Health and safety in the workplace;

- Job safety when the employer sells or transfers ownership of the business to another person;

- Redundancies;

- Dismissals; and

- Minimum notice.

This chapter also contains a brief discussion of the rights of young workers and part-time employees.

THE ENTITLEMENT TO A STATEMENT OF CONDITIONS

The Terms of Employment (Information) Act, 1994, was enacted in order to comply with an EC Directive (Council Directive 91/533/EEC) which required that certain information must be provided to employees concerning their contracts of employment. Section 3 of the Act provides that not later than two months after the commencement of an employee's employment, the employer must provide a statement in writing to the employee setting out the following details in relation to the employee's employment:

- The full names of the employer and the employee;

- The address of the employer;

- Either the place of work or a statement specifying that the employee is required or permitted to work at various places;

- The title of the job or nature of the work for which the employee is employed;

- The date of commencement of the employee's contract of employment;

- In the case of a temporary contract of employment, the expected duration thereof, or, if the contract of employment is for a fixed term, the date on which the contract expires;

- The rate or method of calculation of the employee's remuneration;

- The length of the intervals between the times at which remuneration is paid;

- Any terms or conditions relating to hours of work;

- The times and duration of (and any other conditions relating to) rest periods and breaks provided for by the Organisation of Working Time Act, 1997;

- Any terms or conditions relating to incapacity for work due to sickness or injury, and paid leave, as well as any terms or conditions relating to pensions and pension schemes;

- The period of notice which the employee is required to give and entitled to receive, or the method for determining the length of such notice periods;

- A reference to any collective agreements which directly affect the terms and conditions of the employee's employment.

The employee must be notified in writing of any change occurring in relation to any of the particulars furnished within one month of such change occurring.

Section 6 provides that, in the case of contracts of employment entered into before the commencement of the Act, an employer must, on request by the employee, furnish the employee with a statement containing the required particulars.

WAGES, WAGE SLIPS AND DEDUCTIONS FROM WAGES

The Payment of Wages Act, 1991, affords employees three basic rights in relation to their wages:

1. The right to a readily negotiable mode of wage payment;

2. The right to protection against unlawful deductions from their wages; and

3. The right to written statements of their wages detailing their gross pay and the nature and amount of any deductions.

Section 2(1) of the Act sets out the ways in which wages can be paid (i.e. by way of cheques, bills of exchange, drafts, money orders, postal orders or cash). Only one method of payment can be used, although section 2(2) of the Act provides that if there happens to be a bank strike, the employer may pay in another non-cash mode if the employee consents. In recognition of the notion of collective bargaining, the Act also provides that if there is to be any change in the form in which employees are to be paid, both the employer and employees must consent.

Section 5 of the Act details deductions which an employer is allowed to make from wages, such as tax or other deductions authorised by statute or deductions made with the consent of the employee. An employer can also make deductions of a compensatory nature in lieu of acts or omissions of an employee or in respect of goods given to an employee, but any such deductions must be authorised by the employee's contract and they must be both fair and reasonable having regard to the amount of the wages of the employee. The employee must be given a copy of the Act or notice in writing of section 5 at least one week before any such deduction is made.

WORKING HOURS

The Organisation of Working Time Act, 1997, was introduced in order to give effect to the EU Working Time Directive (Council Directive 93/104/EC) but also deals with a number of matters not referred to in the Directive, as well as repealing and replacing some relatively outdated protective legislation. The following categories of employees are expressly excluded from the application of the Act:

- Members of the Garda Síochána and the Defence Forces;

- Persons engaged in sea fishing or other work at sea;

- Doctors in training;

- Persons employed by relatives;

- Persons who determine their own working time.

Section 15 of the Act provides that an employer may not permit an employee to work more than an average of 48 hours in a seven-day period. The average number of weekly working hours is calculated, in most cases, over a period of four months. In situations where, for example, the employee's work is subject to seasonality or a foreseeable surge in activity, the averaging may be carried out over a period of six months. Exceptionally, the averaging may be carried out over a full 12 months where the parties agree and their collective agreement is approved by the Labour Court.

The legislation also requires that employees be given 11 consecutive hours' rest in each period of 24 hours; a 15-minute break after working for four hours and 30 minutes (or 30 minutes during a six-hour period of work); and 24 hours' consecutive rest in each seven-day period.

HOLIDAYS AND OTHER LEAVE

The Organisation of Working Time Act, 1997, also sets out the minimum statutory holiday entitlements of employees. Significantly, the Act increases the minimum entitlement from the previous level of 15 working days to four working weeks from 1999 on. Part-time employees have an equivalent entitlement to eight per cent of the hours they worked in a leave year. Employers should, however, remember that employees in occupations covered by Labour Court Employment Regulation Orders or Registered Employment Agreements may have a legally enforceable entitlement to more generous terms. In other words, the Act merely sets a minimum entitlement to holidays below which one cannot go.

The time at which annual leave may be taken is determined by the employer, provided that they consult the employee or their trade union at least one month beforehand. Regard must also be had to the employee's opportunities for rest and relaxation.

Maternity Leave

The Maternity Protection Act, 1994 guarantees women the right to take maternity leave and the right to return to work having taken such leave. It does not, however, confer on them any right to obtain pay while on maternity leave. Rather, the Department of Social Welfare is responsible for the payment of employees who fulfil the required PRSI contribution conditions.

The Act entitles women to take 14 consecutive weeks' maternity leave. An employee must take at least four of the 14 weeks before the end of the week in which her baby is due, and four weeks after that week. She may also take up to four additional weeks of unpaid leave immediately after her maternity leave.

Adoptive Leave

The Adoptive Leave Act, 1995, entitles an adopting mother (or a sole male adopter) who is in employment to:

1. A minimum of ten consecutive weeks of adoptive leave from work, beginning on the date of placement of the child; and

2. Up to four weeks additional unpaid leave.

The ten-week period of adoptive leave attracts a social welfare benefit in most cases.

Parental Leave

The Parental Leave Act, 1998, implemented an EU Directive (Council Directive 96/34/EC) on the matter, which aims to further the reconciliation of working and familial obligations by granting parents an entitlement to up to 14 weeks' unpaid leave to enable them to take care of their young children. The Act provides that:

- Parents are entitled to leave where they have been in the continuous employment of their employer for at least one year (although a reduced entitlement is acquired by parents once they have completed three months' continuous service) and their child was born after 3 June 1996;

- Both the mother and father are entitled to 14 weeks' leave each for every qualifying child. Parents may not, however, transfer their leave entitlements to each other;

- The leave must be taken before the child reaches five years of age (although the entitlement may be taken later where the child is one who has been adopted when aged between three and eight);

- Parents may take their leave entitlements at the one time or, where such is agreed with their employers, in separate blocks. Alternatively, the parties may agree that the leave entitlement be satisfied by way of a reduction in working hours.

Force Majeure Leave

The Parental Leave Act, 1998, also entitles employees to paid leave when their presence is required at the location of a relative to whom the Act relates for urgent family reasons owing to illness or injury. The relatives to whom the Act relates are:

- Children of the employee (or persons in respect of whom the employee is *in loco parentis*);

- The employee's spouse or a person with whom the employee is living as husband or wife; and

- The employee's parents, grandparents, brothers and sisters.

The provisions relating to *force majeure* leave are subject to some limitations, in that an employee cannot take such leave on more than three days in any 12-month period or five days in any three-year period.

ADDITIONAL RIGHTS OF YOUNG EMPLOYEES

The Protection of Young Persons (Employment) Act, 1996, has the effect of regulating the employment of persons who have not attained the age of majority. Whereas the common law has traditionally classed all persons under the age of 18 as "minors" or "infants" and dealt with their legal capacity and affairs in a consistent manner regardless of age, the 1996 Act subdivides the larger classification into two groups: "children" and "young persons". For the purposes of the Act, a child is defined as "a person who is under 16 years of age or the school-leaving age, whichever is the higher". A young person, on the other hand, is "a person who has reached 16 years of age or the school-leaving age (whichever is higher) but is less than 18 years of age" (section 1(1)).

The Act imposes a blanket ban on the employment of children. The ban is, however, subject to a number of exceptions. So, for example, children over the age of 15 may be employed to do light work for up to eight hours a week during school term-time. Similarly, children who are over the age of 14 may, according to section 3(4), be employed to do light work as long as:

- The work is not undertaken during school term-time;

- Such work is not harmful to the safety, health and development of the child;

- The child has a break from work of at least 21 days over their summer holidays; and

- The child is not required to work for more than seven hours a day or 35 hours a week.

The employment of 13-year-olds is permitted only where the Minister for Enterprise and Employment introduces regulations authorising such employment:

> . . . in cultural, artistic, sports or advertising activities which are not harmful to the safety, health or development of children and which are not likely to interfere with their attendance at school, vocational guidance or training programmes or capacity to benefit from the instruction received (section 3(3)).

The Act also imposes a blanket ban on the employment of young persons except where:

- The employment lasts no longer than 8 hours a day or 40 hours a week;

- The young person is not required to work between 10.00 p.m. and 6.00 a.m. (or between 11.00 p.m. and 7.00 a.m. "where the Minister is satisfied . . . that there are exceptional circumstances" which arise in relation to the area or kind of work in question);

- The young person is afforded a minimum rest period of at least 12 hours in every 24-hour period;

- The young person is allowed a minimum of two days off in any seven-day period;

- The young person is not allowed to work for more than four-and-a-half consecutive hours without being given at least a 30-minute break.

Where an employer decides to employ either a child or a young person, they are obliged to obtain a copy of the prospective employee's birth certificate or some other "satisfactory evidence" of their age before the child or young person commences employment. In the case of a child, the employer must also obtain written permission from one of the child's parents or legal guardians.

HEALTH AND SAFETY IN THE WORKPLACE[1]

The Safety, Health and Welfare at Work Act, 1989, imposes duties on both employers and employees in relation to ensuring safety, health and welfare at work. The main duties imposed on employers by the Act are:

- To ensure, so far as is reasonably practicable, the safety, health and welfare of employees;

- To provide and maintain a place of work which is safe and without risk to health;

- To provide safe means of access to and egress from each place of work;

- To provide and maintain plant and equipment which is safe and without risk to health;

- To provide systems of work that are safe and without risk to health;

---

[1] See also Chapter 22 for additional information on occupational health and safety.

- To provide the information, instruction, training and supervision necessary for safe and healthy working;

- To provide and maintain suitable protective clothing or equipment where hazards cannot otherwise be controlled;

- To prepare adequate emergency plans;

- To prevent risks to health and safety in relation to the use of articles or substances;

- To provide welfare facilities;

- To provide (when necessary) the services of competent persons to ensure the safety and health at work of employees;

- To prepare a safety statement and to bring it to the attention of persons affected by its terms; and

- To consult with employees on promoting and developing health, safety and welfare at work.

Employers, however, are not the only persons who are responsible for the maintenance of a safe and healthy working environment. In recognition of that fact, the Act also imposes a number of duties on employees. The primary duties in question are:

- To take reasonable care for their own safety, health and welfare and that of others who may be affected by their acts or omissions;

- To co-operate with their employer in relation to compliance with statutory requirements;

- To use protective equipment, clothing or other means for securing safety, health and welfare; and

- To report, without delay, defects in workplace plant, equipment or systems of work which may lead to danger.

THE RIGHTS OF PART-TIME EMPLOYEES

The Worker Protection (Regular Part-time Employees) Act, 1991, extends the benefits of a range of protective legislation to regular part-time employees. Section 1 of the Act defines "regular part-time employee[s]" as being those who are in the continuous employment of the employer for not less than 13 weeks, are normally expected to work not less than eight hours a week and who, but for the Act, would be excluded from benefits under the legislation which the Act amended. The Act extended (to regular part-time employees) the benefits of, *inter alia*, the:

- Unfair Dismissals Act, 1977;

- Minimum Notice and Terms of Employment Acts, 1973 and 1984;

- Redundancy Payments Acts, 1967 to 1990; and

- Protection of Employees (Employers' Insolvency) Acts, 1984 and 1990.

RIGHTS OF EMPLOYEES WHEN A BUSINESS IS SOLD

Before 1977 the courts in most EU member states regarded the sale or transfer of a business as effecting the termination of the contracts of employment of all those employed by the original owner of the business. The Acquired Rights Directive (Council Directive 77/187/EC) was issued by the EEC that year in order to ensure that employees were afforded some protection where their employers sold or transferred the businesses in which they worked. Article 3(1) of the Directive provides that:

> The transferor's rights and obligations arising from a contract of employment or from an employment relationship existing on the date of a transfer . . . shall, by reason of such transfer, be transferred to the transferee. . . .

In like manner, Article 4 provides that:

> The transfer of an undertaking, business or part of a business shall not in itself constitute grounds for dismissal by the transferor or the transferee. This provision shall not stand in the way of dismissals that may take place for economic, technical or organisational reasons entailing changes in the workforce.

The Acquired Rights Directive was implemented in Ireland by way of the European Communities (Safeguarding of Employees' Rights on Transfer of Undertakings) Regulations, 1980. In determining when those regulations apply, Blayney J held, in *Bannon* v *The EAT and Drogheda Town Centre Ltd.* ([1993] 1 IR 500), that the relevant test has two distinct parts. The regulations will, he stated, apply if:

- The business retained its identity; and

- There was a change in the legal or natural person responsible for carrying on the business regardless of whether or not ownership of the business was transferred.

Having so determined, Mr Justice Bannon concluded that a security guard who had been employed by the defendant shopping-centre management company was entitled to regard his contract as having been transferred to the security company to which his previous employers had out-sourced his work.

In the case of *Ayse Suzen* v *Zehnacker Gebaudereinigung* (Case C-13/95, [1997] IRLR 255), however, the European Court of Justice limited the application of the Directive (and, therefore, the regulations), holding that:

> . . . the transfer only of an activity from one sub-contractor to another was not a transfer of an "entity" under the Directive. To qualify as the transfer of an "entity" there must be the transfer not only of an activity but also of the assets necessary to the conduct of the undertaking, which may include the transfer of a significant part of the workforce. The simple loss of a service contract to another contractor would not suffice to attract the protection of the Directive (Bourn, 1997: 1040).

Case Example 18.1: Transfer of Undertakings: Betts *v* Brintel and KLM

In Betts *v* Brintel and KLM *([1997] IRLR 361) the English Court of Appeal was called upon to consider the situation where KLM won the contract to supply helicopter services to North Sea oil rigs (owned and operated by Shell) from Brintel. KLM only took over the contract from Brintel. There was no transfer of helicopters, personnel or helicopter bases. On the basis of the decision in the* Suzen *case, the Court held that there was no transfer of an undertaking.*

Interestingly, as Bourn (1997: 1040) explains:

> *Whilst* Betts *v* Brintel and KLM *was a "second generation" transfer on the expiry of an existing sub-contract, Kennedy LJ saw no reason why the same logic should not apply to "first generation" transfers.*

In other words, Kennedy LJ would seem to be suggesting that he would not regard the Acquired Rights Directive as applying in cases such as Bannon. *Were an Irish judge to reach such a conclusion, it would constitute a significant change in the law in this country. That having been said, it is arguable that the UK courts have consistently interpreted the Directive in a narrower fashion than their Irish and European counterparts. In light of the* Suzen *decision, however, it would seem that they are no longer as far removed from the position adopted by their judicial brethren elsewhere as they have been in the past.*

While the next case to reach the superior courts in Ireland on the matter will be of considerable interest it seems to be a matter of common consensus in this country that the application of the Acquired Rights Directive is no longer as restrictive as it has been in the past. In that context, it would seem likely that companies' freedom to out-source may increase significantly in the short- to medium-term future.

REDUNDANCIES

The Redundancy Payments Acts, 1967 to 1979, provide that when a qualified employee is made redundant their employer must pay them a lump-sum, the amount of which is calculated as follows:

- A half week's pay for each year of employment continuous and reckonable between the ages of 16 and 41 years;

- A week's pay for each year of employment continuous and reckonable over the age of 41 years;

- In addition, the equivalent of one week's normal pay, subject to the statutory ceiling.

An employer who has made a lump-sum payment to an employee may obtain a rebate of part of the lump sum from the Social Insurance Fund at the rate of 60 per cent of the lump sum if the minimum period of two weeks' notice of dismissal is given to the employee. If an employer fails to comply with any provision concerning redundancy notice, the Minister for Enterprise and Employment may, at his/her discretion, reduce the amount of the rebate payable to that employer to 40 per cent of the lump sum.

Exclusions under the Redundancy Payments Acts
A substantial proportion of the Irish labour force is precluded from relying on the provisions of the Redundancy Payments Acts, 1967–1979. The Acts expressly exclude, *inter alia*, the following groups:

- All those who are neither employees within the meaning of the 1967 Act nor apprentices;

- All those who have not been in the continuous employment of their employers for at least 104 weeks;

- All those who have not been insured for all benefits under the Social Welfare Acts for at least four years;

- All those employed by close relatives in domestic situations;

- All those who normally work less than eight hours per week for the same employer;

- All those who have reached pensionable age under the Social Welfare Acts;

- All those ordinarily working outside the State who, at the time they are dismissed, are outside the State.

Dismissals

As Fennell and Lynch point out, historically, Irish workers have had little legal protection against arbitrary dismissal (Fennell and Lynch, 1993: 205). Because of the lack of a means of obtaining legal redress against employers who unfairly dismissed workers, a significant number of strikes disrupted Irish workplaces in the 1960s and 1970s. In 1975, for example, 116,000 working days were lost because of strikes resulting from dismissals and related matters. For that reason, Michael O'Leary, TD, the then Minister for Labour, introduced the first Unfair Dismissals Act in 1977. The main provisions of the 1977 Act and the Unfair Dismissals (Amendment) Act, 1993, which amended and updated it, are outlined below.

Exclusions

The 1977–1993 Acts preclude a significant number of categories of employees from claiming to have been unfairly dismissed. The main categories of employees excluded are:

- Those who have less than one year of continuous service with the employer who dismissed them (except where the employee concerned was dismissed because of their involvement in trade union activities, pregnancy or matters related thereto);

- Those who have reached the normal retiring age for employees of the same employer in similar employment;

- Civil servants;

- Officers of health boards and VECs;

- Persons employed by close relatives, who are members of their employer's household and are employed at a private dwelling-house or a farm in or on which both the employee and the employer reside;

- Members of the gardaí and permanent defence forces;

- FÁS trainees.

Unfair Reasons for Dismissal

The 1977–1993 Acts provide that dismissals for certain specified reasons are deemed automatically to be unfair. The reasons in question are as follows:

- Dismissals resulting wholly or mainly from the religious or political opinions of the claimant are deemed to be automatically unfair. The section in question does not appear to have been considered very often either by the Employment Appeals Tribunal or the courts. In *Merriman* v *St. James' Hospital* (unreported, Circuit Court, 24 November 1986), however, a nurse's aide who refused, for reasons of conscience, to bring a crucifix and a candle to a dying patient was found to have been unfairly dismissed.

- Similarly, dismissals resulting wholly or mainly from the claimant's race, colour, sexual orientation, age or membership of the travelling community are unfair.

- Dismissals prompted wholly or mainly by the fact that the employee is or will be a party to civil proceedings against the employer or the fact that the employee was or is likely to be a witness in proceedings against the employer. Likewise, a dismissal is unfair if caused by criminal proceedings against the employer (whether actual, threatened or proposed) in relation to which the employee has made, proposed or threatened to make a complaint or statement to the prosecuting authority or in which the employee was or is likely to be a witness.

- Dismissals resulting wholly or mainly from pregnancy "or matters connected therewith", except where the employee has proven to be unable, because of the pregnancy, to do adequately the work for which she was employed. For an employer to be able to sustain such a defence, however, they must prove that there was not, at the time of the dismissal, any vacancy that might suitably be filled by the employee, or that the employee refused their offer of alternative employment on equally favourable terms and conditions.

- A dismissal resulting from an employee's participation in a strike or other industrial action if other employees who took part in the industrial action were not also dismissed for that reason, or if another employee who was dismissed for taking part in the action is subsequently offered reinstatement or re-engagement and the claimant is not.

- Dismissals resulting wholly or mainly from the claimant's membership of a trade union, or their engaging in activities on behalf of a union. While it has been held that the mere fact that a claimant is a trade union member does not mean that any dismissal of them is unfair (*A La Française* v *Monaghan*, UD 13/1977), the Employment Appeals Tribunal held in 1989 that the dismissal, for poor work performance, of trade union members is unfair where the employer is prepared to tolerate similar poor performance from non-union members (*McElhinney* v *Sheridan*, UD 470/1989).

Fair Reasons for Dismissal

If an employer is to avoid liability under the Unfair Dismissals Acts, they must be able to prove to the Tribunal that the dismissal resulted "wholly or mainly" from reasons relating to the employee's capability, qualifications, competence, conduct, redundancy, or other substantial grounds.

Dismissals for reasons relating to "capability" usually arise in the context of employees having problems in relation to regular attendance at work. Thus, employees who fail to attend work regularly, who are persistently late, or who are absent for long periods may be regarded as being incapable of performing the work they were employed to do. In both *Reardon* v *St Vincent's Hospital* (UD 74/1979) and *Bevan* v *Daydream Ltd.* (UD 31/1978), therefore, employees who were out of work due to illness for periods close to the equivalent of one-third of the working year were found not to have been unfairly dismissed.

Similarly, an employee will be deemed to have been fairly dismissed if the employer can prove that the dismissal came about because the employee lacked necessary qualifications. In *Flynn* v *CIE* (UD 254/1980), for example, a road freight driver was successfully dismissed when he was disqualified from driving because he committed a road traffic offence.

As has been pointed out above, employers may also dismiss employees for reasons relating to the employee's lack of competence. It has traditionally been the case that the issue of competence arises when poor work performance is alleged. In *Kearns* v *Levi Strauss Ireland* (UD 527/1981), for example, it was held that the failure of an employee to meet reasonable targets set by the employer provides grounds for dismissal. It was, however, pointed out in *McGinlay* v *Disabled Aid Ltd.* (UD 773/1983) that an employee cannot be legally dismissed because of alleged poor performance if no targets have been set for them.

The most common ground on which employers seek to rely when attempting to justify a dismissal is that of misconduct. The nature of the misconduct must be such that it undermines the relationship of trust necessary between an employer and their employee. Even minor acts of misconduct may suffice if they breach that relationship. In pleading misconduct on the part of the employee, an employer will usually seek to pin the dismissal on a single act of gross misconduct or a series of less significant acts followed by a series of warnings.

Not surprisingly, a dismissal will also be deemed to be in compliance with the Act if it results wholly or mainly from the necessity to make an employee redundant. As the Employment Appeals Tribunal pointed out in *Hogan* v *Keadeen (Carlow) Ltd.* (UD 307/1982), however, the employer must be able to prove that a genuine redundancy situation existed. For that reason, in *O'Connell* v *Healy* ([1990] ELR 36) the employer's attempt to justify the claimant's dismissal on the basis of redundancy failed because his business was actually improving.

Section 6(4) of the 1977 Act allows for other substantial grounds to justify dismissals. Without attempting to tightly define the ambit of section 6(4), however, one can justifiably describe it as a catch-all provision designed to deal with unusual cases where the dismissals in question are morally justifiable but cannot be excused under one of the other headings detailed above.

Wrongful Dismissals

Given the limited ambit of the Unfair Dismissals Acts, 1977–1993, employees will often find themselves having to challenge the legality of their dismissals on other bases. Such challenges usually involve an allegation that the impugned dismissal was carried out in breach of the employee's contract or in breach of what lawyers refer to as the "principles of natural justice". Both of these types of legal challenges are briefly discussed below.

Dismissals in Breach of Contract

Dismissals in breach of contract are those dismissals that are inconsistent with one or more of the terms of an employee's contract. Such dismissals can be challenged in the civil courts and are usually deemed to have been "wrongful". In *Gunton v Richmond-upon-Thames London Borough Council* ([1981] Ch 448), for example, the plaintiff was held to have been wrongfully dismissed because the defendant employer had failed to comply with the procedure for dismissal expressly provided for in the plaintiff's contract of employment.

Dismissals and the Principles of Natural Justice

In disciplinary and dismissals scenarios, the courts usually imply minimum standards of fair procedures consistent with the rules of natural justice. The two rules in question are:

1. *Audi alteram partem* (both parties must be heard); and

2. *Nemo iudex in causa sua* (no person may judge his own case).

In an employment context, the first of these rules is more important. *Audi alteram partem* does not simply require that employees be given a hearing by their employer prior to dismissal. It can also extend to giving them time to prepare for the hearing, allowing them to call witnesses and showing them any relevant documents or written accusations against them. As Lord Wilberforce has pointed out in the House of Lords, the very possibility of a dismissal occurring without reasons being given is an action which may vitally affect a person's career or their pension. For that reason, it is all the more important that they be able to "state their case" (*Malloch* v *Aberdeen Corporation* [1971] 1 WLR 1578). The Irish Supreme Court has adopted a similar stance in relation to dismissals and the rules of natural justice. In *State (Gleeson)* v *The Minister for Defence* ([1976] IR 280), for example, Private Gleeson was dismissed from the Army in accordance with section 73 of the Defence Act, 1954. He was given no information in respect of the proceedings and was given no opportunity of being heard. For those reasons, Henchy J held that the dismissal was not in line with the principles of natural justice and was, therefore, unlawful.

MINIMUM NOTICE

The Minimum Notice and Terms of Employment Act, 1973, lays down minimum periods of notice to be given by employers and employees when terminating contracts of employment. Section 4 of the 1973 Act provides that if an employee has been in "continuous service" with the same employer for at least 13 weeks, they are entitled to a minimum period of notice before the employer may dismiss them. The period of notice to which an employee is entitled depends on the length of their service with the employer. The appropriate minimum periods of notice are set out in Table 18.1 below.

Table 18.1: Minimum Notice Periods under the 1973 Act

Length of Service	Minimum Notice
13 weeks to 2 years	1 week
2–5 years	2 weeks
5–10 years	4 weeks
10–15 years	6 weeks
15 years +	8 weeks

In contrast, section 6 of the Act provides that an employer is entitled to only one week's notice from an employee who has been
employed by them for 13 weeks or more and who proposes to resign from their position. The contract, however, may require that
the employee give the employer a greater period of notice before
leaving their employment.

Any provision in a contract of employment for periods of notice shorter than the minimum periods stipulated in the Act has
no effect. Despite the provisions of the Act, however, the employer is at all times entitled to dismiss an employee without notice if that employee has been guilty of gross misconduct.

CONCLUSION

While an employee's contract of employment is still the primary
factor regulating the relationship between an employee and their
employer from a legal perspective, it is increasingly the case that
legislation prescribes what can and cannot be provided for in that
contract. The legislation in question not only prescribes the ambit
of the contract but also, on occasion, intervenes to amend or supplement it. In that context, employers seeking to protect themselves from a legal perspective must not only attain a degree of
familiarity with employment legislation but also seek to keep
themselves attuned to legislative developments in the area.

While these may seem to be heavy demands, it is worth remembering that compliance with the legislation in question does lead to a number of benefits. From the perspective of recruitment in the modern, international job market, for example, the rights afforded to Irish and other European employees are considerably more extensive (and, therefore, more attractive) than those afforded to their counterparts in the US and elsewhere. In addition, from the perspective of employee relations or collective bargaining, it is undoubtedly the case that greater legislative intervention has had the practical advantage of reducing the need to spend long hours negotiating with employees or their trade union representatives. In that context, it may just be that, in an era when employees are viewed as human resources, protective legislation should be viewed by employers as being of benefit (because it protects those assets) rather than simply as a costly nuisance.

References

Bourn, C. (1997), "Redundancy and the Transfer of Undertakings", *New Law Journal*, Vol. 147, pp. 10–40.

Fennell, C., and I. Lynch (1993), *Labour Law in Ireland*, Dublin: Gill & Macmillan.

Twomey, A.F. (1997), "Employment Law", in N. Harvey, *The Challenge of Supervisory Management*, Oak Tree Press, Dublin.

Further Readings

Bercusson, B. (1996), *European Labour Law*, London: Butterworths.

Byrne, R. (1990), *The Safety, Health and Welfare at Work Act, 1989: A Guide*, Dublin: NIFAST.

Department of Enterprise and Employment (1999), *Guide to Labour Law*, Dublin: Department of Enterprise and Employment.

Forde, M. (1992), *Employment Law*, Dublin: Round Hall Press.

Irish Business and Employers Confederation (IBEC) (1996), *A Guide to Employment Legislation*, 6th Edition, Dublin: IBEC.

Madden, D. and A. Kerr (1996), *Unfair Dismissal: Cases and Commentary*, 2nd Edition, Dublin: IBEC.

Meenan, F. (1994), *Working within the Law*, Dublin: Oak Tree Press.

Murphy, T. (1987), "The Impact of the Unfair Dismissals Act on Workplace Industrial Relations", *Journal of the Irish Society for Labour Law* Vol. 6, p. 36.

Twomey, A.F. (1998), "Terms of Engagement", *Gazette of the Incorporated Law Society of Ireland*, May, p. 30.

CHAPTER 19

COLLECTIVE LABOUR LAW: TRADE UNIONS AND THE LAW

Adrian F. Twomey

INTRODUCTION

The history of Irish and British trade union law is littered with clashes between the legislature and the judiciary. Between 1824 and 1906, Parliament at Westminster introduced a series of increasingly progressive pieces of legislation which were, by and large, favourable to the cause of trade unionism. In the same period, the judiciary handed down a series of blatantly anti-union decisions.

In 1824, for example, Parliament passed the Combination Laws Repeal Act, which had the effect of removing the taint of illegality from trade unions. Significantly, it also provided that individuals who participated in strikes were no longer to be deemed to have committed certain criminal offences. In the three decades that followed, however, the courts effectively undermined the 1824 Act by convicting a number of groups of trade union members on charges of criminal conspiracy and finding the unions themselves to be acting in unlawful restraint of trade.

This process of legislative development followed by defeats for the unions in the courts continued well into the twentieth century. Arguably the most significant development, however, occurred in

1906 when the Dunedin Royal Commission on Trade Disputes and Trade Combinations reported, recommending the enactment of "a comprehensive labour law code with positive rights and obligations" (Kerr and Whyte, 1985: 249). Remarkably, the trade unions opposed the introduction of such a Code and instead supported the minority recommendations, which suggested that legislation based on a series of immunities should be introduced. The resulting Trade Disputes Act, 1906, adopted this immunities-based approach, in that it granted trade unions blanket immunities from suit in specified circumstances.

FREEDOM OF ASSOCIATION: TRADE UNIONS AND THE CONSTITUTION

Article 40.6.1° of the 1937 Constitution (Bunreacht na hÉireann) guarantees

> [t]he right of citizens to form associations and unions. Laws, however, may be enacted for the regulation and control in the public interest of the exercise of the foregoing right.

As with many of the other rights guaranteed by the Constitution, the meaning of Article 40.6.1°(iii) has been clarified by a series of decisions handed down by the High Court and the Supreme Court over the years. Among the rights which, it has been suggested, are protected by Article 40.6.1°(iii) are those discussed below.

The Right to Join Trade Unions

In *Nolan Transport Ltd.* v *Halligan* ((1998) 9 ELR 177: 201) O'Flaherty J of the Supreme Court effectively summarised the constitutional position in relation to the right of workers to join trade unions, stating that "no worker can be denied his right to join a trade union which is prepared to accept him". The position is, however, quite different where the union in question refuses to accept an individual as a member. In *Tierney* v *Amalgamated Soci-*

ety of Woodworkers ([1959] IR 254), for example, the plaintiff, a woodworker, applied for membership of the defendant union and was refused because he could not prove that he had an apprenticeship. Because he was not a union member, Tierney was unable to obtain employment as a woodworker. In the High Court he argued that because his right to work was protected by Article 40.3 and he was unable to obtain work unless he had a right to join the union, he must have such a right. Budd J refused to accept that the right in question was implicitly guaranteed by Article 40.6.1°(iii) and held for the union.

In *Murphy* v *Stewart* ([1973] IR 97) the Supreme Court took a similar approach to the matter, holding that Article 40.6.1°(iii) does not implicitly guarantee a right to join a trade union. Walsh J, however, went on to suggest that a union cannot refuse membership if their intention in so doing is solely to injure the applicant. He also implied that if work in a particular profession is exclusively controlled by a union, they have to have very strong grounds for refusing membership.

The Right to Dissociate: the Right to Not Join a Trade Union
The courts have consistently held that Article 40.6.1°(iii) implicitly guarantees the right to dissociate or the right not to have to join a union. That right becomes particularly important in the context of a closed shop, where the relevant union has reached an agreement with management that no worker will be hired unless they are a union member. The legal position changes depending on the type of closed shop agreement in place. For the purposes of constitutional law there are two basic types of closed shop agreement: *pre-entry closed shops* and *post-entry closed shops*.

Pre-entry Closed Shops: Pre-entry closed shops are those that require that one be a trade union member before being hired. It would appear that such closed shops are lawful and do not infringe on an individual's right to dissociate. In *Buckley* v *Rooney* ([1950] Ir Jur Rep 5), for example, O'Connor J of the Circuit Court held that a pre-entry closed shop agreement did not violate Article 40.6.1°(iii).

Post-entry Closed Shops: A post-entry closed shop agreement is one that is concluded after the initial employment of staff. Such agreements are unconstitutional in effect when concluded in workplaces that contain non-unionised employees.

Case Example 19.1: Post-Entry Closed Shops — Educational
Company of Ireland *v* FitzPatrick (No. 2)

In Educational Company of Ireland *v* FitzPatrick (No. 2) *([1961] IR 345) unionised employees were unwilling to work with non-union members and sought to conclude a post-entry closed-shop agreement with the company. The effect of the agreement would have been to force non-union members either to join the union or resign from their jobs. The company refused to agree to any such arrangement. The union took industrial action on foot of this refusal. The company responded by applying for an injunction to prevent the union from striking.*

In the Supreme Court, Budd J held that Article 40.6.1°(iii) protects the right to dissociate (the right not to be forced to associate). The strike was therefore unconstitutional in that it was aimed at coercing non-union members to forego their constitutional right.

The Right to Participate in the Decision-Making Processes of a Trade Union

It has been held by the courts that the right of members to participate in the decision-making process of a trade union is a corollary of the right to form trade unions, where the rules of the union involved make it clear that the decision in question can only be made by those affected by it. In *Rodgers* v *ITGWU* (unreported, 15 March 1978), for example, Finlay P held, in the High Court, that it is a necessary corollary of the primary right guaranteed by Article 40.6.1°(iii) that members be entitled to take part in the democratic processes provided by trade unions. In particular, he added, the right must encompass taking part in the decision-making processes provided for in the trade union's rules.

Similarly, in *Doyle* v *Croke* ((1988) 7 JISLL 150) Costello J held that if a union meeting is to be held which will be making a decision on an issue affecting members, those members should be invited to attend the meeting and be forewarned about the terms of any resolutions affecting them which would be proposed at the meeting.

The Right to Freedom of Choice of Union

In 1941, the Government of the time enacted the Trade Union Act, section 34(3) of which provided that a majority union in any class of workers could get exclusive negotiating rights for that class for a five-year period. The Government's aim was to streamline the trade union movement by reducing the number of small trade unions. The trade union movement was, generally speaking, in favour of the legislation. In *NUR* v *Sullivan* ([1947] IR 77), however, the constitutionality of section 34(3) was challenged. The majority decision of the Supreme Court was delivered by Murnaghan J, who stated that any limitation on negotiating rights, such as that contained in the 1941 Act, effectively deprived citizens of a free choice of persons with whom they would associate. Any such deprivation could not constitute the mere controlling or regulating of the exercise of the right of freedom to associate, but, rather, a denial of that right altogether. The Act was, for that reason, found to be unconstitutional.

The "Right" to Recognition for Negotiating Purposes

It has been held by McWilliam J in *Abbott and Whelan* v *ITGWU & the Southern Health Board* ((1982) 1 JISLL 56) and by Hamilton J in *Dublin Colleges ASA* v *City of Dublin VEC* ((1982) 1 JISLL 73) that Article 40.6.1°(iii) does not implicitly impose any duty on employers to negotiate with the trade unions representing their employees. Given that such is the case, a trade union that is refused recognition by an employer will, very often, take the alternative approach of seeking a Labour Court recommendation that the employers change their stance on the matter. It is, however, clearly the case that employers are under no legal obligation to recognise unions for negotiating purposes.

The "Right" to Strike

The Irish Courts have not clearly determined whether the constitutional guarantee of freedom of association provided by Article 40.6.1°(iii) of Bunreacht na hÉireann also implicitly protects activities undertaken in furtherance of the lawful objects of the association (Kerr and Whyte, 1985: 23). It is, however, arguable that the Constitution is capable of protecting picketing and the withdrawal of labour. In *Brendan Dunne Ltd.* v. *Fitzpatrick* ([1958] IR 29: 34), for example, Budd J indicated that the Constitution protected, *inter alia*, the right of the employer and employee respectively

> . . . to deal with and dispose of their property and labour as they will without interference unless such interference be made legitimate by law.

In the subsequent case of *Educational Co. of Ireland Ltd.* v *Fitzpatrick* (No. 2) ([1961] IR 345: 397) Kingsmill Moore J referred to the right to dispose of one's labour and to withdraw it as a "fundamental personal right". Moreover, it should be noted that the majority of the Supreme Court in *Becton Dickinson & Co.* v *Lee* ([1973] IR 1) adopted the "suspension theory" view of strike action — a theory that is consistent with the existence of a constitutional right to strike (see later, pp. 618–19).

COLLECTIVE BARGAINING AND THE LAW

As Gunnigle et al. (1995: 23) define it, a collective agreement is "the result of collective bargaining between employers and workers (or their respective representatives) over terms and conditions of employment". The purposes of collective bargaining, according to Kahn-Freund (1972: 55), are relatively easy to summarise:

> . . . by bargaining collectively with organised labour, man-
> agement seeks to give effect to its legitimate expectation that
> the planning of production, distribution, etc., should not be
> frustrated through interruptions of work. By bargaining col-
> lectively with management, organised labour seeks to give ef-
> fect to its legitimate expectations that wages and other
> conditions of work should be such as to guarantee a stable
> and adequate form of existence and as to be compatible with
> the physical integrity and moral dignity of the individual, and
> also that jobs should be reasonably secure.

It has been estimated that, in the UK, three-quarters of all employees have their terms and conditions of employment determined by collective agreements (Carr and Kay, 1994: 47). In such a
context, it is obviously of considerable importance to be able to
determine the legal status of such agreements and to be able to
determine the nature of their impact on individual employees'
contracts of employment. Before one can do so, however, one
must analyse the issue of the enforceability of collective bargaining agreements as between the negotiating parties (employers and
trade unions).

The Enforceability of Collective Agreements by Employers and Unions

In 1894, the Fifth and Final Report of the Royal Commission on
Labour concluded that collective agreements were not legally enforceable at the time (Kerr and Whyte, 1985: 153), in part because
trade unions were generally regarded as lacking the necessary
legal capacity to contract. In *Taff Vale Railway Co.* v *Amalgamated
Society of Railway Servants* ([1901] AC 426), however, the House of
Lords held that trade unions did have the necessary legal capacity
and, as Kerr and Whyte (1985: 153) note, "the issue of the non-
enforceability of collective agreements had to be reconsidered".
Even then, however, it remained the case that collective agreements were, in general, regarded as not being contractually
binding because they were seen as not being attended by the nec-

essary intention to create legal relations. In 1969, for example, in the case of *Ford Motor Co. Ltd.* v *Amalgamated Union of Engineering and Foundry Workers* ([1969] 2 All ER 481), the Court of Appeal held that collective agreements are not enforceable because they lack the necessary characteristics of a contract. In particular, the Court noted, such agreements were not characterised by an intention on the part of the parties to the agreement to create legal relations in the contractual sense. As Kahn-Freund (1972: 132) explained three years later:

> This lack of contractual intent is not due to the caprice of the parties. It is rooted in the history, and, more importantly, in the structure of British collective bargaining, and especially in the "institutional" or "dynamic" method of collective bargaining, the impact of "custom and practice," and also the multiplicity of bargaining levels. Owing to these (and perhaps other) factors, it will be very difficult to press collective agreements into the mould of legal contracts.

Kahn-Freund's analysis of the position in England would seem to be equally applicable in this jurisdiction. In Ireland, most industrial relations practitioners, in line with their general antipathy towards legal intervention in the labour relations arena, are opposed to the idea of collective agreements being legally enforceable. In 1981, for example, the Commission of Inquiry on Industrial Relations (1981: 248) reported that:

> The evidence would suggest ... that probably all trade unions and many employers would be opposed to any legislative step to give collective agreements the status of legally binding contracts. Accordingly, we recommend against making collective agreements legally binding by statute.

Even if such were not the case and there was no problem in relation to the intentions of the parties, a second obstacle has still to be surmounted. The nature of the obstacle in question is highlighted by Kahn-Freund (1972: 132), who states that:

> Even if the parties intend, or, . . . if the law imputes to them an intention, to give contractual force to their agreements, they could not in many cases do so unless they changed their bargaining methods. The language of so many agreements is so vague that a court may have to hold them "void for uncertainty".

However, where a collective bargaining agreement is attended by the necessary intention to create legal relations and its terms are both clear and certain, the law would seem to place few obstacles in the path to its enforcement. In *Ardmore Studios* v *Lynch* ([1965] IR 1), for example, the plaintiffs entered into an agreement with a trade union that electricians would be drawn only from a "seniority list" of union electricians. The plaintiffs subsequently hired electricians who were not on the list. The plaintiffs sought an injunction to restrain the defendants from picketing their premises. The company argued that the agreement had been terminated before the electricians who had been the cause of the dispute had been hired. At the trial of the action McLoughlin J stated that in his view the agreement was not binding because of the uncertainty of its terms. According to Clark (1992: 76), however, "had the agreement been clear and specific the collective agreement would have possessed contractual effect".

In the 1980s, Barrington J handed down two decisions on the matter in the High Court that are worth noting at this juncture. The first of the two cases in question was *O'Rourke* v *Talbot Ireland Ltd.* ([1984] ILRM 587), in which Barrington J "reserved the discretion to hold a collective agreement to be binding if the necessary characteristics of a contract did exist" (Fennell and Lynch, 1993: 21). In the second case, *Nolan* v *Telecom Éireann* (*ex tempore*, Barrington J, High Court, 27 June 1985), the plaintiff employees were paid by cheque, as provided for by the terms of a collective agreement. They sought to obtain an injunction compelling the defendant to pay them in cash. In an *ex tempore* judgment at interlocutory stage, Barrington J reportedly indicated that he regarded the collective agreement as being binding in its effect.

Collective Agreements and Contracts of Employment

In the English case of *Marley* v *Forward Trust Group Ltd.* ([1986] ICR 891) the plaintiff was employed as a field supervisor in the company's Bristol office. His terms and conditions of employment incorporated the terms of a collective agreement with ASTMS, and included both a mobility and redundancy clause, the latter allowing a six-month trial period. However, the final clause of the agreement stated that the agreement was "binding in honour only". The company closed their Bristol office and the plaintiff worked in London, under the terms of the agreement, for a trial period. He found the job unsuitable and sought a redundancy payment. Both the Industrial Tribunal and the Employment Appeals Tribunal rejected his claim on the ground that the agreement was stated to be "binding in honour only" and was accordingly unenforceable. The Court of Appeal rejected that line of reasoning and held that the terms of an unenforceable collective agreement can be incorporated into contracts of employment and are then enforceable by individual employees. According to the Court, the unenforceable nature of the agreement was limited to the parties to the agreement; in this case the employer and the union.

In Ireland, it is generally accepted that where persons commence working in an establishment in which a collective agreement regulates some or all of the terms and conditions of employees in their category, the courts will readily imply the agreement's terms into their employment contracts, on the grounds that this is, almost certainly, what the parties intended. Similarly, the terms of a collective agreement are legally enforceable where the agreement is one that is registered with the Labour Court in line with section 25 of the Industrial Relations Act, 1946.

THE INDUSTRIAL RELATIONS ACT, 1990

As has already been explained, the courts have not clearly recognised the existence of a constitutional right to strike in Ireland. As a result, both employees and trade unions face potential legal liability for their actions if they participate in or organise strikes. For that reason, the 1990 Act provides immunities from suit to trade unions and workers where there is a dispute

> . . . between employers and workers which is connected with the employment or non-employment, or the terms or conditions of or affecting the employment of any person.

According to Murphy J of the Supreme Court:

> . . . the Industrial Relations Act, 1990, is of historic importance. It repealed in whole the Trade Disputes Act, 1906, which had for nearly a century provided the legal framework by which industrial action had been governed. Whilst many of the concepts enshrined in the 1906 Act were preserved and much of the detail re-enacted, significant amendments have been made to the previous legislation. Clearly, the legislature sought to achieve a greater degree of responsibility by unions and their members in pursuing industrial action; additional protections for trade unions which acted with that sense of responsibility; and a degree of discipline within the trade union movement which would ensure that settlements negotiated with employers would be observed by all trade unionists (*Nolan Transport (Oaklands) Ltd.* v *Halligan and others* (1998) 9 ELR 177: 194–195).

Immunities Attaching to the Trade Union

Section 13 of the 1990 Act effectively provides trade unions with an immunity against tort actions which might otherwise be instituted against them where they have acted "in contemplation or furtherance of a trade dispute". More limited immunities attach to individuals (such as members or officials) where they are acting within similar parameters (pursuant to sections 10, 11 and 12). In order to qualify for the immunities, however, the union must, as has already been pointed out, be acting "in contemplation or furtherance" of such a dispute. The terminology in question is familiar to both lawyers and trade union officials, having been used in a range of earlier legislation, including the Trade Disputes Act, 1906. The so-called "golden formula" has also been interpreted and applied by the courts in a number of cases. In *Esplanade Pharmacy* v *Larkin* ([1957] IR 285), for example, the Irish Supreme Court stated that the mere anticipation of a possible dispute at some time in the future is not enough to constitute "contemplation". In the earlier English case of *Conway* v *Wade* ([1909] AC 506) Lord Shaw stated that to "contemplate" a trade dispute is to have before the mind some objective event or situation but does not mean a contemplation in regard to something as yet wholly within the mind and of a subjective character.

On the other hand, one will, according to Lord Diplock (*Express Newspapers Ltd.* v *McShane* [1980] AC 672), be regarded as acting in "furtherance" of a trade dispute if one honestly thinks at the time of committing the impugned act that it may help one of the parties to the trade dispute to achieve their objectives and one does the act in question for that reason. The test would, therefore, seem to be a subjective one. As Lord Scarman explained in the McShane case, it would be a

> . . . strange and embarrassing task for a judge to be called upon to review the tactics of a party to a trade dispute and to determine whether . . . the tactic employed was likely to further or advance the party's side of the dispute.

Picketing

Section 11 of the 1990 Act effectively affords workers a statutory right to picket their employer where:

- They are acting on their own behalf or on behalf of a trade union;

- They are acting in contemplation or furtherance of a trade dispute;

- They are picketing at, or where that is not practicable, at the approaches to, a place where their employer works or carries on business; and

- The purpose of the picket is merely to peacefully obtain or communicate information or to peacefully persuade others to work or abstain from working.

Where the picket is, for example, violent or otherwise fails to comply with the requirements of section 11 it will not be protected by the Act. It should, in particular, be noted that pickets comprised of excessive numbers of people may be regarded by the courts as going beyond what is needed for the mere communication of information.

Secondary pickets (pickets placed on premises other than the employer's) are afforded less substantial protection by the Act. Such pickets are only afforded the protection of the statutory immunities where it is reasonable for the picketers to believe (throughout the duration of the picket) that the employer being picketed has directly assisted their employer for the purpose of frustrating their industrial action.

Secret Ballots

One of the most significant features of the Industrial Relations Act, 1990 is the inclusion in it of a section (section 14) requiring trade unions to include in their rules a provision requiring them to conduct a secret ballot of their members prior to engaging in strike action. The introduction of secret ballots was a development that the trade union movement had resisted for many years. They eventually agreed to its introduction in return for the inclusion in the Act of a section curtailing the freedom of employers to seek injunctions against them where they had instigated pickets on workplaces. Section 14 was central to the long-running and controversial litigation in the *Nolan Transport* case, which is discussed below.

Case Example 19.2: Secret Ballots — Nolan Transport Ltd. *v* Halligan

---

In Nolan Transport (Oaklands) Ltd. *v* Halligan and others *([1998] 9 ELR 177) the plaintiff employed approximately 55 drivers, some of whom wished to join SIPTU. The employer was a family-owned business. The father of the family, who played no part in the management of the company, was employed by it (primarily as a labourer). In January 1993, he purported to dismiss three employees. Despite the fact that the father had no authority to dismiss employees, the workers in question believed that their employment had been terminated.*

Twenty-three union members were subsequently balloted for industrial action. In the High Court ([1995] 6 ELR 1), Barron J (whose finding on the matter was subsequently upheld by the Supreme Court) concluded that the ballot was "rigged". In any case, a picket was placed on the company's premises. While the Union submitted that the picket had been placed because of the purported dismissal of its members, the company contended that the picket was, in reality, put in place by the union in order to further its own ambitions in recruiting members at Nolan Transport.

In the Supreme Court, Murphy J found that there were two key issues to be determined. The first of those issues was whether or not there was a "trade dispute" within the meaning of the Act. In finding that there was such a "trade dispute" in the instant case, Murphy J stated ([1998] 9 ELR 177: 193–194) that:

> *In the circumstances I believe that the dispute between the [workers] and the company was bona fide in the sense that Mr Halligan had an honest belief for which there were reasonable grounds and further that the dispute was genuine in the sense that it represented the immediate quarrel between the parties. . . .*

> *If . . . a bona fide trade dispute does exist between an employer and workers, some of whom happen to be members of a trade union, the trade union is entitled, within the constitution and the law, to support its members who are in dispute. That, in doing this, it may be partly motivated by the aim of impressing its members and other workers and enhancing its own reputation and membership appears to me to be quite irrelevant, as long as it acts within the law and does not attempt to infringe the constitutional right of each worker to join or not to join a trade union as he himself thinks best.*

> *It follows that the appellants were entitled to the statutory immunities conferred on those engaged in activities in furtherance of a trade dispute save in so far as those privileges were removed or restricted by the Industrial Relations Act 1990.*

The second key issue highlighted by Murphy J was whether or not SIPTU were entitled to authorise strike action in light of the "rigged" ballot. Crucially, he held that:

> It has been said that section 14 requires that industrial action should be authorised by a secret ballot but such a statement is misleading. The statute requires that the rules of the trade union should contain certain provisions in relation to such ballots and imposes sanctions for the failure either to have such rules or to observe them. On the face of it, the participation by a trade union in or its support for a strike or other industrial action without the authority of a secret ballot of its members would be a matter of internal management of the affairs of the union and constitute a breach of contract between the executive of the union and the membership rather than a breach of statutory duty. This interpretation is confirmed by section 14(3), which expressly provides that the rights in relation to a ballot are "conferred on the members of the trade union concerned and no other person".

That is not to say that the Court regarded third parties (such as employers) as being without any comeback when a union fails to comply with its own rules in relation to balloting. As Murphy J explained, in such circumstances

> . . . it would not forfeit the immunity conferred upon it by section 13. Instead it would risk the loss of its negotiating licence in accordance with the provisions of section 16 of the 1990 Act.

In addition, the individual members engaged in the industrial action would lose the immunities otherwise afforded to them by the Act.

Labour Injunctions

Prior to the introduction of the 1990 Act, many strikes were effectively frustrated by employers who sought and obtained interim or interlocutory injunctions prohibiting picketing until such time as the legality of the pickets in question could be assessed at a full hearing. In exchange for their acceptance of secret balloting requirements, trade unions were afforded some protection against such injunctions by the Industrial Relations Act, 1990. Section 19 of the Act provides that where a ballot has been conducted in accordance with the rules of the union and a minimum of one week's notice has been given to the employer, the latter will not be entitled to obtain an *ex parte* injunction (an injunction granted on the strength of the employer's submission without the relevant union receiving notice of the application). Similarly, the employer will not be entitled to obtain an interlocutory injunction if the union can establish a fair case that it was acting "in contemplation or furtherance of a trade dispute". In considering the application of Nolan Transport for an interlocutory injunction in 1994, Keane J stated (*Nolan Transport* v *Halligan*, unreported, High Court, 22 March 1994) that:

> Before a trade union is afforded the protection of section 19 and, conversely, an employer is deprived of the protection that he would normally have at common law in relation to the obtaining of an injunction in circumstances where his business is or could be affected . . . the court must be satisfied . . . that section 14 has been complied with.

Similar sentiments have been expressed by Laffoy J (*G&T Crampton Ltd.* v *Building and Allied Trades Union* [1998] ILRM 430) and by Murphy J (*Nolan Transport Ltd.* v *Halligan* [1998] 9 ELR 177).

STRIKES AND THE CONTRACT OF EMPLOYMENT

Strike action on the part of an employee has traditionally been viewed at common law as a breach of the contract of employment. The principle was, perhaps, most clearly enunciated by Donovan LJ, who, in *Rookes* v *Barnard* ([1963] 1 QB 623: 682), stated that:

> There can be few strikes which do not involve a breach of contract by the strikers. Until a proper notice is given to terminate their contract of service, and the notice has expired, they remain liable under its terms to perform their bargain.

In *Parkin* v *South Hetton Coal Co.* ((1907) 97 LT 98), Darling J had viewed the matter as being even more clear-cut; a person's refusal to work, he held, was "repugnant to the very contract of service itself". The dictum of Darling J does little more than reflect the generally acknowledged judicial dislike of trade unions and industrial action prevalent during the late nineteenth and early twentieth centuries. By the time *Rookes* v *Barnard* was decided in 1963, legal principles inspired by the doctrine of *laissez-faire* had been firmly cemented into place by the operation of the doctrine of precedent. It came as little surprise to trade unionists, then, when later that year, in *Stratford & Son* v *Lindley* ([1965] AC 269), Lord Denning held that a "strike notice" is "nothing more or less than a notice that . . . men will not come to work. In short, that they will break their contracts." So to hold, however, was, according to Grunfeld (1966: 333):

> . . . surely a perversion of the strike and strike notice intention. The intention of due strike notice is to ensure that the economic pressure constituted by the withdrawal of labour should be lawful pressure. To put it the other way, due strike notice is given with the intention of avoiding breach of contracts of employment.

Two years after the Court of Appeal had handed down its decision in *Stratford & Son Ltd.* v *Lindley*, Grunfeld suggested an alternative approach. He argued that if it was desired to bring legal theory into line with industrial practice, it would be necessary for the law to recognise a special unilateral suspensory notice for strike purposes (Grunfeld, 1966: 334). Lord Denning was convinced. In *Morgan* v *Fry* ([1968] 2 QB 710) he reapplied himself to the question of the relationship between strikes and the contract of employment. This time, he was of the opinion that

> if a strike takes place, the contract of employment is not terminated. It is suspended during the strike: and revives again when the strike is over ([1968] 2 QB 710: 728).

Of the judgment he had delivered in the Stratford case only three years earlier, Denning MR admitted that:

> . . . there must have been something wrong with it: for if [it was] correct, it would do away with the right to strike in this country. It has been held for over sixty years that workmen

> have a right to strike . . . provided that they give sufficient no-
> tice beforehand.

Under what has subsequently come to be known as the "suspension theory", the effect of the taking of strike action by employees
has been to suspend rather than breach their contracts of employment. According to Kerr and Whyte (1985: 209), the "suspension theory" has the effect of excusing

> . . . each party from the execution of the main obligation that is
> imposed upon him by the contract. It releases the employee
> from his duty to perform work and it releases the employer
> from his duty to pay wages.

The theory in question has not gained general acceptance
amongst the English judiciary (Twomey, 1993).

In Ireland, the traditional view was similar to that prevalent in
England. In *Becton Dickinson v Lee* ([1973] IR 1), however, Walsh J
elected to implant the "suspension theory" into Irish law, stating
that he

> would agree with the view expressed by Lord Denning that
> there is to be read into every contract of service an implied
> term that . . . to take action on foot of [a] strike notice would
> . . . not be a breach of the contract.

Such an implied term, according to Walsh J, was not to be read
into the contract of employment where there was an express term
to the contrary or where it was necessary to imply a provision to
the contrary into the contract. He did, however, add the following
caveat:

> An express no-strike clause in a contract is itself such an un-
> usual feature of a contract of employment and is such an ap-
> parent departure from the long-established right to strike that
> a court would be slow to imply it where it is not expressly in-
> cluded in a contract or where it is not a necessary implication;
> a court would probably only do so in cases where there was
> some particular provision for machinery to deal with disputes,

the provision being so phrased as to give rise to the implication that it had been agreed between the parties that no other course would be adopted during the currency of the contract.

Walsh J's dictum has since been relied on by the Supreme Court when assessing the impact of strike action on the contract of employment in *Bates* v *Model Bakery Limited* ((1992) 3 ELR 193). In that case, the general secretary of the Bakery and Food Workers' Amalgamated Union had called an official strike due to the failure of the employer to pay arrears of wages, due for several months, following a Labour Court recommendation (LCR 11095). The defendant subsequently wrote to each of the plaintiffs, stating that due to the "unauthorised withdrawal" of their labour, they had effectively frustrated their contracts of employment.

O'Flaherty J, with whom the other members of the Court concurred, held that, in light of the decision in *Becton Dickinson Ltd.* v *Lee*, the plaintiffs had neither frustrated nor repudiated their contracts of employment simply by taking strike action. He stated that:

> . . . there is to be read into every contract of employment an implied term that the service of a strike notice to terminate the contract of a length not shorter than would be required for notice to terminate the contract would not in itself terminate the contract and would not in itself constitute a breach of the contract and that to take action on foot of the strike notice would likewise not be a breach of the contract.

Therefore, the taking of strike action on the part of an employee, at least when supported by proper notice, does not, in Irish law, amount to a breach of the contract of employment.

CONCLUSION

After a long, protracted battle between the legislature and the judiciary in relation to collective labour law, it is undeniably the case that the trade union movement has made considerable progress. From the perspective of trade unionists, however, much remains to be done. They have won constitutional recognition of the rights to join trade unions and to have a free choice of unions as well as legislative protection for strikes in limited circumstances. From the judiciary, they have acquired recognition of the notion that participation in strike action does not necessarily constitute a breach of contract. On the other hand, however, the Courts have steadfastly refused to recognise the existence of a right to recognition for the purposes of collective bargaining, and post-entry closed shops are clearly regarded as being unconstitutional.

The most interesting developments in trade union law over the coming years are most likely to relate to the ongoing judicial interpretation of the Industrial Relations Act, 1990. After a series of setbacks in that regard between 1990 and the early part of 1998, the trade union movement won a significant battle in the *Nolan Transport* case. It would, however, seem likely that the war will continue to be waged in the courts as well as at negotiating tables over the coming years.

References

Carr, C.J. and P.J. Kay (1994), *Employment Law*, 6th Ed., London: M+E.

Chubb, B. (1978), *The Constitution and Constitutional Change in Ireland*, Dublin: Institute of Public Administration.

Clark, R. (1992), *Contract Law in Ireland*, Dublin: Sweet & Maxwell.

Commission of Inquiry on Industrial Relations (1981), *Report of the Commission of Inquiry on Industrial Relations*, Dublin: Stationery Office.

Courtney, U. (1992), "The Role of the Law in Industrial Relations", 10 (229) IR Data Bank 9.

Dáil Debates, 11 May 1937.

Ewing, K.D. (1991), *The Right to Strike*, Oxford: Clarendon.

Grunfeld, C. (1966), *Modern Trade Union Law*, London: Sweet & Maxwell.

Gunnigle, P., G. McMahon and G. Fitzgerald (1995), *Industrial Relations in Ireland: Theory and Practice*, Dublin: Gill & Macmillan.

Kahn-Freund, O. (1972), *Labour and the Law*, Hamlyn Lectures, 24th Series, London: Stevens.

Kerr, A., and G. Whyte (1985), *Irish Trade Union Law*, Oxford: Professional Books.

Miller, R.L. (1996), "Employee Participation and Contemporary Labor Law in the US", *Industrial Relations Journal*, Vol. 27, p. 166.

Pain, P. (1981), "Contract and Contact: The Trade Unionist and the Lawyer", *Industrial Law Journal*, p. 137.

Pitt, G. (1995), *Employment Law*, 2nd Edition, London: Sweet & Maxwell.

Twomey, A. (1993), "'Macho Management', Moral Outrage and the IBOA: Limited Industrial Action and the Law", *Irish Student Law Review*, Vol. 3, p. 131.

Wedderburn, Lord (1995), *Labour Law and Freedom: Further Essays in Labour Law*, London: Lawrence & Wishart.

Further Readings

Purcell, P. (1998), "Industrial Relations, the Right to Picket and Restrictions of Right to Injunction", *Bar Review*, Vol. 3, p. 239.

CHAPTER 20

EQUAL OPPORTUNITIES IN IRISH WORKPLACES

Adrian Twomey

INTRODUCTION

The process of recruiting staff inevitably requires employers to discriminate between applicants. The discrimination in question may be based on educational qualifications, relevant work experience, skills or abilities. The aim of employment equality legislation, and of equal opportunities policies designed to ensure compliance with such legislation, is not to prevent such discrimination. Rather, it is simply to ensure that employers do not pursue practices that discriminate in a manner which is perceived as being either unfair or socially unacceptable. So, for example, one may not discriminate on the basis of sex or marital status. In that context, the aims of this chapter are:

- To outline the relevant provisions of Irish employment equality legislation;

- To offer guidance as to the practical impact of those provisions; and

- To make suggestions as to how employers can best ensure compliance with anti-discrimination law.

While this chapter places primary emphasis on employment equality law, it is advisable to remember that a commitment to workplace equality on the part of employers and managers can bear fruit not only in terms of ensuring compliance with legislation, but also in relation to the economic wellbeing of their companies. As has been explained elsewhere, companies that discriminate either directly or indirectly against older or disabled people, women or ethnic minorities are effectively limiting the size of the pool of talent available to them (Torrington and Hall, 1998). They are also less likely to retain talented and experienced staff who leave because of a lack of career development or a failure to facilitate flexible or family-friendly working patterns. Finally, they are missing out on the marketing opportunity to present themselves to potential clients as equal opportunities employers.

THE DEVELOPMENT OF EQUAL OPPORTUNITIES LAW

Irish employment equality law has made remarkable strides since Ireland's accession to the EEC in 1973. In the four years following that event, the Oireachtas passed two landmark pieces of legislation which significantly improved the legal position of women workers. The first of those statutes was the Anti-Discrimination (Pay) Act, 1974. As its title suggests, that Act was intended to tackle the problem of gender-based discrimination in relation to pay. While the struggle for equal pay has not yet been successfully concluded, the passing of the 1974 Act was a significant development. According to Curtin (1989: 112):

> The entry into force of the Anti-Discrimination (Pay) Act, 1974, combined with the refusal by the European Commission to permit any derogation by the Irish Government from its European Community obligations, heralded, to borrow James Connolly's terminology, the beginning of the end of the "martyrdom" of Irish women workers.

The second legislative landmark was the Employment Equality Act, 1977, which made it unlawful to discriminate between individuals on grounds of sex or marital status in recruitment for employment, conditions of employment (other than remuneration or pension schemes), training or work experience, or in opportunities for promotion. While the 1977 Act was aimed primarily at eliminating discrimination by employers, it also outlawed discrimination in activities which are related to employment — such as discrimination by organisations providing training courses, trade unions or employment agencies, as well as prohibiting the display or publication of discriminatory advertisements.

While the Oireachtas subsequently legislated for the provision of maternity leave, parental leave and adoptive leave, the recent enactment of the Employment Equality Act, 1998, clearly constitutes the most significant development in the area of Irish employment equality law in more than twenty years. While the new Act was signed by the President during the summer of 1998, it will not come into effect until such time as the Minister for Justice, Equality and Law Reform makes a commencement order or orders. At the time of writing, the Minister has given no firm commitment on the matter. Understandably, it will take some time to set up and staff the Equality Authority and the Office of the Director of Equality Investigations established by the Act. It would seem unlikely that any commencement orders will be made until such time as those organisations have been housed and staffed. It is, however, expected that the Act will be introduced on a phased basis with some provisions coming into effect before others. The Minister has indicated that he expects to make the first commencement orders in the first half of 1999. In the meantime, the 1974 and 1977 Acts continue to regulate employment-related discrimination in this jurisdiction.

THE EMPLOYMENT EQUALITY ACT 1998

The Employment Equality Act, 1998, repeals and replaces the Anti-Discrimination (Pay) Act, 1974, and the Employment Equality Act, 1977. In the process of so doing, it significantly broadens the area to which domestic employment equality law applies, by outlawing previously permissible discrimination on a wide range of grounds. The Act also expressly prohibits sexual harassment for the first time as well as tackling a number of other forms of harassment.

Grounds on which Discrimination is Prohibited

Until the introduction of the new Act, employment-related discrimination was only prohibited where it was related to the sex or marital status of the victim. Section 6 of the 1998 Act, however, provides that it shall be discriminatory to treat a person "less favourably than another is, has been or would be treated" on the basis of their:

- Gender;
- Marital status;
- Family status;
- Sexual orientation;
- Religious belief;
- Age;
- Disability;
- Race, colour, nationality, ethnicity or national origins; or
- Membership of the travelling community.

Gender Discrimination

The prohibition of gender-based discrimination by the 1998 Act is largely just a continuation of the ban on such discrimination originally implemented via the Anti-Discrimination (Pay) Act,

1974, and the Employment Equality Act, 1977. The 1998 Act does not, however, simply deal with gender-based discrimination alongside all of the more recently recognised forms of discrimination. Rather, it is dealt with separately and specifically in Part III of the Act. Significantly, section 24 of the Act also expressly permits what it describes as "positive action" in favour of women. The issue of positive action is discussed later in this chapter.

Discrimination based on Marital Status

Discrimination based on marital status is the second kind of discrimination prohibited by section 6. For the purposes of the legislation, there are five distinct categories of marital status:

- Single;
- Married;
- Separated;
- Divorced; and
- Widowed.

Therefore it is, for example, unlawful for an employer to treat an employee who is divorced differently to their single and married colleagues simply because of that employee's divorce.

Discrimination based on Family Status

The first really new "ground" introduced by the 1998 Act is that relating to family status. Section 6(2)(c) of the Act prohibits discrimination between individuals on the basis that "one has family status and the other does not". According to section 2(1), one is regarded as having "family status" where one has responsibility:

a) As a parent or as a person *in loco parentis* in relation to a person who has not attained the age of 18 years; or

b) As a parent or the resident primary carer in relation to a person of or over that age with a disability which is of

> such a nature as to give rise to the need for care or support
> on a continuing, regular or frequent basis . . .

The inclusion in the Act of such a provision is of particular benefit to lone parents, among others, who would not previously have been protected against employment-related discrimination arising as a result of their status as parents.

Discrimination based on Sexual Orientation

Section 6(2)(d) of the Act prohibits discrimination between individuals on the basis that "they are of different sexual orientation". The enactment of the provision in question is consistent with a number of steps taken by the State in recent years to protect the rights of homosexuals. The Unfair Dismissals (Amendment) Act, 1993, for example, has the effect of deeming "unfair" the dismissal of an individual because of their sexual orientation. The need for the extension of that kind of policy into the area of anti-discrimination law was highlighted by cases such as *McAnnellan* v *Brookfield Leisure Limited* (EEO12/93). In that case, the claimant was allegedly dismissed because of her sexual orientation. She was unable to pursue a case under the Unfair Dismissals Acts, however, because she had not completed the necessary one year in the continuous service of her employers. Similarly, the Labour Court was unable to be of assistance to her when she brought a claim before it under the Employment Equality Act, 1977, because that Act did not prohibit discrimination based on sexual orientation (Twomey, 1994).

Religious Discrimination

Section 6(2)(e) of the Act prohibits discrimination between individuals on the basis that "one has a different religious belief from the other, or that one has a religious belief and that the other has not". The term "religious belief" is defined as including "religious background or outlook".

Age Discrimination

Among the more important changes effected by the 1998 Act (from a practical perspective) is the prohibition of age discrimination introduced by section 6(2)(f). For example, paragraph (f) prevents companies from pursuing recruitment policies that are designed to attract younger workers. Similarly, it prevents employers from eliminating large numbers of applicants for posts on the basis of age.

A legislative development of this nature obviously has significant implications for personnel and human resource management practitioners in Ireland. In that context, the Act imposes some limits on the application of the ban. So, for example, section 34(3) provides that discrimination based on age will not be unlawful "where it is shown that there is clear actuarial or other evidence that significantly increased costs would result if the discrimination were not permitted in those circumstances".

In addition, the Act provides that an employer will not be regarded as having acted unlawfully if they discriminate against a person over the age of 65 or under the age of 18.

Discrimination based on Disability

In 1996, the then Minister for Equality and Law Reform introduced a Bill which was very similar in its provisions to the 1998 Act. The inclusion in that Bill of a ban on discrimination based on a person's disability was one of the factors that contributed to its downfall. In holding the Bill to be unconstitutional, the Supreme Court held that:

> The Bill has the totally laudable aim of making provision for such of our fellow citizens as are disabled. Clearly it is in accordance with the principles of social justice that society should do this. But, prima facie, it would also appear to be just that society should bear the cost of doing it. . . . [T]he difficulty with the section now under discussion is that it attempts to transfer the cost of solving one of society's problems to a particular group. The difficulty the Court finds with the section

is, not that it requires an employer to employ disabled people, but that it requires him to bear the cost of all special treatment or facilities which the disabled person may require to carry out the work unless the cost of the provision of such treatment or facilities would give rise to "undue hardship" to the employer. . . . It therefore appears to the Court that the provisions of the Bill dealing with disability, despite their laudable intention, are repugnant to the Constitution (*In the Matter of Article 26 of the Constitution of Ireland and In the Matter of the Employment Equality Bill 1996* (1997) 8 ELR 132).

In the immediate aftermath of the Supreme Court's decision, there was some concern that the Government's response would simply be to omit the provisions on disability from the expected redraft of the Bill (Barry, 1997). Section 6(2)(g) of the 1998 Act however, does prohibit discrimination between individuals on the basis that "one is a person with a disability and the other either is not or is a person with a different disability".

The word "disability" is very broadly defined for the purposes of the Act. It includes:

a) The total or partial absence of a person's bodily or mental functions, including the absence of a part of a person's body;

b) The presence in the body of organisms causing, or likely to cause, chronic disease or illness;

c) The malfunction, malformation or disfigurement of a part of a person's body;

d) A condition or malfunction which results in a person learning differently from a person without the condition or malfunction; or

e) A condition, illness or disease which affects a person's thought process, perception of reality, emotions or judgment or which results in disturbed behaviour;

and shall be taken to include a disability which exists at present, or which previously existed but no longer exists, or which may exist in the future or which is imputed to a person. . . . (section 2(1)).

While the definition used in the 1996 Bill was even broader, it might well be remarked that one would have to be a remarkably healthy specimen in order to fall outside of even the new, narrower definition transcribed above. In that context, the obligations imposed by section 16(3) on employers in relation to persons with disabilities would seem to be particularly onerous. That section provides that:

a) For the purposes of this Act a person who has a disability shall not be regarded as other than fully competent to undertake, and fully capable of undertaking, any duties if, with the assistance of special treatment or facilities, such person would be fully competent to undertake, and be fully capable of understanding, those duties.

b) An employer shall do all that is reasonable to accommodate the needs of a person who has a disability by providing special treatment or facilities to which paragraph (a) relates.

c) A refusal or failure to provide for special treatment or facilities to which paragraph (a) relates shall not be deemed reasonable unless such provision would give rise to a cost, other than a nominal cost to the employer.

The reference to "nominal" costs in section 16(3) is presumably designed to rectify the flaws highlighted by the Supreme Court and to avoid having the 1998 Act running into constitutional problems in the future. The rigour of the provisions relating to disabilities is also limited by section 34(3) which provides that discrimination based on disability will not be unlawful:

> where it is shown that there is clear actuarial or other evidence that significantly increased costs would result if the discrimination were not permitted in those circumstances.

The Act gives no clear guidelines as to what is to be regarded as "a nominal cost" or "significantly increased costs". There are two possible approaches that may be taken by the courts in interpreting these concepts. The first is to indicate a set figure, above which costs will be regarded as being more than merely "nominal". The second option is to determine the appropriate figures on the basis of the size and wealth of the company involved. In such a scenario, large, wealthy multinational companies might reasonably be expected to bear costs that are significantly in excess of those to be imposed on small, local employers. For larger enterprises with substantial profit margins, once-off costs running to hundreds of thousands of pounds might, for example, be classed as "nominal", whereas the expenditure of a sum of several hundred pounds could be regarded as "significantly" increasing costs for the owner of a suburban corner-shop.

Discrimination based on Race, Colour, Nationality or Ethnic or National Origins

Section 6(2)(h) prohibits discrimination between individuals on the basis that they are of "different race, colour, nationality or ethnic or national origins". None of these terms is defined in the Act, although it would seem unlikely that the absence of definitions will give rise to serious and persistent problems.

While there is little evidence to suggest that such forms of discrimination have constituted a particular problem in Irish workplaces in the past, it would seem almost inevitable that the number of problems in this area encountered by Irish employers will increase as the workforce becomes increasingly diverse in terms of race, ethnicity and so on.

Discrimination based on Membership of the Travelling Community

Finally, the Act specifically prohibits discrimination between individuals on the basis that "one is a member of the traveller community and the other is not". It does not, however, include any definition of the term "traveller community". The potential difficulties that may arise on foot of the lack of such a definition are significant. According to the Travellers' Youth Service:

> The Traveller population in Ireland is at least 24,000. The figure given by the [Central Statistics Office] of 10,891 has been acknowledged by the CSO, the Task Force on Travellers and the Government [as not being] a true representation, as the CSO figures only took Travellers to be people living in Trailers/Caravans on the roadside, they did not include Travellers living in group housing, or County Council/Corporation provided housing. All groups involved in the study agreed it was at least 24,000, if not more (Travellers' Youth Service, 1998).

An obvious question is prompted by such comments. If the State is unclear as to when one may or may not be classed as a member of the "traveller community", how are employers to make the distinction with any reasonable degree of certainty? Such a question is unlikely to be satisfactorily resolved until some guidance is obtained from the courts. In the meantime, employers would seem to be well advised to be as inclusive as possible in terms of who they classify as being afforded protection by the Act.

PAY-RELATED DISCRIMINATION

Discrimination in relation to pay is dealt with under two headings in the 1998 Act. The first is gender-based discrimination in relation to pay. The second is pay-related discrimination based on any of the other grounds.

Gender-based Pay Discrimination

Section 19(1) requires the inclusion in contracts of employment of a term entitling employees to remuneration equal to that being paid to employees of the opposite sex who are doing "like work". Where such a term is not expressly included in the contract, it is inserted by section 20(1). Where there is an express term included in the contract and that term conflicts with or contradicts the term implied by the Act, then the term implied by the Act is to be taken as overriding the express term.

While section 19(1) and section 20(1) combat direct pay-related sex discrimination, section 19(4) is designed to counter indirect discrimination. The subsection in question refers to "A" and "B" where "A" and "B" are two persons of opposite sexes and provides that:

> Where a term of a contract or a criterion applied to employees (including A and B):
>
> a) Applies to all the employees of a particular employer or to a particular class of such employees (including A and B);
>
> b) Is such that the remuneration of those employees who fulfil the term or criterion is different from that of those who do not;
>
> c) Is such that the proportion of employees who are disadvantaged by the term or criterion is substantially higher in the case of those of the same sex as A than in the case of those of the same sex as B; and
>
> d) Cannot be justified by objective factors unrelated to A's sex;
>
> Then, for the purpose of subsection (1), A and B shall be treated as fulfilling or, as the case may be, as not fulfilling the term or criterion, whichever results in the higher remuneration.

Section 19(4) would seem to suggest that requirements imposed by employers which must be satisfied by employees in order to qualify for higher rates of pay are null and void where they disadvantage a substantially greater proportion of women than men or vice versa. The section in question would seem to echo the tone of European Court of Justice decisions, such as those in *Enderby* v *Frenchay Health Authority* (C-127/92, 27 October 1993) and *Jenkins* v *Kingsgate Clothing Productions* (Case 96/80, [1981] ECR 911).

Case Example 20.1: Indirect Pay-Related Discrimination — Enderby *v* Frenchay Health Authority

---

In the Enderby *case, the claimant was a female speech therapist who claimed that her profession was not as well paid as comparable male-dominated professions because it was heavily dominated by females. In arriving at its decision, the European Court of Justice stated that while the burden of proving the existence of discrimination based on sex rested with the claimant, the situation is different*

> *. . . where the statistics seem to disclose an appreciable difference in pay between two jobs of equal value, [in which case] a prima facie case of discrimination will have been made and the onus is on the employer to justify it objectively.*

Notably, in *Jenkins* v *Kingsgate Clothing Productions* (Case 96/80, [1981] ECR 911), the Court of Justice held that a difference in pay between full-time and part-time workers is not *per se* contrary to Article 119, "unless it was in reality an indirect way of reducing the pay of part-time workers on the ground that the group of workers was composed exclusively or predominantly of women".

Pay-Related Discrimination on the Grounds other than Gender

Pay-related discrimination based on grounds other than gender is essentially dealt with in a similar manner to gender-based pay discrimination. Section 29(1) requires the inclusion in contracts of employment of a term entitling employees to remuneration equal to that being paid to other employees who are doing "like work" regardless of age, marital status, sexual orientation and so on. Where such an equal remuneration clause is not expressly included in the contract, it is inserted by section 30(1). Where there is an express term included in the contract and that term conflicts with or contradicts the term implied by the Act, then the term implied by the Act is to be taken as overriding the express term.

Indirect discrimination is dealt with in section 29(4). The subsection in question provides that requirements imposed by employers, which must be satisfied by employees in order to qualify for higher rates of pay, are null and void where they disadvantage a substantially greater proportion of a protected group.

Pay-Related Discrimination and the Concept of "Like Work"

Section 7 of the Act deals with the concept of "like work", a notion familiar to Irish employment lawyers and human resource managers from the old Anti-Discrimination (Pay) Act, 1974. As has already been explained, claimants under the Act who are seeking to combat pay-related discrimination must show that they and their comparators are engaged in "like work". Effectively, the term "like work" is defined by section 7 as including work that is the same, similar or of equal value:

> . . . for the purposes of this Act in relation to the work which one person is employed to do, another person shall be regarded as employed to do like work if:
>
> (a) both perform the same work under the same or similar conditions, or each is interchangeable with the other in relation to the work;
>
> (b) the work performed by one is of a similar nature to that performed by the other and any differences between the work performed or the conditions under which it is performed by each either are of small importance in relation to the work as a whole or occur with such irregularity as not to be significant to the work as a whole; or
>
> (c) the work performed by one is equal in value to the work performed by the other, having regard to such matters as skill, physical or mental requirements, responsibility and working conditions.

It would seem likely that section 7(1) will be interpreted in a similar way to section 3 of the 1974 Act. If such proves to be the case, paragraph (a) will apply where the actual work performed by the claimant and the conditions under which it is performed are the same as, or similar to, that performed by the comparator. If there is a difference of practical importance between the jobs or conditions under which they are performed, the employer can legitimately pay different rates of remuneration. The Court hearing the case will, however, closely scrutinise any misleading "labelling" of a job which may constitute an attempt on the part of the employer to disguise the payment of different rates for the same work.

Section 7(1)(b) covers those situations where the work performed by the claimant is of a broadly similar nature to that performed by the comparator. As Curtin explains, it follows "that differences which occur only infrequently or which are of small importance in relation to the work as a whole will not result in a claim failing. . . ." (Curtin, 1989). Paragraph (b) is not merely a narrow extension of paragraph (a). Rather, it permits frequent differences between the jobs being compared, so long as those differences are of little importance in relation to the work as a whole. So, in *Dowdall O'Mahoney and Co. Ltd.* v *Nine Female Employees* (EP 2/1987, DEP 6/1987) for example, the Labour Court determined that:

> Both claimants and comparators perform general operative factory work. It is the view of the Court that it is the intention of [paragraph (b)] to cover claims from persons employed in such situations as opposed to persons employed on the same work which is covered by [paragraph (a)], e.g. two bus conductors, or work that is not the same or similar which is covered by [paragraph (c)] e.g. a clerical worker and a general operative worker.

The Court went on to explain that in deciding whether differences between the jobs being compared were of small importance, one needed to examine whether the differences:

> . . . were of such importance that they would normally be used as the basis for establishing a different grade, salary scale or rate of pay irrespective of the sex of the workers concerned.

The formulation of section 7(1)(c) focuses attention on the content of the job rather than on the monetary value of the employee's work (in terms of revenue generated) to the employer. Its purpose is to allow jobs that are radically different in content to be the basis of a claim, if it can be demonstrated that the work performed by the claimant and the comparator are equally demanding. The basic premise behind this paragraph is that women, for example, should be able to substantiate a claim for equal pay by showing that their jobs and those of their male colleagues are of equal value in terms of the demands made on them. Among the factors which the Labour Court have considered in carrying out such a balancing exercise are:

- The degree of skill involved in performing the job;

- The number of operations required of the employee in the course of performing the job;

- The conditions under which the job is performed (such as heat, cold or noise);

- The physical demands involved in the performance of the work;

- The mental demands attaching to the work;

- The amount of responsibility attaching to the job.

In *Waterford Glass Ltd.* v *ITGWU* (EP 15/1977), for example, the Equality Officer found that the degree of skill, dexterity and concentration required of female workers balanced out against the "high level" of physical strength and endurance expected of male general workers. Similarly, in the English case of *Hayward* v *Cammel Laird Shipbuilders Ltd.* ([1988] ICR 464) the job of a female cook was found to be of equal value to those of male painters, joiners and thermal insulation engineers on the basis of an analysis of the various jobs under five categories: physical demands; environmental demands; planning and decision-making; skill and knowledge required; and responsibility involved.

Work of Greater than "Equal Value"

As Curtin observed in relation to the Anti-Discrimination (Pay) Act, 1974:

> It emerged early on that an equal pay claim would only succeed where the work was of more or less precisely "equal" value. "Equal" was interpreted so strictly that women were denied equal pay if their work was of greater value than that of the man (Curtin, 1989).

Section 6(3) of the 1998 Act corrects that anomaly, providing that:

> In any case where:
>
> (a) the remuneration received by one person ("the primary worker") is less than the remuneration received by another ("the comparator"), and
>
> (b) the work performed by the primary worker is greater in value than the work performed by the comparator . . .
>
> then . . . the work performed by the primary worker shall be regarded as equal in value to the work performed by the comparator.

One might argue that the primary worker should not only be able to make a claim for equal pay but also one for greater pay based on a comparative analysis of the values of the jobs in question. The complexities involved in making such analyses would, however, obviously make it extremely difficult for the Courts to apply any legislative provision to that effect.

GENDER-BASED DISCRIMINATION IN RELATION TO MATTERS OTHER THAN PAY

Discrimination based on gender in relation to matters other than remuneration is primarily dealt with via the insertion into employment contracts of a gender "equality clause" by section 21. The gender equality clause has the effect of rendering null and void any term in an employee's contract (other than one relating to remuneration or pension rights) which is less favourable than the comparable term in the contract of a comparable worker of the opposite sex. Similarly, the gender equality clause has the effect of inserting into one's contract favourable terms which are included in the contracts of comparable workers of the opposite sex but are not expressly included in one's own contract. Section 21(3) limits (to some extent at least) the impact of the gender equality clause, providing that:

> A gender equality clause shall not operate in relation to a difference between A's contract of employment and B's contract of employment if the employer proves that the difference is genuinely based on grounds other than the gender ground.

It should, however, be noted that the burden of proof rests on employers in such cases: a fact that may make it difficult to defend many claims.

Indirect Discrimination on the Gender Ground

Section 22(1) has the effect of classing as indirect discrimination any requirement, practice or other provision made by an employer, where it disadvantages a substantially higher proportion of one sex than another and where it cannot be justified by objective factors unrelated to the sex of the claimants. The rule in relation to indirect discrimination enunciated in section 22(1) also applies in relation to discrimination based on marital or family status.

Excluded Categories

The Act applies to all employees (both men and women) except, in some circumstances, members of the Garda and the prison services. Section 25 of the Act, however, provides that discrimination by an employer is not unlawful where it can be shown that a person's sex is a genuine occupational qualification for the job, as is the case with, for example, models and actors. Essentially, one may discriminate where:

- The essential nature of the job requires a man (or woman) for reasons of physiology (not including strength or stamina) or authenticity in entertainment;

- The nature or location of the employment requires the employee to live in premises which do not have separate sleeping and sanitary facilities for men and women;

- The duties of the post involve personal services and it is necessary to have persons of both sexes engaged in such duties;

- The job is likely to involve duties outside the state in a country whose laws and customs are such that those duties could not be performed by a man (or woman, as the case may be).

The ambit of such exceptions should not be overestimated. In the case of *Brady* v *Irish TV Rentals Ltd.* (EE 5/1985, DEE 8/1985), for example, the employer discriminated in favour of male applicants for a position as a salesperson on the basis that male staff would be more effective in deterring thieves. The Equality Officer, however, held that being male was not essential in order to deter thieves and that being male was not, therefore, an occupational qualification for the job.

Employers' Defences
The main grounds upon which employers have attempted to rely until now when seeking to justify apparent discrimination on objective non-gender-based grounds have tended to relate to matters such as:

- Experience and educational qualifications;

- Red circling;

- Grading structures;

- The need to do night-work; or

- The fact that one of the parties is working on a part-time basis.

General guidance is, however, provided by the *Enderby* case (C-127/92, 27 October 1993). In arriving at its decision in that case, the Court of Justice stated that while the burden of proving the existence of discrimination based on sex rested with the claimant, the situation is different:

> . . . where the statistics seem to disclose an appreciable difference in pay between two jobs of equal value, [in which case] a prima facie case of discrimination will have been made and the onus is on the employer to justify it objectively (Hyland, 1994).

The Court went on to explain that while the validity of so-called "objective justifications" for apparent discrimination is a matter for national courts to assess, such courts could:

> . . . take into account economic grounds, including the shortage of candidates for jobs in particular professions, and the need to attract them by paying higher rates. Other factors that may be taken into account [include] a worker's flexibility, adaptability to hours or places of work, training, or length of service (Hyland, 1994).

Positive Action

Article 2(4) of the European Equal Treatment Directive (Directive 76/207) elaborates an exception to the Directive's general prohibition on sex discrimination in respect of measures "intended to promote equal opportunity for men and women, in particular by removing existing inequalities which affect women's opportunities".

Article 2(4) of the Directive is reflected in section 24(1) of the 1998 Act, which provides that:

> The provisions of this Act are without prejudice to measures to promote equal opportunity for men and women, in particular by removing existing inequalities which affect women's opportunities in the areas of access to employment, vocational training and promotion, and working conditions.

In interpreting Article 2(4), the Court of Justice of the European Communities has stated that:

> That provision is specifically and exclusively designed to allow measures which, although discriminatory in appearance, are in fact intended to eliminate or reduce actual instances of inequality which may exist in the reality of social life. . . .

It thus permits national measures relating to access to employment, including promotion, which give a specific advantage to women with a view to improving their ability to compete on the labour market and to pursue a career on an equal footing with men (*Kalanke* v *Freie Hansestadt Bremen* [1996] 1 CMLR 175).

Case Example 20.2: Positive Action – Marschall *v* Land Nordrhein-Westfalen

---

In Marschall *v* Land Nordrhein-Westfalen (Germany) *(Case 409/95) the plaintiff, Herr Marschall, was a teacher employed by the defendant. Local law provided that where there were fewer women than men in higher grade posts in a sector of the civil service, women were to be given priority for promotion where male and female candidates were equally suitable. Herr Marschall applied for a promotion in 1994 and lost out because of the application of the local law. The Court of Justice stated that:*

> *. . . in general, men tend to be promoted in preference to women where they have equal qualifications. This "glass ceiling" exists due to deep-rooted prejudices and from stereotyping the role and capacities of women. Thus, the fact that a male and a female candidate are equally qualified does not mean that they have the same chances.*

For this reason, a legal provision such as the German law may help to reduce instances of inequality by introducing an additional criterion for promotion – status as a woman. This can be in conformity with the directive, provided that it does not give automatic priority over men. If women had been given absolute and unconditional priority, this would have contravened the directive. The saving clause, allowing ". . . a male candidate's special qualities to be taken into account meant that this law did not run counter to the directive" (Anonymous, 1998).

DISCRIMINATION IN RELATION TO MATTERS OTHER THAN PAY ON GROUNDS OTHER THAN GENDER

The 1998 Act deals with discrimination based on grounds other than gender in a manner similar to that employed in relation to gender-based discrimination. In other words, the Act provides for what it refers to as "equality clauses" and also prohibits indirect discrimination.

The Equality Clause (Non-Gender Issues)

Section 30 inserts an equality clause into contracts of employment where they do not expressly or otherwise contain one. The equality clause has the effect of rendering null and void any term in an employee's contract (other than one relating to remuneration or pension rights) that is less favourable than the comparable term in the contract of a comparable worker of, for example, another marital status or age. Similarly, the equality clause has the effect of inserting into one's contract favourable terms that are included in the contracts of comparable workers of, for example, a different age or sexual orientation but are not expressly included in one's own contract. The defence provided for employers in section 30(3) is similar to that discussed earlier in relation to gender-based discrimination, in that the section in question states that:

> A non-discriminatory equality clause shall not operate in re-
> lation to a difference between C's contract of employment and
> D's contract of employment if the employer proves that the
> difference is genuinely based on grounds which are not
> among those specified in paragraphs (a) to (h) of section 28(1).

Once again, it should be noted that the burden of proof rests on employers in such cases: a fact that significantly increases the difficulty involved in defending claims. On the other hand, there are a range of very specific exemptions from liability spelled out in Part IV of the Act; many of which have been dealt with earlier in this chapter.

Indirect Discrimination on Grounds other than Gender

Section 31(1) has the effect of classing as indirect discrimination any requirement, practice or other provision made by an employer where it disadvantages a substantially higher proportion of one group than another and where it cannot be justified as being reasonable in all the circumstances of the case.

Positive Action

Section 33(1) of the Act permits programmes of positive action to improve the position/integration of:

- Persons who have attained the age of 50 years;

- Persons with disabilities; or

- Members of the travelling community.

Such programmes will, however, only attract the protection of section 33 where they are "intended to reduce or eliminate the effects of discrimination" against the groups in question.

DISCRIMINATION IN SPECIFIC AREAS

Section 8(1) of the Act specifies the following five areas in relation to which an employer may not discriminate against an employee or prospective employee:

- Access to employment;

- Conditions of employment;

- The provision of training or experience;

- Promotion or re-grading;

- Classification of posts.

Access to Employment

Section 8(5) prohibits discrimination against employees or prospective employees in relation to access to employment. An employer will be deemed to have acted in contravention of the Act if he discriminates:

- In any arrangement he makes for selection purposes; or

- By specifying entry requirements for one set of applicants which are not applied in respect of another class of applicants for the same job.

Discriminatory questioning at the interview stage of a recruitment process, or discriminatory short-listing, are just two examples of the kind of activity that this provision serves to counter.

Conditions of Employment

Section 8(6) of the Act provides that an employer will be regarded as discriminating against an employee in respect of that employee's conditions of employment if they discriminate in relation to:

- Terms of employment (other than remuneration and pension rights);

- Working conditions;

- Overtime;

- Shift work;

- Short time;

- Transfers;

- Lay-offs;

- Redundancies;

- Dismissals; or

- Disciplinary measures.

Provision of Training or Experience

Section 8(7) provides that an employer will be regarded as discriminating against an employee in respect of that employee's training or experience if they refuse:

> to offer or afford to that employee the same opportunities or facilities for employment counselling, training (whether on or off the job) and work experience as the employer offers or affords to other employees.

Promotion or Re-grading

Section 8(8) provides that an employer will be regarded as discriminating against an employee in respect of promotion if, on any of the discriminatory grounds, they refuse or deliberately omit to afford the employee access to opportunities for promotion where another eligible and qualified person is getting such an opportunity.

Discriminatory Advertising

Section 10 of the Act deems it unlawful to publish or display (or cause to be published or displayed) an employment advertisement which:

- Indicates an intention to discriminate; or

- Might reasonably be understood as indicating such an intention.

In particular, an advertisement will be taken as indicating an intention to discriminate if it includes a word or phrase that indicates that the employer is looking for a person of, for example, a particular sexual orientation or religion, unless the advertisement indicates a contrary intention. It is, therefore, more important than ever for employers placing job advertisements to indicate in those advertisements that they are equal opportunities employers. Even where they do so, they should eliminate any extraneous material which might indicate an intention to discriminate.

SEXUAL HARASSMENT

The 1998 Act is the first Irish piece of legislation to expressly deal with the issue of sexual harassment. In the absence of legislation dealing expressly with sexual harassment it has, at least until quite recently, been left to the Labour Court to map out the contours of sexual harassment law in this jurisdiction. For that reason, the inclusion of express provisions in the Act is a significant development. Section 23(3) defines "sexual harassment" as:

a) Any act of physical intimacy by B towards A,

b) Any express request by B for sexual favours from A, or

c) Any other act or conduct of B (including, without prejudice to the generality, spoken words, gestures or the production, display or circulation of written words, pictures or other material)

. . . if the Act request or conduct is unwelcome to A and could reasonably be regarded as sexually, or otherwise on the gender ground, offensive, humiliating or intimidating to A.

Such conduct is classed as discrimination on the gender ground if in the course of an individual's employment, they are sexually harassed and either:

- The victim and the harasser are both employed in the same place or by the same employer; or

- The harasser is the victim's employer; or

- The harasser is a client, customer or other business contact of the victim's employer and the circumstances of the harassment are such that the victim's employer ought reasonably to have taken steps to prevent it.

The Labour Court and Equality Officers have traditionally recognised employers as having a valid defence to an action where the employer has, for example, implemented and enforced an adequate sexual harassment policy and complaints procedure and provided the necessary training to members of their staff (Harvey and Twomey, 1995; see also the sample policies in Chapter 15). In 1991, for example, one of the Equality Officers stated that:

> . . . if the employer took all reasonabl[y] practicable steps to ensure that each of its employees enjoyed working conditions . . . free from sexual harassment, the discrimination carried out by its . . . employees would not constitute a contravention by the employer of the [Employment Equality Act, 1977] (*An Employer* v *One Female Employee*, EE22/1991).

The existence of the defence in question is of benefit in two main respects. Firstly, it ensures that responsible employers who are not to blame for any sexual harassment suffered by their employees are not held liable under the legislation. Secondly, the existence of the defence acts as an incentive for employers to draft and implement sexual harassment policies and complaints procedures and to provide appropriate training. Subsection (5) enshrines this defence in the Bill, stating that:

> If, as a result of any act or conduct of B, another person ("the Employer") who is A's employer would, apart from this subsection, be regarded by virtue of subsection (1) as discriminating against A, it shall be a defence for the Employer to prove that the Employer took such steps as are reasonably practicable:
>
> a) In a case where subsection (2) applies, to prevent A being treated differently in the workplace or otherwise in the course of A's employment and, if and so far as any such treatment has occurred, to reverse the effects of it, and
>
> b) In a case where subsection (1) applies (whether or not subsection (2) also applies) to prevent B from sexually harassing A (or any class of persons of whom A is one).

BULLYING

While the Act does not expressly prohibit bullying *per se*, it does outlaw harassment based on an individual's family status, race, sexual orientation, age and so on. The provisions dealing with such forms of harassment are very similar to those relating to sexual harassment.

CONCLUSION

The introduction of the Employment Equality Act 1998 has a number of significant implications for Irish employers — particularly in the context of recruitment and selection. It is, however, worth remembering that the primary focus of the Act is on the prevention of forms of discrimination that are generally regarded as being both morally questionable and potentially economically detrimental to modern businesses. In that context, employers should bear in mind the fact that if they do not actively intend to discriminate, they are unlikely to encounter legal difficulties. One should not, of course, rely simply on one's own *bona fides* in recruiting and selecting to avoid potential liability. Rather, employers should ideally introduce, implement and monitor employment equality policies; provide appropriate training to all staff; and deal with any problems as and when they arise.

References

Anonymous (1998), "Court Upholds Affirmative Action Programme", *Gazette of the Incorporated Law Society of Ireland*, Vol. 92, p. 32.

Barry, E., (1997), "A Briefing from the Editor", *Employment Law Reports*, Vol. 8, p. ix.

Curtin, D. (1989), *Irish Employment Equality Law*, Dublin: Round Hall Press.

Harvey, N. and A.F. Twomey (1995), *Sexual Harassment in the Workplace*, Dublin: Oak Tree Press.

Hyland, N. (1994), "Equality Update", *Eurlegal*, Vol. 39, p. 1.

Torrington, D., and L. Hall (1998), *Human Resource Management*, Fourth Edition, London: Prentice Hall Europe.

Travellers' Youth Service (1998), http://www.connect.ie/tribli/facts.htm#TravellersInIreland

Twomey, A.F. (1994), "McAnellan could have got Legal Redress in Civil Courts", *Cork Examiner*, 7 February 1994.

Further Reading

Meenan, F. (1994), *Working within the Law*, Dublin: Oak Tree Press.

Hervey, T.K. and D. O'Keeffe (ed.) (1996), *Sex Equality Law in the European Union*, Chichester: Wiley.

PART SIX
EMPLOYEE WELFARE

CHAPTER 21

WORK AND FAMILY ISSUES

Eugenie Houston

INTRODUCTION

The growing number of people at work has pushed the issues surrounding the balance between work and home commitments into the spotlight. Although matters concerning care for the disabled and elderly are also relevant to this discussion, attention in this chapter is focused mainly on issues relating to children and childcare. This chapter examines the growth of the workforce, the resultant family-related issues and a variety of initiatives implemented at government, company and community level to address the issues raised. Extensive coverage is devoted to case studies of organisations that are leading the way with best practices in family-friendly initiatives. An enormous amount of research has been carried out in this area by organisations concerned with equal opportunities and by feminist scholars and campaigners. Given that the traditional role of women has been perceived as being in the home, the work of pioneers in championing equal opportunities and family-friendly initiatives has been instrumental in changing the workforce to what it is today. The Colloquium on Families and Work, which was held in Dublin in 1998, recognised the relative lack of corresponding analysis of men's position vis-à-vis work and family issues. If the following examples appear to have a bias towards women, this is because the initiatives have had to focus on this area to achieve the progress that has been made thus far.

RECONCILIATION OF WORK AND FAMILY LIFE

To the casual observer, the year 1998 witnessed what may have appeared to be a sudden surge of interest in work and family issues, although in reality the groundwork had been taking place over a number of years. The Parental Leave Bill was published on 8 June 1998 and came into law on 3 December 1998. The Minister for Justice, Family and Law Reform announced details of a £5.2 million Equal Opportunity Nationwide Childcare programme to enhance the accessibility and affordability of childcare, something which the National Women's Council of Ireland and the Employment Equality Agency have been advocating for some years. The terms of Partnership 2000 included the establishment of an Expert Working Group on Childcare. Overall, there appears to be a desire to see a more balanced "quality of life", increasingly important as many employers face skills shortages and must endeavour to attract and retain high quality employees. The European Commission launched a Green Paper in late 1997 entitled *Partnership for a New Organisation of Work*. In its 1997 Annual Report, the Employment Equality Agency highlighted that among the main conclusions from the debate were the recognition that people's private lives must be reconciled with the interests of the workplace; the need to change the perception that flexible working hours relate only to women in the workplace instead of both women and men; and the need to change the misconception that a management position is incompatible with working part-time (Employment Equality Agency, 1997).

The number of women at work has grown rapidly over the past 25 years, far outpacing the growth in male employment. Women's employment has grown most rapidly in the 1990s, the increase between 1991 and 1996 almost equalling the growth of the previous 20 years. By 1996, women accounted for almost four in ten of all those at work (see Chapter 2).

The changes are particularly marked in relation to the number of married women at work. In 1971, the 38,000 married women at work accounted for only 14 per cent of the female workforce. Over the following 25 years, the number of married women at work grew by 203,000 and by 1996 about half the female workforce was married.

Changes in the *work situations of couples* between 1986 and 1991 included:

- Number of couples (either married or cohabiting) increased from 666,200 to 708,900.

- Number of couples with both partners aged under 35 decreased — from 163,900 in 1986 to 136,900 in 1991 and 124,700 in 1996.

- Couples with both partners aged 35 to 54 has grown from 243,600 in 1986 to 277,300 in 1991 and 310,300 in 1996.

- Couples in which only the man is at work has fallen steeply, from 354,700 in 1986 to 276,000 in 1996; the number in which both couples are in paid employment has more than doubled from 108,000 to 226,900.

- There are relatively few couples in which the female is the only one in paid employment: 31,500 or 4.4 per cent of all couples in 1996.

- Couples in which neither partner is in paid employment have fallen slightly since 1985: 174,000 such couples in 1996, and in almost 61 per cent of these, both partners were aged 55 or over.

- In 1991, a quarter of all mothers were in the labour force. About a third of mothers with one or two dependent children were in the labour force, compared with just over a fifth of mothers with three or more dependent children.

• In 1996, the participation rate of mothers was higher, in line with overall increases in the labour force. Overall, 36.6 per cent of mothers were in the labour force. About 43 per cent of mothers with one or two dependent children and 33.2 per cent of mothers with three of more children were in the labour force in 1996.

Table 21.1: Labour Force Participation Rate of Mothers by Number of Dependent Children, 1991 and 1996

Number of Dependent Children	1991 (%)	1996 (%)
One	33.1	42.6
Two	30.2	43.2
Three or more	21.6	33.2
All Mothers	*25.7*	*36.6*

Source: Labour Force Survey, 1996

ATTITUDES TO WORK AND FAMILY

When it comes to sharing the caring of children, statistics published by Eurostat, the EU's central statistics office, show that, in all countries, working mothers look after children more than working fathers do (*Equality News*, 1998). This is particularly the case in Greece, Portugal, Luxembourg, Ireland, Italy and Spain, where under 50 per cent of men said they looked after their children, compared to 80 per cent of women. For those parents who said they do spend time with their children, 32 per cent of men and 6 per cent of women said they spend fewer than 2 hours a day looking after them, while 69 per cent of women and 27 per cent of men spend four hours a day.

When asked about combining work and family life, more women (48.5 per cent) than men (47.2 per cent) felt that women are forced to choose between having children and a career. More women also believed that women can combine work and children (48 per cent against 45.6 per cent of men). Eurostat's statistics show that, when asked which measures could make it easier for women to reconcile their working and family lives, 48.5 per cent indicated better childcare and services and 45.9 per cent opted for financial incentives to stay at home. Nearly twice as many women (53 per cent) as men (28 per cent) said they would be prepared to apply for unpaid leave to bring up a child and nearly 1.5 times more women (43 per cent) than men (29 per cent) would take such leave to look after an older relative.

In Autumn 1998, AIB's *Women in Business Task Force Report* was launched in response to the anticipated rapid rise in the percentage of women in the Irish workforce into the twenty-first century. According to the Central Statistics Office, women accounted for almost 37 per cent of the workforce in 1996, close to the CSO's original projections for the year 2001, by which time the percentage of women in paid employment is now expected to reach 45 per cent. AIB Group undertook the research across the 32 counties to determine the requirements and needs of women in business. The research included public submissions invited through national press advertisements, detailed primary qualitative and quantitative research, which included 20 focus groups, a number of in-depth one-to-one interviews and 450 one-to-one telephone interviews with a representative sample of women. Comparative male groups were also researched to ensure that issues of gender were correctly identified as such.

The report states in its findings that people generally believe that women come to the workforce at a disadvantage to men. This may be a result of having children and the related need to organise childcare or it may result from the perceived greater female responsibility to provide meals and run the home as well. Despite the evolution of traditional family roles, as the figures above show, most of the respondents to AIB's research felt that the home, the family and often bill-paying remain the primary responsibility of women rather than men, whether they are in paid employment or not. They recognised that, even today, children are still cared for by women and that this is true even of relatively young women, for whom the "mothering" role remains more important at an emotional level than their work outside the home.

AIB's quantitative research revealed that almost 90 per cent of all respondents feel that childcare presents special difficulties for working parents and that this view is held particularly strongly by women returning to work. The solutions proposed in the report for addressing this issue include:

- Reducing the costs of acquiring adequate quality day-care/crèche facilities (45 per cent);

- Tax relief/financial allowances to offset the cost of childcare (35 per cent);

- Corporate crèches to be provided by bigger companies (19 per cent);

- A more sympathetic attitude when child-related problems arise (12 per cent).

FAMILY-FRIENDLY INITIATIVES

An increasing number of companies are recognising the benefits to both the company and the employee in implementing flexible working arrangements and are introducing a range of family-friendly initiatives. The examples given below are mainly from larger companies. However, many of the initiatives are not necessarily linked to increased costs and could also be adopted by smaller organisations. As the childcare case studies show, partnership with other organisations can work very well. An important point to remember in introducing family-friendly initiatives is the need to practice equality, for example by pro-rating benefits proportionally to the number of hours worked for job-sharers.

FLEXIBLE WORKING

Flexible working arrangements take a number of different forms and concern the facilitation of working patterns that differ from the traditional work pattern. As the following examples show, flexible working arrangements can include variable hours, job-sharing, career breaks, telecommuting and other initiatives.

Case Example 21.1: AIB Choices

AIB Bank introduced its Choices Programme in 1996 in recognition of the ways in which changes in employees' personal lives can affect their working lives. Prior to introducing Choices, AIB already offered career breaks and enhanced maternity leave to its employees. Since Choices was introduced, 609 employees have participated in the programme. Participation is dependent on each business unit's needs, so realistically the numbers able to take part are bound to vary. At 609, this is ten per cent of AIB Bank's workforce. The AIB Choices available are:

Job-Sharing

This involves two employees sharing one full-time position and equally dividing the responsibilities, hours of work, duties and their individual benefits. The position is split on a 50/50 basis so that each job-sharer is paid at 50 per cent of their normal salary. AIB Bank employees up to and including Assistant Manager level with six or more years completed service may apply for job-sharing. Since its introduction, 86 employees have participated or continue to participate in this option. Job-sharing is a permanent arrangement, although participants do have a once-off opportunity after three years to opt to change back to full-time employment, provided six months notice is given to the Bank.

Personalised Hours

These apply where employees wish to vary their contracted hours from the existing norm of 36.25 per week. Employees can apply for any combination of hours between 14.5 and 31.25. Salary and benefits are pro-rated in direct proportion to the number of hours worked. Personalised hours contracts are permanent, although, as with job-sharing, participants do have a once-off opportunity to revert back to full-time hours after three years' completion.

Currently, 172 of the 609 Choices participants are on personalised hours contracts.

Career Breaks
Employees can apply for a continuous leave of absence for a minimum of 6 months and a maximum of 5 years. This can be a single break or alternatively a combination of breaks. Employees with three or four years' completed service can apply for career breaks equal in length to their service; employees with five or more years can apply for a break of up to five years. Employees are not permitted to work for competitor financial institutions during their career break, although they can take up other employment with the Bank's written permission. For pension purposes, an employee's accrued pension is preserved at the start of the career break and each year spent on a career break can be re-credited for pension purposes by completion of a full year on return to work.

Special Short-term Career Breaks
This is a leave of absence, from three months to one year, available to permanent employees with two years' completed service in the following situations:

A Short-Term Responsibility Break *is available to employees who need to spend time with their family at particular times of need, such as illness or when children are starting school.*

A Caring Leave Break *is available to employees with personal caring responsibility who need to take time off to care for elderly, sick or disabled relatives.*

A Family Short-Term Break *is to facilitate employees who wish to spend extended periods of time with their families.*

Of the 609 Choices participants, 287 are on career breaks.

Case Example 21.2: VHI − A Family-Friendly Employer

The VHI has 459 employees, 68 per cent of whom are female. A total of 85 per cent of the workforce are based in VHI's head office in Dublin, 12 per cent work from branch offices, 3 per cent are based in hospitals or work from home. In recognition of the need to retain valued and highly trained em-

ployees, maintain employee motivation, reduce stress levels and improve productivity, the VHI offers its employees a range of family-friendly options. These include:

Flexible Working

Flexitime has been offered since the 1970s and employees can select from a number of options. The VHI has a dedicated group of part-time workers who are typically unavailable to work during normal office hours because of family or study commitments and who work instead in the evenings between 4 and 8pm. Three per cent of the VHI's employees are based at home or in hospitals and a small number are pure teleworkers from home. Twelve per cent of the total workforce either job-share or have personalised hours contracts. In addition, provided they stay within the provisions of the Working Time Act, employees can accumulate up to an additional 13 days off per year through working flexitime.

Special Leave Arrangements

Career breaks are available to employees with three years' completed service. About half of one per cent of the workforce apply for career breaks each year and 54 per cent of all those who have availed of this option have returned to work. One day's leave is given to fathers on the birth of a child and fathers also have the option of taking an additional three days through working flexitime. All employees have the right to take up to five days' emergency leave per year. In practice, relatively few employees need to avail of this option; however, it is commented on favourably in employee feedback. One day's marriage leave is given to attend the weddings of immediate family members.

Flexitime

Flexitime is an arrangement where the employer and employees agree hours of work that are beneficial to both. Some companies offer this flexibility through working a compressed week. An example of this is Intel Ireland, where certain groups of employees in its manufacturing operations work three 12-hour shifts weekly. Typically, companies operating flexitime specify core hours when the employee must be present in work, after which starting and finishing times and the number of days over which the working week is spread are flexible. Siemens Nixdorf and Amdahl Ireland Ltd. are examples of companies that operate flexitime. The following is Amdahl Ireland's Working Day Guideline, which outlines the company's flexitime policy and which is an excellent model policy for other companies considering introducing flexitime.

Case Example 21.3: Amdahl Ireland Ltd.'s Working Day Guideline

---

Working Day Definitions

1. **Hours of Business** 08.30am – 5.00pm

2. **Standard Working Day** 08.30am – 5.00pm
   The hours which must be worked by an employee from whom the benefits of the Flexible Working Day have been removed.

3. **Standard Working Week** 39 hours

4. **Flexible Working Week** *Employee must work a minimum average of 39 hours per week over a 4-week period, i.e. 156 hours minimum over 4 weeks rolling period (Benefits of Flexible Working Week available to employee only if operation of business is not impacted).*

5. **Minimum Working Week** *Employee must work minimum of 35 hours each week.*

6. **Coretime** *The Coretime is the minimum hours an employee must work each working day. Coretime is as follows:*
   Monday–Thursday 09.30–16.00
   Friday 09.30–15.00

7.	**Time Off**	*Where an employee's role involves substantial time and commitment, the employee may be allowed, at their manager's discretion, Time Off without impacting vacation.*
8.	**Lateness**	*Lateness is that standard time from the beginning of Core Time (or Standard Working Day, if applicable) to the time the employee arrives at work.*
7.0	**Corrective Action**	*Corrective Action should be considered where there is any pattern of concern to the Manager in relation to the employee's personal management of the Working Day.*
7.1	**Benefits**	*The benefits of the Flexible Working Week are always at the discretion of the Company.*
7.2	**Removal of Benefits**	*Removal of benefits of the Flexible Working Week will occur when 2 or more of the Corrective Action steps applied for are for breaches of the guidelines outlined in this Working Day Policy.*
7.3	**Reinstatement of Benefits**	*Reintroduction of the benefits of the Flexible Working Week will occur when less than 2 of the current Corrective Action Steps being applied for are for breaches of the guidelines outlined in this Working Day Policy.*

Reproduced with the kind permission of Amdahl Ireland Limited.

Time Off

Employees who are exempt from overtime still tend to work additional hours through choice. Increasingly, organisations are formalising their policies to enable such employees to take additional time off, not necessarily on an hour-for-hour basis but rather in recognition of the employee's extensive hours worked in their personal time. At Amdahl Ireland, employees are paid at the standard rate while availing of time off. Managers use their discretion in giving time off using the following guidelines:

- Where an employee has worked extra hours into the night, with the manager's prior approval, and in line with business requirements, they may take some extra time off the following morning. (Guideline: if an employee works planned extra hours up to 11pm, with prior approval they may start work up to 1pm the following day.)

- Where an employee has worked Saturday/Sunday to meet deadlines, and where the schedule permits, the manager may use discretion in designating Monday/Tuesday as time off for employee.

Teleworking

Teleworking includes working full-time from home, desk-sharing or hot-desking, mobile working, splitting working time between home and the office, or working remotely, for example at a client's premises. Managers in Support of Telework (MAST), a group which includes Telecom Éireann, Hewlett Packard, Ericsson, Aer Rianta, Cork Teleworking, the National College of Ireland and the Irish Institute of Training and Development, have introduced an ADAPT programme, supported by the European Social Fund, to promote telework practice in medium to large firms. As part of the MAST ADAPT programme, The Work Research Centre (1998) released the results of the first survey of teleworking in large Irish companies, conducted among 165 companies with a combined workforce of 104,159 people. Their results show that, within the definition of teleworking given above, 4.3 per cent of the workforce in medium to large companies telework. The report predicts that the number of teleworkers could double within the next two years. Twenty of the companies surveyed either have a formal teleworking policy in place or expect to implement a policy within two years. One such company is Aer Rianta, which plans to launch a pilot teleworking scheme for up to 15 people from 1999. The Work Research Centre plans to introduce a programme to assist organisations that wish to introduce teleworking policies.

Case Example 21.4: Telecommuting at Intel

Intel defines telecommuting as working from home on a structured basis, usually for part of the week. As part of its "alternative working patterns" guidelines, Intel determines the kinds of tasks that can be carried out away from the office, such as data entry, research, writing, reading, word processing, meetings via teleconference, telephone support. The guidelines stipulate the criteria that applicants for telecommuting need to demonstrate: self-motivation, good time management skills, results orientation, good organisational skills, high level of job knowledge and skills, flexibility, PC literacy and a strong performance record, including having demonstrated that they need little supervision. The company sets out the following ground rules for telecommuters, which make a very good model for other companies. They include:

- *Childcare arrangements must be made during scheduled working hours (i.e. telecommuting is not a substitute for childcare).*

- *Set work hours must be established when the employee is available for meetings, telephone calls, e-mail.*

- *The employee and manager should establish at the outset the number of days that the employee is required to come into the office, generally 1–3 days for full-time employees. This can be reviewed at a subsequent date.*

The company helps with the home set-up for telecommuters, by supplying the appropriate PC configuration, together with appropriate ergonomic equipment such as a footrest and document holder, and by paying for the installation of a telephone line with direct bill to the company. The employee is responsible for supplying their own furniture. Part of the agreement with telecommuters is that they use a workstation rather than a dedicated office when they are at a company location. This approach helps eliminate wasted costs on idle offices.

Companies considering making this working pattern available to their employees should note that Intel has in place a highly sophisticated employee communications programme. Communication is an area that could suffer in a telecommuting programme and companies need to agree with their telecommuting employees in advance how two-way communication will take place. In addition, it is important to issue your telecommuting employees with health and safety guidelines, as you would to employees in the workplace. Intel advises its telecommuters on adequate space, lighting, heating and ventilation and fire safety. Should they suffer an accident while working for the company from home, employees are required to report this to their manager for entry in the site accident book in the normal way.

Intel's Telecommuting Tips for Employees

- *Pick a work location away from distractions. Don't work in front of the TV or at the dining room table.*

- *Establish a work routine and stick to it. Begin and finish work at the same time every day and make sure you have a few breaks during the day.*

- *Replace the ritual of getting ready for the office with another ritual such as taking a morning walk or other exercise, playing specific music, going for a coffee and reading the newspaper, having a shower and dressing for work.*

- *Establish a system for organising your work at home. Identify where work will be kept, e.g. filing cabinets.*

- *Develop a to-do list of work assignments to be completed on telecommuting days. Make sure you have the necessary resources and information to complete the list, review the list at the end of the day, stick to deadlines.*

- *Maintain contact with the office and your manager. Check regularly for messages on voicemail and e-mail and return calls promptly. Try to establish a "buddy" system with a co-worker or administrator, who you call once per day. Keep your manager informed of work status, for example through weekly meetings.*

- *Establish an end-of-day ritual, for example by taking exercise, turning on the radio or TV, changing your clothes.*

Reproduced with the kind permission of Intel Ireland.

Part-time Working

The ILO classification of employment and unemployment, which is used for international comparisons, distinguishes between part-time and full-time jobs. According to the CSO, between 1991 and 1996 the number of women in employment, using the ILO classification, increased by 106,000 to 507,000. There were an additional 65,000 women in full-time employment and 42,000 more in part-time employment. The majority of women in part-time employment are classified as part-time, *not underemployed*, which means that they are working part-time through choice and are not seeking additional or alternative employment.

Term-time Working

This provides employees with the opportunity to take unpaid leave during their children's school holidays. Boots the Chemist are an example of a company that provides this option. In Ireland, the Government announced in 1997 the introduction of a pilot scheme of term-time working in the public service, where short-term vacancies created as a result would go to a person on the live register. The option to avail of this scheme has subsequently been extended throughout the Civil Service.

Virtual Assignments

At a time when traditional international assignments continue to increase, companies are becoming more innovative in their use of staff as they enter markets overseas. According to Pricewater-houseCoopers, in addition to the well-established three- to five-year expatriate assignments, there is a greater use of short-term and "virtual" assignments. This new thinking in expatriate management is reported in PWC's third biannual survey, *International Assignments: European Policy and Practices* (1997), conducted amongst 184 companies based in 15 countries and employing 33,000 expatriates. Seven out of ten companies surveyed said they have so-called *virtual assignees* — that is, employees who do not have to relocate themselves and their families but have international job responsibilities which they manage from their home country. Such arrangements are not necessarily new, according to the report. However, where they do exist, 43 per cent have been agreed in place of expatriate assignments.

Whilst half of the companies surveyed reported that the cost of sending employees on expatriate assignments has caused them at times to cancel proposed assignments, almost half experience difficulty in persuading employees to accept international assignments, with many reporting that this problem has become more pronounced over the past five years. Almost 90 per cent of the companies surveyed reported cases of employees turning down the offer of an overseas assignment. The most common reasons for assignment refusals are family concerns and dual careers, although unacceptable locations, perceived career risks and unattractive remuneration packages are also factors.

The issue of dual careers in international assignments has generated considerable discussion over the last few years. A review of the statistics given above for the number of couples in the workforce in Ireland illustrates the point well. Where virtual assignments are not practical, companies offer extra incentives to accommodate the family. Both jobsearch assistance and education support are offered by about a quarter of the companies surveyed, although the number of companies offering jobsearch assistance declined from 41 per cent in 1995 to 26 per cent in 1997, a reflection of the practical difficulties encountered. Given the importance of family in determining whether to accept an assignment, it is hardly surprising that flexibility is shown in accepting the definition of "family" when it comes to expatriate assignments. While 34 per cent of the companies surveyed by PricewaterhouseCoopers restrict the definition of "partner" to a married spouse, 66 per cent include live-in partners of the same sex and 24 per cent a live-in partner of the same sex.

LEAVE ARRANGEMENTS[1]

Maternity Leave

Statutory maternity leave in Ireland, at 14 weeks, is one of the lowest in the EU. Seventy per cent of earnings are paid from the Social Insurance Fund, with the option of an extra four weeks' unpaid leave. However, family-friendly employers can offer benefits above the minimum and among those who do in Ireland are the ESB, which provides employees with the option of taking a total of six months in additional unpaid leave, and Esat Telecom, which pays employees their full salaries less the statutory allowances while on leave, which effectively leaves them better off financially than when they are at work, because of the tax relief on the maternity allowance.

Paternity Leave

Paternity leave is short-term leave for fathers on the birth of a baby. While there is presently no statutory entitlement to paternity leave, some organisations do provide it; for example, the Sunday World Newspaper provides two weeks' paid leave (Employment Equality Agency, 1996), Aer Rianta provides three days and the VHI up to four days.

Adoption Leave

The Adoptive Leave Act, 1995, provides for a minimum of ten consecutive weeks of paid adoptive leave and up to four addi-

---

[1] The legislation relating to maternity, adoptive, parental and *force majeure* leave is discussed further in Chapter 18.

tional weeks unpaid to adopting mothers or a sole male adopter who is in employment. The employee must fulfil mandatory notification requirements.

Parental Leave

The Parental Leave Act, 1998, allows for 14 weeks' unpaid leave entitlement in respect of children born on or after 3 June 1996, which was the date the original EU Parental Leave Directive came into force. The Act provides that employees must normally have one year of service before they are entitled to take parental leave; however, it also provides that employees who have not served this year before their child goes over the age threshold of 5 years but who have completed three months of service are entitled to parental leave of one week for every month that they have been in continuous employment with their employer at the time the leave commences. Both parents are entitled to the leave, but it is non-transferable; i.e. the mother cannot take the father's leave and vice versa. It can be taken as a continuous block or, by agreement between employer and employee, as a number of broken periods, or even as a shortened week. Although the leave is unpaid, employees will retain other employment rights such as service during the period of leave. Existing social welfare rights will be protected by the award of credited contributions during the period of leave, where necessary. The Act also gives all employees a right to limited time off for family emergencies caused by injury or illness (*force majeure* leave). Disputes about entitlements under the Act may, in general, be referred to a Rights Commissioner.

Eldercare

The Employment Equality Agency's *Introducing Family-Friendly Initiatives in the Workplace* (1996) makes the point that relatively little attention has been given to eldercare. However, the Irish population is ageing and people are living longer. The EEA reports that 42 per cent of male carers and 16 per cent of female carers are in paid employment. The EEA report quotes an American AARP study, *National Survey of Caregiving* (1989) on the effects of eldercare on the performance/work situation of employees, which showed that:

- One-third of the employed carers reported that they had lost time from work or had to come in late as a result of their duties;

- Nine per cent of full-time and seven per cent of part-time workers said that they had to take leave of absence;

- Fourteen per cent had to go from working full-time to part-time;

- Between one and five per cent had to take early retirement;

- Twelve per cent had to give up work entirely.

The Irish case studies included in this chapter of companies whose family-friendly programmes facilitate arrangements for eldercare are AIB, VHI and Our Lady's Hospital for Sick Children (see pp. 683–5 below). International examples of companies who have introduced measures to support employees with care responsibilities include Johnson and Johnson, who have introduced a "Work and Family Programme" where employees are allowed one year's unpaid leave of absence to care for an elderly relative, with the right to return to the same position if the leave is shorter than three months. Philip Morris have given US$100,000 to the New York City Department of Ageing to set up a partnership for eldercare. Both IBM and AT&T have established funds to support the development of community services for eldercare. In the UK, the BBC has a formal eldercare policy which includes career breaks, paid and unpaid leave and support groups. Ford Motors (UK) also offers flexibility to employees with eldercare responsibilities and operates a referral service between employees and public and private support organisations (EEA, 1996).

Care for People with Disabilities

The National Rehabilitation Board estimates that there are 350,000 people in Ireland with disabilities. Its 1997 publication, *Positive to Disability*, provides comprehensive guidelines for employers about providing opportunities. Organisations which have been awarded the excellence symbol in recognition of their policies in promoting equal opportunities for people with disability include Aer Lingus, AIB Group, ESB, Environmental Protection Agency (EPA), SmithKline Beecham, Waterford Crystal, KARE and the Irish Council of People with Disabilities.

EMPLOYMENT BREAKS

The Institute of Personnel and Development has coined the term "employment break" in place of "career break", which it says is "usually associated with professionally qualified women and their child care needs" (IPD, 1993). Whichever term you choose to use, an increasing number of organisations, details some of whom are included in the case studies in this chapter, recognise the value of flexibility in allowing breaks from employment. Telecom Éireann offers a scheme of substitution leave where up to 100 days' leave per annum can be taken with the cost of substitution deducted from the employee's salary, calculated at the minimum of the appropriate pay scale. Substitution leave counts as service for seniority, increments, pension entitlements, annual leave and promotion.

SECONDMENTS

A secondment is the temporary loan of an employee to another organisation or a different part of the same organisation for a specific purpose or period of time. The length of a secondment can vary. Secondments can be used for the professional development of the employee, as a transition to retirement or to demonstrate an organisation's commitment to the community or voluntary sector.

CHILDCARE

Background

After a number of years of campaigning for accessible and afford-able childcare by organisations such as the National Women's Council of Ireland and the Employment Equality Agency, the 1990s have seen slow but steady progress towards the provision of nationwide childcare. In 1994, the Department of Justice, Equality and Law Reform initiated a Pilot Childcare Initiative as an equal opportunity measure to assist women and men in disadvantaged areas to avail of work, training and education opportunities. The Department of Justice, Equality and Law Reform has been working in partnership with Area Development Management Ltd. (ADM) since 1994 to deliver the pilot initiative. ADM is an intermediary company established by the Irish Government and the European Union to support local social and economic development in 38 Area Based Partnerships and 33 Community Areas throughout Ireland. Through ADM's work with the Department of Justice, Equality and Law Reform, the Area Partnership Boards have begun to advance childcare as an equal opportunity measure in their areas and the case study of the Galway City Partnership joint childcare project (Case Example 21.6, pp. 681–2) is a good example.

Equal Opportunities Childcare Programme

The Department of Justice, Equality and Law Reform has responsibility for the Partnership 2000 Expert Working Group on Childcare, which is expected to report in December 1999. The Expert Working Group was given a budget of £200,000 and the task of drawing up a National Framework for the development of childcare services. It has already submitted to the Government pre-budget proposals for tax relief for childcare.

In the first half of 1998, the Minister for Justice, Equality and Law Reform announced a £5.2 million nationwide Equal Opportunities Childcare Programme aimed at developing childcare facilities to assist parents to reconcile family and work life. The programme is managed by ADM. This is a very significant equality measure, designed to support local communities and employers who are trying to facilitate women and men who have childcare responsibilities while accessing training, education and employment. It is aimed particularly at parents in disadvantaged areas and those on low pay who cannot access training, education and employment opportunities due to lack of affordable good quality childcare. The Department is developing a database on childcare services to assist in the co-ordination and planning of childcare facilities. Once developed, the database will be a source of information for parents seeking information in relation to childcare provision in Ireland. The database is being developed with the support of the European Social Fund and is expected to be of benefit in trying to bring a sense of strategy and coherence to the whole childcare area.

Ireland has one of the lowest rates of childcare provision when compared with other member states in Europe. The Government has recognised that the provision of a quality childcare system is central to the future development of equal opportunities in this country and that the key to reconciling work with family life is the provision of a national childcare system that is professionally run and properly supervised.

The Equal Opportunities Childcare Initiative has three strands:

1. Capital Infrastructure

This fund will be targeted at community childcare projects to enable them to upgrade/enhance their facilities or establish new purpose-built facilities for those who need childcare while they are at work or availing of training. Under the Capital Infrastructure strand, 90 community projects across the country will receive funding to assist them in providing or improving premises for their childcare services. A total of £2.2 million has been made available for capital infrastructure over the years 1998 and 1999.

2. Community Support

In this strand, £2 million is being made available over two years to 25 flagship projects which have been selected as having the potential to meet the following criteria within two years:

- Operating a childcare service over a full working day;

- Managed as a community-based, non-profit childcare service;

- Operating within quality premises meeting the requirements of the Childcare (Pre-school Services) Regulations, 1996;

- Operating with trained staff and linked to further training with an educational and development pedagogical approach;

- Demonstrating a good quality programme which is child-centred and developmentally appropriate;

- Demonstrating strong management and financial capacity;

- Showing innovation and demonstration characteristics;

- Linked to a strategy of local development or to an equal opportunities action in a non-disadvantaged area.

Each of the 25 projects will receive £40,000 per annum over two years to assist with staffing, administration and evaluation costs to assist them in developing sustainable and affordable childcare. FÁS has agreed that these projects will receive priority assistance under the Community Employment Programme. The participants involved will be given specialised childcare training. It is expected that the majority of them will qualify as professional childcare workers and will proceed to careers in this area.

3. Employer Demonstration Childcare Initiative

This was developed in partnership with IBEC to stimulate employer interest and involvement in supporting equal opportunity childcare facilities. IBEC contacted employers in the first quarter of 1998 and presented the proposals to them. The criteria for selection of Employer Demonstration Projects was based on a number of geographical and demographic factors, including employer knowledge and commitment to childcare. The purpose of this initiative is to look at employer childcare support from two distinct perspectives:

- By enhancing the ability of an enterprise to attract new employees into the labour market to meet potential labour/skills shortage;

- By enhancing the ability of enterprises to retain skilled staff when employees have difficulty reconciling work and family life.

Models for Childcare
The Employer Demonstration Initiative suggests a number of models of providing childcare; interested employers were encouraged to consider the following kinds of projects:

- Network of after-school childcare projects;

- Day care centre to be used by a cluster group of local employers within an industrial estate;

- Out-of-school project to respond to the needs of employees during school holidays;

- Upgrading of community services;

- Shared information and support unit to link employees with local childcare provision;

- Partnership with local communities for the provision of a service for employees.

The total budget available for the Employer Initiative over the period 1998–99 is £1 million from the EU, exchequer and employer sources. A total of 21 employers will be involved in eight demonstration projects over this period and the outcome will be closely evaluated by the Department. A total of 16 applications for funding were received and eight groups were selected.

The following are a number of case studies selected to show the application of the different models in practice. The Elan Pharmaceutical model (Case Example 21.5) is an example of a company-subsidised childcare facility from an organisation whose core values emphasise the importance of family and the balance between work and family life. The Galway City Partnership case (Case Example 21.6) is an example of community/industry partnership in establishing a childcare facility on an industrial estate. This project has received approval for funding under the Equal Opportunities Childcare programme and is at the stage of finalising plans and implementing them at the time of writing. The *NOW*-funded models (Case Example 21.7) are community-based projects designed to assist women and men in gaining access to training and employment (as lack of childcare facilities or funds to pay for childcare is often given as a reason why some low earners don't take up job offers). Our Lady's Hospital for Sick Children (Case Example 21.8) identified the establishment of an on-site crèche as a means of attracting and retaining scarce skills (while the hospital did receive funding under the IBEC co-ordinated strand of the Equal Opportunities Childcare Initiative, this was an added bonus rather than the impetus for starting the crèche). In the case studies that follow, all of the organisations involved highlight the importance of well-trained, experienced staff. Most of the following case studies include costings, which should be of assistance in providing an indication of costs to other companies considering establishing a childcare project.

All of the applicants had an opportunity to review the success of the Elan Corporation childcare facility, described below.

Case Example 21.5: Elan Pharmaceutical Technologies

Elan Pharmaceutical plc is a highly successful and profitable multinational operating in a niche area within the pharmaceutical market. Now publicly traded on the New York, London and Dublin Stock Exchanges, Elan was founded in Ireland and its corporate headquarters are in Dublin. Until recently, the company's headquarters was located at its main manufacturing facility in Athlone and the company's founder, Don Panoz and his wife Nancy spent much of their time in Athlone until their retirement in 1995. Nancy Panoz actively promoted employee involvement and benefits within the organisation, adopting a "nice to have" rather than a "need to have" approach. Today employees enjoy a significant benefits package, including a company crèche, gymnasium, sports hall, share options, generous sick and pension schemes and a subsidised canteen. However, it is the company crèche, named Rainbows, which employees rate as one of the most attractive benefits. Elan was fortunate in that a residential home became available close to the company's facilities and this was purchased in 1994 for the purpose of establishing a crèche.

Elan lists the benefits of the Rainbows Crèche as:

- *High profile, high quality, award-winning facility;*

- *Has proven to be excellent PR, both internally and externally;*

- *Highly appreciated by staff;*

- *Reduced parental anxiety;*

- *Contributing factor to low staff turnover, although it is recognised that the overall terms and conditions, together with career development opportunities, are also important contributing factors.*

Based on its experiences of subsidising and successfully managing the Rainbows Crèche, Elan recommends that companies considering providing a crèche should think about the following points:

- *Requirement for professionally trained staff, who are medically aware and have significant childcare experience;*

- *Staff should be trained to refuse to take children who are ill, in the interests of the health of the other children present, despite the difficulties that this can cause parents;*

- *Professional advice should be sought when planning facilities and space requirements for a crèche.*

Staff/Children Ratios and Costs

Elan's Rainbows Crèche requires one staff member to every three babies, one to every five toddlers and one to every eight pre-school children. The company charges £44.00 per week for the first child and £33.60 each for the second and subsequent children. The revenues do not meet the operating costs and the company provides a subsidy as shown in the figures below.

Initial Costs	£	Annual Costs	£	£
Overheads (1994)		Profit & Loss		
Building	58,635	+ Revenues		45,000
Redesign	41,472	– Labour	63,500	
Furniture & Fittings	23,264	– Sundry	4,900	
Total	123,681		68,400	
		Operating Subsidy		(23,400)
		(excluding depreciation)		

Reproduced with the kind permission of Elan Pharmaceuticals plc.

Case Example 21.6: Galway City Partnership in Conjunction with Local Employers

In recognition of the importance of developing a childcare strategy for Galway City, Galway City Partnership formed a Childcare Working Group in 1998 and has dedicated a permanent part-time worker to the implementation of its strategies. The Partnership company applied under all three strands of the Equal Opportunities Childcare Programme, 1998, and were allocated a grant of £150,000 under the Employer Demonstration Initiative for the development of a childcare centre in conjunction with local employers. The centre is to include:

- *A nursery for 0–1 year olds (6 places)*
- *A crèche for 1–3 year olds (24 places)*
- *A pre-school/Montessori school, catering for 3–5 year olds (20 places).*

The Galway City Partnership is developing the childcare facility in conjunction with local companies. In researching the business case for a childcare facility, the Partnership arranged for five local companies to survey their employees with the following results:

- *The total number of employees in the five companies is 2,216;*

- *There are more females employed (54 per cent) than males (46 per cent);*

- *The workforce is young, with the majority of employees in the 18–35 years age group;*

- *There are 956 child dependants amongst employees of the five companies;*

- *The majority of employees surveyed said they would consider using the crèche and or/ Montessori and would require full-day care.*

- *Typical opening hours would be from 8am to 6pm*

The time frame for opening the crèche is mid-1999. It will be managed by a company set up for that purpose, the board of directors of which will be made up of company representatives of all of the consortium participants, parent representatives, and nominated directors from local agencies such as the Western Health Board and the Galway City Corporation. The company will seek charitable status once registered.

The number of places open to each company will be determined by the Board of Directors, and will be based on individual company requirements and contribution towards start-up costs and/or ongoing operational costs.

Between 1995 and 1997, Employment *NOW* Ireland undertook four childcare projects to develop the childcare sector in the provision of professional employment opportunities for women and to develop childcare facilities that provide flexible, quality and affordable childcare services. The models used in these projects are described briefly in the following case study.

Case Example 21.7: Employment NOW Ireland

During the period 1995 to 1997, NOW funded four model childcare facilities in different regions of Ireland. West Limerick Resources used NOW funding to establish a mobile Playbus that provided childcare to women re-

turning to education and training in a rural area where neither transport nor local training facilities were easily accessible. Waterford Childcare is a commercial childcare facility designed to serve the needs of working parents in the city. Muintearas provides a flexible, Irish language crèche for women in the Gaeltacht area who are retraining. Muintearas has provided both the training and the childcare service to allow women to progress in the field of childcare and other areas of employment. The Ronanstown Women's Group were granted capital funding to construct a full-day care facility in a disadvantaged area of West Dublin. The National Women's Council of Ireland commissioned the Iris Research Group at the Centre for Women's Studies in Trinity College Dublin to study the childcare models and make policy recommendations for establishing a national childcare strategy based on the successful NOW-funded models. The report Caring for all Our Futures *is available from the National Women's Council of Ireland. Many of the issues highlighted in the report are being addressed through the Equal Opportunities Childcare Initiative – for example, the scarcity of information about and funding for in-service training; the need for core funding for staffing and premises; and the need for a government commitment to a long-term childcare strategy. The report also highlights a particularly salient point – namely, the dependence on short-term Community Employment staff due to a lack of funding for full-time positions.*

An organisation that has already conducted its own extensive research into establishing a childcare facility and is a most worthwhile beneficiary of the Childcare Initiative is Our Lady's Hospital for Sick Children, Crumlin.

Case Example 21.8: "Kiddies Kingdom" in Our Lady's Hospital for Sick Children, Crumlin

Our Lady's Hospital for Sick Children was established in 1956. It is the largest paediatric hospital in Ireland and the main specialist referral centre for all of Ireland. Specialities include cardiology, oncology, neonatal surgery, urology and all of the major sub-specialities. The provision of this range of specialist services requires very highly skilled staff. Given the skills shortage in hospitals in Ireland, the difficulties in recruitment, and the scarcity of quality childcare facilities, the management of Our Lady's Hospital made the decision to provide a childcare facility to assist in attracting and retaining essential high quality staff. The hospital employs 1,055 people. The majority (85 per cent) are female, and 52 per cent of the females are in the 18–36 age group. More than 40 employees go on maternity leave each year. The hospital's existing family-friendly measures included flexitime, job-sharing and part-time work in most departments. Our Lady's Hospital is supportive, where possible, of staff who wish to take leave to care for sick or elderly relatives, or who wish to take career breaks.

A staff survey elicited a 16 per cent response rate, confirming the very high level of interest in an on-site childcare facility and, following a detailed planning and redesign phase, Kiddies Kingdom was opened on 31 August 1998. The crèche is a 227 metre square building which can accommodate 34 children on a full-time basis and boasts among its extensive facilities a substantial outside play area, a baby room, toddlers' room and a fully equipped Montessori centre.

Staff/children ratios and costs

The staff ratios are 1:3 for babies, 1:6 for toddlers and 1:8 for pre-school children. Kiddies Kingdom aims to become self-financing over a period of time, although its initial capital investment of some £200,000 will not be recouped, apart from the award of an £85,000 capital grant through the IBEC co-ordinated strand of the Equal Opportunities Childcare Programme.

Companies considering establishing a crèche should be aware that this relatively modest capital cost was achieved by modifying existing buildings and building a link to a new portacabin. The result is a model childcare facility. The weekly cost of full-day care at the crèche (which opens from 7.30am to 6pm) is £70 per child. Parents using the crèche on a part-time basis are charged a minimum of £45 per week.

The following is a breakdown of the costs of establishing Kiddies Kingdom:

(a) Construction/Adaptation of premises

	£
Building costs/fit-out	89,000
Electrical	16,000
Portacabin	52,500
Flooring	5,500
Painting	5,000
Planning/architects' Fees	7,000

(b) Other Costs	
	£
Equipment/furniture	*16,000*
Blinds	*3,000*
Phones/security intercom	*2,000*
Job advertisements	*1,500*
TOTAL	**£197,500**

Reproduced with the kind permission of Our Lady's Hospital for Sick Children, Crumlin.

Our Lady's Hospital's Kiddies Kingdom is an excellent example of what can be achieved in childcare provision at an affordable cost with the best use of available resources.

OTHER FAMILY-FRIENDLY INITIATIVES

Employee Assistance Programmes

These provide employees with advice, counselling and support for a variety of problems. This important family-friendly initiative is covered extensively in Chapter 22.

Parenting Workshops

Barnardo's provides in-house workshops on all aspects of parenting and raising children. Companies who have found this beneficial include An Post and the VHI.

Family Days

Many companies organise family activities as a way of acknowledging the support families give to employees. The VHI organises an annual Family Day, while Intel runs a number of activities, including a Children's Christmas Party.

Health Care

Organisations offering additional health care services for their employees include the VHI, which provides lifestyle workshops on diet and health screening.

CONCLUSION

It is clear that a great deal of work and debate has taken place around the integration of work and family issues. The question generating the greatest attention is certainly childcare. Although some action has been taken at Government level, the onus appears to be on companies and individuals to balance work and family commitments. In the early part of this chapter, we reviewed the very significant increase in the numbers, both of women and of couples, at work. Credit must be given to the companies who have taken the lead in implementing family-friendly policies. The examples used in the chapter illustrate the success of the companies under study in facilitating *the integration of more people into the workforce* — for example, by providing crèche facilities — and at the same time, *the integration of more workers into family life* — for example, through flexible work practices such as teleworking and telecommuting.

Whilst all of these are extremely positive measures, the shortage of childcare places in Ireland has now been dubbed a crisis. The enforcement of necessary registration rules by the health boards is one of the reasons for the sudden shortage, as many established childcare facilities find that they need to increase staff ratios, reduce the number of children they can care for, or modify their premises. However, as these measures are for the good of the children being cared for, the only grounds for criticism can be the absence of accompanying financial resources. The solution is perhaps best summarised in the results of the survey conducted by AIB's Women in Business Task Force — namely, by reducing the costs of quality day-care and crèche facilities; by providing tax relief/financial allowances to offset the cost of childcare; by providing corporate crèches ; and finally, by adopting a more sympathetic attitude when child-related problems arise.

References

AARP (1989), *National Survey of Caregiving*, USA: AARP.

Allied Irish Bank (1998), *AIB Women in Business Task Force Report*, Dublin: AIB.

Central Statistics Office (1997a), Labour Force Survey, Cork: CSO.

Central Statistics Office (1997b), "Women in the Workforce", Statistical Release, Cork: CSO, 22 September.

Department of Employment (UK) (1991), *The Best of Both Worlds*, London: Department of Employment.

Drew, E. (1994), "Employment Prospects of Carers and Dependent Adults", Unpublished paper presented at Working and Caring Conference, Bonn.

Employment Equality Agency (1996) *Introducing Family-Friendly Initiatives in the Workplace*, Dublin: EEA.

Employment Equality Agency (1997), Annual Report, Dublin: EEA.

Employment Equality Agency (1998), "Attitudes to Work and Family", *Equality News*, Number 13, Spring, p. 15.

European Foundation for the Improvement of Living and Working Conditions (1998), *Aspects of Families and Work*, Report of Colloquium on Families and Work, Ireland, Dublin: EFILWC.

Hannelore, J. (1993), *Women: Working and Caring for their Elderly Parents*.

Institute of Personnel and Development (1993), *Employment Breaks*, London: IPD.

IRIS Research Group (1998), *Caring For All Our Futures*, Dublin: National Women's Council of Ireland/IRIS Research Group, Centre for Women's Studies, Trinity College, Dublin.

National Rehabilitation Board (1997), *Positive to Disability*, Dublin: NRB.

PricewaterhouseCoopers (1997), *International Assignments: European Policy and Practices*, Dublin: PCW.

Work Research Centre Ltd. (1998), "MAST ADAPT Teleworking Survey", Dublin: Work Research Centre Ltd.

CHAPTER 22

MANAGING OCCUPATIONAL HEALTH AND EMPLOYEE WELFARE ISSUES

Thomas N. Garavan and *Anne Morgan*

INTRODUCTION

Many Irish organisations now recognise the importance of health and welfare issues in facilitating and encouraging employees to attend work regularly and perform to the optimum. There is evidence that Irish companies do not attach importance to these issues solely because of legislative requirements or altruism. The 1997 Report of the Irish Health and Safety Authority (HSA, 1998) suggests that companies recognise that a healthy workforce makes a significant contribution to employee and business performance. Issues such as smoking, HIV/AIDS, violence and stress now fall within the ambit of contemporary occupational health and welfare. They are generally considered sensitive issues and some would argue that they are not the concern of employers at all. However, it is argued here that organisations that recognise these issues, and address them in a positive manner, can anticipate enhanced levels of employee performance. This chapter addresses the following aspects of occupational health and welfare:

- The importance of managing occupational health and welfare and the benefits to the employer and employee;

- The issues surrounding smoking, alcohol misuse and drug abuse in the workplace;

- The range of employment issues relating to HIV/AIDS;

- The nature, extent and responses to violence and bullying at work;

- The causes of stress and possible strategies that can be adopted by organisations to manage stress;

- The nature and value of work-based counselling.

INVESTING IN OCCUPATIONAL HEALTH AND WELFARE

Research conducted by the Institute of Personnel and Development (IPD, 1996) in the UK, which included Irish companies, revealed that employers who organised and implemented occupational health and "wellness" programmes incurred annual employment costs of between St£1,333 and St£2,910 less per employee than employers who did not. This suggests that consideration of health and welfare issues has quantifiable benefits for organisations. Irish health and safety law requires employers to provide a safe and healthy work environment. However, it is not legislative requirements alone that place concern for health issues high on the agenda. The importance of such issues is also significantly influenced by changing social attitudes and employee expectations. Better-educated and informed employees expect employers to consider new research and changing lifestyles and have these reflected in positive occupational health and welfare policies and practices.

The Safety, Health and Welfare at Work (General Application) Regulations, 1993, mandate employers to take responsibility for employee health as well as for physical safety. The legal provisions are based on the premise that if employees are the organisation's most valuable asset, investing in them through proactive health and welfare policies is a worthwhile exercise. The law

firmly believes that effective occupational health and welfare policies provide a mechanism for managing health-related issues.
Companies such as the Electricity Supply Board and Guinness
have for some time recognised that health screening, health education and employee assistance programmes can contribute to the
proactive management of employee health and welfare. Large
companies such as Intel and Hewlett Packard have implemented
advanced and sophisticated health policies.

The 1993 Regulations advocate that systematic health screening
can enable the monitoring of the health of the entire workforce
and aid identification of health difficulties before they develop
into more serious problems that may result in long-term absence.
There is likewise evidence that systematic health screening may
encourage healthy lifestyles on the part of the employees. Health
education programmes on specific topics such as diet and exer-
cising can inform the workforce about health issues and the associated risks. Other issues emphasised include ergonomics,
smoking, violence, bullying and alcohol/drug abuse.

SMOKING IN THE WORKPLACE

The issue of smoking at work is a sensitive one, requiring tact and
understanding on the part of management to avoid potentially
serious employee relations issues. The arguments of both sides in
the debate are strong. On the one hand, smoking, including pas-
sive smoking, has long been recognised as a serious health haz-
ard, so non-smokers are justified when not wanting to be exposed
to such a risk. On the other hand, the smoker may feel discriminated against by strict anti-smoking regulations, which can often
appear as an attempt to restrict the smoker's individual freedom.

Until 1990, restrictions on smoking at work in Ireland were
generally applied in the interests of safety (e.g. where inflamma-
ble substances were in use). However, the Tobacco (Health Protection and Promotion) Regulations, 1990, expanded the
restrictions to cover primary public amenities, such as transport,

educational institutions, public offices and recreational facilities. Shortly after the introduction of these Regulations, a consultative committee was established to investigate further possible legislative provisions on smoking for all workplaces. The Committee's recommendations resulted in the publication of a voluntary code of practice, which was deemed to be a more appropriate way of dealing with potentially divisive issues.

The code of practice has since been revised, and is now entitled "Working Together for Cleaner Air". In it, employers, employees, and their unions are encouraged to develop a policy on smoking that is tailored to suit the needs of their workplace. Guidelines are provided on how best to achieve this, the main points of which are outlined below. The process is broken down into stages of preparation, consultation, policy formulation, implementation, enforcement and monitoring. Figure 22.1 presents a summary of issues that employers should consider when formulating a smoking policy.

Figure 22.1: Formulating a Smoking Policy – Some Guidelines

---

1. Preparation

Treat the issue as a health and safety matter, stressing the positive rather than negative aspects.

- Be informed — gather information on health risks policies of other companies;

- Assess the views of the workforce, ensuring that employees are involved;

- Make sure that action taken does not appear arbitrary, or is viewed as taken against smokers themselves.

2. Consultation

Involve employees and their representatives throughout policy formulation, implementation and development by gathering employee views via questionnaire or direct consultation.

---

3. Policy Formulation

The policy should be clear about what actions are being taken, why they are being taken and what the penalties for non-compliance are. The following issues should be considered:

- Decide on type of policy, e.g. total ban on smoking, partial ban, restrictions in certain areas, etc.;

- A complaints procedure;

- Disciplinary action;

- Rationale for policy, e.g. legal, fire safety, hygiene, or product image reasons.

4. Implementation

- *Timing*: a realistic period should be allowed for both policy development and implementation, to allow smokers to adjust their smoking patterns. In each case, three months is a reasonable time period for medium to large enterprises.

- *Consistency*: the policy must be implemented evenly across the organisation.

- *Briefing*: all employees should be thoroughly informed of the policy to be implemented.

Facilities may also be made available to help smokers adjust to the new policy, such as information on controlling or indeed giving up the habit if they wish to do so.

5. Enforcement and Monitoring

To a large extent, employees will enforce the policy through self-regulation. However, if breaches do occur, procedures outlined in the policy should be applied consistently. Reviews should also take place to encourage feedback and to promote equity in awkward situations.

Smoking as a health and safety issue is extremely sensitive in organisations with high proportions of smokers and any policy formulation effort will require discussion on issues such as individual freedom, fire hazards, cleaning costs, time lost for smoking breaks and action for non-compliance. An effective policy on smoking will typically try to explain the reason for the policy, specify where employees can and cannot smoke, and state the penalties for violation. Some policies also address the issues involved in resolving disputes between smokers and non-smokers.

While some organisations have implemented strategies to stop smoking, this is often not given explicit recognition in many smoking policies. Examples of strategies include access to "quit" programmes, the distribution of health promotion and lifestyle literature and the provision of medical interventions such as smokers' patches. Human resource managers and safety specialists are usually involved in formulating smoking policies and the subsequent application of discipline or counselling strategies.

Workforce attitudes towards smoking at work should be considered and it is essential to seek the opinions of the employees in developing policy. A joint working party is a useful way of examining the policy options and the composition of this group should include representatives of management and employees who are smokers and non-smokers. The group needs clear terms of reference to enable it to draw conclusions and make recommendations to management.

Smoking Policy Options

Four basic options are available to the organisation in terms of a smoking policy:

Smoking in Designated Areas

This can be an effective option, particularly when a policy is first introduced. It allows for a pragmatic and progressive approach, which, coupled with health education, can enable the organisation to work toward more extensive coverage. Specific issues are associated with this option:

- What is meant by designated areas? If smoking is allowed in enclosed personal space — for example, individual offices — this may be seen as unfair and divisive because only more senior employees are likely to have their own enclosed space.

- Designated areas may be distant from the individual's place of work and taking time off for smoking may adversely affect productivity. Tensions may be created in employee relations with non-smokers feeling aggrieved about the perceived preferential treatment of smokers.

- Designated areas need ventilation to avoid the recirculation of air to non-smoking areas. Designated areas can magnify the problems of litter, a polluted atmosphere and fire risk.

Smoking at Designated Times

This allows for a relatively smoke-free work environment during specific periods of the day. Key issues can be identified and agreed with the non-smoking population and with tolerance and education, this may be implementable. However, it concentrates the problem and can be stressful for non-smokers, if smokers all smoke at the same time. It is very much a compromise option.

Freedom for Individual Work Areas to Decide

This may appear to be a fair and reasonable option, but the organisational status of the smoker may put non-smokers under pressure to accept a smoking environment, or vice versa. The basis for the decision needs to be specified and can present difficulties: will it be a simple majority, a certain percentage of the employees affected, or consensual?

A Total Ban

This creates problems for smokers who find it difficult to curtail or cease smoking. The reasonableness of a total ban could be challenged because of a "custom and practice" right to smoke at work. Therefore, a reasonable period of notice, of perhaps three months or more, may be necessary to allow smokers to adjust to the new working arrangements. Failure to give reasonable notice may lead to allegations of unfairness and ultimately to constructive dismissal if the employee feels unable to continue working. A total ban raises enforcement issues and consideration should be given to how infringements of the policy will be dealt with, as disciplinary action may be necessary. Smokers are innovative in creating refuge areas when faced with smoking bans and the risk of fire and litter pollution increases if employees congregate and smoke in remote or obscure places.

Some smokers would prefer not to smoke but, because of the addictive properties of nicotine, find it difficult or even impossible to cease. A reasonable employer will acknowledge this and offer support. Support mechanisms that can help smokers to adjust and to change behaviour include health education, counselling or self-help groups, and assistance in reducing nicotine dependence, through the provision of patches or chewing gum.

Regular and well-publicised support sessions for smokers send a strong message to the workforce that the organisation is committed to a healthy, smoke-free environment and also that it is supportive of employees who are adjusting to the new policy. Case Example 22.1 presents a sample smoking policy.

Case Example 22.1: A Sample Smoking Policy

Purpose
To protect the health of all employees, avoid conflicts between smoking and non-smoking workers, and ensure accommodation for non-smokers' preferences when necessary.

Guidelines
- *Smoking is permitted outdoors or in designated sections of the cafeteria and employee lounges and break areas.*
- *Smoking is prohibited in all meeting rooms, classrooms, rest rooms, hallways, lifts and other common-access areas.*

- *Employees who do not smoke have the right to post a no-smoking sign on their desk or at their workstation and co-workers who smoke must honour these requests. Employees who have objections to smoke in their work area must submit a written statement to their supervisor outlining the basic reasons for their objections, along with possible solutions to the problem.*

- *Work units or departments may formulate smoking policies for their work area designed to accommodate the preferences of smokers and non-smokers. All employees in a unit shall be allowed to vote on any such policy. If differences cannot be resolved, the manager of the unit or department will be responsible for trying to fashion a reasonable accommodation, such as ventilation modifications, the use of filtering devices such as air purifiers or cleaners or the relocation of workstations. The cost of purchasing filtering devices will be borne by employees who request them.*

- *Supervisors who receive a written statement of objections to smoking from a worker will meet with the employee to discuss possible accommodation. Employees should be asked if devices such as air purifiers or filters would satisfy their objections. The supervisor should consider the feasibility of separating the workstations of smokers and non-smokers if this would resolve the problem. If no mutually acceptable solution can be found, the supervisor must accommodate the non-smoker by designating the work area as a non-smoking zone.*

- *Employees may enrol in either a work site smoking-cessation programme or outside programme sponsored by local agencies and organisations. The work site programme will be free of charge to participants and one-half of the time spent in the sessions will be paid time. The company will reimburse employees for three-quarters of the cost of participating in an offsite smoking-cessation programme. Employees who successfully quit smoking for a one-year period will be eligible for a one-time £50 bonus.*

- *The company will be responsible for supplying all no smoking signs, notices and postings used on the premises.*

Violators of the smoking restrictions set forth in this policy will be subject to the standard disciplinary penalties, i.e. first offences will elicit an oral warning, second offences a written warning, etc.

ALCOHOL AND DRUG-RELATED PROBLEMS

A common cause of absenteeism in Irish industry is connected with employees suffering from alcohol and other drug-related problems. According to the Irish Business and Employers Confederation (IBEC) this form of absenteeism can occur at any level within the organisation, and can be costly to employers in terms of disruption, poor morale, reduced output and safety problems.

It is estimated by IBEC that at least one in ten employees may suffer from alcohol abuse at some stage in their employment history, with male employees being three times more likely to be at risk than female employees. O'Brien and Dufficy (1988) estimate that some 75 per cent of problem drinkers and 25 per cent of problem drug abusers are male employees. These problems can manifest themselves in even the smallest organisations and management should have a planned procedure to aid employees experiencing difficulties.

Alcohol-related employment problems fall broadly into two categories. First, the employee who occasionally drinks inappropriately and may be unable to work for the odd day; and second, the employee who often drinks inappropriately, who may have an alcohol dependency and whose availability to attend work regularly or to perform effectively is severely affected. The first category can be treated as misconduct and dealt with through counselling and through the disciplinary procedure. The second category may indicate alcohol dependency and require treatment as an ill health issue.

O'Brien and Dufficy (1988) suggest numerous benefits to be gained from adopting a systematic approach to alcohol and substance abuse. They highlight benefits such as fewer accidents, less time-off as a result of alcohol- and drug-related sickness, better work relationships, improved decision-making and greater quality and quantity of production.

Means (1996) suggests the following guidelines when formulating an alcohol policy:

- The organisation should produce a written policy that deals specifically with alcoholism alone.

- This policy should be known to all employees and it should clearly set out a positive policy aimed at helping the substance abuser to recover.

- The organisation should develop specific procedures covering such issues as the handling and referral of employees experiencing problems and line managers ensuring compliance with procedures.

- The policy should include an effective referral system. It should incorporate provisions relating to qualified substance diagnostic facilities.

- The policy should be underpinned by an effective medical record-keeping system. This record-keeping system should assure confidentiality to the individual employee, while at the same time having the capacity to provide evidence of the policies.

The policy should focus on establishing and articulating the managerial attitude towards alcohol use and misuse. A precise statement of the rules is required to govern alcohol consumption in the workplace and attendance at work when unfit due to the effects of alcohol. Work arrangements that encourage alcohol consumption, such as access to lunchtime drinking, customer hospitality and availability of alcohol on premises, are powerful influences on employee "norms" of behaviour, and the implementation of an alcohol policy without addressing these arrangements is less likely to succeed. An effective policy can lead to a safer, healthier and more motivated workforce through identifying problems, dealing fairly with employees and offering assistance to treat and rehabilitate where appropriate.

However, management must note the pitfalls when handling employees with a substance abuse problem, as the issue has wide-ranging disciplinary and industrial relations implications, and often causes a great deal of stress for the employees involved. Nonetheless, properly handled, the situation can have positive outcomes for employees, acting as the first step towards their re-habilitation.

To avoid conflict over the issue, it is important to remember that dealing with the problem is a management responsibility, and that a consistent procedure for handling employees must be in place. IBEC suggest that this should consist of four main steps. Figure 22.2 presents the main guidelines.

Figure 22.2: Handling Employees with Alcohol and Drug-Related Problems

---

1. Identify possible problems among employees

Common indicators are:

- Regular absences from work, often with a variety of excuses;

- Poor timekeeping and missed deadlines;

- Poor work performance;

- Disimproved personal appearance;

- Disimprovement in personal relationships with colleagues;

- Uncharacteristic irritability and/or depression;

- Money problems — continued borrowing from colleagues;

- Obvious signs of substance abuse at work.

2. Confirm that a suspected employee has a problem

Gather facts — not rumours — about the following:

- Work performance — examine quality, behaviour, timekeeping, absenteeism;

- Conduct interviews with the relevant supervisors;

- Analyse medical data for any deterioration that is substance abuse related.

---

3. Act on the problem

If there is substantial hard evidence to show that the employee may have a problem, then interview the employee as soon as possible, taking the following into account:

- Give the employee the opportunity to have a colleague/ representative present;
- Present all the gathered evidence to the employee regarding poor performance;
- Allow the employee to put forward an explanation for the poor performance;
- If the explanation is unsatisfactory, advise of the seriousness of the situation, and management's unwillingness to let it continue;
- Directly state to the employee the belief that they are suffering from a substance abuse problem, and suggest appropriate referral to professional help.

If the employee acknowledges the problem, written clarification should be provided regarding:

- Specific performance improvement criteria;
- Potential disciplinary consequences if these are not met;
- Agreement to referral for professional help, where appropriate.

If the employee denies the problem, then they should be advised of the disciplinary consequences, and a continued denial will result in the procedure moving forward to the final stage.

4. Disciplinary action

This should take the form outlined in the company rulebook, or in its absence, according to custom and practice. When carrying out disciplinary action, management should note that:

- It may be helpful to provide a list of sources of professional help;
- The issue has serious industrial relations repercussions, and the employee has the right to refer the issue to:
  - A Rights Commissioner
  - The Labour Court
  - The Employment Appeals Tribunal.

A major issue in the US employment context, and increasingly in Ireland, relates to testing for controlled substances. This issue has not yet received a significant degree of attention in Ireland but there is some evidence that US multinationals operating in Ireland are giving it consideration. Testing for controlled substances is mandatory for federal employment in the US and is becoming increasingly common in the private sector, especially amongst larger employers. Brookler (1992) suggests a range of guidelines for companies considering mandatory testing:

- An employee who tests positive should be referred to an employee assistance programme (EAP — see later section);

- If the employee occupies a sensitive position, the individual should be removed immediately from that position;

- It is recommended that it should be at the employer's discretion whether the employee is returned to that position;

- The severity of action taken will depend on the circumstances of each case and the laws on dismissal.

Testing options available to companies include:

- Random testing: each employee has a chance of being tested;

- "With cause" testing, whereby employers can require an employee to be tested if an alcohol problem is suspected;

- Post-treatment testing to assess the situation on returning to work;

- Pre-employment testing to identify potential problems.

A sample alcohol policy is outlined in Case Example 22.2.

Case Example 22.2: A Sample Alcohol Policy

This policy has been developed in consultation with employee representatives and has the full support of management. This policy applies to all employees and to contractors working on organisation premises. Alcohol consumption or possession in the workplace is prohibited. The breaking of this rule will result in disciplinary action.

The organisation has a duty to protect all employees and others, and alcohol misuse or addiction may affect employee health, safety and performance. The purpose of this policy is to protect employees from the dangers of alcohol and to encourage those with a problem to seek help. The organisation recognises that alcohol dependency may be an illness and can be treated in the same way as any other long-term illness.

The organisation is committed to supporting and assisting in the treatment of those with an alcohol problem. Help is available from your manager, the occupational health department or through the Employee Assistance Programme. The employee has a right to confidentiality in all aspects of health care.

The employee is entitled to occupational sick pay while undergoing recognised and agreed treatment and has the right to return to work following effective treatment, subject to the approval of the occupational health practitioner. Employees will be supported during treatment. However, where treatment is unsuccessful and the employee is not able to return to their job, suitable alternative employment will be sought, but if it is not available, termination of employment on the grounds of ill health will need to be considered.

HIV AND AIDS IN THE WORKPLACE

Acquired Immune Deficiency Syndrome (AIDS) and Human Immuno-Deficiency Virus (HIV), the precursor to full-blown AIDS, are features of modern society. HIV can be transmitted through blood products, through unprotected sexual activity, by an infected mother to the unborn child and through intravenous drug use. HIV cannot be contracted through normal social contact and most workplace situations present no risk of cross-infection. An individual with the virus (HIV+) is normally able to attend work regularly and work performance is unaffected. A person living with full-blown AIDS may develop AIDS-related complex (ARC) and contract various illnesses and infections that will seriously impact on attendance and performance. This distinction between the two conditions was recognised in 1986.

Ignoring the HIV and AIDS issues until a case arises is not a sensible managerial option, as decisions taken under pressure may be inappropriate. Cases of HIV and AIDS raise different issues to those associated with other life-threatening illnesses. Distinctive HIV and AIDS issues include:

- Prejudice, which leads to discrimination;

- Anxiety and fear among employees about contracting the disease;

- A lack of knowledge about the disease;

- A lack of sympathy towards AIDS sufferers because of stereotypical assumptions and inaccurate perceptions about HIV transmission.

The advantage of investigating and addressing HIV and AIDS issues at work is in objectively defining the managerial approach prior to a case occurring in order to facilitate the handling of a case when it does. HIV and AIDS are emotive and emotional subjects, which are characterised by misinformation and stereotypical assumptions and this may test the ability of the most objective manager to handle a case fairly and consistently. Banas (1992), in a frank and readable account of the difficulties of actually *managing* the employment of staff who are living with AIDS, highlights the difficulties and the unpredictability of individual responses. HIV and AIDS are illnesses and an employee with an illness should be dealt with through the sickness and absence management policies and procedures. However, the distinctive issues relating to HIV and AIDS may justify further measures, including a specific policy, to ensure fair, reasonable and equitable treatment.

The language of the HIV and AIDS policy and the message it communicates are critical in setting the tone for the management of HIV and AIDS in the workplace. An analysis of AIDS policies by Goss and Adam-Smith (1994) identified the emergence of two distinct policy types:

- *The Defensive Policy*: this may include a strong introductory statement that discrimination against people affected will not be tolerated, but further investigation of the policy detail identifies a shift that introduces a "sense of uncertainty" about the differential treatment of people with HIV and AIDS. Statements are ostensibly written in language that conveys protection for the AIDS sufferer, but in practice they are used for exclusion in order to "defend" the organisation from AIDS sufferers.

- *The Constructive Policy*: this is more focused on the normalisation of HIV and AIDS as a lethal matter. As a positive consequence, it diverts attention from the stereotyping of and discrimination against the person living with AIDS.

There are many benefits to be gained from an employer approaching the issue of HIV/AIDS in a proactive manner. These include:

- Prevention of new infection among employees by educating them about how HIV is and is not transmitted;

- Informing managers and supervisors of the legal issues raised by HIV infection in the workplace;

- Preventing discrimination by fearful, ill-informed employees;

- Laying the groundwork and preparing managers and supervisors to consider requests from employees disabled by HIV infection;

- Facilitating improvements in morale and preventing fear and anxiety.

With regard to occupational hygiene, many organisations will not have to protect directly against the risks of HIV contamination, except for basic prophylactics in first aid situations. However, certain organisations, such as those involved in the provision of medical care, often require specific measures to prevent the spread of HIV infection. In all cases, organisations should consider indirect hygiene steps (such as education programmes) to lessen the risk of employees contracting HIV outside the workplace. Education programmes may also have a secondary beneficial effect in reducing stress levels among the workforce, by removing fears and prejudices about the issue.

The most effective method for an organisation to treat employees with HIV or AIDS fairly is to implement a clear, non-discriminatory policy on the issue. A definite policy statement not only promotes equal opportunities; it also constitutes good management practice and makes economic sense. It can protect employee rights by providing confidentiality, and prevents discrimination in areas such as job security and promotion opportunities. It also gives managers clear guidelines on how to cope with the sensitivities involved, and can have positive repercussions for both employee relations and customer image.

Some organisations argue that AIDS does not merit this specific attention, especially where resources are tight, and argue that policies for non-occupational diseases are unnecessary. However, because of the sensitivity of the issue, it can create strong reactions, among both employees and the media, justifying the need for a policy. Medium- to large-scale organisations, in particular, need to prepare for the emergence of the issue, as sooner or later they are likely to have an employee with HIV or AIDS.

Aikin (1994) suggests that a HIV/AIDS policy should include the following elements to maximise its fairness:

- It should address HIV and AIDS separately, recognising that they are separate conditions and providing appropriate responses to each;

- It should integrate the policy into other equal opportunity policies;

- It should not tolerate discrimination towards HIV or AIDS from any employee or any aspect of company activity;

- It should outline discipline and grievance procedures for those found breaching the terms of the policy;

- It should state that AIDS will be treated in the same manner as other progressive or debilitating illness;

- It should cover areas such as retraining, redeployment, flexible working and compassionate leave;

- It should be reinforced by an equal opportunities stance on sexual orientation.

In addition to these elements, a HIV/AIDS policy should contain a commitment to some form of educational programme for employees. As formal education programmes, in the form of seminars or workshops, can be both expensive and viewed with reluctance by staff, an alternative is to mail all employees with relevant information. Unfortunately, this method can lead to the issue becoming shrouded with secrecy, with staff perceiving the organisation as sweeping AIDS under the carpet. It is nonetheless a useful way to introduce the issue, and ideally should be backed up with open information systems. This allows employees to improve their knowledge of HIV/AIDS, should they wish to do so.

Employees have a right to confidentiality in health matters and this should be respected in the case of HIV and AIDS. There is no strict obligation for an infected person to tell their employer. HIV and AIDS are not notifiable diseases, and sufferers are advised by representative bodies not to reveal their illness. However, employees have a contractual duty of care and an infected employee in a "sensitive" job has a responsibility to ensure that risks of transmission are assessed and minimised. A sample HIV/AIDS policy is presented in Case Example 22.3.

Case Example 22.3: HIV/AIDS Policy Guidelines

An effective policy should:

- Address HIV and AIDS as separate conditions, because different issues are associated with each.

- Make an opening statement to specify the organisational attitude to HIV and AIDS and state that, as illnesses, any cases will be dealt with through the sickness procedures.

- Make clear that HIV-infected employees are able to work normally and that employees with full-blown AIDS who are no longer able to work normally, in line with all employees with long-term illness, will be considered for redeployment, retraining, flexible working, home working, reduced hours or compassionate leave. Ideally, the policy should extend these options to the carers of AIDS sufferers.

- Assert that discrimination against employees with HIV and AIDS is unlawful and will not be tolerated.

- State that applicants for employment will be assessed on their ability to do the job and that, in conformance with the spirit of the legislation, reasonable adjustments will be made where appropriate.

- Reassure infected employees of confidentiality and provide guidance on support and counselling services.

- Nominate organisational support workers so that the employee can elect to talk to the most appropriate person and not be forced to talk to their immediate manager.

- Commit to the HIV and AIDS education of employees and managers.

VIOLENCE AT WORK

It is important to define what is meant by violence in the context of work. A narrow view encompasses just physical violence, but the requirement in Irish health and safety law is for the employer to provide for the "health, safety and welfare" of people at work and the definition of violence should recognise this wider responsibility.

Violence is therefore defined as any physical or verbal action or threat of action that causes physical or psychological harm to the recipient. The Irish Health and Safety Authority generally defines violence at work as situations where individuals are verbally abused, threatened or assaulted in circumstances relating to their work. The European Commission, on the other hand, has defined violence at work as:

> incidents where persons are abused, threatened or assaulted in circumstances relating to their work, involving an implicit or explicit challenge to their safety, well-being or health.

There is evidence that employers may perceive violence differently. Research evidence suggests that many employers only regard physical attack with a weapon as constituting violence, but the experts agree that violence at work does not involve only physical attacks but also includes threats of attack or simple abuse. The research also demonstrates that violence may arise from two sources:

- *External*: customer/patient/client attack;

- *Internal*: a staff member assaults a colleague.

Violence at Work — Considerations

- *Risk Assessment.* This is fundamental to establishing the threat of violence and to identifying appropriate managerial responses. The complex interplay between the nature of the work, the characteristics of the work situation, the work environment itself and the personal characteristics of staff contribute to defining the violence risk.

- *The Nature of the Work.* There is evidence that this contributes to the risk of violence. Public sector and service sector organisations have a higher violence risk. Local authority employees, advisers to job seekers, social welfare officers, teachers, nurses and others who provide public services come into contact with the public in sometimes frustrating and confrontational situations. The combination of frustration, anger and an inability by the employee to meet "customer demands" can lead to loss of temper (customer rage) and increase the risk of violence. Jobs that involve cash handling also carry higher risk and bank staff, post office staff and retail sales staff are at risk from theft and associated violence.

- *The Work Situation Itself.* Characteristics of the work represent a major contributor to the likelihood of violence. Occupations where staff work alone, such as nurses, social workers and bus and taxi drivers, present particular challenges and need special consideration. Employees who work outside normal hours may be at greater risk and work systems should ensure that staff are not permitted to work without adequate security arrangements.

- *The Work Environment.* Characteristics of both the internal and external work environment contribute to the risk of violence. The internal environment needs to be assessed for the availability of "weapons", such as items of equipment, and the need for protective devices such as screens and alarms. The external environment is influenced by the geographical location of the employer's premises and the incidence of local crime. Systems for the safety of employees entering and leaving the building may be required.

- *The Personal Characteristics of the Individual.* The evidence suggests that some employees are better equipped to deal with confrontational and potentially violent situations, but all staff should be trained to recognise potentially difficult situations and to respond accordingly. A survey of interactions between staff and customers can indicate triggers for frustration and anger and causes of violent exchanges. An analysis of these incidents informs managerial action, which may include changes in systems of work, the reduction of waiting time or the provision of a more amenable customer environment. Employees who are adequately trained to assess and control violent situations are less likely to be the victims of attack than employees who are unable to manage emotional exchanges, or cannot provide relevant information, or who lack skills and confidence in difficult encounters with customers.

Prevention of Violence

Porteous (1997) argues that responses to violence need to be informed by a careful collection of facts and systematic analysis. It is generally accepted that most violence arises through an escalation process. Much violence can therefore be avoided if staff are well-trained in recognising the warning signs.

The first step in establishing a preventative policy is to find out if there is a problem. Four ways to find the answer suggest themselves:

1. Consider if some or all of the organisation's operations are in the "most at risk" category;

2. Look at the organisation's accident records and see if any were the result of violence;

3. Record all incidents;

4. Classify these incidents.

The results of such an analysis should reveal if there is a problem, and if there is whether it is global within the organisation or manifests itself in certain areas of activity. Cox (1987) described three levels of intervention to tackle the problem:

- First, prevention should deal with the problem by organisation and work design or through staff training. It should seek to remove or reduce exposure to potentially violent situations and/or their detrimental effects on staff.

- Second, timely reaction should deal with the problems as they arise, ensuring a rapid and appropriate response.

- Third, rehabilitation should deal with the aftermath of violence through enhanced staff support to help employees cope with and recover from incidents.

The Services, Industrial, Professional and Technical Union (SIPTU) suggest a range of measures including training, emergency procedures, alarm/assistance procedures, support for employees subject to violence, personal protective equipment and safety standards.

BULLYING IN THE WORKPLACE

Bullying represents another dimension of violence in the workplace and there is evidence that it is on the increase. The most effective way of dealing with bullying at work is to have an agreed policy which sets out clearly what is acceptable behaviour and what is not, and which sets out the sanctions that will be invoked if people go beyond the bounds of acceptable behaviour. The policy may be part of an overall policy on harassment or it may be a specific policy on bullying. It may be helpful to have a separate policy that names bullying and deals with it specifically so that people recognise that it is a specific, undesirable form of behaviour and is an important issue in its own right. However, some employees will prefer to include it in an overall harassment policy to avoid a proliferation of procedures. If this is the case, the policy should include a separate clear definition of bullying and the form it takes.

It is important that the policy sets out not only the procedures for dealing with individual cases of bullying but also what measures the employer will put in place to identify and remove organisational causes of bullying.

Content of Bullying Policy

A policy on bullying must:

- Have commitment from the very top;

- Be jointly drawn up and agreed by management and trade unions;

- Recognise that bullying is a serious offence;

- Apply to everyone;

- Guarantee confidentiality;

- Guarantee that anyone complaining of bullying will not be victimised;

- Be implemented.

The policy should set out:

- A clear definition of bullying and the forms it takes;

- A statement that bullying is unacceptable behaviour and will not be tolerated at any level of the organisation;

- A statement that bullying will be treated as a disciplinary offence.

Assessment of the Risks of Workplace Bullying

The policy should include a commitment from management to assess the risk of bullying occurring in the workplace and to rectify organisational deficiencies that could give rise to bullying.

Although risk assessment should be a key part of any policy on bullying, it will often be the area which employers find the most difficult to address, particularly where bullying is rooted in the organisation's own culture and value system. However, employers should review their organisation in a systematic way so that they understand in what circumstances bullying can arise and can determine the steps needed to reduce that risk, such as improved human resource management training, better lines of communication, etc.

Procedures for Complaining about Incidents of Bullying

In common with other interpersonal conflicts, such as sexual or racial harassment, dealing with complaints of bullying requires confidentiality, sensitivity and speed. Standard grievance procedures are generally not suitable for this type of complaint. Such procedures may not provide for a complaint to be made over the heads of a supervisor or line manager, which creates a problem in cases where it is that person who is the alleged bully. Furthermore, standard procedures may be lengthy, leaving the complainant vulnerable to further bullying.

Confidentiality

It is essential that confidentiality is guaranteed and that people likely to be involved in implementing the complaints procedures understand that breach of confidentiality may itself be a disciplinary offence. This means that clear information and training must be provided to all concerned, i.e.:

- Counsellors
- Line managers

- People involved in the investigation

- Complainants

- Alleged bully.

Even if a bullying policy exists, whether to use the complaints procedure may still be a difficult decision for many people to take. If confidentiality is not seen to be respected, then people will not make use of the system and the policy will be ineffective.

Training

A prerequisite for the successful implementation of a bullying policy is training. The policy must provide for all employees to be given appropriate information and training. Staff must be given information about the policy so that they understand the nature of bullying, why it is unacceptable, why the policy was needed, what the procedures are for complaining and what disciplinary action will be taken against those who do not comply. Information about the policy should be included in induction training. Additional training should be provided to those involved in implementing the policy, i.e. counsellors, line managers, personnel officers, those conducting investigations and those hearing appeals. The training must emphasise that senior staff are not exempt form the policy and that if they bully, action will be taken to deal with them just as vigorously as action is taken against more junior staff.

WORKPLACE STRESS

Stress is about pressure on the individual and may be physical, intellectual, emotional or social in manifestation. Pressure becomes distressing when the individual perceives it to be either excessive and beyond their ability to cope, or alternatively insufficient to provide stimulation. It is therefore *distress* that is potentially harmful and distress that ought to be the focus of organisational and individual attention. Using the term distress distinguishes it from positive pressure at work (termed *eustress*). Whereas distress is about an imbalance between the level of pressure and the individual ability to cope, eustress represents the equilibrium pressure point, where the level of pressure on an individual is neither too much, nor too little, but just right.

The relationship between pressure and performance suggests that insufficient pressure as well as too much pressure causes distress. Identifying the eustress point for an individual is problematic. It will vary over time because the whole individual needs to be considered and the level of pressure will be determined by a combination of work stress, life stress and event stress. *Work stress* includes workload, deadlines, work relationships, the nature and extent of change, the degree of control, working conditions and levels of security. *Life stress* describes the pressures of day-to-day living and will include personal finance, emotional relationships, family responsibilities and personal health. *Event stress* describes significant events such as getting married, buying a house, the birth of a child or coping with bereavement.

Individual vulnerability to distress is influenced by a range of factors, including:

- Individual personality differences — for example, type A or type B personality;

- Internal or external locus of control — the extent to which individuals feel able to influence their own destiny;

- The extent of personal support networks;

- The capacity of personal coping strategies;

- The ability to act on own perceptions of stress;

- The compatibility of job experience, knowledge and skills with current job demands.

Figure 22.3 presents a list of potential sources of stress.

Figure 22.3: Sources of Stress in the Organisation

Sources of Stress in Organisations

- Work overload or underload (repetitive work, unrewarding work);
- Poor job design (ergonomically, environmentally, lacking in autonomy or variety);
- Role ambiguity or role conflict;
- Poor quality leadership or supervision;
- Lack of participation in decision-making;
- Poor quality of relationships (horizontally, vertically or externally);
- Responsibility for people or for achieving targets and objectives;
- Organisational change;
- The organisational climate;
- Being subjected to bullying or harassment;
- Pay, conditions and job insecurity.

Personal Sources of Stress

- Unhealthy eating, sleeping or exercise;
- General health and whether it is abused;
- Family and social relationships;
- Significant life events;
- Conflicting personal and organisational demands.

Sources of Stress in the Environment

- The general economic situation;
- Political uncertainty;
- Social change and threats to personal values and standards;
- Concern with the natural environment;
- The pace of technological change;
- Changing male and female role perceptions.

Implications of High Stress Levels

Harmful pressure or stress manifests itself in a wide range of psychological, physiological and behavioural consequences. The main indicators under each heading include the following.

Psychological implications include:

- Anxiety, irritability, frustration, depression;
- Inability to concentrate, procrastination, decision paralysis, inaccurate recall, feelings of unreality;
- Job dissatisfaction, suppressed motivation;
- Disturbed sleep patterns.

Physiological implications include:

- Muscular tension, headaches, palpitations;
- Heart disease, high blood pressure;
- Digestive problems, irritable bowel;
- Increased susceptibility to colds, influenza and respiratory infection.

Behavioural implications include:

- Sub-optimum performance and productivity;
- Higher levels of absence, labour turnover and accident rates, and poor timekeeping;
- Tobacco, alcohol, caffeine and other substance abuse;
- Negative personal appearance and hygiene changes, weight loss or gain;
- Less effective personal and professional relationships.

These three areas are not mutually exclusive, as some of the consequences overlap and feed each other. It is unlikely that one individual will suffer all of these potential outcomes of stress.

Managing Work Stress

It is generally recommended that an assessment of the sources and consequences of stress is an essential prerequisite to taking focused organisational and individual actions. Strategies need to focus both on reducing individual vulnerability and acting on the sources of stress. There is a general tendency to concentrate on reducing individual vulnerability to stress at the expense of addressing the sources. Therefore, an organisation runs the risk of addressing only the symptoms rather than the underlying causes and this has the effect of shifting the burden of responsibility from the organisation to the employee.

Strategies to reduce individual vulnerability include:

- Counselling services, referral systems and the development of support networks;

- The encouragement of healthy habits, diet, sleep and exercise;

- The development of coping techniques — assertiveness, time management, the creation of safety zones, allowing time for leisure;

- The use of relaxation techniques — massage, aromatherapy, yoga;

- The displacement of ventilation of negative feelings through legitimate means — rigorous physical exercise, catharsis, a "bug" list;

- The development of skills, knowledge and competencies in line with job demands.

Strategies for acting on the stressors include:

- Workload re-balancing, role clarification, job redesign;

- Critical evaluation of communication and change processes;

- Critical evaluation of the quality of leadership, management and supervision;

- Critical evaluation of intrinsic and extrinsic rewards;

- Provision of training and development opportunities to enhance job skills;

- Evaluating the physical work environment;

- Educating managers to recognise and respond to distress.

EMPLOYEE ASSISTANCE PROGRAMMES

Employee Assistance Programmes (EAPs) are an effective tool for assisting managers in restoring poor work performance that is affected by personal/social problems. The programmes work by using poor performance as a means of identification and referring the employee to sources of professional help for assessment and rehabilitation.

An EAP is a systematic, organised and continuing provision of counselling, advice and assistance, provided or funded by the employer and designed to help employees and their families with problems arising from work-related or external sources.

In the Irish and UK context, EAPs tend to have two main objectives:

- To help the employee who is distracted by a range of personal problems, be they emotional, stress, relationships, alcohol, drug, financial or legal-related, to cope;

- To assist the organisation in the identification and elimination of performance problems in employees whose job performance is adversely impacted by personal problems.

In terms of the essential elements that distinguish an EAP, Davis and Gibson (1994) and Lee and Gray (1994) suggest the following as core elements:

- A systematic survey of the organisation to determine the nature, causes and extent of problems perceived by individuals;

- A continuing commitment on the part of top management to provide counselling, advisory and assistance services to problem employees on a no-blame, no-cost, totally confidential basis;

- An effective programme of promotion and publicity of the EAP within the organisation;

- A systematic education and training programme on the philosophy, goals and methods used within the EAP programme;

- A procedure for contact with the EAP and referral to counselling;

- An outline of problem assessment procedures, including issues of confidentiality, time-scales, counsellor training and expertise and diagnosis of services;

- A protocol explaining the extent of short-term counselling, long-term treatment and assistance;

- An outline of how the EAP programme links with other services in the organisation and community;

- A procedure for follow-up and monitoring of employees subsequent to their use of the EAP service;

- A mechanism for the feedback of activities;

- A procedure to evaluate individual and organisational benefits.

These characteristics help to make EAPs distinct from other forms of workplace counselling.

A key issue in the operation of the EAP is the selection and placing of the EAP within the organisation. The wrong choice of person to administer the programme may do more harm than good and the programmes should be placed at the highest level within the organisation. If an external programme is used, then the service provider must be able to demonstrate a high code of professional standards and ethics.

An Employee Assistance Programme will:

- Assist employees and their families in resolving personal problems that may have a negative influence on work performance;

- Provide managers/supervisors/unions with a professional resource for the resolution of performance problems caused by employees' personal or health problems;

- Manage and improve the quality of health care of employees and the company;

- Develop prevention activities for employee health care.

It will typically deal with the following types of problems: alcohol and other drugs; compulsive gambling, eating disorders; work stress, marital and family problems; depression, anxiety and mental health; legal, financial and career; grief, bereavement; post-traumatic stress disorder.

The type of EAP chosen will depend on many factors, including size of organisation, structure, culture and resources available. Indeed, in many large organisations a pilot programme is carried out initially. Costs and benefits can then be evaluated prior to enlargement and extension.

WORKPLACE COUNSELLING

Traditionally, counselling was narrowly viewed as a reactive device in response to specific employee problems. There is now an increased awareness of the value of counselling skills in a business context. It is advocated as a positive intervention that helps organisations and employees to overcome problems and difficult situations and it promotes the emotional and physical wellbeing of the employees. Indeed, research shows that employees often report improved mental and physical wellbeing in comparison to that experienced before the counselling intervention. Summerfield and Van Oudtshoorn (1995) suggest that counselling is firmly rooted in good management practices and is not merely used as a device to overcome specific problems.

The increase in the provision of counselling services in Irish companies may be linked to changes in management style and the way work is organised. In modern organisations, empowered team-oriented structures may benefit from the introduction of a counselling service, which can promote a culture of continuous improvement by helping overcome learning blockages in order to realise developmental goals. There may be many motives for providing a counselling service; these can range from organisational self-interest to a purely altruistic motivation that has the welfare of the employee in mind. Research by Highley and Cooper (1995) in the UK illustrates the rationale advanced by employers for the provision of a counselling service. The findings illustrate that the most frequently cited reasons are to provide support to staff members and to create a positive image of a caring employer. Helping employees adapt to organisational change and to cope with stress were also cited less frequently. The motives expressed by organisations introducing a counselling service were also economic, where the role of the counsellor is to maintain the employees' wellbeing so that absenteeism and turnover are controlled and do not adversely affect productivity.

Benefits of Workplace Counselling

It is intuitively appealing that both the organisation and employees benefit from the provision of counselling. However, there have been very few evaluations of the impact of workplace counselling. Sonnenstuhl and Trice (1986) suggest that this may be attributed to several factors, namely the expense and time-consuming nature and the issue of confidentiality. Organisations who provide workplace counselling put forward anecdotal evidence for the direct benefits they have experienced. These include:

- Enhanced work performance through employee wellbeing, motivation and morale, which can foster commitment and loyalty to a firm;

- Enhanced work performance achieved through lower absenteeism rates, turnover, stress-related illnesses and accidents;

- Facilitates effective change management, fostering a culture of employee empowerment, continuous improvement and self-development;

- Conveys a positive image of the organisation as a caring firm.

- Indirect benefits may include the effective and efficient accomplishment of management functions, as employees' personal/social problems can distract a manager's attention from accomplishing the organisational objectives.

- Counselling has the potential of rehabilitating employees, allowing their work to contribute to the effectiveness of the organisation.

Approaches to Counselling

There are a number of approaches in which employees can provide counselling and related services. Employers may choose to set up a counselling service within the organisation, whereby qualified counsellors are employed by the organisation. Alternatively, counselling services can be contracted out to an external counselling specialist; this counselling agency acts as an intermediary between the organisation and the employees. There are advantages and disadvantages associated with both internal and external counselling and these vary depending on the context in which they are provided (Carroll and Walton, 1997). The greatest advantage of contracting out a counselling service is the perception of greater confidentiality by employees, which may result in a more open discussion and counselling session with the employee.

Table 22.1: Advantages of Internal and External Counselling

Advantages of External Counselling	*Advantages of Internal Counselling*
• The counsellor is not immersed in organisational politics • It can challenge the paradigm of the organisation • A wide range of issues covered • Individual's confidentiality may be secured • Set-up and development cost minimised • Specialist expertise that could be lacking in the organisation • The organisation is not responsible for malpractice of counsellors.	• The counsellor may have a greater appreciation of the culture, policies and procedures of the organisation. This may facilitate greater understanding of problems. • The counsellor is a visible face, an insider • The counsellor has flexibility to adapt to clients' needs • Greater control and accountability of the counselling programme • The counselling service may have greater credibility • The counsellor can provide a multiplicity of roles including trainer, welfare officer, home-visitor, information giver, personnel adviser, organisational change-agent, in addition to the traditional counselling role of consultation with individual clients

Source: Carroll (1997)

Some organisations, such as Intel, the ESB, Waterford Crystal and Hewlett Packard, provide an integrated model of internal and external counselling whereby management and HRM specialists may provide limited counselling services as well as working in partnership with external counsellors. There is controversy on what issues of counselling managers and human resource specialists should provide. Wells and Spinks (1997) suggest that the counselling that can be undertaken by managers should be confined to narrow bounds, related directly to work. They suggest that disciplinary counselling, grievance counselling and performance appraisal counselling is suitable/appropriate for a manager to tackle.

Problems experienced by the employee may exceed the existing experience of managers, and in this situation the employee should be given access to advice, information and support from another source.

There is an onus on management to monitor employee behaviour that may signal the need for counselling. Sidney and Phillips (1990) propose indicators for the provision of counselling:

- People not performing to their usual standard;

- Tardiness;

- Inability to communicate clearly;

- Inability to act as part of a team;

- Unusual or changed behaviour;

- Inability to take or make decisions;

- Change in personal circumstances;

- Change in work circumstances.

When to Use Counselling

There are many diverse issues encountered in present-day employment that could benefit from counselling. Problems arise both in a formal work context and also in a social sense. Problems can also be caused by the work organisation acting on the individual. Employees also experience problems that are principally non-work-related but that may have an impact on the employees' work performance. A number of these issues may affect employees at any one time and some work-related problems may exacerbate some non-work issues. The types of work and non-work issues that counselling may address are presented in Table 22.2.

Table 22.2: Types of Work and Non-work Issues that Counselling May Address

Work-Related Issues	Non-Work-Related Issues
• Discipline	• Marital and relationship problems
• Redundancy	
• Stress	• Bereavement
• Performance appraisal	• Suicide
• Grievance and disciplinary handling	• Disability or chronic sickness
	• AIDS
• Relocation stress	• Mental health
• Change management	• Substance abuse
• Career advice	• Alcohol abuse
• Sexual harassment	
• Retirement	

CONCLUSIONS

This chapter has argued that a positive approach to employee health and welfare issues can benefit the employer through enhanced levels of performance, lower absenteeism and a greater capacity to recruit and retain employees. Legislative changes, medical research and changing employee expectations have brought a wide range of sensitive issues to the fore, including smoking, alcohol misuse, drug abuse, HIV and AIDS, workplace violence, bullying and stress.

Alcohol misuse and drug abuse may considerably impact on employee absenteeism and work performance. Such a situation demands a systematic approach to such issues, including the provision of counselling and support to employees in addition to training and backing to managers who have to deal with such issues.

Many organisations have or are about to adopt smoking control policies. A range of options are available to employers. It is important to solicit employee opinion, otherwise it may lead to problems between smokers and non-smokers. Effective policies in this area can minimise many of the problems that arise.

HIV and AIDS are features of modern employment and are likely to remain so for some time to come. Since the early 1990s, the formulation of AIDS policies has become more common. Such policies are intended to address issues related to discrimination, employee education, equitable benefits, guarantees of medical confidentiality and assurances of continued employment.

The research reveals clearly that the nature of the work determines the likelihood of violence at work. Such violence may be threatened or real, verbal or physical. Irish employers have a statutory duty to assess the risks of violence and take appropriate steps to reduce or eliminate the possibility of it occurring. Similar concerns and duties exist in respect of bullying. Failure to address issues of violence and bullying can result in a situation where actions for constructive dismissal may be brought against employers.

The costs of excessive stress levels in the workplace are considerable for both individual and organisation. Effective management of stress requires strategies to address the stressors, as well as promoting individual coping strategies. An effective stress policy should address the stigma associated with stress, enable systematic assessment of stress, and implement appropriate action plans, monitoring and review systems.

References

Aiken, L. (1992), *Psychological Testing and Assessments*, London: Allyn & Bacon.

Aikin, D. (1994), "Procedure for Staff Dismissal", *Personnel Management*, March, pp. 55–6.

Anderson, I. (1996), "Cheers All Round for Employee Counselling", *Professional Manager*, Vol. 5, No. 1, January.

Banas, G. (1992), "Nothing Prepared Me to Manage AIDS", *Harvard Business Review*, July/August.

Brookler, R. (1992), "Industry Standards in Workplace Drug Testing", *Personnel Journal*, April, pp. 123–32.

Carroll, M. and M. Walton (1997), *Handbook of Counselling in Organisations*, London: Sage Publications.

Charlesworth, K. (1996), "Are Managers Under Stress? A Survey of Management Morale", London: Institute of Management Research Report.

Clark, H., J. Chandler and J. Barry (1997), "Gender and Work Stress: Experience, Accommodation and Resistance", *Occasional Papers in Organisational Analysis*, University of Portsmouth.

Cox, T. (1987), "Stress Coping and Problem-Solving", *Work and Stress*, No. 1, pp. 4–14.

Cranwell-Ward, J. (1990), *Thriving on Stress*, London: Routledge.

Davis, A. and L. Gibson (1994), "Designing Employee Welfare Provision" in J.R. Berridge and C.C. Cooper (eds.), "The Employee Assistance Programme: Its Role in Organisational Coping", *Management Review*, Vol. 23, No. 7, pp. 33-45.

Goss, D. and D. Adam-Smith (1994), "Empowerment or Disempowerment? The Limits and Possibilities of Workplace AIDS Policy", in P. Agglerton et al. (eds.), *AIDS: Foundations for the Future*, London: Taylor and Francis.

Health and Safety Authority (1998), 1997 Report of the Irish Health and Safety Authority, Dublin: HSA.

Highley, C. and C. Cooper (1995), "An Assessment and Evaluation of Employee Assistance and Work Place Counselling Programmes in British Organisations", Unpublished Report for the Health and Safety Executive.

Honey, P. (1993), "Managing Unwanted Stress", Seminar Paper, Wessex: IPD.

Hough, L.M. and P. Mayhew (1983), *The British Crime Survey*, London: HMSO.

Incomes Data Services (1991), *Smoking at Work*, Study 474.

Incomes Data Services (1993), *AIDS Returns to the Agenda*, Study 528, April.

IPD (1996), *Occupational Health and Organisational Effectiveness: Key Facts*, London: IPD.

Jones, T. and B. Kleiner (1990), "Smoking and the Work Environment", *Employee Relations*, Vol. 12, No. 4, pp. 29–31.

Judge, L. (1996), "What Safety Practitioners Think about Stress", *Safety and Health Practitioner*, Vol. 14, No. 4, pp. 8–20.

Lee, C. and J.A. Gray (1994), "The Role of Employee Assistance Programmes" in C. Cooper and S. Williams (eds.), *Creating Healthy Work Organisations*, Chichester: Wiley.

Littlefield, D. (1996), "Stress Epidemic Hits Modern Workforces", *People Management*, October.

McKee, V. (1996), "Working to a Frenzy", *The Guardian*, October.

Means, R. (1996), "Alcohol, Alcohol Problems and the Workplace" in K. Dovgan and R. Means (eds.), *Alcohol and the Workplace*, Bristol: SAUS.

Megranahan, M. (1989), *Counselling: A Practical Guide for Employers*, London: Institute of Personnel and Development.

Newell, S. (1995), *The Healthy Organisation: Fairness, Ethics and Effective Management*, London: Routledge.

O'Brien, O. and H. Dufficy (1988), "Alcohol and Drug Policies" in F. Dickenson (ed.), *Drink and Drugs at Work*, London: IPM.

Painter, R. (1990), "Smoking Policies: The Legal Implications", *Employee Relations*, Vol. 12, No. 4, pp. 17–21.

Porteous, M. (1997), *Occupational Psychology*, London: Prentice Hall.

Sidney, E. and N. Phillips (1990), *One to One Management: Counselling to Improve Job Performance*, London: Pitman Publishing.

Sonnenstuhl, W.J. and H.M. Trice (1986), *Strategies for Employee Assistance Programmes: The Crucial Balance*, Key Issues No. 30, ILR Press, New York State, School of Industrial and Labour Relations, Cornell University.

Summerfield, J. and Van L. Oudtshoorn (1995), *Counselling in the Workplace*: London, Institute of Personnel Development Publishing.

Wells, B and N. Spinks (1997), "Counselling Employees: An Applied Communication Skill", *Career Development International*, Vol. 2, No. 2.

INDEX